Children and Adults
with Learning Disabilities

Tom E. C. Smith
University of Arkansas at Little Rock

Carol A. Dowdy
University of Alabama at Birmingham

Edward A. Polloway
Lynchburg College

Ginger E. Blalock
University of New Mexico

Allyn and Bacon

Boston   London   Toronto   Sydney   Tokyo   Singapore

Executive Editor: Raymond Short
Editorial Assistant: Christine Svitila
Marketing Manager: Kris Farnsworth
Editorial Production Service: Elm Street Publishing Services, Inc.
Manufacturing Buyer: Megan Cochran
Cover Administrator: Linda Knowles

Copyright ©1997 by Allyn & Bacon
A Viacom Company
Needham Heights, MA 02194

Internet: www.abacon.com
America Online: keyword: College Online

Library of Congress Cataloging-in-Publication Data
Children and adults with learning disabilities / Tom E.C. Smith . . . [et al.].
       p. cm.
    Includes bibliographical references and index.
    ISBN 0-205-19431-1
    1. Learning disabilities—United States. 2. Learning disabled children—Education—United States. 3. Learning disabled—Education—United States. I. Smith, Tom E.C.
LC4705.C45 1997
371.91—dc20
                                                                      96-9108
                                                                      CIP

Photo Credits:
©Will Faller: Pages 1, 12, 31, 43, 68, 105, 121, 142, 183, 256, 301, 330, 358, 381, 393, 404, 412
©Jim Pickerell: Pages 21, 54, 59, 159, 167, 188, 193, 209, 270, 299, 344, 432
©Stephen Marks: Pages 118, 232, 247, 285, 328, 365, 386, 423
©Brian Smith: Pages 219, 333

Printed in the United States of America
10 9 8 7 6 5 4 3 2 1   01 00 99 98 97 96

For the children, adolescents, and adults with learning disabilities who have been our best teachers, and to children significant in our lives: Jake, Alex, Suni, Cameron, Meredith, Lyndsay, Barbara, and Sam.

Contents

CHAPTER 3   ASSESSMENT   59

CHAPTER 8   LEARNING DISABILITIES IN ADULTHOOD   256

by Craig A. Michaels

CHAPTER 11   WORKING WITH FAMILIES OF STUDENTS
WITH LEARNING DISABILITIES   358

CHAPTER 12   CONCOMITANT EXCEPTIONALITIES   386

Preface

The field of learning disabilities has been evolving for more than three decades, and there is still a great deal of controversy over such issues as definition, eligibility, and educational services. This field, more than any other in special education, has been and remains controversial in many aspects. In some critiques, it has been called nebulous, unfocused, and even nonexistent. Unfortunately, such critiques fail to account for the very real challenges that individuals with learning disabilities face both within and beyond the school setting.

For children of school age, learning disabilities account for more students in special education than all other disabilities combined. The overwhelming number of children with a learning disability, as well as their unique needs, makes this disability category noteworthy of study for special educators, general educators, counselors, and professionals in many related disciplines.

During the past few years there has been an increasing interest in adults with learning disabilities. Learning disabilities are not simply a child's disorder that will vanish when an individual leaves high school. They remain an ever-present part of that person's life, often causing considerable problems in social and vocational areas. This realization has led to increased services by adult service agencies as well as increased opportunities for college students with learning disabilities.

For the most part, textbooks that introduce learning disabilities have followed similar organizational formats. While the content in these texts has changed over time, the basic organization has remained similar. This text takes an alternative approach to introducing the reader to the field of learning disabilities. Its emphasis on the nature of learning disabilities serves as a basis for understanding the needs of individuals with this disability. As such, it focuses on a developmental approach, presenting information about individuals with learning disabilities at different life periods. It does not include a primary emphasis on intervention models, leaving that content to textbooks that focus on curriculum and instructional methods. Instead, the text provides information that presents a comprehensive picture of learning disabilities and how they impact on people at different points in their lives, thus serving as a foundation for further inquiries into appropriate interventions.

The text is organized into thirteen chapters, including introductory chapters that provide a general orientation to learning disabilities; chapters that focus on the impact of learning disabilities during preschool and elementary years, adolescence, and adulthood; and special topics such as legal and family issues and concomitant disabilities. Each chapter includes opening objectives as well as a summary.

The text provides a broad conceptualization of learning disabilities. This is reflected in the focus of several chapters. For example, in the chapter on concomitant disabilities, we do not present the view that learning disabilities can only occur alone and not be associated with other problems, but rather that learning disabilities and these instances must be examined and understood. The chapter on etiology also adopts a broader conceptualization of learning disabilities by focusing on causative factors often overlooked in other texts but which clearly may result in learning disabilities. The also includes a unique chapter on diversity, which is such an important reality in our culture.

▶ ACKNOWLEDGMENTS

We would like to acknowledge several individuals who played important roles in the development of this text. These include Ray Short, our editor at Allyn and Bacon who encouraged us to pursue this project; Martha Beyerlein, the project editor for Elm Street Publishing Services, Inc., who was always willing to give us "one more day"; and Kevin Seeley and Phyllis Lane for their assistance in manuscript preparation. Particularly significant are the contributions made to individual chapters by Diane Bassett, Helen Rucker, and Craig Michaels. We would also like to thank our families for their support and encouragement, especially our "significant other," Bonnie, Jim, Carolyn, and Eloy. Finally, we want to acknowledge the individuals who reviewed the manuscript and provided helpful feedback that was incorporated into the final manuscript. These included: Janis Bulgren,; The University of Kansas; Rhoda Cummings, University of Nevada–Reno; Debra Harley, University of Kentucky; John Wasson, Moorhead State University; Barbara Priddy Guyer, Marshall University; John M. Dodd, Montana State University–Billings.

TECS, CAD, EAP, GEB

Chapter 1

LEARNING DISABILITIES:
An Introduction

The objectives for this chapter are as follows:

▶ To understand the role of early researchers in the development of the field of learning disabilities.

▶ To know the importance of brain research in adults to the development of the field of learning disabilities.

▶ To describe several prominent researchers who made a significant contribution to the field of learning disabilities.

▶ To describe the process approach for dealing with children with learning disabilities.

▶ To list laws that had a significant impact on the development of the field of learning disabilities.

▶ To describe the major activities since 1963 that have affected the field of learning disabilities.

▶ To describe some of the emerging issues that will affect the field of learning disabilities over the coming years.

Learning Disabilities Are Difficult to Identify

Billy's mother always thought that the school was simply not doing its job. Billy is a nine-year-old, awkward boy who has difficulties in school with school work and his behavior even though he is obviously very bright. He can take his things apart and put them back together even better than his father, who is a contractor. His mother began worrying about Billy when he was about five years old. He was awkward, did not seem to pay attention, and was always what she called *overactive*. In kindergarten, Billy constantly got into trouble. He had a habit of just getting up and wandering around the room at all times, even when the teacher was reading an interesting story. He simply could not pay attention to the teacher for a very long period of time. By the time Billy finished first grade he was already behind his peers. He had trouble reading even the simplest words. The second grade was a disaster. Billy's behavior became much worse, and he was actually suspended from school twice for acting inappropriately to the teacher. His grades were always near the failing level. Now in the third grade, Billy's mother does not know what to do. Billy is continuing to have behavior problems and makes very poor grades. He frequently states that he is dumb and will not ever learn to read very well.

Billy may well have a learning disability. Many children with learning disabilities begin school excited about learning only to enter into a failure cycle that results in low self-esteem and behavior problems. The field of learning disabilities has evolved incredibly fast over the past few decades and is continuing to find itself in the field of disabilities.

The field of learning disabilities is a much discussed, much maligned category of disabilities. It is one of the newest, largest, and most difficult to understand disability categories currently recognized by professionals in the field of disabilities. In addition, it is also the most debated disability category in this country (Moats and Lyon, 1993). The category of *learning disabilities* was not even recognized until the 1960s. Prior to this time there were numerous disabilities identified and served in schools and by other agencies, including mental retardation, speech impairment, cerebral palsy, and emotional disturbance. Even autism, another *modern* disability, was recognized.

The fact that learning disabilities was not a recognized category did not mean that some children with these kinds of problems were not provided services. Some children with *brain injury* or *minimal brain dysfunction* were identified. However, services for these children were very limited and many children who did not exhibit significant learning problems were not identified and provided services. As recently as the 1970s, many children with unusual *learning characteristics* were often left without any formal special education services because they did not fit into one of the recognized disability categories (Moats and Lyon, 1993). Many children currently recognized as having learning disabilities exhibited these kinds of unusual problems.

Some children who experienced learning disabilities were served with such labels as brain-injured, minimally brain-injured, or minimally brain-damaged; however, such terms were not conducive to large numbers of children being identified. Many parents did not want their children identified with the label brain injury, or any term suggesting damage to the brain. The term also suggested a strong medical model for intervention, another reason for limited numbers of children identified and served. Once learning disabilities became recognized as a disability without direct association with brain injury, one barrier to the identification of children as having a learning disability was removed.

Learning disabilities is a category of disabilities that has often been misunderstood by educators, adult service providers, family members, and even individuals with learning disabilities. "The field has been, and continues to be, beset by pervasive and, at times, contentious disagreements about definitions, diagnostic criteria, assessment practices, teaching or intervention procedures, and educational policy" (Moats and Lyon, 1993, p. 282). One result of these disagreements has been the rapid increase in the number of students with learning disabilities, many of whom are actually underachieving students identified as learning disabled. The growth rate was so phenomenal in the 1970s that the federal government proposed to limit the number of children it would allow for reimbursement with P.L. 94-142 funds to 2 percent of the student population (*Federal Register,* 1976). As a result of the comments received in response to this proposal, attempts to cap the number of children with learning disabilities who were supported with federal special education funds were dropped. Currently the learning disabilities category represents by far the largest group of children served in special education programs, accounting for more than fifty percent of all students receiving special education services (U.S. Department of Education, 1995).

Not only has defining and identifying children with learning disabilities proved difficult, but the determination of appropriate services and intervention programs has also encountered a great deal of controversy. From sensory-motor intervention and dietary management to the more current intervention approaches used, persons involved in developing programs for these students have often found themselves adhering to one or more overriding philosophical views that may or may not have had a validated research base. Unfortunately, conflicting theories about learning disabilities and intervention approaches have resulted in major disagreements among professionals trying to meet the needs of this unique group of individuals. These conflicts have only added to the confusion in the field of learning disabilities.

Many changes have occurred during the rapid growth of learning disabilities. Learning disabilities has evolved from a category surrounded by the aura of medicine and neurological problems to one that is often applied to children and adults who may not display many of the characteristics originally thought to be critical of the disability. It has gone from a field designed to provide services to a finite number of children with a specific type of problem, to one in which, seemingly, many children are referred simply because the teaching-learning process breaks down or because students are achieving below average (Moats and Lyon, 1993).

Regardless of numerous problems and growing pains, the field of learning disabilities has evolved significantly and will continue to evolve. As research findings add more valid information to the pool of knowledge about this disability, better definitions will be developed, eligibility criteria will be tightened, and services will be more appropriate. The next several years will undoubtedly see continued changes in this very exciting disability area. As noted by Swanson (1991), "As professionals in the field, we have some serious thinking to do if we are to capture the complexity of a learning disability" (p. 250). There remains a great deal of work to do.

❱ HISTORY OF LEARNING DISABILITIES

The history of learning disabilities is reflective of the controversial nature of the category. It is a complex chronology of events, partly because of the wide variability of interests in the field. Neurologists, child development specialists, speech/language therapists, educators, pediatricians, family physicians, vocational rehabilitation counselors, and psychologists are just some of the professional groups involved in identifying and serving children and adults with learning disabilities. As a result, the history of the field of learning disabilities has taken many different turns in getting to the present.

There are many different ways to organize the history of learning disabilities in the United States. Hammill (1993) started with the *Foundations phase,* which covers some of the early research and work with individuals with brain trauma and poststroke patients in the 1800s. In concurring with Hammill on some of the early foundations of learning disabilities, Richardson (1992) noted that the field has roots in studies of aphasia in the nineteenth century. From this beginning came an interest in studying the brains of people who had experienced strokes or trauma as a result of wars or accidents. The majority of research and intervention in the early years of learning disabilities was related to neurology (Richardson, 1992). The realization that some children, without apparent brain injury, displayed similar characteristics as adults with known brain injury was an important step in the field of learning disabilities (Hammill, 1993).

The foundations phase of learning disabilities was followed by the phase Hammill (1993) labeled the *Early Years of the LD Movement*. This period began in earnest in the 1960s with a focus on children with brain injury. This period was followed in 1990 by the *Modern phase*. Several issues dominate this phase, including the stabilization of the numbers of children identified with learning disabilities, the recognition that many different types of learning disabilities can be identified, and the movement to provide all educational services in general education classrooms. It is also during this period that adults with learning disabilities were first recognized as needing services.

Foundations Phase

Hammill (1993) described the foundations phase as the period when various theoretical positions about learning disabilities were first established. The period began in the 1800s when a great deal of work was done in the area of aphasia. This early work led to more expanded research in neurology and formed much of the basis for the initial knowledge about learning disabilities (Richardson, 1992). The focus of much of this early work was on clinical observations by physicians of adults with sustained brain injury. The first systematic investigations started around 1800 when Franz-Joseph Gall, a German neurologist, examined adults with head injuries who maintained their intellectual level but lost the ability to communicate through speech (Opp, 1994).

Gall's early work led him to conclude that specified localization of brain function existed, a theory that was later adopted by many of his followers. Unfortunately, Gall lost favor with many of his colleagues with his later promotion of phrenology, or the study of bumps on a person's head (Richardson, 1992). Still, Gall's early efforts laid a strong foundation for the next generation of researchers interested in the brain and the results of brain damage (Opp, 1994).

Gall's work was a very important beginning for learning disabilities. When comparing Gall's early observations with current definitions of learning disabilities, it is likely that if the conditions described by Gall were currently found in a child, the child would be classified as having a learning disability and would be eligible for special education services. Gall, therefore, helped lay the foundation for the field of learning disabilities although his intent was to study adults whose head injuries resulted in their loss of certain functions (Hammill, 1993).

Following Gall were several European scientists who continued to do research that helped lead to an understanding of the relationship between the brain and various body functions. One such scientist was Frenchman Pierre Paul Broca. In the early 1860s, Broca described motor aphasia in an individual and identified the location of the defect in the individual's brain. This person and others described by Broca had command over language and understood the correct relationships between symbols and ideas and also displayed intact auditory and motor systems. However, they exhibited significant problems with verbal expression (Savage, 1994).

On April 4, 1861, Broca showed the brain of a person known as Tan who had died of gangrene. The patient had lost his speech twenty-one years before his death. Broca's demonstration revealed that Tan's brain had severe lesions in the area of the left temporal lobe now known as Broca's area. By 1863, Broca and his colleagues had found twenty similar cases, leading him to conclude that pathological alterations of the left side of the brain could result in speech and language problems (Mann, 1979).

Broca's research findings were critical for the further development of neurology. Before his research, scientists and physicians had no idea why individuals experienced these kinds of problems (Mann, 1979). Broca's findings were truly revolutionary and were "the beginning of a long (as judged from a contemporary perspective), fruitful scientific controversy about localistic versus wholistic concepts of brain function" (Opp, 1994, p. 10).

Another scientist during this period who made a major contribution to the field of learning disabilities was the German neurologist Carl Wernicke. In 1874 Wernicke located the auditory speech area in the superior temporal convolution on the left side of the brain. He believed that the front half of the brain dealt with movement, and the back half focused on sensory areas. As such, Wernicke believed that a lesion or damage to the back half of the brain would affect the understanding of speech, as well as the ability to read and write (Richardson, 1992). Wernicke was one of the first scientists to understand the complexity of speech. He described speech in terms of pathways, stimuli, and functional centers, believing that disruptions in pathways and centers resulted in aphasia (Opp, 1994). Out of Wernicke's work "grew the distinction between receptive aphasia, due to disturbances in the sensory aspects of language, and expressive aphasia (Broca's aphasia), due to disturbances or defects in the motor areas of the cortex" (Mann, 1979, p. 415).

Wernicke's work was further expanded by Lichtheim, who described seven disturbances of speech that resulted from interruptions in neural pathways. Lichtheim "differentiated among the functions of volitional speech, repetition of words, reading aloud, volitional writing, writing according to dictation, understanding of spoken words, understanding of written words, and the faculty of copying" (Opp, 1994, p. 12). He thus expanded Wernicke's work to include areas of reading and writing. In doing so, he theorized that written language is related to the association between sound and images of letters. These theories were critical for later understanding of learning disabilities.

As previously noted, early work in the area of aphasia spread to include more than just auditory language. Disorders of reading and writing began to be linked to the same neurological problems associated with aphasia. One of the first scientists to make this assertion was the Englishman, Sir William Broadbent. Broadbent described several individuals who could not read, but who did not appear to have any other types of problems. These observations provided an important beginning in the study of dyslexia (Richardson, 1992).

Broadbent's work was followed by several other scientists who began to study the relationships between neurological problems and functions such as reading. In the late 1870s, Kussamaul noted that reading problems can be present even though individuals have intact intellectual, visual, and speech abilities (Richardson, 1992). A German ophthalmologist, Berlin, began using the term *dyslexia* in 1887 to describe these kinds of problems. Berlin's work resulted in a better understanding of individuals who experienced reading problems but did not have any visual problems. He considered dyslexia another problem related to other aphasias. In his research, Berlin found that the size of print, and whether or not the person read out loud or silently, did not affect the reading difficulty, further establishing the relationship between brain functioning and reading (Richardson, 1992).

In the 1890s, an important area in research opportunities opened up when researchers began extensive study of the brains of individuals in postmortem examinations. This gave scientists a first-hand look at the brains of individuals who had exhibited various functional dysfunctions. Following such an examination of an individual who lost his ability to read but not his ability to write, Dejerine concluded that the cause of the reading disability was the result of a disconnection of two parts of the brain—the right side of the visual cortex from the left angular gyrus. About this same time, Morgan published the first article in the medical literature about children with word blindness (Richardson, 1992). This article continued to link reading problems with neurological dysfunction.

Regardless of the early work on dyslexia prior to the twentieth century, it was not until Hinshelwood, a Scottish ophthalmologist, reported on word-blindness in the medical literature that much attention was paid to the condition. Hinshelwood defined word-blindness as an inability to accurately interpret what a person's eyes are seeing (Wiederholt, 1974). In other words, there was nothing wrong with a person's vision, but the process broke down between when the eye "saw" something and when the brain interpreted the image.

Hinshelwood is best remembered for his distinction of congenital word-blindness (Mann, 1979). In an article in 1917, he noted that more than one case of *word-blindness* was often present in families. Hinshelwood also noted that the characteristics of children with this condition were very similar to adults who had sustained brain injury. After drawing this analogy, Hinshelwood concluded that dyslexia was due to either injury, or to an underdevelopment in the lower parietal lobe on the left side of the brain, and that such a condition could be due to disease, birth injury, or abnormal development (Richardson, 1992).

One of Hinshelwood's concerns was that word-blindness might be confused or associated with mental deficiency. In an attempt to clarify the differences between these two distinctly different characteristics he made the following statement in 1917.

When I see it stated that congenital word-blindness may be combined with any amount of other mental defects from mere dullness to low-grade mental defects, imbecility or idiocy, I can understand how confusion has arisen from the loose application of the term congenital word-blindness to all conditions in which there is defective development of the visual memory center, quite independently of any consideration as to whether it is strictly local defect or only a symptom of a great injustice to the children affected with the pure type of congenital word-blindness, a strictly local affection, to be placed in the same category as others suffering from generalized cerebral defects, as the former can be successfully dealt with, while the latter are practically irremediable. (Richardson, 1992, pp. 42, 93–94)

While it is clear that mental deficiency and dyslexia are very different conditions, there remains confusion about their inter-relatedness.

During this same period, Goldstein studied men who had been injured during World War I. His studies of men who had suffered brain damage led him to conclude that brain injury would result in the development of a variety of problems rather than specific behavioral disturbance. Strauss and Werner would later expand the work of Goldstein to children and develop a subset of individuals with Strauss syndrome (Myers and Hammill, 1990).

Still another researcher during the early 1900s was Samuel T. Orton, a neuropathologist. Orton agreed with some of Hinshelwood's theories while disagreeing with him regarding etiology and intervention methods (Hammill, 1993). In a report written in 1925, Orton wrote that word-blindness (1) varies in degree of severity, (2) is not related to mental deficiency, (3) is due to brain irregularities, and (4) can be corrected with proper methods that are implemented early (Richardson, 1992). Orton believed that word-blindness could be due to both hereditary as well as environmental factors.

Orton realized that listening, speaking, reading, and writing are all interrelated functions. As a result, he understood that problems in any of these functions could be affected by neurological dysfunction. He identified five different syndromes related to these functions (Richardson, 1992):

1. developmental aphasia (word-blindness)
2. developmental word deafness (auditory aphasia)
3. special difficulty in writing
4. motor speech delay
5. stuttering

Orton agreed with Hinshelwood that educational intervention was the best method of dealing with children with these types of disabilities. "His recommended training procedures aided the establishment of phoneme-grapheme association and emphasized the appropriate sequencing of written and auditory symbols" (Richardson, 1992, p. 42). Orton also advocated the use of reinforcement and the use of all sense modalities to reinforce and strengthen weak memory (Richardson, 1992). One of the overriding beliefs of Orton was the role played by lateral dominance, or cerebral dominance (Smith and Luckasson, 1995). If a child had not established cerebral dominance, Orton believed that they would experience "hemispheric competition" when attempting to read. He labeled this strephosymbolia, meaning twisted symbols (Myers and Hammill, 1990). As a result, Orton advocated dominance training for students with problems related to cerebral dominance (Smith and Neisworth, 1975). Many of Orton's ideas have been adopted as part of intervention programs for the past fifty years.

The latter part of the foundations phase focused on attempts to convert theories into practice. Orton, Hinshelwood, and other early scientists in learning disabilities focused their attention on adults. This focus changed dramatically during the period between 1930 and 1963, when the emphasis shifted to children. Areas of research included methods of evaluating children with learning problems and appropriate intervention techniques with learning problems. It was also during this period that several psychologists and educators emerged as early leaders in the field of learning disabilities (Hammill, 1993).

Two prominent researchers during the early 1940s who were instrumental in the expanding knowledge about children with learning disabilities were Alfred Strauss, a neuropsychiatrist, and Heinz Werner, a developmental psychologist. Strauss and Werner, using Goldstein's work as a basis, described children who manifested a variety of learning problems concomitant with certain behavior and psychological problems. These children were later classified as having a condition referred to as *Strauss syndrome*. Children with Strauss syndrome supposedly had brain damage, and were comparable in many ways with World War I veterans studied by Goldstein (Smith and Luckasson, 1995). The characteristics typically displayed by these children included (1) short attention span, (2) high distractibility, (3) problems with reading and other academic tasks, (4) poor motor coordination, and (5) hyperactivity. In 1947, Strauss and another colleague, Laura Lehtinen, published a classic book, *Psychopathology and Education of the Brain-Injured Child*, which described these children and emphasized structured academic and behavioral programming. The presumption was made by Strauss and Lehtinen that these children had neurological deficits. Strauss and his colleagues had a major impact on the field of learning disabilities (Kavale and Forness, 1985). Their work influenced many later professionals, especially many who advocated perceptual-motor training. These included Sam Kirk, Ray Barsch, Marianne Frostig, Gerald Getman, and Newell Kephart (Hallahan, Kauffman, and Lloyd, 1996; Mann, 1979).

In addition to Strauss and Lehtinen, many other early theorists' ideas were used as a basis for intervention techniques. Orton's ideas resulted in efforts of Gillingham and Stillman in the late 1960s and early 1970s to remediate reading disabilities using a remedial phonics method. At about the same time, Fernald developed a remedial approach for reading and spelling disorders that was based on using a multisensory model. This program was called V-A-K-T, standing for visual-auditory-kinesthetic-tactile approach (Hammill, 1993). Many of the techniques developed by Gillman, Stillman, and Fernald are still used to teach students with learning disabilities and other academic problems.

The foundations phase of the learning disabilities movement was filled with a great deal of new knowledge about the brain and different functions associated with the brain. This knowledge, while not always validated with later research, laid a firm foundation for the development of the field of learning disabilities. Table 1.1 summarizes some of the important events during this period.

Early Years of the Learning Disabilities Movement

Hammill (1993) noted that the early years of the learning disabilities movement started at a 1963 conference sponsored by a group of parents who founded the Association for Children with Learning Disabilities (ACLD). At this conference, Samuel Kirk, a noted leader in the field of special education, used the term *learning disabilities* to describe children that had previously been classified

TABLE 1.1

Summary of Important Activities in the Foundations Phase

- Gall (neurologist) examined adults with head injuries who had lost capacity to express feelings and ideas through speech (about 1800).
- Gall concluded that localization of brain functions existed and linked various parts of the brain with specific functions.
- Broca further identified sites in the brain responsible for various functions, particularly language (about 1880).
- Wernicke (neurologist) located the auditory speech area in the brain; he believed that a lesion in the brain would affect language skills (1970s).
- Lichtheim expanded on Wernicke's work and described seven different disturbances resulting from interruptions in the neural pathways (1880s).
- Kussamaul noted that reading problems could exist in individuals with intact intelligence, vision, and speech (1870s–1880s).
- Berlin used the term dyslexia in 1887 to describe reading problems without other obvious difficulties.
- Hinshelwood (ophthalmologist) noted that more than one case of word-blindness could be present in the same family (1917).
- Orton (neuropathologist) believed that word-blindness could be due to heredity or environment, and could be remediated; he identified five different syndromes.
- Strauss and Werner began working with children and described children with Strauss syndrome (1940s).
- Gillingham, Stillman and Fernald developed remedial programs for students with these kinds of problems (1960s–1970s).

with a variety of labels, including perceptually handicapped, brain-damaged, minimally brain-damaged, brain-injured, minimally brain-injured, and hyperactive. Beginning with this conference, more and more professionals interested in children with these types of disabilities banded together under the rubric of learning disabilities. Their aim was "to gain educational leverage for a group of children who were overlooked or excluded from basic educational services" (Moats and Lyon, 1993, p. 283).

In addition to Kirk, several other individuals became prominent in the field of learning disabilities during this period. They included William Cruickshank, Marianne Frostig, Newell Kephart, and Gerald Getman. Cruickshank was a leader in the field of special education when learning disabilities began to become recognized. In the third edition of his text, *Education of Exceptional Children and Youth* (1975), he referred to learning disabilities and noted that between the first and third editions "a whole new field of special education has developed" (p. 242). Cruickshank described children with learning disabilities as those who had been labeled as having Strauss syndrome, hyperactive, hyperactive-emotionally disturbed, perceptually disabled, and brain-injured. He noted that "Motor training for the child with specific learning disabilities appears to be of value as an integral part of the daily educational program" (p. 287). He went on to add that a minimum of thirty minutes daily should be devoted to motor training.

Marianne Frostig focused on the need to remediate deficits in visual-perceptual skills. She developed the *Frostig Developmental Test of Visual Perception* (Frostig, et al., 1964) which measured five areas of visual-motor coordination—eye-motor coordination, figure-ground perception, perception of constancy, perception of position in space, and perception of spatial relationships (Becker and Sabatino, 1973). Frostig also developed a remedial program related to her evaluation instrument (Frostig, 1967). Gerald Getman, an optometrist, was also notable in the field of special education during this period. Getman focused on visual-motor training in his intervention programs for children with brain injury and later for those classified as having a learning disability (Cruickshank, 1967). In 1960, Kephart published *The Slow Learner in the Classroom,* and described in detail an educational program based on a process orientation. A detailed description of Kephart's program will be presented later in the chapter.

Following the 1963 conference described earlier, learning disabilities began to be a more focused disability category for research, advocacy, and services. In Hammill's 1993 review of the history of learning disabilities, he noted that five major aspects can be used to describe the field since 1963. These include (1) the formation of professional and parental organizations that focus on learning disabilities, (2) legislation affecting individuals with learning disabilities, (3) the rise of educational services for students with learning disabilities, (4) the inclusion of diverse interest groups, and (5) the resolution of the major paradigm dispute in the field of learning disabilities.

Rise of Organizations A key element in the rapid expansion of learning disabilities was the development of professional and advocacy organizations. These organizations brought focus to advocates and professionals in their efforts to expand and improve services for children and later adults with learning disabilities. There are five major organizations dealing with learning disabilities that currently impact the field, and have made major contributions during the past thirty years. In 1967, in a meeting in St. Louis, the Council for Learning Disabilities (CLD) was formed as a division of the Council for Exceptional Children (CEC) (Wiig, 1989). This organization was primarily composed of teachers and teacher educators and had the primary purpose to "promote the education and general welfare of persons with learning disabilities." In 1982 the membership of CLD voted to disassociate with CEC and became an independent organization. Currently approximately four thousand individuals belong to CLD (Hammill, 1993); it remains a significant professional association for individuals interested in learning disabilities.

As a result of CLD disassociating itself from CEC, another organization, the Division for Learning Disabilities (DLD), was formed in 1982. This organization continues to be a division of CEC and currently has more than 14,000 members, mostly teachers and teacher educators. The Orton Dyslexia Society, Inc., the oldest organization that focuses on learning disabilities was formed in

The Individuals with Disabilities Education Act guarantees the right of children with learning disabilities to a free appropriate public education.

1949 and named for Samuel Orton. This group includes an educational as well as a medical focus on individuals with dyslexia. This organization includes both professionals and parents (Hammill, 1993).

The Learning Disabilities Association of America (LDA), primarily a parent organization, was formed in 1963 at the meeting where Kirk coined the term *learning disabilities*. Originally the Association for Children with Learning Disabilities (ACLD), the organization currently has a membership of approximately fifty thousand, making it by far the largest professional or advocacy group that focuses on learning disabilities. LDA remains primarily a parent organization, although it does include some professional involvement.

To facilitate coordination among the organizations focusing on learning disabilities, the National Joint Committee on Learning Disabilities (NJCLD) was organized in 1975. This group, made up of the American Speech-Language-Hearing Association, Association on Higher Education and Disability, Council for Learning Disabilities, Division for Children with Communication Disorders, Division for Learning Disabilities, International Reading Association, Learning Disabilities Association of America, National Association of School Psychologists, and the Orton Dyslexia Society, works on national issues affecting the field of learning disabilities and attempts to present a united front on problems facing the field (Hammill, 1993). NJCLD publishes position papers, develops consensus definitions, and attempts to coordinate the collaboration of all of its members.

The growth of organizations focusing on learning disabilities is representative of the rapid growth of the entire field. While the numbers of parents, professionals, and other advocates for learning disabilities increased dramatically, so did the number of children with learning disabilities served in school programs. Concomitantly, the number of states providing services for adults with learning disabilities also grew during this period, indicating that the expansion of organizations very likely had an impact on the expansion of services.

Legislation and Learning Disabilities   One area that professional and advocacy organizations impacted was legislation affecting persons with learning disabilities. Since the mid-1960s several federal legislative acts have had a major impact on services for children and adults with learning disabilities. Acts specifically involving this population include (Podemski, Marsh, Smith, and Price, 1995):

- P.L. 89-10, Elementary and Secondary Education Act, 1965
- Section 504 of the Rehabilitation Act of 1973
- Public Law 94-142, the Education for All Handicapped Children Act
- Individuals with Disabilities Education Act (IDEA), the 1990 reauthorization of the Education for All Handicapped Children Act
- P.L. 101-336, The Americans with Disabilities Act (ADA)

Each of these acts resulted in an increase in services or protections for children and adults with learning disabilities. For children, they mandate appropriate educational programs, accommodations in general education classes, and modifications that are necessary to ensure that students with learning disabilities have equal opportunities to access the entire educational service array (Podemski, et al., 1995). For adults, these acts require employers, state and local governments, and even private businesses to be nondiscriminatory in their interactions and provision of opportunities. Table 1.2 describes the major components of these laws. Various components of IDEA will be discussed in several chapters of the text. Chapter 10 provides a more in-depth description of Section 504 and the ADA.

Educational Services   As a result of legislation and litigation, educational services for children with learning disabilities have expanded dramatically since the late 1970s. Bateman (1992) noted that a key result of the passage of P.L. 94-142 in 1975 was the movement of learning disabilities "from the clinic to the classroom" and the corresponding growth in the numbers of children with learning disabilities receiving services. During the 1976–1977 school year, only 1.8 percent of students served in special education were classified as having a learning disability. The latest Report to Congress on the Implementation of IDEA indicates that during the 1992–1993 school year, 2.3 million students with learning disabilities, ages six through twenty-one, were served in special education. This represented 55.4 percent of all children served in special education programs (U.S. Department of Education, 1995), an incredible increase since 1976. Public Law 94-142, more than anything else, propelled the identification and services of children with learning disabilities, *validating* the existence of this particular disability among school-age children.

TABLE 1.2

Legislation Affecting Individuals with Learning Disabilities

- *P.L. 89-10, Elementary and Secondary Education Act of 1965*   was the first massive legislative aid to education passed by Congress. Although focusing on disadvantaged children, the law included many provisions for students with disabilities.

- *Section 504 of the Rehabilitation Act of 1973*   This act primarily focused on adults with disabilities and their equal opportunities in entities receiving federal funds. During the past few years, the importance of Section 504 to schools and to students with disabilities has become more obvious. Many children not covered under P.L. 94-142 (e.g. some children with learning disabilities) are covered under Section 504.

- *P.L. 94-142, Education for All Handicapped Children Act, 1975*   This legislation was the most important piece of legislation passed for children with disabilities and resulted in an expansion of services and the full recognition of students with disabilities as eligible for special education services.

- *Revisions of the Education for All Handicapped Children Act, 1983, 1990*   Congress re-authorizes P.L. 94-142 approximately every five years. These reauthorizations have expanded services for some groups of children and added requirements such as transition planning and programming.

- *P.L. 101-336, The Americans with Disabilities Act (ADA)*   The law is basically civil rights legislation for individuals with disabilities, including those with learning disabilities. The ADA, unlike Section 504 which only affects entities receiving federal funds, covers just about every group in this country including private businesses, service groups, and private schools.

Prior to the passage of P.L. 94-142, educational opportunities for students with learning disabilities were very limited. In fact, as noted by Smith and Neisworth in 1975, the year P.L. 94-142 was passed, placement options for children with learning disabilities were likely in classes developed for students classified as educable mentally retarded (EMR). This option was not appropriate for many of these children because teachers had only been trained to teach students with mental retardation.

Inclusion of Diverse Groups Another factor affecting the growth of learning disabilities was the increase in the diversity of individuals and professions interested in learning disabilities. As noted earlier, learning disabilities was predominantly an area of interest of physicians and psychologists in the early history of the field. However, as a result of the rapid growth of learning disabilities in schools, educators and other school-related personnel became heavily involved in the development and implementation of programs for students with this disorder.

The sheer number of educators involved in programs for students with learning disabilities is incredible. During the 1991–1992 school year, 97,805 teachers were employed in public schools in this country to provide special education services to children with learning disabilities, ages six through twenty-one. At the same time it was reported that an additional 8,003 teachers were still needed for this group of students. The latest data from the U.S. Department of Education indicate that teachers who serve students with learning disabilities represent almost one-third of all special education teachers in the United States (U.S. Department of Education, 1995).

In addition to teachers, the involvement of speech-language pathologists has also expanded significantly. Because of the language-base of many learning disabilities, the role of speech-language pathologists has been central in the evolution of identification and services for these students. Since the early 1960s, this involvement has become even more important, with many of the leaders in the field coming from speech and language backgrounds (Hammill 1993). The field of vocational rehabilitation has also become involved in providing services to individuals with learning disabilities. This will be discussed later in the chapter and in Chapter 8 which focuses on adults.

Researchers have also become more involved in the learning disabilities field. These include field researchers, who are constantly attempting to determine better ways to identify and educate students with learning disabilities and researchers who continue their efforts to find the causes of learning disabilities, including whether or not a genetic link exists with learning disabilities. Finally, neuropsychologists have continued to be involved in the field of learning disabilities. Physicians and, in particular, neurologists were involved in early work with people with learning disabilities. Their findings of relationships between brain anomalies and reading disabilities, language, and motor skills helped promote an understanding of the etiology of learning disabilities, as well as a better understanding of how the brain affects various body functions. Work to develop a better understanding of the relationship between brain development and functioning continues to be a focus, not only for physicians, but also for neuropsychologists. Recently many neuropsychologists are expanding their interest in learning disabilities to include intervention methods as well as etiology (Hammill, 1993).

Resolution of Theoretical Dispute During the 1960s and 1970s, the predominant theory related to learning disabilities focused on a process approach to assessment and intervention for children with this disorder. It was hypothesized that certain "basic learning processes," including auditory, visual, tactile, motoric, vocal, attention, sequencing, and memory processes, were necessary for learning. And it was further hypothesized that if there were deficits in any of these processes, learning would likely be impaired. Some professionals took this orientation to the extreme and advocated remediating learning deficits through perceptual-motor training; some even supported such training over academic remediation (Mann, 1979). For example, Kephart stated the following in his classic 1960 text, *The Slow Learner in the Classroom:*

> It is logical to suppose that even in "pure thought" activities, the muscular basis of behavior is not lost but still provides the foundation for these higher activities. Pure thought activities are based on the ability of the organism to respond mus-

cularly just as the lower responses of simpler experimental tasks are based on motor abilities. There is evidence that the efficiency of the higher thought processes
can be no better than the basic motor abilities upon which they are based. (p. 81)

As was noted earlier, Cruickshank (1975) advocated a minimum of thirty minutes of motor training daily for students with learning disabilities.

The result of this orientation was intervention programs based on remediating
the deficit processes. Many classes for students with learning disabilities focused
on remediating deficits in the basic learning processes and their related skill areas
rather than directly remediating the academic deficit. It was thought that once
these basic processing areas were remediated, then the student would be able to
benefit from academic instruction. Classes were used where students would work
not on their academic deficit areas but on their basic learning processing deficits
(Hammill, 1993). Some of the activities used included students walking up and
down a balance beam, visually tracking a ball on the end of a string, and using
visual-motor paper-pencil work sheets to work on visual motor skill deficits.
Connecting dots and replicating geometric designs are examples of activities
related to such paper-pencil tasks. These types of activities were used to remediate processing deficits of students identified as having learning disabilities.

Kephart (1971) promoted an intervention program using such an approach.
In his focus on perceptual-motor training, Kephart suggested the following
types of activities:

• *Walking board.* Students would walk on a walking board, or balance
beam, to improve their general balance. Students would walk forward, back-
ward, and sidewise. Finally the student would learn how to turn and even
bounce on the board.

• *Balance board.* A balance board is a 16" x 16" board that was used to help
students "pinpoint the center of gravity of his body, and through requiring him
to maintain both fore-and-aft and left-to-right balance, we can offer him a more
dynamic problem" than posed with the walking board. Students would rock the
board in all directions, enabling them to develop a better sense of balance.

• *Trampoline.* A trampoline was used to help students develop coordination
and muscular control. It was thought that using the trampoline would also help
the student develop balance and develop a body image of himself.

• *Angels-in-the-snow.* This activity would require students to lie on their
backs and move their arms and legs in various sequences. The purpose of the
activity was to help students learn laterality and increase body image.

In addition to these activities, Kephart (1971) advocated that students work
on their hand-eye coordination, first learning to follow their hand visually, then
learning how to trace and scribble using large hand movements. Kephart also
thought that teachers should remediate the ocular control of students, using
such activities as having the child visually follow the eraser on a pencil. Finally,
Kephart encouraged teachers to use chalkboard training, where the child works
at the chalkboard on activities that supposedly assist him in developing directionality, copying, and fine motor skills. These types of activities advocated by

Kephart were all based on his theory that the foundations of achievement were motor and the way to remediate problems experienced by children, including academic problems, was in working with their perceptual-motor deficit areas.

Many leaders in the field of learning disabilities advocated the process approach. These included Marianne Frostig, Gerald Getman, Newell Kephart, and Ray Barsch (Johnson and Myklebust, 1967). Table 1.3 summarizes some of the contributions made by these individuals. One result of the process approach was the development of tests, remediation materials, remediation kits, and teacher training programs that focused on process intervention. One test used a great deal that resulted in many different training materials developed to coincide with the components of the test was the Illinois Test of Psycholinguistic Abilities (ITPA). The ITPA, developed by Kirk, et al. (1968) was an individually administered, norm-referenced test designed to "measure a child's relative ability to understand, process, and produce both verbal and nonverbal language" (Salvia and Ysseldyke, 1985).

The ITPA consisted of twelve subtests, including (Anderson and Novina, 1973):

1. Auditory reception
2. Visual reception

TABLE 1.3	
Contributions Made by Some Early Professionals in Learning Disabilities	
Kephart	• wrote *The Slow Learner in the Classroom*
	• emphasized large motor activities
	• described the perceptual-motor match
	• provided numerous activities for children
	• developed the Purdue Perceptual Motor Survey
Frostig	• focused on fine motor activities
	• developed the Developmental Test of Visual Perception
	• developed numerous activities and worksheets aimed at improving perceptual-motor skills
Barsch	• developed his movigenic theory in 1967 based on belief that learning was related to motor skills
	• developed curriculum that focused on movement education
Getman	• targeted vision problems and their relationship to learning problems
	• developed a visumotor intervention model
	• focused on visual development and learning
	• learning tasks very sequential and interdependent

3. Auditory association
4. Visual association
5. Verbal expression
6. Manual expression
7. Grammatic closure
8. Auditory closure
9. Sound blending
10. Visual closure
11. Auditory sequential memory
12. Visual sequential memory

Many programs for students with learning disabilities were based on performances on the ITPA. The ITPA was administered and remedial programs were developed that focused on student's strengths and weaknesses. Giles and Bush (1969) even developed a book of activities keyed to subtest items of the ITPA. In addition to the ITPA-related activities and materials, Frostig-Horne work sheets were used extensively in classes for students with learning disabilities (Hammill, 1993).

Although accepted by most professionals, a few leaders in the field of special education began to question the efficacy of process training. In the late 1960s and early 1970s, Lester Mann took the unprecedented step of questioning the validity of process training. He was soon joined by many more colleagues with research data that tended to support his views (Becker and Sabatino, 1973; Belmont, Flegenheimer, and Birch, 1973; Bibace and Hancock, 1969). As could be expected, the publication of these research studies, as well as other articles that pointedly questioned the use of process training, resulted in a major polarization of the field of learning disabilities. Professionals found themselves either supporting process training or questioning the approach.

The debate over process training raged through the 1970s, but had largely subsided by the early 1980s. The result of the debate was a reversal of the use of process interventions. Tests, materials, and methods based on the process training approach were rapidly replaced by more direct instruction methods related to specific academic deficits. The resolution of this debate was no small factor in the field of learning disabilities; indeed, the resolution of this controversy allowed the field of learning disabilities to move forward. It created a situation where the field could be viewed as more legitimate, after having undergone such self scrutiny.

Although many of the process-oriented approaches were replaced by other approaches (Kavale and Mattson, 1983; Mann, 1971; Ysseldyke, 1973), the contribution of those advocating these methods to the field of learning disabilities cannot be underestimated. Don Hammill, one of the leaders in raising questions about many of their methods, said about this group of individuals, "There would have been no field of learning disabilities without those people."

Furthermore, he stated, that "it was only their efforts that brought us this far through the 60's and 70's" (Hammill, 1979). The lesson learned from the debate over process training was that conflicts that develop in a particular field do not have to be totally destructive. In the case of learning disabilities, the conflict resulted in a stronger field of study.

The early years of the learning disabilities field included a great deal of activity that attempted to develop a better understanding of the science of learning disabilities. Although the period ended with continued confusion over definition, etiology, and intervention approaches, the period was probably most characterized by the widespread adoption of the process-training approach followed by intense scrutiny and eventual decline of this methodology. Criterion-referenced testing and task analysis began to be used in place of processed approaches. This shift, plus the passage of major federal legislation had a profound impact on further development of the field of learning disabilities. Table 1.4 summarizes some of the actions that occurred during this period.

Modern Phase

The 1990s have seen a continuously changing landscape regarding the education and training of individuals with learning disabilities. Changes have occurred related to the way students with learning disabilities are educated in public schools, as well as the initiation and expansion of working with adults with learning disabilities in employment and other areas. There are several areas where significant changes continue to be made in the field of learning disabilities, and other issues that appear to be emerging that will impact on learning disabilities over the next several years.

TABLE 1.4

Summary of Important Activities in the Early Development Phase

- Samuel Kirk coined the term learning disabilities in 1963.
- Following 1963, the field became more focused on research, advocacy, and services.
- Professional and advocacy organizations grew rapidly (CLD, 1967; DLD, 1982; Orton Dyslexia Society, 1949; LDA, 1963; NJCLD, 1975).
- Legislation was passed that played a major role in services for individuals with learning disabilities (P.L. 94-142, 1975; Section 504, 1973; ADA, 1990).
- Educational services were significantly expanded.
- A wide variety of different professionals became involved in the field of learning disabilities.
- The resolution of a paradigm dispute related to process training was accomplished.

Generic services Beginning in the 1980s, and gaining momentum during the past several years, was the change from categorical to noncategorical or generic services for children with disabilities. Special education has long been a system based on *categories of disabilities*. Children have been identified and served on the basis of their having mental retardation, learning disabilities, emotional disturbance, or other specific category of disability. Public Law 94-142 and its subsequent re-authorizations (e.g. IDEA) was originally, and remains to a large extent, a categorical law. Children are served as a result of their being identified as having a recognized disability, under the law. Children who may need special education, but who do not fit into one of the recognized disability categories, are generally not eligible for special education services funded by IDEA.

Although children have to meet the categorical eligibility requirement of IDEA to be eligible for special education services, once they are determined eligible, they may be served noncategorically. Many states have moved to this type of service delivery system where students are provided services based on their needs rather than clinical labels. Reasons cited by proponents of a generic services model include (Smith, Price, and Marsh, 1986):

1. *Confusing definitions.* Many definitions used to describe learning disabilities, as well as some other disabilities, are confusing. As noted earlier in this chapter, confusing and vague definitions of learning disabilities have been one of the reasons for the problems besetting the learning disabilities field. If definitions of different categorical groups of disabilities are confusing, advocates for generic services argue that they should not be used to distinguish services.

2. *Similar etiologies.* Many of the causes of learning disabilities are the same as causes for mild mental retardation and other disabilities. Neurological dysfunction, an assumption made as the basis for learning disabilities, can also result in mental retardation, cerebral palsy, and a variety of other conditions.

3. *Social and behavioral characteristics.* When reviewing the characteristics of students with learning disabilities, the similarity of these characteristics with students who have other disabilities becomes apparent. Below average academic achievement, poor social skills, and behavioral problems are common among students with learning disabilities and several other disabilities.

4. *Similar instructional methods.* Many of the instructional methods that are effective for children classified as having a learning disability often work very well with children with other disabilities, as well as children without disabilities. Many of the methods that are effective with children with learning disabilities, such as a multisensory approach, are also effective with other students.

The trend to provide services for children based on needs rather than clinical label will likely continue. Section 504 of the Rehabilitation Act of 1973, and the Americans with Disabilities Act, two major federal legislative acts, define disabilities and determine eligibility for services and protections using a functional rather than a categorical definition of disability (Streett and Smith, 1996).

*The social and behavioral characteristics of stu-
dents with learning disabilities are similar to those
with other types of disabilities.*

Inclusion A current movement having a significant impact on services to children
with learning disabilities is inclusion. Beginning in the 1980s many professionals
and advocates for students with learning disabilities called for more fully including students with disabilities in general education classrooms. The movement,
named the Regular Education Initiative (REI), called for dismantling the dual
system of education, one for students with disabilities and another for students
without disabilities. The REI differed significantly from the mainstreaming model
which was implemented in the late 1970s as a result of Public Law 94–142.
Mainstreaming called for students with disabilities to be educated with their
nondisabled peers as much as appropriate. This represented a major shift from
previous service systems which had segregated students with disabilities from
their nondisabled peers most of the time. Still, the mainstreaming model suggests
that students with disabilities are placed in special education programs and *mainstreamed* into general classrooms as much as is appropriate (Smith, et al., 1995).

The REI model, which later evolved into the current inclusion movement,
emphasized that the student should be placed in the general education setting
and served in that setting with special supports whenever appropriate. The
emphasis was on the assumed placement of the student. With mainstreaming
the focus was the special education classroom; with inclusion the focus is the
general education classroom.

The inclusion movement has created major controversy in the field of learning disabilities. Many professionals and advocates for students with learning disabilities argue that these students will get *lost* in general education classrooms and that the gains made during the past twenty years will quickly evaporate. Regardless of the ultimate outcome of the inclusion movement, it continues to be a major force in placement and education of children with learning disabilities and will likely expand in the future (Smith, et al., 1995).

New Educational Models

The Modern phase has seen the adoption of several contemporary models for teaching students with learning disabilities. These include the cognitive, or information processing model, cognitive-behavioral model, and constructivist model. The cognitive model, heavily influenced by Piaget, focuses on the mental processes and the student's ability to manipulate these processes. Proponents of cognitive intervention "emphasize (1) guiding students while they are learning, (2) relating instructional activities to students' prior experiences, and (3) encouraging students to use strategies for solving problems" (Hallahan, et al., 1996, p. 144). The use of rehearsal and mnemonics are two examples of techniques used in the cognitive model.

The cognitive-behavioral model applies behavior analysis to the cognitive approach. It stresses self-control, including self-monitoring, self-assessment, self-recording, and self-reinforcement (Hallahan, et al., 1996). Barkley (1990) noted that regarding the use of cognitive-behavioral approach with children with attention deficits, teachers should encourage students to talk to themselves regarding immediate problems and the generation of solutions to those problems. The constructivist model, often referred to as the holistic approach, stresses learning going from the whole to parts of the whole (Poplin, 1988). Therefore, a common approach to teaching reading using this model would be to use children's literature, not basal readers.

▶ EMERGING ISSUES AND DIRECTIONS

The field of learning disabilities is at a "critical juncture" (Moats and Lyon, 1993). Numerous issues remain controversial and crucial to the continued success of the learning disabilities movement that need to be resolved. Without resolution, the field of learning disabilities could change dramatically or even cease to exist. The following discussion presents several of the issues that need to be addressed by professionals, advocates, and persons with learning disabilities.

Defining Learning Disabilities

One of the most confusing areas of learning disabilities that needs to be resolved is *definition*. Moats and Lyon (1993) concluded that the definition of learning disabilities used in Public Law 94-142 was extremely vague and confusing. In their discussion about the definition, they noted that the definition "is impotent with respect to providing objective guidelines and criteria for distinguishing individuals with LD from those with other primary handicaps or generalized learning difficulties." (p. 284) They further stated that "our persistent use of vague, ambiguous, exclusionary, and nonvalidated definitions of LD continue to get us into trouble in this regard." (p. 283) These kinds of issues result in very little consensus among interested parties in defining learning disabilities, and result in a wide variety of answers to the question: What is learning disabilities? (Kavale, Forness, and Lorsbach, 1991).

Although better definitions continue to evolve, a new definition of learning disabilities needs to be developed and adopted by the majority of professionals providing services to individuals with this disability. Schools, vocational rehabilitation agencies, and other groups must develop a definition that is less vague, less ambiguous, and less exclusionary. The definition should be one that can easily be understood not only by the various groups of individuals involved in learning disabilities, including members of the medical profession, teachers, vocational rehabilitation counselors, parents, and individuals who have learning disabilities. Chapter 2 provides an extensive discussion of the definition of learning disabilities and presents a number of different ways to define the disability.

Identification of Individuals with Learning Disabilities

A direct result of the nebulous definitions of learning disabilities is the lack of a systematic method for identifying individuals with this disability. The current overidentification of students who are underachievers reflects the need for better ways of defining and identifying students with learning disabilities. Since each state can develop its own operational criteria for identifying students with this disability, students may be classified as having a learning disability in one state, only to lose such a classification in another (Moats and Lyon, 1993). Similarly, an adult may be provided vocational rehabilitation services in one state and lose those services after moving to another state and being determining ineligible. Until a uniform method of defining and identifying individuals with learning disabilities is developed, the field will remain in a state of confusion. Although the field has seen incredible growth over the past twenty years, "it is unlikely to continue unabated unless there is a more logical rational means of defining LD." (Kavale, Forness, and Lorsbach, 1991, p. 257)

A key element in finding an acceptable definition for learning disabilities is to establish a method for differentiating learning disabilities from underachievement. Until this is accomplished, continuous problems will beset the field. For example, much of the research that purports to focus on learning disabilities actually targets learning problems. "Failure to differentiate underachievement caused by neurological dysfunctioning from that caused by other factors has been cited specifically as a major deterrent to important lines of research and theory and is certainly a threat to the very integrity of the LD field." (Adelman, 1992, p. 17)

A problem in the differentiation between learning disabilities and underachievement that does not have a neurological basis is assessment of central nervous system dysfunction. Instruments that supposedly measure such dysfunction simply lack the validity necessary to make such a diagnosis. The result is that many persons are classified as having a learning disability, not because of a valid assessment of neurological dysfunction, but because of severe underachievement. This means that many of the children and adults classified as learning disabled may not actually have a learning disability (Adelman, 1992). Chapter 3 presents information regarding the assessment and identification of individuals with learning disabilities.

Generic/Noncategorical Movement

As noted above, during the 1980s, a movement to identify and provide services to students with disabilities that de-emphasized clinical categories was initiated. Continued emphasis on generic or noncategorical identification could have a major impact on the field of learning disabilities. In many states, the learning disabilities category has already been absorbed into a generic disability category considered to be *mildly disabled*. This trend has occurred even though some students with learning disabilities might be considered to have a severe disability. While the continuation of this trend could result in learning disabilities losing its identity as a distinct category, development of the *science* of learning disabilities to include a validated process for identifying individuals and providing appropriate intervention services will support the continuation of the learning disability category.

Intervention

Following problems of definition and identification comes issues related to intervention. As noted earlier, there have been many different approaches to remediating learning disabilities. Many of these approaches have been "zealously promoted, summarily attacked, and sometimes discredited for failing to produce miracle cures" (Moats and Lyon, 1993, p. 283). Table 1.5 lists some of the major approaches that have been promoted and their corresponding professional advocates. Many of these intervention models have been discarded while others continue to be used.

Related to the instructional methods used with students with learning disabilities is the issue of educational placement. Currently, inclusion is the trend for placing students with all types of disabilities, including learning disabilities. It appears that this trend will continue to be debated and implemented. No doubt inclusion will have an impact on learning disabilities. Chapter 4 discusses programming and placement issues for students with learning disabilities, including inclusion.

Preventive Intervention

Although the genetic nature of learning disabilities is only beginning to be realized, a possible future direction for the field will target preventive intervention for young children with a family history of learning problems even before problems develop (Moats and Lyon, 1993). Preventive intervention is the identifica-

TABLE 1.5	
Major Intervention Approaches and Their Professional Advocates	
Approach	**Professional Advocates**
Perceptual-motor training	Ayres, 1972; Cratty, 1973; Frostig and Maslow, 1973; Kephart, 1971
Psycholinguistic prescription based on ITPA	Bush and Giles, 1969; Kirk and Kirk, 1971
Interactional analysis	Bryan and Bryan, 1978; Kronick, 1976
Criterion-referenced testing and task analysis	Bateman, 1971; Frank, 1973; Siegel, 1972
Holism	Heshusius, 1989; Poplin, 1984
Constructivism	Reid and Stone, 1991

Source: Moats and Lyon, 1993

tion of children who are at-risk for developing learning disabilities and the provision of interventions to help reduce the likelihood for developing these problems. This approach serves numerous purposes, including: (1) reducing the need to label children with any disability label, including learning disability; (2) reducing the number of students identified as having a learning disability; and (3) reducing the need for students to receive specialized intervention throughout their school time. While preventive intervention will not always alleviate the problem, it is possible that the process may result in many children being spared from unnecessary identification and labeling, while still having their needs met.

Differentiation of Science and Public Policy

Moats and Lyon (1993) suggested that in the future, leaders in the field of learning disabilities differentiate between science and public policy. An example they give is in the area of terminology. Whereas the umbrella term, *learning disabilities*, might be appropriate in areas regarding policy, for scientific purposes, specific disorders should be identified and utilized. For example, general policies can easily be focused on large groups of individuals with generic learning problems. Legislation mandating services, policies for services by rehabilitation agencies, and procedures used in public schools to identify and provide services for children are examples. However, regarding research issues, the category of learning disabilities is so diverse that more specific descriptions of populations need to be provided. Due to the great diversity of persons with learning disabilities, research results can only be generalized cautiously. Defining the specific population in studies will enable consumers of the research information to apply the results to an appropriate group of individuals. This will facilitate a more valid research agenda, with results being more germane to the field of learning disabilities.

Research in Treatment Effectiveness

Unfortunately, there still is no *science of learning disabilities*. This is because of many of the problems previously discussed, such as definition and eligibility criteria (Swanson, 1991), assessment procedures, and not differentiating between underachievers and those with neurological dysfunction. Regardless of the reason, a science of learning disabilities needs to be developed that can have an impact on treatment and intervention. Teachers need to know that specific methods are likely effective with children who display a particular specific disability or deficit. Moats and Lyon (1993) noted that until a science of intervention for children with "well-defined" learning disabilities is available, then intervention methodologies without any scientific basis will continue to proliferate, costing children and adults with learning disabilities, and professionals in the field, a great deal of time and effort. For example, had there been a more valid science of learning disabilities, it is unlikely the field would have adopted, so universally, the process training approach used in the 1970s.

Although there is no science of learning disabilities, largely because of definitional and eligibility problems, there is a large set of intervention approaches available, many of which are effective with some children labeled as learning-disabled. These include an information processing model, cognitive-behavioral model, and task-analytic model (Hallahan, et al., 1996). Therefore, rather than having to invent or discover new methods, what is needed is for educators and researchers to determine which methods are effective with children who display specific needs, put those into understandable formats, and disseminate them to practitioners (Lovitt, 1992).

One approach to the development of effective intervention methods would be to adopt the continuum of programs for children with learning disabilities provided by Adelman (1992). In this continuum, a variety of different activities are listed as they apply to a stage on the intervention continuum. Adelman's view is that regardless of the specific intervention, social, economic, political, and cultural factors must always be a consideration. Table 1.6 depicts Adelman's continuum.

Teacher Training

Teacher training has long been considered a critical component in any specialized area of education or teaching. "The successful preparation of teachers and clinicians to address the needs of individuals with learning disabilities is dependent to a large extent on our ability to identify and define the declarative and procedural knowledge required of practitioners for producing learning and generalization in children" (Moats and Lyon, 1993, p. 290). Until this is accomplished, teacher preparation for students with learning disabilities will remain in some confusion.

Another factor influencing teacher training is the movement toward noncategorical services. The result of this trend is that many teacher training institutions only train teachers to work with *mildly disabled* students rather than students specifically diagnosed as having learning disabilities. The continuation of this

A Continuum of Programs for Learning, Behavior, and Socioemotional Problems

Continuum	Types of Activities
Prevention ↑	I. Primary prevention to promote and maintain • safety • physical and mental health (beginning with family planning)
Early-age Intervention	II. Preschool programs • day care • parent education • early education (encompassing a focus on psychosocial and mental health problems)
	III. Early school adjustment • personalization in primary grades • parent participation in problem solving • comprehensive psychosocial and mental health programs (school-based)
Early-after-onset Intervention	IV. Improvement of ongoing regular support • specified remedial role for regular classroom teachers • parent involvement • comprehensive psychosocial and mental health programs (school-based—all grades)
	V. Augmentation of regular support • academic (e.g., reading teachers, computer aided instruction, volunteer tutors) • psychosocial (e.g., staff and peer counselors, crisis teams)
	VI. Specialized staff development and interventions prior to referral for special education and other intensive treatments • staff training/consultation • short-term specialized interventions
Treatment for Chronic Problems ↓	VII. System change and intensive treatment • rehabilitation of existing programs • special education services • referral to and coordination with community mental health services

Source: Adelman, H.S. (1992). LD: The next 25 years. *Journal of Learning Disabilities*, 25, p. 21. Used with permission.

trend makes it imperative that teacher educators include in their coursework topics specifically related to successful intervention programs for students with learning disabilities. While these strategies might also work for students with other disabilities, they must be included in generic teacher training programs to ensure that teachers are prepared to teach students with learning disabilities.

Early Identification and Intervention

Early identification of children with disabilities followed by appropriate interventions is acknowledged as an excellent method of dealing with problems created by learning disabilities. Efforts at identifying young children with learning disabilities are relatively new because of the nature of the disability. However, there is a trend to develop better means of determining risk factors for some children and appropriate interventions. Chapter 6 provides an extensive review of methods to identify and provide appropriate services for young children with learning disabilities.

Transition Services

The 1990 amendments to Public Law 94-142, the Individuals with Disabilities Education Act (IDEA), requires schools to implement transition programming for students with disabilities, including those with learning disabilities. The need for planning for the future of individuals with disabilities has been a focus of special education and adult service providers for many years. However, there has been little focus on transition for students with learning disabilities. As noted by Blalock and Patton (1996), a missing piece in services for students with learning disabilities has been "the systematic consideration of what students need to functional successfully as adults" (p. 7).

Transition planning for students with learning disabilities has lagged behind planning for students with other disabilities for a variety of reasons. These include the myths that young adults with learning disabilities do not experience difficulties, that this group of individuals can achieve basic academic competencies, that the intellectual functioning level for this group is average to above average, and the fact that learning disabilities are "hidden" disabilities (Dunn, 1996). Many of these myths are finally being set aside, and transition planning for students with learning disabilities is being realized as more important. Evidence of this current interest can be seen in a two volume special edition of the *Journal of Learning Disabilities* which focuses on transition (see volume 29, numbers 1 and 2). Interest in transition planning will likely continue to increase over the next several years. Chapter 7 on adolescents and transition will provide a great deal of information on this very important practice for students with learning disabilities.

Adult Services

Adults with learning disabilities have not always been involved with vocational rehabilitation or any other adult service agency. In fact, "until relatively recently, most services afforded to persons with learning disabilities terminated when they exited from high school" (Patton and Polloway, 1996, p. 9). For example, although federal vocational rehabilitation programs have provided services to individuals with disabilities to assist them with employment for more than seventy years, it was not until 1981 that such services were made available for adults with learning disabilities. Similarly, postsecondary educational opportunities and social service supports were not available for adults with learning disabilities until recently.

For most of the twentieth century, students with learning disabilities interested in attending postsecondary education and training programs found it very difficult because of their disability. While many universities continue to expect students with learning disabilities to succeed "on their own," more and more universities, as well as other postsecondary educational institutions, have developed programs to address the specific needs of students with learning disabilities (Patton and Polloway, 1996). The response is that more and more individuals with learning disabilities are pursuing postsecondary education. While this is due, in part, to the field recognizing the needs of these students, it is also the result of Section 504 of the Rehabilitation Act of 1973, which mandates equal opportunities for persons with disabilities (Brinckerhoff, Shaw, and McGuire, 1996), and the Americans with Disabilities Act, passed in 1990 (Smith, et al., 1995).

Rehabilitation services for this group of individuals, similar to postsecondary educational services, were not provided until recently. Rehabilitation services were originally developed to serve disabled World War I veterans through the Soldier's Rehabilitation Act of 1918 (Smith, Price, and Marsh, 1986). From this legislation evolved the current vocational rehabilitation services which focus their efforts on individuals with physical disabilities and mental retardation. Learning disabilities was not considered a disability covered by vocational rehabilitation until the 1980s. Between 1983 and 1988, the number of vocational rehabilitation *clients* with learning disabilities actually tripled (Dowdy, Smith, and Nowell, 1996).

Since beginning to provide such services, the Federal Rehabilitation Services Administration (RSA) has experienced some of the same problems experienced by schools in their efforts to meet the needs of this group. RSA has struggled in its efforts to define learning disabilities, determine diagnostic criteria, develop appropriate eligibility requirements, and establish policies for its counselors to use (Dowdy and Smith, 1994; Dowdy, Smith, and Nowell, 1992). Although much work needs to be done in the area of vocational rehabilitation and learning disabilities, the future trend appears to be the continued recognition by RSA of the unique needs of this population and continued services.

The future for adults with learning disabilities continues to evolve. Shifts of policies in the 1980s regarding this population will likely continue into the 1990s and beyond. However, although gains by this group of individuals will likely continue, they will undoubtedly be challenged. One result of such challenges will be the expansion of self-advocacy among adults with learning disabilities. Self-advocates, as well as others who advocate for them, will continue to push for improved services for this group of individuals. Chapter 8 focuses entirely on adults with learning disabilities.

SUMMARY

This chapter has provided a general introduction to the field of learning disabilities. The following points summarize the major areas included in the chapter:

- Learning disabilities was not recognized as a disability category until the 1960s.
- A variety of labels, including brain-damaged, brain-injured, and minimal brain dysfunction were used to classify children before the term learning disabilities was adopted.
- Many parents did not want their children labeled with a term that included a reference to brain damage.
- In the 1980s, efforts were made to cap the number of children eligible for federal funds through P.L. 94-142.
- The history of learning disabilities can be traced to early studies of aphasia in the early nineteenth century.
- Brain injured veterans of wars served as subjects for much of the early research related to brain functions.
- Gall, Broca, and Wernicke were early scientists who drew important conclusions about the relationship of parts of the brain and certain brain functions.
- In 1917, Hinshelwood, a Scottish ophthalmologist, first reported on word-blindness in the medical literature.
- An early concern was that people would confuse dyslexia and mental deficiency.
- Strauss syndrome was a condition described by Strauss and Lehtinen that dealt with children who were hyperactive, distractible, and had motor and academic problems.
- Sam Kirk coined the term learning disabilities in 1963 to bring consolidation among different groups interested in children with these types of problems.
- The development of professional and advocacy organizations facilitated the LD movement.
- Public Law 94-142 had a profound, positive impact on learning disabilities.
- A major paradigm shift in the 1970s, away from process-oriented theories, gave validity to the field of learning disabilities.
- The movement to generic over categorical services has impacted and will continue to impact learning disabilities.
- Better methods of defining and determining eligibility for programs for individuals with learning disabilities need to be developed.
- Adult services for individuals with learning disabilities have expanded greatly over the past ten years and will continue to evolve.

Chapter 2

CONCEPTUAL ISSUES IN DEFINING LEARNING DISABILITIES

The objectives for this chapter are as follows:

▶ To know the early definitions of learning disabilities.

▶ To understand the differences of early definitions of learning disabilities.

▶ To know the current definition used in the Individuals with Disabilities Education Act (IDEA).

▶ To describe the concerns expressed by many professionals about the federal definition of learning disabilities.

▶ To understand the reason for the National Joint Committee on Learning Disabilities Definition to develop its own definition of learning disabilities.

▶ To know the NJCLD and LDA definitions of learning disabilities.

▶ To know the revised NJCLD definition of learning disabilities.

▶ To describe the common factors found in the majority of definitions of learning disabilities.

▶ To know the prevalence of learning disabilities.

What the Experts Say

Before studying this chapter on the theoretical development of the definition of learning disabilities, listen to the experts! Read what successful adults with learning disabilities say when asked, "What is a learning disability?"

"It is any interruption in the learning process that makes it difficult for that person to achieve goals."

"When the brain is not programmed to process information like most people's brains are programmed."

"It is an inability because of natural causes with a person to accomplish thought processes, speech and language processes, educational processes."

"Not mental retardation, higher IQ, processing problem, you work hard and you fail."

"Someone who can't concentrate on more than one thing at a time. Difficult time breaking your train of thoughts, analyzing different things."

"Not able to learn in the conventional way because of a technical problem in their brains that makes them unable to visually or orally remember or both."

"Difficult time with written word, comprehension, handling numbers... time factor... slow reader, poor decoding, poor writing."

"Difficulty with learning."

"A difficulty, sometimes with an inability, to achieve at one's potential."

"Smarter than can illustrate to others."

"Not learning disabled, it's learning different."

"Not a learning disability, but a teaching disability."

"Some areas of the brain of the neuropathways are jumbled, missing, in a mess, kind of stretched."

The definitions above were selected from an article by Reiff, Gerber, and Ginsberg (1993). Definitions of learning disabilities from adults with learning disabilities: The insiders' perspectives. *Learning Disabilities Quarterly, 16* pp. 115–125.

The history of learning disabilities discussed in Chapter 1 reveals a complex evolution of theories proposed by individuals from a variety of professional backgrounds. Each professional group typically proposed a definition and expected characteristics to explain the *unexpected underachievement* in the individuals they were studying. Minimal brain dysfunction, brain injury, dyslexia, psychoneurological learning disorders, and perceptual handicaps were some of the terms used to describe the condition now referred to as a learning disability. Even though the history of learning disabilities can be traced back to these early works of physicians and other professionals, the term learning disabilities and the definitions proposed to define that term really began in the 1960s with a definition proposed by Samuel Kirk (1962).

In comparison to other areas of disabilities, the field of learning disabilities has had a relatively short history. During the last thirty years there have been a series of lively debates on a number of issues, keeping learning disabilities a dynamic, exciting profession. However, a recent investigation by Hammill (1990) suggests that consensus is finally near on the issue of definition.

Hammill studied twenty-eight textbooks dealing with learning disabilities and discovered eleven different definitions of learning disabilities cited. He suggests that the four definitions developed since 1977 (those developed by the United States Department of Education, the National Joint Committee on Learning Disabilities, the Learning Disabilities Association of America, and the Interagency Committee on Learning Disabilities) are in fundamental agreement on the basic components. A review of recent literature on definition finds Hammill's substantive work in this area to be extensively cited (Shaw, Cullen, McGuire, Brinkerhoff, 1995; Reiff, Gerber, Ginsberg, 1993; Swanson and Christie, 1995, Doris, 1993); therefore, Hammill's study will be used as the primary source to study the development of the definition of learning disabilities. This chapter will briefly trace the early definitions that contributed to the current definitions, focus on the strengths and limitations of each of the four most recent definitions, and identify the basic primary elements or characteristics that appear across these definitions. This chapter will fully explore the most defensible, current definition of learning disabilities and will address the current issues surrounding the definition of learning disabilities.

▶ EARLY DEFINITIONS

The two most influential early definitions of learning disabilities were written by Kirk (1962) and Bateman (1965). Each of these contained elements that strongly influenced later definitions; however, the definitions as a whole were criticized and eventually the authors themselves ceased to advocate their adoption (Sentura, 1985; Hammill, 1990). The influence that these definitions had on the field of learning disabilities makes it important to discuss the content and the strengths and limitations of each.

In 1962 Kirk defined learning disabilities in his textbook, *Educating Exceptional Children*. This definition stated

> A learning disability refers to a retardation, disorder, or delayed development in one or more of the processes of speech, language, reading, writing, arithmetic, or other school subjects resulting from a psychological handicap caused by a possible cerebral dysfunction and/or emotional or behavioral disturbances. It is not the result of mental retardation, sensory deprivation, or cultural and instructional factors. (Kirk, 1962, p. 263)

The concepts which continued to appear in later definitions include references to delays in processes and the manifestation of those delays in speech, language, and academic subjects. Kirk also referred to the etiology of learning disabilities as cerebral dysfunction and the exclusion of other factors such as mental retardation as the cause of learning disabilities. These concepts continue to be incorporated in a general sense in more recent definitions.

When Kirk became the first director of the then Division for Handicapped Children in the U.S. Office of Education, he chaired the National Advisory Committee on Handicapped Children (NACHC), a committee created to guide the funding of special education programs. His influence as leader of that committee resulted in the development of a definition for learning disabilities in 1968 that closely resembles Kirk's early definition. This definition was important because it was incorporated into federal law in the Learning Disabilities Act of 1969 and was used as the model in most states as they began to serve children with learning disabilities. It was also the basis for the 1977 United States Office of Education (USOE) definition cited originally in Public Law 94-142. The NACHC definition reads

> Children with special (specific) learning disabilities exhibit a disorder in one or more of the basic psychological processes involved in understanding or in using spoken and written language. These may be manifested in disorders of listening, thinking, talking, reading, writing, spelling, or arithmetic. They include conditions which have been referred to as perceptual handicaps, brain injury, minimal brain dysfunction, dyslexia, developmental aphasia, etc. They do not include learning problems that are due primarily to visual, hearing, or motor handicaps, to mental retardation, emotional disturbance, or to environmental disadvantage. (NACHC, 1968, p. 34)

There were three important differences between Kirk's early definition and the NACHC definition. The word "children" was added to the NACHC definition, targeting this group for funding and services. "Thinking disorders" were included with academic and language deficits as manifestations of learning disabilities, and "emotional disturbance" was moved from being a cause of learning disabilities as in Kirk's definition (1962) to being *excluded* as a primary cause in this definition.

Another important early definition was proposed by Barbara Bateman (1965). Her definition contained the innovative concept of a discrepancy between aptitude and achievement. The Bateman definition states

> Children who have learning disorders are those who manifest an educationally significant discrepancy between their estimated intellectual potential and actual level of performance related to basic disorders in the learning process, which may or may not be accompanied by demonstrable central nervous system dysfunction and which

are not secondary to generalized mental retardation, educational or cultural deprivation, severe emotional disturbance, or sensory loss. (Bateman, 1965, p. 220)

This definition introduced the concept of *unexpected underachievement* in
children. Bateman also referred to a disorder in learning processes; however,
she noted that there may or may not be a central nervous system dysfunction
that is measurable. Bateman also included an exclusion clause. Although her
definition was not widely accepted, the concept of a significant discrepancy was
used extensively in the criteria for identification of learning disabilities later
proposed by the U.S. Office of Education (Hammill, 1990).

▶ CURRENT DEFINITIONS

In 1976 the U.S. Office of Education attempted to improve the NACHC definition by combining components from that definition with Bateman's concept of
a severe discrepancy. It is repeated below to demonstrate the significant change
that occurred between this definition and the one finally approved and published the next year. This proposed definition reads

> A specific learning disability may be found if a child has a severe discrepancy between
> achievement and intellectual ability in one or more of several areas: oral expression,
> written expression, listening comprehension or reading comprehension, basic reading
> skills, mathematics calculation, mathematics reasoning, or spelling. A "severe dis-
> crepancy" is defined to exist when achievement in one or more of the areas falls at or
> below 50 percent of the child's expected achievement level, when age and previous
> educational experiences are taken into consideration. (USOE, 1976, p. 52405)

This definition led to proposed regulations identifying a complex formula to
be used for calculating the discrepancy between intelligence and achievement.
The proposed definition was presented across the nation during a year-long
period of public hearings. During this time there was heated debate and criticism for applying a mathematical formula to the identification process. Over
nine hundred written statements were received. Finally, these proposed regulations were dropped and the result was a significantly different definition proposed by the federal government in 1977.

The U.S. Office of Education Definition (1977)

This definition published in the *Federal Register* reads

> The term "specific learning disability" means a disorder in one or more of the ba-
> sic psychological processes involved in understanding or in using language, spo-
> ken or written, which may manifest itself in an imperfect ability to listen, speak,
> read, write, spell, or to do mathematical calculations. The term includes such con-
> ditions such as perceptual handicaps, brain injury, minimal brain dysfunction,
> dyslexia, and developmental aphasia. The term does not include children who
> have learning disabilities which are primarily the result of visual, hearing, or mo-
> tor handicaps, or mental retardation, or emotional disturbance or of environ-
> mental, cultural, or economic disadvantage. (USOE, 1977, p. 65083)

Basically this same definition was first incorporated into the Learning Disabilities Act of 1969, into Public Law 94-142, the Education for All Handicapped Children Act of 1975, and into the reauthorization of the Education of the Handicapped Act of 1986. Mercer, King-Sears, and Mercer (1990) suggest that the 1977 federal definition continues to be the most widely used across the states. This is probably because it is the one used repeatedly by federal funding agencies. However, Hammill (1990, p. 77) proposes that this definition was developed primarily to guide funding practices for the federal government and was never intended to serve as a "comprehensive theoretical statement about the nature of learning disabilities."

In 1977 an issue of the *Federal Register* was published to operationalize the definition of learning disabilities and to provide the specific criteria for the identification of a learning disability. The criteria published relied heavily on the concept of a discrepancy between ability and achievement as proposed by Bateman. The criteria for identification of specific learning disability are included in Figure 2.1.

FIGURE 2.1

Criteria for Identification of a Specific Learning Disability

Criteria (Section 300.541)

(a) A team may determine that a child has a specific learning disability if—

   (1) The child does not achieve commensurate with his or her age and ability levels in one or more of the areas listed in paragraph (a)(2) of this section, when provided with learning experiences appropriate for the child's age and ability levels; and

   (2) The team finds that a child has a severe discrepancy between achievement and intellectual ability in one or more of the following areas—

      (i) Oral expression;

      (ii) Listening comprehension;

      (iii) Written expression;

      (iv) Basic reading skill;

      (v) Reading comprehension;

      (vi) Mathematics calculation; or

      (vii) Mathematics reasoning.

(b) The team may not identify a child as having a specific learning disability if the severe discrepancy between ability and achievement is primarily a result of—

   (1) A visual, hearing, or motor impairment;

   (2) Mental retardation;

   (3) Emotional disturbance; or

   (4) Environmental, cultural or economic disadvantage. (USOE, 1977, p. 65083)

The fact that the federally published definition of learning disabilities and the federally published criteria for identification of learning disabilities are not parallel have led to confusion in the field. For example, the concept of psychological processing (i.e., auditory perception, visual perception, perceptual motor) that is prominent in the NACHC definition was not addressed at all in the identification procedures. In addition the concept of spelling included in the definition was dropped in the criteria; however, written expression was substituted. Also, a reference to children that had been omitted in the definition was included in the criteria, suggesting that only children can be identified and thus served. Because the criteria for identification (USOE, 1977) were used to determine eligibility for placement, they appear to have had more impact on the field than the actual definition that was published with it (Hammill, 1990). The methods often used to implement these criteria for identification will be described and discussed further in Chapter 3.

Although the appearance of the definition in the federal law added an "aura of officiality" (Hammill, et al., 1988, p. 218) to the field, there was still widespread disagreement and controversy regarding the issue of definition. Finally, in 1981 a group of individuals representing professional organizations having a major interest in learning disabilities organized and formed the National Joint Committee on Learning Disabilities (NJCLD). As noted in Chapter 1, the committee is currently comprised of representatives from nine organizations including the American Speech-Language-Hearing Association (ASHA), the National Association of School Psychologists (NASP), the Association for Children and Adults with Learning Disabilities (ACLD) renamed Learning Disabilities Association of America (LDA), the Council for Learning Disabilities (CLD), the Division for Children with Communication Disorders (DCCD), the Division for Learning Disabilities (DLD) of the Council for Exceptional Children (CEC), the International Reading Association (IRA), the Association on Higher Education and Disability (AHEAD), and the Orton Dyslexia Society (ODS). The representatives agreed that a theoretical statement was needed to specify the characteristics of the conditions called learning disabilities. The NJCLD believed that the federal definitions including the 1968 NACHC definition and the modification of that definition appearing in Public Law 94-142 (1977) had many weaknesses that made it an unacceptable definition to be used as an explanation for the complex condition of a learning disability. In 1981, the NJCLD published a position paper that was revised in 1990 defining the limitations of the federal definition. These issues provided the motivation to create the NJCLD definitions (1981; 1990). The concerns include

1. The federal definition was noted to be frequently misinterpreted. This misinterpretation has led to the erroneous assumption by too many people that individuals with learning disabilities were a homogeneous group and could be assessed and taught in a singular approach. The NJCLD urge the view of LD as a heterogeneous population comprised of various subgroups.

2. The NJCLD was very concerned with the reference to the term "children" appearing in the 1968 definition and again in the criteria for identification of

learning disabilities published in the *Federal Register* in 1977. It is widely accepted that learning disabilities may occur in individuals of all ages. The position paper points out that several organizations have actually changed their name in order to embrace the entire population of individuals with learning disabilities. For example, the parent organization originally named the Association for Children with Learning Disabilities (ACLD) became the Association for Children and Adults with Learning Disabilities and later the Learning Disability Association of America (LDA). Similarly the Division for Learning Disabilities in the Council for Exceptional Children was originally called the Division for Children with Learning Disabilities.

3. The phrase "basic psychological processes" included in the definition generated extensive debate. The intent of the phrase was to acknowledge the intrinsic nature of learning disabilities without emphasizing the neurological focus that had dominated the early study of learning disabilities. The NACHC was attempting to differentiate between unexpected underachievement caused by internal factors (e.g. psychological or neurological) from underachievement which might be the result of poor instruction or cultural deprivation. Unfortunately, the phrase "psychological processes" became synonymous with perceptual motor ability and mental processes that were proposed to be developed or remediated prior to academic instruction. Advocates of this viewpoint were training students' processing abilities such as visual perception, auditory perception, sequencing, etc. By the early 1970s, the literature began to suggest that the direct instruction approach of teaching in the specific areas of underachievement such as writing, reading, and listening was the most effective method (Hammill and Wiederholt, 1974).

4. The reference to spelling in the 94-142 definition is also criticized. It was felt that spelling should be subsumed under the larger concept of written expression and should not be mentioned as a separate area of achievement.

5. The NJCLD felt that the sentence in the earlier definition alluding to a number of conditions that should be included under the term learning disabilities (e.g., perceptual handicaps, brain injury, minimal brain dysfunction, and dyslexia) was no longer necessary. When this definition was developed in the 1960s, so many phrases and terms were being used by different professionals that it was important to state that the term "learning disabilities" would be an umbrella term including all of these various concepts. However, years later, it was confusing to include terms which were no longer being used as an explanation of what LD meant. The NJCLD felt that to include those terms would only invite further controversy, misinterpretation, and confusion in regard to etiology or cause of LD. The NJCLD supported the idea that the basis for learning disabilities is the notion of central nervous system dysfunction.

6. The NJCLD was also concerned about the wording of the NACHC's definition's final sentence, which has been referred to as the *exclusion clause*. This sentence is often misinterpreted to mean that learning disabilities cannot occur in conjunction with other handicapping conditions or in the presence of "environmental, cultural, or economic disadvantage." Although that may not be the orig-

inal intent, it has been widely interpreted in this way. If each word is carefully considered, the current interpretation would be made that a learning disability cannot be the *primary* result of the conditions listed. However, it is then possible for those conditions to exist as a *secondary* condition. For example, an individual with cerebral palsy might demonstrate difficulties in written expression in legibility primarily due to motor difficulties; however, if the individual had difficulty with sentence structure and subject/verb agreement, the written expression deficits would not be explained by the motoric difficulties associated with cerebral palsy. (The concept of concomitant disabilities is discussed extensively in Chapter 12.)

The 1981 National Joint Committee on Learning Disabilities Definition

Although the deliberations of the National Joint Committee on Learning Disabilities included extensive discussions of shortcomings of earlier definitions of learning disabilities, the five listed above were considered the most critical. To address these concerns, the National Joint Committee on Learning Disabilities proposed its first definition in 1981. It was not intended to provide operational criteria for identifying learning disabilities; however, it was proposed as a statement needed to specify the characteristics of the conditions called learning disabilities. This definition reads

> Learning disabilities is a generic term that refers to a heterogeneous group of disorders manifested by significant difficulties in the acquisition and use of listening, speaking, reading, writing, reasoning, or mathematical abilities. These disorders are intrinsic to the individual and presumed to be due to central nervous system dysfunction. Even though a learning disability may occur concomitantly with other handicapping conditions (e.g., sensory impairment, mental retardation, social and emotional disturbance) or environmental influences (e.g., cultural differences, insufficient/inappropriate instruction, psychogenic factors), it is not the direct result of those conditions or influences. (Hammill, et al., 1981, p. 336)

After many years of debate and study, this definition was unanimously approved by the NJCLD in 1981 and was distributed to the members of the organizations in NJCLD for consideration for adoption. Subsequently all organizations represented in the development of the definition approved it except the Learning Disabilities Association of America, the national parent organization. A discussion of the Learning Disabilities Association definition follows.

The Learning Disabilities Association of America Definition

After the leaders of LDA studied and rejected the 1981 NJCLD definition, the organization developed and published the following new definition of its own in the 1986 issue of *ACLD Newsbriefs*.

> Specific learning disabilities is a chronic condition of presumed neurologic origin which selectively interferes with the development, integration, and/or demonstration of verbal or nonverbal abilities. Specific learning disabilities exists as a dis-

tinct handicapping condition and varies in its manifestation and in degree of severity. Throughout life, the condition can affect self- esteem, education, vocation, socialization, and/or daily living activities. (ACLD, 1986, p. 15)

Although this definition basically agrees with the NJCLD definition, according to Hammill (1990) it does differ on two important points. First, the manifestations of the learning disability (e.g., reading, listening, writing) are omitted. The ACLD definition refers to learning disabilities in general as problems of "verbal and/or nonverbal abilities." The explanation for the use of this term suggests that they wanted inclusive terms that would include academic problems as well as conceptual and thinking problems and motor problems. However, Hammill notes (1990) that the omission of math problems, ambiguous vocabulary (i.e., nonverbal abilities and integrating problems), awkward sentence structure, and unusual punctuation make the interpretation very difficult.

Another important omission in the LDA definition is that of an exclusion clause. Without this concept in the definition, it is difficult to determine whether LDA believes in a multihandicapping nature of learning disabilities. It is not clear whether they believe that learning disabilities can coexist with mental retardation, emotional disturbance, or environmental disadvantage. While the definition has good qualities, it is not considered to be a threat to replace either the 1977 U.S. Office of Education definition or the NJCLD definition due to its vagueness in critical areas (Hammill, 1990).

The Interagency Committee on Learning Disabilities Definition (ICLD)

Also in reaction to the NJCLD definition, the ICLD was developed in 1987 to design an improved definition. This committee was constituted by 12 agencies in the Department of Health and Human Services and the Department of Education. Their definition was a modification of the NJCLD definition; the primary difference between the NJCLD definition and the ICLD definition was the addition of social skills to the list of manifestations of the specific learning disabilities in the first sentence. It reads:

Learning disability is a generic term that refers to a heterogeneous group of disorders manifested by significant difficulties in the acquisition and use of listening, speaking, reading, writing, reasoning, or mathematical abilities, or of social skills. These disorders are intrinsic to the individual and presumed to be due to central nervous system dysfunction. Even though a learning disability may occur concomitantly with other handicapping conditions (e.g., sensory impairment, mental retardation, social and emotional disturbance), with socio-environmental influences (e.g., cultural differences, insufficient or inappropriate instruction, psychogenic factors), and especially attention deficit disorder, all of which may cause learning problems, a learning disability is not the direct result of those conditions or influences. (Interagency Committee on Learning Disabilities, 1987, p. 222)

The public reaction to the addition of social skills in a definition of learning disabilities was significant. Concerns were summarized by Silver (1988) as he noted that "someone with significant difficulties with social skills but without deficits in one or more of the other six areas should not be considered learning disabled" (p. 79). It was felt that the addition of social skills was not supported or refuted by research (Gresham and Elliott, 1989). The National Joint Committee on Learning Disabilities did not view the insertion of "social skills" into their definition as an improvement, and responded quickly with a letter to the director of the National Institute of Child Health and Human Development. The following is an excerpt from that letter.

> ...while the NJCLD does not support addition of the phrase "or social skills" to the definition, we do support efforts to clarify the relationship between learning disabilities and social learning problems. We recognize that learning disabilities may significantly affect the individual's patterns of social development and interaction, self-esteem, and activities of daily living. However, the NJCLD does not support the argument that these problems of social and personal adaptation constitute a separate and unique learning disability.
>
> We also are concerned that the designation of social skills as a separate manifestation of learning disability invites the inclusion and the category of individuals with significant psychiatric illness. Such a conclusion will only complicate problems relating to identification, diagnosis, and intervention of children, youth, and adults with learning disabilities. (S. Dublinske, Personal Communication, March 2, 1988)

Hammill (1990) points out that the definition proposed by ICLD was not adopted by the Department of Education for three reasons. First, including social skills would necessitate a rewording in P.L. 94-142. Second, it would increase confusion over eligibility and third, it might serve to increase the number of students placed as learning disabled. Although neither this definition nor the LDA definition is considered a serious contender for national acceptance, they did serve an important function in stimulating NJCLD to reconsider its own definition and make important changes related to the issue of social skills which was brought up by these two groups.

The Revised NJCLD Definition

In 1988 the 1981 NJCLD definition was modified in response to changes in the knowledge base and in reaction to the ICLD definition. The revised definition has been adopted by all organizations in the NJCLD except the Division of Learning Disabilities which has taken no action. This definition reads

> Learning Disabilities is a general term that refers to a heterogeneous group of disorders manifested by significant difficulties in the acquisition and use of listening, speaking, reading, writing, reasoning, or mathematical abilities. These disorders are intrinsic to the individual, presumed to be due to central nervous system dysfunction, and may occur across the lifespan. Problems in self-regulatory behaviors, social perception, and social interaction may exist with learning disabilities but do not by themselves constitute a learning disability. Although learning disability may occur concomitantly with other handicapping conditions

(for example, sensory impairment, mental retardation, serious emotional disturbance) or with extrinsic influences (such as cultural difference, insufficient or inappropriate instruction), they are not the result of those conditions or influences. (NJCLD, 1988, p. 1)

Hammill (1993) provides a phrase by phrase discussion of the new definition of the NJCLD to avoid misinterpretation. Following is a summary of his explanations.

- *"Learning disabilities is a general term"*   The NJCLD believes that learning disabilities is a global term that can be used to group a variety of specific disorders. Most professionals agree that an individual with learning disabilities actually has a specific deficit in one or more ability areas but not in all areas. For example a child might have severe problems in math but be very competent in reading and spoken language. Another individual might have a specific underachievement in the area of reading but have adequate or excellent skills in mathematics and written language.

- *"that refers to a heterogeneous group of disorders"*   This phrase confirms that the disabilities referred to by the umbrella term learning disabilities are actually specific and different (e.g. heterogeneous). This phrase also suggests that the disorders may be caused by many dissimilar things.

- *"manifested by significant difficulties"*   In this phrase the NJCLD emphasizes the belief that the presence of a learning disability can be just as debilitating as mental retardation, blindness, cerebral palsy, or any handicapping condition. The purpose of this phrase is to take exception with many school personnel who mistakenly use the term learning disability synonymously with mildly handicapped. This phrase suggests that the effect of a learning disability is highly detrimental and that it is a serious handicap which limits performance of some key ability to a significant extent. By adding this phrase, the committee aligns itself with professionals who believe that the label learning disability should only be applied to hard core cases with serious limitations.

- *"in the acquisition and use of listening, speaking, reading, writing, reasoning, or mathematical abilities."*   In this phrase the NJCLD reflects the widely accepted point that a learning disability is a serious impairment in one or more of the abilities listed. This suggests that the final goal of instruction for individuals with learning disabilities is to "facilitate more efficient performance in reading, listening, speaking, arithmetic or other specified abilities." (p. 5)

- *"these disorders are intrinsic to the individual,"*   This phrase means that the cause of the disorder or disability is found within the individual. The unexpected underachievement is not a result of economic deprivation, poor parenting, ineffective school instruction, outside pressures of society, or cultural difference, etc. When these factors are present they certainly complicate the education and treatment, but they are not considered the primary cause of the learning disability.

- *"presumed to be due to central nervous system dysfunction"*   This phrase reinforces the belief that the learning disability is intrinsic to the individual. The etiology or cause of the learning disability may be a known central nervous system dysfunction or the cause may be a presumed central nervous system dysfunction. The dysfunctions may be the result of inherited factors, biochemical imbalances or insufficiencies, traumatic damage to tissues, or other similar conditions which might affect the central nervous system. The NJCLD clearly questions the structure and functional integrity of the central nervous system in this phrase.

The NJCLD was careful to clarify the fact that the cause for a learning disability is most often not obvious. In a situation where an individual shows marked reduction in proficiencies such as the loss of language skills after a stoke or brain injury; the difficulty could be attributed to an acquired central nervous system dysfunction. However, the vast majority of cases are considered developmental. These developmental problems (i.e., oral language differences, difficulties in social interactions and written expression) emerge slowly and appear only as the child attempts to master a skill, generally during school years. For example, a learning disability may not be apparent in a child until first or second grade, when he or she fails to develop developmentally appropriate reading skills.

Because of the difficulties involved in acquiring hard evidence of organicity (e.g., central nervous system damage or dysfunction), the NJCLD proposed that a neurological diagnosis did not have to be present; however, they did propose that no individual should be labeled with a learning disability unless central nervous system dysfunction was presumed to be the cause. In fact, the committee stated that if the cause is known or thought to be something other than central nervous system dysfunction, the diagnosis of learning disability should not be made. However, a study by Frankenberger and Fronzaglio (1991) showed that only 52 percent of the states include the neurological component in their definition.

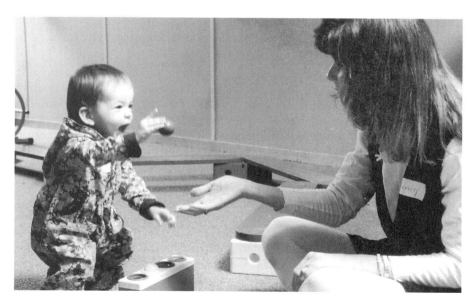

Learning disabilities are not restricted to school-age children but are thought to be manifested in people of all ages.

- *"and may occur across the lifespan"*   The committee uses this phrase to confirm that a learning disability is not restricted to children in school. In fact, a learning disability is thought to be manifested in people of all ages.

- *"problems in self-regulatory behaviors, social perceptions, and social interactions. . . do not by themselves constitute a learning disability"*   This phrase is a change from the NJCLD definition proposed in 1981. The definition was modified to reflect current beliefs that an individual with learning disabilities might demonstrate problems in their ability to self-regulate their behaviors and problems in social perception and social interaction. However, the NJCLD maintained that even though the presence of these difficulties need to be addressed in the definition as well in treatment programs, the presence of these problems would not constitute a learning disability in and of themselves. This committee felt that it was important to add a statement regarding diagnosis to alleviate confusion which might occur between the distinction of the category learning disability with emotional disturbance.

- *"Although learning disabilities may occur concomitantly with other handicapping conditions . . . or with extrinsic influences. . . ,"*   This is an important clause suggesting that learning disabilities may be found among all kinds and types of people. This would include individuals with other handicapping conditions, those from all socioeconomic groups, and from ethnic and racial groups. NJCLD felt that this was an inclusionary clause—as opposed to the earlier exclusionary clause—because it recognizes that individuals may be learning-disabled and also be deaf, blind, and/or mentally retarded. They may be learning-disabled and have experiences in a significantly different culture or have experienced extreme economic deprivation. In summary the definition formally recognized that individuals with learning disabilities may be considered multiply disabled. Issues related to cultural variance and concomitant disabilities are discussed at length in Chapters 9 and 12.

- *"they are not the result of those conditions or influences."*   In this last phrase the committee states the belief that although learning disabilities may coexist with other disabilities, they are distinctly different from other disabling conditions. Hammill notes that a "person may have a learning disability in addition to another disability, but they may not have a learning disability because of another disability" (Hammill, 1993, p. 6).

The advantage of the NJCLD definition is that it was developed from a number of professional and parent organizations who have officially adopted it as their definition. This is an improvement over the definitions that were created by a single government agency, association, or individual. NJCLD notes that the definition is not perfect yet, but they believe that it is a substantial improvement over other existing ones. When NJCLD began to address the problem of definition, they did not believe they would write the perfect definition, only a better one. Hammill notes that the NJCLD definition may never replace the 1977 U.S. Office of Education definition in legal documents; however, he suggests that it is important for parents and professionals to unite around one definition so we can have a consensus that "this is what we mean when we say learning disabilities" (Hammill, 1993, p. 7).

▶ COMMON FACTORS IN DEFINITIONS

Hammill (1990) reviewed eleven definitions cited throughout the twenty-eight textbooks on learning disabilities. His research cited the following nine important conceptual elements that can be used to discriminate among the eleven definitions.

1. Underachievement determination.   All eleven definitions referred to the idea that an individual with a learning disability is an underachiever. Most of the definitions use wording that specifically notes the manifestations of a learning disability in "one or more" ability areas. These definitions refer to uneven patterns of development. For example an individual might be skilled in written language but show deficits in the area of mathematics.

Other definitions describe the concept of underachievement through discussion of a discrepancy of ability or aptitude in achievement. In these definitions reference is made to intellectual ability and the contrasting underachievement in one or more areas of learning disabilities. For example, if an individual has an average IQ but is shown on a test of written language to be performing significantly lower than their ability as predicted by the IQ, then the presence of a learning disability would be supported. The requirement for an IQ and achievement discrepancy is being widely questioned. This debate will be explored further in this chapter and Chapter 3.

2. Central nervous system dysfunction etiology.   The eleven definitions differed on this with some of the definitions remaining silent on etiology and others suggesting that the assumed cause of the problem is in the central nervous system.

3. Process involvement.   While some definitions make no mention of process dysfunction, others suggest that the learning disability "disrupts the psychological processes that make proficient performance possible in some skill or ability area" (Hammill, 1990, p. 80). A process or language component is included in about 88 percent of the definitions in the United States (Frankenberger and Fronzaglio, 1991).

4. Being present throughout the lifespan.   Most definitions avoid reference to any specific age, therefore suggesting that learning disabilities can be traced throughout the lifespan. Other definitions reference the developmental level of children, especially those of school age, usually in the beginning of the definition.

5. Specification of spoken language problems as potential learning disabilities. Some definitions omit a reference to spoken language problems while others specify problems in listening and speaking, or spoken language problems.

6. Specification of academic problems as potential learning disabilities. Some of the eleven definitions studied by Hammill do not specifically mention academic problems while others specify the specific areas in which a learning disability might be manifested (e.g., reading, math, or writing). The federal definition lists seven areas in the criteria for identifying LD (e.g., reading skills, reading comprehension, math calculation, math reasoning, oral language, written expression and listening). According to Frankenberg and Fronzaglio (1991) all fifty states list academic problems in their definitions.

7. Specification of conceptual problems as potential learning disabilities. Some definitions do not address this concept while others mention conceptual problems such as reasoning and thinking.

8. Specification of other conditions as potential learning disabilities.   Some definitions propose that problems in areas like motor abilities and social skills may constitute a learning disability while other definitions omit this area.

9. Allowance for the multihandicapping nature of learning disabilities. Hammill (1990) noted there are three possibilities in references for this area. First, the definition may distinguish between primary and secondary learning problems, noting that learning disabilities can exist concomitantly with other disability areas such as emotional disturbance and sensory and motor impairment. For example, an individual who is blind might not be able to read print primarily because of the blindness; however, the same child might have a spoken language disability that is secondary to the blindness. Second, the definition can be written to totally exclude the possibility of a learning disability coexisting with other handicapping conditions. In this scenario, for example, it would be impossible for a person with mental retardation to have a learning disability. Third, some definitions may not refer to the concept of multihandicapping conditions at all. Frankenberg and Fronzaglio (1991) report that about 96 percent of the states in the United States have the exclusion component in their definition. Chapter 12 will deal extensively with this issue.

Table 2.1 presents the status of each of the eight definitions discussed in this chapter on the nine elements compared. After Hammill documented the characteristics of the definitions, he studied the percentage of agreement among the definitions on the nine elements. These data are presented in Table 2.2 for each of the definitions discussed in this chapter.

TABLE 2.2

Percentage of Agreement Among the Eleven Definitions on the Nine Elements

Definitions	1	2	3	4	5	6	7	8	9	10	11
1. Kirk	—	44	78	56	56	56	67	100	78	56	67
2. Bateman		—	44	67	67	67	78	44	22	0	11
3. NACHC			—	56	56	56	67	78	78	56	67
4. 1976 USOE							—	67	44	22	33
5. 1977 USOE								—	78	56	67
6. NJCLD									—	78	89
7. ACLD (LDA)										—	78
8. ICLD											—

Source: Adapted from Hammill, D.D. (1990). On defining learning disabilities: An emerging consensus. *Journal of Learning Disabilities, 23* (2), p. 81.

TABLE 2.1

Status of Definitions Relative to Definitional Elements

Definitional Elements

Definition	Underachievement Determination	CNS Dysfunction	Process Clause	Life Span	Language	Academic	Thinking	Other	Allows for Multihandicap
Kirk (1962)	Intraindividual	Yes	Yes	Yes	Yes	Yes	No	No	Yes
Bateman (1965)	Aptitude-Achievement	No	Yes	No	No	No	No	No	Yes
NACHC (1968)	Intraindividual	Yes	Yes	No	Yes	Yes	Yes	No	Yes
USOE (1976)	Aptitude-Achievement	No	Yes	No	Yes	Yes	No	No	Yes
USOE (1977)	Intraindividual	Yes	Yes	Yes	Yes	Yes	No	No	Yes
NJCLD (1988)	Intraindividual	Yes	No	Yes	Yes	Yes	Yes	No	Yes
ACLD (1986)	Intraindividual	Yes	No	Yes	Yes	Yes	Yes	Integration; Motor	—[a]
ICLD (1987)	Intraindividual	Yes	No	Yes	Yes	Yes	Yes	Social Skills	Yes

[a]Definitions silent on this element.

Adopted from Hammill, D.D. (1990). On defining learning disabilities: An emerging consensus. *Journal of Learning Disabilities, 23*(2), p. 81.

When singling out the four definitions that have the most professional impact today (i.e., the 1977 USOE, the NJCLD, the LDA, and ICLD definitions), Hammill (1993) reported an overall agreement of 74 percent. He stated that this represents a strong relationship among the viable definitions and indicates that consensus in the field is finally near.

Hammill went on to propose that the NJCLD definition is the best of the four viable choices. After an extensive review of LD research, Doris (1993) agreed that the NJCLD has the essential element described in the literature for a definition of LD. The NJCLD definition has also been endorsed as appropriate for the adult population with learning disabilities (Brinkerhoff, Shaw, and McGuire, 1993). Shaw, Cullen, McGuire, and Brinkerhoff (1995), citing Hammill's study (1990), also agreed that the NJCLD is gaining momentum as the best theoretical explanation of learning disabilities. They cited the following reasons:

- it is the most descriptive definition of learning disabilities;
- it is in line with the concept of intraindividual differences across areas;
- it specifies that learning disabilities exist throughout the life span;
- it deals with learning disabilities as the primary condition, while acknowledging possible concomitant disability conditions;
- it does not rule out the possibility that learning disabilities can occur in people who are gifted and talented; and
- it has support from a broad range of professional constituencies (p. 591).

In justifying his recommendation of the NJCLD definition, Hammill cited the limitations of the other three major contenders. He proposed that the primary limitation of the 1977 USOE definition is the inclusion of the vague and misleading reference to psychological processes. Reference to psychological processes is considered a throwback to the early history in which professionals in learning disabilities trained these processes before educating children in the areas of their disability (i.e., reading, math, and written language). Hammill noted that a more modern interpretation of that term might be more easily defended; however, the research at this time is not sufficient to justify the inclusion of this clause in the definition. He proposed that when this research becomes valid and useful, the NJCLD definition might be revised or a new definition developed. Another limitation of the 1977 USOE definition cited is the inconsistency between the contents of the federal definition and the operational criteria specified to identify a specific learning disability. This discrepancy will be discussed further in Chapter 3. The 1977 USOE definition also omits any reference to problems with thinking cited in the other three most recent definitions of learning disabilities.

Hammill (1993) also described the limitations of the LDA and ICLD definitions. The primary limitation of the LDA definition is its overall vagueness, its lack of specificity regarding what constitutes a learning disability, and its ambiguity regarding the relationship between other handicapping conditions and learning disabilities. The main limitation of the ICLD definition is the reference to social skills as constituting a primary learning disability. Neither of the other three definitions specifically target social skills as an example of a learning disability. Hammill pointed out that since the NJCLD definition and the USOE definition specifically omit social skills and LDA's definition is vague on social skills, the Department of Education has been reluctant to endorse the ICLD definition because of the reference to social skills. Thus the ICLD definition is an unlikely contender for wide acceptance in the field. This leaves the NJCLD definition as the most viable definition to unite the field at this time.

Hammill (1990) pointed out that the time has come for professionals to come together in many of the areas we have debated so strongly in the past. The financial climate in Washington is such that individuals are trying to cut services for students with learning disabilities, and they use as justification the lack of agreement on critical issues such as definition. While consensus is growing on the theoretical definition of learning disabilities, many issues remain in the operationalization of the definition.

▶ THE DEBATE GOES ON!

Regardless of Hammill's important work in finding consensus among the most widely accepted theoretical definitions, and his challenge to unite behind one of these definitions, debate and controversy continued. As an example of progress, one area that has been seemingly resolved is the debate on the issue of social skills. The importance of adding social skills to the definition was argued for at least ten years. The current resolution seems to be inclusion of social deficits and self-regulatory behaviors as important characteristics but not raising these deficits to the level of constituting a learning disability in isolation (NJCLD, 1988). Following is a brief summary of other definitional issues that continue to stimulate debate. The wording of an actual definition seems to no longer be on the forefront for debate; the new issues primarily relate to how best to *operationalize* the definition of learning disabilities.

Should IQ Be Used to Define Learning Disabilities?

The guidelines in the *Federal Register* (1977) specify the discrepancy between ability and achievement as the first criterion for identifying a learning disability. Most states have automatically associated the measurement of ability with the assessment of intelligence and do this by obtaining an intelligence quotient or IQ. In fact, the concept of learning disabilities in many states has become synonymous with a discrepancy between IQ and achievement (Mather and Roberts, 1994). According to Frankenberger and Fronzaglio (1991), the concept and utilization of aptitude-achievement discrepancy in defining learning disabilities is actually increasing. However, the *Federal Register* does not specify that ability necessarily equates to IQ. Many professionals in the field are now calling for a new interpretation of ability (Chalfant, 1989; Keogh, 1988; Mather and Healey, 1990; Berninger, Hart, Abbott, and Karovsky, 1992; Zigmond, 1993).

Chalfant (1989) proposed that the use of intelligence as the measure of potential does not differentiate underachievers from LD, and he cited this as the reason the prevalence figures have risen so dramatically. Chalfant proposed that intraindividual differences between psychological processes (ability) be used to document the severe discrepancy between ability and achievement; however, he acknowledges the following difficulties that have been experienced in assessing processing deficits:

- consensus does not exist as to identify the most important psychological processes needed to be measured;
- no single theoretical base for defining psychological processes is embraced by the field;
- there is a lack of reliable and valid instruments for measuring processing dysfunctions;
- cognitive abilities are not easily understood and cannot be directly observed.

One option is to continue to administer the psychological processing tests available and validate the scores of those tests by observing behavior during intelligence tests and, more importantly, in classroom functioning (Chalfant, 1989). The practice of observing and prompting behavior during assessment (e.g., dynamic assessment) will be explored further in Chapter 6. Chalfant challenges the field to continue to explore the use of psychological processes in the identification of LD rather than giving up the task because it is difficult. Important research by cognitive theorists is currently ongoing in this area. For further study refer to researchers such as Swanson (1993), Torgeson (1993), and Meltzer (1994).

Meltzer (1994) provides a good example of an alternative to aptitude (IQ) and achievement discrepancy in the identification of reading disability. She proposed that "these measures emphasize the end product of learning while largely ignoring the processes and strategies that students use to approach various learning and problem-solving situations" (p. 581). To assess the "product" of deficits in reading, Meltzer suggested an assessment of general aptitude but also other factors such as listening, phonetic awareness, and speed in word recognition. This type of reinterpretation of the discrepancy concept should also be followed closely in the future.

Another concern regarding the current emphasis on IQ and academic discrepancy criteria is the possibility that the learning disability can adversely affect a student's performance on either the aptitude test or the measure of academic achievement. When this happens, a student may not demonstrate a discrepancy between ability and achievement because the scores obtained are actually an underestimate of his ability. From this perspective, it can be reasoned that a student may have a learning disability but may not demonstrate a significant discrepancy (Mather and Healey, 1990; Swanson, 1993).

Mather and Roberts (1994) pointed out another alarming consideration in the emphasis of the discrepancy concept, that is, the fact that this assessment procedure is based on school failure. Children have to have been in school for a significant period of time achieving at unsuccessful levels to come to the attention of a concerned teacher. Often, in younger children particularly, these children have to fail for several years until their academic levels become low enough to substantiate a discrepancy between ability and achievement. This has led many to be concerned about the definition and identification of learning disabilities in young children. Early identification is explored further in Chapter 6.

Shaw, et al., (1995) discussed five alternatives that have been proposed to address the issues on defining learning disabilities through an achievement-aptitude discrepancy. These include

- making the discrepancy model more stringent
- redefining psychometric discrepancies as intraindividual discrepancies
- deemphasizing eligibility criteria in favor of clinical judgment
- shifting focus of assessment to information processing
- providing services on a noncategorical basis (p. 588)

These alternatives will be discussed more extensively in Chapter 3.

Are Separate Definitions Needed for Adult Populations?

As more and more adults with learning disabilities request services in postsecondary institutions, literacy programs, and employment, the issue of an operational definition for this population is becoming more prominent. Legal rights and services are protected under the Americans with Disabilities Act of 1990 and Section 504 of the Rehabilitation Act of 1973, but a definition is not included in these laws. Agencies are searching for an operational definition that can be used to target the recipients of services and help determine the range of services needed (Shaw, Cullen, McGuire, and Brinkerhoff, 1995).

The problem is exacerbated by the fact that many adults were not diagnosed in childhood and come to the agency many years after their formal school training. Since most of the definitions and criteria for identification were designed to be used with students in a school setting, the use of the existing criteria has been questioned in the adult population. Brinkerhoff, Shaw, and McGuire (1993) have proposed an operational definition for adults with learning disabilities based on the definition proposed by the NJCLD (1988). This definition incorporates four levels of investigation and provides a broader base to assess many of the characteristics of adults with LD that may impact their success in postsecondary educational settings and employment. This operational interpretation is provided in Figure 2.2.

With the increased dissatisfaction regarding the narrow focus of the current criteria for the identification of learning disabilities, the model proposed by Brinkerhoff et al. (1993) may also provide a basis for a more extensive and effective method of identifying students (K–12) with learning disabilities (Coutinho, 1995; Tomlan and Mather, 1996).

FIGURE 2.2

An Operational Definition of Learning Disabilities Across the Age Span

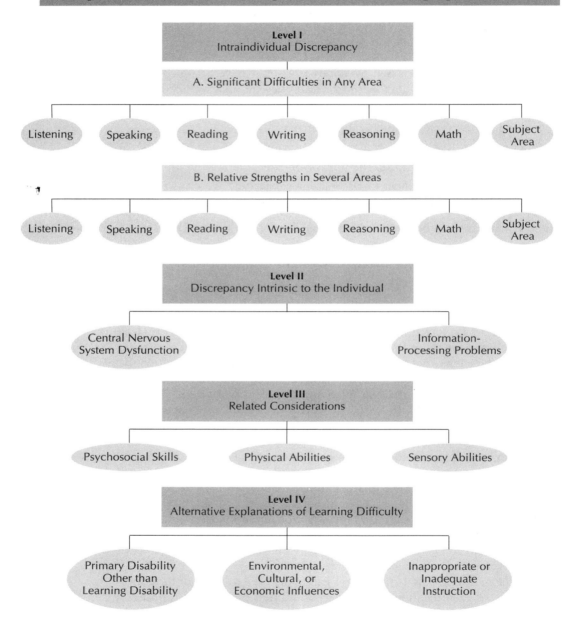

Source: *Promoting Postsecondary Education for Students with Learning Disabilities: A Handbook for Practitioners* by L. Brinkerhoff, S. Shaw, & J.McGuire, 1993, pp. 74–75. Austin, TX: PRO-ED. Copyright 1993 by PRO-ED. Adapted with permission.

Are Learning Disabilities Equal to Mild Disabilities?

One radical method of solving the problem of identifying a learning disability is to do away with the term entirely or develop and use new noncategorical terminology. Many states have moved toward an emphasis on noncategorical approaches and often students with learning disabilities are grouped with mental retardation and/or emotional conflict. This category is often referred to as mild learning handicaps. As Mather and Roberts (1994) suggested, any disability exists on a continuum that includes mild to severe cases. The thinking behind the use of the term mild disability seems to be an attempt to distinguish this group of students from those with severe and profound or multiple disabilities. However, anyone who has spent time with adults with learning disabilities who have failed multiple attempts in postsecondary settings (e.g., technical school, community college) and changed jobs many times during the period of a few months will contend that there is nothing mild about the limitations that create these handicaps. Mather and Roberts (1994) proposed the following difficulties with the term mild leading to false assumptions:

- if the learning disability is not considered severe, students do not require the systematic intensive structure to learn;
- because specialized methods are not necessarily required, the regular classroom can be used to teach all children with learning disabilities;
- if the students can be taught in general education classrooms, teachers with specialized training regarding learning disabilities are not required.

Mather and Roberts also noted that taking away the term mild would improve the label but not solve the problem of providing appropriate special education services.

If the purpose of assessment could be focused on identifying the needs of students in order to increase their success in the learning process, instead of providing a label to automatically separate students, the issue of assessing for identifying a label could be deemphasized. Mather and Roberts (1994) urged the field to begin to evaluate students to identify the capabilities and needs of students instead of labeling their conditions.

▶ PREVALENCE OF LEARNING DISABILITIES

Another major concern in the area of learning disabilities has been the increasing number of students labeled as having a learning disability. Each year, the U.S. Department of Education reports the percentages and numbers of children and youth receiving special education and related services. The data is collected from child count statistics submitted to the federal government by all territories and states. Since the numbers were first reported in the 1976–1977 school year, the percentage of students with disabilities labeled as learning-disabled has risen from 1.79 percent to 52.4 percent. The data from 1992–1993 school year suggest that 2,333,571 students or 52.4 percent of the students

Children with learning disabilities account for more than 50 percent of all students served in special education programs.

with disabilities between age six and twenty-one who were served under Part B were learning-disabled. The next largest category is speech or language impairment with 22.2 percent. Mental retardation is third with 10.9 percent. Figure 2.3 displays the distribution in child count from 1976–1977 to 1992–1993. The number of children with learning disabilities served by each state and the changes in those numbers is demonstrated in Table 2.3. Future trends in this area are discussed further in Chapter 13.

The literature suggests that variations in definitions, terminology, and assessment practices have resulted in an unstable foundation for accurate estimates of the prevalence of learning disabilities. Since there is no absolute criteria for identification, the figures vary depending on the stringency of the criteria used in each state to determine eligibility for services in a class for children with learning disabilities (Mercer, 1993). Mercer also noted that if more stringent criteria were used, the overall prevalence might be as low as 1.5 percent. The differences in the criteria and prevalence figures between states will be demonstrated in Chapter 3.

Henley, Ramsey, and Algozzine (1993) suggested the continued trend of increases in learning disabilities can be attributed to the vagueness of the federal definition for learning disabilities and the preference and social acceptance for the classification of learning disabilities (favored over behavior disorders or mental retardation). Sigmon (1989) cited the differing criteria used by states for qualification of services. Finlan (1992) added the large number of under-achieving children who need help and Hallahan (1992) noted that social changes such as an increase in poverty that might result in greater risk for

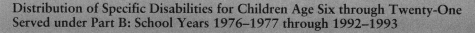

FIGURE 2.3

Distribution of Specific Disabilities for Children Age Six through Twenty-One Served under Part B: School Years 1976–1977 through 1992–1993

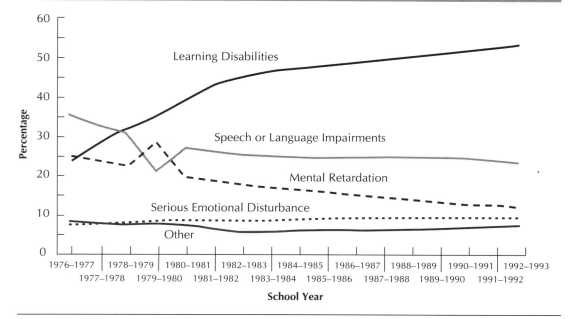

Source: U.S. Department of Education, Office of Special Education Programs, Data Analysis System (DANS). *16th Annual Report to Congress.*

poor health care and nutritional deficiencies during pregnancy and after birth might result in central nervous system damage. The Children's Defense Fund (1994) published statistics on the increase in hunger and health concerns due to poverty as well as the breakdown of the nuclear family and the increase in drug-exposed infants. That study suggests that increases can be expected in the students served in special education.

A study by Gartner and Lipsky (1987) reported that between 1977 and 1985, while there was a 16 percent increase overall in students with disabilities, the number of students specifically classified as learning disabled rose 119 percent! Although the growth has evened out since 1985, the large numbers of children identified as learning disabled is causing difficulties for administrators as they try to find appropriate placements and services to meet the needs of these students. As resources become more and more limited for special education, this rapid increase and variability of prevalence rate in the area of learning disabilities is causing great concern for legislators as well as educators (Mercer, 1993). The development of effective assessment procedures and eligibility criteria is becoming critical.

TABLE 2.3

Number and Change in Number of Children Age Six–Twenty-One Served Under IDEA, Part B

| | Specific Learning Disabilities | | |
| | Number Served | Change in Number Served | Percentage Change in Number Served |
State	1976–1977	1993–1994	1976–1977 to 1993–1994	1976–1977 to 1993–1994
Alabama	5,407	38,208	32,801	606.64
Alaska	3,873	7,953	4,080	105.34
Arizona	17,161	36,222	19,061	111.07
Arkansas	5,061	25,768	20,707	409.15
California	73,416	293,650	220,234	299.98
Colorado	16,360	32,954	16,594	101.43
Connecticut	19,065	32,450	13,385	70.21
Delaware	4,345	7,384	3,039	69.94
District of Columbia	1,591	1,531	−60	−3.77
Florida	31,687	118,123	86,436	272.78
Georgia	15,558	36,061	20,503	131.78
Hawaii	4,867	7,254	2,387	49.04
Idaho	5,551	11,865	6,314	113.75
Illinois	51,644	102,991	51,347	99.42
Indiana	5,381	48,692	43,311	804.89
Iowa	17,173	26,620	9,447	55.01
Kansas	8,240	19,523	11,283	136.93
Kentucky	7,399	22,927	15,528	209.87
Louisiana	10,662	34,467	23,805	223.27
Maine	7,125	12,224	5,099	71.56
Maryland	28,938	42,591	13,653	47.18
Massachusetts	17,795	77,838	60,043	337.42
Michigan	27,226	77,869	50,643	186.01
Minnesota	21,236	34,124	12,888	60.69
Mississippi	2,728	30,947	28,219	1,034.42
Missouri	21,988	56,106	34,118	155.17
Montana	2,765	9,866	7,121	257.54
Nebraska	5,360	14,864	9,504	177.31
Nevada	4,646	13,754	9,108	196.04
New Hampshire	3,059	11,596	8,537	279.08
New Jersey	32,680	93,248	60,568	185.34
New Mexico	6,137	20,287	14,150	230.57
New York	33,880	184,602	150,722	444.87
North Carolina	17,501	54,960	37,459	214.04
North Dakota	2,378	5,607	3,229	135.79
Ohio	32,334	77,875	45,541	140.85

(continued)

TABLE 2.3

continued

	Specific Learning Disabilities		
	Number Served	Change in Number Served	Percentage Change in Number Served
State	1976–1977	1993–1994	1976–1977 to 1993–1994	1976–1977 to 1993–1994
Oklahoma	14,776	34,808	20,032	135.57
Oregon	10,905	29,701	18,796	172.36
Pennsylvania	19,451	86,685	67,234	345.66
Puerto Rico	972	14,477	13,505	1,389.40
Rhode Island	4,430	12,948	8,518	192.28
South Carolina	10,777	30,669	19,892	184.58
South Dakota	1,166	6,806	5,640	483.70
Tennessee	34,923	56,750	21,827	62.50
Texas	48,469	222,109	173,640	358.25
Utah	13,194	26,318	13,124	99.47
Vermont	1,925	4,162	2,237	116.21
Virginia	15,928	60,631	44,703	280.66
Washington	10,016	41,053	31,037	309.87
West Virginia	5,713	17,914	12,201	213.57
Wisconsin	14,199	28,603	14,404	101.44
Wyoming	3,034	5,546	2,512	82.79
American Samoa	37	113	76	205.41
Guam	148	1,034	886	598.65
Northern Marianas	0	109	109	100.00
Palau	257	221	−36	−14.01
Virgin Islands	176	434	258	146.59
Bur. of Indian Affairs	0	3,787	3,787	100.00
U.S. and Outlying Areas	782,713	2,407,899	1,625,186	207.63
50 States, D.C., and P.R.	782,095	2,402,201	1,620,106	207.15

Source: U.S. Department of Education (1995). *17th Annual Report to Congress.*

SUMMARY

This chapter has presented an extensive discussion of various definitions of learning disabilities. Major definitions that have existed over the past thirty years were presented and compared. Finally, the prevalence of learning disabilities was presented. The following points summarize the major areas included in the chapter:

• Kirk (1962) and Bateman (1965) authored two of the most influential early definitions of learning disabilities.

- Early definitions included references to delays in processes.
- Kirk's definition referred to the etiology of learning disabilities as cerebral dysfunction.
- Kirk was influential in developing the first definition of learning disabilities incorporated into federal law.
- Federal regulations published in 1977 to operationalize the definition of learning disabilities emphasized a discrepancy between ability and achievement.
- In 1981, the National Joint Committee on Learning Disabilities was organized, partly because of perceived weaknesses in the prevailing definitions of learning disabilities.
- The NJCLD proposed its own definition of learning disabilities in 1981.
- In reaction to the NJCLD, the Interagency Committee on Learning Disabilities was created in 1987 to develop its definition.
- In 1988, the NJCLD revised its definition, in response to new knowledge about learning disabilities and the ICLD definition.
- Regardless of the numerous definitions for learning disabilities, there are many common factors.
- Underachievement is referred to as a factor in most definitions of learning disabilities.
- Most of the definitions avoid putting age restrictions on learning disabilities, thereby suggesting that this is a life-long disability.
- Definitions that appear to have the most commonality include the 1977 federal definition, NCJLD definition, LDA definition, and ICLD definition.
- The debate regarding the definition of learning disabilities seems to be nearing consensus; the current focus for debate centers around operationalizing the definition.
- Learning disabilities represents the largest category of children served under the Individuals with Disabilities Education Act.

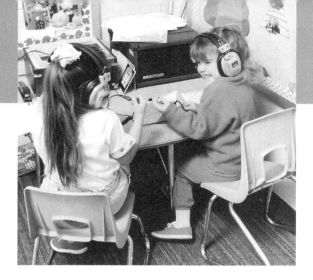

Chapter 3

ASSESSMENT

The objectives for this chapter are as follows:

▶ To know the major purposes of assessment.

▶ To describe the screening process.

▶ To describe the mandated parental rights regarding assessment.

▶ To understand the basic requirements of nondiscriminatory assessment.

▶ To know the specific requirements for assessment of students with learning disabilities.

▶ To describe the observation requirements for assessing students with learning disabilities.

▶ To know how to evaluate assessment instruments that are used with students with learning disabilities.

▶ To know the difference between formal and informal assessment.

▶ To describe the differences between norm-referenced and criterion-referenced tests.

▶ To define portfolio assessment.

▶ To describe the components of the assessment process.

▶ To discuss the different models for determining eligibility for learning disabilities.

Frank: A Case Study

Frank was an eight-year-old second grader when he arrived at Hunter School. Because of a September birthday, Frank was six when he started kindergarten. His progress report from kindergarten showed satisfactory performance in all areas. He had age-appropriate social skills, demonstrated above-average number skills, named all the letters, knew all of the consonant sounds, and had adequate fine motor skills. He was promoted to first grade.

In first grade Frank had an integrated reading program that combined whole language practices (big books, predictable readers), a basal reading series (group skill lessons), and a systematic phonics curriculum. His initial progress reports in the first grade, the teacher's comments, and work samples indicated that Frank enjoyed reading activities, participated enthusiastically, and made satisfactory progress. He seemed to prefer to read familiar or predictable storybooks over and over. His sight vocabulary included 80 percent of the basic word list taken from the basal series. However, in the second semester, reading became more difficult for Frank. His teacher checked "Needs Improvement" on his report card, and her comments revealed difficulty with blends and vowels. Samples of Frank's daily journal and spelling tests supported this. Frank's report card also showed "Needs Improvement" in listening and following directions. Mathematics skills were still above average, and Frank's behavior was satisfactory. Frank was promoted to second grade and over the summer his family moved to a different state.

When second grade began, Frank was in his new school. He seemed to adjust, made friends quickly, and was able to successfully handle the work for about nine weeks. The overall instructional program was similar to his previous one, and Frank managed. At a parent conference in late October, Frank's mother reported that he was beginning to complain of stomachaches and asking to stay home. His teacher, Mrs. Principi, shared that she had noticed Frank was starting to experience a little frustration and was not finishing some of his work, usually phonics. Mrs. Principi felt that it was normal because the difficulty of the work was increasing, and Frank was probably still adjusting to the school change. They agreed to watch him closely and to stay in contact.

Over the next nine weeks Mrs. Principi tried to work individually with Frank each day with his reading skills. She observed that he was basically a sight reader and avoided text containing multisyllable words. He tried to use phonetic skills, but did not know many of the sounds and patterns. He appeared to understand the text when he knew the words but his guesses when he did not know the words were often incorrect. He seemed more and more embarrassed to read in this mid-level reading group so she moved him to the lower group where he might feel more comfortable. After this change, Mrs. Principi noticed that Frank seemed happier, but he started clowning around in the new group. She continued to give him the regular classwork so he would not feel different. She did notice that she was having to provide additional directions and explanations to help Frank complete his activities. Frank was a real "star" in math, and Mrs. Principi gave him many chances to show his ability. She shared her concern for Frank with other teachers and they encouraged her to keep trying and reevaluate Frank's progress at midyear.

Frank's story of unexpected underachievement is representative of many students who try unsuccessfully to keep up with their peers in school. Luckily for Frank, he has a concerned teacher watching and evaluating his progress. Later in this chapter you will learn more about Frank and the help he receives as his struggle in school continues.

Note: The authors would like to thank Nancy Dunavant, M.Ed., learning disabilities teacher, Homewood School District Birmingham, AL for sharing Frank's story.

Assessment is an integral part of the identification and education of students with learning disabilities. Although much of what educators do in assessment is mandated by law, significant variation exists across the country. Differences are found in the types of assessment procedures used by school districts, the specific instruments selected for use, and the criteria applied to the results for decision-making purposes. These differences raise issues that continue to divide professionals in the field. This chapter will discuss the purpose of assessment, the legal mandates regarding assessment, the range of assessment techniques and instruments commonly employed, and the assessment process from identification to instructional design and program evaluation. The issue of cultural diversity as related to assessment will also be explored.

▶ PURPOSE OF ASSESSMENT

Assessment guides the decision-making process throughout the identification and education of students with learning disabilities. Taylor (1993) described the following five major purposes of assessment.

1. *Initial identification or screening.* This is the first level of assessment to identify children who might require special education or other special services. These procedures may consist of an informal observation of the student in the classroom or a review of class work. Formal testing of intelligence or achievement may also be used.

Frequently during the screening phase, all children in a specific grade, school, or district are administered the same test to determine which ones score in a range that would indicate the need for additional, more in-depth testing. These tests are typically norm-referenced and group administered (Salvia and Ysseldyke, 1991). When all children in the target group are being treated—or tested—equally, special parental permission is not required.

In summary, this level of assessment identifies students who are in need of additional assessment. The initial assessment might identify students at risk for future problems; their academic progress and/or emotional stability need to be closely monitored by a concerned teacher. For some students, the need for more formal testing and immediate modification of classroom demands will be readily apparent.

2. *Determination and evaluation of teaching programs and strategies.* This is one of the most important uses of assessment; it can serve four purposes. First, this type of assessment can assist general education teachers in deciding what should be taught and how it should be taught. Second, assessment can evaluate the success of a particular strategy or program. Implementation of assessment at this level may result in more effective intervention strategies which could negate the need for a special education referral.

For example, if a teacher is not satisfied with the progress a student is making in reading, through assessment the teacher could determine that the student lacks ability to use phonetic cues to decode new words. This might be remediated with carefully planned mini-skill lessons, and progress could continue to be monitored over time. If reading improves to an acceptable level, a referral to special education might be totally avoided. If the method was not successful, important documentation of the effect of a prereferral intervention strategy would be available.

This leads to the third use, the documentation of the need for a formal special education referral. On the referral form, the teacher is asked to describe the student's problems in the class and to record assessment data for documentation. Fourth, if students are eventually found eligible for special education, the information gathered at this level can be used to develop the individualized education program (IEP). Information documenting effective and ineffective teaching strategies are particularly relevant.

3. *Determination of current performance level and educational need.* In order to proceed with special education eligibility, a child must be found to have needs clearly identified as not being met by his or her current placement in general education (P.L. 94–142, 1975). The results of the initial screening and the evaluation of classroom performance or behavior is reviewed to structure the comprehensive testing that is completed by a qualified evaluator. This testing is individualized and may include formal tests such as the Wechsler Intelligence Scale for Children-Revised (Wechsler, 1991) or informal tests such as interviews or records of classroom behavior. (These types of tests will be discussed later in the chapter.) Because the child is being singled out for further testing, parental permission is required by law.

The purpose of this additional testing is to document that adequate progress has not been made. All areas of suspected problems should be assessed including but not limited to social, preacademic, or academic skills. According to Taylor (1993), the purpose of this stage of the assessment process is

- to determine the deficit areas needing remediation
- to establish specific strengths and weaknesses
- to identify the potentially effective remedial approaches and teaching strategies

4. *Decisions about classification and program placement.* During this phase the results of the individualized testing are reviewed by a multidisciplinary team to determine the student's eligibility for special education programming. This stage is the most controversial because a label or classification is attached to the student to justify eligibility for special education services. Parents are informed of the results and, if the student is determined eligible, the parents are invited to attend the meeting to plan instruction.

5. *Development of the individual education program.* The results of all assessment data are reviewed by a team including general and special education teachers, administrators, parents, and when appropriate, the student, to determine instructional goals and objectives for the next year. Decisions are also made as to the type of educational environment that would be least restrictive.

Assessment is also critical in the on-going process of monitoring student progress. Effective teachers continue to evaluate their students' progress on a daily or weekly basis and to make appropriate adjustments in short-term objectives and instructional methods. This type of assessment is usually informal. A more formal assessment and review of the annual goals and student progress is made annually by teachers, parents, and a representative of the public agency.

Several of the assessment procedures described above and the practices for implementation are mandated by law. In some cases litigation and philosophical trends have led to legislation, and in other cases legislation has led to changes in philosophy and litigation. A discussion of the legal aspects of assessment and the special education process follows.

▶ LEGAL MANDATES AND SPECIAL EDUCATION ASSESSMENT

The most powerful legislation affecting all special education policy, including assessment, is the Education for All Handicapped Children Act (Public Law 94-142), and the amendments to that law, including the one which changed the name of the original law to the Individuals with Disabilities Education Act (IDEA). Many of the mandates appeared in the original laws, and others were published in the *Federal Register,* a government publication published daily to provide the rules and regulations related to specific legislation. The two areas addressed by IDEA that have the most direct relevance to assessment are parent participation and nondiscriminatory evaluation (Taylor, 1993). The *Federal Register* (United States Office of Education, 1977) also mandates specific procedures for evaluating a student with a learning disability. Following are the regulations regarding each of these areas.

Parent Participation

A child's parents have the right to review all educational records regarding the identification, evaluation, and educational placement of their child in a free, appropriate, public education setting. According to Taylor (1993), the parents should receive written notification which includes

1. the name of the person requesting an evaluation and the reason for the testing;
2. the instruments that will be used and the procedures for the evaluation. The parents may evaluate the instruments if requested;
3. an explanation of their right to refuse the evaluation, including the possibility that their refusal might result in an impartial hearing to determine the outcome;
4. an explanation of their right to obtain an outside evaluation which must be considered in the determination of eligibility.

As stated above, if the parents do not agree with the process or the results, they may obtain an independent educational evaluation. If requested, the public agency must provide information about where an independent evaluation may be obtained by a qualified examiner. The examiner recommended may not be employed by the public agency responsible for the education of the child in question. Parents have the right to obtain the evaluation at public expense, if they disagree with the results obtained by the public agency. However, to avoid these expenses, the public agency may initiate a hearing to show that its evaluation is appropriate.

If the hearing officer rules that the school's evaluation is appropriate, parents may still obtain an independent evaluation but the school is not required to cover the expenses. If the parent does obtain an outside evaluation, the results of the evaluation must be considered by the school in any decision related to the provision of a free, appropriate, public education; it may also be used in any future hearings (USOE, 1992).

The parent must give written consent to allow the individualized evaluation to determine eligibility for placement to take place. They must also give written consent before their child's initial placement in a special education classroom. Due process safeguards specified in the *Federal Register* (USOE, 1992) ensure that

1. parents are fully informed of all information relevant to the activity for which consent is sought, in his or her native language, or other mode of communication;

2. the parent understands and agrees in writing to carrying-out of the activity for which consent is sought, and the consent describes that activity and lists the records (if any) that will be released and to whom; and

3. the parent understands that the granting of consent is voluntary and may be revoked at any time (p. 44819).

If the parent *refuses* to give consent, the state law may include procedures that allow the local education agency to obtain a court order to proceed with the evaluation. If state law is not specific relative to the parent's lack of consent, the local education agency may use the due process hearing procedures in the *Federal Register* (USOE, 1992) to override a parent's refusal to consent. If this is done and the hearing officer rules in favor of the agency, then the agency may evaluate or initiate special education placement without parental consent (p. 44820). A more detailed description of parents' rights and impartial due process hearings are included in Chapter 10.

Nondiscriminatory Evaluation

After consent is obtained, an evaluation is scheduled. The *Federal Register* (USOE, 1992) specifies that an "evaluation" means procedures to determine whether a child has a disability and the nature and extent of services that the student needs. In the special education law, the term refers to procedures used selectively with an *individual* child; it does not include group administered tests or procedures used with all children in a school, grade, or class (p. 44819).

The *Federal Register* (USOE, 1992) also contains very specific processes related to evaluation which State Education Agencies (SEAs) and Local Education Agencies (LEAs) must ensure. These include, at a minimum, that

A. Tests and other evaluation materials

   1. are provided and administered in the child's native language or other mode of communication, unless it is clearly not feasible to do so;

   2. have been validated for the specific purpose for which they are used; and

3. are administered by trained personnel in conformance with the instructions provided by their producer.

B. Tests and other evaluation materials include those tailored to assess specific areas of educational need and not merely those that are designed to provide a single general intelligence quotient (e.g., an IQ test).

C. Tests are selected and administered so as best to ensure that when a test is administered to a child with impaired sensory, manual, or speaking skills, the test results accurately reflect the child's aptitude or achievement level or whatever other factors the test purports to measure, rather than reflecting the child's impaired sensory, manual, or speaking skills (except where those skills are the factors that the test purports to measure).

D. No single procedure is used as the sole criterion for determining an appropriate educational program for a child.

E. The evaluation is made by a multidisciplinary team or group of persons, including at least one teacher or other specialist with knowledge in the area of suspected disability. This team is generally referred to as the Multidisciplinary Evaluation Team or MET.

F. The child is assessed in all areas related to the suspected disability, including (if appropriate) health, vision, hearing, social and emotional status, general intelligence, academic performance, communicative status, and motor abilities (p. 44822).

The *Federal Register* (USOE, 1992) also specifies that a reevaluation is mandatory every three years or more frequently if the child's teacher or parents make a request, or the conditions warrant a reevaluation (p. 44822). In interpreting evaluation data and in making placement decisions, the *Federal Register* mandates that each public agency is to

1. draw on a variety of sources, including aptitude and achievement tests, teacher recommendations, physical conditions, social or cultural background, and adaptive behavior;

2. ensure that information obtained from all of these sources is documented and carefully considered;

3. ensure that the placement decision is made by a group of persons, including persons knowledgeable about the child, the meaning of the evaluation data, and the placement options; and

4. ensure that the placement decision is made within the guidelines for placement in the least restrictive environment (p. 44822).

Regulations for Learning Disabilities

In addition to these general guidelines, the *Federal Register* (USOE, 1975; 1992) specifies very significant additional procedures for evaluating children with specific learning disabilities. These include

Additional Team Members (Section 300.540)

1. Each agency shall include on the Multidisciplinary Evaluation Team the child's regular teacher or if the child has no general education teacher, a general education classroom teacher qualified to teach a child of his or her age; and,

2. At least one person qualified to conduct individual diagnostic examinations of children, such as a school psychologist, speech-language pathologist, or remedial reading teacher.

Definition (Section 300.541) As reported in Chapter 2, the *Federal Register* published to provide regulations for P.L. 94–142 (USOE, 1977) contained the federal definition of specific learning disabilities. This definition states

> The term "specific learning disability" means a disorder in one or more of the basic psychological processes involved in understanding or in using language, spoken or written, that may manifest itself in an imperfect ability to listen, think, speak, read, write, spell, or to do mathematical calculations. The term includes such conditions as perceptual disabilities, brain injury, minimal brain dysfunction, dyslexia, and developmental aphasia. The term does not apply to children who have learning problems that are primarily the result of visual, hearing, or motor disabilities, of mental retardation, of emotional disturbance, or of environmental, cultural, or economic disadvantage. (USOE, 1977, p. 65083)

However, the USOE felt that this definition lacked the specificity needed to identify students as eligible for special education services. Therefore, in the November, 1977 *Federal Register,* criteria were published for the identification of a specific learning disability. The differences between the definition and the criteria for identification were discussed in Chapter 2. The criteria are repeated below for further study of the implications in the assessment process:

Criteria (Section 300.541)

(a) A team may determine that a child has a specific learning disability if

   (1) The child does not achieve commensurate with his or her age and ability levels in one or more of the areas listed in paragraph (a)(2) of this section, when provided with learning experiences appropriate for the child's age and ability levels; and

   (2) The team finds that a child has a severe discrepancy between achievement and intellectual ability in one or more of the following areas

   (i) Oral expression;

   (ii) Listening comprehension;

   (iii) Written expression;

   (iv) Basic reading skills;

   (v) Reading comprehension;

   (vi) Mathematics calculation; or

   (vii) Mathematics reasoning.

(b) The team may not identify a child as having a specific learning disability if the severe discrepancy between ability and achievement is primarily the result of

(1) A visual, hearing, or motor impairment;

(2) Mental retardation;

(3) Emotional disturbance; or

(4) Environmental, cultural or economic disadvantage (USOE, 1977, p. 65083).

The team that reviews the results of the evaluation and determines if the child is eligible for services in special education is generally referred to as the Multidisciplinary Eligibility Determination Team (MEDT). These individuals have been given the difficult task of applying the set of criteria listed above to individual children struggling in school. They know the children need help, yet they also know the negative impact labeling can have on a child's life. The team's dilemma is complicated by the fact that the criteria really have no specific guidelines that define the magnitude of discrepancy or recommendations regarding the tests or measures that should be used to demonstrate the discrepancy. The various ways states have developed policy to guide the MEDT's in their determination of eligibility will be discussed later. Following is a discussion of the federal mandates for observation and a written report that provides additional structure to the process.

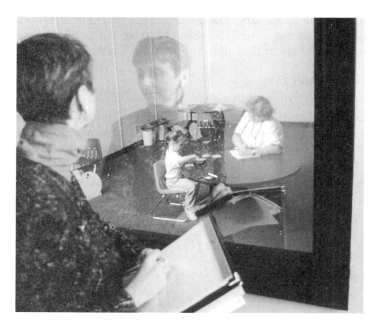

Part of the formal assessment includes an observation of the child completed by someone other than the child's teacher.

Observation (300.542)

(a) At least one team member other than the child's regular teacher shall observe the child's academic performance in the regular classroom setting.

(b) In the case of a child of less than school age or out of school, a team member shall observe the child in an environment appropriate for a child of that age.

Written report (Section 300.543)

(a) The team shall prepare a written report of the results of the evaluation.

(b) The report must include a statement of

(1) Whether the child has a specific learning disability;

(2) The basis for making the determination;

(3) The relevant behavior noted during the observation of the child;

(4) The relationship of that behavior to the child's academic functioning;

(5) The educationally relevant medical findings, if any;

(6) Whether there is a severe discrepancy between achievement and ability that is not correctable without special education and related services; and

(7) The determination of the team concerning the effects of environmental, cultural, or economic disadvantage.

(c) Each team member shall certify in writing whether the report reflects his or her conclusion. If it does not reflect his or her conclusion, the team member must submit a separate statement presenting his or her conclusions. (USDE, 1977)

These technical procedures and legal mandates can be overwhelming when you are first introduced to them. Remember that the purpose is to provide *minimum* standards to ensure that underachieving students throughout the country have an opportunity to receive special education services, if a team of professionals and their parents agree that it is appropriate. Professionals in some states argue that the standards are too restricting, while others request more stringent guidelines!

The Multidisciplinary Evaluation Team must use a variety of assessment techniques and instruments to address the criteria reported above. The following section provides a discussion of the types of instruments that might be used in the process of determining eligibility for specific learning disability services. The special education process will then be discussed step by step, and you will see how the regulations are applied to Frank, the student introduced in the opening vignette.

▶ ASSESSMENT BATTERY

Multidisciplinary Evaluation Teams and teachers are faced with selecting assessment tools which are the most accurate, efficient, and effective means of data collection. These include formal or norm-referenced tests and informal measures such as observation reports, criterion-referenced assessment, curriculum-based assessment, portfolio assessment, and classroom assessment. The assessment battery must be comprehensive, but unnecessary duplication must be avoided. McLoughlin and Lewis (1990) provided the following questions and discussion to address the evaluation of assessment tools.

1. *Does the instrument fit the purpose of assessment?* It is particularly important to select assessment measures that can address the reasons for a referral. If the goal is to answer questions about how a student compares to his or her peers, then a norm-referenced measure would be appropriate. If the question relates to classroom behavior, observational techniques would be adequate. If the teacher is questioning the mastery of specific academic skills, criterion-referenced tests, informal inventories, and teacher-made tests would provide the most valuable information. These types of tests will be defined later in this chapter.

It is also important to consider the types of results that are available from the assessment instrument. If the Multidisciplinary Evaluation Team is determining *eligibility,* percentile ranks or standard scores may be required to provide a comparison of this student's achievement to his peers across the country. To answer other questions, a simple frequency count of an undesirable behavior might be all that is necessary to answer the question.

Other considerations include the scope or content of the instrument. For example, if a Multidisciplinary Evaluation Team is trying to measure written expression in a student, a test such as the *Kauffman Test of Educational Achievement* (1995), that only includes a spelling subtest in the writing domain, would not be comprehensive enough to answer the referral question. The purpose of the assessment must be clearly identified before selecting the most appropriate assessment instrument. As a general rule, a test that is administered to groups of children should only be used if screening information is being gathered. When interpreting a low score on a test administered in a large group, it is difficult to determine if the score is a true reflection of ability or the result of distraction, lack of time, lack of motivation, etc. If it is determined that two procedures or instruments are equally appropriate to answer the referral question, the most efficient instrument should be the one selected.

2. *Is the evaluation instrument appropriate for the student?* The needs and abilities of the student must be considered in selecting assessment instruments or strategies. If standardized tests are used, the student's characteristics must be represented in the norm group on which the test was standardized. The examiner should look at the method of item presentation to determine if the test will be fair in assessing the student's actual ability in that area. For example, is the student asked to read, to listen, or to attend to a demonstration? It is possible that the child might have the knowledge or ability being assessed, but not be able to efficiently respond in the method required. For example, children are often asked to read a word problem and solve the problem to demonstrate un-

derstanding of a math concept. In this case, the math *ability* may be significantly affected by a reading *disability.*

The response mode is also important to consider in order to confirm that the student has the skills to perform the tasks required such as speaking, darkening of squares, writing sentences, or pointing to the correct response. When possible, students who have poor written expression ability should be allowed to provide oral responses during a test unless the purpose of the test is to study written expression. Also, some listening tests will require the child to listen to information and then circle one of four sentences that best summarizes what they have just heard. In this example the child's "listening" ability can only be measured if the child can "read" the summaries. Time factors must also be considered in terms of the student's capacity to attend for the required length of time as well as the impact on the student's stress level under timed conditions.

The assessment instrument should not discriminate against the student on the basis of race, culture, gender, language, or disability. Tests may contain language or concepts to which students from different races or cultures or with certain disabilities have not been exposed. This critical issue will be fully discussed in the section on formal tests.

3. *Is the tool appropriate for the evaluator?* McLoughlin and Lewis (1990) suggested that the potential for bias goes farther than the careful selection of assessment instruments. Bias can also be introduced into testing when the professional administering the test is not adequately trained. Professionals should be educated as to the individual differences of the students they assess, particularly when students are from different cultures or have handicapping conditions which may impact test performance.

No assessment instrument should be administered by an individual who has not been adequately trained to administer and score the test and interpret the test results. The skills of the professional must match the administration requirement of the testing device.

4. *Is the tool technically adequate?* Before teachers and Multidisciplinary Evaluation Team members adopt an instrument to make decisions regarding placement or teaching effectiveness, the quality of that instrument must be validated. The techniques used to design the instrument must be sound, and the instrument must be shown to be reliable and valid.

The two primary issues of technical adequacy are reliability and validity. **Reliability** refers to a test's ability to provide consistent results. For example if a child were administered a reliable test repeatedly, the scores would basically remain the same with little fluctuation. A reliability coefficient of .60 is generally recommended as a minimal level of acceptance for group data, and a coefficient of .80 is recommended for any data that will influence screening decisions. For data that will be used to make important decisions such as special education placement, a coefficient of .90 is recommended (Salvia and Ysseldyke, 1991).

The **validity** of an assessment instrument refers to whether it actually measures what it is reported to measure. Again, if a test claims to be a measure of written language but only includes spelling, this would be considered an invalid measure of written language because of the narrow focus. Judging the validity of a test is not as direct, with no set rules for judging the minimum standards for a validity coefficient. However, Anastasia (1988) stated that when the correlation with a repeated, parallel test is used, the correlation should at least be statistically significant.

Information on technical data for tests is generally found in the test manual or in a technical supplement. It is always available on a highly respected standardized instrument and is generally available on informal measures such as rating scales, criterion-referenced tests, inventories, and checklists. Review of this information is critical before test adoption.

5. *Is the tool an efficient data-collection mechanism?* With the amount of paperwork required in all aspects of teaching and special education service delivery, the need for efficient methods for data collection is critical. Without sacrificing quality, the evaluator must select an efficient device which gives the important information with a minimum expenditure of effort and time. Factors to consider include preparation time needed by the tester, time in test administration, difficulty in scoring results, and time required for data interpretation. More difficult administrative requirements often take longer and introduce a greater possibility of error. These are some of the advantages and disadvantages to formal, or norm-referenced tests and informal assessment measures and strategies. Following is a discussion of these instruments.

▶ FORMAL TESTS

The more traditional or formal type of test, used to determine eligibility for special education programming, is the **norm-referenced** or **standardized test.** These tests mandate specific procedures for administration, scoring, and interpretation (McLoughlin and Lewis, 1990). In a norm-referenced test, the student's performance is compared to the performance of a specific group that is a comparable population of children in the United States, in the child's school, or in a special population. The norm refers to the typical performance of the group to whom the child is being compared. The comparison is made by using a statistical procedure to convert the child's raw score or number of items correct into a derived score that indicates the child's standing relative to the norm group. The derived scores are needed for comparative purposes because a raw score is not very meaningful by itself. Knowing that a child answered fifteen out of twenty questions correctly may be of little use unless you know how other similar children performed on the same test.

The derived scores that may be obtained on norm-referenced measures include age- and grade-equivalent scores, percentile ranks, and standard scores.

Age-equivalent and grade-equivalent scores are generally considered to be misleading and have poor statistical properties. For example, when a student in the fourth grade scores a 2.5 grade equivalent on a reading test, it means that the fourth grader's *raw score* was scored most frequently by students in the second grade-fifth month. The score does not mean that the student actually read material written on a second grade-fifth month level during the test.

Percentile ranks can be useful in making educational decisions since it compares the child's position in relationship to the comparative sample. For example, if a student scored at the seventy-fifth percentile on a reading test, it means the student's raw score was the same or better than 75 percent of the students taking the test to which he was compared. It also means 25 percent scored as well or better than he or she scored. However, percentiles are often misinterpreted as percent correct and can really alarm parents. For example, if a student scores at the fiftieth percentile, the raw score was average—with 50 percent of students in the norm group scoring equal to or above and 50 percent scoring equal to or below. This average score does not suggest a deficit at all, but parents and students seeing these numbers may think they failed the test with a score of 50 percent correct!

The preferred derived scores are standard scores such as Z scores, T scores, and deviation quotients (Sattler, 1990). Standard scores have a constant mean and a standard deviation across all ages included in the normative sample. For example the mean of the *Wechsler Intelligence* scales is 100 with a standard deviation of 15. An intelligence score of 100 on a Wechsler intelligence scale places the student at the fiftieth percentile and suggests no deficit. Table 3.1 demonstrates the relative standing of various standard scores to percentile ranks. You may want to refer to this table again as you study Chapter 4 on Educational Service Options.

Figure 3.1 depicts the position of various standard scores compared to the normal curve. This is helpful in reviewing standard test scores with varying means. For example a T-score of 50 on a test has the same relative standing of a Wechsler IQ score of 100. The figure also provides a visual of the normal range (e.g., + or − 1 standard deviation). Notice that a percentile score of 25 is still in the normal range (e.g., less than 1 standard deviation from the mean).

The type of derived score selected will depend on the purpose for obtaining the score. For example, the criteria for eligibility developed by a State Department of Education or local school district may require a standard score or a grade equivalent score. Typically, important norm-referenced instruments used in the eligibility process for students with LD include the determination of aptitude, usually measured by an IQ test, and the standard scores that reflect their levels of performance in reading skills, reading comprehension, math calculations, math application, written expression, oral language, and/or listening. Scores should be obtained for any of these areas noted as problematic on the referral form.

Norm-referenced or formal tests are typically used to identify a student with a learning disability because they (1) provide information regarding the child

TABLE 3.1

Relation of Various Standard Scores to Percentile
Rank and Each Other

			Standard Scores			
Percentile Rank	Quotients	NCE Scores	T-Scores	Z-Scores	Stanines	Deficit
99	150	99	83	+3.33	9	
99	145	99	80	+3.00	9	
99	140	99	77	+2.67	9	
99	135	99	73	+2.33	9	
98	130	92	70	+2.00	9	
95	125	85	67	+1.67	8	
91	120	78	63	+1.34	8	none
84	115	71	60	+1.00	7	
75	110	64	57	+0.67	6	
63	105	57	53	+0.33	6	
50	100	50	50	+0.00	5	
37	95	43	47	−0.33	4	
25	90	36	43	−0.67	4	
16	85	29	40	−1.00	3	mild
9	80	22	37	−1.34	2	
5	75	15	33	−1.67	2	moderate
2	70	8	30	−2.00	1	
1	65	1	27	−2.33	1	
1	60	1	23	−2.67	1	severe
1	55	1	20	−3.00	1	

Source: From "The Role of Standardized Tests in Planning Academic Instruction" (p. 377) by D.D. Hammill and B.R. Bryant, 1991, in H.L. Swanson (Ed.), *Handbook on the Assessment Assembly of Learning Disabilities* (pp. 373–406). Austin, TX: PRO-ED. Copyright 1991 by PRO-ED, Inc. Reprinted by permission.

referred in comparison to his or her peers and (2) are mathematically adequate to be employed in complex calculations required for identification and eligibility in most states (Strawser, 1993). Although formal tests have been a major component of the special education process for many years, there has been much controversy over their use. Significant legislation and litigation regarding assessment practices in special education occurred during the 1970s and 1980s. Major concerns were raised that norm-referenced instruments were not adequately valid and reliable, that they were not culturally fair, and they were not relevant to instructional planning and implementation.

In selecting a test, the evaluator should determine that the child being evaluated is comparable to the normative group that was used to develop derived

FIGURE 3.1

Relationship of Normal Curve to Various Types of Standard Scores

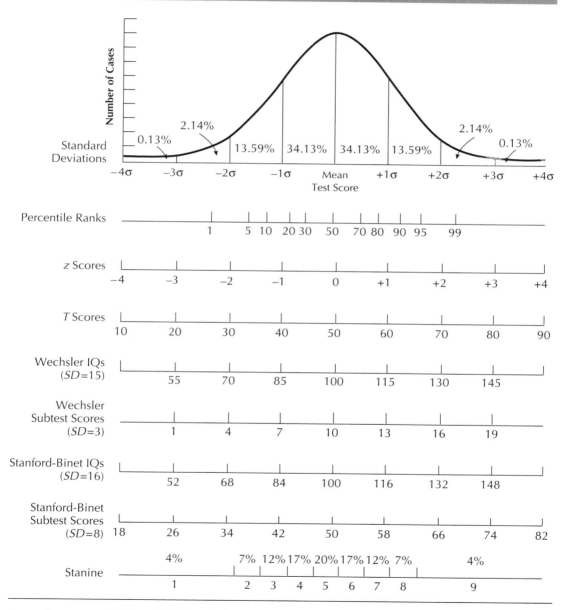

Source: Assessment of Children (3rd Ed., p. 17) by J.M. Sattler, 1990, San Diego: Jerome M. Sattler Publisher. Copyright 1981 and 1990. Reprinted with permission of the author.

scores for the test. In addition the test should be evaluated to determine that the population used to represent the demographic characteristics of the population as a whole is representative of the types of persons with whom the test will be used. This would include age and grade levels, gender, ethnicity, geographic regions, and socio-economic status. The normative data should also be reviewed to determine that an adequate number of each group of subjects was included in the norm group (McLoughlin and Lewis, 1990).

Although difficult to identify, a nondiscriminatory and unbiased assessment battery must be rigorously pursued. A standardized test may be unfair and biased to persons from cultural minorities if items on the test relate primarily to middle-class values and attitudes from a largely Caucasian population. Norm-referenced tests typically do not reflect the unique experiences and the individual language, thinking, and cultural styles and values from a minority population. McLoughlin and Lewis (1990) propose the following considerations to minimize bias in assessment.

1. Assessment measures should be translated into languages other than English (although this can affect the validity of the test if translations depart from the format of original items).
2. Interpreters should be used for non-English speaking students.
3. Culture-fair or culture-free measures should be developed to minimize items which might lower the performance of minority students.
4. Separate norms should be developed for minority students when using traditional assessment devices.
5. Informal procedures should be used to assess a student's performance as opposed to standardized tests with more formal procedures.
6. Although a controversial recommendation, it has been suggested that standardized testing be abolished.

The following questions are recommended to be addressed in evaluating an assessment tool in terms of nonbiased testing.

1. Is the normed group or other standard of comparison appropriate for the student in terms of race, culture, and gender?
2. Are test items free from cultural bias?
3. Is the language of the measure appropriate for the student?
4. Does the measure bypass the limitations imposed by the disability? (McLoughlin and Lewis, 1990; p. 67)

It is also important that the evaluator have appropriate beliefs and attitudes about the groups that they are testing. For example, if an examiner believes that girls do not excel in science, this bias may be reflected in test administration and scoring practices. Rapport is also important to develop between the student and the evaluator. If the evaluator is from an unfamiliar culture, it may take extra time to put the students at ease in the testing situation. Bias should also be avoided during the interpretation of test results. Standardized procedures for scoring and interpretation of test scores must be strictly adhered to.

Also problematic is the frequency with which formal assessment measures can be administered. Since these tools are generally recommended to be administered no more than once or twice a year, teachers, depending only on standardized tests, miss the systematic monitoring that can be on-going when using more informal types of measurement. Informal assessment techniques are also more effective for making instructional decisions because they are more sensitive to curricular differences and academic gains. They can provide frequent documentation for greater accountability and serve to document student progress within the curriculum. There has been a movement away from the more formal methods of norm-referenced assessment and towards a more informal assessment strategy that would provide direct, curriculum-based measures of student performance (Monda-Amaya and Reed, 1993).

INFORMAL TESTS AND MEASUREMENT

McLoughlin and Lewis (1990) defined **informal assessment** as procedures without rigid administration, scoring, and interpretation rules. They noted that through informal assessment, a student's performance in the existing curriculum in the natural learning environment can be evaluated. Informal assessment devices can be used to

- provide information about current levels of performance;
- aid in the selection of goals and objectives;
- point to the need for instructional modifications;
- document student progress; and
- suggest directions for further assessment (Monda-Amaya and Reed, 1993, p. 109). The following is a discussion of four types of informal assessment: curriculum-based, criterion-referenced (CBA), observation, and interviews, checklists, and questionnaires.

Curriculum-Based Assessment (CBA)

Deno (1987) defined **curriculum-based assessment** as "any approach that uses direct observation and recording of a student's performance in a local school curriculum as a basis for gathering information to make instructional decisions" (p. 41). The goal is to analyze the curriculum and determine the instructional mismatch that occurs between the skills of the student and the curriculum (Gickling and Thompson, 1985). This type of assessment is particularly important now that there is an increase in teaching students with learning disabilities in the general education setting. However, curriculum-based assessment is also useful in all stages of the special education process from the initial screening to program evaluation (Monda-Amaya and Reed, 1993).

During the initial screening, CBA provides a mechanism for documenting student performance and the degree that it deviates from the performance of peers. This is much like the information provided by norm-referenced instruments with the benefit of assessing the child's abilities in relation to a relevant curriculum as opposed to the abilities of other children with similar backgrounds. If the deviation is significant, additional justification for the referral would be available.

Monda-Amaya and Reed (1993) also noted that CBA is advantageous during eligibility decisions because the focus can be redirected from labeling in terms of an exceptionality to identifying instructional deficits that can be addressed through teaching the areas of deficit in relation to the classroom curriculum. Curriculum-based assessment procedures can be used repeatedly over time, they can be applied to any subject area, and they are sensitive to small changes in progress toward accomplishing a goal. Monda-Amaya and Reed (1993) discussed the following six types of curriculum-based assessments.

Curriculum-based Measurement

In curriculum-based measurement "teachers specify long-term academic goals, conduct on-going assessments that monitor student progress toward that goal, evaluate the adequacy of student progress and the instructional plan, and develop instructional changes that increase the probability of goal attainment" (Fuchs, Allinder, Hamlet, and Fuchs, 1990, p. 42). An example of a procedure to measure a student's skill in the area of math might be described by the following: Given division problems from the fifth grade math textbook, Cameron will perform the calculations at a rate of fifteen problems correct per minute with no more than two errors per minute. Cameron will be given a test with thirty questions typical of items found in the text. The teacher will time Cameron's performance. The following decisions could then be made

- How appropriate is the objective?
- How adequate is the student's progress?
- Does modification of instruction need to take place?
- Which parts of the intervention have worked effectively? (Fuchs, et al., 1991).

Response and Error Analysis

Another type of CBA is a thorough review and analysis of student work samples. In the example above the teacher would review not only the correct or incorrect number of Cameron's response but the process that was used to answer the questions. This is particularly important for students with learning disabilities. Deficits in areas like sequencing and reasoning are often problematic, but if a student has difficulty asking questions these inefficient methods may continue until the teacher analyzes the problem. Figure 3.2 demonstrates the type of information that may be obtained from an item analysis in math.

FIGURE 3.2

Examples of Selected Error Types

Conceptual Errors

20 −13 —— 10	inappropriate concept of zero

13 +4 —— 8	no concept of a multidigit number

$\dfrac{1}{2}$
$+$
$\dfrac{1}{5}$
——
9   no concept of fractions; adds all numbers

Procedural Errors

3¹2
+83
——
16   adds from left to right

41
−28
——
27   subtracts smaller number from larger number

5¹8
−35
——
23   unnecessary regrouping

2
35
x 5
——
255   adds regrouped number before multiplying

14
3⟌123
12
——
3   records answer from left to right

$\dfrac{1}{4}$
$+$
$\dfrac{3}{5}$
——
$\dfrac{4}{9}$ adds numerators and denominators

Source: *Assessment: The Special Educator's Role* by C. Hoy and N. Gregg. Copyright © 1994 Brooks/Cole Publishing Company, Pacific Grove, CA 93950, a division of International Thomson Publishing Inc. By permission of the publisher.

Other products that teachers may evaluate include student journals, class assignments, projects, tests, homework assignments, and oral responses to questions. Spelling errors might be analyzed to look for errors involving initial consonants, vowel teams, suffixes, vowel plus *r*, vowel plus *n*, final *e*, and blends (Fuchs et al., 1990). In the area of reading, a student's oral reading might be analyzed for common miscues including omissions, insertions, substitutions, reversals, and syntactically and semantically unacceptable responses (Adams, 1990). Figure 3.3 provides an example of the information provided by the analysis of student's miscues (e.g., errors during oral reading).

FIGURE 3.3

Example of an Analysis of Oral Reading

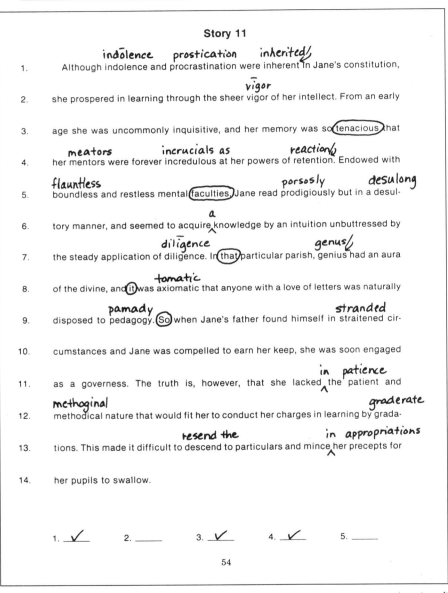

Story 11

1. Although indolence and procrastination were inherent in Jane's constitution,
indolence   prostication   inherited

2. she prospered in learning through the sheer vigor of her intellect. From an early
vigor

3. age she was uncommonly inquisitive, and her memory was so tenacious that

4. her mentors were forever incredulous at her powers of retention. Endowed with
meators   incrucials as   reactiony

5. boundless and restless mental faculties, Jane read prodigiously but in a desul-
flauntless   porsosly   desulong

6. tory manner, and seemed to acquire knowledge by an intuition unbuttressed by
a

7. the steady application of diligence. In that particular parish, genius had an aura
diligence   genusy

8. of the divine, and it was axiomatic that anyone with a love of letters was naturally
tomatic

9. disposed to pedagogy. So when Jane's father found himself in straitened cir-
pamady   stranded

10. cumstances and Jane was compelled to earn her keep, she was soon engaged

11. as a governess. The truth is, however, that she lacked the patient and
in patience

12. methodical nature that would fit her to conduct her charges in learning by grada-
methoginal   graderate

13. tions. This made it difficult to descend to particulars and mince her precepts for
resend the   in appropriations

14. her pupils to swallow.

1. ✓   2. ____   3. ✓   4. ✓   5. ____

54

(continued)

Academic Probes

When a specific academic behavior is measured in a time sample, the measurement technique is called a probe. The purpose of an academic probe is to assess

FIGURE 3.3

continued

EXAMINER'S WORKSHEET

Student's Name **Dori**

Form _____ Oral Reading Level **11**

NO.	LINE	TEXT WORD	MISCUE	Meaning Similarity	Function Similarity	Graphic/Phonemic Similarity	Multiple Sources	Self-Correction
1	1	indolence	indolence	0	0	1	0	0
2	1	procrastination	prostication	0	0	1	0	0
3	1	inherent	inherited/ɹ	1	1	1	1	1
4	2	vigor	vigor	0	0	1	0	0
5	4	mentors	meators	0	0	1	0	0
6	4	incredulous	incrucials	0	0	1	0	0
7	4	at	as	0	1	1	1	0
8	4	retention	reaction/ɹ	0	1	1	1	1
9	5	boundless	flauntless	0	0	1	0	0
10	5	prodigiously	porsosly	0	0	1	0	0
11	5	desultory	desulong	0	0	1	0	0
12	7	diligence	diligence	0	0	1	0	0
13	7	genius	genus/ɹ	0	0	1	0	1
14	8	axiomatic	tomatic	0	0	1	0	0
15	9	pedagogy	pamady	0	0	1	0	0
16	9	straitened	stranded	0	1	1	1	0
17	11	patient	patience	0	1	1	1	0
18	12	methodical	methoginal	0	0	1	0	0
19	12	gradations	graderate	0	0	1	0	0
20	13	descend	resend	0	1	1	1	0
21	13	to	the	0	1	1	1	0
22	13	precepts	appropriations	0	1	1	1	0
23								
24								
25								
TOTAL YES				1	8	22	8	3
TOTAL NO				21	14	0	14	19

OTHER MISCUES

Type

Omissions O ☐
Additions ∧ ☐
Dialect ∨ ☐
Reversals ~ ☐

OTHER OBSERVATIONS

Type

Slow reading rate ☐
Word-by-word reading ☐
Poor phrasing ☐
Lack of expression ☐
Pitch too high or low; voice too soft or strained ☐
Poor enunciation

Type

Disregard of punctuation ☐
Head movement ☐
Finger pointing ☐
Loss of place ☐
Nervousness ☐
Poor attitude
Other _____ ☐

55

Adapted from Formal Reading Inventory (pp. 54-55) by J.L. Wiederholt, 1985, Austin, TX: PRO-ED. Reprinted with permission.

acquisition, fluency, and maintenance of a specific behavior. McLoughlin and Lewis (1990) noted that an academic probe can be used to determine the effectiveness of a specific instructional strategy since performance can be evaluated repeatedly under standard conditions. An example of an academic probe would be a worksheet with basic multiplication facts listed. The student could either be timed to see how long it would take him or her to complete the task or given a certain time period (e.g., two minutes) to see how many he or she can answer in the specified period. The scores are calculated with the percentage correct and the number of errors, and the results are charted. This can be excellent feedback to reinforce progress in the acquisition and fluency of solving basic facts. With delayed responses and slow work rate being common characteristics of students with learning disabilities, a poor grade may be a reflection of these characteristics and not a measure of their actual knowledge. Targeting rate of response for improvement may be more beneficial in the long run than automatically offering accommodations that do not provide a challenge to increase productivity. A probe for knowledge of single consonant sounds is pictured in Figure 3.4.

Task Analysis

Task analysis has been defined by Maag (1989) as a process of identifying, breaking down and sequencing the components of a target behavior and evaluating a student's progress towards the mastery of those subcomponent skills. In designing a task analysis or administering a task assessment, the teacher identifies the target behavior or task and writes a terminal objective. The teacher then breaks down the targeted behavior into teachable subtasks and describes each in measurable terms. Once the subtasks have been identified, the teacher develops an assessment tool containing questions measuring each of the subobjectives. This becomes the assessment device and as the data are collected, it is used to identify deficit skill areas, and to plan and implement instruction.

Often when a student with learning disabilities is failing, it is because the instruction has been provided in increments too large for him or her to comprehend. With task analysis skills, a teacher can segment an academic process into small steps and identify the specific task or step that is problematic. In summary, task analysis is particularly helpful in identifying

- a student's entry level for a particular skill;
- specific deficit skills within an academic area; and
- monitoring the student's progress through the mastery of subtasks leading to a terminal objective.

Teacher-Made Tests

Teacher-made tests are a simple type of curriculum-based assessment. Since the teachers know how a skill is taught, it is more appropriate for them to develop a test to accurately reflect student knowledge. Teacher-made tests are frequently criterion-referenced so that a preset criteria is established to determine whether the student has demonstrated mastery. Since many students with learning disabilities have difficulty generalizing, it may be important for the teacher to develop a test that measures the skill in the format used during instruction.

FIGURE 3.4

Teacher Probe Sheet For Single Consonant Sounds in Isolation

Name _____

Date _____

Mastery: Yes   No

Correct: _____

PROBE SHEET

Single Consonant Sounds in Isolation: Form A

Objective: Given 100 consonant letters in isolation, the student will verbally identify the 23 sounds associated with 21 single consonant letters.

Directions: On the sheet I have given you, read the *sounds* that the letters stand for. Read the sounds from left to right and from the top of the page to the bottom of the page (demonstrate on student probe sheet). You will have 1 minute to read as many possible sounds as you can.

b	v	k	t	f	c	r	f	j	t	10
v	y	v	l	d	h	z	t	w	s	20
y	d	c	s	g	n	w	k	z	m	30
m	w	f	g	k	q	d	d	r	q	40
r	g	x	y	l	f	x	j	p	h	50
v	l	q	f	h	c	n	t	d	m	60
s	g	p	b	l	r	g	n	z	p	70
b	j	h	c	w	c	p	y	g	r	80
p	l	m	x	k	b	h	q	k	z	90
n	b	y	w	m	s	j	x	c	n	100

(Accept hard or soft c & g sounds in all cases. If the student does not use all 4 sounds at some time, note in comment section and reattach as appropriate.)

Number of sounds read per minute: _____   Comments:

Number of sounds read correctly: _____

Number of sounds read incorrectly: _____

Mastery = 70 sounds per minute with 2 or less errors.

Note: This sheet and the student probe sheet would have alternative forms.

Source: *Curriculum-Based Assessment in Special Education* by M.E. Kings-Sears, 1992. San Diego, CA: Singular Publishing Company. Reprinted with permission by Singular Publishing Group, Inc.

For example, if a teacher uses vertical math problems to teach single-digit addition, the student with learning disabilities might become frustrated with a test presenting horizontal addition problems. The teacher would lose valuable information, not knowing whether the child understood the concept or was "tricked" by the change in format.

Portfolio Assessment

As educators look for alternatives to standardized testing procedures, many have been drawn towards the concept of authentic assessment or demonstrating knowledge and understanding through a product, performance, or exhibition (Wiggins, 1989). Archibald and Newman (1988) defined portfolio as "a file or folder containing a variety of information that documents a student's experiences and accomplishments" (p. 29). Tindal (1991) suggested that authentic assessment includes

- items that relate directly to the curriculum;
- criteria used in assessment procedures;
- self-evaluation by students; and
- a presentation by students of work that they select.

This type of assessment has been compared to a review of an artist's work in which the portfolio or collection of art work of the artist is collected. The use of portfolios in the assessment of students with learning disabilities has been very enthusiastically received. While the idea of portfolio assessment has been used in regular education extensively, it is particularly effective as a means to document progress towards meeting the goals and objectives of an individual educational plan. The *Portfolio News* (Staff, 1990) lists over thirty-five potential purposes of portfolios for classrooms. Some of these include

- documenting improvement in students' writing over time;
- involving students in self-evaluation;
- documenting effective teaching practices;
- improving communication between teachers and parents;
- serving as a portfolio for college applications;
- replacing competency exams;
- motivating students by providing ownership, participation and sense of accomplishment;
- assessing needs in the curriculum;
- connecting thinking, reading, and writing;
- aiding in conferences with parents.

While guidelines for developing and implementing portfolio assessment are beyond the scope of this chapter, you are encouraged to study additional references for further information in this important area. (Walsh and McCabe, 1995; Carpenter, Ray, and Bloom, 1995; Swicegood, 1994).

Criterion-Referenced Assessment

Another form of informal assessment is the criterion-referenced test (CRT). McLoughlin and Lewis (1990) defined CRTs as assessment devices that measure skill mastery and compare student performance to a set of standards or preset criteria on items developed from the curriculum. CRTs may be teacher-made or developed commercially. These tests are typically linked to a more general instructional curriculum or scope and sequence of skills, although they may be developed from the local school curriculum. An example of commercially available CRTs are the *Brigance Inventories* and the *Enright Inventory of Basic Arithmetic Skills*. These and other CRTs are described more fully by Taylor (1993). Care should be taken to determine whether the CRTs being used are reliable and a valid measure of the curriculum being taught. Figure 3.5 provides an example of a teacher-made, criterion-referenced assessment that includes a weekly assessment with an increase in skills projected.

FIGURE 3.5

Sample Criterion-Referenced Assessment for Written Language

**Written Language
Curriculum-based Assessment**

Sentence Writing

Objective:
　Given a writing topic, the student will write 10 related sentences using complete sentence structure 80% of the time (8 out of 10 sentences are related to the topic and complete) in a weekly writing sample.

Directions:

_____ Choose a writing prompt.

_____ Assign the prompt to a student.

_____ Allow one class period for draft and rewrite.

_____ Allow use of visuals and word lists.

Assessment is to be done weekly.

Mastery level = 80% to 100%

Maintenance Mastery level to attain by June = 100%*
* student will be able to write 10 complete sentences on a topic in a weekly writing sample

Source: *Curriculum-Based Assessment in Special Education* by M.E. King-Sears, 1992. San Diego, CA: Singular Publishing Company. Reprinted with permission by Singular Publishing Group, Inc.

Observation

Direct observation of a student's performance in educational settings continues to be one of the most widely used techniques in assessment. It is used to

- detect student's problems early;
- validate information from other measurement strategies;
- collect information on a student's performance across a variety of situations;
- evaluate instructional interventions; and
- identify relationships between a student's behavior and the environmental stimuli (Bailey and Wolery, 1989).

Care should be taken to collect observational data in a systematic, objective manner. Training in this type of assessment is important, particularly if the information is to be used to determine eligibility as is the case for students with learning disabilities.

Data from the observation can be charted or summarized as an anecdotal record report. Anecdotal records should contain factual information regarding the interaction between the student's behavior and the environment. Using this observation technique, an evaluator can examine the antecedent or what was happening in the classroom prior to the behavior occurring as well as the consequences to a behavior in the natural classroom setting (Monda-Amaya and Reed, 1993).

Interviews, Questionnaires, and Checklists

Interviews, questionnaires, and checklists are informal assessment tools for data collection that provide teachers an opportunity to ask questions and obtain reactions to assist in determining areas of further assessment (Tindal and Marston, 1990). This data collection procedure is generally face-to-face, personal interaction. When personal interactions are not feasible, a written questionnaire may be used. Questionnaires may contain structured multiple choice items, true/false items, or open-ended questions (McLoughlin and Lewis, 1990).

A checklist provides a different format on which lists of descriptive statements regarding characteristics, behaviors, skills, interests, knowledge concepts, or traits are provided to the respondent who is asked to verify whether the statements are true or not true of the student being evaluated. When adopting interviews, questionnaires, and checklists, care should be taken to verify that the evaluator and the respondent are providing data that is non-biased and that the questions used are fair and appropriate for the situation.

▶ COMPONENTS OF THE ASSESSMENT PROCESS

Swanson (1991) defined assessment as "a goal-directed problem-solving process that uses various measures within a theoretical framework" (p. 4). As noted in Chapters 1 and 2 on the history and definitions of LD, many theoretical frameworks and definitions of learning disabilities have been proposed by individuals with LD and their families, professionals, and government agencies. Kavale and Forness (1985) called LD a "victim of its own history" (p. 39) because each phase of the relatively brief history of LD has introduced a theoretical framework with its own terminology and definition. Each of these perspectives has in some way influenced the assessment and identification process (Strawser, 1993).

The assessment process is also complicated by the nature of learning disabilities which covers a complex range of problems and includes a heterogeneous group of characteristics. School personnel are faced with the challenge of developing assessment procedures that are comprehensive enough to address the wide variation of characteristics and problems yet are not so extensive that timelines cannot be met and financial resources are not exhausted. Figure 3.6 displays the assessment process commonly used in special education programs. This process represents the logical flow in assessment procedures from the initial screening or prereferral to final outcome.

FIGURE 3.6

The Assessment Process for Special Education

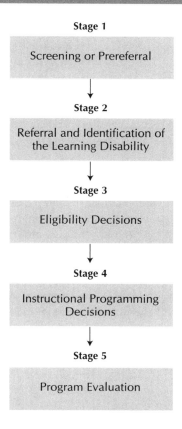

Stage 1

Screening or Prereferral

Stage 2

Referral and Identification of the Learning Disability

Stage 3

Eligibility Decisions

Stage 4

Instructional Programming Decisions

Stage 5

Program Evaluation

To provide an example of the application of each stage in the special education process, you will follow the story of Frank who was introduced at the beginning of the chapter. Frank began to have needs that were not being met in the general education classroom at the beginning of second grade. The following discussion of the special education process will include information on Frank as his case evolves.

▶ STAGE 1: SCREENING OR PREREFERRAL

This is the beginning of the special education process in which a teacher or parent realizes that there is a problem. Strawser (1993) pointed out that learning problems may be caused by any number of things including medical problems, poor nutrition, lack of motivation, cultural differences, excessive absences, poor teaching, or a disability. Questions which Strawser (1993) suggested might be asked during this initial exploration phase include

- Is there a problem in classroom performance or is the child not learning?
- Can we determine what is causing the problem?
- Can something be done to help the problem?
- Is specialized testing and possibly special education indicated?

A study by Algozzine, Christenson, and Ysseldyke (1982) suggested that if a child is referred, there is a 92 percent chance that the child will be tested and a 73 percent chance that the child will be placed in a special education program. This high rate of acceptance of referrals and placement in special education continued to be reported throughout the 80s. In response to this trend, there is increased emphasis on the techniques and processes used during screening and intervention that can be tried prior to referral (e.g., prereferral intervention phase). Prereferral intervention requires the concerned teacher to modify some aspect(s) of the learning environment or teaching procedures to determine if the referral for special education services can be avoided.

Carter and Sugai (1989) surveyed state departments and found that prereferral interventions were recommended in eleven states and required in twenty-three states. In many states the prereferral interventions are generated as part of a teacher support team or child study team. This team approach represents a collaborative technique for systematic problem solving which has resulted in schoolwide changes. These teams have developed interventions for implementation in general education classrooms that are very responsive to the needs of children with learning and behavior problems (Graden, 1989).

During the child study team meeting, teachers present concerns regarding individual students to a group typically composed of master teachers from general education, an administrator, and a special education teacher. After considering the difficulties that the child is experiencing in the general education classroom, the team begins to explore the possible causes and solutions for the problems. Specifically, the team should consider

- the student's medical status and visual and auditory acuity;

- differences in cultural or ethnic expectations or language spoken in the home;
- educational history including absenteeism;
- the classroom environment;
- the complexity of the language and vocabulary used to deliver instruction and give directions;
- the curriculum being used;
- the match between the child's skills and the curriculum requirements;
- the techniques for delivering instruction; and,
- the strategies for reinforcing good performance (Smith, 1991; Salvia and Ysseldyke, 1991; Taylor, Willits, and Richards, 1988; Strawser, 1989).

After exploring these areas, the team will recommend specific interventions or accommodations to solve the problem in the general education classroom or in other programs that may be available in the school to assist children at risk for academic failure. Generally, the team agrees on a specified time period, such as six to nine weeks, for trying the interventions. Figure 3.7 (p. 91) contains a form to document various prereferral interventions. The Child Study Team might reject the traditional approaches included on the form and choose to create interventions more specifically addressing the individual child's needs. Blanks are left in each category for the team's creative solutions.

Read the information in Box 3.1 to follow Frank's case as it is presented to the Child Study Team. Figure 3.8 (p. 92) contains the form completed by Frank's teacher to present information on Frank to the team. The prereferral intervention strategies implemented for Frank are documented on the Referral Form in Figure 3.8.

▶ STAGE 2: REFERRAL AND IDENTIFICATION OF THE DISABILITY

At this point in the special education process, the teacher and/or the Child Study Team determines that the prereferral interventions are not successfully meeting the educational needs of the student, and the parents are notified that a referral is being made. Figure 3.9 (p. 93) provides the referral form completed by Frank's teacher to begin the evaluation process needed to determine if Frank will be eligible for special education services.

Figure 3.10 (p. 95) contains a sample of a parent's rights form given to parents to sign as a record that their rights were received and understood. This is the form Frank's parents received. The permission form to be signed by Frank's parents giving the school permission to begin Frank's individualized assessment is included in Figure 3.11 (p. 99).

After the necessary permission forms have been obtained, the assessment process begins. At this point the Multidisciplinary Evaluation Team (MET) is activated and a variety of specialists may participate in obtaining the necessary information to eventually determine whether a child will be eligible for special

| Box 3.1 | *Prereferral Intervention for Frank* |

At the semester parent conference, Mrs. Principi and Frank's parents agreed that Frank was struggling with his reading and that he might need some more accommodations or modifications. Mrs. Principi said she would like to present her concerns about Frank to the school-based Child Study Team to get some assistance. The parents agreed. Mrs. Principi put Frank on the agenda for late January. She completed the appropriate form (shown in Figure 3.8), copied records, and collected work samples to share with the team.

At the Child Study Team meeting, Mrs. Principi shared her concerns and all the pertinent information. The team agreed that Frank needed additional interventions to progress. It was suggested that the special education consultant teacher help Mrs. Principi put together some individualized phonic material to review skills he had not mastered. Frank's parents could help him work through the material at home. It was also suggested that Frank have a fifth grade peer helper to read with him three days a week. This student would encourage and help Frank read simple chapter books selected by Mrs. Principi with Frank's input.

The counselor agreed that she would talk with Frank about his move and try to determine if he was adjusting. The special education consultant said she would like to observe Frank in the regular class to watch him work independently, to observe his reading group, and to see how Frank interacted with other students. This could be done during her weekly consult time for second grade. Mrs. Principi also agreed to have Frank restate oral directions after they were given to increase comprehension. The Child Study Team scheduled a follow-up on Frank for the second week in March. Suggested interventions were implemented.

In March the Child Study Team met to evaluate Frank's progress. Mrs. Principi reported that Frank enjoyed the attention from the peer tutor, but continued to struggle with any text multisyllable words. He continued to select storybooks to read instead of progressing to simple chapter books. The counselor felt that Frank had adjusted to his school change but she reported Frank said that "the work is harder here." Frank completed the phonics work at home with great difficulty even with significant help from parents. His parents and Mrs. Principi agreed that Frank had mastered short vowel patterns, but could not apply them to decode larger words like "understand." The special education consultant noted that Frank worked quickly and accurately to complete math work. However, he dawdled and tried to talk with friends instead of completing his reading work. She agreed that he was probably the weakest reader in his group. Mrs. Principi said that having Frank restate directions seemed to make him focus more, but he continued to need to have instructions repeated frequently.

The Child Study Team recommended that a Special Education referral should be made to determine if Frank might be eligible to receive services. It was agreed that the referral should be done so that if Frank did qualify for special education, no time would be lost in third grade. Mrs. Principi volunteered to contact the parents and was given a referral form to complete and return to the team. (See Figure 3.9)

Mrs. Principi called Frank's parents to share the recommendations of the Child Study Team. Both parents were concerned, but pleased that a referral would be made. Mrs. Principi completed the referral form and the Child Study Team accepted the referral. The Parental Rights and Permission to Evaluate forms were signed by Frank's parents. These are included in Figure 3.10 and 3.11.

education. Each assessment battery should be developed around the referral problem indicated by the teachers and Child Study Team. Formal, standardized tests administered individually are usually employed to identify the disability. The individuals that conduct the evaluations must be qualified to administer any examination assigned to them.

FIGURE 3.7

Form to Document Prereferral Interventions within the Regular Classroom

The following prereferral intervention strategies will be implemented for _____ beginning _____. The results of these strategies will be reviewed on _____ by the Child Study Team.

	No. of days Attempted	Problem Better	No Change	Problem Worse
Teaching Strategies				
Taped or oral presentation/testing	_____	_____	_____	_____
Modeling	_____	_____	_____	_____
Preteach vocabulary	_____	_____	_____	_____
Slower pace	_____	_____	_____	_____
Alternative/additional materials	_____	_____	_____	_____
Tutoring-peers, volunteers, paraprofessionals	_____	_____	_____	_____
Guided practice	_____	_____	_____	_____
Special grouping	_____	_____	_____	_____
Task Requirements				
Change criteria for success	_____	_____	_____	_____
Break into smaller steps	_____	_____	_____	_____
Provide prompts	_____	_____	_____	_____
Clarify directions	_____	_____	_____	_____
Behavior Techniques				
Behavior management (Attach explanation)	_____	_____	_____	_____
Student Contract	_____	_____	_____	_____
Consultation with _____	_____	_____	_____	
Sessions with school counselor	_____	_____	_____	_____
Other (Describe) _____	_____	_____	_____	_____
_____	_____	_____	_____	_____
_____	_____	_____	_____	_____
_____	_____	_____	_____	_____
_____	_____	_____	_____	_____

Team Members Present: _____

_____

_____

FIGURE 3.8

Child Study Team Data Form

Child Study Team Student Data Form

Student's Name _Frank P._____

Teacher _Mrs. Sally Principi_ Date _Jan. 24, 1995_____

Parent(s) Name_Mr+Mrs. Frank P._____

Address __100 Oak Street_____

Home Phone_967-9097____   Work Phone_934-8335___

Birthdate___9-10-86_____   Grade___2nd_____

Reason for CST review: __✓__Academic   __✓__Emotional

_____Behavior   _____Environmental

_____Social   _____Other

Please give a brief description of the problem(s).

Frank is new to Hunter School. He is having difficulty with reading decoding which is impacting his comprehension. He can't decode or spell 2-3 syllable words accurately. He requires that directions be repeated or explained individually. He seems to be more and more frustrated by this. Many assignments are going undone.

Please attach copies of any pertinent information to share with the CST. (Examples: report card, SAT scores, work samples, anecdotal notes about behavior, etc.)

In referring to the *Federal Register* (USOE, 1977) "Criteria for Identifying a Learning Disability" for direction in terms of the types of tests needed to determine eligibility, it becomes clear that at a minimum the child's mental ability, achievement, and socioemotional behavior must be determined. The most common measure for determining ability is the intelligence test. The test most frequently used are the *Wechsler Intelligence Scale for Children-III* (1991) or the *Stanford-Binet Intelligence Scale* (1986). Table 3.2 (p. 100) contains a description of these and other standardized measures used to measure aptitude.

FIGURE 3.9

Student Referral Form

Referral was made by:
Phone _____
Mail _____
Conference _____
Referral Form _____
on _____ (date). **THE 90-DAY TIMELINE BEGINS WITH THE DATE IN THIS BOX.**

STUDENT REFERRAL FORM

Student's Complete Legal Name   *Frank P.*
Person Referring *Mrs. Sally P.*   Position *2nd teacher*
Social Security No. _____   Sex *M*   Grade *2nd*   Race *W*
Date of Birth   *9-10-86*   School/Service Provider *Hunter School*
Parent's Name(s) *Mr. + Mrs. Frank P.*
Address *100 Oak Street*   Home Phone *967-9097*
                                             Work Phone *934-8335*
Primary Language in Home   *English*   Work Phone _____
Reason for Referral (List specific concerns)
Frank has difficulty decoding words in text using phonics.
He avoids text with multi-syllable words. Directions have to be
repeated frequently. He is not completing reading work. He
is becoming quite frustrated. He can't spell multi-syllable words
in his writing.

Have the parents been informed of the reason for this referral? *Yes*   If no, please explain. _____
_____
_____

PREREFERRAL INTERVENTIONS WITHIN THE REGULAR PROGRAM

For school-based referrals only, indicate below, or briefly describe the interventions you have used over a six-weeks period of time in response to this student's problem(s).

Teaching Strategies	No. of days Attempted	Problem Better	No Change	Problem Worse
Taped or oral presentation/testing				
Modeling				
Preteach vocabulary				
Slower pace	30+	✓		
Alternative/additional materials	30+		✓	
Tutoring-peers, volunteers, paraprofessionals	30+		✓	
Guided practice	30+			
Special grouping				
Task Requirements				
Change criteria for success				
Break into smaller steps				
Provide prompts				
Clarify directions *(restate)*	30+	✓		

4/7/94

(continued)

However, the need for a more global view of determining aptitude is also being investigated. For example Spring and French (1990) suggested that a more accept-

FIGURE 3.9

continued

Name _Frank P._____ School Year _95_ Page _2_

PREREFERRAL INTERVENTIONS WITHIN THE REGULAR PROGRAM (Con't)

	No. of days Attempted	Problem Better	No Change	Problem Worse
Behavior Techniques				
Behavior management (Attach explanation)	_____	_____	_____	_____
Student Contract	_____	_____	_____	_____
Consultation with _____	_____	_____	_____	_____
Sessions with school counselor	_2_	✓	_____	_____
Other (Describe)_____	_____	_____	_____	_____
_____	_____	_____	_____	_____
_____	_____	_____	_____	_____
_____	_____	_____	_____	_____

ADDITIONAL INFORMATION

1. Attach copies of relevant evaluations.
2. Attach the most recent BCT, HSBSE (Exit Exam), Stanford Achievement Test and/or Otis Lennon results.
3. Attach copies of cumulative records containing grades and attendance.
4. Has the student ever repeated a grade? _no *_ If so, which one(s)_____ How many times? *_late birthday - Frank didn't start until he was 6._
5. Attach current work samples.
6. Attach current report card.
7. Has the student received other services? _no_ If so, what _____
8. Does the student wear glasses?   Yes _____ No ✓
9. Does the student wear a hearing aid?   Yes _____ No ✓
10. Does the student have a health problem?   Yes _____ No ✓ If yes, what _____
11. Does the student have an orthopedic problem?   Yes _____ No ✓ If yes, what _____
12. Does the student take any medication regularly? Yes _____ No ✓ If yes, what _____
13. Other relevant information. _new to Hunter School_

MULTIDISCIPLINARY EVALUATION TEAM (MET) RECOMMENDATIONS

DATE
_3-21-95_ **ACCEPTED FOR EVALUATION.** Send *Notice and Consent for Initial Evaluation/Large Print Rights/Parents-Partners in Special Education.*

_____ **NOT ACCEPTED FOR EVALUATION.** Send *Notice of Intent Not to Evaluate/Large Print rights/Parents-Partners in Special Education.*

MET MEMBERS	POSITION	DATE
Mrs. Sally Principi	Teacher	4-25-95
Julia Williams	Principal	4-25-95
Mrs. D. Castro	Counselor	4-25-95
Nancy Armount	special ed.	4-25-95
Mrs. Lee Brown	psychometrist	4-25-95

4/7/94

---

able measure of aptitude for reading skills is listening. Ongoing research is needed to advance the understanding of the concept and use of aptitude assessment.

FIGURE 3.10

Rights in Special Education

To Parent(s) of: _Frank P._ _____ (Child)   _3-21-95_ _____ (date sent)

Please read, sign and return this copy of *Rights in Special Education* no later than (Date) _3-28-95_
to (Name) _Mrs. D. Castre'_ (Address) _Hunter School_ _____

I understand the Rights in Special Education	
_3-25-95_	_Mr and Mrs Frank P_
Date	Parent's Signature

If you have questions, please contact _Mrs. Castre'_ _____
_____ at (telephone) _942-4767_

RIGHTS IN SPECIAL EDUCATION

Federal and state laws create specific rights for eligible students and responsibilities of parents to protect those rights. The following is an explanation of those rights and the procedural safeguards available to ensure that school systems and parents exercise their responsibilities in ensuring those rights. If you would like a further explanation of any of these rights you may contact your school principal, your superintendent of schools, the special education coordinator in your school system or the Division of Special Education Services, 50 North Ripley Street, Montgomery, AL 36130, telephone: 1-800-392-8020 or (334) 242-8406 (TDD).

PRIOR NOTICE TO PARENTS
Your education agency must provide you with prior written notice each time it proposes or refuses to initiate or change the identification, evaluation or educational placement of your child or the provision of a free appropriate public education to your child.

The notice must include (a) a full explanation of all of the procedural safeguards available to you; (b) a description of the action proposed or refused by the education agency; (c) an explanation of why your education agency proposes or refuses to take the action; (d) and a description of any options considered and the reasons why those options were rejected; (e) a description of each evaluation procedure, test, record or report the education agency uses as a basis for the proposal or refusal; and (f) a description of any other factors which are relevant to the education agency's proposal or refusal.

The notice must be written in language understandable to the general public, and provided in your native language or other mode of communication, unless it is clearly not feasible to do so. If your native language or other mode of communication is not a written language, your education agency must take steps to ensure that the notice is translated orally or by other means to you in your native language or other mode of communication; that you understand the content of the notice, and that there is written evidence that these requirements have been met.

PARENTAL CONSENT
Your education agency must obtain your consent before conducting a preplacement evaluation or initial placement of your child in a program providing special education and related services. Except for preplacement evaluation and initial placement, consent may not be required as a condition of any benefit to you or your child. Your education agency may require parental consent for other services and activities if it establishes and implements effective procedures to ensure that a parent's refusal to consent does not result in a failure to provide the child with a free appropriate education.

Where State law requires parental consent before a child with disabilities is evaluated or initially provided special education and related services, State procedures govern your district in overriding your refusal to consent. Where there is no State law requiring consent before a child is evaluated or initially provided special education and related services, the education agency may use the Federal procedures for due process hearings to determine whether your child may be evaluated or initially provided special education and related services without your

1   2/1/95

(continued)

The *Federal Register* also suggests that seven academic areas may be involved as the manifestation of the learning disability. These include oral expression, listening comprehension, written expression, basic reading skills, reading comprehension,

FIGURE 3.10

continued

consent. If the hearing officer upholds your education agency, it may evaluate or initially provide special education and related services to your child without your consent, subject to your rights to appeal the decision and to have your child remain in his or her present educational placement during the pendency of any administrative or judicial proceeding.

INDEPENDENT EDUCATIONAL EVALUATION
You have the right to an independent educational evaluation at public expense if you disagree with an evaluation obtained by your education agency. However, your education agency may initiate a due process hearing to show that its evaluation is appropriate. If the final decision is that the evaluation is appropriate, you still have the right to an independent educational evaluation, but not at public expense. If you obtain an independent educational evaluation at private expense, the results of the evaluation must be considered by your education agency in any decision made with respect to the provision of a free appropriate public education to your child, and may be presented as evidence at a due process hearing regarding your child.

If an impartial due process hearing officer requests an independent educational evaluation as part of a hearing, the cost of the evaluation must be at public expense.

Each education agency shall provide you, on request, information about where an independent educational evaluation may be obtained.

Whenever an independent evaluation is at public expense, the criteria under which the evaluation is obtained, including the location of the evaluation and the qualifications of the examiner, must be the same as the criteria which the education agency uses when it initiates an evaluation.

IMPARTIAL DUE PROCESS HEARING
You or your education agency may initiate a due process hearing regarding the education agency's proposal or refusal to initiate or change the identification, evaluation or educational placement of your child or the provision of a free appropriate public education to your child.

The hearing must be conducted by the SEA or the education agency directly responsible for the education of your child.

The education agency must inform you of any free or low-cost legal and other relevant services available in the area if you request the information or you or the education agency initiate a due process hearing.

A hearing may not be conducted by a person who is an employee of the education agency which is involved in the education or care of your child, or by any person having a personal or professional interest which would conflict with his or her objectivity in the hearing. A person who otherwise qualifies to conduct a hearing is not an employee of the education agency solely because he or she is paid by the education agency to serve as an impartial due process hearing officer.

Each education agency shall keep a list of the persons who serve as impartial due process hearing officers. The list must include a statement of the qualifications of each of those persons.

The education agency shall ensure that a final hearing decision is reached and mailed to the parties within 45 days after the receipt of a request for a hearing, unless the hearing officer grants a specific extension at the request of either party. The decision made in an impartial due process hearing is final, unless a party to the hearing brings a civil action in State or Federal Court.

Any party to a hearing has the right to (a) be accompanied and advised by counsel and by individuals with special knowledge or training with respect to the problems of children with disabilities; (b) present evidence and confront, cross-examine and compel the attendance of witnesses; (c) prohibit the introduction of any evidence at the hearing that has not been disclosed to that party at least five days before the hearing; (d) obtain a written or electronic verbatim record of the hearing; (e) obtain written findings of fact and decisions. After deleting any personally identifiable information, the education agency shall transmit those findings and decisions to the State advisory panel and make them available to the public. In addition to the rights in a - e, you have the right to have your child present, open the hearing to the public and have the hearing conducted at a time and place which is reasonably convenient to you and your child.

2   2/1/95

(continued)

math calculations, or mathematics reasoning. The assessment team should consider the referral information to determine which of the areas above need an indi-

FIGURE 3.10

continued

CIVIL ACTION
Any party aggrieved by the findings and decision made in an impartial due process hearing has the right to bring a civil action in State or Federal Court.

CHILD'S STATUS DURING PROCEEDINGS
During the pendency of any administrative or judicial proceeding regarding a complaint, unless you and your education agency agree otherwise, your child must remain in his or her present educational placement. If the hearing involves an application for initial admission to public school, your child, with your consent, must be placed in the public school program until the completion of all the proceedings.

AWARD OF ATTORNEYS' FEES
In any action or proceeding brought under Part B of the Individuals with Disabilities Education Act, the court may award reasonable attorneys' fees to the parents of a child with disabilities if they are the prevailing party.

SURROGATE PARENTS
Each education agency shall ensure that an individual is assigned to act as a surrogate for the parents of a child when no parent can be identified; the education agency, after reasonable efforts, cannot discover the whereabouts of a parent; or the child is a ward of the State under the laws of the State. The agency must have a method for determining whether a child needs a surrogate parent and for assigning a surrogate parent to the child.

The education agency may select a surrogate parent in any way permitted under State law, but must ensure that a person selected as a surrogate is not an employee of a education agency which is involved in the education or care of the child, has no interest that conflicts with the interest of the child he or she represents, and has knowledge and skills that ensure adequate representation of the child. An individual is not disqualified as a education agency employee from appointment as a surrogate solely because he or she is paid by the agency to serve as a surrogate parent.

The surrogate parent may represent the child in all matters relating to the identification, evaluation, and educational placement of the child, and the provision of a free appropriate public education to the child.

ACCESS TO RECORDS
Your education agency must permit you to inspect and review any education records relating to your child with respect to the identification, evaluation and educational placement of your child, and the provision of a free appropriate public education to your child, which are collected, maintained or used by the education agency under Part B. The education agency must comply with a request without unnecessary delay and before any meeting regarding an individualized education program or hearing relating to the identification, evaluation or placement of your child, and in no case more than 45 days after the request has been made.

Your right to inspect and review education records includes (a) your right to a response from the participating agency to reasonable requests for explanations and interpretations of the records; (b) your right to have your representative inspect and review the records; and (c) your right to request that the education agency provide copies of the records containing the information if failure to provide those copies would effectively prevent you from exercising your right to inspect and review the records.

The education agency may presume that you have authority to inspect and review records relating to his or her child unless the education agency has been advised that you do not have the authority under applicable State law governing such matters as guardianship, separation and divorce.

If any education record includes information on more than one child, you have the right to inspect and review only the information relating to your child or to be informed of that specific information.

The education agency must provide you, on request, a list of the types and locations of education records collected, maintained or used by the education agency.

The education agency must keep a record of parties obtaining access to education records collected, maintained or used (except access by parents and authorized employees of the participating agency), including the name of the party, the date access was given, and the purpose for which the party is authorized to the records.

3

2/1/95

(continued)

vidualized, comprehensive assessment. Table 3.3 (p. 101) contains a description of instruments frequently used to measure the array of academic deficiencies.

FIGURE 3.10

continued

FEES FOR SEARCHING, RETRIEVING, AND COPYING RECORDS
The education agency may not charge a fee to search for or to retrieve information under this part, but may charge a fee for copies of records which are made for you under this part if the fee does not effectively prevent you from exercising your right to inspect and review those records.

AMENDMENT OF RECORDS AT PARENT'S REQUEST
If you believe that information in education records collected, maintained or used is inaccurate, misleading or violates the privacy or other rights of your child, you may request that the education agency that maintains the information to amend the information.

The education agency must decide whether to amend the information in accordance with your request within a reasonable period of time of receipt of the request. If the education agency decides to refuse to amend the information in accordance with the request, it must inform you of the refusal and of your right to a hearing.

The education agency shall, on request, provide an opportunity for a hearing to challenge information in education records to ensure that it is not inaccurate, misleading or otherwise in violation of the privacy or other rights of your child.

If, as a result of the hearing, the education agency decides that the information is inaccurate, misleading or otherwise in violation of the privacy or other rights of your child, it must amend the information accordingly and so inform you in writing.

If, as a result of the hearing, the education agency decides that the information is not inaccurate, misleading or otherwise in violation of the privacy or other rights of the child, it must inform you of the right to place in the records it maintains on your child, a statement commenting on the information or setting forth any reasons for disagreeing with the decision of the education agency. Any explanation placed in your child's education records must be maintained by the education agency as part of the education records of your child as long as the record or the contested portion is maintained by the education agency. If the records of your child or the contested portion is disclosed by the education agency to any party, the explanation must also be disclosed to the party.

DEFINITIONS
Consent means that (a) you have been fully informed in your native language or other mode of communication of all information relevant to the activity for which consent is sought; (b) you understand and agree in writing to the carrying out of the activity for which your consent is sought and the consent describes that activity and lists the records (if any) that will be released and to whom; and (c) you understand that the granting of consent is voluntary on your part and may be revoked at any time prior to the preplacement evaluation of the student or the student's receipt of special education for the first time; thus, for parental consent, the parent's right to revoke ceases once the preplacement evaluation and the initial placement have occurred.

Evaluation means procedures used to determine whether a child is disabled and the nature and extent of the special education and related services that the child needs. The term means procedures used selectively with an individual child and does not include basic tests administered to or procedures used with all children in a school, grade or class.

Independent educational evaluation means an evaluation conducted by a qualified examiner who is not employed by the education agency responsible for the education of the child in question.

Independent education evaluation at public expense means that the education agency either pays for the full cost of the evaluation or ensures that the evaluation is otherwise provided at no cost to you.

Personally identifiable means that information includes (a) the name of the child, parent or other family member; (b) the address of the child; (c) a personal identifier, such as the child's social security number or student number; or (d) a list of personal characteristics or other information that would make it possible to identify the child with reasonable certainty.

4   2/1/95

Because of the exclusion clause in the *Federal Register* (USOE, 1977), the team must also differentiate between LD and other disabilities. To determine that the learning disability is not primarily the result of a vision or hearing deficit, a thorough evaluation needs to be completed to determine sensory

FIGURE 3.11

Notice and Consent for Initial Evaluation

3-23-95 (Date Sent)

NOTICE and CONSENT for INITIAL EVALUATION

Dear Parents:

We are asking for your permission to conduct a comprehensive evaluation of your child, _____ Frank P. _____. The Multidisciplinary Evaluation Team believes an evaluation will help the school better meet your child's educational needs. Your child will be considered for possible eligibility for special education services.

We would like to evaluate your child for the following checked reasons:

[ ] Above grade level in basic skills   [ ] Increased rate of progress   [ ] Behavior inconsistent with age
[ ] Below grade level in basic skills   [✓] decreased rate of progress   [ ] Speech/language inconsistent with age
[ ] To determine developmental level   [ ] _____   [ ] _____

We propose to evaluate the following checked areas:

[✓] Vision   [✓] Achievement   [ ] _____   [ ] _____
[✓] Hearing   [ ] Speech/Language   [ ] _____   [ ] _____
[✓] Intelligence [ ] Developmental   [ ] _____   [ ] _____
[✓] Behavior   [ ] Gross/Fine Motor   [ ] _____   [ ] _____

Your written permission is required in order to conduct an evaluation. Please check one of the following boxes, sign and date the form.

[✓]   I **GIVE PERMISSION** for you to evaluate my child.

[ ]   I **DO NOT GIVE PERMISSION** for you to evaluate my child.

_____   3-25-95
Parent's Signature Mr. & Mrs. Frank P.   Date

If you have information about your child that can assist in this evaluation or if you have questions please contact:
Name N. Dunnavant _____   Telephone: 942-4767

Please return this form to: Mrs. D. Castro _____

My signature below verifies that parents who require notice and an explanation of their rights in their native language have been accommodated to ensure their understanding.

Sinderely,

Mrs. Alberta Newnun
Education Agency Official

Enclosure: *Special Education Student and Parent Rights/Parents-Partners in Special Education*
8/1/93

TABLE 3.2

Standardized Instruments: Intelligence Domain

Test	Ages	Score	Domains/Subtests
Wechsler Intelligence Scale for Children-Revised (WISC-III) (1991)	6-0 to 16-6	Full Scale IQ	Verbal IQ; Performance IQ
Wechsler Preschool and Primary Scale of Intelligence-Revised (WPPSI-R) (1989)	3-0 to 7-3	Full Scale IQ	Verbal IQ; Performance IQ
Wechsler Adult Intelligence Scale-Revised (WAIS-R) (1981)	16 to 74	Full Scale IQ	Verbal IQ; Performance IQ
Stanford-Binet Intelligence Scale: Fourth Edition (SB:FE) (1986)	2-6 to 23-11	Composite, Standard Age Score (SAS)	Verbal Reasoning, Abstract/Visual Reasoning, Quantitative Reasoning, Short-term Memory
Kaufman Assessment Battery for Children (K-ABC) (1983)	2-6 to 12-5	Mental Processing, Composite score	Sequential Processing Scale, Simultaneous Processing Scale
Woodcock-Johnson Psycho-educational Battery (1977)	3-0 to 80+	Broad Cognitive Ability score	Reading, Mathematics, Written Language, and Knowledge Aptitude
Woodcock-Johnson Psycho-educational Battery, Revised (WJ-R) (1989)	2-0 to 90+	Broad Cognitive Ability score	Oral Language, Reading, Mathematics, Written Language, Knowledge Aptitude;8 additional processing scales
Detroit Tests of Learning Aptitude (DTLA-3) (1991)	6 through 18	General Intelligence Quotient	Linguistic, Cognitive, Attentional, and Motoric domains
Differential Ability Scales (DAS)	2-6 to 17	Cognitive Ability score	Speed of information processing; verbal, nonverbal, quantitative reasoning; spatial imagery; perceptual matching; memory
Hiskey-Nebraska Test of Learning Aptitude (HNTLA) (1966)	3 to 16	Deviation Learning Quotient	Twelve subtests of verbal labeling, categorization, concept formation, and rehearsal (no verbal direction of responses required)

Source: S. Strawser (1993). Assessment and Identification Practices in W.N. Bender (Ed.) *Learning Disabilities: Best Practices for Professionals*. Austin: PRO-ED.

TABLE 3.3

Standardized Instruments: Achievement Domain

Test	Grade/Age	Areas/Subtests
Wechsler Individual Achievement Test (WIAT) (1992)	Level I: 5-0 to 11-11; Level II: 12-0 to 74-11	Basic reading, reading comprehension, math reasoning, numerical operations, listening comprehension, oral expression, spelling, written expression
Peabody Individual Achievement Test Revised (PIAT-R) (1989)	5 through adult	Mathematics, reading recognition, reading comprehension, spelling, written expression, general information
Test of Academic Progress (1988)	Grades K–12	Mathematics, reading, spelling
Kaufman Test of Educational Achievement (KTEA) (1985)	Grades 1–12	Reading decoding, reading comprehension, mathematics applications, spelling
Kaufman Assessment Battery for Children-The Achievement Scale (K-ABC) (1983)	2-6 to 12-5	Expressive Vocabulary, Faces and Places, Arithmetic, Riddles, Reading/Decoding, Reading/Understanding
Woodcock-Johnson Psycho-educational Battery Part II, Tests of Achievement (1977)	3-0 to 80+	Reading, mathematics, written language, knowledge (science, social studies, humanities) clusters
Woodcock-Johnson Psycho-educational Battery, Revised (WJ-R), WJ-R Tests of Achievement (1989)	2-0 to 90+	Reading, mathematics, written language, knowledge, and skills clusters
Woodcock Reading Mastery Tests-Revised (WRMT-R) Forms G and H (1987)	K through college	Word Identification, Word Attack, Word Comprehension, Passage Comprehension, Visual-Auditory Learning, Letter Identification
KeyMath Diagnostic Arithmetic Test-Revised (KM-R) (1988)	Grades K–9	Basic Concepts (numeration rational numbers, geometry) Operations (addition, subtraction, multiplication, division, mental computation), Applications (measurement, time and money, estimation, interpreting data, problem solving)
Test of Adolescent and Adult Language-3 (1994)	Grades 6–12	Listening, speaking, reading, writing, spoken and written language, vocabulary, grammar, expressive and receptive language

(continued)

TABLE 3.3		
continued		

Test	Grade/Age	Areas/Subtests
Test of Language Competence-Expanded Edition (TLC-Expanded) (1988)	Level 1: 5 to 9 Level 2: 9 to 19	Scores in expressing and interpreting intents, screening composite, and expanded composite; subtests: ambiguous sentences, listening comprehension, oral expression, figurative language
The Test of Language Development-Intermediate (TOLD-2) (1988)	8-6 to 13	Sentence combining, vocabulary, word ordering, grammatic comprehension, and malapropisms
Test of Written Language-3 (TOWL-3) (1996)	Ages 7-6 to 17-11	Thematic maturity, word usage, style, spelling, vocabulary, handwriting

Source: S. Strawser (1993). Assessment and Identification Practices in W.N. Bender (Ed.) *Learning Disabilities: Best Practices for Professionals*. Austin: PRO-ED.

acuity. The test of intelligence or aptitude may also be used to rule out mental retardation as the primary cause for the learning disability.

To determine that an emotional disturbance is not the cause of the learning disability, typically a behavior rating scale will be administered. According to Strawser (1993), this is one of the most difficult determinations to make for several reasons. First, it is difficult to determine if a child is acting out or having other social problems because of academic failure or if the child is failing to achieve because of overriding emotional disturbances or behavioral disorders. Second, many of the characteristics associated with learning disabilities, such as impulsivity and difficulty relating to peers or teachers, may be misinterpreted as the primary problems. Finally, if the origin of the learning difficulties is not clear, the label of LD is more likely to be accepted than that of behaviorally disordered. Table 3.4 contains standardized instruments frequently used to assess the behavioral domain. Chapter 12 discusses in detail the relationship between learning disabilities and emotional and behavioral disorders (E/BD).

The team must also investigate the environmental, cultural, or economic disadvantage status of the child. Various checklists have been developed; however, a well-informed teacher, counselor, or administrator who knows the family is probably the best judge of the impact of socioeconomic factors. This area of exclusion continues to be one of the more controversial. The MEDC must review the information regarding culture, socio-economic level, and the community and home environment to determine if the child has been given opportunity and encouragement to learn. For example, a parent living in poverty may not be able to afford books, writing material, scissors, etc. They may be too proud to borrow materials or fear that the books, etc. might get lost or damaged, and they would

TABLE 3.4

Standardized Instruments: Behavior Domain

Test	Ages	Domains/Subtests
Behavior Evaluation Scale-2 (BES-2) (McCarney and Leigh 1990)	Grades K–12	Learning problems, interpersonal difficulties, inappropriate behaviors, unhappiness, depression. T.
Behavior Rating Profile-2 (Brown and Hammill 1983)	Grades 1–12	Home, school peers. S-Pa-T-Pe.
Burks' Behavior Rating Scales (Burks 1977)	Grades 1–9	Self-blame, dependency, withdrawal, anxiety, social conformity, sense of identity, impulse control, attention, physical fears/symptoms. T.
Coopersmith Self Esteem Inventories (Coopersmith 1981)	Elementary grades	Self-perception in social, academic, & personal contexts. S.
Revised Behavior Problem Checklist (BPC) (Quay and Peterson 1987)	Grades K–12	Personality disorders, inadequacy-immaturity, socialized delinquency, conduct disorders. T.
Social Skills Rating System (Elliott 1989)	3–18	Social skills, problem behaviors, & academic competence. S-Pa-T.
Walker Problem Behavior Identification Checklist (Walker 1983)	Pre-K–6	Acting out, withdrawal, distractibility, disturbed peer relations, immaturity. T.
Weller-Strawser Adaptive Behavior Scale (Weller and Strawser 1981)	K–12	Task orientation, social coping, pragmatic language. T.

Forms available: S = self, Pa = Parent, T = teacher, Pe = peers.

Source: S. Strawser (1993). Assessment and Identification Practices in W.N. Bender (Ed.) *Learning Disabilities: Best Practices for Professionals.* Austin: PRO-ED.

not have the money to replace the items. Children from these situations do not enter school with the rich or even adequate experiences so important in linking new information to previous knowledge. Their lack of achievement or lack of progress commensurate with their peers would be expected and might be interpreted as the *primary* cause of the learning deficits. Of course, it is also possible that the child could have central nervous system dysfunction that is *primarily* the cause of the learning deficits. The MEDC does not want to label a child inappropriately, yet this child does need help. Often federal programs are available in schools in low socio-economic communities to provide the enriched experience-based education needed by these children. Placement in these programs may be tried first at the prereferral intervention level.

The *Federal Register* (USOE, 1977) also requires that at least one team member other than the child's regular teacher observe the child's performance in the general education classroom. This type of evaluation is informal but critical in documenting or verifying that the learning disability is in fact manifested in the academic setting. Remember that no single procedure can be used as the sole criteria for determining the educational placement of the child. The multidisciplinary team must assess the child in all areas related to the suspected disability including if appropriate health, vision, hearing, social and emotional status, general intelligence, academic performance, communicative status, and motor ability (USOE, Federal Register, 1992, p. 44822).

Although not required by the *Federal Register* "Regulations for Identification of Learning Disabilities" (USOE, 1977), the definition of learning disabilities specified in P.L. 94-142 (1975) refers to the basic psychological processes involved in understanding or in using spoken or written language. Initially, states performed evaluations in the psychological processing areas of visual perception and auditory perception; however, there was much controversy about evaluations in this area. A more recent interpretation of psychological processes that may impact sig-

FIGURE 3.12

An Operational Definition of Learning Disabilities

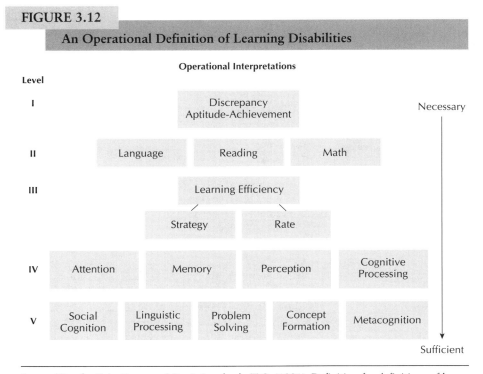

Source: Kavale, K.A., Forness, S.R., & Lorsbach, T.C. (1991). Definition for definitions of learning disabilities, *Learning Disabilities Quarterly*, 14, p. 204. Reprinted with permission of the Council for Learning Disabilities.

nificantly the educational success of children with learning disabilities includes the evaluation of a child's attention, memory, and other cognitive processing abilities (Kavale, Forness, and Lorsbach, 1991). Figure 3.12 provides a pictorial representation of an operational definition of learning disabilities proposed by these investigators. The model specifies areas that may be assessed to complete the investigation of the presence of a learning disability and predict deficiencies which may impact learning efficiency and successful classroom functioning.

▶ STAGE 3: ELIGIBILITY DECISIONS

When the multidisciplinary team evaluations are completed, the Multidisciplinary Eligibility Determination Committee (MEDC) must specify in a written report whether the child has a learning disability, the basis for determining the presence of a learning disability, the relevant behaviors and academic functionings, and the existence of the severe discrepancy as well as the impact of environmental, cultural or economic disadvantage. Each team member must certify in writing whether they agree or disagree with the conclusions of the team.

As discussed in Chapter 2, the task of determining eligibility or operationalizing the definition of learning disabilities is especially controversial in the field of learning disabilities. Because of the dramatic increase in prevalence noted in Chapter 2, some school districts are making the criteria so stringent for eligibility that some children with learning disabilities are not receiving needed ser-

The task of determining which children are eligible for special education because of a learning disability is very controversial.

vices. No criteria or criteria that were too lenient can result in overidentification; this situation is just as problematic, draining resources to serve inappropriately placed students (Adelman, 1989).

Mercer (1992) cited the following six obstacles that may be impeding the search for better ways to identify students with learning disabilities.

1. The various definitions of learning disabilities make consensus on identification procedures difficult. Each definition suggests a different set of criteria. Mercer, King-Sears, and Mercer (1990) found that even when states were establishing identification criteria based on the same definition (e.g., the federal definition), there was significant variation in criteria.

2. The primary criteria for identification cited in the *Federal Register* (USOE, 1977), the discrepancy factor, has been difficult to operationalize. Some states have chosen to use a specified number of standard score units below I.Q.; others may use a specified grade equivalent deficit (e.g., two years below grade placement). These options will be discussed further in the next section of this chapter.

3. Many standardized tests used to identify students with learning disabilities lack acceptable standards for reliability and validity (Shepard and Smith, 1981).

4. The heterogeneity of children with learning disabilities makes it difficult to establish a single set of identification criteria. The criteria must be broad enough to include children with very different characteristics and abilities.

5. Services to disruptive and low-achieving students are often not adequate to provide the general educator support for these students. Often these students and others who might be culturally different or mildly mentally retarded are misplaced in classes for children with learning disabilities. The mandates of Public Law 99-457 and its emphasis on serving preschool children considered at-risk for academic failure will increase the likelihood that young children will be misdiagnosed as learning disabled. Trying to apply the federal criteria to these young children will only increase the confusion.

6. Often members of the multidisciplinary team have not been adequately trained to identify children with and without learning disabilities. Communication is also frequently difficult across the professional jargon of each discipline.

Despite these limitations, professionals must make decisions daily regarding the identification of a learning disability and the eligibility for special education services. Although not the sole criteria, many states depend heavily on the determination of an existence of a discrepancy between aptitude and achievement. Strawser (1993) provided the following overview of the most commonly used discrepancy models.

Grade Level Deviation Models

When a grade level deviation model is used, the referred individual's achievement scores are compared to individuals in their current grade placement. The MEDC might note that Frank was two years below grade level, if the team was using the grade level deviation model. Usually a state will site a constant or fixed number of years, for example one to two years, as the cutoff indicating a severe deviation from grade level. Systems may also use a graduated deviation model, so as children get older the discrepancy or fixed grade level deviation increases. For example in elementary schools, the deviation grade level cut off might be one year, whereas a high school senior might need to lag behind two to three years to be considered for placement.

Although this deviation model is easiest to calculate and explain, it has many associated conceptual problems and potential for measurement error. For example, a child theoretically must fail several years to be considered for placement in this model. Also the model does not consider the importance of aptitude or an individual's expected achievement level. It only evaluates under-achievement relative to the expected achievement for the current grade placement. This model would tend to overidentify slow learners or those achieving below grade level but achieving at a level consistent with their own capacity, while underidentifying those with higher levels of ability.

Expected Formula Models

These models identify a discrepancy by (1) determining the expected academic performance of a student based on his or her intellectual ability, using IQ or mental age scores and/or years in school; and (2) determining the difference between the expected achievement and the actual achievement to document the degree or severity of the discrepancy. Several formulas for determining expected achievement are available; however, Algozzine, Forgone, Mercer, and Trifiletti (1979) noted that students might be identified by one formula as learning disabled but not by another. Although these methods seem to be an improvement over the grade level deviation model because of the use of age and intellectual aptitude or potential, they are frought with mathematical weaknesses and are generally not recommended (Salvia and Ysseldyke, 1991).

Standard Score Comparison Models

To combat the problems encountered when using grade equivalences to determine discrepancies, the standard score comparison model has been recommended. In this model the raw score is converted to a standard score. Standard score values are available for IQ tests as well as achievement measures, and the comparisons between standard scores on these tests is considered a more mathematically defensible procedure than comparing the standard score from an IQ test to the grade equivalent from an achievement test. The weaknesses of the standard score comparison model were noted by Mercer et al. (1990) as problematic due to the lack of consideration of the technical differences between tests and the lack of agreement on the criteria to determine a severe discrepancy.

Regression Inclusion Models

The models mentioned above are based on the concept that intelligence scores predict academic success; however, this prediction is invalidated by the statistical phenomenon called *regression toward the mean*. When scores on intelligence measures are higher or lower than average, the academic achievement predicted by the intelligence quotient will not be accurate. Students whose IQs are above the mean tend to score lower than expected on measures of academic achievement as they regress toward the mean, and students whose IQs are below average tend to score higher than expected on academic measures (Cone and Wilson, 1981).

The discrepancy models based on a regression equation are an improvement as they control for this type of error. The National Joint Committee on Learning Disabilities (1987) recommended that standard scores be used to describe performance because they have the highest degree of comparability across tests and that any formula used to calculate severe discrepancy between ability and achievement must include a correction for regression. Critics of this method however suggest that the accuracy of the discrepancy still depends on the reliability and technical soundness of the tests used (Reynolds, 1985). Because of the sophisticated nature of the equations used in this model, extensive training or support is necessary for school personnel to understand them. In most cases the MEDC is provided a regression equation chart generated by a computer to use in determining severe discrepancy between aptitude and achievement controlling for the regression phenomenon.

Professional Judgment Models

In light of the criticism applied to each of the discrepancy models used above, Strawser (1993) proposed that the professional members of the MET should be allowed to look at the assessment data and make a decision as to whether the child is eligible without stringent criteria. This process is referred to as using professional or clinical judgment. Research has demonstrated that teachers and other educational personnel can be very accurate in their recommendations (Weller, Strawser, Callahan, Pugh, and Watanabe, 1990).

Clinical judgment should be based on a review of all of the available data including the individual's ability to benefit from instructional efforts (McLeskey and Waldron, 1991). It should be noted that applying any of the discrepancy models discussed above or documenting intraindividual differences through clinical judgment models may result in one child being eligible for services in one area and not eligible for services in a nearby district or state.

The prevalence rates vary considerably from state to state. The 1993–1994 data from the federal government (U.S. Department of Education, 1995) show that Georgia reported the lowest percentage of students with LD (2.25 percent) served under IDEA and Massachusetts reported the highest (7.17 percent). Table 3.5 demonstrates this variability across states. A study by Finlan (1992) suggests that of the sixteen states reporting the highest percentages of students with LD in 1989, eleven were states with no precise, structured definition. Two of these sixteen states used the standard score model and only one of the states used the regression formula. Finlan suggested that if a state wanted to reduce the number of students misclassified as LD, the use of an operational definition of severe dis-

TABLE 3.5

Percentage (Based on Estimated Resident Population) of Children Age Six to Twenty–One Served Under IDEA, Part B and Chapter 1 of ESEA (SOP) by Disability During the 1993—1994 School Year

State	All Disabilities	Specific Learning Disabilities	State	All Disabilities	Specific Learning Disabilities
Alabama	9.30	3.92	New Mexico	9.68	4.93
Alaska	9.89	6.20	New York	8.46	4.96
Arizona	6.89	4.04	North Carolina	8.05	3.64
Arkansas	8.06	4.50	North Dakota	7.14	3.61
California	6.97	4.26	Ohio	8.10	3.10
Colorado	7.38	4.13	Oklahoma	8.55	4.48
Connecticut	9.83	5.19	Oregon	8.40	4.43
Delaware	8.91	5.58	Pennsylvania	7.39	3.50
District of Columbia	6.60	3.92	Puerto Rico	.	.
			Rhode Island	10.27	6.50
Florida	9.65	4.43	South Carolina	8.39	3.61
Georgia	6.92	2.25	South Dakota	7.34	3.73
Hawaii	5.23	2.85	Tennessee	9.46	5.01
Idaho	6.65	3.98	Texas	8.43	5.02
Illinois	8.68	4.41	Utah	8.00	4.51
Indiana	8.70	3.71	Vermont	7.14	3.36
Iowa	8.62	4.05	Virginia	8.41	4.35
Kansas	7.35	3.30	Washington	7.28	3.45
Kentucky	7.52	2.58	West Virginia	9.38	4.30
Louisiana	6.92	3.15	Wisconsin	7.32	2.42
Maine	9.54	4.42	Wyoming	8.36	4.39
Maryland	8.30	4.14	America Samoa	.	.
Massachusetts	11.72	7.17	Guam	.	.
Michigan	7.34	3.55	Northern Marianas	.	.
Minnesota	7.38	3.23			
Mississippi	8.49	4.51	Palau	.	.
Missouri	8.77	4.69	Virgin Islands	.	.
Montana	7.83	4.76	Bureau of Indian Affairs	.	.
Nebraska	8.58	3.82			
Nevada	7.68	4.80	50 States and D.C.	8.19	4.19
New Hampshire	8.52	4.77			
New Jersey	10.77	5.86			

The sum of the percentages of individual disabilities may not equal the percentage of all disabilities because of rounding. Percentage of children served is based on U.S. Census Bureau estimated resident population, by state, for July, 1993. Data as of October 1, 1994.

Source: U.S. Department of Education (1995) *17th Annual Report to Congress.*

crepancy might be effective. Even when provided the criteria, the determination of eligibility for learning disabilities is a serious challenge for the MEDC.
States have a very important decision to make as they adapt policy for determining eligibility procedures for identifying students with LD.

Figure 3.13 contains the Multidisciplinary Eligibility Determination Committee's report on Frank. Refer to Box 3.2 for the outcome of Frank's evaluation process. The *Wechsler Individual Achievement Test* (WIAT, 1992) was used as the primary tool for determining academic deficits. Please note that Frank's assessment battery included tests to validate vision and hearing acuity, to determine aptitude and behavior status, and to validate the academic levels obtained on the WIAT. Other areas assessed were only those identified as problematic on the referral. As noted in Box 3.2, Frank's parents signed the permission form to place Frank in a special education program; the permission form used is included in Figure 3.14 (p. 115).

▶ STAGE 4: INSTRUCTIONAL PROGRAMMING DECISIONS

The methods of assessment for identification of the disability should be comprehensive enough to yield important information about the student to use in designing an appropriate educational plan. If a sequence of skills is automatically taught or a method is routinely used without regard for the student's unique learning differences, the outcome could be wasted educational time or actually harmful to the student (Lerner, 1993). The team of individuals that develops the educational

| Box 3.2 | *Identification of Frank's Learning Disability and Determination of Eligibility* |

Frank's evaluation took place over the next month. The evaluation included vision and hearing screening, an individual intelligence test, individual academic achievement tests, a behavior rating, and a classroom observation. When testing was complete, a meeting of the Multidisciplinary Eligibility Determination Committee (MEDC) was scheduled to review the results to determine if Frank qualified for service under any special education category. The results of Frank's evaluation are recorded on the MEDC Report form in Figure 3.13. Using a regression analysis discrepancy formula provided in the Wechsler Individual Achievement Test (WIAT) manual, Frank was found to have a discrepancy between his ability as measured by the Wechsler Intelligence Scale for Children-Revised and his scores in the areas of basic reading skills, written expression, specifically spelling, and listening. The MEDC determined that Frank was eligible for special education services for students with learning disabilities.

Mrs. Principi, the counselor, and the special education teacher scheduled a conference with Frank's parents to go over test results and recommendations. At that time the parents consented to special education placement and signed the Permission to Place form included in Figure 3.14. A meeting was scheduled for next week to prepare Frank's Individualized Educational Program (IEP). Frank's IEP will be discussed in Chapter 4.

FIGURE 3.13

Multidisciplinary Eligibility Determination Committee (MEDC) Report

initial _____
reevaluation _____

MULTIDISCIPLINARY ELIGIBILITY DETERMINATION COMMITTEE (MEDC) REPORT

NAME _Frank P._   SCHOOL _Hunter_

BIRTHDATE _9-10-86_ MEETING DATE _4/25/95_ REFERRAL DATE _3/21/95_ GRADE _2_

PERMISSION-TO-EVALUATE/STUDENT-PARENT RIGHTS DATE _3-25-95_

AREA	DATE	ASSESSMENT INSTRUMENT-SCORES-RESULTS
VISION	4-4-95	Passed - Snellen
HEARING	4-4-95	Passed - Pure tone audiological
INTELLIGENCE	4-10	Wechsler Intelligence scale for Children III Verbal- 107, Performance- 111 Total 109 ±3
ADAPTIVE BEHAVIOR		
BEHAVIOR RATING SCALES	3-27	Bunkes Behavior Rating Scale Significant - poor ego strength, inattention
ACHIEVEMENT/ DIAGNOSTIC		
ORAL EXPRESSION	4-11	WIAT- (Wechsler Individual Achievement test) Oral expression 111 Total 84
WRITTEN EXPRESSION	4-19	Test of Written Spelling Predictable 81 Spelling 78 Unpredictable 96 WIAT- Written expression 97 Writing Composite 80
LISTENING COMPREHENSION	4-11	WIAT - Listening 88
BASIC READING SKILLS	4-17 / 4-11	Elkwall Reading Inventory Reading Words - 1st grade level WIAT - Basic Reading 81 Reading Total 83
READING COMPREHENSION	4-11	WIAT Reading Comprehension 96

8/1/93

(continued)

FIGURE 3.13

continued

Name *Frank P.*   MEDC REPORT - Page 2

AREA	DATE	ASSESSMENT INSTRUMENT-SCORES-RESULTS
MATHEMATICAL CALCULATION	4-11	WIAT - Numerical Operations - 113 Math total - 112
MATHEMATICAL REASONING	4-11	WIAT - Math Reasoning - 110
WORK SAMPLES	April 95	poor spelling, incorrect comprehension responses on reading sheets-unable to read text.
FINE MOTOR GROSS MOTOR PERCEPTUAL MOTOR		
DEVELOPMENTAL SCALES		
ARTICULATION		
VOICE		
FLUENCY		
LANGUAGE		
MEDICAL		
VISUAL PERCEPTION		
AUDITORY PERCEPTION		
OBSERVATION	4-7	Frank had difficulty completing his reading work and reading orally in this group. poor spelling
FAMILY INTERVIEW		ATTACH COPY

8/1/93

(continued)

FIGURE 3.13

continued

Name _Frank P._   MEDC REPORT - Page 3

AREA	DATE	ASSESSMENT INSTRUMENT-SCORES-RESULTS
DOCUMENTATION OF EMOTIONAL IMPAIRMENT		N/A
ENVIRONMENTAL, CULTURAL, AND/OR ECONOMIC CONCERNS CHECKLIST	3-19	No problems or areas of concern.
OTHER		

L.D. ONLY

1. There is a severe discrepancy between the student's educational performance and/or achievement for his/her age and ability level in one or more of the following: oral expression, written expression, basic reading skills, reading comprehension, mathematical calculation, listening comprehension and/or mathematical reasoning. Yes ✓ No ____

2. For educationally relevant behaviors noted during the classroom observation(s) and educationally relevant medical findings (if any), please refer to page two of the MEDC Report.

3. Relationship of the educationally relevant behaviors to the student's academic functioning is: _Reading problem is interfering with classroom performance!_

4. The following factors have been ruled out as the primary cause of the impairment: (check all that apply)
   [✓]   Environmental/Cultural/Economic Concerns
   [✓]   Mental Retardation   [✓] Emotional Conflict
   [✓]   Visual/Hearing Disabilities   [✓] Motor Disabilities

8/1/93

(continued)

FIGURE 3.13

continued

Name **Frank P.**   MEDC REPORT - Page 4

CONCLUSIONS OF THE
MULTIDISCIPLINARY ELIGIBILITY DETERMINATION COMMITTEE

ELIGIBLE   YES [✓]   NO [ ]
AREA OF DISABILITY: PRIMARY   *Specific Learning Disability*
                           SECONDARY   _____
                           SECONDARY   _____

EXPLANATION (IF NEEDED)

Frank is currently discrepant in the areas of basic reading skills, written language, specifically spelling and listening.

	NAME	POSITION	DATE
I AGREE with the conclusions written in this report.	Mrs. Sally Principi	classroom teacher	4-25-95
	Mrs. Lee Brown	psychometrist	4-25-95
	Mr. D. Castle	counselor	4-25-95
	N. Dunnavant	sp.ed.	4-25-95
	J. Williams	Principal	4-25-95

	NAME	POSITION	DATE
I DO NOT AGREE with the conclusions written in this report. The attached statement represents my conclusions in this area.			

8/1/93

FIGURE 3.14

Permission for Temporary Placement in Special Education

_5-5-95_ (Date Sent)

PERMISSION FOR TEMPORARY PLACEMENT IN SPECIAL EDUCATION

Dear Parents:

A temporary educational placement in ___Frank P.___ (area(s) of disability) has been proposed for your child, _____. The temporary placement is based on previous special education placement in another school and/or is part of the evaluation process for special education. Continued placement depends upon a review of your child's studnet records to determine if he/she qualifies for special education services under the Alabama Exceptional Child Act and P.L. 91-230, as amended. This temporary placement **MAY NOT EXCEED THIRTY (30) CALENDAR DAYS. WITHIN TEN (10) CALENDAR DAYS AFTER ENROLLMENT IN THE EDUCATION AGENCY, AN IEP MUST BE DEVELOPED.**

Your written permission is required in order to provide special education services. Please check one of the following boxes, sign, date and return the form.

[✓] I **APPROVE** the placement.

[ ] I **DO NOT APPROVE** the placement.

_____   _5-8-95_
Parent's Signature   Date

If you have questions or wish to arrange a conference to discuss this placement, please call:

NAME _N. Nunnavant_   TELEPHONE _942-4767_

Please return this form to _Mrs. Castre'_ by _5-15-95_.

My signature below verifies that parents who require notice and an explanation of their rights in their native language have been accommodated to ensure their understanding.

Sincerely,

Ms. Alberta Newman
Education Agency Official

Enclosure: _Special Education Student and Parent Right_

8/1/93

plan, referred to as the Individualized Educational Program (IEP) Committee, has a critical job. This committee's composition and the requirements for the IEP are discussed in Chapter 4. Frank's IEP is also included in Chapter 4.

▶ STAGE 5: PROGRAM EVALUATION

An effective teacher evaluates her or his program daily or weekly to determine if satisfactory progress is being made to achieve IEP goals and objectives. If progress is not being made as proposed in the IEP, (e.g., either too little progress or progress that means the IEP will not be completed before the year is out) the teacher should reconvene the committee to revise the IEP. Changes may be needed in the curriculum, the tasks, or teaching strategies.

Although ethically the teacher is expected to make a good faith effort to meet the goals and objectives of the IEP, the *Federal Register* (USOE, September, 1992) does state that the teacher, agency, or other person is not held accountable, if a child does not achieve the growth projected in the annual goals and objectives. This does not negate parents' rights to register a complaint, to request changes in the IEP, or to begin due process procedures if they feel adequate effort is not being made (p. 44816). Frequent communication and collaboration between IEP team members is the key to maintaining an effective educational program and positive relationships between team members.

SUMMARY

This chapter has presented information regarding the assessment of students with learning disabilities. The following points summarize the major areas included in the chapter:

- Assessment is primarily designed to guide the decision-making process for students with learning disabilities.
- Initial identification or screening is the first level of assessment to identify children who might need special services.
- Assessment is used to determine the current functioning level of students.
- Assessment information helps professionals make decisions regarding program eligibility.
- The development of an IEP is based in large part on assessment data.
- Parent involvement in the assessment process is mandated by federal law.
- Schools are required to use nondiscriminatory assessment procedures when evaluating students.
- When determining if a student is eligible for services because of a learning disability, schools must observe the student in a natural environment.
- A team of individuals makes the decision regarding program eligibility for students with learning disabilities.

- Assessment of students must be comprehensive.
- Formal tests are generally norm-referenced or standardized tests.
- Norm-referenced tests enable schools to compare students with a normative sample.
- Curriculum-based assessment determines a student's performance relative to the school's curriculum.
- Academic probes focus on specific academic behaviors.
- Task analysis allows teachers to evaluate students on specific steps in an overall activity.
- Portfolio assessment requires school personnel to look at a broad picture of the student, not just quantitative data.
- Observation is a critical component of assessment for students with learning disabilities.
- The assessment process includes screening, referral, determining eligibility, designing programs, and program evaluation.
- Each stage of the assessment process requires extensive collaboration.
- Several models are currently used to determine eligibility for learning disabilities.

Chapter 4

EDUCATIONAL PLANNING AND SERVICE DELIVERY OPTIONS

The objectives for this chapter are as follows:

▶ To describe the membership of the individualized educational program (IEP) committee.

▶ To describe the components of an IEP.

▶ To describe the continuum of placement options in special education.

▶ To discuss the advantages and disadvantages of each placement option.

▶ To discuss the Regular Education Initiative (REI).

▶ To discuss the concepts of least restrictive environment (LRE), inclusion, full inclusion, and responsible inclusion.

▶ To describe the placement options most often used for students with learning disabilities.

Two Tales of Inclusion

Two mothers having lunch during the early days of summer were having a conversation about the school year and how it had been for their two children with learning disabilities. One mother, enthusiastic about the successful year her son had experienced, said, "You will not believe the difference in Michael's personality! He is a different child and all because of a change in the way his LD teacher taught this year. Instead of pulling Michael out of the general education class, his LD teacher came into his classroom. If Michael was having problems, she was able to work with him right there. Sometimes she worked with other children who also needed special help. He never had to leave the room and explain to the other children where he was going or why he was leaving. Michael's self-concept has improved so much—he is willing to try new things and has even made some new friends."

Another mother sat quietly by during Michael's mother's report. She shook her head and sadly said, " I wish I could say the same thing about Meredith. Her school quit having special time in the resource class this year. Her LD teacher now teaches her in the general education classroom. Meredith says she stands over her and watches her do her work. Then when she makes a mistake, the teacher corrects her in front of all the other children. Sometimes she even takes her to a special table in the back of the room and teaches her separately. Meredith said that last year, when she left the room for the resource room, at least the other children really didn't know where she was going. Now her self-concept is worse than ever. She is so embarrassed about the other children knowing how dumb she is. She seldom has any friends over, and she hates going to school. I hope this summer will help her make up for her miserable year."

These two stories represent both the best and the worst about inclusion. Sometimes students with LD fare extremely well in general education classrooms, while others do not do as well. Remember these two tales as you read about the important decisions that have to be made by the Individual Educational Program Committee and service delivery options described in this chapter.

After the Eligibility Determination Committee (described in Chapter 3) reviews the assessment data and decides that a student is eligible for special education services, another important step occurs in the special education process. The parents are notified of the availability of services and invited to participate in a committee meeting to develop an individualized educational program (IEP) for their child. This is a team effort. All members of the IEP committee come together to focus on the needs of one student. This intense educational planning is part of what is special about special education.

▶ EDUCATIONAL PLANNING

The educational planning process is considered so important that the composition of the committee and the basic components of every child's IEP are specified by IDEA (U.S. Office of Education, 1992). The legal mandates in these two important areas are discussed below.

Members of the IEP Committee

The IEP committee must meet within a reasonable time (normally around 30 days) from the determination of eligibility and develop the educational plan that will guide the education of the student for the following year. This committee must include:

1. A representative of the public agency (other than the child's teacher) who is qualified to provide or supervise the provision of special education. (This individual is often the coordinator of special education services for the school system or the principal of the school.)

2. The child's teacher must be included. If there is more than one general education teacher involved in the child's education, they should all be invited to attend.

3. One or both of the child's parents should attend. (IDEA has several specific mandates regarding the participation of parents; these will be discussed below.)

4. If appropriate, the child should attend. This option should be considered for all age groups; however, it is a required invitation for students age 16 and above. These students must be involved in planning the services and educational program that will lead to their successful transition from high school to postsecondary programs or employment. More information on transition programming is included in Chapter 7.

5. Other individuals may be invited at the discretion of the parent or agency. Parents may feel more comfortable bringing another family member, a close friend who is a teacher, or in some cases, a lawyer.

6. If the child has been evaluated for the first time, a member of the evaluation team or the child's teachers or an individual knowledgeable about the evaluation procedures used and the results of the evaluation must attend

(USOE, 1992, p. 44814). This is important because the IEP is developed around the student's strengths and weaknesses determined during the assessment process. This may also be the first time the parents are given the specific assessment results presented during the eligibility determination meeting.

The importance of parents attending and participating in this meeting cannot be overemphasized. The Rules and Regulations of IDEA (USOE, *Federal Register*, September, 1992) mandate that steps be taken to ensure parents are at the IEP meeting or afforded the opportunity to participate. Recommended actions include

- notifying parents early enough to ensure that they will be able to attend;
- scheduling meetings at an agreed-upon time;
- documenting the purpose, time, and location in writing as well as who will be attending; and
- if the parents cannot attend, phone calls should be made to obtain parental input (p. 44814).

Contents of the IEP

The IEP should be developed solely on the needs of the student as identified through the comprehensive assessment. The IEP should not be limited by the resources of the school or the materials owned by the teacher. According to Polloway and Patton (1993), IEPs have three primary purposes. First, the IEP

The student's individualized educational program should focus on many different components of the child's school program.

can serve to provide *direction* through well-written goals and objectives. Second, the IEP can function as an *evaluation* to mark the success of the agreed upon program. And third, the IEP can serve as a *communication* tool for all concerned with the education of the student. The contents of the IEP are also specified by IDEA. The IEP should include:

1. A statement of the child's present levels of educational performance;
2. A statement of annual goals, including short-term instructional objectives;
3. A statement of the specific special education and related services to be provided to the child and the extent that the child will be able to participate in regular educational programs;
4. The projected dates for initiation of services and the anticipated duration of the services; and
5. Objective criteria and evaluation procedures and schedules for determining whether the short term instructional objectives are being achieved.

Each of these components will be discussed below.

Present Levels of Performance This section of the IEP should include strengths and weaknesses across the student's skill levels. The data may be obtained from both formal and informal measures. Each of the weaknesses listed should generally be addressed with a goal or objective in the educational plan. For a student with a learning disability, the areas of reading skills and comprehension, math calculation and reasoning, listening, oral expression, written expression, and social skills might be expected to be addressed depending on the referral information.

The strengths are especially important in designing appropriate accommodations or strategies for teaching in the general education classroom. For example, if a student had a deficit in reading, the team might determine that oral instructions would be a reasonable accommodation. However, if the student did not have skills in listening comprehension, the accommodation would be as ineffective as asking the child to read. The next set of figures depict part of the IEP planning process for Frank, discussed in Chapter 3. Note the many details that have to be included in these documents. The summary of Frank's present levels of performance is shown in Figure 4.1.

Annual Goal and Objectives The annual goals and short-term objectives must be stated positively, be stated in a way that can be measured, be student-oriented, and be a relevant, direct need of the student (Polloway and Patton, 1993). A measurable goal can be evaluated. For example, if an objective stated that a student would recognize basic sight vocabulary, that objective might cause a problem because it cannot be measured—recognize is not a measurable goal. Is it when the student's eyes widen as if in recognition, when the student points to the correct word, etc? A measurable goal in reading would be: Given fifteen primer-level Dolch words, John will read them with 90 percent accuracy.

FIGURE 4.1

Individualized Education Program

INDIVIDUALIZED EDUCATION PROGRAM

NAME Frank P.
BIRTHDATE 9-10-86 GRADE 2nd + 3rd
SCHOOL YEAR 95-96
IEP FROM 5/14/95 TO 6/2/95
FROM 8/25/95 TO 5/10/96

AREA(S) OF DISABILITY
PRIMARY Specific Learning Disability
SECONDARY _____
SECONDARY _____
SECONDARY _____

PRESENT LEVEL OF PERFORMANCE SUMMARY

DATE	ASSESSMENT INSTRUMENTS & SCORES	STRENGTHS	NEEDS
4-11-95	Wechsler Individual Achievement Test Basic Reading 81 Reading Comprehension 96 Spelling 78 Written Expression 97 Writing Composite 80 Listening 88 Oral Expression 111 Math Composite 112 Test of Written Spelling predictable 81 unpredictable 96 Total 84 Ekwall Reading Inventory Graded word lists and passages read orally at first grade level	Math Skills Spelling sight-words oral expression	Reading decoding skills writing/ spelling predictable phonetic words Listening

8/1/93

Annual goals must be broken down into short-term objectives. This process of identifying a series of objectives listed in a logical, sequential order is called task analysis. The short-term objectives should "add up" to the annual goal.

Often skill sequences and checklists are used to develop individual plans. Frank's annual goals and objectives in reading skills, written expression, and listening are included in Figure 4.2. A skill sequence that might be used for reading comprehension and written language is included in Figure 4.3 (p. 128).

Special and Regular Education Placement and Services A major decision of the IEP committee is to specify the environment in which the student with a learning disability will receive his or her education and any special services needed (e.g., transportation, counseling, modified physical education). The continuum of options available and the pros and cons of each is discussed later in this chapter. This section of the IEP documents the amount of time the student will benefit from instruction in the general education classroom. Statements regarding the accommodations to be made in the general education classroom are also important here. This page of Frank's IEP is included in Figure 4.4 (p.130). A guide that was used to identify accommodations for Frank in the general classroom is included in Figure 4.5 (p. 131). Note that different accommodations are needed in Frank's three classes. Other components of an IEP might include the degree to which a student will participate in the general education testing program and any accommodations needed in that situation. Frank's participation in the testing program and the accommodations agreed upon by his IEP committee are included in Figure 4.6 (p. 135). The final page of Frank's IEP (see Figure 4.7, p.137) includes the Least Restrictive Environment (LRE) identified, justification for the LRE, and the signatures of the committee members. The committee determined that the LRE for Frank was the resource room. A description of this service delivery option and others that were available to Frank are described later in the chapter.

Projected Dates and Duration of Services The IEP generally is written to cover one full school year. It must be in effect at the beginning of each school year, before special education and related services are provided to a student. If the IEP meeting is scheduled during the school year, the services should be implemented as soon as possible after the meeting. The only exception is when there is a short delay due to circumstances such as arrangements for transportation (USOE, 1992, p. 44814). Projected dates for the short term objectives are also listed on the IEP. These dates provide structure to the teaching process and help establish a pace. If the teacher realizes that the learning process is proceeding significantly ahead or behind the anticipated schedule, the IEP committee will need to meet to revise the IEP.

The first page of Frank's IEP (Figure 4.1) shows that his plan is written to cover the last month of school, skip the summer months, and begin the following year. Pages two through four of his IEP show the projected dates that the teacher is planning to use to cover the short-term objectives (see Figure 4.2). The projection of dates for the short-term objectives is one of the most difficult decisions to make for new teachers who have not experienced the pressure of time limits. It is also difficult to establish time periods for students who are new to your classroom, because their learning pace is relatively unknown.

FIGURE 4.2

IEP Goals and Objectives

* Page ___2___

STUDENT'S NAME _Frank P._   SCHOOL YEAR _95 - 96_

AREA _Basic Reading Skills_

	Type Of Evaluation or Agency Responsible	Projected Check Date or Initiation Date	Date/Degree Of Mastery or Completion Date

ANNUAL GOAL _Frank will improve decoding skills to a 2.9+ level_

Objective _Given a targeted phonetic pattern, Frank will decode words with the pattern 8/10 times._ — _WIAT Ekwall Reading Inventory new patterns ongoing every 6 weeks._

Objective _Given a common decoding cluster, Frank will decode 1, 2, +3 syllable words with cluster 8/10 times._ — _1-2 syllable – Jan. 96 3 Syllable – May 96_

Objective _Given text with unknown words, Frank will apply a "skip/predict" strategy and confirm with phonetic features 8/10 times._ — _Jan. 96_

Objective _Frank will locate a 1 and 2 syllable unknown word in a dictionary and use pronunciation symbols to decode 5/10 times._ — _May 96_

Objective _Frank will read a page of phonetically predictable 2nd grade text (Merrill Readers) with 85% accuracy including self-corrections._ — _May 96_

Objective _____ _____ _____

* Add additional pages if needed.

8/1/93

(continued)

FIGURE 4.2

continued

* Page _3_

STUDENT'S NAME _Frank P._   SCHOOL YEAR _95-96_

AREA _Written Expression /Spelling_

ANNUAL GOAL _Frank will improve his spelling of phonetically regular words._

	Type Of Evaluation or Agency Responsible	Projected Check Date or Initiation Date	Date/Degree Of Mastery or Completion Date
Objective	WIAT Test of written spelling Weekly spelling tests Grades.		
Objective _Given 10-20 words/week which apply targeted phonetic patterns, Frank will spell the words with 80% accuracy._		Checks will occur weekly & grades will be given every 6 weeks	
Objective _Given 10 2 syllable words using a pattern or word family, Frank will write the word in syllables 80% accuracy._		All goals ongoing Aug. 95 to May 96	
Objective _Given 3 choices of spellings, Frank will select the correct spelling of a phonetically regular word 8/10 times._			
Objective _Using samples of his own journal writing, Frank will identify and correct 50% or more of the_			
Objective _misspelled words._			
Objective			

* Add additional pages if needed.

8/1/93

(continued)

FIGURE 4.2

continued

* Page 4

STUDENT'S NAME Frank P.   SCHOOL YEAR 95-96

AREA Listening

	Type Of Evaluation or Agency Responsible	Projected Check Date or Initiation Date	Date/Degree Of Mastery or Completion Date

ANNUAL GOAL Frank will improve listening skills as measured on the Wechsler Individual Achievement Test

WIAT
Teacher Observation

Objective When oral directions are given by teacher, Frank will face and maintain eye contact with speaker 8/10 times.   Oct 95

Objective After listening to oral directions, Frank will follow the directions with no repetition 8/10 times.   Jan 96

Objective After hearing a word pronounced twice, Frank will tell how many syllables and say the word in syllables 8/10 times.   Jan 96

Objective After hearing a word, Frank will indicate if the word contains a targeted sound 8/10 times.   ongoing May 95+ Aug 95-May 96

Objective After listening to a 1-5 paragraph passage, Frank will answer 5 questions concerning the   May 96

Objective passage with 80% accuracy.

* Add additional pages if needed.

8/1/93

FIGURE 4.3

Skill Sequence for Reading Comprehension and Language Skills

Area: Reading Comprehension

Annual Goal: _____
will improve reading comprehension
scores to the _____ grade level.

Reading instruction will be designed to develop
the literal and inferential comprehension skills
below. Given text on an instructional level, the
student will read orally and/or silently and complete specified comprehension tasks with
75–80% accuracy.

Objectives:

___1. The student will use literal comprehension
skills below to gain meaning from a vari-
ety of text.
___Follow printed directions
___Recognize and generate main ideas
___Recall and restate details
___Locate information to verify
___Identify basic text elements
(5 Ws, characters, setting, plot, etc.)
___Define new vocabulary
___Understand homonyms, antonyms,
and synonyms
___Identify facts and opinions

___2. The student will use inferential compre-
hension skills below to gain meaning from
a variety of text.
___Use contextual cueing systems
___Predict outcomes
___Draw conclusions
___Make inferences
___Recognize cause/effect relationships
___Identify character traits and motives
___Identify theme and mood
___Understand idioms and figures of
speech

___3. _____
_____
_____
_____
_____

Evaluation:
Gates-MacGinitie
K-TEA
Ekwall
WIAT
Observation

Progress will be monitored every
nine weeks and documented on
progress report.

(continued)

FIGURE 4.3

continued

Area: Written Language

Annual goal: _____will generate written work that demonstrates mastery of writing skills appropriate for the _____ grade level.

Written activities will focus on targeted skills specified below. The student will perform writing tasks successfully 4 out of 5 times or with 80% accuracy.

Objectives:

___1. The student will express an idea in a complete sentence.

___2. The student will construct an organized paragraph with a topic sentence, 3–5 details, and a concluding sentence.

___3. The student will write pieces in a variety of genre including:
___narrative   ___expository   ___letters
___descriptive ___sequential   ___poetry
___persuasive ___research/   ___other:
                  reports

___4. The student will demonstrate use of skills appropriate for the _____ grade level in the following areas:
___capitalization   ____correct usage of
___punctuation   words
___types of sentences   ____handwriting
___: other as

___5. The student will use editing skills to edit written work with attention to:
___capitalization   ____word usage
___punctuation   ____legibility
___spelling   ____: other as

___6. The student will apply knowledge to engage in the writing process—prewriting, drafting, revising, editing, and publishing. A minimum of _____ piece(s) will be completed each six weeks

___7. _____
     _____
     _____

Evaluation:
WIAT
TOWL
Woodcock-Johnson
Writing samples
Observation

Progress will be monitored every nine weeks and documented on progress report.

Source: Dunavant, N. (1993) Homewood School System, Birmingham, Alabama.

FIGURE 4.4

Regular Class Participation

Name **Frank P.**   School Year **94-95; 95-96**   Page **5**

REGULAR CLASS PARTICIPATION (_32 1/2_   HOURS PER WEEK)

MODIFICATIONS IN THE REGULAR EDUCATION PROGRAM

If modifications to the regular education program are necessary to ensure the student's participation in that program, those modifications must be described in the student's IEP. Any modification to the regular education program must be indicated by writing the letter(s) of the modification description on the line beside the area.

	MODIFICATION		MODIFICATION		MODIFICATION
READING	A, D, E	LANGUAGE ARTS		HOMEROOM	
ENGLISH		SOCIAL STUDIES	A, D, G	LUNCH	
SPELLING	A, D	VOCATIONAL ED		LIBRARY	
MATH	D	HEALTH		ART	
SCIENCE	A, D, G				
MUSIC					

MODIFICATION DESCRIPTIONS

A. Modify presentation   D. Modify materials   G. _Read test aloud_
B. Modify environment   E. Use groups and peers   H. _____
C. Modify time demands   F. Use paraprofessionals   I. _____

The following TESTING MODIFICATION(S) is/are made in the special education program.

AREA   MODIFICATION
Science   _Read tests aloud_
Social Studies   _Read tests aloud_
_____   _____

CHECK ONE OF THE FOLLOWING ITEM:

_____   This **IS NOT** a stat testing program year for this student.
_✓_   This **IS** a state testing program year for this student. See attached documents.

PHYSICAL EDUCATION   Regular _✓_ Modified ___ Special ___ NA ___

TRANSPORTATION   Regular _✓_ Special ___ NA ___

RELATED SERVICES

SERVICE   HR/WK   PERSON(S) RESPONSIBLE
none
_____   _____   _____
_____   _____   _____

8/1/93

Objective Criteria and Evaluation Procedures IDEA (1992) mandates the specification of the methods the teacher will use for evaluating whether the short-term objectives are being met. The criteria for success is generally written into

FIGURE 4.5

Modifications for Regular Classes

MODIFICATIONS FOR REGULAR CLASS

NAME ___Frank P._____ SCHOOL YEAR ___95-96___

It may be necessary that modifications be made in your classroom for students because P.L. 91-230, as amended, provides that all students with disabilities, including those in public or private institutions or other care facilities, are educated with children who are not disabled, and that special classes, separate schooling, or other removal of students with disabilities from the regular education environment occurs only when the nature or severity of the disability is such that an education in regular classes with the use of supplementary aids and services cannot be achieved satisfactorily."

DIRECTIONS: Check each modification made.

Name of Course
1. _Social Studies/Science_   Regular Teacher _____
2. _Math_ _____
3. _Reading/Spelling_ _____

Courses

1	2	3		
			A.	**MODIFYING THE PRESENTATION OF THE MATERIAL**
—	—	—	1.	Break assignment into segments of shorter tasks.
—	—	—	2.	When content mastery is questionable, investigate the use of concrete concepts BEFORE teaching abstract.
—	—	—	3.	Relate information to student's experiential base.
—	—	✓	4.	Reduce the number of concepts introduced at any one time.
—	—	—	5.	Provide student with an overview of the lesson BEFORE beginning the lesson. (Tell student what student should expect to learn and why.)
✓	—	—	6.	Monitor the level of language you use to communicate ideas. (Are you using vocabulary and complex sentence structures that are too advanced?)
✓	—	—	7.	Schedule frequent, short conferences with student to check for comprehension.
✓	—	✓	8.	Provide consistent review of any lesson BEFORE introducing new information.
			9.	Allow student to obtain and report information utilizing:

   ✓ cassette/tape recorders   ___ projects   ___ dictation   ___ typewriters
    ___ computers   ✓ films   ✓ interviews/oral reports ___ calculators

1	2	3		
—	—	—	10.	Highlight important concepts to be learned in text or material. (Color code key points; outline; student guides.)
—	—	—	11.	Space practice and drill sessions over time.
—	—	—	12.	Monitor the rate in which you present material. (Do you talk too fast or give too much material at one time?)
—	—	—	13.	Give additional presentations.
—	—	—		a. repeat original presentation.
—	—	✓		b. provide more complete/simpler explanation.
—	—	✓		c. give additional examples.
—	—	✓		d. model skills in several ways.
—	—	—	14.	Provide additional guided practice.
—	—	—		a. require more responses.
—	—	—		b. lengthen practice sessions.
—	—	—		c. schedule extra practice sessions.
✓	—	—	15.	Make consequences more attractive.
—	—	—		a. increase feedback.
—	—	—		b. provide knowledge of results.
—	—	—		c. chart performance.
—	—	—		d. reward approximations.
—	—	—		e. give incentives to begin and to complete.

-1-   8/1/93

(continued)

the objective. For example, Figure 4.8 (p. 138) contains a sample IEP in Reading Decoding that specifies the objectives must be met at 75–80% accuracy at a minimum. The teacher has also specified the formal and informal assessment measures that will be used. Since the school is on a nine-week reporting system,

FIGURE 4.5

continued

16.	Recognize and give credit for student's oral participation in class.
17.	Make arrangements for homework assignments to reach home with clear, concise directions.
18.	Assign tasks at the appropriate level (lower reading/difficulty level).
19.	Give tests orally.
20.	Other: _____
21.	Other: _____

1 2 3   **B. MODIFYING THE ENVIRONMENT**

1.	Use study carrels.
2.	Use proximity seating.
3.	Seat student in area free from distractions.
4.	Let student select the place which is best for him to study.
5.	Help keep student's space free of unnecessary materials.
6.	Use checklists to help student get organized.
7.	Use notebook for organized assignments, materials, and homework.
8.	Provide opportunities for movement.
9.	Other: _____
10.	Other: _____

1 2 3   **C. MODIFYING TIME DEMANDS**

1.	Increase amount of time allowed to complete assignment/tests. (Contract with student concerning time allotment.)
2.	Reduce amount of work or length of tests (as opposed to allowing more time).
3.	Teach time management skills (use of checklists, prioritizing time, prioritizing assignments).
4.	Space short work periods with breaks or change of task.
5.	Set up a specific routine and stick with it.
6.	Alternate quiet and active time (short periods of each).
7.	Give student a specific task to perform within specific time limits.
8.	Other: _____
9.	Other: _____

D. MODIFYING THE MATERIALS

1 2 3   1. Visual Motor Integration

a.	Avoid large amount of written work (both in class and homework).
b.	Encourage student to select the method of writing which is most comfortable. (cursive or manuscript)
c.	Set realistic and mutually agreed upon expectations for neatness.
d.	Let student type, record, or give answers orally instead of writing.
e.	Avoid pressures of speed and accuracy.
f.	Provide student with carbon copy of lecture notes produced by teacher or peer.
g.	Reduce amounts of boardwork copying and textbook copying: provide student with written information.
h.	Other: _____
i.	Other: _____

1 2 3   2. Visual Processing

a.	Highlight information to be learned (color coding, underlining, etc.).
b.	Keep written assignments and work space free from extraneous/irrelevant distracters.
c.	Avoid purple dittos.
d.	Worksheets should be clear and well-defined.
e.	Go over visual task with student and make sure he has a clear understanding of all parts of the assignment <u>BEFORE</u> beginning.
f.	Avoid having student copy from the board. (Provide him/her with a written copy of the material. May copy teacher's manual or lecture notes).

-2-   8/1/93

(continued)

the IEP goals will be evaluated each nine weeks. Typically the short-term objectives are measured by informal assessment procedures and the annual goals are measured at the end of the IEP period using formal assessment procedures.

FIGURE 4.5

continued

___ ___ ___   g. Other: _____
___ ___ ___   h. Other: _____

1   2   3   3. Language Processing

✓ ___ ✓   a. Give written directions to supplement verbal directions.
___ ___ ✓   b. Slow the rate of presentation.
✓ ___ ___   c. Paraphrase material using similar language.
✓ ___ ___   d. Keep statements short and to the point.
___ ___ ___   e. Avoid use of abstract language (metaphors, idioms, puns, etc.).
___ ___ ___   f. Keep sentence structures simple. Gradually introduce more complex sentences as student masters
    the ability to comprehend them.
✓ ___ ___   g. Encourage feedback from student to check for understanding.
    (Have student restate what you have said in his own words).
___ ___ ___   h. Familiarize student with any new vocabulary BEFORE the lesson.
    (Make sure student can use this vocabulary not just recognize it).
___ ___ ___   i. Reduce amount of extraneous noise such as conversations, TV, radio, noises from outside, etc.
✓ ___ ___   j. Alert student's attention to key points with such phrases as, "This is important. Listen
    carefully."
✓ ___ ✓   k. Ensure the readability levels of the textbooks used in class are commensurate with student's
    language level.
___ ___ ✓   l. Utilize visual aids to supplement verbal information.
    (Charts, graphics, pictures, etc., can be used to illustrate written and spoken information).
___ ___ ___   m. Utilize manipulative, hands-on activities whenever possible. Establish the concrete experience
    base BEFORE teaching more abstract concepts.
___ ___ ___   n. ALWAYS demonstrate to student how the new material relates to material he/she has
    previously learned.
___ ✓ ___   o. Other: *Read word problems aloud* _____
___ ___ ___   p. Other: _____

1   2   3   4. Organizational

✓ ___ ___   a. Establish a daily routine and attempt to maintain it.
___ ___ ___   b. Make clear rules and be consistent enforcing them.
___ ___ ___   c. Contract with student, using a reward for completion of the contract.
___ ___ ___   d. Provide notebook with organized sections such as:
    ___ assignments due   ___ calendar   ___ homework   ___ time management
    ___ prioritized to-do lists   ___ study guides ___ class notes   schedules
___ ___ ___   e. Avoid cluttered, crowded worksheets by utilizing techniques such as:
    blocking - black assignments into smaller segments.
    cutting - cut worksheets into fourths, sixths, or eighths and place one problem in each square.
    folding - fold worksheets into fourths, sixths, or eighths and place one problem in each square.
    color coding, highlighting, or underlining important information on which student needs to
    focus.
___ ___ ___   f. Hand out written assignments with expected dates of completion typed or written on one corner.
___ ___ ___   g. To prevent misplaced assignments, provide student with file folders, notebooks or trays in which
    he/she can immediately place his/her work BEFORE it is lost.
___ ___ ___   h. Set aside a specific time for cleaning desks, lockers, organizing notebooks, etc.
___ ___ ___   i. Teach goal-setting skills.
___ ___ ___   j. Teach decision making/prioritizing skills.
___ ___ ___   k. Teach time management skills.
___ ___ ___   l. Other: _____
___ ___ ___   m. Other: _____

1   2   3   E. **USE OF GROUPS AND PEERS**

✓ ___ ___   1. Utilize cooperative learning strategies when appropriate.

-3-   8/1/93

(continued)

Overview of Service Delivery Systems

Before the passage of Public Law 94-142, if special education was available for
students with learning disabilities, it was primarily delivered in separate, self-

FIGURE 4.5

continued

✓	—	—	2. Assign a peer helper to:
✓	—	—	a. Check understanding of directions.
—	—	—	b. Read important directions and essential material.
—	—	—	c. Make carbon copies of lecture notes.
—	—	—	d. Drill work.
—	—	—	e. Summarize important textbook passages (on tape or in person).
—	—	—	f. Record material dictated by student.
			g. Model appropriate responses.
✓	—	—	3. Other: *practice reading Keywords*
—	—	—	4. Other: _____

1 2 3 F. **USE OF A PARAPROFESSIONAL**

—	—	—	1. _____
—	—	—	2. _____
—	—	—	3. _____
—	—	—	4. _____
—	—	—	5. _____

1 2 3 G. **OTHER (SPECIFY)**

✓	—	—	1. *read tests aloud*
—	—	—	2. _____
—	—	—	3. _____
—	—	—	4. _____
—	—	—	5. _____
—	—	—	6. _____
—	—	—	7. _____
—	—	—	8. _____
—	—	—	9. _____
—	—	—	10. _____

-4   8/1/93

contained, special education classrooms. Under this model children with learning disabilities had only limited contact with students who were not disabled and special education teachers rarely interacted with general education teachers (Hallahan and Kauffman, 1995). When P.L. 94-142 was passed, it contained a

FIGURE 4.6

Alabama State Testing Program

BASIC COMPETENCY TEST (BCT)
HIGH SCHOOL BASIC SKILLS EXIT EXAM (EXIT EXAM)
Accommodations Checklist

When completed by the IEP/504 Committee, this checklist becomes part of the student's IEP/504 Plan.

Name: _Frank P._____   School Year: _95-96_

A.   Scheduling Accommodations: Tests will be administered:

___   1.   At time of day most beneficial to student.

___   2.   In periods of ___ minutes followed by rest breaks of ___ minutes.

___   3.   Until, in the administrator's judgment, the student can no longer sustain the activity due to physical disability or limited attention span

___   4.   With other accommodations needed due to the nature of the disability and nature of the assessment. **SDE APPROVAL ONLY.**

B.   Setting Accommodations: Tests will be administered:

___   1.   In a small group.

___   2.   In a carrel.

___   3.   In the special education classroom.

___   4.   At the student's home.

___   5.   With student seated in front of classroom.

✓   6.   With teacher facing student.

___   7.   By student's special education teacher.

___   8.   Using an interpreter during the time oral instruction is given to the student. (Interpreter may only interpret directions--interpreter may not clarify or offer interpretation of items.)

___   9.   Individually.

___   10.   With other accommodations needed due to the nature of the disability and nature of the assessment. **SDE APPROVAL ONLY.**

C.   Format and/or Equipment Accommodations: Tests will be administered in keeping with the student's IEP/504 Plan format and/or equipment modifications which are commonly used in instruction and/or other test situations such as:

___   1.   Large print.

___   2.   Braille.

___   3.   Mathematics subject-area test read aloud by test administrator.

✓   4.   Language subject-area test read aloud by test administrator.

___   5.   Student using magnifying equipment.

___   6.   Student using amplification equipment (e.g., hearing aid, auditory trainer).

___   7.   Student wearing noise buffers.

___   8.   Templates and/or graph paper.

___   9.   Abacus.

___   10.   Other accommodations needed due to the nature of the disability and nature of the assessment. **SDE APPROVAL ONLY.**

D.   Recording Accommodations:

___   1.   Student will mark answers in test booklets.

___   2.   Student's answers will be recorded by proctor or assistant.

___   3.   Student will mark answers by machine.

___   4.   Other accommodations needed due to the nature of the disability and nature of the assessment. **SDE APPROVAL ONLY.**

Revised 9-1-95   18

(continued)

powerful requirement of providing special education services in the least-restrictive-environment (LRE). This means that students with disabilities should remain with their nondisabled, chronological-age peers as much as possible.

FIGURE 4.6

continued

Name: **Frank P.**   **ALABAMA STATE TESTING PROGRAM**   School Year: **95-96**

✓ **BASIC COMPETENCY TEST (BCT), Grade 9**
  1. Student will participate.
  ___ 2. No accommodations are required for student to participate.
  ✓ 3. Accommodations are required for student to participate. (See attached accommodations.)
  ___ 4. Student will not participate.
  ___ 5. Justification for the committee decision:
  _____
  _____

HIGH SCHOOL BASIC SKILLS EXIT EXAM (EXIT EXAM)
  1. Student will participate . . .
  ___   in the eleventh grade.
  ___   in the twelfth grade.
  ___ 2. No accommodations are required for student to participate.
  ___ 3. Accommodations are required for student to participate. (See attached accommodations.)
  ___ 4. Student will not participate.
  ___ 5. Justification for the committee decision:
  _____
  _____

STANFORD ACHIEVEMENT TEST
  ___ 1. Student will participate.
  ___ 2. No accommodations are required for student to participate.
  ___ 3. Accommodations are required for student to participate. (See attached accommodations.)
  ___ 4. Student will not participate.
  ___ 5. Justification for the committee decision:
  _____
  _____

DIFFERENTIAL APTITUDE TESTS (DAT)
  ___ 1. Student will participate.
  ___ 2. No accommodations are required for student to participate.
  ___ 3. Accommodations are required for student to participate. (See attached accommodations.)
  ___ 4. Student will not participate.
  ___ 5. Justification for the committee decision:
  _____
  _____

CAREER INTEREST INVENTORY (CII)
  1. Student will participate in the. . .
  ___   eighth grade (Level 1).
  ___   tenth grade (Level 2).
  ___ 2. No accommodations are required for student to participate.
  ___ 3. Accommodations are required for student to participate. (See attached accommodations.)
  ___ 4. Student will not participate.
  ___ 5. Justification for the committee decision:
  _____
  _____

GRADE-LEVEL CRITERION-REFERENCED TEST (Specify) _____
  ___ 1. Student will participate.
  ___ 2. No accommodations are required for student to participate.
  ___ 3. Accommodations are required for student to participate. (See attached accommodations.)
  ___ 4. Student will not participate.
  ___ 5. Justification for the committee decision:
  _____
  _____

If the school is chosen to participate in piloting of a new assessment and/or edition, the student will participate unless the IEP/504 Committee is reconvened. Students needing special formats will participate in pilots only if special formats are available.   Revised 9-1-95

17

The law specifically requires students with disabilities to be educated with their nondisabled peers "to the maximum extent appropriate." The law further mandates that removal of students with disabilities from general education

FIGURE 4.7

Least Restrictive Environment Justification

Name **Frank P.**   School Year **May 95 ; 95-96**   Page _____

The student will have the opportunity to participate as appropriate in NONACADEMIC and EXTRACURRICULAR activities unless the IEP states otherwise. Reasons for nonparticipation, if appropriate, are as follows: _____

CHECK THE APPROPRIATE LEAST RESTRICTIVE ENVIRONMENT

[✓] 01 Regular (less than 6 hrs. per week)   [ ] 05 Private Day School   [ ] 08 Hospital
[ ] 02 Resource (6-21 hrs. per week)   [ ] 06 Public Residential   [ ] 09 Corrections
[ ] 03 Separate (over 21 hrs. per week)   [ ] 07 Private Residential   [ ] 10 Private School
[ ] 04 Public Day School   [ ] 08 Home   (placed by parents)

JUSTIFICATION FOR THE LEAST RESTRICTIVE ENVIRONMENT IS AS FOLLOWS:

In the third grade, Frank will receive individualized instruction in the resource room 30 minutes/day to strengthen the areas of decoding, spelling, and listening. All other programming will take place in the regular 3rd grade class with accommodations and/or modifications. For the remainder of 2nd grade, Frank will go to the resource room only 3 times/week to adjust to the routine.

THE FOLLOWING PERSONS ATTENDED THE IEP MEETING

IEP COMMITTEE MEMBER'S SIGNATURE	DATE	POSITION
Mr. Frank P.		PARENT
Julia Williams	5/13/95	LEA REPRESENTATIVE
Mrs. Sally Principi	5/13/95	TEACHER
		STUDENT
Ms. L. Castri	5-13-95	*Counselor*
Nancy Pemerant	5-13-95	*Sped teacher*

SOURCES OF ADDITIONAL INPUT

NAME   POSITION

_____   _____

_____   _____

8/1/93

settings to special classes, separate schools, or other placement should only happen when students cannot be successfully served in regular education class-rooms, even provided supplementary services and aids. The burden of deter-

FIGURE 4.8

Sample IEP in Reading Decoding

Area: Reading Decoding

Annual goal: _____will improve
reading decoding scores to the _____ grade level.

Reading instruction will be designed to improve
word recognition skills and strategies in the areas
below. Given a variety of level-appropriate text,
the student will apply decoding knowledge to
complete tasks with 75–80% accuracy.

Objectives:
___1. Use Context Clues
   ___Apply "skip/substitute" strategy
   ___Predict based on logical meaning
   ___Predict based on sentence structure
   ___Predict based on prior knowledge
   ___Confirm based on word features

___2. Use Phonetic Elements
   ___Consonants ___Diagraphs
   ___Short Vowels ___Vowel Combinations
   ___Long Vowels ___Consonant Variations
   ___Blends   ___Silent Letters

___3. Use Word Analysis Strategies
   ___Recognize and construct word families
   ___Identify base words
   ___Identify prefixes and suffixes
   ___Apply syllabication rules

___4. Recognize High-Frequency Vocabulary
   ___Dolch Word List _____
   ___Building Sight Vocabulary _____
   ___Alabama Competency List _____
   ___Other: _____

___5. Use Information Sources
   ___Locate words in dictionary/glossary
   ___Use technology sources
   ___Request help of others

___6. _____
   _____
   _____

Evaluation:
Gates-MacGinitie
K-TEA
Ekwall
WIAT
Work Samples
Observation

Progress will be monitored every
nine weeks and documented on
progress report.

Source: Dunavant, N. (1993) Homewood School System, Birmingham, Alabama

mining the most appropriate placement for students is placed by law with each student's IEP committee. The law requires a full continuum of placement options for students, ranging from the isolated, special education setting to full inclusion in regular classrooms.

While several models have emerged to define the continuum of placement options, most are based on Evelyn Deno's cascade system (1970). This model, displayed in Figure 4.9, pictures the continuum of services ranging from the most restrictive to the least restrictive. This model also most closely parallels the services and regulations defined in Public Law 94-142. Since the terminology, such as self-contained classrooms, resource rooms, and organizational structures of special education, reflects the general concepts proposed by Deno's cascade, this model will be used to describe the continuum. Following are several of the positive aspects of the continuum as described in the literature:

1. A conceptualization of a continuum of services is provided for service providers and administrators to develop their own service delivery system (Podemski, Price, Smith, and Marsh, 1984).

2. A basic list of service options for students with varying abilities and disabilities is proposed (Merulla and McKinnon, 1982).

3. The focus of special education services is not on the mechanical aspects of placement or the physical plant. The focus is on the the child's needs, not on how they fit into existing space (Reid and Hresko, 1981).

4. The model emphasizes a flexible continuum of appropriate special education assignments, suggesting that students can advance toward regular class placement (Cegelka and Prehm, 1982).

Even though the model of services described in Deno's cascade has contributed significantly to the understanding and evolutionary process of least restrictive environment, the following criticisms are noted:

1. Although the original intent of Deno was to suggest a flexible model that allows movement freely along the continuum, schools have developed rules and organizational procedures that are strict and may provide barriers to advancing in the continuum (Smith, Finn, and Dowdy, 1993).

2. The implementation of Deno's procedures is considered limiting due to the disagreement about the precise nature of the levels of disabilities (McMillan, 1977).

3. Some educators have questioned the distinctions proposed by the model (e.g., the amount of integration described in each level, the disabilities of the students served, variation in the distribution of time by teachers).

Since Deno's Levels I, II, III, and IV are the most commonly used to educate students with learning disabilities, these will be described briefly below.

Level IV: Full-time Special Class This type of service delivery is often called the self-contained classroom. Smith, Price, and Marsh (1986) provided the following characteristics of these classrooms:

FIGURE 4.9

Cascade of Services

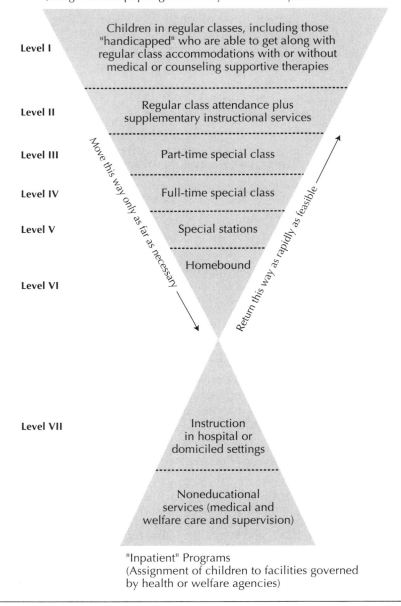

"Outpatient" Programs
(Assignment of pupils governed by the school system)

Level I — Children in regular classes, including those "handicapped" who are able to get along with regular class accommodations with or without medical or counseling supportive therapies

Level II — Regular class attendance plus supplementary instructional services

Level III — Part-time special class

Level IV — Full-time special class

Level V — Special stations

Level VI — Homebound

Level VII — Instruction in hospital or domiciled settings

Noneducational services (medical and welfare care and supervision)

Move this way only as far as necessary

Return this way as rapidly as feasible

"Inpatient" Programs
(Assignment of children to facilities governed by health or welfare agencies)

Source: "Special Education as Developmental Capital" by E. Deno, *Exceptional Children*, 1970, 37, 229–237. Copyright 1970 by the Council for Exceptional Children. Reprinted with permission.

1. The primary responsibility for delivering instruction is provided by a certified special education teacher;

2. The majority of the instruction for students is delivered within one classroom;

3. Support services such as physical education, art, speech, and music may be provided by the special education teacher as well; and

4. The skill and motivation of the special education teacher and the richness of materials available in the classroom determines the degree of individualized instruction delivered to students.

Reynolds (1973) suggested that the self-contained, special class was the preferred service delivery option for educating students with less severe disabilities during the period of 1950–1970. Parents and educators were beginning to question the desirability of this approach prior to P.L. 94-142. During this time the parents began to be concerned regarding the impact of the isolation of their children from the regular activities within the school and the lack of research demonstrating the effectiveness of self-contained classes (Hallahan and Kauffman, 1995). Table 4.1 contains the advantages and disadvantages of the self-contained classroom model.

Level III: Part-time Special Class   The desire for a more normalized educational environment led to the widespread development of part-time special classrooms that represented a significantly more integrated special education program than

TABLE 4.1

Summary of Possible Advantages and Disadvantages of the Self-Contained Classroom Model

Advantages

1. Full-time interaction with the teacher may allow more scheduling flexibility.

2. Students are able to spend more time in small groups with peers, which may foster friendships.

3. Parents may form closer relationships with one teacher than if they deal with several teachers.

4. Grouping for instruction may be easier to accomplish.

5. It may be easier for one teacher to assume complete responsibility for the student's performance.

Disadvantages

1. The student's opportunities to interact with peers and other adults are restricted.

2. Teachers may be isolated from other staff members.

3. Opportunity is limited for special education students to have experiences with students of other ability levels.

Source: Cegelka, P.T. and Prehm, H.J. (1982) *Mental retardation: From categories to people.* Columbus, OH: Merrill Co.

the self-contained classroom. This class became commonly called the "resource room." This placement was considered less stigmatizing and offered a bridge between full-time inclusion in a regular classroom and placement in a self-contained class. In this model, students receive direct instruction for a part of the day and spend the remainder of the day in a general education setting. The U.S. Department of Education (1990) described a resource room as a setting where students "receive special education and related services for 60 percent or less of the school day and at least 21 percent of the school week. This may include resource rooms with part-time instruction in the regular classroom" (p. 19).

Although resource rooms vary greatly, they frequently have a wide variety of materials designed to support teaching of the regular classroom curriculum. They typically have a variety of learning areas which might include a reading center, small group work areas, areas for individual study, and a listening center. Smith, Finn, and Dowdy (1993) proposed several purposes for the resource room:

1. To provide intensive instruction to assist students in maintaining the pace of the regular classroom;
2. To provide direct instruction for remediation of basic skills such as math, written expression, and reading; and
3. To provide direct instruction in skills not typically addressed in the general classroom such as social skills, strategies, or development of employability skills.

Figure 4.10 demonstrates a form of recordkeeping that the resource teacher might use to provide regular feedback to the parents and general education

Regular classroom placement with support services for students with learning disabilities is a very common option.

FIGURE 4.10

Resource Progress Report

Name: _____ Year: _____

Grade: _____ Teacher: _____

Performance Code: Comments

S—Satisfactory/Consistent   N—Needs Improvement/   U—Unsatisfactory
I—Improving/Developing   No progress   X—Not applicable

Reading Skills	1	2	3	4	5	6
Understands what is read						
Uses context cues						
Uses letter/sound cues						
Reads orally with expression						
Self-corrects when reading						
Responds to text: oral, written						

Writing Skills	1	2	3	4	5	6
Participates willingly in writing						
Writes for a variety of purposes						
Expresses ideas clearly						
Applies grammar/ punctuation						
Applies standard spelling						
Uses legible handwriting						

Spelling Skills	1	2	3	4	5	6
Spells high frequency words						
Spells phonetic words						
Generalizes to other subjects						
Completes weekly work						

Math Skills	1	2	3	4	5	6
Numeration and place value						
Addition						
Subtraction						
Multiplication						
Division						
Knowledge of basic facts						
Fractions/Decimals						
Measurement/ Geometry						
Problem solving strategies						

Work Habits/Behavior	1	2	3	4	5	6
Comes to class prepared						
Listens in class						
Follows directions						
Works independently						
Completes work						
Obeys class rules						
Shows self-control						
Respects others						

Please call the school if you would like to schedule a conference (942-8607).

Source: Dunavant, N. (1993). Homewood School System, Birmingham, AL.

teachers regarding progress. Communication is always critical to the success of any educational model. The advantages and disadvantages of the resource room are noted in Table 4.2.

Level II: Regular Class Placement with Supportive Services   One of the strategies used to provide supportive services in the regular classroom is the use of an itinerant teacher who travels across several schools providing minimal direct services. An itinerant teacher might provide direct instruction via a regular schedule with two to three sessions per week. The itinerant teacher might work with individual students or small groups of children with similar educational needs. Communication is very important in this model. Figure 4.11 provides a form developed by a teacher to obtain feedback on the behavior and progress in the general education classroom of students with learning disabilities. A section at the bottom of the form provides the special education teacher a space to document the response made to provide assistance to the general education teacher regarding the concern noted above.

TABLE 4.2
Advantages and Disadvantages of Resource Rooms

Advantages

1. Students receive specialized instruction and related services from special education professionals.
2. Students receive portions of their educational services in regular classrooms with nondisabled peers.
3. Students with disabilities have nondisabled role models.
4. Students with disabilities have opportunities for developing appropriate social skills in a natural setting (regular classroom).
5. Students without disabilities have the opportunity to interact with students who are disabled.
6. Regular classroom teachers and special education teachers share the responsibility of students with disabilities.

Disadvantages

1. Some students may require more intensive services than are provided in a resource room.
2. Scheduling students in and out of regular classes often presents problems.
3. Close collaboration between the resource room teacher and regular classroom is difficult to accomplish and may result in confusion for the student.
4. Students may feel stigmatized by having to leave the regular classroom for services.

Source: Table from *Teaching Students with Mild Disabilities* by Tom E.C. Smith, David M. Finn, and Carol A. Dowdy, copyright 1993 by Holt, Rinehart and Winston, Inc., reproduced by permission of the publisher.

FIGURE 4.11

Six Week Monitoring Documentation

Name: _____ Date: _____

Teacher _____ Grade: _____

Six Weeks Grades: _____Reading
                     _____Spelling
                     _____English
                     _____Writing
                     _____Math
                     _____Social Studies
                     _____Science
                     _____Music, Art, P.E.

Has this student had any behavior problems this six weeks? _____
If so, please comment.

Has this student had problems with work habits?
If so, please comment._____

Are there specific areas of concern that need to be addressed for this student to perform more successfully next six weeks? _____
If so, please comment._____

Consult service was documented on the following dates: _____

_____

Regular Class Teacher: _____

Resource Teacher: _____

_____

Source: Dunavant, N. (1993). Homewood School System, Birmingham, AL.

Many schools also offer a service delivery model in which a special education teacher works parallel with a regular education teacher on a daily basis
(West and Idol, 1990). In this model, the regular education teacher is usually
primarily responsible for providing instruction in the regular curriculum.
Special education teachers provide assistance to those who need it, modify the
existing curriculum, develop adapted tests, etc.

This relatively new option for providing instructional support for children
with learning disabilities in a regular classroom is often called the collaborative
teaching model. The Council for Exceptional Children defines collaboration as
a generic term used to describe a style of interacting in which persons with
diverse backgrounds/expertise voluntarily agree to work together to generate
creative solutions to mutually defined problems. It is characterized by a mutual
trust and respect, open communications, and parity of contributions. The goal
of collaboration is to more effectively meet the unique educational needs of
exceptional students (Council for Exceptional Children, 1991). This approach

is often called a "plug-in" model since special educators work within the regular classroom directly with students with learning disabilities.

Phillips and McCullough (1990) suggested the following as principles of an effective collaborative approach:

1. All professionals jointly share responsibility and concern for all students.

2. There is joint accountability and problem solving, and resolution of problems is mutually completed.

3. The cooperative teachers believe that pooling resources and talents is mutually advantageous with the following benefits: (a) the range of solutions generated is increased; (b) there is greater diversity of expertise and resources on hand to attack the problem; and (c) the solutions generated are superior to those that would be developed by a single teacher working alone.

4. There should be a belief that solving problems related to students with disabilities is worthy of expenditure of energy, time, and resources.

5. There should be a belief that collaboration results in important and desirable outcomes including better teacher morale, increased knowledge or creative decision making, and more effective design of alternative classroom interventions (p. 295).

This model is being carefully studied as to the effects on instructional outcome as well as issues of self-esteem. Fuchs and Fuchs (1992) caution that there is no research currently available that supports the effect of this model on student learning. Research does suggest that it is an extraordinarily complex process and its success is largely dependent on the teachers' mutual respect and compatibility (Reeve and Hallahan, 1994).

Level I: Regular Classroom Placement with Minimal Support Services   This organizational arrangement allows for the maximum integration of students with disabilities in a regular classroom. Under this model, the regular classroom teacher is primarily responsible for delivery of instruction to students with disabilities. The special education teacher would not provide direct service to students; however, assistance could be provided through a consulting arrangement between the special education teacher and the general education teacher. Figure 4.12 provides an example of an IEP for a student with a learning disability receiving instruction in the general education classroom.

There has been some concern that administrators faced with economic limitations might resort to this approach as a means to lighten the stress of financial obligations. If students are capable of benefiting from instruction in the regular classroom, however, this would be the most desirable placement in terms of least restrictive environment. It should be considered as the first option for all students with learning disabilities.

Regular Education Initiative (REI) and Inclusion

In the 1980s Madeline Will, then Assistant Secretary of Education, Office of Special Education and Rehabilitative Services, proclaimed her intent to merge

FIGURE 4.12

IEP for Student with Learning Disability in the General Education Classroom

Student Name _____Year _____Page _____

Area: Regular Classroom Placement

Annual Goal: _____will maintain average

or above average grades in all regular _____grade academic classes.

Objectives:

1. _____will participate in regular class activities 5 of 5 days per week.

2. _____will complete regular class assignments on time 5 of 5 days per week.

3. _____will complete homework assignments 4 of 5 days per week.

4. _____will average 70% or higher on tests taken in the regular academic classes.

5. _____will self-evaluate progress by meeting with a resource teacher a minimum of once per grading period.

Type of Evaluation _____

Projected Check Date _____

Date/Degree of Mastery _____

Progress will be monitored every nine weeks and the report card will document the meeting of objectives.

Note: This student_____does/ _____does not require classroom modifications.

Source: Dunavant, N. (1993) Homewood School System, Birmingham, Alabama.

special education into regular education. This proposal, although perpetuated by the Office of Special Education, has come to be called the Regular Education Initiative (REI). This initiative has evolved into the right of students with disabilities to receive an education in the same environment as their nondisabled peers. The proponents of REI, or inclusion, criticize the dichotomous nature of the public education system, one for regular education students and one for students with disabilities. Advocates of inclusion propose that many special education programs are turning out students with disabilities who have not learned successfully. They propose that the pull-out model of service delivery, in which students are taken out of the general education classroom to receive special education, is failing miserably. Will (1986) also commented on the need to conserve scarce resources in order to address critical financial needs.

Friend and Bursuck (1996) summarized the literature in terms of the advocates of inclusion and those individuals who support inclusion only under certain conditions. The early push for inclusion came primarily from parents, professionals, and advocates for individuals with severe disabilities other than learning disabilities; however, some parents and advocates for individuals with learning disabilities do support inclusion. The arguments of these advocates of inclusion include:

1. Students with disabilities have a basic human right to attend school with their age peers (Stainback and Stainback, 1984).

2. With assistance, all students can benefit from education in regular classrooms. Even students who do not need the traditional academic curriculum being provided in the regular classrooms benefit by learning social skills observed in the appropriate behaviors of other students (Stainback and Stainback, 1988).

3. In the regular classroom, students with disabilities feel like full class members, not second-class citizens whose deficits require that they leave the inclusive environment (Hahn, 1989). Advocates of full inclusion cite the stigma felt by students who leave the general education classroom to go to a special education environment (Lilly, 1992). Friend and Bursuck (1996) also noted that children with disabilities miss important information presented in the regular classroom when they are receiving instruction in a separate class.

4. Algozzine, Morsink, and Algozzine (1988) proposed that the teaching approaches in special education classrooms are very similar to those provided in general education classes. They also proposed that learning opportunities and techniques in regular education classes may be superior in some instances. As an example, they cited the laboratory equipment available in a regular education biology class that might not be available in a special education biology classroom.

Friend and Bursuck (1996) also summarized the beliefs of individuals who believe in inclusion but only under certain conditions. These include:

1. The Council for Exceptional Children (1993) proposed that to suggest all students with disabilities should be educated in general education settings denies the unique needs and characteristics of students with disabilities. Treating all students in the same educational environment denies the right to an individualized education and in doing so violates the federal special education law. They noted that many students with disabilities do require specialized materials and a structured environment which may not be available in a regular classroom. In the special education classes, students may learn more and at a faster rate. They noted that many of the specialized services, such as speech therapy for articulation problems, cannot be provided in regular education classes without disrupting the regular education classroom and calling attention to the student with disabilities.

2. An argument made by Semmel, Abernathy, Butera, and Lesar (1991) was that many teachers in general education classrooms are not trained to manage the educational needs and individual behaviors of students with disabilities. They also cited the large class sizes and pressures for rigorous academic standards advocated by the education reform being felt across the nation.

The themes in the inclusion debate focus generally on philosophical issues, social issues, economic issues, and instructional issues. While the collaborative teaching model is considered an effective way of educating most students with

TABLE 4.3

Position Paper on Full Inclusion of All Students with Learning Disabilities in the Regular Education Classroom, January, 1993

The Learning Disabilities Association of America, LDA, is a national not-for-profit organization of parents, professionals and persons with learning disabilities, concerned about the welfare of individuals with learning disabilities. During the 1990-91 school year 2,117,087 children in public schools in the United States were identified as having learning disabilities. This is more than fifty percent of the total number of students identified in all disability categories.

"Full inclusion," "full integration," "unified system," and "inclusive education" are terms used to describe a popular policy/practice in which all students with disabilities, regardless of the nature or the severity of the disability and need for related services, receive their total education within the regular education classroom in their home school.

The Learning Disabilities Association of America does not support "full inclusion" or any policies that mandate the same placement, instruction, or treatment for ALL students with learning disabilities. Many students with learning disabilities benefit from being served in the regular education classroom. However, the regular education classroom is not the appropriate placement for a number of students with learning disabilities who may need alternative instructional environments, teaching strategies, and/or materials that cannot or will not be provided within the context of a regular classroom placement.

LDA believes that decisions regarding education placement of students with disabilities must be based on the needs of each individual student rather than administrative convenience or budgetary considerations and must be the results of a cooperative effort involving the educators, parents, and the student when appropriate.

LDA strongly supports the Individuals with Disabilities Education Act (IDEA) which mandates:

- a free and appropriate public education in the least restrictive environment appropriate for the students' specific learning needs.

- a team approved Individualized Education Program (IEP) that includes current functioning levels, instructional goals and objectives, placement and service decisions, and procedures for evaluation of program effectiveness.

- a placement decision must be made on an individual basis and considered only after the development of the IEP.

- a continuum of alternative placements to meet the needs of students with disabilities for special education and related services.

- a system for the continuing education of regular and special education and related services personnel to enable these personnel to meet the needs of children with disabilities.

LDA believes that the placement of ALL children with disabilities in the regular education classroom is as great a violation of IDEA as is the placement of ALL children in separate classrooms on the basis of their type of disability.

LDA urges the U.S. Department of Education and each state to move deliberately and reflectively in school restructuring, using the Individuals with Disabilities Education Act as a foundation. . . mindful of the best interests of all children with disabilities.

Source: Reproduced with permission of the Learning Disabilities Association of America.

disabilities in the general education classroom, Friend and Bursuck (1996) caution that a continued commitment of finances and other resources must be maintained to ensure a quality education for students with disabilities.

The various professional and parent organizations in the area of learning disabilities have debated the full inclusion model and have published position papers regarding this issue. These have been included in Tables 4.3, 4.4, and 4.5.

▶ IMPACT ON PLACEMENT FOR STUDENTS WITH LEARNING DISABILITIES

Nearly 80 percent of identified students with learning disabilities spend all or part of a day in general education classrooms, with 35 percent of these fully included using special education consultative services as the sole support. Table

TABLE 4.4

Council for Learning Disabilities Position Statement, April 1993

The Council for Learning Disabilities (CLD) recognizes that any process as dynamic as educating individuals who have LD must continuously be evaluated. Such an evaluation allows for a critical review of current practices and promotes positive change and growth. Presently, advocates for people with LD have the opportunity to engage in such an evaluation in response to recent calls for school reform.

As part of these efforts, the Board of Trustees of the Council for Learning Disabilities recently approved a position statement addressing the issues of least restrictive environment and full inclusion. This position statement appears below.

Concerns About the "Full Inclusion" of Students with Learning Disabilities in Regular Education Classrooms

The Board of Trustees of the Council for Learning Disabilities (CLD) SUPPORTS school reform efforts that enhance the education of all students, including those with learning disabilities (LD). The Council SUPPORTS the education of students with LD in general education classrooms *when deemed appropriate* by the Individual Education Program (IEP) team. Such inclusion efforts require the provision of needed support services in order to be successful. One policy that the Council CANNOT SUPPORT is the indiscriminate full-time placement of ALL students with LD in the regular education classroom, a policy often referred to as "full inclusion." CLD has grave concerns about any placement policy that ignores a critical component of special education service delivery. Program placement of each student should be based on an evaluation of that student's individual needs. The Council CANNOT SUPPORT any policy that minimizes or eliminates service options designed to enhance the education of students with LD and that are guaranteed by the Individuals with Disabilities Education Act.

Source: Reprinted with permission of The Council for Learning Disabilities.

TABLE 4.5

Providing Appropriate Education for Students with Learning Disabilities in Regular Education Classrooms (This position paper was developed by the National Joint Committee on Learning Disabilities (NJCLD) and approved by the member organizations, January 1991.)

Many children and youths with diverse learning needs can and should be educated in the regular education classroom. This setting is appropriate *for some, but not all,* students with learning disabilities. More than 90% of students with learning disabilities are taught in regular classrooms for some part of their school day. When provided appropriate support within this setting, many of these students can achieve academically and develop positive self-esteem and social skills. *The regular classroom is one of many educational options but is not a substitute for the full continuum necessary to assure the provision of an appropriate education for all students with learning disabilities.*

In this Paper, the NJCLD Will Identify

a. those factors necessary for an effective educational program for students with learning disabilities

b. the problems related to serving students with learning disabilities in the regular classroom, and

c. the recommendations for actions required at the state, school district, and school building level to effectively educate students with learning disabilities within the regular education classroom.

Factors Related to Effective Education of Students with Learning Disabilities

As early as 1982, the NJCLD took the position that "providing appropriate education for individuals must be the principal concept on which all educational programs and services are developed." The NJCLD reaffirms its commitment to and support for the following:

• The educational, social, and emotional needs of the individual, the types of disabilities, and the degree of severity should determine the design and delivery of educational programs and services.

• A continuum of educational placements, including the regular education classroom, must be available to all students with learning disabilities and must be flexible enough to meet their changing needs.

• Specialized instructional strategies, materials, and appropriate accommodations must be provided as needed.

• Because the educational, social, and emotional needs of students with learning disabilities can change over time, systematic and ongoing review of the student's progress and needs is essential to make appropriate adjustments in the current educational program and related services.

• Because learning depends on the quality of the programs and services provided, systematic and ongoing evaluation of programs and their effectiveness in producing desired long-term outcomes is essential.

(continued)

TABLE 4.5

continued

• Due to the chronic nature of learning disabilities and the changes that occur across the life span of the individual, coordinated educational and vocational planning are required. Therefore, provisions must be made to facilitate transitions that occur at all major junctures in the student's education.

• Social acceptance has a significant impact upon the self-esteem of students with learning disabilities. Social acceptance of these students requires the sensitivity of the entire school community.

• To ensure effective mainstreaming of students with learning disabilities, the building principal must set the tone for a positive and accepting learning environment for all children.

Problems

The NJCLD acknowledges the following problems related to the education of students with learning disabilities in regular education classrooms. Some of these problems are encountered by the teacher in the classroom while others are related to administrative policies and procedures. All of these problems must be addressed by public and private education agencies as plans are developed and implemented for the education of students with learning disabilities.

• The regular education teacher is required to deal with multiple factors including an increasing number of students with diverse cultural and linguistic backgrounds, developmental variations, disabilities, family and social problems, and large class size. The co-occurrence of these factors compounds the situation.

• Many regular education teachers are not prepared to provide the kinds of instruction that benefit a wide diversity of students in the classroom.

• The characteristics of individuals with learning disabilities and the ways in which they interact with curricular demands are not understood by all school personnel.

• Adequate support services, materials, and technology often are not available for either the teacher or the student with learning disabilities.

• Time and support for the ongoing planning and assessment that are needed to make adjustments in students' programs and services are often inadequate.

• Schools rarely have a comprehensive plan to evaluate the effectiveness of programs and services provided for students with learning disabilities, especially those served in regular classrooms.

• Coordinated planning is lacking for students with learning disabilities as they make transitions from home to school to work, across levels of schooling, and among educational settings.

• Communication concerning students with learning disabilities among administrators, teachers, specialists, parents, and students is often insufficient to facilitate the development and implementation of effective programs.

(continued)

TABLE 4.5

continued

Recommendations

Implementation of the following recommendations is essential to provide appropriate education for students with learning disabilities in regular education classrooms. Specifically, public and private education agencies should:

- Establish system-wide plans for educating students with learning disabilities in the regular classroom when such placement is appropriate. The responsibility for developing plans must be shared by regular and special educators, parents, and student consumers of the services. Once developed, a plan must be supported at all levels of the educational system.

Source: The National Joint Committee on Learning Disabilities.

4.6 provides these data as well as a comparison between placement of students with learning disabilities and those with other disabilities. Table 4.7 demonstrates the differences in educational placements across states.

Much discussion continues on the advantages and disadvantages of full inclusion. Inclusion for students with learning disabilities has yielded mixed results. Students with LD who spend a greater proportion of time in general education class-

TABLE 4.6

Percentage of Students with Disabilities Age Six through Twenty-one Served in Different Educational Environments, by Disability: School Year 1992–1993

Disability	Regular Class	Resource Room	Separate Class	Separate School	Residential Facility	Homebound/ Hospital
Specific learning disabilities	34.8	43.9	20.1	0.8	0.2	0.2
Speech or language impairments	81.8	10.7	6.0	1.4	0.1	0.1
Mental retardation	7.1	26.8	56.8	7.9	0.9	0.5
Serious emotional disturbance	19.6	26.7	35.2	13.7	3.5	1.3
Multiple disabilities	7.6	19.1	44.6	23.6	3.4	1.8
Hearing impairments	29.5	19.7	28.1	8.3	14.0	0.4
Orthopedic impairments	35.1	20.0	34.1	6.7	0.6	3.5
Other health impairments	40.0	27.4	20.6	2.5	0.5	9.1
Visual impairments	45.5	21.1	18.0	5.6	9.4	0.5
Autism	9.0	9.6	50.0	27.6	3.2	0.6
Deaf-blindness	12.3	9.7	31.4	21.2	24.6	1.0
Traumatic brain injury	16.4	19.8	28.4	28.4	4.4	2.6
All disabilities	**39.8**	**31.7**	**23.5**	**3.7**	**0.8**	**0.5**

Source: U.S. Department of Education, Office of Special Education, Data Analysis Systems (DANS).

TABLE 4.7

Percentage of Children Age Six–Twenty-one Served in Different Educational Environments Under IDEA, Part B and Chapter 1 of ESEA (SOP) During the 1992–1993 School Year

Specific Learning Disability

Percentage

State	Regular Class	Resource Room	Separate Class	Public Separate Facility	Private Separate Facility	Public Residential Facility	Private Residential Facility	Homebound Hospital Environment
Alabama	53.35	37.56	8.85	0.06	0.02	0.02	0.03	0.11
Alaska	50.65	41.52	7.29	0.22	0.05	0.06	0.18	0.02
Arizona	7.21	75.28	17.15	0.05	0.19	0.03	0.01	0.08
Arkansas	38.64	54.20	6.65	0.06	0.10	.	0.09	0.26
California	46.23	32.70	20.40	0.07	0.37	.	0.04	0.18
Colorado	17.02	77.57	4.64	0.06	0.01	0.49	0.15	0.07
Connecticut	56.44	26.71	15.26	0.38	0.89	0.01	0.20	0.11
Delaware	29.65	44.22	24.22	1.80	.	0.08	.	0.03
District of Columbia	7.68	35.46	46.70	2.76	7.41	.	.	.
Florida	29.05	45.67	24.92	0.18	0.09	0.05	.	0.04
Georgia	49.09	38.41	12.46	0.01	0.01	.	.	0.02
Hawaii	37.58	47.92	14.15	.	.	.	.	0.34
Idaho	69.47	26.93	3.21	0.18	0.03	0.12	0.01	0.05
Illinois	4.05	64.02	31.20	0.41	0.19	0.08	0.01	0.03
Indiana	57.78	23.75	18.23	0.09	.	0.07	0.01	0.07
Iowa	0.93	95.98	2.89	0.03	.	0.08	0.03	0.06
Kansas	49.74	42.57	7.33	0.16	.	0.14	0.03	0.04
Kentucky	22.75	68.89	7.52	0.27	0.01	0.21	0.01	0.34
Louisiana	22.23	32.30	43.76	0.80	0.26	0.33	0.02	0.32
Maine	45.30	49.36	5.00	0.17	0.06	.	0.06	0.06
Maryland	43.61	25.78	29.28	0.85	0.31	0.02	0.04	0.11
Massachusetts	70.01	18.55	10.10	0.51	0.66	.	0.10	0.08
Michigan	39.59	41.17	19.00	0.17	.	0.01	0.04	0.02
Minnesota	57.15	39.37	2.84	0.30	0.09	0.15	0.04	0.05
Mississippi	14.24	57.30	28.21	0.02	.	.	0.02	0.20
Missouri	25.13	61.85	12.40	0.21	0.34	0.00	0.01	0.05
Montana	52.21	43.04	4.19	0.05	.	0.21	0.16	0.14
Nebraska	63.00	31.25	5.21	0.13	0.04	0.23	0.04	0.10
Nevada	20.02	67.34	10.65	1.85	0.01	0.03	.	0.10
New Hampshire	57.47	25.68	15.31	0.15	0.58	0.10	0.65	0.07
New Jersey	8.36	45.91	42.24	1.55	1.69	0.03	0.01	0.20
New Mexico	40.83	35.12	23.83	.	.	0.16	0.04	0.02
New York	25.13	35.86	36.89	1.46	0.39	0.04	0.07	0.16

(continued)

TABLE 4.7

continued

	Specific Learning Disability							
	Percentage							
State	Regular Class	Resource Room	Separate Class	Public Separate Facility	Private Separate Facility	Public Residential Facility	Private Residential Facility	Homebound Hospital Environment
North Carolina	59.22	32.43	7.99	0.06	0.01	0.06	.	0.24
North Dakota	86.13	12.33	0.99	0.28	0.02	0.05	0.09	0.10
Ohio	32.04	55.60	9.51	0.15	2.45	0.18	.	0.07
Oklahoma	45.79	48.58	5.26	0.06	0.05	0.08	0.04	0.13
Oregon	65.18	31.96	1.99	0.10	0.53	0.05	0.03	0.16
Pennsylvania	25.13	45.57	28.52	0.53	.	0.23	.	0.02
Puerto Rico	6.82	75.43	16.11	1.02	0.17	0.23	0.02	0.21
Rhode Island	51.56	22.23	25.18	.	0.51	.	0.36	0.16
South Carolina	13.50	66.60	19.60	0.08	.	0.07	.	0.14
South Dakota	65.93	31.88	1.90	0.12	0.03	0.12	0.02	.
Tennessee	44.73	41.78	12.87	0.22	0.22	0.04	0.00	0.14
Texas	25.56	46.58	24.76	0.99	0.06	0.56	0.01	1.48
Utah	39.17	45.62	14.96	0.17	.	0.01	.	0.06
Vermont	94.98	2.37	1.24	0.13	0.56	0.02	0.50	0.20
Virginia	31.89	45.39	22.03	0.09	0.25	0.21	0.09	0.06
Washington	49.48	40.85	9.41	0.09	0.06	0.02	0.01	0.08
West Virginia	10.23	74.69	14.74	0.12	.	0.15	0.01	0.05
Wisconsin	28.15	64.90	6.72	0.11	.	0.08	.	0.05
Wyoming	42.73	50.52	5.68	0.12	0.12	0.60	0.18	0.06
American Samoa	94.97	5.03	.	.	.	.	.	.
Guam	28.10	47.68	23.84	0.38	.	.	.	.
Northern Marianas	90.65	2.88	2.16	.	4.32	.	.	.
Palau	.	.	.	.	.	.	.	.
Virgin Islands	43.04	43.04	13.04	0.87	.	.	.	.
Bureau of Indian Affairs	36.53	57.87	5.60	.	.	.	.	.
U.S. and Outlying Areas	34.83	43.93	20.06	0.44	0.34	0.12	0.04	0.24
50 States, D.C., & P.R.	34.83	43.91	20.08	0.44	0.34	0.12	0.04	0.24

Source: U.S. Department of Education (1995) *17th Annual Report to Congress.*

rooms tend to be higher functioning and from higher income, two-parent house-holds (Wagner et al., 1991). Inclusion is also a powerful factor in increasing social affiliations and group participation. Students with LD in inclusive settings tend to attend postsecondary schooling at a higher rate (the same is true of those who take vocational education classes). However, grade point averages are significantly lower for students with LD across all general education courses as opposed to those students taking only special education courses. One third of all LD students taking general education courses fail at least one course. According to Wagner and her colleagues, 60% of students with LD attend schools where no accommodations are made at all, yet students are expected to keep up. Wagner et al. (1991) terms inclusion into general education a "sink or swim" environment. Students with LD who succeed in general education classrooms demonstrate more positive academic, vocational, and social outcomes. In contrast, students with LD who fail in general educational settings evidence higher absenteeism, failing grades, and an increase in dropout rates that negatively correlates with strong postschool outcomes. Guterman (1995) found that nine adolescents with LD viewed the inclusion movement as unrealistic, at least partially due to general educator's inability and unwillingness to adapt to individual student needs.

If student with learning disabilities are to succeed in general education, then responsible inclusion should become the rule, not the exception. Vaughn and Schumm (1995) define "responsible inclusion" as that which provides for appropriate resources, teachers willing to participate in the inclusive process, and consideration of student and family needs over placement. With the implementation of standards-based education, we must ensure that students with learning disabilities can succeed in both academic and vocational courses through the instructional expertise of teachers, adaptations in methods and materials, accommodations and modifications in acquiring content and in subsequent assessment, and alternative ways of demonstrating mastery. Open and active collaboration between general and special educators is an absolute necessity in order to provide both the content and appropriate accommodations for successful learning.

While the debate is still ongoing, it is important to remember that the individual characteristics of children with disabilities should drive the decisions made to provide the legal mandate of special education services in the least restrictive environment. These important characteristics and the ways in which they impact success in learning will be discussed in future chapters. Table 4.8 provides a checklist that may be used to evaluate each school in terms of best practices in the inclusion movement.

SUMMARY

This chapter has presented information regarding the educational planning and service delivery options for students with learning disabilities. The following points summarize the major areas included in the chapter:

TABLE 4.8

Inclusion Checklist for Your School

1. Do we genuinely start from the premise that each child belongs in the classroom he or she would otherwise attend if not disabled (or do we cluster children with disabilities into special groups, classrooms, or schools)?

2. Do we individualize the instructional program for all the children whether or not they are disabled and provide the resources that each child needs to explore individual interests in the school environment (or do we tend to provide the same sorts of services for most children who share the same diagnostic label)?

3. Are we fully committed to maintenance of a caring community that fosters mutual respect and support among staff, parents, and students in which we honestly believe that nondisabled children can benefit from friendships with disabled children (or do our practices tacitly tolerate children teasing or isolating some as outcasts)?

4. Have our general educators and special educators integrated their efforts and their resources so that they work together as integral parts of a unified team (or are they isolated in separate rooms or departments with separate supervisors and budgets)?

5. Does our administration create a work climate in which staff are supported as they provide assistance to each other (or are teachers afraid of being presumed to be incompetent if they seek peer collaboration in working with students)?

6. Do we actively encourage the full participation of children with learning disabilities in the life of our school, including co-curricular and extracurricular activities (or do they participate only in the academic portion of the school day)?

7. Are we prepared to alter support systems for students as their needs change through the school year so that they can achieve, experience success, and feel that they genuinely belong in their school and classes (or do we sometimes provide such limited services to them that the children are set up to fail)?

8. Do we make parents of children with disabilities fully a part of our school community so they also can experience a sense of belonging (or do we give them a separate PTA and different newsletters)?

9. Do we give children with disabilities just as much of the full school curriculum as they can master and modify it as necessary so that they can share elements of these experiences with their classmates (or do we have a separate curriculum for children with disabilities)?

10. Have we included children with disabilities supportively in as many as possible of the same testing and evaluation experiences as their nondisabled classmates (or do we exclude them from these opportunities while assuming that they cannot benefit from experiences)?

This checklist may help school personnel in evaluating whether their practices are consistent with the best intentions of the inclusion movement. Rate your school with a + for each item where the main statement best describes your school and a 0 for each item where the parenthetical statement better describes your school. Each item marked 0 could serve as the basis for discussion among the staff. Is this an area in which the staff sees need for further development? Viewed in this context, an inclusive school would not be characterized by a particular set of practices as much as by the commitment of its staff to continually develop its capacity to accommodate the full range of individual differences among its learners.

Source: Rogers, J. (1993). *Research Bulletin.* Bloomington, IN: Phi Delta Kappa, Center for Evaluation, Development, and Research. Used with permission.

- The IEP is developed by a committee composed of a representative of the public agency, the child's teacher, one or both parents, the child if appropriate, and other individuals invited by the parent or the agency.
- It is essential to include the parents in the IEP committee meeting.
- The IEP should contain present levels of educational performance, annual and short term instructional goals, special education and related services provided, projected dates of services, and criteria for evaluation. The student's strengths and weaknesses must also be documented on the IEP.
- Objectives should be stated positively, be student oriented, and stated in a way that can be measured.
- Special services might include transportation, counseling, or modified physical education.
- The IEP must contain the amount of time the student will spend in the general education classroom and the accommodations needed for success in that environment.
- The IEP is generally written to cover one year.
- The teacher must specify how each short-term objective will be evaluated.
- The least restrictive environment (LRE), mandated by the federal government, provides for students to remain with their nondisabled, chronologically aged peers to maximum extent appropriate.
- The law requires a full continuum of placement options, ranging from full-time special education settings to full inclusion in regular classrooms.
- The special education placement options most often used with students with learning disabilities include full-time special class, part-time special class, regular class placement with supportive services, and regular classroom placement with minimal support services.
- The Regular Education Initiative proposed that students with disabilities have the right to be educated in general education classrooms with their nondisabled peers.
- The Regular Education Initiative led to the full inclusion movement.
- There is a significant debate between professionals and advocacy groups regarding the advantages and disadvantages of inclusion.
- Many individuals believe that inclusion should be one placement option available under specific conditions.
- The professional and advocacy groups associated with learning disabilities have published position papers indicating their support for a full continuum of services for students with learning disabilities.
- Nearly 80 percent of students with learning disabilities spend all or part of their day in general education classrooms.

Chapter 5

ETIOLOGY: BIOLOGICAL AND ENVIRONMENTAL CONSIDERATIONS[1]

The objectives for this chapter are as follows:

- To understand the complexities of the etiology of learning disabilities.

- To identify developmental periods for specific causes.

- To generally understand the concept of brain dysfunction.

- To identify possible chromosomal disorders which may be associated with learning disabilities.

- To identify representative single gene disorders which may lead to learning disabilities.

- To discuss the concept and implications of substance exposure in utero.

- To identify and evaluate perinatal and postnatal causative factors.

- To evaluate the relative contributions of biological and environmental factors.

- To identify preventative measures that can impact on learning disabilities.

[1] This chapter was co-authored by Helen Rucker.

A Mother's Story About Fragile X Syndrome

My daughter was born one sunny summer afternoon. The labor went well, and we were pleased to present our families with their first grandchild. Everything about her was perfectly average in the doctor's eyes, but, in our eyes, everything about her was perfectly exceptional.

I kept a close eye on her development, reading every book I could get my hands on. She reached her developmental milestones within the average age range but tended toward the late end. At sixteen months she was assessed and her scores were slightly below average.

Preschool began for her at age three. The school was excellent; the environment was rich and stimulating, the teachers warm and accepting. She made friends easily, participated fully in all the classroom activities, and related well to adults.

In kindergarten, I began to receive calls from the teacher asking me if Elise was sleeping well, or if there had been stressful changes at home. The concern was that she was unable to pay attention in class, that she was spacy. Her handwriting was poor, and she couldn't figure out which of the lines . . . to write on. We considered having Elise repeat kindergarten but were advised to send her on . . .

In the first grade we were told that she was having difficulty in both reading and math. We were told that she was math-phobic and lacked self-confidence. She began to show signs of stress and our concerns increased.

The second grade brought a huge jump in reading ability, to slightly above grade level, but mathematics remained an area of low achievement. Our daughter began to request that she be allowed to move to a quiet corner of the classroom to do her work. She often positioned herself so that she was as far away from others as possible with her face to the wall. She seemed to be trying so hard and achieving so little. Concerned, we approached the teacher about having her tested for a learning disability but were assured that (she) was just young for her age. Finally, we sought out a private assessment.

The results of the test solidly confirmed . . . a learning disability. As is often typical, she also was beginning to develop a poor self–concept.

Although we were pleased that we could now label Elise's problem and provide her with much needed help, we felt overwhelmed. Our child seemed too much like the other children her age to require all this specialized help. Wouldn't all this therapy take her away from time that would be better spent growing up doing the same things other children her age were doing?

A letter arrived not long after Elise's learning disability was identified, explaining that my uncle, who was mentally retarded, had been diagnosed as having Fragile X syndrome and it could be inherited by other relatives. It was recommended that Elise be tested since she was experiencing academic problems.

I began to reflect on members of my family and realized, not for the first time . . . (that) most of us had experienced some academic difficulty . . ., but three of my cousins . . . had encountered special problems. One cousin was diagnosed as mentally retarded before she entered school. Two others completed public school and went on to technical school. Academic, social, and physical difficulties rolled in and out of their lives regularly.

The phone call came on my birthday. "We want you to know that the results of your daughter's blood test are in. She is positive for Fragile X syndrome." I was shocked . . . Would Elise's now normal IQ decline and would she eventually become mentally retarded? Have our younger children inherited Fragile X also? Will they ever be able to have children of their own? She inherited the gene from me. What will my husband think? All at once, everything that we had planned took on a new light.

It was several months later that we came across an article describing females with Fragile X syndrome who were not mentally retarded or autistic. Here we read about girls who were . . . functioning adequately in school, but having problems in math, self-expression, distractibility, and with making and keeping friends.

Perhaps the most devastating characteristic of Fragile X in girls is the effect it has on social skills development. Her real problems began in first and second grade when children began to play cooperatively, inventing spoken or unspoken rules for play. She was unable to discern the rules of play and was therefore often excluded. Likewise, she had difficulty picking up on the rules of everyday behavior—to chew with a closed mouth, to make eye contact when someone is speaking to you, to wait your turn before you speak. She did not realize that her interactional style and interests were more like her peers' younger siblings than like those of her own age group.

Elise's situation has been a real test of my own fiber. I have wanted to run and hide in embarrassment as Elise inappropriately responds to polite questions from my friends. I feel sadness for unachievable dreams, frustration for not being able to change my daughter, and guilt for wanting to. More often, however, I have a sense of pride for how well my daughter is doing. Despite her disabilities, she remains motivated in school. Despite rejection, she is not bitter or angry. Despite many failures, she still tries. I believe that Elise has taught me more about personal strength and fortitude than any sermon I have heard or any book I have read. She is truly a blessing.

Source: Adapted from Neely, C. (1991). LD Newsbriefs, 2, (4), p. 3–4, 6.

The search for cause is a complex task in the field of learning disabilities. The assumption that some causative factor is operative is reflected in the definition of the National Joint Committee on Learning Disabilities (1990) with its reference to learning disabilities as "intrinsic to the individual, presumed to be due to [central] nervous system dysfunction" (p. 1). However, this definitional assertion has remained a promise of the potential discovery of causes of individual cases, a goal which continues to be an elusive one. In fact, the most striking revelation of the search for cause in this field is the fact that specific etiology is typically so difficult to identify. As Hallahan and Kauffman (1991, p. 127) stated, "in most cases the cause of a child's learning disabilities remains a mystery." The purpose of this chapter is to explore potential representative causes which may lead to learning disabilities.

▶ MODEL FOR CAUSATION

The myriad of potential causes of learning disabilities can be conceptualized as falling along a developmental sequence that acknowledges the fact that learning disabilities can manifest throughout the developmental period. Figure 5.1 outlines the developmental period and provides a context for viewing, in particular, the possible biological basis of learning disabilities. The periods reflected in the figure and representative etiological examples include:

- *hereditary* genetically based disorders (e.g., neurofibromatosis);
- *innate* conditions present from conception (e.g., Klinefelter syndrome);
- *congenital* biological influences originating during gestation (e.g. fetal alcohol syndrome); and
- *constitutional* biological factors inclusive of the prenatal, perinatal, and postnatal periods (e.g., brain injury).

The above outline and Figure 5.1 provide an overview of biological causes that may result in learning disabilities that are "intrusive to the individual." Subsumed within the model are a number of specific causes (e.g., fetal alcohol syndrome, Fragile X syndrome) which have more frequently in the past been associated with mental retardation. However, given the positive effects of early intervention and consequent to the more inclusive concepts of learning disabilities, they are of increasing importance as causes of learning disabilities and are often also associated with concomitant problems such as attention deficit and hyperactivity.

In addition to biological causes, it is important to consider the role of environmental events in the development of the child. In some instances these can be conceptually isolated as specific and primary causative agents. However such an effort remains an empirical challenge and presents a conceptual dilemma within the constraints of current definitions of learning disabilities. In other instances, environmental considerations are best considered as complementary

FIGURE 5.1

Developmental Model of Biological Causation

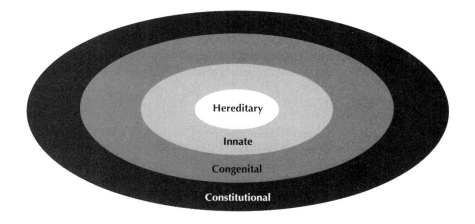

to potential biological factors and work in complementary fashion to either increase a child's risk of learning disabilities or to prevent or ameliorate his or her learning disabilities. Such a view would reflect a transactional model of causality in the field of learning disabilities (Adelman, 1992) by integrating environmental and biological factors.

The remainder of the chapter thus highlights possible causative factors in learning disabilities. Specific foci include genetic considerations, prenatal and perinatal factors, postnatal causes, environmental considerations, and prevention. The discussion is founded in an overview of the brain and brain dysfunction. The reader is cautioned throughout to recall that, in spite of these diverse etiological factors, cause remains most often unknown—or at least unspecifiable—in the majority of cases of learning disabilities.

▶ BRAIN AND BRAIN DYSFUNCTION

Many professionals in the field of learning disabilities consider brain dysfunction to be the central underlying cause of learning disabilities (Cotman and Lynch, 1988; Hynd, Marshall, and Gonzalez, 1991). In fact, as noted in Chapter 1, such a focus was critical to the emergence of the field through the work of preeminent researchers such as Goldstein, Strauss, Lehtinen, and Cruickshank (see Wiederholt, 1974, and Hammill, 1993, for a further discussion of this relationship). A variety of factors which cause brain damage or brain dysfunction potentially could lead to a learning disability; these factors are discussed later in the chapter. The purpose of this section is to provide a brief overview of the central nervous system as it relates to normal development, thus providing a foundation for subsequent discussions.

The Brain and Spinal Cord

The central nervous system (CNS) is composed of the brain and the spinal cord. The spinal cord transmits and receives information and thus serves as a link between the brain and the body. The key components of the brain are the brain stem, the cerebellum, and the cerebrum (see Figure 5.2).

Each region is a complex subsystem which serves specialized functions. The brain stem primarily controls both heartbeat and respiration, while the cerebellum plays a significant role in the coordination of voluntary muscular movements. The largest part of the brain is the cerebrum. It is here that higher-level cognitive processes such as memory, learning, and reasoning occur. The cerebrum consists of right and left hemispheres which are joined by the corpus callosum. The crossing of nerve fibers in the corpus callosum is a key reason why each hemisphere is "wired" to the opposite side of the body. Consequently, sensorimotor responses related to the left side of the body are a function of the right hemisphere, whereas the right side of the body is controlled by the left hemisphere.

Each cerebral hemisphere is associated with different forms of learning. For example, functions generally related to the left hemisphere include language

FIGURE 5.2

The Brain

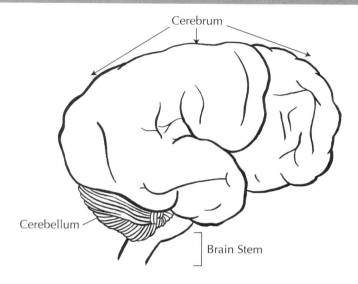

Source: This figure was drawn by John Davies and is used with permission.

skills, logic, and organization. On the other hand, the right hemisphere is typically concerned with functions such as spatial orientation and creativity. These distinctions give rise to the common, oversimplified observations of individuals being, for example, dominated by creative versus logical thinking, and thus referred to as a "right brain" person or such. However, it should be noted that the apparent specialization of hemispheric functions is not clearly defined in some individuals (Westman, 1990).

Neurons

Neurons, or nerve cells, are key components of the central nervous system. Neurons generally consist of a cell body, numerous dendrites (i.e., projections which conduct impulses to the cell body), and an axon (i.e., projection which conducts impulses away from the cell body) (see Figure 5.3). Dendrites and axons of adjacent neurons "communicate" at synaptic gaps (i.e., junctions in the neural pathway) via the transmission of chemical signals. The fact that each nerve cell has contact with thousands of other neurons clearly serves to demonstrate the complexity of the central nervous system. The chemicals which are chiefly responsible for the interaction among neurons are called neurotransmitters. The release of specific neurotransmitters may result in either an increase or a decrease in neuronal activity. Significantly, for example, some

FIGURE 5.3

An Illustration of Neurons

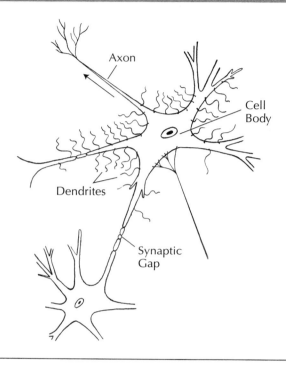

Axon

Cell
Body

Dendrites

Synaptic
Gap

Source: This figure was drawn by John Davies and is used with permission.

interventions designed to decrease hyperactivity (a common behavioral accompaniment to learning disabilities) include medications which affect neurotransmitter activity (Westman, 1990). Jordan (in press) noted that research on the neural pathways of individuals with learning disabilities have demonstrated the presence of incompletely developed brain cells, particularly in the language processing areas of the brain. Such changes necessarily prevent the vital transmission of neurotransmitters along affected pathways, thus leading to deficits in language processing.

▶ GENETIC CONSIDERATIONS

It has been a common observation that learning disabilities tend to run in families (e.g., Johnson, 1988; Tallal, 1988). However, such an observation begs for clarification. Specifically, the key issue is whether the transmission of such disabilities is due to specific single genes, the complex interaction of multiple genes, chromosomal aberrations, or a combination of genetic and environ-

Learning disabilities tend to run in families suggesting a genetic link in the disability.

mental influences. While specific genetic causation can be established in some cases of learning disabilities, the issue of heritability remains only proposed or assumed in other cases.

Because many genetically-influenced learning disabilities are associated with specific patterns of cognitive deficits, the continuing hope of accurate diagnoses may lead to more appropriate and timely educational interventions (Smith, 1986). The discussion below highlights examples of possible disorders linked to learning disabilities that operate within the genetics domain.

Chromosomal Disorders

Each human somatic cell contains forty-six chromosomes, which are arranged in twenty-three pairs. Individuals receive one chromosome of each pair from their mother while the other comes from the father. Thus, 50 percent of the genetic information received by the embryo is maternally derived and 50 percent is of paternal origin.

The twenty–three pairs of human chromosomes are classified according to their shapes, banding patterns, and sizes, with the first pair being the largest pair and the other pairs numbered in a general sequence reflecting a decrease in size. The first twenty-two pairs are called autosomes, which refers to the fact that each member of the pair contains the same genes. The last pair of chromosomes are the unmatched sex chromosomes, commonly labeled X and Y. The larger X chromosome contains a significant amount of genetic information, whereas the smaller Y chromosome mainly serves to determine the male sex. Females have two X chromosomes (one derived from each parent), while males have one X chromosome (derived from the mother) and one Y chromosome (derived from the father).

Chromosomal abnormalities can be associated with either autosomes or sex chromosomes and have traditionally been discussed in connection with mental retardation. A prime example, and by far the most common autosomal anomaly, is Down syndrome, most often the result of a trisomy (i.e., three chromosomes) on the twenty-first pair. Down syndrome is considered among the two most prevalent specific causes of mental retardation (Polloway and Smith, 1994). On the other hand, sex chromosomal anomalies are of greater concern for the field of learning disabilities. Such abnormalities can be related to either the X or Y chromosome and thus will have variant implications for males or females. While individuals with autosomal chromosome abnormalities typically have mental retardation, those with sex chromosome abnormalities are more likely to exhibit learning disabilities (Bender, Puck, Salbenblatt, and Robinson, 1986).[2]

In the discussion below, three specific chromosomal anomalies which have increasingly been associated with learning disabilities are discussed. Each of the three are related to an abnormality in the sex chromosomes.

Turner Syndrome   Turner syndrome is a chromosomal abnormality in which the female has only a single X chromosome, often referred to as an XO pattern (see Figure 5.4), or in which a portion of the X chromosome is missing. In the former case, it represents the rare phenomenon of a fetus surviving to term with only 45 chromosomes in each cell. Turner syndrome occurs in approximately 1 in 2,500 (female) births (Rovet, 1993). A variety of features is often noted. Physical characteristics include short stature, webbing of the neck, underdeveloped sexual maturation, and possibly hearing, vision, and cardiac problems.

In recent years, an increasing amount of attention has focused on the cognitive characteristics that may be associated with Turner syndrome. Although historically the syndrome has been discussed primarily in relation to mental retardation, it is only associated with this disability in 20 percent or fewer of cases. Rather, it is far more commonly associated with learning disabilities, with specific deficits in the areas of visuospatial skills, memory, and arithmetic abilities being most commonly cited (Downey, et al., 1991; Rovet, 1993). Attention deficits and hyperactivity have also been noted to occur with increased frequency among females with Turner syndrome (Bender, Puck, Salbenblatt, and Robinson, 1984) and poor social competence and lower self-esteem are also potential problems (Rovet, 1993).

Klinefelter Syndrome   The most frequently exhibited sex chromosome abnormality among males is Klinefelter syndrome, which occurs in approximately 1

---

[2]This equation is far from a perfect one. For example, Prader-Willi syndrome, an autosomal disorder related to chromosome 15, and associated with a biological predisposition to overeating, has been commonly identified as a causative agent for both learning disabilities and mental retardation (Scott, 1995).

FIGURE 5.4

Turner Syndrome (45, XO)

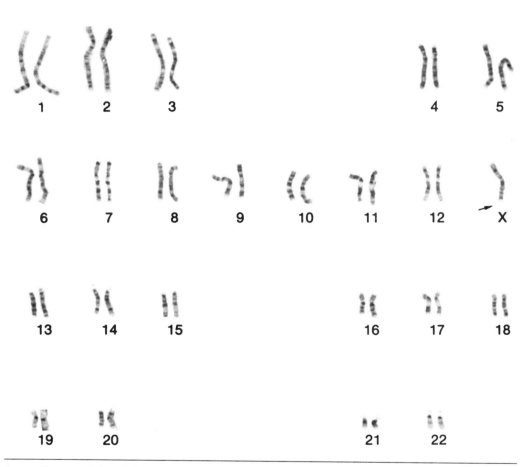

TURNER SYNDROME
45,X

Source: Greenwood Genetic Center (1984). *Counseling aids for geneticists*. Greenwood, SC: Author (p. 13). Used with permission.

in 500 live births. This condition results when males receive an extra X chromosome, hence having an XXY sex chromosome complement (see Figure 5.5). Typical features of Klinefelter syndrome include underdevelopment of male secondary sex characteristics with a concomitant increase in female secondary sex characteristics, sterility, behavioral problems (often linked to a poor self–image related to the physical stigmata of the syndrome), and learning dif-

FIGURE 5.5

Klinefelter Syndrome (47, XXY)

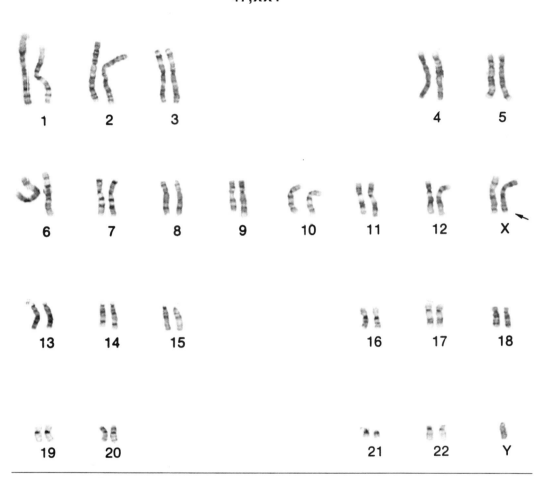

**KLINEFELTER SYNDROME
47,XXY**

Source: Greenwood Genetic Center (1984). *Counseling aids for geneticists*. Greenwood, SC: Author (p. 11). Used with permission.

ficulties. Specific learning deficits have been noted in the areas of speech and language (Plumridge, Barkost, and LaFranchi, 1982), with particular difficulty in the development of reading skills (Bender, et al., 1986).

Klinefelter syndrome, like Turner syndrome, has often been discussed in relation to mental retardation although it appears that only a small minority of individuals with the condition may experience retardation, primarily in the mild range. Rather school difficulties more associated with learning disabilities are the more common pattern. In rare instances, additional X chromosomes (i.e., XXXY, XXXXY) have been reported and are associated with more severe disabilities.

Fragile X Syndrome Fragile X syndrome is a relatively recently identified chromosomal condition, first described by Martin and Bell in 1964. It is likely to be the most common hereditary cause of mental retardation, present in as many as 1 in 1500 live male births (Lachiewicz, Harrison, Spiridliozzi, Callanan, and Livermore, 1988). The name refers to the identification of a fragile site on the X chromosome (see Figure 5.6).

Previously, many cases of Fragile X have gone undiagnosed, particularly because of the lack of reliable testing methods. However, direct diagnosis of

FIGURE 5.6

Fragile X Syndrome

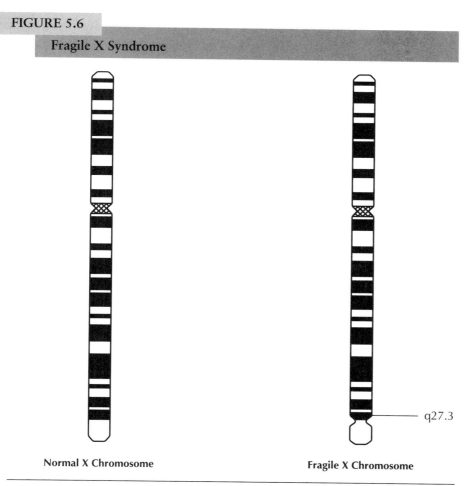

Normal X Chromosome

Fragile X Chromosome

q27.3

Source: Greenwood Genetic Center (1984). *Counseling aids for geneticists.* Greenwood, SC: Author (p. 25) Used with permission.

Fragile X by DNA analysis is now available (Rousseau, et al., 1991; Sutherland, et al., 1991).

Common physical characteristics include broad forehead, elongated face, large ears, and macroorchidism (i.e., large testicles). Behavioral traits often include self–stimulatory behavior (such as hand-flapping) and other autistic-like behaviors, attention deficits, and reduced eye contact or gaze aversion. Speech and language problems are common. While often discussed in relation to mild or moderate mental retardation, some Fragile X males are not accurately labeled as mentally retarded, but rather may experience problems associated with learning disabilities. Other males may have the fragile site but otherwise not reflect the behavioral or cognitive characteristics of the syndrome.

Much of the discussion on Fragile X and learning disabilities concerns the characteristics of females who carry the gene for the condition. Lachiewicz et al. (1988) estimated that about l in 750 women carry the gene with about 50 percent exhibiting either mental retardation or learning problems. The presence of learning disabilities appears to be a common finding (e.g., Smith, 1993; Wilson and Mazzocco, 1993). Females may exhibit characteristics such as short attention span, hyperactivity, and autistic–like behaviors, as well as some of the physical features described above which are typical of Fragile X syndrome in males.

The relationship between Fragile X and learning disabilities has only recently been understood and responded to. In the beginning of this chapter, a mother's poignant perspective on Fragile X was presented which reflects this process of understanding and response.

Single Gene Disorders

Humans likely have billions of genes in every cell nucleus, although only an estimated 50,000 genes are expressed as specific traits (e.g., hair color, eye color) (Van Dyke and Lin–Dyken, 1993). Located at specific sites on the forty-six chromosomes, genes contain the blueprints for physical and mental development. Genes are functional parts of chromosomes situated in specific loci. They supply the body with the information necessary for development. Although the function and location of many genes is unknown, researchers, particularly through the Human Genome Initiative, have recently successfully mapped numerous genes to specific chromosome sites. Because many conditions can be traced to defects in single genes, the nature of transmission of genes from one generation to the next provides significant information regarding the heritability of such conditions.

In order for a dominant genetic condition to be manifested, only one of the two genes in a specific pair needs to have a defect. This occurs because the information on the dominant gene "overrides" the information provided by its gene partner (see Figure 5.7). Conversely, recessive genetic conditions occur only if both genes in a specific pair contain the same defect (see Figure 5.8). A discussion of several examples of single gene disorders that may be associated with learning disabilities follows.

FIGURE 5.7

Segregation of Autosomal Dominant Trait (One Parent Affected)

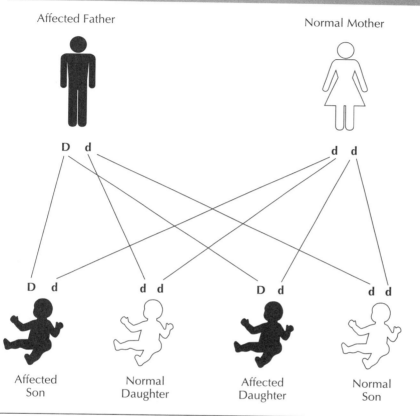

Affected Father   Normal Mother

D d   d d

D d   d d   D d   d d

Affected   Normal   Affected   Normal
Son   Daughter   Daughter   Son

Source: Greenwood Genetic Center (1984). *Counseling aids for geneticists.* Greenwood, SC: Author (p. 33). Used with permission.

Autosomal Dominant Conditions

Neurofibromatosis Neurofibromatosis (most commonly, NF-type 1) is an auto-somal dominant condition occurring with a frequency of approximately 1 in 3,000 births. Gene mapping has localized the neurofibromatosis gene to chromosome 17. Neurofibromatosis is also known as von Recklinghausen's disease, after the distinguished German pathologist who first described the previously unrecognized disorder in 1882 (Gripp, 1995). However, it is most commonly known as "Elephant Man's disease," after its association with Joseph (a.k.a. John) Merrick, of nineteenth-century England play and film fame.

The distinguishing features of NF include neurofibromas (nerve cell tumors) of the skin and central nervous system, cafe–au–lait (light brown) spots, axillary freckling, additional types of tumors, and seizures. Wide variability in the

FIGURE 5.8

Segregation of Autosomal Recessive Trait (Both Parents Carriers)

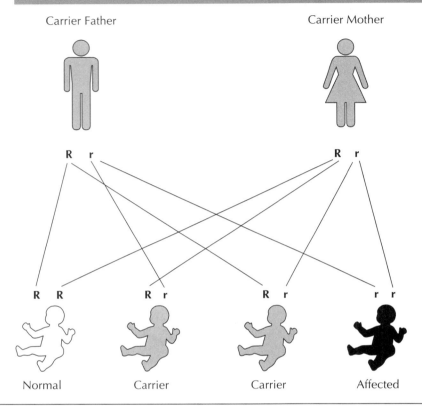

Source: Greenwood Genetic Center (1984). *Counseling aids for geneticists*. Greenwood, SC: Author (p. 37). Used with permission.

expression of these characteristics is an integral component of the neurofibromatosis pattern (Nativio and Belz, 1990) with a range from severe manifestations (as with John Merrick) to mild, undiagnosed forms (Gripp, 1995).

A variety of cognitive and learning characteristics have been investigated in individuals with NF with up to 40 percent having learning disabilities (Natirio and Belz, 1990). Eliason's study (1986) of children with NF revealed that 56 percent exhibited isolated visual perceptual deficits, while 30 percent experienced these deficits in conjunction with language or memory problems. In contrast, only 6 percent of children with learning disabilities in the general population were seen to manifest isolated visual perceptual deficits. A subsequent study by Eliason (1988) indicated that children with NF more often displayed nonverbal difficulties, which interfered with written language and organization. Conversely, unaffected children with learning disabilities more typically exhibited verbal language or memory deficits, which impacted on their reading abilities. Anderson (1992) noted that the presence of attention deficit hyperactivity disorder is a significant factor in the diagnosis of neurofibromatosis among both children and adults.

Achondroplasia   Individuals with achondroplasia are most easily identified by their short stature. Although primarily considered a skeletal system abnormality of the body, this autosomal dominant condition also significantly affects craniofacial development. Typical characteristics include megalocephaly (i.e., large head), depressed nasal bridge, midface hypoplasia, and a small foramen magnum (i.e., opening in skull which the spinal cord passes through). While intellect is most often reported to be within the normal range, individuals with achondroplasia commonly exhibit learning disabilities. There is some suggestion that such learning difficulties may occur secondary to abnormal development of the cranium and face (Shprintzen and Goldberg, 1986).

Autosomal Recessive Conditions

A large number of autosomal recessive conditions may directly or indirectly result in disabilities, although the more common association is with mental retardation rather than learning disabilities. In fact, it is within this category of genetics-based disorders that the most numerous (perhaps thousands) of etiologies have been identified or hypothesized. Most common is phenylketonuria (PKU), a disorder related to the metabolism of the amino acid, phenylaline. There has been limited research conclusively linking autosomal recessive genes with learning disabilities. However, several disorders have been associated with speech and language deficits, as well as other learning problems. These include lysosomal (i.e., conditions related to deficiencies of certain enzymes) storage diseases such as Morquio syndrome, Maroteaux-Lamy syndrome, Scheie syndrome, Hurler-Scheie syndrome, and pseudo-Hurler syndrome (Shprintzen and Goldberg, 1986).

Proposed Genetic Influences

Dyslexia, or severe reading disability, is characterized by extreme difficulty in learning to read among individuals who apparently have no clear neurological, intellectual, or emotional deficits, nor lack the educational experiences of their peers (Flowers, 1993). Estimates of prevalence range significantly with some as high as 5 percent of the population (Pennington, 1990).

A number of researchers have suggested that a genetic basis, or at least some degree of heritability, exists for dyslexia. Based on a study of children with reading disabilities and their first degree relatives, Decker and DeFries (1980) concluded that a familial component was indeed present, although any familial component can be evaluated from an environmental perspective as well. Later, DeFries, Fulker, and LaBuda (1987) examined the issue of reading disability among twins and presented evidence of a genetic basis for its occurrence. Phonological coding (i.e., detecting letter-sound correspondences) deficits, which are considered key factors in severe reading disabilities (see Vellutino, 1987), in particular have been shown to exhibit a high degree of heritability (Cardon, DeFries, and Fulker, in press; Olson, Wise, Conners, Rack, and Fulker, 1989).

Recent research has focused on determining specific genes which may be related to the manifestation of dyslexia. After examination of available data, Pennington (1990) concluded that dyslexia is genetically heterogeneous (i.e., there is no one single cause but rather there are a number of different genes associated with its expression). However, an association between one form of severe reading disability and a region of chromosome 6 has been suggested by Cardon et al. (in press). Additionally, Jordan (in press) reviewed research in this area and noted the linkage of one form of dyslexia to chromosome 15. Such preliminary observations represent exciting areas of research in the near future.

Some research has focused on the significance of specific anomalies in the brain which may result in learning disabilities such as dyslexia. Flowers (1993) reported an association between physiological anomalies in the left hemisphere and language deficits as seen in individuals with dyslexia, while also noting concurrent evidence of heritability factors. Perhaps one of the most elaborate hypotheses associating structural brain anomalies and dyslexia was established through the work of Geschwind and Behan (Galaburda, 1990; Geschwind and Behan, 1984). This hypothesis proposes that an abnormal surge of testosterone during the prenatal period may lead to a trilogy of left-handedness, diseases of the immune system, and learning disabilities, the latter due to delayed development of the left hemisphere of the brain. It was speculated by these researchers that the unusual surge of testosterone may be related to genetic factors.

The research in this area continues to be subjected to review and refinement and cannot yet be accepted as empirically resolved. For example, Shaywitz, Escobar, Shaywitz, Fletcher, and Makuch (1992) proposed that dyslexia is not a distinct entity at all, but rather lies on the lower end of a continuum which includes all degrees of reading ability.

Interaction of Genetic and Environmental Factors

Genetic factors certainly provide the foundation for the developmental process, yet the complex interaction of genetics and environmental influences (both prenatally and postnatally) cannot be overlooked. Recognizing that specific types of cognitive deficits are associated with certain genetic conditions is a significant consideration, yet individual differences that may have either another biological basis or an environmental genesis must also not be overlooked.

▶ PRENATAL FACTORS

The prenatal or gestational period focuses on possible congenital influences on fetal development during pregnancy. A teratogenic agent is one that negatively affects prenatal development, thus resulting in damage to the central nervous system, as well as other developing systems. Critical periods of development for various body systems (e.g., limbs, heart) have been delineated and are defined as occurring during the time of the organs' most rapid cell division. However, it must not be concluded that the effects of teratogens are limited to these developmental time periods.

Development of the brain begins at approximately the third embryonic week. Although the CNS is most highly sensitive to teratogens between the third and sixth embryonic weeks, the critical period of development extends through infancy (Moore, 1982).

Substance Exposure in Utero

Recent years have witnessed a phenomenal increase in research on the effects of substance abuse on the fetus, driven by an unfortunate societal explosion in the occurrence of such incidents. For example, May, Kundert, and Akpan (1994) reported in their review that over 260,000 children are born annually with low birth weight due to prenatal exposure to drugs and/or alcohol. Much of the research had its origin in the study of alcoholic mothers and the characteristics of their children, which eventually lead to the identification of the condition which has more recently been labeled fetal alcohol syndrome.

Fetal Alcohol Syndrome   Fetal alcohol syndrome (FAS) was popularized as a specific syndrome when research clearly demonstrated the effects of drinking, particularly excessive drinking, during pregnancy. The term was coined by Jones, Smith, Ulleland, and Streissguth (1973), who recognized a pattern of congenital malformations and developmental disabilities among children of chronically alcoholic mothers. Fetal alcohol syndrome has been commonly estimated to occur in 1 to 3 births per 1,000 (Warren and Bast, 1988) although more recent data (i.e., 1993) from the Centers for Disease Control and Prevention indicate an incidence of 6.7 births per 1,000 (ARC, 1995).

The distinguishing characteristics utilized in the diagnosis of FAS include central nervous system dysfunction, including cognitive impairments, growth retardation in the prenatal and/or postnatal periods, and facial malformations (Griesbach and Polloway, 1990; Johnson and Scruggs, 1981). Major problems facing children with FAS as defined by Ouellette (1984) include feeding difficulties, emotional problems, and learning problems. Indeed, Ouellette suggested that learning difficulties, distractibility, short attention span, and hyperactivity may lead to the initial diagnosis of FAS among school–aged children.

Although central nervous system involvement associated with FAS historically has been linked most often to mild to severe mental retardation (Griesbach and Polloway, 1990), the presence of learning disabilities among such children is receiving increased attention. For example, a review of the literature by Gold and Sherry (1984) revealed that maternal alcohol use may be related to learning disabilities, attention deficit disorder, hyperactivity, impulsiveness, and behavioral problems. As noted earlier, the positive effects of early intervention programs can ameliorate some effects thus increasing the association of fetal alcohol syndrome with learning disabilities (versus mental retardation).

A more recent term, which was coined to describe a less severe form of FAS, is fetal alcohol effects (FAE). FAE refers to any abnormalities which are related to maternal use of alcohol, including the clinical features observed in FAS children, as well as learning and developmental disabilities, attention deficit disorder, and failure to thrive. Continuing research attention to the more subtle FAE is quite likely to reveal increased risk for learning disabilities.

The teratogenic effects of alcohol may encompass a wide range of overt physical malformations and cognitive deficits. Ouellette (1984) noted that one of the most tragic factors regarding FAS is that it is totally preventable. Labeling of alcoholic beverages and public information campaigns have attempted to promote prevention. However, as the data noted above indicate, the results to date have been discouraging.

Fetal Cocaine Exposure Another potential teratogen which recently has gained extensive attention is cocaine. However, while there are numerous studies reporting the effects of alcohol on the fetus, information regarding fetal exposure to cocaine is relatively sparse. There are several reasons that such information is not readily forthcoming. First, many mothers who may expose their child to cocaine do not limit their drug use, but rather use a combination of drugs such as alcohol, cigarettes, marijuana, and heroin. Therefore, it is difficult to isolate the specific effects of cocaine. Secondly, effects of cocaine on the fetus may be influenced by factors such as method of drug use, maternal health, and the age of the fetus (Brooks-Gunn, McCarton, and Hawley, 1994; Singer, Garber, and Kliegman, 1991; van Baar and de Graaff, 1994). Finally, accurate identification of mothers who use cocaine during the prenatal period has proven to be a difficult task (Brooks-Gunn, et al., 1994; Singer, et al., 1991), in part due to its illicit nature.

Prenatal exposure to cocaine may result in intrauterine growth retardation, premature birth, and decreased birth weight. A literature review by Brooks-Gunn et al. (1994) indicates that long–term effects of prematurity and low birth weight include intellectual and cognitive deficits, significant neurosensory difficulties (i.e., hearing, sight), school failure, and other health problems. Additionally, because one of the consequences of cocaine use is reduced availability of oxygen to the fetus, it has been hypothesized that this phenomenon may have negative effects on the fetal nervous system (Singer, et al., 1991).

Maternal Smoking Because nicotine also has the effect of reducing the oxygen-rich maternal blood flow to the fetus, intrauterine growth retardation often results from heavy maternal smoking (i.e., twenty or more cigarettes per day). Such oxygen deprivation may negatively affect mental development in the fetus (Moore, 1982).

Nichols and Chen (1981) reported that children of mothers who smoked twenty or more cigarettes per day were at increased risk for hyperactivity, impulsivity, neurological soft signs, and learning disabilities. Childhood attention deficits also have been reported to be related to maternal smoking (Streissguth, et al., 1984).

Early Amniotic Rupture

One example of a prenatal teratogen which occurs sporadically and is not associated with in utero substance abuse such as in the case of FAS, is the ADAM sequence (i.e., amniotic disruptions, amputations, mutilations). This condition occurs when the membranes surrounding the fetus rupture prematurely. The most common malformations associated with this sequence include limb and craniofacial defects, with cognitive deficits occurring secondary to the latter dysmorphology. Specific learning disabilities and language delay are also frequently exhibited (Shprintzen and Goldberg, 1986). Research on the ADAM sequence is ongoing and promises to elucidate further aspects of the results of this phenomenon.

▶ PERINATAL FACTORS

Perinatal events are those which occur during the time of birth. Prematurity and low birth weight are often classified as perinatal factors. As described in the above section, the long–term effects of these occurrences include cognitive and neurosensory deficits, failure to achieve success in school, and other health problems. For example, Sell, Gaines, Gluckman, and Williams (1985) reported that 43 percent of the children in their prospective study of premature infants who were admitted to the neonatal intensive care unit later had school problems. Specifically, 23 percent of the study group were receiving special services for problems related to learning disabilities.

Of particular concern are young mothers. Specifically women under the age of eighteen are 90 percent more likely to have a premature child than are women, for example, in their early twenties. These data take on special meaning given that over a million teenagers become pregnant per year. The fact that two–thirds of the girls are unmarried further increases risks related to adequate care and medical attention (Leigh, Huntze, and Lamores, 1995).

Trauma at birth is another area of concern at the perinatal stage. Both prolonged delivery and a twisted umbilical cord can result in decreased fetal oxygen supply. This traumatic perinatal occurrence, referred to as anoxia or hypoxia, may have significantly negative effects on the central nervous system and subsequent cognitive development. The possible relationship to learning disabilities is an apparent one that continues to be under study.

▶ POSTNATAL FACTORS

Numerous events may occur after birth which may cause injury to the brain. Consequently, children and adults who previously had no history of learning disabilities may, subsequent to such brain injury, develop a variety of "symptoms" which parallel those of individuals who are considered to be learning disabled, yet who have no documented history of CNS trauma.

Head Injuries

Head injuries may occur as the result of such incidents as falls, motor vehicle accidents, bicycle accidents, and child abuse and/or neglect. While all are theoretically preventable, the latter are particularly troublesome given estimates ranging from 480,000 to over 2,000,000 instances of abuse annually. Often, medical attention is not sought for mild head injuries, perhaps due to the rapid recovery from related symptoms or, in some instances, even to evade criminal charges stemming from abuse. Although the prevalence of mild head injuries is reported to be 3 percent for those sixteen years of age and younger, Segalowitz and Lawson (1995) suggest that the figure may be closer to ten times that level with the discrepancy due to the lower reporting rate.

The effects of brain trauma vary according to the location and extent of the injury, as well as the age of the affected individual (Obrzut and Hynd, 1987). While left hemisphere damage generally affects verbal skills, damage to the right hemisphere is associated with visual-spatial deficits. However, Selz and Wilson (1989) noted that because the development of the brain is a continual process through middle childhood or even the mid-twenties, cognitive deficits may not be as easily defined during this time. Additionally, whereas brain injury among young children typically affects knowledge acquisition (e.g., language skills), adults who suffer brain damage often experience deficits in problem solving and adaptive skills.

Segalowitz and Lawson (1995) reported that mild head injuries may be associated with attention deficits, as well as difficulties in speech, language, and reading. More serious injuries have been associated with more comprehensive affects on language and academic ability.

Lead Exposure

The toxic effects of lead have been observed for some time and are noted to include retardation, convulsions, drowsiness, irritability, and gastrointestinal problems (Pueschel, Kopito, and Schwachman, 1972). Lead poisoning has been most notably linked to children's ingestion of lead-based paint found on the walls of older residences. Although legislation has addressed the issue of safe levels of lead in paint, concern still exists for children living in areas of high lead exposure (e.g., certain industrialized regions).

While significant levels of lead may produce the clinical signs described above, other types of difficulties have also been linked to lead exposure. Needleman et al. (1979) conducted a classic study in which the effects of non-symptomatic (i.e, presenting no noticeable signs) lead levels were assessed. The degree of lead exposure among a group of children was determined by analysis of shed deciduous teeth. It was found that children with relatively higher lead levels demonstrated deficits in verbal performance, auditory processing, and attention. Further, increased distractibility, poor organizational skills, and inability to follow directions were noted among this group of children. The effects of exposure to low levels of lead remain under study (Ernhart, 1987; Needleman, 1987).

Diet

A third hypothesized postnatal cause of learning disabilities is in the area of diet. Perhaps the most well–known proponent of diet restriction to control hyperactivity is Benjamin Feingold (1976). Feingold's Kaiser-Permanente (K-P) Diet calls for the omission of artificial colors and flavors, as well as foods containing salicylates, as a method of reducing hyperactivity and other behavioral problems that may be associated with learning disabilities. Feingold reported that 30 to 50 percent of children who adhered to the K-P diet experienced behavioral improvements. Interestingly, Feingold also posited that such food additives may have teratogenic effects on the developing fetus, thus resulting in learning disabilities and behavioral problems later in life.

Other researchers (e.g., Rapp, 1978) have suggested that foods which may be allergenic, such as milk, wheat, and eggs, are associated with increased levels of activity. Rapp further noted that the incidence of allergies among hyperactive children included in her study was much greater than that in the general population.

The presumption of dietary factors as causative agents clearly has an intuitive appeal. For many people, the association of specific foods and certain outcomes (e.g., headaches, increased energy, mood swings) have been commonly accepted. However, the reader is cautioned not to accept as validated the existence of a clear relationship between diet and a comprehensive and complex phenomenon such as learning disabilities. Further research is clearly indicated.

▶ ENVIRONMENTAL CONSIDERATIONS

The above discussion has focused on the potential influence of biological factors in causing learning disabilities and related learning and behavioral difficulties. However, in spite of the presumption of learning disabilities being intrinsic to the individual, a variety of environmental factors may result in learning difficulties either collectively or in combination with biological risk factors. These are briefly outlined below.

Home and Child Rearing Factors

Numerous child rearing and home variables have been associated with cognitive disabilities and school achievement problems. While research on the effects of a specific variable remains elusive, a cluster of variables have been identified which collectively have been associated with risk for subsequent school problems. Thus, while a variety of factors are often identified as potentially causative, it would be inaccurate to isolate one factor and hypothesize an effect (e.g., father-absent homes causing a learning disability). The common cluster of factors include those listed in Table 5.1 (Polloway and Smith, 1994; Ramey, et al., 1985; Whitman, Borkowski, Schellenbach and Nath, 1987). A special area of concern is teen mothers who run increased risk themselves of poor health

TABLE 5.1	
	Environmental Correlates of Risks for Learning Problems

- Authoritarian parenting (e.g., external control parenting practices)
- Reliance on punishment
- Lack of structure and organization in home
- Lack of stimulation
- Excessive, chaotic stimulation
- Absence of mediation of the environment by parents
- Large number of children
- Single parent home
- Practical daily dilemmas interfere with time with child
- Necessary focus on present precludes attention to future planning
- Teenage mothers
- Lack of parenting preparation or readiness
- Personality and social adjustment of parent(s)
- Cognitive limitations of parents
- Social support system for family

and nutrition, substandard housing, and limited education (May, et al., 1994), each of which may have significant implications for their children.

An encouraging area of study has been in the investigations into resiliency in children from high-risk backgrounds (e.g., Werner and Smith, 1992; Wang and Gorden, 1994). The focus of this research is on determining why some children seem "invulnerable" to the causative agents associated with learning problems and school failure when compared to their peers or even their siblings. Table 5.2, based on Viaderos' (1995) review of research in this area, highlights variables that have been associated with resilience in children. These lines of research promise to provide a more comprehensive perspective on the nature of the effects of poverty and possible directions for the prevention of its deleterious effects.

A variety of cultural factors further complicates the consideration of environmental factors. These are addressed within the context of cultural influences in Chapter 9.

Educational Factors

It is important to consider that some learning problems have their basis in, or are exacerbated by, a child's school experiences. To reflect this possibility, the concept of "dyspedagogia" was introduced by Cohen (1971), who used the term perhaps somewhat facetiously to identify a common cause of reading problems. Essentially the concept served a useful purpose in raising the issues

TABLE 5.2

Resilience Variables in Children

Child Variables

average intellectual level
positive temperament as infants ("cuddlers")
sense of self-efficacy
sense of self-control

Environmental Variables

supportive parents
supportive surrogate (e.g., teacher, coach)
high degree of attention in early childhood
participation opportunities (e.g., sports, youth groups)
opportunities for responsible work in childhood

School Variables

effective schools
goal-setting and futures planning for students
differentiated instruction
focus on academic-engaged time (time spent learning)

Some learning problems are either caused by or exacerbated by school experiences.

of poor teaching or curricular inadequacies to a pseudo–scientific level as a basis for providing educators with food for thought on the causation of learning difficulties.

The consideration of the concept of dyspedagogia presents an automatic paradox. Specifically, the definition of learning disabilities is based on an assumption of CNS dysfunction. However, it is worth considering this sequence of assumptions:

- Proof of CNS dysfunction is generally not achieved in most instances of learning disabilities.
- The vast majority of students are identified as learning disabled after school entrance and without proof of CNS damage.
- The basis for identification in most cases is evidence of school failure.
- Poor teaching is clearly a precursor or correlate of numerous cases of school failure.
- Poor teaching may inevitably be at least a secondary etiological agent in many cases of learning disabilities.

While "dyspedagogia" cannot rival chromosomal disorders as a specifiable cause of certain learning problems, it remains a major consideration. This concern is further exacerbated by the possible mismatch between the focus of the school curriculum and the learning needs of an individual child. For example, recent debates in the area of reading concerning the value of a whole language orientation versus decoding and direct instruction approaches have highlighted the views of persons who suggest negative implications for the child when the focus of the curriculum is not sensitive to the needs of the child (see Mather, 1992; Polloway and Patton, 1997).

▶ PRINCIPLES OF PREVENTION

The ongoing research on etiology will be most notable for its contributions to prevention and treatment. While the burgeoning scientific body of knowledge is inherently significant in its own right for an understanding of the nature of disabilities, the key element will be the translation of this information into effective preventative strategies.

Perhaps the foremost spokesperson for models for the prevention of disabilities is Crocker (1992). While his primary work is in the field of mental retardation, a number of his principles have clear legitimacy for the field of learning disabilities as well. In Table 5.3, relevant preventative strategies, adapted from Crocker's (1992) work, are presented. Of particular note are the varied approaches inherent in a comprehensive program of prevention. Elements necessary include, for example, consideration of family planning, public information, and early intervention.

TABLE 5.3

Prevention Strategies

Prenatal Considerations

- family planning and timing of pregnancies
- genetic counseling
- testing of genetic carriers
- adequate prenatal care
- prenatal diagnosis
- reduction in teenage pregnancy rates
- reduction in births out of wedlock
- diagnosis and response to pregnancy complications
- avoidance of alcohol during pregnancy
- avoidance of other teratogenic substances during pregnancy

Perinatal Considerations

- screening of newborns for disorders
- screening of newborns for diseases (e.g., HIV)
- early intervention for at-risk infants (e.g., prematurity)

Postnatal: Preschool Considerations

- enrollment in early intervention programs
- parental education and support
- avoidance of lead in environment
- avoidance of hazards associated with brain injury
- reduction in occurrences of child abuse and neglect
- use of safety restraints in vehicles
- immunizations for diseases
- proper medical care and treatment
- appropriate transition to school programs

Postnatal: School Considerations

- student-centered curriculum
- effective instruction
- parental involvement in education
- family life curriculum

(continued)

TABLE 5.3

continued

General Societal Considerations

- reduction in poverty
- reduction in prevalence of homelessness
- public information campaigns
- sufficient support for comprehensive prevention programs
- universal health care programs
- sufficient support for preventative research

Cautionary Concerns

Society in general, and the field of learning disabilities in particular, vitally needs to embrace a comprehensive view of prevention. At the same time, it is also critical that caution be exercised in the preventative measures and treatment approaches that are considered since unfortunately the field of learning disabilities has hosted an inordinate number of purported cures and treatments. While not all of these have direct relevance to etiology (i.e., many are nonvalidated educational treatments), clearly a number of efforts have focused on medical and health aspects. Worrall (1990) cautioned that professionals in the field must be vigilant in their selection of approaches which have proven validity. Further, he identified a useful approach to considering these cures and treatments by encouraging an "FDA–type" approach to evaluating their possible effectiveness. Specifically, he suggested that professionals caused the use of the following considerations as a vehicle for recognizing fraud or quackery:

- If it sounds too good to be true, it probably is.
- Be suspicious of therapy that claims to treat many illnesses.
- Be wary of treatments offering a "cure." Cures are few and far between.
- Do not rely only on testimonials from users. They rarely can be confirmed.
- Be cautious of promises labelled: "complete," "immediate," "effortless," "safe," or "guaranteed."
- Legitimate researchers do not use words such as "amazing," "secret," "exclusive," "miracle," and "special."
- Be skeptical if a "doctor" claims a treatment is being suppressed (i.e., by the FDA) (p. 212).

SUMMARY

This chapter has presented information about the causes of learning disabilities. While many cases of LD have no known cause, there are many etiological factors that can result in this condition. The following points summarize the major areas included in the chapter:

- Often, the cause of specific learning disabilities may not be ascertained.
- The current definition of learning disabilities suggests that central nervous system dysfunction is the underlying mechanism.
- The search for substantial evidence to support this view is still underway.
- There are a number of factors which are known to be related to learning disabilities.
- Genetic etiological concerns include possible problems in chromosomal patterns on dominant and recessive inheritances.
- Prenatal factors include the effects of teratogens such as prenatal alcohol exposure.
- Perinatal considerations include trauma that occurs at the time of birth.
- Postnatal factors may include a variety of deleterious factors such as those associated with child abuse.
- Environmental influences are critical to development and warrant more careful considerations in the field of learning disabilities.
- Preventative strategies must be employed in a comprehensive fashion to combat the effects of learning disabilities.

Chapter 6

PRESCHOOL AND ELEMENTARY STUDENTS

The objectives for this chapter are as follows:

▶ To describe the dilemma surrounding diagnosis of learning disabilities in preschoolers.

▶ To discuss the offerings that preschool programs make available in many communities.

▶ To recommend strategies for successful transitions from preschool to kindergarten and from elementary to middle school programs.

▶ To describe the cognitive/academic, language, personal/social, and mathematics performance characteristics found in many elementary students with learning disabilities.

▶ To discuss prevailing characteristics among elementary age children with learning disabilities.

▶ To describe major intervention approaches recommended for these elementary age students in general learning, personal/social, language, and mathematics areas.

▶ To identify a philosophy about supporting the development and well-being of students with learning disabilities.

Larry: The Beginning of Problems

Larry had already had a vague feeling that things weren't going the way they should; he knew that kind of hanging-around-kinda-yucky-not-really-sick feeling very well. What was wrong? Well, his teacher had spent some extra time with him last week, asking questions about what he was learning and the best way for him to learn. This was after a spell of his not doing well with his schoolwork. And his parents had sat down and worked with him on how to do things like filling out the library card application and feeding the animals at a certain time each day. He knew how to do those things! Sometimes he did just great! It's just that sometimes he couldn't figure them out on his own. OK, so those things weren't so bad, but having to go through that testing session yesterday was awful; *nobody* has to sit through something like that unless they think something is wrong! He had to sit there way too long, and he was missing a big basketball game and he couldn't think of answers for half the questions, plus the lady had on a stinky perfume and they were in a little cubbyhole . . . it was the *pits*. And *then,* nobody would tell him how he did or why the testing—that must mean that something was *really* wrong with him . . . . Maybe it's just best to leave well enough alone; it's probably better not to know! There's still enough that he can do and likes to do in school that he's not too worried . . . yet.

Young children between the ages of three and eleven are in the midst of a great adventure as they approach formal schooling and learn to navigate systems and being around lots of peers. Preschool programs and elementary schools offer a vast array of learning experiences, with varying degrees of support for those who might learn differently. The primary grades, while full of wonder and hope, may also begin the nightmare of dashed hopes for a child's success when a family is told that a disability is suspected or confirmed. The majority of students who are identified with learning disabilities engage in the diagnostic process during the elementary years, although some youth are not assessed until their teens. McLeskey (1992) found in his state that more children are identified in first and second grades than any other time, with 76 percent diagnosed by the end of fifth grade. Students identified during elementary school tended to have more serious problems than older students, but older students also tended to have lower Full Scale IQ scores than younger students. Academic scores also have differed across age groups, with reading improving but mathematics decreasing over time; retention has been tried with over half of those later diagnosed with learning disabilities (McLeskey, 1992). Most of those about to be labeled find themselves facing daunting academic tasks, without the strategies, clues, or supports they need to unravel the assignments at hand during the late primary or intermediate school period. Behavior problems, often due to frustration with school tasks, also emerge at this time.

The preschool and elementary years are a period of rapid growth—physically, intellectually, and emotionally. Physical and motor development continue to evolve, but now language and cognitive development link together to allow learning to practically explode. Four critical competencies essential for movement from preschool programs to the primary grades were described by Polloway (1987): (1) basic readiness to maximize academic achievement, (2) prosocial and age-appropriate social skills, (3) appropriate responsiveness to various instructional styles, and (4) appropriate responsiveness to new and different environmental structures.

As students enter kindergarten, their cognitive or academic language begins to develop in their native language and continues to grow and refine if given the opportunity to be used in formal education. Given appropriate levels of nutrition and normal exercise, children will demonstrate steady physical growth and motor coordination will mature during these years. Elementary age students will learn to assume appropriate social roles, such as team members in class and in sports, members of families and neighborhoods, and part of groups of friends.

Professionals in education and parents have long discussed the types of foundations that must be laid in preschool and elementary programs. Comprehensive educational programs include not only instruction in academics but also sports and other recreational activities, as well as fine arts and other creative experiences and socialization activities. Most kindergarten and elementary programs now include instruction in the initial use of computers to support learning, and some innovative schools are beginning to incorporate service learning into their curricula. At these ages, instruction in critical thinking, social and self-help skills, and career awareness occurs informally (typically) in general education and should occur with more precision in special education. Figure 6.1 depicts Brolin's (1995) K–12 model which portrays the evolution of a comprehensive career education program that allows a self-sufficient adult learner to emerge at the end of formal schooling. The model illustrates for students, parents, and educators the necessity of building carefully throughout the relatively short years that students are in school.

▶ EARLY CHILDHOOD YEARS AND LEARNING DISABILITIES

Learning disabilities are not typically diagnosed until kindergarten or first grade at the earliest, due to a number of factors that will be discussed later in this sec-

FIGURE 6.1

Life-Centered Career Education Curriculum Model

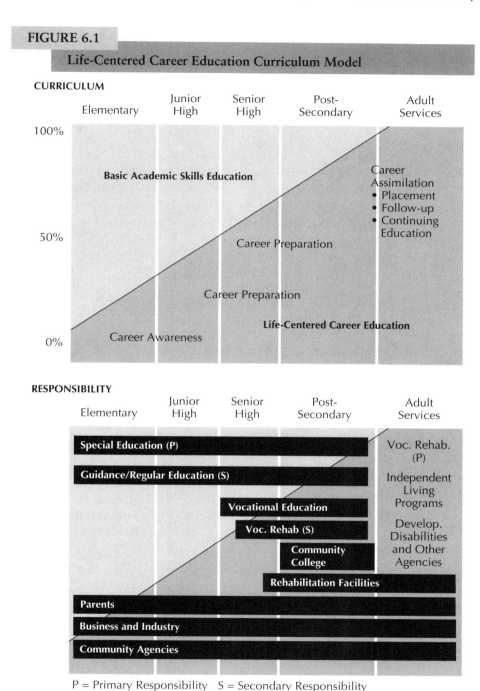

Source: *Career Education: A Functional Life Skills Approach* by Brolin, D.E., ©1995. Reprinted by permission of Prentice-Hall, Inc. Upper Saddle River, NJ.

tion. As a result, generic information about early intervention programs for children with disabilities and those at risk for failure will be initially presented as a frame of reference. These programs are supported in the United States by Part H of the IDEA and by other agencies such as Health and Human Services and the Developmental Disabilities system. The impressive outcomes generated in the past twenty years by early intervention programs have clearly demonstrated their efficacy over the life of the individual with disabilities. As the field has matured, the value of *integrated* early intervention/early childhood special education has become widely recognized (Wolery, Werts, and Holcombe, 1994). Substantiated successes of young children have been attributed to carefully designed family-centered programs planned by multidisciplinary teams and implemented during the peak developmental stages. As a result, federal and state mandates and funding for early intervention services continue to build. States reported serving 76,449 infants and toddlers (birth to two years old) with disabilities under Chapter 1 (state-operated programs) in 1992–1993, a 15 percent increase over the prior year. Under non-Chapter 1 programs, 66,943 infants and toddlers received services. The child's home continues to be the most frequent service delivery site for early intervention services (34 percent during 1992–1993), followed by the early intervention classroom (33 percent) and the specialized center (29 percent) (U.S. Department of Education, 1994).

The number of preschool children, ages three to five, in special programs increased 10.8 percent during fiscal year 1993. The large increases are attributed in part to better accounting procedures evolving with improved early intervention systems (U.S. Department of Education, 1994). Problems still remain, however, in full implementation of early intervention services in states, such as "... the volume of policy decisions, challenging fiscal situations, . . . lack of direct authority or power by the lead agency" (pp. xxv-xxvi). The result is continued and serious "fragmentation, duplication, and overlap in services" (p. xxvi). For preschoolers, providing services in the least restrictive environment (LRE) has become a national concern. One problem is that many districts do not offer preschool programs at all for the general population, particularly for three-year-olds. In addition, problems exist in collecting data regarding services in inclusive preschool settings.

The number of children in preschool programs for children with disabilities who will eventually be diagnosed as having a learning disability is unknown, but likely very small. This is because most students in preschool special education programs have disabilities that are more obvious than learning disabilities. Mental retardation, visual and hearing impairments, and physical disabilities are much more readily identified in young children than learning disabilities. Children who are eventually classified as having a learning disability are frequently thought to be only slightly slow during their preschool years, with parents and others frequently saying that "he'll grow out of it."

Early Identification Issues and Procedures

Hallahan, Kauffman, and Lloyd (1996) presented a cogent argument, echoed by many in the field, against early identification of learning disabilities. They

The early identification of students with learning disabilities is difficult because of the nature of the disability.

based their case on two major problems. The first are the inherent difficulties of diagnosing learning disabilities at early ages, including the inadequacy of current testing tools and procedures. Existing diagnostic instruments do not have the norms needed to determine an IQ/achievement discrepancy in preschoolers. The mitigating influences of diverse cultures, languages, and educational experiences at that age may be impossible to filter out in the diagnostic process. The second is the risk of misdiagnosing the presence of learning disabilities in a young child when in fact none exist. That situation creates unnecessary stigma and anxiety for the child and the family that may last for an entire lifetime and create an expectation for failure.

Mercer, Algozzine, and Trifiletti (1988) summarized the advantages and disadvantages of various early identification approaches and considered a range of prediction models that might help agencies and families ward off potential failure in school. They echoed the complicating factors that make early identification so complex, such as lack of precision in definitions of learning disabilities and in test instruments. They also shared some recommendations for identification of young children with learning disabilities:

- Assess in preacademic or readiness areas (rather than language or motor, for example).

- Teacher perceptions are better predictors at the preschool level than tests.

- Administration of predictive measures seems to work better during spring of the kindergarten year, rather than fall.

- Effects of misdiagnosis of LD can be minimized through ongoing progress monitoring and open-entry, open-exit placement options.
- Parental involvement can enhance identification and intervention.
- Early identification instruments and procedures should be selected and evaluated on the basis of the full prediction matrix they recommended.

Other researchers have questioned the need to identify learning disabilities in preschoolers since early intervention programs can use more generic terms such as "developmental delay" (Haring, et al., 1992). The most important point is that if delays are present in the preschool years, early intervention can make a significant favorable difference.

Early Interventions and Their Relevance to Learning Disabilities

Since 1974, Head Start programs have been mandated to serve children with disabilities to the level of 10 percent of their total enrollment (Wolery, Werts, and Holcombe, 1994). The largest group among that 10 percent served has been children with speech-language impairments. In other surveys of Head Start, public school prekindergarten, public school kindergarten, and community preschool programs (Wolery, Holcombe, et al., 1993), respondents reported enrolling children with four other types of disabilities (mental retardation, behavior disorders, sensory impairments, and physical disabilities); learning disabilities was not mentioned as a category.

Communities or public schools are increasingly offering birth-to-three special programs, while four-year-old programs are becoming more common for all children. Serving more preschool children has led to changes in methods used to identify disabilities. Trends over the past decade in the assessment of preschoolers with disabilities, as summarized by Wolery, Werts, and Holcombe (1994), include movement toward more team-determined, naturalistic, multiple-type assessment procedures and away from standardized tests and procedures. They noted four major assessment and intervention areas in which young children with disabilities receive much more service than young children without disabilities. These areas included (1) depth and breadth of assessment activities, (2) family involvement in assessment, (3) multidisciplinary team members' involvement, and (4) IEP development. All of these components help ensure the development of thoughtful individualized programs for any child at risk of failing. For children from diverse families, they recommended direct observation in natural contexts and using other adults as cultural and language translators or mediators.

Instructional programs for preschool children have also changed. Trends have stressed *adaptation of existing programs* to support the acquisition of critical skills in the child with disabilities, rather than planning an entire program based on identified needs. To that end, Wolery et al. (1994) described two emerging themes: (1) distributing targeted learning and practice opportunities throughout the day as naturally appropriate, and (2) integrating critical skill instruction and application into ongoing activities and routines, or "activity-based instruction" (p. 8). These practices go far in supporting children's learning within the general education environment.

Since many children with disabilities develop academic skills in the same ways that nondisabled children do, as documented by numerous researchers (e.g., Goodman, 1982; Katims, 1991; Reid and Hresko, 1980; Wiederholt and Hale, 1982), then interventions that fit naturally within existing programs are appropriate. Katims (1994) described gains in literacy development of preschoolers with mild and moderate disability levels through a literature-based program. The procedures included multiple daily readings by the adults of a small number of familiar, predictable books, along with structured techniques to facilitate students' independent use of books. These techniques would work well for all children.

Transition from Preschool to Kindergarten

Policymakers, administrators, and other practitioners have been actively working to coordinate the different service delivery systems for young children, since those identified early must move from birth-to-two programs to three-to-five-year-old programs and then again to kindergarten/elementary programs. One federally-funded project, the Kansas Early Childhood Research Institute (KECRI), advocates an "ecocultural niche model" of transition. This model views children as members of families who are part of a broader social and cultural community. KECRI stated several beliefs about transition, including the following:

• Transition is a change in a child's and family's ecocultrual niche, instigated by a change in service providers.

• Transitions are hard because they require accommodations in daily routines for individual families and service providers (e.g., getting transportation or household help) as well as creating systems change (e.g., financial policy changes) for everyone involved.

• The success of a child's (and family's) transition to the next stage depends on the amount of accommodations required and how easily sustained those supports are (U.S. Department of Education, 1994).

Professionals and families can use a number of strategies to assist children in making the transition from preschool to kindergarten programs. Katims and Pierce (1995) argued that natural, literacy-rich classroom environments can readily help children with special needs to learn the essential competencies critical for successful movement to the primary grades. These environments engage students in authentic and individually meaningful language activities that help them acquire the four areas of concepts, or *content*, described earlier. Blalock and colleagues (1994) identified components for a thoughtful transition *process* (i.e., the connecting activities) at this age level (see Figure 6.2).

FIGURE 6.2

Transition Process—Preschool Program to Kindergarten

WHO?	Family Members/Guardian	Service Coordinator
	Current Preschool Teacher	Related Services Personnel
	Kindergarten Teacher	Administrator, Principal, Special Education Director
WHAT?	Identification of appropriate outcomes to allow for continuum of service, skill development including prevocational, self-determination, and healthy relationships	
HOW?	Communication by professionals sharing information with families	
	Transition planning team meets to develop IFSP/IEP	
WHERE?	Elementary campus or preschool campus	
WHEN?	Six months to one year prior to entering kindergarten (must consider family preference)	

CRITICAL CONSIDERATIONS:

1. Information provided on services/resources and eligibility issues (examples of strategies, parent handbook, community directories)

2. Present levels of performance, family's preference and interests

3. Transition activities to meet the outcomes with specific activities (transition activities, goals, and objectives to attain the next level)

4. Most inclusive option based on previous visitations by all team members (e.g., family visits future service sites, and/or receiving agency visits current service site)

5. Community/cultural supports, issues

Source: Blalock, et al., (1994, pp. II-5–II-6).

▶ CHARACTERISTICS OF ELEMENTARY STUDENTS WITH LEARNING DISABILITIES

Elementary students with learning disabilities display a wide range of characteristics. One area that consistently surfaces with these students is academic achievement. Long-range studies of primary grade students have shown that different variables predict long-term achievement for students with learning disabilities than those for average achievers (McKinney, Osborne, and Schulte, 1993). These studies have also indicated that students with LD remain consistently and significantly behind their peers academically. Achievement scores were at the 30th percentile level for the former group, in contrast to 49th percentile for the latter group, in spite of a third of the students with LD being placed full-time in the general education classroom. The variables germane to students with learning disabilities included teacher perceptions of intelligence and task-oriented behavior,

IQ scores, and grade retention. These findings suggest that very *focused interventions* (i.e., specific to the learner's strengths and deficits) will be important to help students with learning disabilities learn to their maximum potentials.

Subtypes of Learning Disabilities in Children

Subtyping or creating subcategories of learning disabilities has been popular among many researchers due to the complexities inherent in this condition. Subtypes offer a way of clarifying the difficult constructs that can help research and development in diagnosis, instructional assessment, and intervention. For example, Little (1993), based on the work of Rourke (1991) and others, described the apparent presence of a nonverbal learning disabilities (NLD) subtype characterized by "(a) poorer visual-motor skills than verbal skills; (b) lower mathematical achievement than sight-word reading ability; and (c) relatively limited success at solving abstract, nonverbal problems" (p. 653). However, disagreement continues about the symptoms that accompany such a subtype (e.g., spelling abilities, reading comprehension levels, verbal problem-solving, and, of special importance, social/emotional traits).

Lyon and Flynn (1991) discussed the common subgroups by which the population with learning disabilities is frequently categorized, based on type of disability (e.g., those with cognitive, oral language disorders, reading, writing, mathematical, and social skill disorders) as a basis for simply beginning to think about classification systems. They cautioned that "because the definitional problems that characterize the field of learning disabilities are not likely to be reduced in the near future, the identification of subgroups and subtypes of learning disabilities can best be accomplished when guided by a developmental longitudinal perspective" (p. 71). In other words, professionals will need to carefully observe students over a long period of time, at different age stages and in diverse settings, to begin to understand what kinds of subgroups are truly present. The following sections provide general profiles of children whose learning disabilities fall within the full range of categories listed above.

Cognitive Characteristics

Several aspects of cognition (i.e., learning and knowing) become important as educators study children with learning disabilities. An initial feature is how these students view themselves and their learning capacities, particularly in relation to their nondisabled peers; these aspects are addressed as "self-perceptions," "locus of control," and "attributions." In addition, the very significant potential to learn among these students may be seriously affected by the capacities involved with information processing and memory, generalization, problem-solving, and related attentional behaviors, which are discussed in the remainder of this section.

Self-perceptions   A hopeful and positive finding has been that children with LD often view themselves very similarly to the way non-LD children view themselves (Butler and Marinov-Glassman, 1994). Children with learning disabilities seem to base their self-perceptions on (1) the same things that one's peer group generally does (e.g., preadolescents become very self-critical), and (2) their educational placement (i.e., being mostly with others of similar or different abilities). Indications are that when these students are with peers much more academically competent than themselves, their academic self-concepts may suffer (Halmhuber and Paris, 1993), a factor that should be considered when programming arrangements are created within schools. Other research has supported the idea that self-worth depends upon the specific domain or context in which it is assessed (Bear, Juvonen, and McInerney, 1993; Bluechardt and Shephard, 1995; Halmhuber and Paris, 1993; Montgomery, 1994), so that differences in self-perceptions occur, for instance, between language arts and math, between global self-worth or social acceptance and academic competence, or between school and home.

Children with learning disabilities tend to view themselves more positively than do the adults in their lives. For example, Halmhuber and Paris (1993) observed that parents and general educators rated the coping skills of nondisabled students or students with physical impairments as higher than students with LD. Montgomery (1994) also reported that teachers generally underestimated the self-concept scores of average achieving students and students with LD while overestimating the self-concepts of high-achieving students.

Locus of Control and Attributions A great deal of research has been conducted on **locus of control** with students with learning disabilities. Locus of control means the perceived source of control over the events in one's life. The general consensus is that children with learning disabilities tend to operate from an external locus of control, having given up responsibility for their actions (especially academic ones). This means that they often view their lives as being controlled by external forces. Such perceptions are manifested in behaviors like those observed by Halmhuber and Paris (1993): (1) failure to seek ways to adjust to setting demands, (2) limited repertoire of strategies, and (3) passive tendencies. The external locus of control in these students may have occurred because professionals in special education assumed excessive control in planning these students' instructional programs (e.g., not explaining how their learning disabilities affected their academic performance, or not allowing students input into planning their instructional programs), or because students with LD did not take advantage of naturally occurring opportunities to make decisions, or a combination of reasons. Recently the field has moved to change that direction, teaching self-determination to increasingly younger students so that they can become much more intrinsically driven.

Related to locus of control are **attributions,** the alleged causes of a person's successes and failures. Research has consistently shown that children with LD attribute their successes to luck, outside help, or unknown causes (Bryan, 1986; Halmhuber and Paris, 1993), and they attribute failures to their own lack of ability or action. This profile creates serious, long-lasting damage to students' self-concepts and self-esteem. The good news, however, is that attribution retraining has proven successful in shifting attributes to more realistic, action-oriented sources (i.e., the self).

Information-Processing and Memory Patterns   The two abilities of information processing and memory are closely linked, as illustrated in the Atkinson-Shiffrin model of memory in Figure 6.3. A continuing debate surrounds the quantitative versus qualitative differences in learning found among students with learning disabilities (Kulak, 1993). In other words, do learners with learning disabilities develop the same learning behaviors as nondisabled learners but at a slower rate (and thus have a developmental lag or a quantitative difference), or is their academic learning different than that of their peers (differences in quality)? Some have suggested that students with mild disabilities experience more of a developmental lag but that those with severe learning disabilities present atypical learning behaviors (Stanovich, 1988).

While conclusions differ about the nature of learning disabilities in this respect, research has consistently shown that students with LD do have different learning outcomes or accomplishments than their non-LD peers. Several studies have shown consistently lower performance in these learning tasks among students with LD:

- cognitive and attentional tasks (Das, Mishra, and Kirby, 1994);
- memory, phonological, and mental addition tasks (Ackerman and Dykman, 1993);

FIGURE 6.3

Atkinson and Shiffrin Model of Memory (1971)

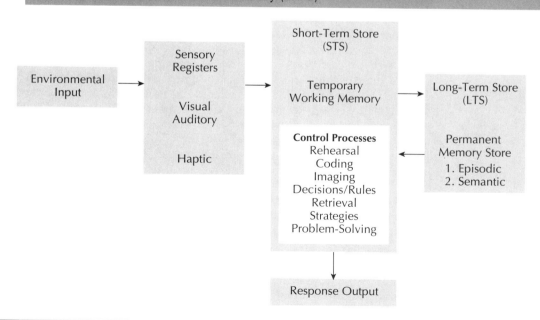

- accessing, organizing, and coordinating incoming information (Swanson, 1989);

- semantically-based memory skills critical for success across content areas (Scruggs and Mastropieri, 1990); and

- efficiency in learning content from reading passages and retention of information (Gettinger, 1991).

Learners with and without learning disabilities also show many similarities. For example, Ackerman and Dykman (1993) found that extraneous noise interrupted working memories for all students, while monetary rewards improved their performance! In another study, Gettinger (1991) observed that students with *and* without LD spent similar amounts of time learning content from reading passages (but with different results, unfortunately).

Differences in cognitive functioning have also been found to be dependent on the specific area of information processing (Fletcher, 1985; Siegal and Ryan, 1989). For instance, children with reading disabilities performed lower on a verbal-memory task, while those with math disabilities did less well on a visual-spatial memory task but showed good working memory for language-related tasks. Swanson (1994) also discovered differences based on subtypes. He analyzed the degree to which differences in working memory (see Figure 6.3) reflected specific or global processes and found that while the LD subtypes compared similarly during initial testing conditions, dynamic testing procedures produced greater gains among children with math disabilities over those with reading disabilities. Dynamic testing procedures are described later in this chapter. Swanson (1994) also discovered that the students with learning disabilities performed worse than average achievers but better than slow learners across working-memory process conditions, thus contradicting suggestions that children with LD and slow learners are alike in their learning behaviors. For educators, these insights about information processing and memory mean that assessment and intervention strategies should be used that point out and build on students' strengths as well as their needs.

Generalization Skills Generalization of learned skills or concepts to new situations has always been a significant area of concern for students with learning disabilities. "Despite average to above-average intellectual potential, students with . . . LD exhibit problem-solving deficits that may negatively affect their ability to recognize structural similarities between problems and subsequently inhibit far transfer" (Brownell, Mellard, and Deshler, 1993, pp. 138–139). "Far transfer" means generalization to very different task situations—tasks with few or no similarities to prior tasks. As a result, many strategic learning approaches now incorporate direct instruction of generalization into their models. For example, students discuss, plan for, and practice applying newly learned skills in novel situations and receive feedback on their performance (e.g., setting up an assignment to ask for help or use mathematics skills in a consumer situation in the community).

Problem-solving Performance Students with learning disabilities have demonstrated difficulty in grasping a structure or set of rules to follow, in order to solve problems (Stone and Michals, 1986). Initial learning of problem-solving strategies seems difficult for many of these students, supporting the idea of developmental lag in this area (Brownell, et al., 1993). Students with LD often fail to effectively use new information to revise their ideas when situational changes occur. For instance, introduction of a new forced choice test format may not trigger the student to think about how that differs from prior test formats and why, so that the best possible answers may be given. Therefore, even when students learn a particular problem-solving strategy they may need support (such as prompts or cues) to generalize the strategy to different situations. Brownell et al. (1993) described a continuum of difficulties in problem-solving that may be linked to a learning disability:

- using feedback to modify problem-solving strategies;
- generating hypotheses for problem solution;
- determining the salient features of a task and ignoring irrelevant details;
- processing the organizational features of information;
- inducing rule structures necessary for problem solution; and
- manipulating multiple processes in working memory necessary to create a problem space for generating problem solutions. (p. 152)

Related Attentional Deficits Years of research have demonstrated that an attention deficit disorder (ADD) does not cause learning disabilities, nor does the severity of ADD directly relate to the severity of a learning disability (Ackerman and Dykman, 1993) even though the two conditions may overlap in some students. Students with LD appear similar to their non-LD peers in initial attentional response and selective focus, but they may have more difficulty with sustaining focused attention on some items. Stanford and Hynd (1994) found that children with attention deficit disorders with hyperactivity were more disruptive than students with ADD without hyperactivity or with LD. Their study, and others, found similarities between the latter two groups on symptoms of withdrawal and impulsivity but differences in attention. For example, students with ADD were consistently viewed as being more disorganized and needing more supervision than even those with ADD with hyperactivity. The relationship between learning disabilities and ADD is further explored in the chapter on concomitant exceptionalities.

Oral and Written Language Characteristics

Listening and Speaking Special education has traditionally focused on the most formal of academic tasks as critical instructional targets (i.e., reading, writing, and mathematics) and neglected oral language skills. It is now known that a significant portion of the problems faced by students with LD are language-based and that receptive and expressive oral language (listening and speaking) are foundational to the higher level language skills of reading and writing. Myklebust proposed a reciprocal, interactive model that portrays all language development as based on experience and proceeding over time toward increasingly higher level skills (see Figure 6.4). Researchers have found that students with LD often display problems with receptive and expressive oral language skills (Roth, Spekman, and Fye, 1995) which, according to Myklebust's model, has implications for reading and writing skill acquisition. In addition, as in the case of students with diverse language backgrounds, educators often assume that adequate conversational skills mean that more sophisticated academic language abilities are also intact, when in fact they may be seriously deficient. For example, students with learning disabilities were significantly different from non-LD students on both receptive and expressive language-based measures in science (Shepard and Adjogah, 1994).

Students with LD typically have not learned how to listen effectively, so they need to be taught strategies to enhance these skills. They need instruction in skills that maximize comprehension of oral exchange, such as categorizing what is heard, seeking verbal and nonverbal cues, identifying main ideas and supporting details, employing memory strategies, and critically evaluating the message.

Common speaking difficulties are also found in students with LD. They include vague and inaccurate use of references (such as pronouns with no clear item or person to whom they refer), staccato and repetitive speech, difficulties

FIGURE 6.4

Hierarchy of Language Development

Expressive Written Language
(Writing)

Receptive Written Language
(Reading)

Expressive Oral Language
(Speaking)

Receptive Oral Language
(Listening)

Experience and Inner Language

Source: Myklebust, H.R. (1965). *Development and disorders of written language, Volume one: Picture Story Language Test.* New York: Grune and Stratton, p. 3. Used with permission.

with naming objects, problems understanding figurative and idiomatic language, and problems taking turns, among others. Students can benefit greatly from instruction that prepares them to communicate with intent (e.g., requesting information or action, making comments, arguing, greeting).

Reading Reading remains the single most problematic area for students with learning disabilities, primarily because most school programs expect students to obtain most of their information from the reading process, both in groups and individually. **Dyslexia** is the *medical* term denoted for significant reading disorders, and some professionals, consumers, and advocates also attribute a composite of other characteristics, mostly neurological in nature, to this label. Flowers (1993) described this condition:

> Students with dyslexia do not learn to read as well as their peers, even though they are given ample opportunity and are neurologically, emotionally, and intellectually healthy. In most cases, some reading ability is present, although it can require great effort and motivation to attain, and still reading may be laboriously inefficient, inaccurate, and unrewarding (p. 577).

Hynd and Cohen (1983), among others, have emphasized the importance of identifying subtypes of reading disabilities in order to learn more about them and provide appropriate interventions. Additional exploration of these subtypes may be found in discussions by Masutto, Bravar, and Fabbro (1994), Boder (1973), and Bakker (1990). Bakker's subtypes included:

1. Linguistic dyslexia—fairly rapid reading speed with numerous errors (e.g., additions, omissions, or substitutions of letters, syllables or words).

2. Perceptual dyslexia—fairly accurate but very slow reading, frequently disrupted by hesitations and repetitions.

3. Mixed dyslexia—includes both types of reading behaviors listed above.

Spear-Swerling and Sternberg (1994) recently described four possible patterns of reading disability as a possible framework when thinking about poor readers. Table 6.1 delineates the differences across their categories of nonalphabetic, compensatory, nonautomatic, and delayed (in descending order of difficulty).

The controversy described earlier in this chapter about the quantitative versus qualitative nature of learning disabilities (i.e., developmental lag versus fundamental difference) certainly receives attention within the reading domain (Kulak, 1993). On the one hand, Felton and Wood (1992) observed that very poor readers in 3rd and 5th grades showed significant deficits in reading nonsense words (i.e., reading phonemes rather than real words, as often found in phonics-based reading programs). Delays in phonological awareness have been linked with verbal short-term memory problems and slower automatic naming tasks, all of which relate to one's ability to acquire early reading skills (Ackerman and Dykman, 1993; Torgeson, 1985; Torgeson, Wagner, and Rashotte, 1994). In other words, problems with oral decoding of phonemes appear to seriously affect one's ability to learn to read, representing a *fundamental* difference in the reading acquisition process from that of non-LD learners.

TABLE 6.1

Characteristics of Various Patterns of Reading Difficulty

Pattern	Characteristics			
	Word-Recognition Skills	Reading-Comprehension Skills	Use of Comprehension Strategies	Disabled Reader
Nonalphabetic	No phonetic skills. Relies heavily on visual cues to recognize words.	Reading comprehension is very low because word-recognition skills are so limited.	None	Yes
Compensatory	Has limited phonetic skills. Relies heavily on compensatory abilities, such as use of sentence context or sight-word knowledge.	May do well with relatively undemanding materials. Has difficulty when comprehension demands escalate because word recognition consumes too many mental resources.	None	Yes
Nonautomatic	Has word decoding skills, but these are effortful, not automatic. May use sentence context to speed word recognition.	May do well with relatively undemanding materials. Has difficulty when comprehension demands escalate because word recognition consumes too many mental resources.	None	Yes
Delayed	Has automatic word recognition, but lags far behind cohort in acquisition of these skills.	Impaired comprehension. Was not "ready" for comprehension instruction at the time it was delivered.	Impaired strategy use.	Yes
Suboptimal	Has automatic word-recognition skills.	Lacks higher-order comprehension skills.	Has at least some basic strategies, but may lack higher level strategies.	No

Source: Spear-Swerling, L., and Sternberg, R.J. (1994). The road not taken: An integrative theoretical model of reading disability. *Journal of Learning Disabilities, 27* (2), p. 96.

In contrast, Seidenberg, Bruck, Fornarolo, and Backman (1985, 1986) documented more *quantitative* differences among students with reading disabilities in their research. Others have documented that accurate, fluent word identification is a core problem in most cases of reading disability (Blachman, 1994; Vellutino, 1991). As a balance, Stanovich and his colleagues (Stanovich, 1988; Stanovich, Nathan, and Vala-Rossi, 1986) have suggested that the *typical* poor reader exhibits a developmental lag but that students with *severe* reading disabilities appear to have specific deficits in phonological processing skills.

Writing   Students with learning disabilities often reveal challenges with one or more broad areas of writing: handwriting, spelling, and written expression. Since expressive written language is the highest level of language development and is an area that can be continually refined throughout one's life, it represents the most difficult area in academics for children, especially those with learning disabilities. Unfortunately, Palinscar and Klenk (1992) noticed that special education teachers frequently limited students' writing tasks to filling out worksheets and copying words, activities which are far from conducive to expanding one's writing skills.

   Dysgraphia is the major *medical* term connected to handwriting disorders and has been defined by Hamstra-Bletz and Blote (1993, p. 690) as:

> . . . a written-language disorder . . . that concerns mechanical writing skill. It manifests itself in poor writing performance in children of at least average intelligence who do not have a distinct neurological disability and/or an overt perceptual-motor handicap. In addition, the child should have had proper instruction in handwriting. Furthermore, dysgraphia is regarded as a disability that can or cannot occur in the presence of other disabilities, like dyslexia . . .

Hamstra-Bletz and Blote (1993) reported that young children maintained their dysgraphic problems as they grew older, demonstrating lower fine-motor ability and structural performance than nondisabled students, but no differences in writing speed. In addition, they showed less stylistic preference than their peers as they moved into higher grades, an issue of choice rather than ability.

   Students with learning disabilities have been noted to have difficulty organizing compositional writing and less awareness of strategies that could help them organize than their peers, such as graphic organizers or brainstorming (Englert and Raphael, 1988). They also have shown less awareness of the text structures or formats that present reading material (Dickson, Simmons, and Kameenui, 1995); this in turn affects their ability to predict, distinguish essential from nonessential information, and summarize (Siedenberg, 1989).

Mathematics Performance

Professionals in the field of learning disabilities have learned over the past twenty years that disorders in arithmetic and mathematics may be as prevalent as those of reading and writing. McLeod and Armstrong (1982) found that nearly two out of three children were getting help in arithmetic and math, although mathematics is an area of substantial strength for some students with

LD. Many of the problems in mathematics relate to language issues (e.g., terms, word problems, directions), while others are linked more to spatial abilities (e.g., place value, location of operational signs). **Dyscalculia** is the *medical* term for disorders in mathematical reasoning, particularly computational skills. Students with LD in math have shown significant problems in a wide range of conceptual and skill areas, including understanding and using one or more of the four operations, concepts of zero, carrying, borrowing, place value, basic mathematical concepts (e.g., one-to-one correspondence, conservation, sets), spatial arrangements, and several facets of word problems.

Kulak (1993) related the deficit versus delay positions discussed earlier to findings about mathematical difficulties, citing evidence by Goldman (Goldman, et al., 1988, 1989) and Geary (Geary and Brown, 1991; Geary, et al., 1991) that indicated *delays* in acquisition of more sophisticated math strategies, rather than fundamental strategies. However, as in reading, *some* evidence supports idiosyncratic or atypical mathematical problem-solving processes (e.g., inability to discriminate numbers and signs, problems with copying geometric designs), even after intervention (Goldman, et al., 1988). Jordan, Levine, and Huttenlocher (1995) found significant differences in learning computation skills across students with three varied patterns of learning abilities: (1) low language/adequate spatial skills, (2) low spatial/adequate language abilities, and (3) general delays; these results also suggest qualitative or fundamental differences in learning patterns, at least among some students.

Social Characteristics

The issue of socioemotional functioning of individuals with learning disabilities has been investigated for almost as long as the field of LD has existed. Some theoreticians have concluded that students with LD appear no different than their non-LD peers (Bruck, 1986), while others concluded that social and emotional areas can also harbor true learning disabilities (Pearl, 1987). Bryan and Bryan (1978) and Gresham and Reschley (1986), among others, have led the field in investigating the social status and social performance of children with LD. They have generally found a diminished social status of these students among peers, teachers, and parents, as well as numerous difficulties in their social behaviors. Trying to relate LD subtypes to socioemotional functioning appears a bit premature at this point (Little, 1993).

Social Status Students with LD frequently have demonstrated lower peer acceptance than non-LD students. For example, Bursuck (1989) reported that students with LD were significantly less accepted by peers than were low-achieving, non-LD students. That study's findings also indicated significantly different ratings for the group with LD than for high achievers on social indicators by peers and teachers. Conderman (1995) found that teacher ratings, self-ratings, and a sociogram completed by peers all showed that students with learning disabilities share lower social status than their nondisabled peers. "Children who are rejected by their peers are at considerable risk for later problems including dropping out of school, adjustment difficulties, and loneliness" (Vaughn, McIntosh, and Spencer-Rowe, 1991, p. 87). In general, Vaughn and Hogan (1994) summarized that peer acceptance of students with LD is related to several variables, including:

- *disability-related factors*—low achievement, information processing problems, expressive language problems;
- *others' perceptions and behaviors*—perceptions of and treatment by peers and by teachers;
- *environmental factors*—removal from classroom for parts of each day, reduced participation in class activities.

Ochoa and Palmer (1991) reported that Hispanic students with LD collectively experienced lower sociometric status than non-LD Hispanic peers, but that half of the group with LD actually were rated with popular or average status. Context (school or play) affected social ratings.

Social Competence   The social competence of students with LD appears to vary considerably. Vaughn and Hogan (1994) reported, through longitudinal research, that students with LD sometimes demonstrated consistently high social competence while others changed dramatically over the elementary years. Some students showed early problem resolution, while others displayed poor problem resolution throughout their childhood and adolescence. Tur-Kaspa and Bryan (1995) found that students with LD received similar behavioral ratings by their teachers as low achievers and that younger students with LD appeared at greater risk for developing social-behavioral problems than their non-LD peers.

Impact on Relationships   The social competence of students with learning disabilities can have a direct impact on their relationships with peers. With more and more of these students being included in general education classrooms for greater parts of the school day, peer relationships becomes more important than ever before. Vaught and Hogan (1994) observed reciprocal friendships among some of their students with learning disabilities, even when they exhibited lowered acceptance ratings. In contrast, other students had long-term acceptance problems and no reciprocal friendships. Some students with LD do not appear to differ in their friendships from their non-LD peers (Bear, Juvonen, and McInerney, 1993). Finally, family relationships have been examined to determine their role in learning disabilities. Results, for the most part have been inconsistent, but have not shown different family organizations to be the cause of learning disabilities (Wadsworth, DeFries, and Fulker, 1993).

▶ ASSESSING CURRICULAR NEEDS OF CHILDREN WITH LEARNING DISABILITIES

The preparation for instruction necessarily begins with finding out where students' abilities are as a place to begin teaching. This "present level of performance" identification is an essential step in the instructional process. Two types of instructional assessment are highlighted below as particularly effective for students with diverse abilities when determining present functioning.

Curriculum-Based Assessment

Educators are finding success in utilizing a **curriculum-based assessment** approach when implementing and evaluating instruction. This model entails the analysis of curricular components in sufficient detail to note milestones or indicators of progress and then to assess the learner's achievements or performance relative to those markers through a variety of informal means. These informal assessment strategies might include observations, interviews, probes, error analysis, checklists, product development, or other techniques. The advantage of such an approach is its close relevance to the instructional content and the instructional process.

Dynamic Assessment

Another assessment model effective for determining performance level is **dynamic assessment.** Palincsar, Brown, and Campione (1991) defined dynamic assessment as testing procedures that try to modify the student's performance level by providing structured cues or instruction with items. Such procedures actually modified favorably children's ability to process information in learning tasks (Swanson, 1994). Dynamic assessment is still in its infancy in many ways but is promising for learning disabilities due to its central beliefs that learners' performance is grounded within social contexts, is flexible and can improve, and that assessment should measure such improvement or changes (Palincsar, et al., 1991). Brownell et al. (1993) described the power of dynamic assessment procedures to differentiate among task performance levels of students with LD, mental retardation, and no disabilities.

▶ MAJOR INTERVENTION APPROACHES

This section outlines and briefly overviews some of the prevailing and core approaches for addressing instructional needs of students with LD in the areas of cognitive, oral language, written language, mathematical, social, and transition skills development. Chapter 7 should also be consulted for descriptions of interventions that are more prevalent among adolescents but which may prove fruitful for some younger students.

Cognitive Instruction

Learning about one's disability in relation to self-identity, self-determination instruction, and numerous self-esteem strategies has been helpful in promoting the personal development of students with learning disabilities. Of critical importance is that students learn what learning disabilities are and put them

Elementary-aged students with learning dis-abilitites require a comprehensive curriculum.

into perspective, rather than continuing a mystique or a silence about them. Teachers are encouraged to help elementary students learn about effective learning behaviors, the basics of learning disabilities, its relative importance within their overall beings, and the importance of action to create desired consequences. Self-determination curricula and instruction are discussed in Chapter 7. Many cognitive strategies presented below have helped students assume greater control over their academic lives.

Metacognitive Techniques   Chapter 7 contains descriptive discussions of various instructional approaches that combine the strengths of behavioral organization with metacognitive activities that actively engage the learner. This kind of approach at an early stage of education cannot be stressed enough. The use of metacognitive techniques can help students with LD avoid the passivity and learned helplessness that has come to be associated with this group of students. **Self-instructional strategies,** such as self-monitoring, self-graphing, self-reinforcement, and self-evaluation, continue to show improvement in academic outcomes (DiGangi, Maag, and Rutherford, 1991). According to Scruggs and Mastropieri (1990) **mnemonic devices** (tools or procedures used to improve memory) have helped many learners recall, comprehend, and feel positive about learning, much more so than any other type of special education intervention researched. They summarized several types of mnemonics which can be used by students to assist in information processing, organization for storage in memory, and retrieval from memory, a few of which include:

- pegwords—using rhyming words to aid recall of numbered or ordered information
- acronyms—the most familiar, where the first letters of each word in a list are combined to create a word or easily retrieved sequence of letters that relates to the target information
- loci methods—linking information to memorized places
- phonic mnemonics—connecting a letter to an object whose first sound is represented by that letter
- spelling mnemonics—creating a device that literally spells out the difficult-to-remember letters while saying something about the word to be spelled
- number-sound mnemonics—linking numbers and letters together in order to retrieve strings of numbers or dates, generating words that can be retrieved
- Japanese "yodai" methods—integrating rhymes and visual imagery to aid learning and retention of new concepts (Scruggs and Mastropieri, 1990).

Remedial readers have benefited most from combining information about the usefulness of a reading comprehension strategy (i.e., being told about its benefits) with how to use and modify the strategy (demonstration and practice) (Schunk and Rice, 1992). Giving explicit (elaborated) feedback, plus active student involvement in receiving and acting on the feedback, significantly increased learning gains (Kline, Schumaker, and Deshler, 1991).

Problem-solving A recently emerged technique that promises success for many students is **scaffolded instruction,** defined by Winn (1994) as "teachers (1) challenging students to engage in tasks that they are unable to complete independently and (2) providing the support needed to enable students to share the teachers' understanding of the tasks and successfully carry them out" (p. 89). Scaffolded instruction is based on teacher-student interactions that eventually lead to students' internalizing new skills and understandings (Winn, 1994) and on the concept of the student's "zone of proximal development" (a Vygotskian term meaning the distance between what one can do by oneself and what one can do with the help of a more knowledgeable other) (Stone and Reid, 1994). As part of an exploratory study of mediated collaborative problem-solving, Winn (1994) used scaffolding to teach self-regulation to students with LD and low achievers as a way to help the learners identify, define, and evaluate strategies for monitoring and controlling their reading.

Task Analytic and Academic Strategies Instruction Students with LD have been very successful with a range of techniques that involve breaking academic or behavioral tasks down into their component steps and devising or using strategies built upon those steps to complete the task. The self-instructional techniques described earlier combine well with the task analysis-to-strategy method, enabling learners to (1) preview what is expected from the list of steps, (2) guide themselves through the task by following the steps or strategy, and (3) evaluate their achievements through specific means.

Acceptable Treatments Students with learning disabilities need to be more actively involved in their educational programs. For example, Bryan and Nelson (1994) indicated that educators need to communicate the rationale for and the benefits of doing homework, as well as listen to student perspectives about homework, if we want them to successfully complete homework. Accommodations in homework, grading, and testing that are acceptable to students and to general educators have been explored by Polloway, Bursuck, Jayanthi, Epstein, and Nelson (1996). These conclusions help educators to remember to include students as active partners in the instructional process.

Oral Language Skills Instruction

Generic strategies to improve listening and speaking skills have been helpful to many students with mild levels of learning disabilities. Wallace et al. (1990) described a series of activities designed to improve listening abilities, including:

- getting organized for listening
- outlining techniques for oral presentations
- directed listening activities
- guided listening procedures.

Improved speaking capacities have resulted from interventions that help students be more intentional in their

- requests for information or action,
- responses to requests,
- statements or comments,
- attention seeking,
- projecting/rejecting and denying, and
- other performatives (Wallace, et al., 1990).

Direct instruction in more explicit descriptions (elaboration) of objects or events also improves speaking skills (Bos and Vaughn, 1994).

Wiig (1990) stressed different reasoning strategies in language intervention as a process component to engage learners and maximize their outcomes. Her Levels of Competence Model supports student advancement toward competence that gradually builds and expands to other situations. Combined with those competence levels are strategic learning behaviors, taught through a variety of approaches that include direct instruction of information, demonstration of basic content and subsequent abstractions, inductive learning, deduction learning, and learning by analogy. Wiig's Process Model for Strategy Development parallels typical steps in problem-solving within a context of developing a language learning strategy (Wiig, 1989). Table 6.2 illustrates those two related models.

Several clinical programs have been developed over the years to help students with LD acquire semantic, syntactic, and pragmatic aspects of language. Examples of these include:

Peabody Language Development Kit-Revised (Dunn and Smith, 1992)

Developmental Syntax Program (Coughran and Liles, 1974)

Clinical Language Intervention Program (Semel and Wiig, 1982)

TABLE 6.2

Wiig's Levels of Competence Model and Process Model for Strategy Development

Levels of Competence Model (Wiig, 1989)

Level	Name	Objectives
1	Basic Training	Develop awareness of significant features and underlying patterns
2	Extension to Pragmatic Uses	Strengthen the awareness of features and patterns and extend the knowledge to real-life uses
3	Extension across Media, Participants, and Contexts	Provide opportunities for generalization of acquired knowledge to complex tasks with more controlling variables or at a higher level of abstraction
4	Self-Directed Training	Foster independent application of knowledge to establish competence

Process Model for Strategy Development (Wiig, 1989)

Step	Major Objective
1	To actively identify features of stimuli and contexts that may or may not be significant in problem-solving
2	To perceive patterns in targeted features of stimuli and contexts
3	To formulate and test hypotheses generated about the significance of the perceived patterns
4	To select and execute a plan of action judged to have high probability for success
5	To self-monitor and evaluate the efficacy of the selected plan of action, and repair or revise as needed

Source: Adapted from Wiig, E.H. (1990). Linguistic transitions and learning disabilities: Strategic learning perspective. *Learning Disability Quarterly, 13* (2), pp. 133, 136. Reprinted with permission, Council for Learning Disabilities.

Reading and Writing Skills Instruction

Torgeson and colleagues (1994) have established the case for "intensive training in phonological awareness coupled with systematic instruction in word-level reading skills" (p. 284). They suggested that phonological awareness instruction prior to reading instruction may significantly reduce reading disabilities among young children. Felton (1993) and her colleagues at the Bowman Gray School of Medicine Learning Disabilities Project have reported significant word identification and spelling gains in first and second graders with problems with sound-symbol correspondence, using a code emphasis (phonics-based) intervention. This method, taught through a basal reading program, stressed instruction of basic decoding skills, in contrast to a meaning-emphasis basal program whose sample participants could not apply their phonetic skills to reading words and who relied on sight word recognition and context or picture cues to identify words. Several recommendations emerged from their longitudinal study, described in greater detail by Felton (1993):

1. Provide direct instruction in language analysis.
2. Provide direct teaching of the alphabetic code.
3. Reading and spelling should be taught in coordination.
4. Reading instruction must be intensive.
5. Teach for automaticity (Felton, 1993, pp. 587-588).

Graham, Harris, and MacArthur (1995) compelled readers to approach writing instruction from a comprehensive base.

> While frequent and meaningful writing is necessary to children's growth as writers, it is not sufficient . . . we need to create learning environments where they take responsibility for initiating and directing their writing efforts; . . . we also believe that teachers need to explicitly teach (within this meaningful context) skills and processes that are essential to the development of effective writing . . . strategies for planning, revising, and regulating the writing process as well as the basic skills needed to produce text. In providing such instruction, it is important that we maintain a reasonable balance among meaning, process, and form (p. 251).

One example of this balanced approach was described by Englert et al (1995). Their Early Literacy Project (ELP) is an integrated reading-writing program that incorporates five major components (described by Graham et al as principles of teaching and learning):

1. meaningful, holistic literacy activities
2. teaching for self-regulated learning
3. using interactive dialogues to strategize about literacy skills
4. teaching responsively in students' zones of proximal development (i.e., scaffolding or temporary supports)
5. community of learners

Several connected activities form the ELP curriculum, which include (Englert, et al., 1995):

- thematic units
- choral reading
- undisturbed silent reading
- partner reading/writing
- sharing chair
- morning news
- story response/discussion
- journal writing
- author's center

The ELP has demonstrated effectiveness in enhancing the reading and writing performance of first through fourth graders with mild disabilities including students with learning disabilities.

Another integrative approach demonstrated significant gains among elementary students with LD by combining word processing, strategy instruction, and a process approach to writing instruction (MacArthur, Graham, Schwartz, and Schafer, 1995). Teachers established a social context for meaningful writing, and the classroom routine supported extended cycles of planning, drafting, editing, and revising. Conferencing and explicit instruction in strategies for writing improvement (in particular, a planning strategy and a reciprocal revising strategy) followed the principles of the self-regulated strategy development model (Harris and Graham, 1992) where strategies are adapted as necessary, depending on students' writing skills.

A critical review of spelling interventions by McNaughton, Hughes, and Clark (1994) generated a repertoire of recommended instructional activities:

1. limiting the number of new words introduced each day
2. facilitating student-directed and peer-assisted instruction
3. directing students to name letters aloud as they are practiced
4. including instruction in morphemic analysis
5. providing immediate error imitation and correction
6. using motivating reinforcers
7. providing periodic retesting and review (p. 183)

Prior spelling research has suggested that, in addition, repeated copying alone fails to ensure automaticity since errors in copying occur and the mind disengages during copying. Rather, study-cover-write-compare methods, combined with the techniques above, are more useful. Polloway and Patton (1997) thoroughly described a range of spelling instruction methods that are easily used by teachers and students.

Multisensory Approaches Multisensory intervention approaches have long been known to be effective with students with LD. Although others were certainly developed in the twenty-five-year history of learning disabilities, the two most widely known multisensory approaches for written language instruction will be discussed here. Fernald's (1943) *V-A-K-T approach* (visual-auditory-kinesthetic-tactile) is a whole-language approach directed by students' choices of words they want to learn to read and spell. Language experience stories, alphabetical word files, writing words as whole units, and using words in context are features of the first stage, as is tracing and then writing words from memory. Stage 2 leads the student through greater writing about topics of interest combined with vocalizations to retain the multisensory emphasis. The last two stages drop the vocalizing and copying but add regular reviews, writing words from memory, and generalizing reading skills to unknown words.

The Orton-Gillingham *Alphabetic Method* (Gillingham and Stillman, 1965) also uses the visual, auditory, and kinesthetic modalities in a very structured sequence of presentations combining two modalities at a time for teaching specified concepts and skills. This program is intended to take the seriously poor reader or nonreader from start to finish in two years; during that time, reading to the student is allowed but s/he should not read outside material due to potential interference with the student's language development. After a discussion of written language and reading/spelling problems, the Alphabetic Method takes the student through reading and spelling with phonetically regular and then irregular words, until students are able to read and spell using words in context or in content areas.

Direct Instruction Hallahan, Kauffman, and Lloyd (1996) described the Direct Instruction materials for remedial reading, the *Corrective Reading Program* or CRP (Engelmann, Becker, Hanner, and Johnson, 1988). Based on prior learning about the alphabetic code, the CRP uses "general-case strategies for attacking and solving types of reading tasks" (Hallahan, et al., 1996, p. 244). Scripted daily lessons teach the skills required for fluent, correct decoding through carefully developed word lists and group and individual reading of very motivating stories. A heavy emphasis on syntax and sequence has led many students with LD to show great improvements in reading abilities.

Miscellaneous Techniques Numerous instructional strategies have been used successfully with students with LD in reading. **Repeated readings** in various forms, where students reread passages for improved reading rates, have produced significant gains in reading fluency (Weinstein and Cooke, 1992). **Neurological impress,** where the teacher leads oral reading with a single student slightly behind her/his ear, enhances comprehension as well as decoding skills through greater practice in reading. Progressive and constant **time-delay** procedures provide opportunities for students to engage more actively in the learning process. **Choral reading** and **audiotaped reading passages** both allow readers to experience fluency while enhancing comprehension.

Mathematics Instruction

Many special educators now rely on the National Council of Teachers of Mathematics (NCTM) Standards for mathematics competencies, and NCTM also publishes curricula for general and special education students. Their methods and materials have helped teachers realize the benefits of structural (discovery of underlying principles) approaches to mathematics instruction over more fundamental methods. Basal mathematics programs have been used with many students with LD, but are limited due to a lack of sufficient practice at each learning stage or targeted skill, a single method of presentation of most concepts or skills, and an overly rapid move to abstract ideas.

As a result of the weaknesses described above, **specific skills approaches** in mathematics have been developed to teach in greater depth the target skills that students with LD need. One example of these programs is The *Computational Arithmetic Program* (CAP) (Smith and Lovitt, 1982). CAP Math teaches the four major operations with whole numbers, through a structured series of worksheets and probes that have identified criteria rates. The Strategic Math Series (Mercer and Miller, 1991) helps students grasp the basic operations and become independent problem solvers via the concrete-representational-abstract (CRA) teaching method and use of manipulatives.

Specialized approaches have also been developed for students with LD. *Project Math* (Cawley, et al., 1976) is based on a structural, discovery method that teaches primary and intermediate levels of the principles underlying mathematics; problem-solving and conceptual understanding are major foci of that curriculum. Okolo (1992) reported significant improvement in math facts proficiency after four sessions of computer-based practice, as well as enhanced motivation of reluctant students due to the computer-assisted instructional game.

Social Skills Interventions

In the past ten years, a wealth of social skills curricula have emerged that allow educators a reasonable level of comfort when targeting skill instruction in this domain. Common elements among these include specific skill instruction, rationales, modeling and demonstration, role-playing, guided practice with feedback, and programming for generalization. Widely used examples at the elementary level are:

Social Skills in the Classroom (Stephens, 1978)

The Social Learning Curriculum (Goldstein, 1974)

The Walker Social Skills Curriculum: Accepts Program (Walker, et al., 1983).

Teaching social skills within context remains an important principle for instruction. Vaughn, McIntosh, and Spencer-Rowe (1991) found that some students with LD experienced increased peer acceptance with a contextualist training model that involved three components: problem-solving (FAST strategy) skills training, informant (trainer/consultant) status, and significant interactions. Teacher acceptance did not seem to make a difference. Bluechardt and Shephard (1995) used an extracurricular physical activity program to enhance social skills of elementary students with LD who showed significant deficiencies in motor performance as well as in social behavior. While gains were shown in motor skills, self-ratings of competence, and teacher ratings of social behaviors, similar gains were seen in control students who received comparable attention through individualized academic instruction, indicating that social skills training could readily occur through any instructional domain. Gains were persistent three months after intervention.

Transition Services and Supports from Elementary to Middle School

Changing from the belongingness perceived with one teacher or team at the elementary level to the apparent lack of connection perceived with a whole cadre of teachers at the middle school or junior high level is tremendously shocking for many students. Such drastic differences between the two levels demands systematic preparation in a wide range of areas. For example, Bryan and Nelson (1994) cautioned that the changes in homework assignments and grading that occur between elementary and junior high school may make those transitions especially hard for students with learning problems. Their survey indicated that teachers give less homework to elementary students in special education than to students in resource and regular education programs, but then "catch up" on such assignments in junior high, creating what appears to be an excessive burden to students. Figure 6.5 captures the basics of a transition process that helps prepare students and families for the next stage.

SUMMARY

This chapter has focused on preschool and elementary students with learning disabilities. Numerous characteristics and instructional suggestions were included in the chapter. The following points summarize the major areas included in the chapter.

- Young children face many challenges as they enter preschool and elementary programs, some of which may be internal (e.g., neurological development) but many of which are external, including school variables, sociocultural variables, economic variables, and others.

- Special education and related fields generally resist diagnosing learning disabilities in very young children, due to the lack of precision in testing instruments and procedures and the potential negative effects for children and their families.

- Students with learning disabilities have demonstrated in many cases a dogged ability to learn in the same ways as typical students, requiring simply that educators afford them the time, attention, and expectations they need to achieve.

FIGURE 6.5

**Transition Process—Elementary Program to
Middle School/Junior High**

WHO?	Student	Current and Receiving Teacher(s)
	Family Members/Guardian	Related Services Personnel
	Evaluation Team Members (if applicable)	Administrator

WHAT?   Identification of appropriate outcomes moving toward self-determination, healthy relationships, pre-employment skills, community involvement, and appropriate academics

HOW?   Communication by district, family, and community partners

Transition planning team meets to develop IEP and informal transition plan

WHERE?   Elementary campus or middle school/junior high campus, or family preference

WHEN?   1. Times vary

2. Annual review (exit IEP meeting) before entering middle school

CRITICAL CONSIDERATIONS

1. Information regarding services and resources, strategies, Community Transition Teams, media resources, handbooks, agency representatives

2. Present levels of performance, family's preference and interests

3. Transition activities (i.e., career exploration, functional curriculum, community involvement, life skill development, social/leisure skill development)

4. Most inclusive option based on student performance levels and interests, cultural/language factors, community options, etc.

Source: Blalock, et al., (1994, pp. II-5–II-6).

- In other cases, students with LD have needed creative alternatives to traditional instruction in order to master certain concepts and skills.

- Most important in the education of these students is professionals' concerted and multidisciplinary efforts to ascertain how each one learns best.

- Researchers and practitioners have responded to learners' needs by developing a range of interventions from several theoretical frameworks (behavioral and cognitive psychology in particular), but the field has been reticent to fully investigate and disseminate findings about current approaches.

ADOLESCENCE AND TRANSITION ISSUES[1]

The objectives for this chapter are as follows:

- ▶ To briefly describe the challenges faced by all adolescents.

- ▶ To summarize the typical characteristics of youth with learning disabilities.

- ▶ To define transition, the legal mandates for transition services, and the implications of transition programs for these students.

- ▶ To describe the range of instructional options that schools should provide for these learners.

- ▶ To summarize the range of services and supports that can enhance success of transitions from school to adulthood.

[1]This chapter was co-authored by Diane S. Bassett.

Chapter 7

From Middle School to Senior High—A Big Step

Sandra is moving from middle to high school and has tremendous anxiety about what will be expected of her and about her ability to measure up to those expectations. School has always been a struggle, and she has worked hard to please the adults in her world, particularly her parents and her teachers. She has found herself this year wanting to please her few friends much more, to fit into a larger crowd, to work harder on her appearance. She feels guilty about the lack of effort she's put into her schoolwork, which landed her mostly Cs and a D. She knows that she needs to put in two or three times as much studying as others, but she doesn't really feel like it's worth it anymore . . . too many other things to think about! She loves her parents, but making them happy with her grades doesn't motivate her like it used to, and that makes her feel guilty too. Her counselor talks about her planning for the future by making good choices with electives, and her teacher is trying to get her ready for high school by cramming in a few more study skills and learning strategies. Is it really worth it? Won't high school be so enormous she'll get lost in the crowd? What difference does it make? Getting through this week is enough to manage.

Research in the field of learning disabilities has taken seriously the issues of adolescents for only twenty years or so (Brolin, 1995b). It is now known that learning disabilities do not disappear with maturity. It is also known that the demands in life, as well as the support systems one might have available, change with age, and therefore the impact of a learning disability may wane or expand or transform. Youth with learning disabilities have difficulty generalizing their skills from one situation to another—thus, the need for individualized interventions at each transition, or movement from one stage in life to the next. Learning about what those school and life demands are, how adolescents with learning disabilities have responded to those challenges, and what supports have been created by families and professionals to assist in the transition process are the emphases of this chapter. Major sections will include:

- a brief description of the hurdles or challenges faced by all adolescents;
- a summary of the characteristics of youth with learning disabilities;

- a description of transition concepts and legal requirements for students;
- an outline of instructional options provided by schools for these learners;
- an overview of transition services and supports.

Readers are encouraged to imagine themselves in the situations faced by youth with learning disabilities or to think about the dilemmas of a particular adolescent while reading this chapter. A sense of urgency arises when the short span of school years is contrasted to the individual's lifespan of opportunities. The fact that we lose many of our students long before twelfth grade, as they drop out or are imprisoned, adds to the urgency. It is the obligation of professionals and advocates to help these students "seize" those moments, if they so choose. To do so means (1) knowing the student well, (2) facilitating the student's global and specific independence, (3) having a wealth of strategies, supports, and resources for these students, and (4) being sufficiently organized to mobilize those services in an efficient and effective manner. This chapter attempts to build a solid foundation for developing those capacities.

▶ CHALLENGES OF ADOLESCENCE

Adolescence has been defined as "that period within the lifespan when most of the person's physical, psychological, and social characteristics are in a state of transition from what they were in childhood to what they will be in adulthood" (Lerner and Galambos, 1984, p. 8). Multiple perspectives of adolescence have been described by Rice (1987) and others: biological, psychoanalytical, sociological, anthropological, and psychosocial. Although adolescence is heavily influenced by one's childhood experiences and in turn strongly affects one's adulthood, its marked transformations warrant study as a separate period of development. The section below describes some of the major changes that occur in this period of transition.

Changing Realities

Adolescents face tough battles, much tougher today than twenty-five years ago. Many youth (especially in urban areas) literally fear for their lives, anticipating harm through either random violence or the dangerous activities they choose. On the other hand, teenagers frequently have access to significant support from the people in their lives (teachers, parents, employers, siblings, friends, extended family members) to learn, to participate in life's myriad events, and to develop their potentials in a variety of life domains. Powerful pressures from the outside, both positive and negative, play important roles in facilitating the teenager's movement through the stages of adolescence. These typically include cultural or community expectations about maturation; school expectations to perform scholastically, artistically, and/or athletically; peer pressure to take part in group-sanctioned behaviors, some of which may be illegal or dangerous; and family expectations to participate emotionally, physically, and perhaps even financially in family activities and dynamics. Many other pressures may also be present.

At center stage, however, are the internal forces that so famously typify adolescence: puberty and emerging sexuality, separation from parents, peer acceptance, and identity development, to mention a few. These inner compulsions may be much more powerful at times than external influences, to the point that they "create" the adolescent's reality (Pipher, 1994).

However, the adolescent experience is not necessarily as full of turmoil as the media (or our own experience) might suggest. Offer (1969) noted three types of journeys through adolescence: (1) "continuous growth" development, in which changes and parental relationships are smooth and which typified most adolescent experiences historically; (2) "surgent growth" movement, involving abrupt change but not necessarily turmoil; and (3) "tumultuous growth" development, characterized by stress and significant problems. The external realities of increasing portions of our population in the United States have undoubtedly greatly propelled the number of teens who experience the "tumultuous growth" type of development, but this reality is not for all. A brief description of the major areas that develop during the adolescent period can help us understand the emerging individual.

Physiological/Physical Development The physiological changes that occur in adolescence are the most visible signs of change. The endocrine glands generate new hormones that first transform primary sexual traits (i.e., the genitals) and next affect secondary sexual characteristics (e.g., pubic hair, breasts in females, facial hair in males). Figuring out what to do with this emerging sexuality becomes a major task, involving all other areas of functioning during this period (Lerner and Galambos, 1984). Spurts of growth characterize most youth, but late developers can experience loss of self-esteem, along with many other physical, cognitive, and social effects associated with lack of development. Weight may become a critical issue for some teens. Many females obsess over excess weight and develop maladaptive ways to deal with it. In the United States, far too many females become obese during adolescence, a condition that is extremely difficult to change. Being underweight is also a concern for some youth, particularly males (Rice, 1987).

Emotional and Social Development Pipher (1994) described the emotional system in early adolescence as immature when emotions are extreme and prone to change easily. Feelings are chaotic and intensive, and teenagers, especially females, can easily lose perspective. This may be one reason why suicides are the leading cause of death among adolescents; no middle emotional ground exists, and one's feelings can take control to the point of losing oneself along the way (Pipher, 1994).

As the adolescent's physical and cognitive development occurs, so does the emotional and social repertoire. For example, ". . . both males and females may have a more negative or positive self-concept, depending upon the age of onset and the duration of puberty. Also physical changes lead to sexual feelings that may influence interactions with the opposite sex" (Lerner and Galambos, 1984, p. 12). Cognitive changes may generate beliefs of invulnerability, which may in turn propel more risk-taking behaviors with one's body or mind.

Cognitive development Other challenges that occur in early adolescence include a tendency to think concretely in extreme black and white terms, to overgeneralize, and to assume others are always watching. Most importantly to those around them, young teens are very egocentric in their thinking, displaying a lack of sensitivity to others' situations (Lerner and Galambos, 1984). If they do not occasionally reflect on their lives and come to understand the changes and forces affecting them, they may not develop an identity that is true to themselves (Pipher, 1994).

In *later* adolescence, the individual develops new thinking capacities. Thinking in hypothetical and abstract terms becomes the norm (Lerner and Galambos, 1984), creating the ability to see the world from a variety of perspectives. Flexibility, logical thinking, systematic problem-solving, and the capacity to symbolize all define Piaget's stage of formal operational thought (Rice, 1987). Youth unconsciously create new relationships with the people in their lives and with society as a whole, with reciprocal influences on each other. At this point, it is natural— and important— that the adolescent and the parents ask, "Who is this person who looks, feels, and thinks so differently? What will the next few years be like, and what will the ultimate outcome be?" (Lerner and Galambos, 1984).

Career/Vocational Development Super (1953) defined the middle level years (ages eleven to fourteen) as a period for career exploration, exploring through fantasy, roleplaying, and information gathering one's "fit" with a variety of occupations. In today's schools, thirteen- or fourteen-year-olds are often asked to decide their life's career path in order to develop their four-year high school course of studies, when, in fact, they may not know by age eighteen exactly what they want to do. "Try-outs" are extremely important throughout this period, but asking youth to commit to a "permanent" role in society may be unrealistic. They must get to know their interests, abilities, values, and goals first in order to define this area of identity. Having a variety of experiences through which to explore these aspects of self is essential to their identification and ultimate "match."

▶ CHARACTERISTICS OF ADOLESCENTS WITH LEARNING DISABILITIES

Youth with learning disabilities present individual profiles like all other youth: emerging personalities and "passions," talented in some respects, not so talented in others, inquisitive about certain areas, heavily focused on peers and their acceptance, and trying to figure out their relations with their families (Dudley-Marling and Dippo, 1995; Bogdan, 1986). Nonetheless, differences such as their academic underachievement do exist that distinguish youth with learning disabilities from non-LD students.

Cognitive Characteristics

Academic Achievements Evidence abounds about how difficult school can be for youngsters with learning disabilities. Hallahan et al. (1996) cited outcome statistics that suggested youth with learning disabilities face serious challenges in completing their secondary academic programs. Among students with learning disabilities who graduate, approximately 20 percent receive certificates of completion rather than diplomas (U.S. Department of Education, 1995), perhaps in part due to diplomas' requirement to pass high school competency exams in most states. Shokoohi-Yekta and Kavale (1994) found that students with learning disabilities achieved lower ACT scores and earned fewer course credits in high school than did their nondisabled peers, outcomes that were not affected by differential diagnoses. Other areas such as foreign language acquisition, have also created difficulties for some students with learning disabilities (Lerner, Ganschow, and Sparks, 1991).

Reflections by a young adult with learning disabilities indicated the magnitude of academic and other challenges that students, and families, face:

> My other proudest moment was when I graduated from high school. I had mixed feelings about it. On the one hand, I was upset about leaving the teachers who were my best friends. On the other hand, I was happy and excited because I got into college. For the first time in a long while, something was going right in our family life. What I mean by this is that my family forgot about all their pain, and we had some happiness in our lives, which I personally did not mind at all. (Lipper, 1995, p. 65)

Cognitive Behaviors Students with learning disabilities are noted for their lack of strategic approaches to academic tasks, which can be circumvented by direct strategy instruction. Montague, Bos, and Doucette (1991) documented that 8th graders with learning disabilities had a poor attitude toward mathematics. In fact, their knowledge of math problem-solving strategies was lower than for high achievers, and their grasp of problem representation strategies appeared less than for average and high achievers. Of great benefit to these learners is to identify their learning behaviors (e.g., "ask for help when unclear," "usually cram for an exam the night before") and to characterize those behaviors as effective or not and efficient or not. When directly taught strategic ways to approach academic or social tasks, these individuals can learn and apply those techniques effectively.

Students with learning disabilities have frequently not developed good reasoning skills but are certainly capable of benefiting from instruction in critical thinking and problem-solving. Swanson, Christie, and Rubadeau (1993) found among twelve- to fourteen- year-old students that those with learning disabilities performed similarly to normally-achieving (NA) students on some types of metacognitive items (e.g., person variables), lower on other types (e.g., knowledge of strategies), and even higher on other types (e.g., knowledge of task variables). No differences were found in analogical reasoning. *Specific* components of metacognitive processing seemed to govern, rather than a global link to metacognitive abilities; this kind of splinter-skills pattern is typical among persons with learning disabilities.

Personal Characteristics

Self-concept/Self-perceptions Educators have learned through research over the years that many students with learning disabilities adjust to their diagnoses by separating their "academic-behavior" self from their "intelligent" self. For instance, Montague, Bos, and Doucette (1991) found that eighth graders with learning disabilities had a low self-perception of ability and achievement in mathematics. And almost all view their LD label negatively (Guterman, 1995). Some continue to experience the stigma associated with their disabilities throughout adolescence, as one student lamented:

> I wish I was somebody besides me. I wish I wasn't so outgoing; too talkable. I take too many things to heart. I can beat myself down mentally and physically to a bloody pulp where I can't stand it anymore. It takes somebody from the outside to tell me, "Hey, look. You're honest, you're great, a spectacular kid." I can't do that to myself. . . . I'm 17 years old. I should be going to parties, doing this and doing that and the other thing. But, my brain is 3 years behind me so I am only 14 years old. Like I said, I'm nobody and that is how it is. (Guterman, 1995, p. 119).

Locus of control/attributions/learned helplessness. A growing body of research indicates that students with learning disabilities are more likely to have maladaptive patterns of attributions than their achieving peers (i.e., the students with learning disabilities attribute success to external factors and failure to internal factors) (Bell, Feraios, and Bryan, 1991). These include such tendencies as less persistence, little creation of strategies, answering fewer problems, spending less time on problems, and pessimism about future achievements—all behaviors that make the adolescent more vulnerable to harm if he or she fails to approach life's challenges proactively.

Autonomous Functioning Lewis and Taymans (1992) asked one hundred families to rate the autonomous functioning skills of their adolescents with learning disabilities. Autonomous functioning in this case was categorized as (1) self and family care, (2) management (i.e., interactions with resources, management of self), (3) recreation, and (4) social and vocational activity (interactions within friendships and jobs). They compared these data to that of 250 nondisabled youth in the same age range. At three ages (fifteen, sixteen, eighteen), mean overall score differences between the two groups were significant. The only separate subscale showing a significant difference was in self-management. Noteworthy was the indication that participants with higher levels of special education services (i.e., more hours) attained lower management subscale scores. Also of interest was that autonomous functioning scores were significantly higher among youth whose parent(s) at home were employed outside the home, in contrast to those whose parent(s) did not work.

Motivation   Students with learning disabilities have frequently demonstrated a serious lack of motivation about their educational programs, possibly associated to the learned helplessness discussed in Chapter 6. Adelman and Vogel (1990) indicated that motivation and attitude toward learning were linked to both educational and employment success. Program components that teach self-determination and self-advocacy beginning in the early years can help counteract the tendency of students to give up on their academic achievements.

Depression   A number of studies have reported the presence of depression among youth with learning disabilities (Forness, 1988; Mokros, Poznanski, and Merrick, 1989; Rourke, Young and Leenaars, 1989). Unfortunately few intervention programs have been developed to deal with this aspect of functioning in schools, and even fewer have been widely disseminated. As a result, depression may go undetected by classroom teachers which puts students at greater risk for suicide and self-destructive behaviors.

Social Characteristics

The field of learning disabilities is currently struggling with the role of social skills deficits, whether they qualify as a primary type of learning disability or simply occur as characteristics (Forness and Kavale, 1991). Although a fair amount of data exists regarding social performance of individuals with learning disabilities, findings seem somewhat contradictory, indicating a need for additional research. Following are some of the general findings about adolescents with learning disabilities in the social skills arena.

About 50 percent of students with learning disabilities emerged as poorly accepted by peers in recent research studies (Stone and La Greca, 1990; Vaughn, et al., 1993; Wiener, Harris, and Shirer, 1990). La Greca and Stone (1990) found students with learning disabilities were neglected (neither sought after nor rejected) more often than average-achieving boys, even when academic achievement was controlled. They found a strong relationship between knowing and liking others, suggesting that students involved in pull-out programs may set themselves up for being neglected since peers have fewer chances to know them (La Greca and Stone, 1990). Another study found that high school students with learning disabilities believed peers thought of them as less capable than nondisabled students, once the LD label was applied. They went to great lengths to avoid classmates from the LD program when they were in general classes (Guterman, 1995).

Mellard and Hazel (1992) investigated several adaptive behavior competencies with over four hundred students with learning disabilities and 618 non-LD students. Significant differences were found in several areas on a majority (over half) of the items, including pragmatics (appropriate use of language in various social situations), use and understanding of humor, peer relations, understanding others' perspectives, and coping with stress. Communication skills, heavily dependent on language abilities, may also create some of the social skills problems shared by some youth with learning disabilities. For example, some of the characteristics noted include an inactive, passive style during communication, few adaptations to one's audience, failure to question inappropriate verbal statements, and failure to "code switch" (i.e., adjust one's vocabulary and speaking style according to the situation at hand). Pearl, Bryan, Fallon, and Herzog (1991) found that seventh and eighth graders with learning disabilities were less likely than nondisabled students to recognize deceptive statements and, in another study, noted that students were willing to conform to peer pressure to engage in antisocial acts (Bryan, Pearl, and Fallon, 1989).

Friendships of adolescents with learning disabilities may or may not be impacted by the disability. Vaughn et al. (1993) found students with learning disabilities did not differ significantly from average or high achievers without learning disabilities in a number of reciprocal friendships; about 90% of their subjects with learning disabilities had a mutual best friend. In contrast, Mithaug and Horiuchi (1983) reported that 42 percent of their post-school adults with learning disabilities were socially inactive. Hoffman et al. (1987) described ongoing social and personal problems among adults with learning disabilities, including an inability to make and maintain friends, problems with initiating and sustaining conversation, impulsive talking and thinking, and inability to use free time well. In another study, Seidel and Vaughn (1991) discovered that dropouts with learning disabilities felt more socially alienated from classmates (while still in school) than did students with learning disabilities who completed high school. The former group lacked affective attachments to classmates and reflected feelings of being perceived unfavorably by others or being excluded from activities.

Functional Outcomes of Youth with Learning Disabilities

The findings generated by numerous follow-up studies of students with learning disabilities (cited below) vary tremendously for a number of reasons (see White, 1992, for a more thorough discussion). Michaels (1994) suggested the following reasons for some of the variability.

- Populations of students with disabilities may not be similar across studies, such as use of the mild disability category versus learning disabilities.

- Sampling procedures might have differed, as with record reviews, telephone interviews with parents, and face-to-face interviews with students.

- Threats to validity may be present due to sampling errors.

- Targeted outcomes may have varied across studies, such as employment versus independent living versus social integration.

- Definitions of similar outcomes might have varied, such as counting sheltered workshops as employment.

- The actual time of sampling may have differed, such as length of time since exiting school.

Generally speaking, many findings from follow-up studies portray poten- tially problematic outcomes. These may reflect the impact of the label or the manifestation of the disability itself. Regardless, many of the results are trou- bling if not shocking. The most comprehensive outcomes study was conducted by Stanford Research Institute (SRI) International under contract to the U.S. Department of Education (Wagner, 1993). The SRI study, called the National Longitudinal Transition Study (NLTS), collected data from three-hundred school districts across the nation, in two major waves: in 1987 when the major- ity of the sample had been out of school for less than two years, and in 1990 when the sample had been out of school from three to five years. Discerning the impact of years of special education programming on students' outcomes is what led Edgar (1987) to initially question the justifiability of secondary special education programs. The findings summarized below indicate that "business as usual" is no longer acceptable.

Unemployment Rates and Underemployment   In the last decade, researchers have concurred that young adults with learning disabilities experience double the unemployment rates (Edgar and Levine, 1987; White, et al., 1983), are employed in lower status jobs (Gajar, 1992; White et al., 1983), and earn lower salaries than their non-LD peers (Edgar and Levine, 1987). Dropping out of school compounds the problem. Edgar (1987) reported that dropouts with learning disabilities/BD were employed at a 30 percent rate, compared to those who completed high school at a 61 percent rate. White (1992) reported a 36 to 87 percent employment rate after high school among individuals with learning disabilities, as well as serious underemployment. Unemployment rates are much higher for females than males (Adelman and Vogel, 1993; Sitlington and Frank, 1990). Underemployment for both males and females within low-level jobs (part-time, service occupations, laborer, etc.) is also common (Gajar, 1992; Haring et al., 1990). Parents apparently play an important role in occupation- al training and employment outcomes (Mellard and Hazel, 1992).

The SRI found somewhat different results. It discovered that students with and without learning disabilities were employed at similar levels two years out of school (about 59 percent) and even more so at three to five years out of school (roughly 70 percent). The difference between the groups was that a significantly greater portion of those without disabilities also were simultaneously engaged in postsecondary education or high school equivalency programs (Wagner, 1993).

Residential Living   No studies have been conducted to examine the actual living conditions within the home among adolescents with learning disabilities. Most studies simply have asked individuals about their living arrangements. Haring, Lovett, and Smith (1990) found 79 percent of twenty-one-year-olds with learning disabilities were living with parents or relatives. In another study, Hoffman et al. (1987) found 48 to 65 percent of young adults who had learn- ing disabilities living with parents, compared to 29 to 55 percent of their nondisabled peers. Messerer and Meyers (1983) discovered that only 5 percent of young adults with learning disabilities said they envisioned themselves relocating geographically within the next ten years, compared to 43 percent of those without disabilities.

In 1993 the U.S. Department of Education reported that 20 percent of adults with learning disabilities who exited school three to five years earlier were not productively engaged outside the home and were living with parents or relatives. Living arrangements are often associated with financial dependence. Spekman et al. (1992) discovered that all but one of the fifty adults with learning disabilities in their study continued to be financially dependent on their family, with few prospects of change and a fair amount of frustration.

Postsecondary/Lifelong Education The National Longitudinal Transition Study (Wagner, 1989) reported that only 16.7 percent of young adults with learning disabilities participated in any type of postsecondary education or training program, and only 9 percent enrolled at two- or four-year colleges. This compares with 50 percent of the general population. Other studies report differing rates of participation. For example, Fourqurean, Meisgeier, Swank, and Williams (1991) reported that 26 percent of their sample completed at least one semester of college or technical school and another 35 percent participated in other types of post-secondary training (e.g., adult-based education, military service, private training, apprenticeships), the highest level in literature. Scuccimarra and Speece (1990) described a 40 percent rate of postsecondary education participants, including 3 percent through vocational rehabilitation and 6 percent at community colleges. In still another study, Shapiro and Lentz (1991) reported that only 15 percent had enrolled in any formal education program within two years of finishing school. Sitlington and Frank (1990) reported that 44 percent of the young adults with learning disabilities in their study engaged in one or more of the various forms of post-school learning. In most of these studies, training (as opposed to education) opportunities were connected to work (Mellard and Hazel, 1992).

Dropping Out *The 17th Annual Report* (1995) reported that the percentage of students with specific learning disabilities graduating with a diploma or certificate each year has remained steady for the most recent five years of data. Zigmond and Thornton (1985) found 54 percent of students with learning disabilities dropped out compared to 33 percent of their nondisabled peers. Subsequent research was somewhat heartening, finding a dropout rate of 36 percent among students with learning disabilities compared to 13 percent for students without disabilities (deBettencourt, Zigmond, and Thornton, 1989). As mentioned earlier, dropping out has been linked to both social alienation from classmates (Seidel and Vaughn, 1991), and to much lower rates of employment (Edgar, 1987). Especially troubling among this group is their relative failure to return for high school equivalency certificates, with less than 10 percent from the SRI study pursuing a diploma equivalent at any time compared to roughly 60 percent of the nondisabled group.

Learning Disabilities and the Criminal Justice System Estimates of juvenile inmates with some type of disability range from 40 percent to 70 percent, with the assumption that the majority of those disabilities are emotional/behavioral disorders or learning disabilities. Wagner (1993) noted a steady increase in the arrest rate for young adults with learning disabilities, rising from 9 percent while in school to 19.9 percent after two years out of school and to 31 percent after five years out of school. Many years ago Schumaker, Hazel, Sherman, and Sheldon (1982) noted that the social behaviors of youth with learning disabilities was much more like their delinquent peers than normally achieving adolescents. These students appear to be at a high risk for delinquency for a number of reasons (Keilitz and Dunivant, 1986). States are finally beginning to respond to the transition programs and services that youth involved in the criminal justice system need in order to make successful adjustments in home schools or adult activities.

▶ TRANSITION CONCEPTS AND LEGAL REQUIREMENTS

Definition of Transition

Transition simply means movement from one life stage or phase to another, or one setting to another. Within special education and rehabilitation, the term has primarily come to signify the passage of adolescents with disabilities from school to adulthood. Transitions from preschool programs to kindergarten, from elementary to middle school, from middle school to high school, and from high school to postsecondary activities are also transitions that students with disabilities must address.

The Division on Career Development and Transition (DCDT) of the Council for Exceptional Children adopted the following definition of transition in 1994:

> Transition refers to a change in status from behaving primarily as a student to assuming emergent adult roles in the community. These roles include employment, participating in post-secondary education, maintaining a home, becoming appropriately involved in the community, and experiencing satisfactory personal and social relationships. The process of enhancing transition involves the participation and coordination of school programs, adult agency services, and natural supports within the community. The foundations for transition should be laid during the elementary and middle school years, guided by the broad concept of career development. Transition planning should begin no later than age fourteen, and students should be encouraged, to the full extent of their capabilities, to assume a maximum amount of responsibility for such planning (Halpern, 1994, p. 117).

The DCDT position statement on transition describes the process of transition planning as having four main components:

• an emerging sense of student empowerment which eventually enhances student *self-determination* within the transition planning process;

• student *self-evaluation*, as a foundation for transition planning;

• student *identification of post-school transition goals* that are consistent with the outcomes of their self-evaluations; and

- student *selection of appropriate educational experiences* to pursue during high school, both in school and within the broader community, that are consistent with their self-evaluations and their post-school goals (Halpern, 1994, p. 118).

DCDT's position paper elaborated on each of these components. Halpern (1994) stressed the importance of evaluating *any* selected transition approach by its match to the criteria above, along with its sensitivity to the five issues listed below, in order to maximize relevance and engage learners:

- the extent to which an instructional program is based on student skills, interests and preferences,
- inclusion of the student within the regular school program,
- provision of community-based learning opportunities when appropriate,
- involvement of adult service agencies as needed, and
- involvement of community organizations, as contrasted with service agencies, in helping students with their transition (p. 121).

Major Federal Initiatives

Limited emphasis was placed on exemplary secondary special education programming during the 1970s and early 1980s. Indeed, transition initiative did not even begin until Madeleine Will (1984) called for increased interventions for youth with disabilities moving into adulthood. Several federal initiatives have been passed during the past five years that have focused on transition activities.

IDEA   The Individuals with Disabilities Education Act (P.L. 101-476, 1990) requires that individualized transition planning for post-school outcomes occur:

- for all students in special education
- no later than age sixteen and earlier for some students who need it
- involving parents, the student, and all pertinent parties.

Provision of transition services is described as a coordinated set of instructional activities, aiming toward an agreed-upon outcome and based on the student's needs, preferences, and interests.

ADA   The Americans with Disabilities Act (1990) prohibits discrimination against people with disabilities in all public arenas of life. Employers cannot discriminate against otherwise qualified job applicants or workers and must provide reasonable accommodations for their employees with disabilities who need them. Public transportation and other public facilities (e.g., libraries, restaurants, stores, theaters) must provide accommodations; schools must have a long-range plan to show their accommodations or strategies to accommodate students.

School to Work Opportunities Act (1994)   This Act authorized $300 million in seed money to states and communities to develop coordinated systems to help youth connect their education to future employment through three major activities:

Nearly eighty percent of adolescents with learning disabilities spend at least part of each school day in general education classrooms.

• *school-based learning,* aimed partially at achieving GOALS 2000's (P.L. 103-227) academic standards in core subjects and at linkages with the workplace, including regular evaluations, career counseling, and choice of career by eleventh grade;

• *work-based learning,* including work experiences, workplace mentors, broad instruction in industry-specific skills, and a continuum of job training experiences focused on mastery of higher level skills; and

• *connecting activities,* including matching students with employers and linking studies with work, ultimately leading to post-school choices of a job, continued education, or another training program (Gugerty, 1994).

Designed for all students, the Act fails to specifically address the needs of youth with disabilities (Hallahan, et al., 1996; O'Neil, 1994). Therefore, each state and community will need to ensure that these students participate and that school-to-work transition programs are not developed in isolation of the transition accomplishments by special education and rehabilitation made over the past thirty years (Halpern, 1994). According to Gugerty (1994), the U.S. Departments of Education and Labor are prepared to provide technical assistance to help states and localities offer opportunities to all students, including those from disadvantaged or diverse backgrounds, the gifted and talented, and those with disabilities and limited English proficiency.

Exclusion of Students with Learning Disabilities from Transition Planning and Services

Individuals with learning disabilities have often been excluded from the discussions about and programming for transitions to post-school settings, with the exception of transitions to postsecondary education. This neglect has occurred from a widespread misconception that learning disabilities belong by their nature within a "mild" disability category and, therefore, that few if any transition services are really needed among those who have this disability, a perception that research consistently contradicts (Reiff and deFur, 1992).

Karge, Patton, and de la Garza (1992) found that high school students with learning problems and the professional educators serving them both perceived a significantly low level of transition instruction and services in contrast to a high level of needs for these services. The study examined the development of skills in several areas: fulfilling the central role in transition planning, job searches, job maintenance, functional academics, self-advocacy, mobility and transportation, and recreation. Other transition needs identified included having paid jobs during high school, individualized transition planning, parent involvement, planning for postsecondary options, and connections with adult agencies.

The needs of many secondary students with learning disabilities are simply not being adequately addressed. Dunn (1996), Mellard and Hazel (1992), Sitlington (1996), and others have provided compelling arguments for schools to revamp programs and services for students with learning disabilities. Mellard and Hazel (1992) noted, "LD has severe consequences for young adults' likelihood of completing secondary education, of participating in postsecondary training and educational experiences, and of obtaining employment in positions offering more than minimum wages" (p. 268). Only through concerted, long-range planning at both the individual and the system levels that results in holistic education appropriate for each student will changes in the currently dismal outcomes data occur. The following section offers hope for that shift through curricular options that promote academic, personal, social, and career development throughout the lifespan.

▶ LEARNER OPTIONS WITHIN THE SCHOOLS

Individualized Planning Frameworks

When the delivery of services to students with learning disabilities began in earnest in the 1960s, it was assumed that, if properly remediated, learning disabilities would impact elementary-aged children only. The profession falsely estimated that these children would be "cured" and could subsequently complete their secondary schooling to enter adulthood as typically functioning adults. As a result of this thinking, those early professionals who followed students with learning disabilities into secondary schools attempted to use the methods and techniques developed for use in elementary settings. While some of the remedial, skill-based techniques can be used with older students, educators have found that adolescents with learning disabilities require a different array of learner and service delivery options if they are to successfully complete their schooling and become productive adults. Brolin's curriculum model portrayed in Chapter 6 shows the range of content and delivery options which a comprehensive career education model for all learners would include.

While the primary responsibility of elementary programs is to prepare students for the rigors of secondary schooling, the ultimate responsibility of middle grades and high schools is to prepare students for transition to the broad spectrum of adult opportunities and responsibilities. As mentioned earlier, these outcomes include employment and education, personal relationships and responsibilities, physical and mental health, home management, community participation, and leisure pursuits (Cronin and Patton, 1993). In order to successfully transition students with learning disabilities to adult lives, secondary programming must provide an array of service delivery options. Optimally, a student should be exposed to a variety of these options throughout one's life so as to best prepare for the range of future challenges. These options should be articulated through the transition planning process and appear within the IEP, taking into account one's broad-based risk and protective factors (Keogh and Weisner, 1993). If students are to be fully included as key participants in their own planning, "self-determination, which includes self-actualization, assertiveness, creativity, pride and self-advocacy, must be part of the career development process that begins in early childhood and continues throughout adult life" (Ward, 1992, p. 389). Finally, steps must be taken to ensure that the strengths, needs, and goals of students are included. Person-centered planning offers a way to accomplish this critical participation.

Person-Centered Planning and Student-Directed IEP Development Person-centered planning began with adult service agencies that wished to include the consumer with disabilities in many or all aspects of life planning. It has since been used by educators in both elementary and secondary schools as a precursor to IEP and transition development. Basically, person-centered planning asks the student, his or her family members, friends, and involved professionals to meet as a team to follow a series of steps culminating in articulation of goals and supports needed to address the goals. A general outline of the steps are listed below:

1. Participants offer their perspectives of the history of the student including home, school, and community variables.
2. Dreams and hopes for the student are shared by all participants, including (and especially) the student.
3. "Nightmares," representing the outcomes that could happen without appropriate supports, are also shared by all.
4. The strengths and needs of the student are shared around the group.

5. Goals are discussed, as well as the obstacles to those goals.

6. A plan is determined that reflects the goals to be met along with the supports needed to overcome the obstacles.

7. The entire process is documented, either through writing, pictorials, or a combination of both.

A number of models exist to support person-centered planning (Dowdy and Smith, 1991; Forest and Pearpoint, 1992). What all share is the premise that the individual is ultimately responsible for his or her goals; our job as educators and family members is to support those goals. Person-centered planning also aids family members in asserting *their* hopes, dreams, and goals for their child through an articulated partnership with committed professionals. It should be noted that the strength of person-centered planning rests not with the development of a plan, but with its ongoing and consistent implementation. Support must be offered actively and effectively by all team members.

Self-directed IEP   Adolescents with learning disabilities tend to respond passively to education and to assuming responsibility in other areas. A belief exists that these behaviors are both intrinsic to students who lack "executive decision-making" abilities as well as extrinsic in the form of "learned helplessness." Regardless of origin, it is critical that we involve students in the decisions affecting their present and future lives. One way of doing this is to actively involve them in the IEP process. The National Joint Committee on Learning Disabilities (NJCLD) (1994) carefully outlined students' roles and responsibilities in the transition planning process, as well as those for parents, secondary educators, and postsecondary staff.

IDEA states that students receiving transition services must be present at their IEP meetings, and if they are not, that another meeting be convened to include them to focus on transitions. Although many schools are now including students with learning disabilities into IEP meetings, students involve themselves minimally and passively. They take a back seat while educators and other professionals dominate the meetings and make decisions on their behalves. We now recognize that, if students are to become active participants in their own transition planning, they must have training and support to accomplish this. The *Self-Directed IEP* (Martin, Marshall, Maxson, and Jerman, 1994) provides students with a structure for assessing their own strengths and needs and forming goals for the IEP. Students are trained to follow an eleven-step process by which to lead their IEPs. Training is supported by video and workbooks, role plays, and debriefings. As evidenced in a video production, students report more engagement with school and a feeling of ownership over their futures.

The Self-Advocacy Strategy   Van Reusen, Bos, Schumaker, and Deshler (1994) developed the *Self-Advocacy Strategy* to provide a strategic way to teach adolescents with learning disabilities how to set goals and articulate them through active participation in the IEP meeting. Although the *Self-Advocacy Strategy* does not prepare students to *lead* the IEP meeting, it directs students on how to be both an active listener and an active participant during the IEP meeting. It provides a detailed format for students to assess their academic and functional strengths and needs, and to identify those areas targeted as goals by the student. Results of strategy training indicate that, before training, only 14 percent of student goals were included in the IEP; after training, 86 percent of student-initiated goals were included. *The Self-Advocacy Strategy* offers another means by which to involve students in their own learning. It must be emphasized that in order to make student involvement in the IEP process effective, professionals will have to relinquish most of the control for the meeting. Thus, we are all in the process of learning how to assist students in assuming responsibility for their lives.

Academic Instructional Approaches

Direct Instruction   Direct instruction has been used as the approach of choice for years by special educators. It has been defined as the direct measurement of a student's performance on a learning task and the accompanying arrangement of instructional programs and procedures for each child (Haring and Gentry, 1976). The tasks are usually academic and are broken into a series of task-analyzed instructional units. Direct instruction relies heavily on teachers assuming responsibility for student learning. The teachers must organize and modify instruction to match students' learning styles. Direct instruction can be very effective with students with severe learning disabilities and is useful for those with the most minimal levels of oral and written language or mathematical skills. Participants' gains have given some researchers the foundation from which to emphasize the importance of keeping remedial curricula in the high school (Polloway, et al., 1986).

Direct Instruction is the system developed by Engelmann and Carnine and colleagues at the University of Washington, a spinoff of the direct instruction model. Direct Instruction has produced significant gains in reading (Polloway, et al., 1986), for example, through the SRA Corrective Reading Program (Engelmann, Becker, Hanner, and Johnson, 1980). A more complete description of Direct Instruction can be found in the strategies for elementary-aged students in Chapter 6.

Metacognition   Metacognition refers to the recognition of the *way* one thinks about and controls his or her cognitive processes. Metacognition includes self-monitoring, predicting, reality testing, and coordinating the processes of studying and learning (deBettencourt, 1990). This instruction is particularly effective with adolescents with learning disabilities who have acquired a sense (albeit accurate or not) of their own learning and are more able to think directly about how they learn and how to apply methods and strategies to assist their learning. Metacognitive processes have been successfully paired with behavior modification to provide an approach which relies on both intrinsic student cognitions and extrinsic teacher-guided structure to change behaviors. Known as cognitive behavior modification

(CBM) (Meichenbaum, 1977), the approach follows several distinct steps. First, a teacher performs a task or instructs while simultaneously modeling the task. Next, the student performs the task under the direction of the teacher. The student then vocalizes the steps and practices the task by herself while the teacher is available for guidance. Finally, the student performs the task independently with no guidance while "talking" herself through it. Two things occur concurrently: the student assumes more responsibility for learning the task or concept as the teacher moves from the role of instructor to facilitator to observer.

CBM has served as the foundation for strategy instruction developed by many researchers (e.g., Hallahan and Sapona, 1983). Its pairing of instruction, cognitive processes, and eventual teacher relinquishment of responsibility for student learning provides an effective process for adolescents with learning disabilities to both acquire skills and generalize them to other settings. Cognitive strategies which call upon self-management and self-directed learning may prove to be successful in maintaining learning and generalizing it to other settings.

Friend and Bursuck (1996) contended that students with learning disabilities may develop "self-strategies" to help perform tasks independently. These strategies include self-instruction, self-monitoring, self-questioning, and self-reinforcement. In self-instruction, students guide themselves through self-talk through a process or task. Self-monitoring requires that students watch and check themselves for things such as time management, on task behaviors, when to use a strategy, etc. When students self-question, they ask themselves questions in their own words to help guide their learning. Students can use self-reinforcement to reward themselves for tasks completed or appropriate behavior. Although many of us use these self-strategies unconsciously to enhance our learning, it is important to note that students with learning disabilities have difficulties with these executive functioning processes and subsequently must be instructed as to how to use them.

"Academic strategy training" (Cullinan, Lloyd, and Epstein, 1981) combines task analysis and self-instruction to assist students with learning disabilities to strategically approach academic tasks. For example, a cognitive task like subtraction with borrowing is task-analyzed into its component steps. The teacher models the steps to complete the task, translating the steps into a "strategy" for tackling the problem. The student is taught the steps (which may include questions or prompts as well as instructions about what to do) prior to actually doing the task. Finally, the student applies the strategy with a representative task, using self-instruction, self-monitoring, self-reward, or other self-strategies as appropriate. Students with LD *can* acquire these internal strategies through the assistance of skilled professionals who can facilitate relevant strategy acquisition. The University of Kansas' Center for Research in Learning (CRL) has been at the forefront of strategy acquisition since 1977. We will explore their Strategies Intervention Model along with other effective strategic methods.

Strategies Intervention Model (SIM) The University of Kansas Center for Research on Learning (KU-CRL) began in 1977 to determine how setting demands differ from elementary to secondary schools for low achieving students and students with learning disabilities. They determined that secondary students spend more time reading for content, listening to lectures, and being responsible for content-laden mastery. They also found that teachers expect students to (1) know *if* they do not understand something, (2) know *when* to ask a question, (3) know *how* to ask the question to receive the answer they need, and (4) know *what* to do with the answer once they have received it. These skills are metacognitive in nature and are sometimes termed "executive functioning" skills because students must know when and how to utilize them. The UK team found that many students with learning disabilities lack executive functioning skills in acquiring knowledge, processing it, and expressing it (e.g., poor time management, poor-test taking skills, etc.).

The Strategies Intervention Model is the product of these empirical findings. It pairs the skills for acquiring content with the executive functioning skills necessary to retrieve and utilize the content. SIM utilizes elements from three contrasting constructs: (1) the reductionist approach, which is reducing cognition and behavior to smaller, more understandable parts to learn it, (2) the constructivist approach, where learning is constructed through active interface with new experiences by learners who bring their own unique backgrounds, and (3) the functionalist approach, which pragmatically selects the best approach to match the person, place, and time (Deshler, Ellis, and Lenz, 1996).

Each strategy incorporates a mnemonic device that "cues" the learner to both the purpose of the strategy and the steps to use it. Ellis, Lenz, and Scanlon (1996) described the components of an effective strategy that incorporates essential elements of learning, listed briefly below:

1. The strategy should contain a set of steps that lead to a specific and successful outcome.

2. The steps of the strategy should be sequenced in a manner that leads to an efficient approach to the task.

3. The steps of the strategy should cue the student to use specific cognitive strategies.

4. The steps of the strategy should cue the student to use metacognition.

5. The steps of the strategy should cue the student to select and use appropriate procedures, skills, or rules.

6. The steps of the strategy should cue the student to perform some type of overt physical action.

7. All of the overt physical actions should be supported by a clear explanation of the associated cognitive actions that need to take place.

8. All of the steps of the strategy should be able to be performed by an individual in a limited amount of time.

9. Unnecessary steps or explanations should be eliminated.

10. Information related to why to use the strategy, when to use the strategy, and where to use the strategy should be included.

11. The strategy should provide guidelines related to how to think and act when planning, executing, and evaluating performance on a task and its outcomes (pp. 9–11).

FIGURE 7.1

Anatomy of a Learning Strategy (Example: The Paraphrasing Strategy)

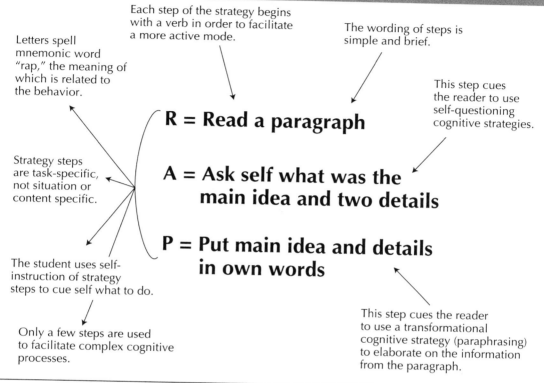

Each step of the strategy begins with a verb in order to facilitate a more active mode.

The wording of steps is simple and brief.

Letters spell mnemonic word "rap," the meaning of which is related to the behavior.

This step cues the reader to use self-questioning cognitive strategies.

R = Read a paragraph

Strategy steps are task-specific, not situation or content specific.

A = Ask self what was the main idea and two details

P = Put main idea and details in own words

The student uses self-instruction of strategy steps to cue self what to do.

Only a few steps are used to facilitate complex cognitive processes.

This step cues the reader to use a transformational cognitive strategy (paraphrasing) to elaborate on the information from the paragraph.

Source: Prepared by Edwin S. Ellis, © 1988

Figure 7.1 provides an example of a reading comprehension strategy.

In order to effectively utilize a strategy, SIM has developed a series of learning stages to instruct and implement strategic use. Figure 7.2 provides an overview of the stages of acquisition and generalization in the Strategies Intervention Model. With few exceptions, instruction in each of the strategies developed within the SIM follows this format.

The KU-CRL continues to research and develop new components of strategic and cognitive interventions. Figure 7.3 provides a limited example of some of the strategies developed to date for reading, writing, and test-taking.

Wong (1994), like the SIM, contended that generalization is the most important factor in strategic acquisition, and the hardest to facilitate. She argued that students with learning disabilities rarely have the time to reflect on the importance or use of the strategy; instead the teacher provides the rationales for the students without allowing for deeper thought and reflection. Wong believes that two components are critical for student transfer of learning strategies: (1) "mediated mindfulness" (p. 112) or engaging the student to want to learn the

FIGURE 7.2

Stages of Acquisition and Generalization—Strategies Intervention Model (SIM)

Stages:

1. **Pretest and Make Commitments**
   - make students aware of specific setting demands in classes, jobs, and community
   - ascertain how students are performing with regard to this demand
   - the existence of alternative approaches to meet this demand
   - students are informed of the results from other students who have used this strategy
   - provide a rationale for learning the strategy
   - obtain written commitment from student to learn strategy

2. **Describe the Strategy**
   - give rationales for using the strategy
   - describe the results that can be expected
   - become aware of the overt and covert processes involved in performing the new strategy
   - become aware of how the steps of the strategy are used
   - see how this strategy is different from previously used strategies
   - become motivated to learn the new strategy

3. **Model the Strategy**
   - demonstrate the entire process by "thinking aloud"
   - involve students in demonstration

4. **Verbal Elaboration and Rehearsal of the Strategy**
   - have students use their own words to describe what each step is designed to do and why it is important to the strategic process
   - have students commit the steps of the strategy via rote rehearsal
   - require mastery

5. **Controlled Practice and Feedback**
   - give students opportunities to practice using "easier" materials largely devoid of classroom demands
   - build the students' confidence and fluency in use of the strategy
   - students gradually take over strategy use from the teacher
   - provide positive and corrective feedback
   - require mastery

6. **Advanced Practice and Feedback**
   - provide a wide variety of grade-appropriate materials from regular coursework
   - structure assignments so that students must adapt the strategy for use
   - fade instructional prompts and cues so students become responsible for using the strategy themselves
   - provide positive and corrective feedback
   - require mastery

7. **Confirm Acquisition and Make Generalization Commitments**
   - confirm and document mastery of strategy use
   - celebrate results of efforts and commitments
   - explain goals of generalization process
   - obtain written commitment to generalize

(continued)

FIGURE 7.2

continued

8. Generalization

Phase One—Orientation
- make student aware of the necessity of applying the strategy in other relevant settings
- explain why strategy transfer and generalization is important
- identify ways in which to adapt the strategy for various settings
- identify cues which might signal use of the strategy

Phase Two—Activation
- prompt the student to use the strategy across settings
- monitor the student's application of the strategy
- prompt appropriate application of strategy when generalization does not occur
- enlist the help of others to solve problems and provide feedback

Phase Three—Adaptation
- discuss how the strategy can be modified to meet other setting demands
- assist student in modifying strategy appropriate to setting

Phase Four—Maintenance
- ensure that student uses strategy across time and settings
- conduct periodic reviews
- identify self-reinforcements and self-rewards

Source: Adapted from *Teaching Adolescents with Learning Disabilities: Strategies and Methods (2nd Ed.)*, pp. 37–55, by D.D. Deshler, E.S. Ellis, and B.K. Lenz (1996). Denver: Love Publishing. Reprinted with permission.

strategy on his or her own volition, and (2) providing structured practice to promote transfer to other settings. She urges educators and researchers to "instruct their students to engage in *reflective abstraction* (italics added) of strategies learned and to attempt transfer-promoting instruction" (p. 118).

Other researchers have also developed many fine metacognitive processes with which to aid students. These include, but are not limited to reciprocal teaching (Palinscar and Brown, 1988); self-monitoring (Hallahan and Sapona, 1983); teaching revision skills through interactive teaching (Wong, Wong, Darlington, and Jones, 1991); teaching reasoning skills (Greenan and Jarwan, 1994); and many others. What all researchers share is the belief that adolescents with learning disabilities must be responsible for their own learning; they must "learn" to see their abilities as intrinsic to themselves, not imposed upon them.

Life Skills Instructional Approaches

Just as educators have recognized the need for adolescents with learning disabilities to assume responsibility for their learning and behavior, educators are also discovering an increasing need for relevant instruction and content.

FIGURE 7.3

Selected Reading, Writing and Test-Taking Strategies From the Strategies Intervention Model (SIM)

Reading Strategy Instruction
1. Paraphrasing Reading Strategy (RAP)
To facilitate reading comprehension by reading, asking what the paragraph was about, then rephrasing it in student's own words
2. Word Identification Strategy (DISSECT)
To apply decoding rules to words including base words, prefixes, suffixes, and stems
3. Text Perusal Strategy (PARTS)
To analyze the major and minor sections of chapter parts and determine questions that might be asked of the reader
4. Strategy for Analyzing Visual Aids (SNIPS)
To learn to use visual aids to aid in reading comprehension

Writing Strategy Instruction
1. Sentence Writing Strategy (PENS)
Students become more fluid in their writing through the acquisition of sentence patterns.
2. Writing Strategy (DEFENDS)
Students look at specific situations, perceive key elements about which to write, and learn to organize their thoughts.
3. Editing and Revising Strategy (SEARCH)
To aid students in effectively monitoring editing and revision processes with a range of written products

Memory and Test-Taking Strategies
1. Key-word Mnemonic Strategy (LINCS)
To "link" a key word used in studying to a visual (a word that sounds like the key word) and to associate the two to assist in retrieval
2. First-letter Mnemonic Strategy (FIRST and LISTS)
Includes one strategy to design a first letter mnemonic list and another strategy to make and memorize lists
3. Objective Test-Taking Strategy (PIRATES)
Designed to assist students in taking objective tests, including time allotment, guessing, reading instruction, reviewing answers
4. Essay Test-Taking Strategy (ANSWERS)
Designed to assist students in organizing better responses to essay exams through outlining, providing details, and writing an introduction with supporting evidence

Source: Adapted from *Teaching Adolescents with Learning Disabilities:* Strategies and Methods (2nd Ed). by D.D. Deshler, E.S. Ellis, & B.K. Lenz, 1996. Denver: Love Publishing. Reprinted with permission.

Instruction which reflects the imminent needs of adulthood engages students and increases not only their achievement but overall success. Wagner et al. (1991) found that occupationally-oriented classes helped to decrease truancy, absenteeism, and drop out rates while raising GPAs and positive statements of schooling by students with disabilities. Providing a link to positive adult outcomes through meaningful content lies at the heart of life skills instruction.

Cronin and Patton (1993) found that few students with disabilities were being prepared for the plethora of adult tasks they faced. Many of these students felt disenfranchised from school and dropped out, ill-prepared to deal with the realities of post-school life. Further, few school programs prioritized life skills instruction as critical for exiting students. Many researchers now believe that schools, at the elementary and secondary levels, must address both the functional and academic needs of students (Clark, Field, Patton, Brolin, and Sitlington, 1994; Edgar, 1987; Halpern, 1994). Based on their identified needs among adolescents, Karge, Patton, and de la Garza (1992) suggested a range of instructional strategies to enhance skills in job seeking and keeping, mobility and transportation, leisure/recreation, and self-advocacy in IEP meetings, among other areas.

Developing a Life Skills Curriculum   Cronin and Patton (1993) have developed a model for developing and infusing life skills into curricula and coursework from elementary through secondary grades. Philosophically, they built a foundation for the integration of life skills by framing all instruction as it applies to future environments. Each instructional moment should count as if it were the student's last scholastic day before entering the adult world.

Six domains represent a holistic view of what adults experience (Cronin and Patton, 1993):

- employment and education
- home and family
- leisure/recreation pursuits
- community involvement
- emotional and physical health
- personal responsibilities and relationships.

Under each of these domains are subdomains or subcategories for understanding the complex tasks of each domain. Major life demands within each subcompetency define the events or activities typically encountered by adults in everyday life. These, in turn, can be supported by life skills instruction in order to successfully negotiate major life demands. Figure 7.4 illustrates the organization of this construct.

Life skills instruction and content can be implemented across grade levels and curricula. They can be taught as a distinct set of courses or as one course (the most popular model in secondary schools). Life skills can also be augmented into core content as a related topical unit that links relevance to traditional coursework. Finally, life skills can be infused into existing content in small, meaningful chunks that immediately provide relevance to the learner without undue effort on the part of the instructor. Table 7.1 offers comparisons of the various options for teaching life skills across grades and content. A number of easy-to-access materials have been developed to accompany a curricular framework for life skills instruction, such as Mannix's (1995) set of secondary life skills activities that range from health and sex education to finding a job.

Life-Centered Career Education Curriculum   Brolin (1993) began development of an extensive K–12 functional curriculum 20 years ago and has been implementing and refining it since that time. *The Life-Centered Career*

FIGURE 7.4

Conceptual Sequencing to Organize for Instruction in Life Skills

PROCESS

EXAMPLE

Adult Domains

Employment/Education
- Home and family
- Leisure pursuits
- Community involvement
- Emotional/physical health
- Personal responsibilities and relationships

Subdomain

General Job Skills
- Employment setting considerations
- Education/training
- Career refinement and re-evaluation

Major Life Demand
Specific Life Skills

Seeking and Securing a Job
- Identifying marketable job skills and interests
- Identifying sources of job possibilities
- Using all sources of available jobs to identify appropriate jobs for the skills you possess
- Sending letters of inquiry or making calls of inquiry regarding the job, its availability, and application procedures
- Locating the site of the prospective job on the map
- Determining transportation needs for prospective jobs
- Obtaining and filling out a job application
- Calling for an interview appointment
- Recording time, place, location, and name of person interviewing for future reference
- Determining appropriate dress for interview
- Practicing interview skills
- Generating list of questions to ask about the job
- Computing weekly or monthly income
- Calculating mileage to work
- Asking about subsequent evaluations of job performance
- Identifying appropriate dress for the job

Source: From M. Cronin and J. Patton (1993). Life skills instruction for all students with special needs (p. 20). Austin, TX: PRO-ED.

TABLE 7.1

Comparison of Various Options for Teaching Life Skills Content

Curricular Option	Nature of Curricular Approach	Appropriateness for		Appropriateness for		Curricular Example
		Regular Education	Special Education	Elementary Level	Secondary Level	
Infusion into existing content	Infusion	Y	Y	Y	Y	Working in a discussion of how to treat athlete's foot when the topic of fungus is covered in a general science textbook
Dedicated portion of course	Augmentation	Y	Y	Y	Y	Unit on "the financial implications of dating" in addition to the regular content of a "consumer math" course
Generic life skills course	Distinct course	(Y)	Y	N	Y	Course entitled "Life 101"
Topical life skills course	Distinct course	(Y)	Y	N	Y	Course entitled "Math in the Real World"
Comprehensive arrangement of life skills courses	Distinct set of courses	Y/N	Y	N	Y	Set of courses such as: Personal Finance Practical Math Health and Hygiene Everyday Science Practical Communications Community Awareness and Involvement Occupational Development Interpersonal Relations

Source: From M. Cronin and J. Patton (1993). *Life skills instruction for all students with special needs* (p. 26). Austin, TX: PRO-ED.

Education (LCCE) curriculum offers assessment and instructional activities in three major domains: personal (self-care, home management), social (interpersonal skills, access of local resources), and occupational (job search, application, and job maintenance) skills. LCCE's implementation is proposed through a variety of activities, including role-playing, cooperative learning, mentorships, community-based instruction, work experiences, and many other techniques linked to real life application. Teachers across the United States find the LCCE competencies (see Figure 7.5) and activities useful for students with mild, moderate, and even severe disability levels. Brolin (1995) presented the entire curricular framework, including the LCCE, within a lifelong learning model.

Career Ladder Program   Siegel and his colleagues (1993) developed the *Career Ladder Program* to meet the needs of older adolescents with severe learning disabilities and others for whom dropping out, unemployment, and other maladaptive activities were the likely outcomes of ineffective educational programs. Designed as a philosophical framework, transition planning procedure, and community-based instructional program, the Career Ladder Program links students with employers for mentorships, job tryouts, training, and work experiences. The community becomes the classroom, with sites and experiences designed to address the individual's interests, goals, capacities, and needs.

TRAC   The *Trade-Related Academic Competencies (TRAC)* program (Minskoff and DeMoss, 1993) is a vocational education model designed for students with learning problems. Work-related behaviors (e.g., safety rules, reading instructions) and specific vocational skills for several common occupations (e.g., accounting, child care, word processing) are documented for preassessment, instruction, and post-testing.

Social Skills Instruction   Two important self-advocacy curricula are described in the individualized planning section, since they deal primarily with advocacy for self within transition and IEP meetings. Another self-advocacy curriculum that teaches prerequisite social skill acquisition is the *Learning with PURPOSE* curriculum by Serna and Lau-Smith (1995). This set of manuals teaches students to self-evaluate, self-direct, network, collaborate, take risks, and deal with stress.

Other curricula which were developed for social skills instruction with students with learning disabilities include:

- *Social Skills for Daily Living* (Schumaker, Hazel, & Pederson, 1988, American Guidance Service)
- *ASSET* (Hazel, Schumaker, Sherman, and Sheldon-Wildgen, 1981, Research Press)
- *ACCESS* (Walker, Todis, Holmes, and Horton, 1988, PRO-ED)
- *Skillstreaming the Adolescent* (Goldstein, Sprafkin, Gershaw, and Klein, 1980, Research Press)

Each of these approaches involves structured, sequential instruction of specific social skills through demonstration and modeling, problem-solving, role-playing, and practice with feedback. However, Elksnin, and Elksnin (1991) reviewed these programs for their generalizability to vocational training programs and jobs and found them to offer varying degrees of these generalizable interpersonal skills.

Work Experiences Students with learning disabilities can and should benefit from structured, supervised work experience programs that rotate through a variety of occupations, preferably over four years or more. Several statewide follow-up studies have discovered that having a paid job during school is one of the most important predictors of employment success after school. These work experiences may even begin in middle school, for an hour a month, and gradually increase to committed work placements by the senior year that may involve as much as 20 hours per week. Service delivery options through which work experiences readily operate include community-based instruction (CBI), vocational education cooperative programs, special education work-study programs, service learning programs, and internships. Local tech prep agreements may provide additional opportunities for connected vocational-technical training that flows between the high school and the community college, through applied academics, linkages with employers, and concurrent enrollment capacities. Recent emphases on preapprenticeship and apprenticeship programs offer yet another arena of great potential value to youth with learning disabilities who select particular occupations.

▶ TRANSITION SERVICES AND SUPPORTS

Dunn (1996) documented, and decried, the lack of opportunity that students with learning disabilities have experienced for carefully examining themselves,

Students with learning disabilities should be involved in planning their own transition programs.

FIGURE 7.5

Life-Centered Career Education Competencies

Curriculum Area	Competency	Subcompetency: The student will be able to:		
Daily Living Skills	1. Managing Personal Finances	1. Count money and make correct change	2. Make responsible expenditures	
	2. Selecting and Managing a Household	7. Maintain home exterior/interior	8. Use basic appliances and tools	
	3. Caring for Personal Needs	12. Demonstrate knowledge of physical fitness, nutrition and weight	13. Exhibit proper grooming and hygiene	
	4. Raising Children and Meeting Marriage Responsibilities	17. Demonstrate physical care for raising children	18. Know psychological aspects of raising children	
	5. Buying, Preparing and Consuming Food	20. Purchase food	21. Clean food preparation areas	
	6. Buying and Caring for Clothing	26. Wash/clean clothing	27. Purchase clothing	
	7. Exhibiting Responsible Citizenship	29. Demonstrate knowledge of civil rights and responsibilities	30. Know nature of local, state and federal governments	
	8. Utilizing Recreational Facilities and Engaging in Leisure	33. Demonstrate knowledge of available community resources	34. Choose and plan activities	
	9. Getting Around the Community	38. Demonstrates knowledge of traffic rules and safety	39. Demonstrate knowledge and use of various means of transportation	
Personal Social Skills	10. Achieving Self-Awareness	42. Identify physical and psychological needs	43. Identify interests and abilities	
	11. Acquiring Self-Confidence	46. Express feelings of self-worth	47. Describe others' perception of self	
	12. Achieving Socially Responsible Behavior— Community	51. Develop respect for the rights and properties of others	52. Recognize authority and follow instructions	
	13. Maintaining Good Interpersonal Skills	56. Demonstrate listening and responding skills	57. Establish and maintain close relationships	
	14. Achieving Independence	59. Strive toward self-actualization	60. Demonstrate self-organization	

3. Keep basic financial records	4. Calculate and pay taxes	5. Use credit responsibly	6. Use banking services	
9. Select adequate housing	10. Set up household	11. Maintain home grounds		
14. Dress appropriately	15. Demonstrate knowledge of common illness, prevention and treatment	16. Practice personal safety		
19. Demonstrate marriage responsibilities				
22. Store food	23. Prepare meals	24. Demonstrate appropriate eating habits	25. Plan/eat balanced meals	
28. Iron, mend and store clothing				
31. Demonstrate knowledge of the law and ability to follow the law	32. Demonstrate knowledge of citizen rights and responsibilities			
35. Demonstrate knowledge of the value of recreation	36. Engage in group and individual activities	37. Plan vacation time		
40. Find way around the community	41. Drive a car			
44. Identify emotions	45. Demonstrate knowledge of physical self			
48. Accept and give praise	49. Accept and give criticism	50. Develop confidence in oneself		
53. Demonstrate appropriate behavior in public places	54. Know important character traits	55. Recognize personal roles		
58. Make and maintain friendships				
61. Demonstrate awareness of how one's behavior affects others				

(continued)

FIGURE 7.5

continued

Curriculum Area	Competency	Subcompetency: The student will be able to:	
	15. Making Adequate Decisions	62. Locate and utilize sources of assistance	63. Anticipate consequences
	16. Communicating with Others	67. Recognize and respond to emergency situations	68. Communicate with understanding
Occupational Guidance and Preparation	17. Knowing and Exploring Occupational Possibilities	70. Identify remunerative aspects of work	71. Locate sources of occupational and training information
	18. Selecting and Planning Occupational Choices	76. Make realistic occupational choices	77. Identify requirements of appropriate and available jobs
	19. Exhibiting Appropriate Work Habits and Behaviors	81. Follow directions and observe regulations	82. Recognize importance of attendance and punctuality
	20. Seeking, Securing and Maintaining Employment	88. Search for a job	89. Apply for a job
	21. Exhibiting Sufficient Physical Manual Skills	94. Demonstrate stamina and endurance	95. Demonstrate satisfactory balance and coordination
	22. Obtaining Specific Occupational Skills		

Source: From D. Brolin (1993). *Life centered career education: A competency-based approach.* Reston, VA: Council for Exceptional Children.

their strengths, their goals, and their needs holistically. The rationales presented by Dunn for transition planning and services for these students set the stage for a series of compelling arguments about transition programming in several areas (Patton and Blalock, 1996). The curricular and instruction areas have been discussed within the "Learner Options" section of this chapter. Addressed in the section below are three major transition supports or services (assessment, individualized transition planning within the IEP, and transition teams), as well as sets of specific transition techniques for movement from one level to the next.

Functional/Career/Transition Assessment

DCDT's position statement on transition included *student self-evaluation* as one of the four major cornerstones of the transition planning process (Halpern,

64. Develop and evaluate alternatives	65. Recognize nature of a problem	66. Develop goal-seeking behavior		
69. Know subtleties of communication				
72. Identify personal values met through work	73. Identify societal values met through work	74. Classify jobs into occupational categories	75. Investigate local occupational and training opportunities	
78. Identify occupational aptitudes	79. Identify major occupational interests	80. Identify major occupational needs		
83. Recognize importance of supervision	84. Demonstrate knowledge of occupational safety	85. Work with others	86. Meet demands for quality work	87. Work at a satis-factory rate
90. Interview for a job	91. Know how to maintain post-school occupa-tional adjustment	92. Demonstrate knowledge of competitive standards	93. Know how to adjust to changes in employment	
96. Demonstrate manual dexterity	97. Demonstrate sensory discrimination			
There are no specific subcompetencies as they depend on skill being taught.				

1994). The shift to student control over the process is congruent with the field's shift toward helping students develop greater independence and self-determination, as well as contributing to one's quality of life (Dennis, Williams, Giangreco, and Cloninger, 1993; Halpern, 1993). "The assessment procedures that accompany transition planning should involve teaching students with disabilities how to evaluate themselves, taking into consideration a variety of assessment areas and findings" (Halpern, 1994, p. 119). The areas in which such self-assessment should occur include academic, vocational, social/behavioral, personal, and independent living goals, interests, and abilities or aptitudes. Ongoing, informal assessment procedures (which students can and should learn much more readily than standardized testing) should be emphasized throughout the students' middle and high school years. Blalock (1996) outlined a possible level system for vocational or functional assessment for students with varying degrees of learning disabilities that specifies information to be targeted and responsible professionals to support that process. A comprehensive review of transition assessment can be found in Clark (1996).

Individualized Transition Planning within the IEP: An Outcomes Orientation that Starts in Elementary School

One of the most powerful tools for ensuring successful transitions from high school to adulthood is transition planning within the IEP. Students with learning disabilities are extremely heterogeneous as a group. Each individual's focus for the future will vary from all the others, so no single approach to transition planning will be effective. By requiring transition planning within the IEP, IDEA's mandate has helped to ensure that an outcomes orientation is closely linked to instructional design and that both are based *on each student's unique strengths, needs, goals, and interests,* as well as on family goals. Reiff and deFur (1992) developed a Transition Services Planning Guide that helps the IEP team identify desired outcomes and link those to annual goals, objectives, and activities (see Figure 7.6).

Individualized transition planning, according to the DCDT position statement (Halpern, 1994), should occur no later than age fourteen for all students with exceptionalities so that each individual has a chance to reach his or her stated goal(s). Transition planning must be based on sound student self-evaluation, discussed above, and should specify the coordinated set of services and curricular options in which the student will participate. The IEP team, when engaged in transition planning, should include all persons involved in the student's current and future life: counselor, administrator, general and special educators, transition or career development coordinator, adult agency staff, postsecondary institution representatives, employer, other social services staff, or correctional staff if applicable. If adult service providers are unable to attend the preliminary transition planning meetings (e.g., in eighth to tenth grade), then (1) the school personnel should forward information about the potential consumer to the agency for advance planning purposes, and (2) the agency should be encouraged to attend the later transition planning meetings (eleventh and twelfth grades).

Transition Teams and School-Community Partnerships: Students, Families, Agencies, Employers

Interagency collaboration is a must if IDEA's mandate for a coordinated set of services is to be realized (Hallahan, et al., 1996). Reiff and deFur (1992) referred to this activity as "intracommunity," with students and families constituting the "centerpiece of the team" (p. 246). Local transition teams also include employers, adult service providers, correctional programs, postsecondary education, and schools. For a more comprehensive review of transition teams, Blalock (1996a) discussed the importance of community transition teams as a foundation for transition services for youth with learning disabilities. Major purposes of such collaboration include:

- development of a continuum of needed services within a community or state

FIGURE 7.6

Transition Services Planning Guide

Based on_____(student's name) interests, aptitudes, and needs, the following desired post-secondary transition outcomes have been identified to date _____:

Desired Post-Secondary Education Outcome(s)	Desired Post-Secondary Employment Outcome(s)	Desired Post-Secondary Community Living Outcome(s)
Adult Education _____	Full-Time Competitive Employment _____	Living Alone, with Friends or Partner _____
Vocational Training _____	Part-Time Competitive Employment _____	Living with Family _____
Community College _____	Full-Time Supported Employment _____	Transportation Independently _____
College or University _____	Part-Time Supported Employment _____	Transportation Support _____
Tech Prep _____	Apprenticeship _____	Independent Living Support _____
Other _____	Sheltered Workshop _____	Community Participation _____
	Other _____	Other _____
Specialized transition services or planning needed in this area? Yes_____ No_____	Specialized transition services or planning needed in this area? Yes_____ No_____	Specialized transition services or planning needed in this area? Yes_____ No_____

Statement of Needed Transition Services:
Based on_____(student's name) interests, needs and desired post-secondary outcomes identified, this IEP team has determined that _____ is in need of specialized transition services and/or support in the following areas:

Desired Long-Range Outcome: _____

Annual Goal: _____

Annual Objective(s) _____

Activities/Resources: _____

Time Line(s): _____ Review Date: _____

Person(s)/Agencies Responsible: _____

Source: From Reiff, H.B. and deFur, S. (1992). Transition for youths with learning disabilities: A focus on developing independence. *Learning Disability Quarterly* 15 (4), p. 243. Reprinted with permission, Council for Learning Disabilities.

- reduction of duplication of efforts
- maximizing limited resources
- helping systems change to better meet individual and family needs
- providing a cadre of helpful people who can provide supports when needed.

In some localities, interagency agreements or memoranda of understanding that specify each partner's responsibilities in the overall transition program have helped clarify roles, strengthen the commitments to the program, and support continuity when turnovers occur.

Parental support of and participation in the transition process is discussed as an essential component of transition programming in every arena where the topic arises. Several sources offer strategies for enhancing family involvement in transition, such as informally assessing their educational and vocational goals for their children about to enter high school (Blalock, 1995); using the IEP as a report card to monitor progress toward goals (Blalock, et al., 1994), and assigning young children chores and rewarding them with a small allowance (Brotherson, Berdine, and Sartini, 1993).

Transitions From Middle to High School

Classroom teachers, with their middle-grade students, can plan a variety of simple, ongoing interventions that will prepare them for the move to high school and that will also serve as informal transition planning. Blalock (1996b) outlined several of those options, such as meeting with students from the ninth and tenth grades to get questions answered, vocational interest assessment, parent inventories about their goals for their child, and development of more sophisticated study and learning strategies.

Transitions From High School to Adulthood

Zigmond (1990) proposed two models for students—one for those aiming for college and the other for those likely to seek employment after graduation. Each model consists of four elements: basic skills instruction, survival skills instruction, completion of required courses for graduation, and planning for life after school. The differences between the models lie in the distribution of courses by general and special educators. For example, the college bound model includes primarily mainstream academic classes; special education support for those courses occurs through monitoring or consultation, and other support is provided through instruction of annual reading, survival skills, and study hall classes. In the non-college-bound model, the vocational educators may be the only general educator instructing the student. Both models pay special attention to the ninth grade load, so that students can start off successfully.

Sitlington (1996) described the neglect which professionals have shown to the aspects of living that also plague young adults with learning disabilities if they enter adulthood unprepared. Her recommendations to the field include research directions (efficacy of approaches that address life skills, more holistic foci of follow-up studies) as well as programmatic guidelines. Infusion of life skills instruction into general education and personnel preparation programs and development of more relevant assessment models were two of her compelling endorsements.

SUMMARY

This chapter has presented information on adolescents with learning disabilities and the transition from school to post-school environments. The following points summarize the major areas included in the chapter:

- Adolescence is a critical juncture for preparing to embrace the rest of one's life; decisions made in eighth or ninth grade may make or break achievement of a post-school goal.

- Consideration by the IEP team for specialized transition services related to physical and emotional health, lifelong learning, interpersonal skills, career development, and community life options is required by law by age sixteen.

- Educational programs at the secondary level must broaden the context within which the person must function to include roles, abilities, experiences, and goals for family, school, work, and community.

- Research findings have demonstrated the efficacy of certain programs and approaches that emphasize student ownership of the educational process: self-awareness, self-determination, self-evaluation, and the self as primary agent in planning.

- Studies have also shown that remedial programs still have a place in secondary special education.

- Specific strategies for preparing for transitions from one school stage to the next, or from high school to adulthood, provide connecting activities that can enhance successful adjustments.

Chapter 8

LEARNING DISABILITIES IN ADULTHOOD[1]

The objectives for this chapter are as follows:

- ▶ To understand that learning disabilities continue into adulthood.

- ▶ To understand the impact of learning disabilities on adult functioning.

- ▶ To appreciate the challenges to our traditional concepts of competency faced by adults with learning disabilities.

- ▶ To understand the general cognitive, educational, psychosocial, and vocational characteristics of adults with learning disabilities.

- ▶ To identify reasons for increased postsecondary enrollment by individuals with learning disabilities.

- ▶ To gain an appreciation of the demands of the postsecondary environment and the

types of accommodations deemed appropriate for students with learning disabilities.

- ▶ To understand conceptually the approach to making an appropriate match between a student's need for services and a postsecondary institution's ability to provide accommodations.

- ▶ To understand the demands of the work environment.

- ▶ To gain an appreciation of Sections 503 and 504 of the Rehabilitation Act of 1973, the Americans with Disabilities Act, and the types of accommodations deemed reasonable for adults with learning disabilities in the workplace.

[1]This chapter was written by Craig A. Michaels

256

▶ To understand conceptually the approach to making an appropriate match within the context of the work environment.

▶ To gain an appreciation of other nondegree postsecondary options for adults with learning disabilities.

▶ To understand the personal functional needs of adults with learning disabilities within the social and independent living areas.

▶ To gain an appreciation of person-centered planning strategies which can be utilized to empower adults with learning disabilities to create positive visions for the future.

What Do Adults with Learning Disabilities Have to Say?

Open your eyes and see, Brian.

You spelled this wrong, Brian.

We're tired of hearing excuses, Brian.

Do you want to fail, Brian?

You are going to need people to help you, Brian.

You are starting to improve now, Brian.

If you would just put in a little extra time you can do it, Brian.

We finally found something you're good at, Brian, math.

You're starting to open your eyes, Brian.

We realize you are capable, Brian.

Soon you will be on your own, Brian.

You can do it, Brian.

Just (if you would) open your eyes!

(Brian Sultzer, February 14, 1996, personal communication)

I am here today because I am a person with specific learning disabilities or SLD. I was not diagnosed with this disability until I was thirty years old. . . . I was diagnosed quite by accident, when my daughter was being tested to see whether she qualified for a gifted school program. I mentioned to the tester how I did poorly on certain segments of the tests my daughter was taking. She asked me if I had trouble spelling and writing, as well as other things. I was quite taken aback as she know [sic] my deep secrets so quickly. The tester informed me that the areas that I was weak in were the areas where persons with learning disabilities were weak. "Learning Disabilities, What's that?" was my response. That day, it was confirmed that my daughter was a genius, and I was in fact not an idiot. . . . My success in turning my life around resulted from what I call the FOUR R's: Recognition, Remediation (or relearning how to learn), Rehabilitation (or appropriate job training), and Reasonable Accommodation (or the effective use of alternative means of displaying knowledge and skills.) The key is recognition. Without the understanding that there is a disability, the knowledge of the specific services and accommodations that help that particular disability, I could not move forward. (Glenn Young, 1995, pp. 4–5)

I AM my learning disability. Buried deep within, there exists a frustration and yes, even a sadness, that others cannot even understand. But there is also a resilience, a buoyancy, a wisdom and sensitivity born from pain that others cannot even have. In addition, there is a compassion for and tolerance of others—a patience and calmness that comes from knowing that all things will improve if nurtured gently and skillfully. These qualities are solely mine. These are gifts to me from my past. Without my learning disability, I would be weaker. I would be less tolerant, less empathetic, less patient and kind. I would be less joyful—for the lows intensify the highs. Because of my learning disability, I have learned to laugh. I have learned to wait. I have learned to take risks. I have learned to persevere. I have learned to stretch myself in many directions at once. I have learned to live minute by minute and to find joy and wonder and goodness in almost everything. . . . Without my learning disability, I would be half of who I am now. I AM my learning disability. We are one. We are inseparable. And, finally, we are friends. (Trudy Winstead, 1995, p. 7)

We now know that learning disabilities are not outgrown in childhood. Learning disabilities continue and, in fact, may even intensify in adulthood as task and environmental demands change (Michaels, 1994a; Michaels, et al., 1988). Learning disabilities present fundamental challenges to our society's basic assumptions and perceptions about success, work, and adulthood that we have yet to deal with. These assumptions are most eloquently stated by Kopp, Miller, and Mukley (1984):

1. Intelligent people are good readers. Poor readers are not very intelligent.

2. Highly motivated people set goals, develop plans, and make efficient use of their time. People who have few goals are disorganized and do not use time wisely; they are unmotivated and generally lazy.

3. The ability to concentrate on a task and learn quickly is an indication of high level of intelligence. People who are easily distracted and learn slowly are not capable of learning very much.

4. People who care about those around them are sensitive to the needs of others. People who are not perceptive of other's feelings do not really care about the needs of other people.

5. People with a good attitude towards work on one job will do well on another job whether they like it or not. People who display a "don't care" attitude on one job will display the same attitude on other jobs (p. 4).

These challenges to our basic assumptions and perceptions about success, work, and adulthood, i.e., competency, are reflections of what Snow (1994) has termed our embracing of "the disability paradigm." From the vantage point of this paradigm, we (as a society) have become convinced that "only young, happy and otherwise perfect people are eligible for fulfillment. Until we attain these three conditions we consider ourselves wounded in our ability to be creative or to make a contribution" (Snow, 1994, p. 13).

As reflected in the personal stories of the adults presented in the opening vignette and the anecdotal life experiences of most adults with learning disabilities, the internal resolution of these assumptions about adulthood and competency is at the heart of the challenges faced by adults with learning disabilities. Transmuting learning disabilities (and society's perceptions of learning disabilities) into a gift which contributes to an individual's uniqueness is the lesson many adults with learning disabilities are somewhere in the process of internalizing. As West pointed out:

> many [adults with learning disabilities] have achieved success or even greatness not in spite of but because of their apparent disabilities. . . . [W]hat is being suggested here is that for a certain group of people the handicap itself may be fundamentally and essentially associated with a gift. For some the handicap and the gift may be two aspects of the same thing. How we perceive it depends entirely on the context (1991, p. 19).

A more realistic picture of the general perception of learning disabilities and the general approach to research on the topic of learning disabilities was presented by Norman Geschwind, a neurologist, in his 1982 address to the Orton Dyslexia Society in which he described the general disbelief among his colleagues as he continued to try to investigate the potential advantages of being learning disabled:

> I had the experience recently of raising the issue [the advantages of the predisposition to dyslexia] at a meeting on the genetics of speech and language disorders

only to find that this suggestion was greeted with incredulity by many of the attendants, who could not conceive what possible advantages dyslexia might confer on its bearer (cited in West, 1991, p. 19).

▶ THE ADULT AGENDA

The realization that learning disabilities continue into adulthood has led to a new agenda in relation to the supports and intervention services that persons with learning disabilities may require across the life span and across educational, employment, and community environments. As Patton and Polloway pointed out, "Not only are [the] individuals with learning disabilities [identified through special education programs created by P.L. 94–142] becoming adults, but the field of learning disabilities has also 'grown up'" (1996, p. 2).

This new framework and growth in the field of adults with learning disabilities is reflected in the 1988 definition proposed by the National Joint Committee for Learning Disabilities (NJCLD) which highlighted the fact that learning disabilities are "intrinsic to the individual, presumed to be due to central nervous system dysfunction, *and may occur across the lifespan* [emphasis added]" (p. 1). In 1985 the NJCLD issued a position paper on adults with learning disabilities which bore the subheading of *A Call to Action*. The recommendations made in their call to action (as summarized in Table 8.1) are still relevant today.

The growth of interest in adults with learning disabilities, or perhaps the field's response to the NJCLD's call for action, is demonstrated in the rise in attention to adult issues in professional journals. Patton and Polloway (1996) indicated that the *Journal of Learning Disabilities* addressed adult issues in about three percent of their articles in 1985. This percentage had grown to 13 percent in 1990. *Learning Disabilities Quarterly* was also addressing adult issues in about three percent of its articles in 1985. By 1990 this percentage increased to about 28 percent.

▶ CHARACTERISTICS OF ADULTS WITH LEARNING DISABILITIES

The General Perspective of Adults with Learning Disabilities

In 1994 the Learning Disabilities Association of America (LDA) conducted a needs assessment of its membership through the Adult Issues Committee (LDA Newsbriefs, 1994). The LDA sample was made up of 587 individuals from 48 states with the majority (more than 57 percent) being adults with learning disabilities. The greatest areas of need (or the highest area of difficulty) for these adults were identified as difficulties with social relations (56 percent), postsecondary education and training (53 percent), and job/career advancement (40

TABLE 8.1

National Joint Committee on Learning Disabilities Recommendations Regarding Adults with Learning Disabilities

1. Programs must be initiated to increase public and professional awareness and understanding of the manifestations and needs of adults with learning disabilities.

2. Selection of appropriate education and vocational training programs and employment for adults with learning disabilities is predicated on a clear understanding of how their condition influences their learning and performance.

3. Throughout the school years, individuals with learning disabilities must have access to a range of program and service options that will prepare them to make the transition from secondary to postsecondary or vocational settings.

4. Alternative programs and services must be provided for adults with learning disabilities who have failed to obtain a high school diploma.

5. Adults with learning disabilities must have an active role in determining the course of their postsecondary or vocational efforts.

6. Consistent with the Rehabilitation Act of 1973 and regulations implementing Section 504 of that Act, appropriate federal, state, and local agencies as well as postsecondary and vocational training programs should continue the development and implementation of effective programs that will allow adults with learning disabilities the opportunity to attain career goals. Also, consistent with Section 504, postsecondary programs, colleges, vocational schools, employers, and governmental agencies should be aware of the nondiscriminatory testing requirements for the handicapped. (It should be noted that these recommendations precede the passing of the Americans with Disabilities Act (ADA) in 1990. The ADA makes the points discussed in item # 6 applicable to the public sector as well.)

7. The development of systematic programs of research that will address the status and needs of adults with learning disabilities is essential for the provision of appropriate services.

8. Curricula must be developed and incorporated in preparation programs for professionals in such disciplines as education, vocational and rehabilitative counseling, social work, psychology, medicine, and law to inform these professionals about the problems and needs of adults with learning disabilities.

9. Mental health professionals must be aware of the unique personal, social and emotional difficulties that individuals with learning disabilities may experience throughout their lives.

Source: National Joint Committee on Learning Disabilities. (1985, February). *Adults with learning disabilities: A call to action.*

percent). In addition to learning disabilities, 39 percent of the sample identified attention deficit disorders (ADD) as a secondary disability. Disorders related to depression or anxiety were also identified by 38 percent and 32 percent of the population respectively.

The types of intervention services and/or treatment received by adults were listed as evaluation (66 percent), tutoring (60 percent), psychological therapy and educational support (47 percent), vocational counseling (33 percent), language therapy (27 percent), and medical services (25 percent). When asked about the services that would be most required either by them or other adults with learning disabilities in the future they reported: job placement services (28 percent); educational support services (27 percent); social and vocational skill training (24 percent); and vocational counseling, support groups, job coaching, peer support services, and advocacy services (22 percent) (LDA Newsbriefs, 1994).

▶ A WORD OF CAUTION

The reader is cautioned at this point that for ease of presentation, the characteristics of an extremely heterogeneous population, namely adults with learning disabilities, will be presented in generalities which might unfortunately imply homogeneity. As Gottesman (1994) noted "In general background and attributes, adults with learning disabilities are as heterogeneous a group as those adults without learning disabilities. Adults with learning disabilities are also far from homogeneous in their symptomatology" (p. 6).

A second caution to the reader is that characteristics will be presented in isolation as if they reside only within the individual. The characteristics of adults with learning disabilities should idealistically be viewed within a context that is both holistic and ecological grounded (Gaylord-Ross and Browder, 1991; Schalock, 1986). This notion of viewing learning disabilities within a framework which is holistic refers to viewing *both* the inherent central nervous process differences of the individual and the role that society plays through the embracing of the disability paradigm (e.g., Snow, 1994) in promoting and inhibiting the development of competency (Michaels, 1997). Society (and more specifically service providers, parents, and the educational system) can play a critical role in the prevention of damage to the developing sense of self and competency among individuals with learning disabilities. Currently, by the time many individuals with learning disabilities reach adolescence and adulthood, their sense of competency, willingness to dream, and ability to actively participate in creating a vision for their future (Mount, 1992) have been severely diminished (Michaels, 1997).

The concept of ecological grounding refers to viewing the processing differences of the individual within the context of a given task within a given environment. Thus, as the characteristics of adults with learning disabilities are presented, the reader should realize that an attempt should be made to consider those characteristics in relation to the functional demands of a variety of "real world" environments in which we expect adults to perform successfully. This notion of an adaptive fit between individuals and the environment (or more specifically between individual needs, experiences, and abilities and environmental demands) is more commonly employed when considering the characteristics and needs of individuals with severe disabilities (e.g., McDonnell, Hardman, McDonnell, and Kiefer-O'Donnell, 1995). McDonnell et al. (1995) pointed out that this concept of adaptive fit is in keeping with the Association for Persons with Severe Handicaps (TASH) definition of severe disabilities which emphasizes the level of support individuals may require to "participate in integrated community settings" (Meyer, Peck, Brown, 1991, p. 19). While learning disabilities are traditionally considered within the mild disability category, this concept of adaptive fit is equally important. Viewing *barriers* (i.e., the mismatch between the individual and the environment) versus *deficits* (i.e., the psychological processing deficits of the individual) is critical to the design of services which will empower adults to compete in a "non-learning disabled world."

The final caution to the reader is that of necessity this type of approach to describing the characteristics of adults will focus solely on weaknesses (the strengths and coping strategies of this population will be virtually ignored). Little research has been conducted to identify the coping strategies or protective factors that individuals with learning disabilities utilize to enhance their chances for success. Available anecdotal reports and personal life stories identify such common features as:

- proactiveness or taking control of one's life;
- distribution of challenges over time, so everything does not hit at once (time management);
- acceptance of one's learning disability and developing an understanding of both strengths and weaknesses;
- development of a positive outlook on life;
- realistic goal setting and goal-directedness;
- positive stress reduction strategies;
- overall perseverance;
- ability to recruit, accept, use, and acknowledge support from others; and
- ability to apply these attributes at the right time, in the right circumstances.

The limited research which has attempted to study the positive characteristics (i.e., strengths) most often associated with adults with learning disabilities identifies control, specifically the ability to take control of one's own life as a predominant theme (Ginsberg, Gerber, and Reiff, 1994). "A set of interacting variables, which we call internal decisions and external manifestations, characterizes control" (Ginsberg, Gerber, and Reiff, 1994, p. 208). Some of these internal and external manifestations of control include adaptability, persistence, the goodness of fit between the adult and his or her environment, learned creativity, the support systems that the adults have created for themselves, the internal desire to succeed, active goal setting, and reframing—reinterpreting the experiences of learning disabilities in a more positive manner (Ginsberg, Gerber, and Reiff, 1994).

Adelman and Vogel (1990) also found motivation and attitude toward learning were related to educational and employment success. However, the interaction of these within-person variables with features of the broader context (family, community, culture) was emphasized by all researchers. External protective factors included significant others (as mentors, guides, supports, etc.) and a family or community ethic that values work, independence, belongingness, and purpose (Spekman, et al., 1993).

Findings from the Kauai Longitudinal Study of people with and without learning disabilities from birth to adulthood (Werner, 1993) indicated that most individuals with learning disabilities made successful adjustments by age thirty-two; in particular, mental health problems and criminal behavior declined from adolescence to adulthood. Werner (1993) attributed these successes to a common core of individuals' dispositions and sources of support:

- temperamental traits that attract positive responses from family, friends, and teachers;
- productivity, planfulness, and self-esteem;
- effective caregivers and other supportive adults (besides parents) who help create a sense of purpose; and
- opportunities to try again (in school, work, church, military, etc.) that generate competence and confidence among learners.

These protective factors reportedly have more impact than do risk factors on learners' outcomes and appear to cross ethnic, socioeconomic, geographical, and historical boundaries (Werner, 1993).

West (1991) felt that an understanding of the strengths, compensatory strategies, and gifts of adults with learning disabilities may (in the near future and certainly in the long run) be more important than an understanding of their limitations. This knowledge

> might shed light on normal but poorly understood human capabilities—modes of thought that may be essential to finding truly effective creative solutions to the complex problems affecting our society. It is not unusual, in the history of medicine or science, to pursue the investigation of what was first thought to be a relatively minor question—merely a puzzling loose end—and end up with a surprising new understanding that at once not only answers the original question but also entirely transforms the former perspective of the whole. (West, 1991, p. 43).

With these caveats in mind, the characteristics of adults with learning disabilities will be presented in terms of cognitive, educational, psychosocial, and vocational characteristics. Cognitive characteristics will be further separated into the areas of language, processing, memory, and attention.

▶ COGNITIVE CHARACTERISTICS

Adults with learning disabilities tend to demonstrate difficulties with all higher order conceptual/linguistic tasks. From the cognitive perspective, it is interesting to note that many of the perceptual linguistic difficulties that may have initially been responsible for an individual's initial referral for a learning disabilities evaluation as a child (e.g., decoding problems) appear to be replaced by conceptual linguistic difficulties in adulthood (e.g., comprehension problems) (Michaels, Lazar, and Risucci, 1995). Table 8.2 (McCue, 1994) presents a comprehensive overview of the assessment domains that should be considered when conducting an evaluation of an adult with documented learning disabilities (i.e., an adult who was previ-

TABLE 8.2

Assessment Domains for Learning Disabilities in Adulthood

Attention

- Ability to attend to auditory and visual information
- Ability to sustain attention sufficiently for task completion
- Freedom from distractibility
- Freedom from impulsivity and behavioral disinhibition

Memory

- Short term recall of spoken, written, and diagrammatical information
- Learning ability (recall through repeated exposure or practice)
- Long term recall
- Prospective memory
- Procedural memory (task recall)

Reasoning and Problem Solving

- Cognitive flexibility
- Ability to describe categorical qualities and see relationships
- Sequential logic
- Ability to derive abstract meaning and form abstract intent
- Insight and self-evaluation
- Ability to appraise a problem situation
- Ability to generate and evaluate alternative solutions
- Ability to generalize from one situation to another, or from the general to the specific
- Spatial visualization, spatial reasoning, and nonverbal problem solving

Executive Functions

- Ability to identify problems and formulate goals
- Ability to plan and organize activities
- Ability to initiate, maintain, and disengage from problem solving activity
- Ability to internally structure
- Ability to self-monitor
- Ability to change in response to failure or feedback

Language Functions

- Ability to understand language (simple–complex, spatially based, grammatically varied, span of comprehension)
- Speech quality, rate, and fluency
- Ability to express ideas through speech (content, form)

(continued)

TABLE 8.2

continued

Functional Literacy

- Reading mechanics, oral reading, and comprehension
- Ability to express ideas in writing (grammar, spelling, content, handwriting)
- Arithmetic calculation and applied math problem solving

Perceptual Motor Skills

- Ability to perceive basic and complex visual, auditory, and tactile stimuli
- Fine and gross motor skills, coordination, and speed
- Ability to guide activity and problem solving from sensory input (e.g., kinesthesis, visuoconstruction)

Source: McCue, M. (1994). Clinical diagnostic and functional assessment of adults with learning disabilities. In P. J. Gerber and H. B. Reiff (Eds.), *Learning disabilities in adulthood—Persisting problems and evolving issues* (pp. 55–71). Austin: PRO-ED.

ously evaluated and classified as "learning disabled") or with presumed learning disabilities (i.e., an adult who has never been formally evaluated).

Language

Within the language area, adults with learning disabilities often have difficulties with semantics. They may not realize when an individual is exaggerating, teasing, joking or using figurative language (Gottesman, 1994). Expressive and receptive language difficulties have also been noted in this population (Michaels, Lazar, and Risucci, 1995). They may have smaller than average vocabularies, have word retrieval problems, use words incorrectly, have poor organization of thoughts, and have difficulties using and/or understanding complex sentences (Blalock, 1987a; Litowitz, 1987; Michaels, Lazar, and Risucci, 1995; Wiig and Fleischmann, 1980).

Processing

Although it has been suggested that many of the perceptual difficulties initially experienced by children with learning disabilities are not problematic for adults, some difficulties in processing and perception have been noted in this population. Gottesman (1994) noted frequent difficulties in spatial relationships, directionality, and time. These individuals may have difficulty with mechanical assemblies, e.g., putting things together, and frequently get lost. Some auditory discrimination problems have also been noted in adults with learning disabilities in relation to discriminating similar sounding phonemes and sound blends (Elliott and Bosse, 1987; Gottesman, 1994).

Memory and Attention

Attention and memory deficits have been noted in adults with learning disabilities. McCue, Shelly, and Goldstein (1986) found that deficits in attention frequently interfere with the ability of adults with learning disabilities to focus and concentrate on new tasks. Michaels, Lazar, and Risucci (1995) indicated that adults with learning disabilities show significant academic achievement deficits in the area of knowledge learned over time, e.g., basic information in the areas of social studies and science. These deficits were assigned to memory storage and retrieval problems.

▶ EDUCATIONAL CHARACTERISTICS

Many of the academic-educational characteristics of children with learning disabilities persist into adulthood. Adults continue to have reading difficulties with all aspects of reading. Gottesman (1994) reported that they continue to have difficulty "in decoding unfamiliar words, and they often complain of slow, labored reading, and poor comprehension and retention of what they read" (p. 7).

Many adults report difficulty with simple math operations (Hoffmann, et al., 1987) and with written communication for reasons of handwriting, spelling, grammar, and organization (Gottesman, 1994; Gregg, 1983; Hoffmann et al., 1987). These academic difficulties result in numerous difficulties in basic skills of daily life which include filling out job applications; reading want ads, newspapers, menus, and street signs; handling money (e.g., dealing with bills, checks, credit cards, calculating tips for service); and following directions (e.g., following a recipe or a manual) (Gottesman, 1994; Blalock, 1987b). Zwerlein, Smith and Diffley (1984) also identified a number of functional academic problems in adults with learning disabilities referred for vocational rehabilitation. These included inability to read job applications, follow written directions, read important signs, follow maps, measure items accurately, handle money or successfully budget, keep track of time, understand or successfully use a calendar, and spell correctly and organize ideas in writing.

▶ PSYCHOSOCIAL CHARACTERISTICS

"The many failures and frustrations experienced by persons with learning disabilities throughout their school years and beyond often leave them with feelings of inadequacy, low self-esteem, lack of confidence, and depression" (Gottesman, p. 7). Price (1993) defined the term *psychosocial* in relation to integral areas in the lives of adults with learning disabilities: "(1) the *psycho* part or psychological aspect (i.e., how one sees oneself or feels about oneself), and (2) the *social* part or social aspect (i.e., how one relates to others in one's everyday environment and communicates with others)" (Price, 1993, p. 141). She described the primary psychosocial issues of adults with learning disabilities in terms of their: "(1) negative self-concept, (2) lack of socialization skills, (3) dependency on others, (4) stress and anxiety, (5) various negative behaviors and feelings, and (6) depression and dependency" (p. 141).

Michaels, Lazar, and Risucci (1995) reported on the psychological adjustment of adults with learning disabilities as measured by the Millon Clinical Multiaxial Inventory, a self-reported personality inventory (Millon, 1983). The adults with learning disabilities in their sample had more clinical symptoms than would be expected of a non-clinical sample. They tended to score higher than anticipated on five scales—schizoid, dependent, narcissistic, paranoid, and paranoid disorders—and lower than would be anticipated on three scales—compulsive, borderline, and alcohol abuse. Michaels, Lazar and Risucci described adults with learning disabilities as a population that tends to distrust others and have difficulty making and maintaining relationships. Simultaneously, these same individuals seem to be in conflict because they also are dependent on others for approval and guidance (1995).

In a survey of adults with learning disabilities, Chesler (1982) found that developing social relationships and utilizing appropriate social skills was an area of critical concern. Adults with learning disabilities tend to be less satisfied with family relationship and less involved socially with others (Farfard and Haubrich, 1981). In addition, these adults tend to participate less in recreational and social activities and in the general life of their communities (White, et al., 1980).

▶ VOCATIONAL CHARACTERISTICS

The impact of learning disabilities in adults often manifests in unemployment, underemployment, and/or frequent job changes (Cronin and Gerber, 1982; Hasazi, Gordon, and Roe, 1985; Mithaug, Horiuchi, and Fanning, 1985; President's Committee on the Employment of People with Disabilities, 1990; White, et al., 1980). Hoffmann et al. (1987) surveyed both individuals with learning disabilities and service providers about the vocational needs of adults with learning disabilities. The adults with learning disabilities identified difficulties filling out job applications, not knowing where to go to find a job, and not knowing how to get the job training they might need as the most significant employment-related issues. Service providers also identified these as serious concerns but felt that difficulties following directions on the job and the lack of interviewing skills were the most significant employment-related issues for adults with learning disabilities (Hoffmann, et al., 1987). Adults with learning disabilities have histories of work behaviors that are counterproductive (Buchanan and Wolf, 1986). They continue to lose jobs for reasons that they are unaware of and as a result continue to take jobs with similar requirements in which they will make the same mistakes (Blalock and Dixon, 1982; Buchanan and Wolf, 1986).

Postsecondary Educational Environments

Today, more and more individuals with learning disabilities are enrolling in both two- and four-year college programs (Astin, et al, 1988; HEATH, 1989; United

States Department of Education, 1987). In fact, most secondary students with learning disabilities state that they are planning to participate in some form of postsecondary education following graduation (Bruck, 1987). According to the American Council on Education (1987), the percentage of students with identified learning disabilities on college campuses has increased from .3 percent in 1983 to 1.2 percent in 1987. This translates to roughly twenty-thousand first-year students with learning disabilities enrolling in colleges across the country in any given academic year (HEATH, 1988). Recently, the National Joint Committee on Learning Disabilities (1996) released a position paper on secondary to postsecondary education transition planning for students with learning disabilities. This position paper articulates the roles and responsibilities of four constituencies—students, parents, secondary school personnel, and postsecondary personnel—to work together to assure the postsecondary success of the student. This position paper states that when coordination, communication, and planning occurs among these constituency groups, the result will be "a student with LD who is confident, independent, self-directed, and in actual pursuit of career goals" (p. 64). Brinckerhoff, Shaw, and McGuire (1992) identified four questions that must be addressed in developing programmatic access and serving students with learning disabilities in postsecondary environments: "(1) How are high school and postsecondary settings different? (2) How are eligibility and access determined? (3) How are 'reasonable accommodations' determined? and (4) How can the independence level of college students be fostered?" (p. 417).

Reasons for Increased Postsecondary Enrollment by Adults with Learning Disabilities

Mangrum and Strichart (1984) identified a number of the critical factors that have contributed to the increase in students with learning disabilities choosing postsecondary education following graduation from high school. These included:

1. Extension of special services from secondary to postsecondary educational settings. Now that learning disabilities are recognized as a "lifelong disability" (e.g., National Joint Committee on Learning Disabilities definition, 1985) more and more students are demanding services for learning disabilities at the postsecondary level.

2. Pressure exercised on colleges and universities by parents, advocates, and professionals to provide access to students with learning disabilities.

3. The increased desire of students with learning disabilities to pursue postsecondary education.

4. The identification of the lack of programs for individuals with learning disabilities and the subsequent growth of new programs.

5. The effect of open enrollment policies. Open enrollment (especially at the community college level) has created the situation in which colleges accept anyone with a high school diploma for matriculation into their programs. Obviously, this covers the vast majority of individuals with learning disabilities

Students with learning disabilities are getting more assistance from colleges and universities than ever before.

who complete secondary education and will receive regular high school diplomas. Most colleges with open enrollment policies do not require the standardized testing typically required by more selective institutions, such as the Scholastic Aptitude Test (SAT) or the American College Test (ACT).

6. Compliance with federal legislation. Section 504 regulations of the Rehabilitation Act of 1973 prevent colleges and universities and other recipients of federal financial assistance from discriminating against qualified persons with disabilities. These sentiments are echoed in the more recent regulations of the Americans with Disabilities Act (ADA) of 1990 as well.

7. College students with learning disabilities are a good source of enrollment and revenue. Most colleges are currently experiencing moderate-to-severe financial crises because of the decreases in enrollment and the increases in operating costs. College students with learning disabilities represent an untapped market with excellent potential.

▶ ACCOMMODATIONS FOR COLLEGE STUDENTS WITH LEARNING DISABILITIES

Section 504 of the Rehabilitation Act of 1973 is the basic civil rights provision that has created access to postsecondary education for "qualified" individuals with disabilities. The law described in detail in Chapter 10, prohibits discrimination against individuals with disabilities.

Subpart E of Section 504 is applicable to all postsecondary education programs. In brief, colleges and universities must be free from discrimination in recruitment, admissions, and treatment of students. Reasonable accommodations in academic programs must be made by all educational institutions to insure maximum participation by all students with disabilities (Brinckerhoff, 1985). Subpart E protects the rights of students (and potential students) with disabilities by:

1. Prohibiting colleges and universities from discriminating against students with disabilities in programs and activities;

2. Identifying practices leading to exclusion of people with disabilities; and

3. Indicating appropriate steps postsecondary institutions should take to ensure equal opportunity (Mistler, 1978).

It must be stressed that the Section 504 regulations of the Rehabilitation Act in no way require colleges and universities to offer special education programs to students with learning disabilities. While all colleges and universities in the United States that recieve any federal funds must demonstrate compliance with Section 504 regulations, approaches to implementation vary greatly from school to school.

Michaels et al. (1988) suggest that the following accommodations be available to postsecondary education students with learning disabilities:

1. Allow students to tape-record lectures.

2. Give students extra time to complete tests.

3. Allow students to dictate answers to a proctor.

4. Allow students to use a calculator in class.

5. Allow students to take a reduced course load without losing full-time student status.

6. Provide students with alternatives to computer-scored answer sheets.

7. Allow students to respond orally to essay questions.

8. Allow students an alternative setting for a proctored exam.

9. Do not penalize students for misspellings.

10. Give students extended deadlines to complete projects.

11. Give students priority registration for classes.

12. Allow proofreaders to correct grammar and punctuation and indicate mistakes so that students may make corrections.

13. Give students partial credit for work shown, even when final answer is incorrect.

14. Allow students to withdraw from class without penalty, even after last regular date for withdrawal.

15. Provide students with copies of the instructor's lecture notes for those classes they attend (p. 46).

While it is important to provide students with the appropriate accommodations as mandated by Section 504 of the Rehabilitation Act (and now also through the Americans with Disabilities Act), our focus must simultaneously be on fostering independence and competency. Table 8.3 (Brinckerhoff, Shaw, and

TABLE 8.3

Postsecondary Service Provider Behaviors That Foster Dependence or Independence

Dependence	Independence
1. Allows student to interrupt or "barge in" to get immediate response to perceived need	1. Uses such occurrences to teach or practice appropriate social skills
2. Takes responsibility for the products and grades of seemingly sincere and hard-working student	2. Maintains focus on helping student learn without taking responsibility for student success or failure
3. Advocates for untimed tests in all subjects	3. Encourages extended time on certain tests in specified courses based upon specific assessment data
4. Helps a student write a paper	4. Provides instruction on how to write a paper
5. Edits and corrects a student's paper	5. Teaches the student how to proofread a paper and/or teaches the use of appropriate computer software
6. Explains the student's disability and needed accommodations to a professor	6. Role-plays discussion with a professor so the student can self-advocate
7. Sends a list of students with learning disabilities to all faculty	7. Discusses with student when, if, and how to disclose a learning disability
8. Mails a letter to faculty requesting test modifications or accommodations	8. Gives a letter to the student that indicates provider's availability to support the student's request for test modifications or accommodations
9. Tells the student that a certain credit load, course, or major is inappropriate or unacceptable	9. Helps a student determine the pros and cons of a particular decision and allows the student to experience the consequences (positive or negative) of that decision
10. Organizes the student and controls his or her environment to ensure success	10. Encourages the student to assess needs, identify problems, and develop compensatory strategies
11. Attempts to meet all student instructional, counseling, advising, and personal needs using resources of LD services	11. Helps student identify and access other campus and community resources

Source: Brinckerhoff, L. C., Shaw, S. F., and McGuire, J. M. (1992). Promoting access, accommodations, and independence for college students with learning disabilities, *Journal of Learning Disabilities, 25*, 417–429.

McGuire, 1992) outlines postsecondary service provider behaviors that foster dependence and suggests alternative solutions that promote independence and competency in students.

▶ MAKING THE RIGHT MATCH BETWEEN STUDENTS AND POSTSECONDARY ENVIRONMENTS

In trying to cope successfully with the demands of the postsecondary environment, students may find that nonacademic areas related to "control" (as described in the characteristics of successful adults with learning disabilities by Ginsberg, Gerber, and Reiff, 1994) and functioning socially are frequently overwhelming. "These [control and social] areas include: (a) problem solving, (b) organizing, (c) prioritizing multiple task completion, (d) studying, (e) self-monitoring, (f) attacking and following though on tasks, (g) managing time, and (h) interacting socially in a variety of new situations" (DuChossois and Michaels, 1994, p. 85).

The average college student should spend about three hours engaged in studying for each hour spent in class. For students with learning disabilities—who may take a longer time reading assigned homework, taking notes on assigned work, and/or understanding the important concepts in a given assignment—the time invested in studying may need to be considerably more (Brinckerhoff, Shaw, and McGuire, 1992; DuChossois and Michaels, 1994).

> If a high school student spends five and one-half hours a day in a classroom 180 days a year, the youngster completes nearly 1,000 hours of instruction annually. This same student in high school may spend as little as 10 hours a week outside of class working on their own (completing homework). In short, high school students spend about two-thirds of their time in class and one-third of their time out of class doing homework. This same student in college will spend about 16 hours a week in class (about three and one-quarter hours for each of 5 classes) for about 26 weeks. This translates to about 416 hours of in-class instruction in an academic year. Based on the above cited statistic of 3 hours out-of-class for each hour in-class, this same student would be expected to spend about 1,240 hours working independently outside of class. (DuChossois and Michaels, 1994, p. 88).

The Demands of the College Environment

In addition to all of the normal adjustments to the newfound freedom and responsibility of college, students with learning disabilities have further new responsibilities, as the nature of many of the supportive services that were provided in high school also change. In most high schools, the institution is responsible for assessment of students and for developing an appropriate educational plan. Subsequent notification of the teaching staff regarding the nature of the learning disability and the appropriate services is then coordinated by the department of special education. The parents and the school provide the advocacy for, planning for, and implementation of services. Students are not expected to initiate the request for services and, in most cases, although informed about the proceedings, are not really involved in the decision-making. The postsecondary environment requires a much greater level of self-advocacy. Students frequently must seek out services on their own, be able to inform their professors about their learning disabilities, and make their own decisions about what services they need to be successful. Again, paralleling the more independent philosophy of the postsecondary environment, the responsibility is given to the student to initiate services and ensure that services are provided (as appropriate) to facilitate success. The more service providers foster independent functioning rather than promote dependence the greater the development of competence and control within the student (see again Table 8.3 [Brinckerhoff, Shaw, and McGuire, 1992]).

Making the Postsecondary Match

Adults with learning disabilities must be prepared for success in postsecondary education. In keeping with the notion of examining "goodness of fit" (Ginsberg, Gerber, and Reiff, 1994) and then analyzing the functional demands of real world environments (e.g., Gaylord-Ross and Browder, 1991; Schalock, 1986), DuChossois and Michaels (1994) stated that:

- The transition from secondary to postsecondary education must be planned in advance.
- The needs and characteristics of the student must be realistically evaluated.
- The college must be an appropriate setting for the student (i.e., the support that the college can provide must match the support that the student will need).

Potential college students with learning disabilities (either with or without the help of parents, friends, teachers, or other service providers) can achieve the following goals by answering *all* the questions about themselves and their study skills in Table 8.4:

1. to plan in advance;
2. to realistically evaluate their needs and characteristics; and
3. to determine the support they will need at college (i.e., make the match).

They can then ask the questions presented in Table 8.5 (p. 278) of the appropriate college representative(s) at the schools they are considering. Students will need to do some real "soul searching" to answer honestly the questions about themselves and their learning needs presented in Table 8.4. DuChossois and Michaels suggested that equipped with this self-knowledge, potential students can then solicit the answers to the questions in Table 8.5 during visits to college campuses and to the college offices that provide support services to students with learning disabilities. By examining the congruence between support needs (as identified through the questions presented in Table 8.4) and the potential support available (elicited through questions in Table 8.5) individuals will maximize the match and their potential to successfully negotiate the postsecondary environment.

TABLE 8.4

Study Skills Questionnaire for Self-Evaluation in Preparation for Postsecondary Education

Time Management

- Do you usually have a well-organized study schedule?
- Do you see yourself as someone who uses time effectively?
- Do you study for one to two hours per day with full concentration?
- Do you usually allow enough time for long-term assignments (e.g., term papers, lengthy reading assignments, etc.)?
- Do you finish your work far enough ahead of time to be able to proofread and to make corrections?
- Do you accurately estimate how long it will take you to get work done?
- How often do you hand assignments in late or ask for extensions?

Notetaking

- Do you understand the notes you have taken in class?
- Do you feel that you can study from your notes (even if the test is two months later)?
- Do you share/compare notes with other students in the class?
- Are your notes legible?
- Have you ever used a tape recorder to supplement your notes?
- Do you date all your notes and class handouts?
- Are you able to keep up with all important information while the teacher is lecturing?
- Is it easy for you to select what information is important while you take notes?

Reading Assignments

- Do you preview or survey your reading material and ask yourself questions before reading (do you establish a purpose for your reading)?
- Do you usually know the main ideas expressed in a reading assignment?
- Do you make a plan to divide a lengthy reading assignment into sections?
- After completing a reading assignment, do you review the lesson to organize what you have learned?
- Do you highlight or take notes when you read?
- Do you use the dictionary when you come across unfamiliar words?
- Do you use charts and graphs to aid your understanding when you read?
- Do you use the overall structure of the textbook to help you approach reading assignments (e.g., table of contents, glossary, heading and subheadings, etc.)?
- Can you concentrate on and comprehend material on topics that you do not find interesting?

Writing Assignments/Essays/Research Papers

- Do you tend to have trouble thinking of words to express your ideas?

(continued)

TABLE 8.4

continued

- Is it harder for you to write as much as other students in your classes?
- Does it take you a lot longer to write than you think it should?
- Do you develop an outline for lengthier writing assignments before you start to write?
- Can you write in clear sentences?
- Is your writing punctuated correctly?
- Do readers find your writing well-organized and logical?
- Do you have trouble with spelling?
- Do you approach writing in stages, first completing a rough draft and then refining your work?
- Can you proofread your own work and find your errors?
- Do you use a word processor or computer with a spellcheck?
- Do you ask others to read your reports and make suggestions?
- Can you use the library effectively to do research and gather information?
- Are you organized about keeping track of references and sources?
- Can you write a paper of a particular length?
- Are the topics you choose appropriate to the assignment length (not too broad, not too narrow)?

Examination Preparation

- Do you find that you have usually studied the right information for tests?
- Do you have strategies for memorizing material for exams?
- Do you feel prepared for most tests?
- Can you anticipate what questions might be on an exam?
- Do you prepare answers to possible essay questions before an exam?
- Do you study with other students in your class?
- Do you retain what you have studied when you get to the test?
- Do you usually begin studying well in advance or do you cram for exams?

Test-Taking Behavior

- Are you ready for exams (e.g., get there early, know the right time and date, have pens/pencils, calculators, etc.) ?
- Do you plan your exam time well (e.g., allow enough time for each section, know the point value of various questions, spend as much time on the end of the test as on the beginning)?
- Do you usually have enough time to check your work (e.g., content, grammar, punctuation, calculations)?
- Do you have strategies for dealing with complex questions (e.g., underlining key words, narrowing down multiple choice options, etc.)?
- Do you accurately read test questions and directions?

(continued)

TABLE 8.4

continued

- Does test anxiety interfere with your performance on exams?
- Is your sense of how well you performed on an exam usually accurate?

General Questions About YOU

- Do you usually recognize when you need help (and are you willing to ask for it)?
- Do you study in a place where you can concentrate?
- Do you have a routine time to study and do work (a time of day when you are most productive)?
- Do you pace yourself well when studying (e.g., take reasonable breaks, get back to work after breaks, etc.)?
- Are you able to make decisions about what you have to study?
- Can you set priorities (or do you generally put off the material you do not like)?
- Would your study habits enable you to be ready for a surprise quiz?
- Do you monitor your own comprehension (do you stop yourself when you are not understanding material)?
- What type of learner are you (do you learn best through visual, auditory, or experiential methods)?
- In what way does your learning disability affect your school work?
- Can you comfortably describe your learning disability to others?
- What are the strategies that help you learn (e.g., books on tape, one-to-one tutoring, study groups, re-reading material, using a study guide, etc.)?
- How much time each week do you get extra help?
- How much time each week do you study?
- Do you prefer small discussion classes or large lecture classes?
- Do you feel that you are aware of what extra help and accommodations you need (or would you find it helpful to explore various options with a learning disabilities specialist at college)?
- Are you easily distracted (and if so, how will you compensate for this in the college living environment)?
- What size school are you interested in?
- What kind of setting would you prefer (e.g., rural or city, commuter or residential, etc.)?
- What extracurricular activities are important to you?
- What area(s) most interest you as possible majors?

Source: DuChossois, G., and Michaels, C. A. (1994). Postsecondary education. In C. A. Michaels (Ed.), *Transition strategies for persons with learning disabilities* (pp. 79–118). San Diego: Singular Publishing Group, Inc. Reprinted with permission by Singular Publishing Group, Inc.

TABLE 8.5

Potential College Evaluation in Preparation for Postsecondary Education

Structured College Interview

Admissions

1. Describe any differences in the application process for students with learning disabilities.
2. Do you require a diagnostic test report (If yes, what must be included)?
3. How recent must the testing be? Who must conduct it?
4. Is an IEP from high school also necessary?
5. What is your policy regarding SATs/ACTs? Untimed? Waived?
6. Do you conduct personal interviews? Are they required or suggested?

Fees

7. What extra charges, if any, are made for services provided to students with learning disabilities?
8. Are there additional charges if I need services during the summer session?

Program Services

9. How many students with learning disabilities are eligible to receive services? How many of those students regularly participate in the services?
10. Would you say that your college provides compensatory services, remediation services, psychoeducational services?
11. Is there a mandatory package of services or does each student receive different services? Who decides?
12. Does each student have specific staff members assigned to work with them?
13. How many times per week does the average first-year student use the services?
14. Who advises students with learning disabilities about courses?
15. Is there a summer orientation for students? Is it mandatory? How long does it last? Are there fees? What topics are covered in this orientation?
16. Are courses offered specifically for students with learning disabilities? What topics do they cover? What department(s) offer these courses? Are these courses offered for credit?

Tutoring Services

17. Is tutoring available? Is this tutoring subject matter or learning strategies oriented?
18. How many times a week is tutoring available?
19. What are the qualifications of the tutors?
20. Do students receive individual tutoring or do they work in small groups?
21. Do students see the same tutor each session?

(continued)

TABLE 8.5

continued

Counseling and Psychological Services

22. Is psychological counseling available for students with learning disabilities?

23. Is career counseling available for students with learning disabilities?

24. Is a student support group available for students with learning disabilities? Who conducts the group? How often does it meet, and what is the purpose of this group?

Accommodations

25. How are test or course modifications arranged?

26. Are any of the following accommodations commonly available for exams: extended time; alternate test formats (e.g., multiple choice in place of essay); use of a word processor; use of calculator or other aids; readers; scribes; separate testing rooms?

27. What accommodations are commonly available for classes?

28. Are students able to take a reduced course load?

29. Are substitutions or waivers of courses ever provided (e.g., foreign language)?

30. Are readers available? How is this arranged?

31. Are notetakers available? How is this arranged?

32. Are taped texts available? How is this arranged?

33. What technological aids are available to students with learning disabilities: word processors with spellcheck; computers; personal reading machines (e.g., Kurzweil); tape recorders? Any other aids available?

Other Campus Resources

34. Are any of the following resources available on campus: writing clinic; academic assistance center; subject tutoring; counseling services; first-year student support; computer facilities; library assistance? Are any other resources available which might be helpful? Do resource personnel have an understanding of the needs of students with learning disabilities?

35. What extracurricular activities are available on campus? Students should ask about their particular interests.

36. What kinds of residence halls are available? Are there single rooms, special interest housing, or quiet halls?

A Final Question

37. What do you think are the unique features or strengths of your services for students with learning disabilities?

Source: DuChossois, G., and Michaels, C. A. (1994). Postsecondary education. In C. A. Michaels (Ed.), *Transition strategies for persons with learning disabilities* (pp. 79–118). San Diego: Singular Publishing Group, Inc. Reprinted with permission by Singular Publishing Group, Inc.

▶ THE WORK ENVIRONMENT

As described earlier in this chapter, now that the first generation of children identified as "learning disabled" and educated through the provisions of P.L. 94-142 in special education has entered the workforce, the view that learning disabilities affect only academic areas is no longer viable. Learning disabilities must be viewed both (1) as a lifelong disability, and (2) as impacting all aspects of life far beyond traditional academic settings (e.g., Blalock, 1981; National Joint Committee on Learning Disabilities, 1985). Zwerlein, Smith, and Diffley identify the following observable characteristics as areas to consider when trying to assess the vocational impact of learning disabilities:

- general attitude toward work
- independent functioning
- distractibility/attention span
- supervisory relations
- co-worker relations
- continuity of performance
- reaction to monotonous tasks
- acceptance of change in work assignments
- coping skills/frustration level
- communication skills
- punctuality
- attendance
- vitality and energy output
- response to own mistakes
- odd or inappropriate behavior
- organization of work (1984, p. 46)

The federal definition utilized in most states to diagnose learning disabilities for vocational rehabilitation and employment-related services mentions 12 functional areas compared to only four that reflect the traditional academic areas mentioned in the P.L. 94-142 definition. The definition used by most state VR offices is:

> A specific learning disability is a disorder in one or more of the central nervous system processes involved in perceiving, understanding, and/or using concepts through verbal (spoken or written) language or nonverbal means. This disorder manifests itself with a deficit in one or more of the following areas: attention, reasoning, processing, memory, communication, reading, writing, spelling, calculation, coordination, social competence, and emotional maturity (Rehabilitation Services Administration, 1985).

Adults with learning disabilities are a relatively new population to receive employment-related services through the state-federal vocational rehabilitation system. While rehabilitation services for adults with learning disabilities were first mandated in 1978 with the amendments to the Rehabilitation Act of 1973 (P.L. 93-112), rehabilitation service providers were extremely uncomfortable and lacked the necessary skills (and professional training) to provide services to this population. It was really not until the medical community also recognized specific learning disabilities as a medical condition in 1980 with the inclusion of "Specific Developmental Disorders" in the *Diagnostic and Statistical Manual-III* (DSM-III) that the rehabilitation community began to take a closer look at learning disabilities. The original DSM-III (AXIS II) guidelines for diagnosing learning disabilities paralleled closely the major components of the special education definition. The DSM-III criteria included the following four points:

1. The disorder of specific areas of development are not due to another disorder (e.g., mental retardation, vision, hearing, or motor handicap);
2. Disorders are related to biological maturation (e.g., not the result of an injury);
3. Performance is significantly below intellectual capacities; and
4. Skill deficits are not accounted for by chronological age, mental age, or inadequate schooling (American Psychiatric Association, 1980).

It was not until about 1984 that the first publications and journal articles devoted to vocational rehabilitation of persons with learning disabilities became available (e.g., Kopp, Miller, and Mulkey, 1984; Zwerlein, Smith, and Diffley, 1984). By 1984, the population of students with learning disabilities served through special education programs in our nation's schools (nine years after the passage of P.L. 94-142 and five years after its full implementation) had already grown to become the largest single population of students served in special education.

Reasonable Accommodations

Section 503 regulations of the Rehabilitation Act of 1973 were the first mandates calling for all employers who receive federal contracts or subcontracts to provide reasonable accommodations for qualified individuals with disabilities. Section 504 regulations require the same for employers receiving federal monies and for colleges and universities. Most recently, the ADA has extended this concept to both smaller employers and employers who are not federal contractors or recipients of federal monies. Chapter 10 provides information on reasonable accommodations, as described in Section 504 and the ADA.

To be protected under the ADA, a person with a disability must be qualified—that is, the individual must be able to perform the essential functions of the job with or without reasonable accommodations. This individual must also have the same education and/or experience that would be required of any other individual in this position. The ADA lists specific learning disabilities as one possible physical or mental impairment, and learning is included as a major life activity" (National Joint Committee on Learning Disabilities, 1992, p. 88).

Table 8.6 presents suggestions from the position paper entitled Learning Disabilities and the Americans with Disabilities Act (ADA) which was issued by the National Joint Committee on Learning Disabilities (NJCLD, 1992). The ADA focuses on the concept of barriers (as described earlier in this chapter) rather than deficits inherent in the individual. Table 8.6 presents examples of potential barriers to employment of individuals with learning disabilities and suggests what could be done to minimize those barriers and/or accommodate individuals with learning disabilities.

Michaels (1989) described reasonable accommodations for individuals with disabilities in a somewhat different format. Michaels (1989) presented job modifications/accommodations as falling into three broad categories: (1) environmental modifications—the removal of architectural barriers; (2) equipment modifications—assistive devices and special tools; and (3) procedural modifications—restructuring tasks, altering work methods, changing work schedules. While most accommodations for potential employees with disabilities fall in categories 1 and 2, modifications for employees with learning disabilities tend to fall mostly into category 3.

Evaluating the "Reasonableness" of Accommodations

Michaels (1989) used a simplified information processing model to divide an employee's (or potential employee's) essential job functioning into three phases, using an analogy borrowed from the personal computer. *Phase One*, the input phase, relates to how an employee or potential employee is expected to receive information for performing the job. *Phase Two* is analogous to the storage phase in keeping with this computer analogy. During this phase of performing the job, the employee or potential employee must internally perform some type of mental operation with the information taken in during phase one. *Phase Three* is the output phase. This is the actual job function the employee or potential employee is expected to perform. If information processing problems occur during any of the three phases, there will be problems with the employee and his or her ultimate job performance.

An employer or potential employer would most often be requested to make procedural modifications for an employee with learning disabilities at phase one (input phase) such as by presenting directions in writing as well as orally, providing feedback on job performance more frequently, or perhaps providing an example of the completed task for the employee to follow.

All modifications during the second stage of the model (the storage stage) should be the responsibility of the employee. These modifications should constitute the compensatory strategies and learning strategies that the individual has developed (or at least should have developed in high school) to be able to negotiate their learning disabilities.

Any modifications in the final stage (the output) *should be* approached with caution. It is important at this point to stress the words *reasonable* and *essential job functions*. If the elimination of essential job functions is required,

TABLE 8.6

Suggestions for Accommodating Workers and Potential Workers with Learning Disabilities

Potential Barriers for Individuals with Learning Disabilities

Physical/environmental barriers:

- Inappropriately designed instruction manuals or testing materials
- Long or complex directions
- Noisy or visually distracting work settings

Attitudinal/behavioral barriers:

- Impatient or inflexible teachers, job supervisors, or peers
- Lack of understanding that individuals with learning disabilities have many capabilities

What Can be Done to Minimize Barriers?

Ways to minimize physical/environmental barriers:

- Provide auxiliary aids and use assistive technology (spelling devices, electronic calculators)
- Reduce visual or auditory distractions
- Change activity site (quieter, fewer distractions)
- Provide international symbols, illustrations, or other signage modifications
- Provide memory aids or cue cards

Ways to minimize attitudinal/behavioral barriers:

- Encourage appropriate attitudes and behaviors of managers and peers
- Use peer coaches or mentors to provide guidance
- Ask students or employees what works best for them
- Encourage individuals to ask questions
- Recognize and use the individual's abilities

What are Possible Task Accommodations and Modifications?

- Analyze the job and develop effective accommodations
- Supplement training and instruction using alternative materials and methods (visual, auditory, manipulative)
- Simplify information
- Clearly spell out expectations
- Organize tasks into meaningful steps
- Demonstrate by example, and provide practice
- Provide both written and spoken instructions
- Allow additional time to complete tasks
- Modify ways to complete tasks
- Modify techniques for evaluating task performance

Source: National Joint Committee on *Learning Disabilities. (1992, September). Learning disabilities and the Americans with Disabilities Act (ADA).*

it most often will indicate an inappropriate job match—in the language of Sections 503, 504, and the ADA.

Making the Employment Match

McCue (1987) criticized the application of traditional psychoeducational, psychological, and vocational assessment batteries for use with adults with learning disabilities, "given the definitional criteria of SLD [specific learning disabilities] adopted by the Rehabilitation Services Administration and the identified range of characteristics of this disorder" (p. 26). McCue stressed the need to assess the broad range of cognitive, behavioral, and emotional characteristics of this population through the application of comprehensive evaluation strategies. Strodden (1980) also warned that standard vocational work samples utilize one-trial learning and thus tend to magnify both learning and strategy deficits. Adults with learning disabilities demonstrate poor task performance on these measures because of poor task-attack (organization) and task follow-through strategies.

This chapter has already described the need to constantly seek to focus on the match (or mismatch) between an individual's skills and the specific demands of a given environment in which we expect that individual to function within successfully (e.g., Gaylord-Ross and Browder, 1991; Schalock, 1986). This approach *both* moves away from the "internal deficit" notion so often associated with disability while simultaneously ecologically grounding the assessment process in real work environments. The situational assessment can give information on performance in different job sites and also provide information on the crucial areas so often left out of traditional evaluation reports, namely the strengths of the individual such as independent strategy usage, coping strategies, task performance improvement with strategy instruction, social skills, and adaptive behavior. Situational assessment has been defined by the Vocational Evaluation and Work Adjustment Association (VEWAA) of the National Rehabilitation Association as a "clinical assessment method utilizing observational techniques in established or created environments" (1978, p. 10). Situational assessment links the performance of an individual with the environment in which performance is required. The situational assessment provides ecologically valid information about performance in various work sites and for potential jobs with various job demands. Michaels, Lazar, and Marsh (1989, as cited in Michaels, 1994c) suggested the use of the *Situational Assessment Behavior Checklist* and the *Situational Assessment Site Description* forms (Tables 8.7 and 8.8) to provide a structure for recording information and monitoring situational job placements.

The *Situational Assessment Behavior Checklist* (Table 8.7) allows an employer to provide information about five key areas that may impact on the eventual employment success of an adult with learning disabilities. Information about skills that may need to be enhanced or developed prior to

Part of the assessment of adults with learning disabilities focuses on interpersonal skills.

full-time placement can also be elicited. Specifically the *Situational Assessment Behavior Checklist* gathers information about:

1. *Instructional needs:* How does the individual best take instruction on the job?

2. *Problem solving:* What does the individual do when faced with a problem on the job?

3. *Attendance to task:* Does the individual demonstrate appropriate attention on the job?

4. *Worker orientation:* Does the individual demonstrate ability to function independently and for a sustained period of time on the job? and

5. *Interpersonal skills:* Does the individual demonstrate appropriate social skills for the job? (Michaels, 1994c, pp. 134-135).

The *Situational Assessment Site Description* (Table 8.8) is the companion form to the behavior checklist. This form is used to describe the actual demands of a specific work environment. It serves as a control to match an individual's strengths and weaknesses in the five areas (assessed by the *Situational Assessment Behavior Checklist*) to the importance of those skills in successfully performing the particular job. This information can be extremely useful in making more appropriate accommodations and in identifying essential and nonessential job demands (as described in the Americans with Disabilities Act).

TABLE 8.7
Situational Assessment Behavior Checklist

Instructions: Please rate the individual on each of the following characteristics on a scale from 1 (Below Average) to 5 (Above Average) in comparison to other workers or trainees. An individual who demonstrates average functioning on a given characteristic should receive a rating of 3 (Average).

Potential Employee's Characteristics

I. Instructional Needs

Functions with oral instructions	1	2	3	4	5
Functions with written instructions	1	2	3	4	5
Functions with modeling of instructions	1	2	3	4	5
Needs well-organized information	1	2	3	4	5

II. Problem Solving

Seeks assistance when needed	1	2	3	4	5
Asks relevant questions	1	2	3	4	5
Knows when assistance is needed	1	2	3	4	5
Accepts constructive criticism	1	2	3	4	5

III. Attends to Task

Functions without special focusing	1	2	3	4	5
Shows sustained attention	1	2	3	4	5
Exhibits an impulsive style	1	2	3	4	5

IV. Worker Orientation

Works efficiently	1	2	3	4	5
Organizes components to complete a project	1	2	3	4	5
Adjusts to changes in demands	1	2	3	4	5
Shows adequate performance	1	2	3	4	5
Shows adequate aptitudes	1	2	3	4	5
Functions without supervision	1	2	3	4	5
Demonstrates competence	1	2	3	4	5
Demonstrates responsibility	1	2	3	4	5

V. Interpersonal Skills

Adjusts to the mood of others	1	2	3	4	5
Exhibits an argumentative style	1	2	3	4	5
Demonstrates social appropriateness	1	2	3	4	5

(continued)

TABLE 8.7

continued

Demonstrates understanding by giving appropriate response	1	2	3	4	5
Demonstrates conversational skills	1	2	3	4	5
Understands figurative language	1	2	3	4	5
Appreciates nuance	1	2	3	4	5
Appreciates and initiates humor	1	2	3	4	5
Demonstrates appropriate affect	1	2	3	4	5
Adjusts social behavior appropriately	1	2	3	4	5

Source: Michaels, C. A. (1994). Employment issues: Transition from school to work. In C. A. Michaels (Ed.), *Transition strategies for persons with learning disabilities* (pp. 119–152). San Diego: Singular Publishing Group, Inc. Reprinted with permission by Singular Publishing Group, Inc.

TABLE 8.8

Situational Assessment Site Description

Instructions: Please rate the specific job on each of the following site demands on a scale from 1 (Not Important) to 5 (Very Important). A site demand that is of average importance should receive a rating of 3 (Somewhat Important).

Potential Site Demands

Functioning without supervision	1	2	3	4	5
Functioning with oral instructions	1	2	3	4	5
Functioning with written instructions	1	2	3	4	5
Functioning with modeling, e.g., with examples	1	2	3	4	5
Functioning with well organized information	1	2	3	4	5
Requesting assistance when needed	1	2	3	4	5
Capacity for sustained attention	1	2	3	4	5
Efficient work habits	1	2	3	4	5
Organization and planning skills	1	2	3	4	5
Capacity to adjust to changes in job demands	1	2	3	4	5
Reliability	1	2	3	4	5
Interpersonal skills	1	2	3	4	5

Source: Michaels, C. A. (1994). Employment issues: *Transition from school to work. In C. A. Michaels (Ed.), Transition strategies for persons with learning disabilities* (pp. 119–152). San Diego: Singular Publishing Group, Inc. Reprinted with permission by Singular Publishing Group, Inc.

▶ SOCIAL AND INTERPERSONAL ENVIRONMENTS

When focusing on adults with learning disabilities, there is a tendency to assign all aspects of an individual's character, personality, and interactions with others to the learning disability. In this way we extricate (or separate) the individual to some degree from him/herself and from the whole host of personality traits we tend to assign to individuals without disabilities. Reiff and Gerber (1994) pointed out that this is somewhat artificial and that adults with learning disabilities face the same social, emotional, and daily living challenges as we all do. They also argue that as with the general population of adults, individuals with learning disabilities (for the most part) tend to develop behavioral repertoires within the social and personal domains that tend to be more or less successful and more or less fulfilling. Simultaneously, however, it is important to realize that for some adults with learning disabilities

> [t]he same complex problems that make learning in a classroom difficult may interfere with acquiring the necessary skills to negotiate social situations and everyday activities. The residual effects of learning disabilities, from frustration about schooling to a lack of satisfaction in one or a number of areas of adulthood, sometimes reverberate in the emotional sphere. For some adults with learning disabilities, a seeming inability to understand why life continues to be a struggle creates a tragic and self-perpetuating cycle of loneliness and despair (Reiff and Gerber, 1994, p. 72).

Wilson (1994) stated that recognition by others contributes to our development of self. Positive recognition, particularly during our formative years, is critical to the development of what Erikson (1968) termed a healthy "ego-identity." Wilson went on to point out that all social interactions are complex and that the beliefs and expectations of others frequently influence our interactions. "If the social recognition becomes one that focuses on lack of skills, such as an inability to speak on one's own behalf, rather than on recognition of the individual, the person may be viewed as less competent and the individual's self-view may become distorted" (Wilson, 1994, p. 156). Thus, the perceptions of others greatly influence our perception of self and impacts our social efficacy (competency). Personality is a changeable dimension of the self which "is by definition a temporal phenomenon, a pattern of experiences and interactions over time, and the only way in which personality can be known is through the medium of interpersonal interactions" (Greenberg and Mitchell, 1983, p. 90).

Michaels (1997) argues that in all our lives, the experiences we tend to classify as our "triumphs" or our "successes" are always fewer than the experiences we euphemistically title our "learning experiences." It seems to be primarily our sense of self, or our belief in our own ability to positively affect change that allows us to continue trying. Based upon the description of the characteristics of adults with learning disabilities it can be inferred that many adults will have difficulty believing in their own ability to positively affect change within their own lives. In addition, many adults with learning disabilities historically tend to experience even fewer triumphs or successes in relation to the proportion of learning experiences and these learning experiences are frequently labelled by educators, parents, significant others, and by the individuals themselves as "personal failures." Each failure is attributed to self (and all too often turned against the self, eroding competency) while the triumphs/successes are attributed only to luck or some external force or agent (Michaels, Thaler, Zwerlein, Gioglio, and Apostoli, 1988). The result is an individual with a poor sense of personal competency who lacks the will to try in pre-anticipation of failure (Michaels, 1997). The diminished sense of personal competency and lack of willingness to try may simultaneously impact quality of life issues.

▶ QUALITY OF LIFE ISSUES

Quality of life is an elusive concept. There tends to be little agreement among professionals as to exactly how to conceptualize or measure an individual's quality of life (Taylor and Bogdan, 1996). Most researchers are, however, in agreement that quality of life must be composed of both objective and subjective components (see Halpern, 1993). Table 8.9 presents a recent conceptualization of the core quality of life dimensions and their indicators (Schalock,

TABLE 8.9

Core Quality of Life Dimensions and Indicators

Dimension	Exemplary Indicators
1. Emotional Well-Being	Safety, Spirituality, Happiness, Freedom from stress, Self-concept, Contentment
2. Interpersonal Relations	Intimacy, Affection, Family, Interactions, Friendships, Supports
3. Material Well-Being	Ownership, Financial security, Food, Employment, Possessions, Social economic status, Shelter
4. Personal Development	Education, Skills, Fulfillment, Personal competency, Purposeful activity, Advancement
5. Physical Well-Being	Health, Nutrition, Recreation, Mobility, Health care, Health insurance, Leisure, Activities of daily living
6. Self-Determination	Autonomy, Choices, Decisions, Personal control, Self-direction, Personal goals/values
7. Social Inclusion	Acceptance, Status, Supports, Work environment, Community integration and participation, Roles, Volunteer activities, Residential environments
8. Rights	Privacy, Voting, Access, Due process, Ownership, Civic responsibilities

Source: Schalock, R. L. (1996). Reconsidering the conceptualization and measurement of quality of life. In R. L. Schalock (Ed.), *Quality of life: Conceptualization and measurement (volume 1)* (pp. 123–139). Washington: American Association on Mental Retardation.

1996). Adults with learning disabilities may need assistance and support from service providers and their natural support systems (e.g., family, community members, and significant others) in order to achieve many of these indicators.

▶ ALTERNATIVE "POSTSECONDARY" ENVIRONMENTS

A variety of alternative programs are available to individuals with learning disabilities under the general rubric of *nondegree programs*. These programs are designed to address the quality of life dimensions and indicators described in Table 8.10. These programs tend to focus on offering the support individuals with learning disabilities need to become independent with a heavy emphasis on social and independent living skills. "Participants learn what it takes emotionally to function as an adult. This process is experiential and situational. Real-life situations tend to become the classrooms in most [nondegree] programs" (Bosch, 1994, p. 226).

While there exist tremendous differences within the types of services and interventions across these nondegree programs, they all "offer a residential component that allows the young to physically move away from home and yet still be in a safe, structured environment" (Bosch, 1994, p. 225). One of the first national models of nondegree programs for individuals with learning disabilities was the Threshold Program at Lesley College in Cambridge, Massachusetts which was established in 1982. This program is described as a nondegree transitional program

> designed to prepare young adults with learning disabilities, who also function in the low-average intellectual range, to become independent, responsible, productive, working citizens. Its three-year, comprehensive curriculum includes vocational preparation for paraprofessional positions in offices or settings with young children or elderly clientele; hands-on independent living training focusing on money management, apartment living skills, and leisure-time planning; creative courses; a variety of emotional support systems; and social skill training, which is reinforced throughout the rest of the program to help students become assertive self-advocates capable of responding appropriately to a broad range of social situations (Roffman, 1994, p. 199).

Bosch described the wide variation of approaches across these nondegree postsecondary programs:

> [t]hey may be apartment-based, on a campus of a regular college, or in a large group home setting. Some offer classes and instruction toward specific types of careers, with others being more individualized. Some have staffing around the clock and others do not. Some run on a school calendar and others are year-round. Some offer long—term support and living arrangements and others expect a transition back to the family home (1994, p. 225).

Table 8.10 presents an adaption of the basic skills of independent living as typically addressed within nondegree programs for adults with learning dis-

TABLE 8.10

The Domains and Curriculum Components of Independent Living Skills Instruction

Money Skills

Basic	Understanding values of currency/coins
Intermediate	Using a checking account, understanding basic banking (deposit, withdrawal, balance)
Advanced	Budgeting, comparison shopping, reconciling and balancing bank statements
Exceptional	Financial planning, preparation of taxes

Food Management

Basic	Knowing utensils, setting a table, ordering in a restaurant
Intermediate	Fixing breakfast or lunch, making a shopping list, basic safety when using kitchen appliances
Advanced	Following instructions for prepared, frozen, and canned foods; planning a menu
Exceptional	Following a recipe from a cookbook, using coupons and comparison shopping

Personal Appearance and Hygiene

Basic	Dresses and bathes self; using personal care products appropriately (deodorant, shampoo, etc)
Intermediate	Bathes regularly, habits of oral hygiene, wears clean clothes
Advanced	Sorts and washes clothes, knows settings and types of laundry products, irons and mends clothes
Exceptional	Demonstrates knowledge of appropriate dress for a variety of environments/occasions; budgets money for clothing and personal care needs

Basic Health Needs

Basic	Knows the parts of the body and their function; understands how to utilize simple medication (e.g., aspirin)
Intermediate	Recognizes and describes basic symptoms and health problems; knows how to get emergency health care
Advanced	Arranges for doctor appointments, appropriately takes care of self when sick; takes medication independently
Exceptional	Understands medical insurance and utilizes preventative health care measures

(continued)

TABLE 8.10
continued

Housekeeping Skills

Basic	Makes bed, washes dishes, and uses cleaning products appropriately
Intermediate	Uses a vacuum cleaner, properly maintains sinks and toilets to prevent clogs
Advanced	Defrosting a refrigerator, cleaning a room/bathroom
Exceptional	Home maintenance, minor household repairs, organizes closets and drawers

Emergency and Safety Skills

Basic	Knows functions of police, fire department, ambulance, etc., and how to contact them
Intermediate	Understands basic fire prevention, recognizes a gas leak and knowing what to do
Advanced	Knows how to use a fire extinguisher, determines when medical assistance is needed
Exceptional	Has mastered first aid and completed CPR training

Transportation

Basic	Rides a bicycle, can make a single trip utilizing public transportation
Intermediate	Uses public transportation with transfers
Advanced	Can obtain travel information, make reservations and arrange all aspects of travel
Exceptional	Can obtain a personal driver's license; read a map; own and maintain a car

Adapted from Bosch, 1994.

abilities. The model presented in Table 8.10 was conceptualized initially by Griffin and Ansell (1989) and divides independent living skills in the domains of money skills, food management, personal appearance and hygiene, basic health needs, housekeeping skills, emergency and safety skills, and transportation skills and identifies basic, intermediate, advanced, and exceptional levels of achievement within each skill domain (cited in Bosch, 1994).

In 1991 as a product of a national research and demonstration project funded by the United States Department of Education which was to address the transition from community college to employment for individuals with learning disabilities, Michaels et al. developed a comprehensive social skills curriculum to address many of the social skills needs of adults with learning disabilities for the world of work and beyond. Michaels et al. (1991) focus on five domains of social skills: interpersonal skills, dealing with feelings, dealing with stress and aggression, planning skills, and negotiating the work environment. The areas within each of the five domains are presented in Table 8.11.

Roffman (1994) suggested that it is critical when developing social skill intervention or teaching strategies that training is provided in both therapeutic or instructional settings and naturalistic settings. Without real instruction in naturalistic settings little transfer or skill generalization is noted. For example, Schumaker and Ellis (1982) found that successful role playing during a training session was not necessarily predictive of the social response

---

TABLE 8.11

Social Skill Domains and Component Skills

Interpersonal Skills

- The Art of Listening
- The Art of Conversation
- The Art of Asking Questions
- Verbal and Non-Verbal Communication

Dealing with Feelings

- Identifying and Expressing your Feelings
- Understanding and Respecting the Feelings of Others

Dealing with Stress and Aggression

- Developing and Using Self-Control
- Asserting Oneself in a Positive Manner
- Dealing with Criticism
- Coping with Change

Planning Skills

- Making Decisions
- Setting Goals
- Task Attack and Follow Through

The Work Environment

- Evaluating Performance
- Understanding the Dynamics of Office Relationships

Adapted from Michaels et al., 1991

or performance of young adults with learning disabilities in the natural environment. Roffman (1994) articulated a seven-step strategy for effective social skills instruction:

1. *Modeling* Modeling provides an opportunity for vicarious learning through direct observation which may then be incorporated into an individual's own behavioral repertoire (Roffman, 1994).

2. *Rehearsal* Following behavioral modeling, controlled playing or acting out of situations with feedback and suggestions should occur. Michaels et al. (1991) pointed out that if video is used at this stage of instruction it promotes the ability of the individuals participating in the role play to self-critique. Without the use of video, the "actors" learn mostly through the feedback and suggestions of others. This practice provides the opportunity to safely test a variety of alternatives without experiencing any potential aversive consequences which might result from the implementing of any of the strategies within naturalistic environments (Roffman, 1994).

3. *Reinforcement* Reinforcement refers to the praising or acknowledging of behaviors in a clear and specific manner. Citing Rose (1977), Roffman noted the benefit of participating in a social skills group on reinforcing behavior: "as a person learns to reinforce others, he or she is reciprocally reinforced by others" (1994, p. 197).

4. *Coaching* While coaching might be viewed as a component of the reinforcement process, Roffman rightfully separated it. Reinforcement serves to increase the occurrence of behavior, while coaching serves to modify and refine behavior. Typically, coaching refers to the corrective feedback which is offered either by the group facilitator or other group members and involves specific recommendations for improving behavioral performance.

5. *Cognitive restructuring* We know that behavior is strongly influenced by the verbal messages (or self-statements) individuals give themselves. Based on the 1977 work of Meichenbaum, Roffman pointed out that traditional behavioral approaches tend to "overemphasize the importance of environmental events (antecedents and consequences) and have underemphasized how individuals perceive and evaluate those events" (1994, p. 198). Individuals can be taught to modify the internal dialogue they engage in, utilizing many of the same strategies used to change overt behavior.

6. *Relaxation* Roffman (1994) pointed out that "the physiological arousal associated with anxiety and anger" (p. 198) may impede or inhibit performance. Social skill training programs should incorporate some form of relaxation training into the program to increase program effectiveness and skill transfer to naturalistic "real life" environments.

7. *Homework assignments* Homework encourages the transfer of skill training in simulated situations and environments to naturalistic life situations and environments. Frequently, real learning occurs when the group re-convenes and participants discuss the effectiveness, i.e., what actually occurred within the naturalistic environment, of a particular strategy or behavioral repertoire.

▶ VOCATIONAL REHABILITATION SERVICES

Vocational rehabilitation services may be an appropriate option from some adults with learning disabilities whose limitations may prevent them from either gaining or sustaining employment. The state-federal vocational rehabilitation (VR) system is operated at the federal level by the Rehabilitation Services Administration which is part of the Office of Special Education and Rehabilitative Services (OSERS) of the United States Department of Education. The overall goal of the state-federal VR system is to assist individuals with disabilities achieve employment. Once a determination of eligibility is made based on a diagnosis of learning disabilities (see the RSA definition provided earlier in this chapter) which is a substantial impediment to employment, an individual may qualify for a broad array of vocationally-oriented services. Dowdy and McCue (1994) described the broad scope of VR services provided to individuals with disabilities:

- assessment to determine eligibility and VR needs;
- vocational counseling, guidance, and referral services;
- physical and mental restoration services;
- vocational and other training, including on-the-job training;
- maintenance for additional costs incurred while the individual is in rehabilitation;
- transportation related to other VR services;
- interpreter services to individuals who are deaf;
- reader services for those who are blind;
- services to assist students with disabilities in transition from school to work;
- personal assistance services (including training in managing, supervising, and directing personal assistance services) while receiving VR services;
- rehabilitation technology services and devices;
- supported employment services; and
- job placement services. (p. 57)

▶ WORKING IN PARTNERSHIPS WITH ADULTS WITH LEARNING DISABILITIES TO CREATE A POSITIVE VISION FOR THE FUTURE

Probably one of the most critical supports educators, advocates, and service providers can provide to individuals with learning disabilities is to willingly agree to take the journey with them. In other words, rather than act in the traditional "professional" manner of trying to convince each person about what is best, service providers need to open their ears (and hearts) in order to listen to the hopes, dreams, and desires of the individuals they serve. Many different systems or approaches have been designed for accomplishing this task, and they are generally referred to under the general rubric of "person-centered planning approaches" (e.g., see Mount, 1992; Pearpoint, Forest, and Snow, 1992; Snow, 1994). Beyond all systems and approaches, the attitude of the service provider is probably most important—*Listen and Support*. The PATH process will be described here (adapted from Pearpoint, O'Brien, and Forest, 1992). The PATH (Planning Alternative Tomorrows with Hope) process requires that an individual or group work together through an eight-step planning process with the assistance of two co-facilitators—one facilitator elicits information while the other primarily serves to graphically record information. The reader is cautioned that only a brief description of the PATH process is provided here and that prior to attempting to facilitate a PATH, additional in-depth training should be pursued. The eight steps of the PATH process are:

1. *Identify the dream* The dream is often described as the "north star" of an individual's life. From this reference point, we are able to orient for the remaining seven steps of the process and in the design and implementation of all future services and interventions.

2. *Develop the goal* While the dream is frequently "out-there" almost like some spiritual ideal, the goal is more concrete and attainable. The goal stems directly from the dream in much the same way as a corporate mission statement might stem from the corporate vision statement. The goal results from having the individual remain focused on the dream while simultaneously "traveling forward" in time to some specified time (e.g., one year down the road) and should be described in as much detail as possible.

3. *Describe the present* Traveling back to the here and now, the individual is asked to describe where they are today in relation to both the dream and the goal. This step helps to capture exactly where the person is currently in his/her life compared to where they would like to be. At this point in the process, a natural tension is created between what is and what could be. The individual must be permitted to experience this tension and then make a conscious commitment to beginning the journey to the goal.

4. *Identify people to enroll in creating change* In this step the individual works to identify people within the immediate family and the extended circles of support (i.e., neighbors, friends, members of the community, etc.) who can be mobilized to support the individual in creating the future (or at least in minimizing potential road blocks along the way). This step is particularly important for young adults with learning disabilities who may have difficulty developing relationships and/or asking for assistance (based upon the personality profile described earlier).

5. *Build strengths* The individual is asked to identify the skills, knowledge, and relationships (people resources) necessary to move from what is current (3) to the goal (2). Frequently, the need for additional education and/or training may be identified at this stage of the process. It is also important to identify the

internal supports, e.g., exercise, meditating, that the individual needs to do for him/herself to remain motivated and vital through the journey.

6. *Set objectives to be accomplished in the next few months* After reviewing the goal again, the individual begins to describe what concrete steps can be taken in the next three to six months. The individual should describe actions to be taken in concrete terms and make sure that those actions are consistent with both the goal and the dream.

7. *Plan for the next month* Describe the immediate steps to be taken in the achievement of the objectives just established (step 6). Eliciting information in answer to *who* will do *what* and by *when* in the next month will help to move the process into action.

8. *Gain commitment to action* The final step of the process requires that the facilitators get the individual to commit to taking the very first step towards the achievement of the goal. As with almost any other change discussed within a counseling milieu, "breaking the grasp of inertia is critical" (Pearpoint, O'Brien, and Forest, 1992, p. 18).

SUMMARY

This chapter has focused on adults with learning disabilities. Problems encountered by adults with learning disabilities, as well as services available for this group were presented. The following points summarize the major areas included in the chapter:

- Children with learning disabilities do not outgrow their problems.

- A new agenda relative to supports for adults with learning disabilities has recently been developed.

- There has recently been a great deal of growth in attention to adults with learning disabilities.

- Adults with learning disabilities often have problems in their jobs.

- Social relations appears to be a very high area of need for adults with learning disabilities.

- Evaluation and tutoring are two of the most frequently found services available for adults with learning disabilities.

- Many adults with learning disabilities learn to compensate for their disability.

- Adults with learning disabilities tend to demonstrate difficulties with all higher order conceptual/linguistic tasks.

- Psychosocial problems are encountered by many adults with learning disabilities.

- Unemployment and underemployment often plague adults with learning disabilities.

- Approximately 20,000 students with learning disabilities enroll in colleges as first-year students annually.
- Section 504 of the Rehabilitation Act of 1973 requires colleges and universities to provide accommodations for students with learning disabilities.
- College demands often result in many students with learning disabilities experiencing major problems.
- Vocational rehabilitation agencies provide many support services for adults with learning disabilities in the work environment.
- Reasonable work accommodations are required by Section 504 for employees with learning disabilities.
- Assessing adults with learning disabilities is very important in establishing a good job match for this group of individuals.
- A variety of alternative programs are available for adults with learning disabilities under the general rubric of nondegree programs.

Chapter 9

DIVERSITY AND LEARNING DISABILITIES[1]

The objectives for this chapter are as follows:

▶ To define the common terms used to describe students with disabilities whose backgrounds are culturally and linguistically different from the mainstream.

▶ To describe the issues and practices linked to identification of students with learning disabilities who come from diverse language and cultural backgrounds.

▶ To describe appropriate interventions to maximize the cognitive and affective development of students with LD from diverse backgrounds.

▶ To describe the factors associated with socioeconomic differences that may impact one's learning abilities, such as poverty and substance abuse.

▶ To apply knowledge about differences between the sexes in aspects such as active learning, participation in school, optimal class size, and other variables.

▶ To describe the role of sexual orientation within the framework of diversity.

▶ To discuss issues related to preparation of personnel to work with students with exceptionalities whose backgrounds are very diverse.

[1]This chapter was co-authored by Diane S. Bassett.

Gilbert: Trying to Bridge the Cultural Gap

Gilbert arrived at the rural elementary school in a new community, bringing with him a short lifetime of experiences and individual characteristics. His family's dominant language is not English, but he speaks only English due to television and to older siblings who have acculturated quickly. His father works at a minimum wage position while his mother works hard to care for the five children and the home. The teacher believes the parents have low expectations for Gilbert's achievements now *and* in the future based on their failure to attend meetings or to actively participate when they are there. No matter how hard the teacher tries, Gilbert never asks for help, even when it is obvious he does not understand the directions. As the school year has progressed, his performance has gotten increasingly worse in almost all of his school subjects. He does well in science (during hands-on experiments), physical education, and art.

He looks uncomfortable when other students compete for leadership roles or top scores in the classroom or on the playground. The teacher notices that, rather than gradually joining in with his peers, Gilbert appears increasingly withdrawn and absences are occurring more frequently.

- What might be significant factors in Gilbert's reactions?
- How could school personnel have better prepared Gilbert for the shock of this new situation?

Many educators, parents, and advocates are attempting to eliminate the term "normal" from their comparative descriptions about students, with good reason. The profiles of students in the U.S. educational system now are quite disparate from any traditional stereotypes, which means that adults involved in educating children and youth must be prepared to learn more thoroughly about each student's situation and refrain from making assumptions. Parents from diverse groups hold expectations that schools will broaden the scope of education to address the needs of their children, including the use of diverse languages, acceptance of diverse cultures, support for ethnic identities, and support services for families as well as students (Weismantel and Fradd, 1989).

This chapter describes ways in which students might differ from each other in an attempt to help educators understand the numerous interrelated dimensions that might affect learning so they can provide the appropriate educational services which communities expect. Differences can include culture and language, socioeconomic, gender, and sexual orientation. The presence of a learning disability adds yet another dimension which may interact with these traits in very minor or sometimes very significant ways. Each of the conditions discussed in this chapter may be inherently intertwined with a number of other intrapersonal, interpersonal, and environmental elements that will not be separately addressed but which may compound the complexities of the diversity issues presented.

▶ CULTURAL AND LINGUISTIC DIVERSITY AND LEARNING DISABILITIES

The scope and length of this chapter disallow discussions about the origins, natures, or futures of diverse cultural and language groups within the U.S. educational system. The purpose here is to see how these aspects of diversity relate to learning disabilities. A brief section on demographic characteristics, followed by definitions, will help the reader know a little about students in these groups. Then follows the major educational components in which cultural and language differences critically relate to learning disabilities, including assessment for identification, program planning, instructional implementation, and personnel preparation.

Demographic Characteristics

Approximately five percent of the school population is identified with learning disabilities. At the same time, cultural or language diversity is present among

Cultural and linguistic diversity is a factor for students with learning disabilities.

rapidly growing numbers of students (Gersten and Woodward, 1994; Smith and Luckasson, 1995). Thus, it follows that diverse students will comprise a substantial, and possibly growing portion of students identified with learning disabilities. In one study, Baca and Almanza (1991) noted that approximately one million students with diverse language backgrounds have already been identified as learning disabled. Adding to the problem is that some districts and states *misdiagnose* students from diverse backgrounds with learning problems, an issue addressed later in this chapter. The following summarizes the diversity of many states.

> Today in twenty-five of the country's largest cities and metropolitan areas, at least half the student population is from culturally and linguistically diverse groups (American Council on Education, 1988). The states with the largest LEP populations are California, Texas, New York, and Florida. In three states—California, New Mexico, and Mississippi—minority students are the majority, and Texas will soon join them (Quality Education for Minorities Project, 1990). The largest and fastest-growing group is Hispanic, currently with 75 percent of all children of limited English proficiency . . . We can estimate conservatively that at least 1.5 percent of children are culturally and linguistically diverse and have special education needs (Smith and Luckasson, 1995, pp. 48–49).

Cultural pluralism and language differences clearly do not create exceptionalities, nor should they be viewed as risk factors for children. For example, extensive research evidence asserts that bilingualism can enhance intellectual utility and flexibility through augmenting creativity and strengthening the capacity to produce phonemes (sounds) from diverse languages (Bozinou-Doukas, 1983). In spite of such benefits, however, three forces continue to link culturally diverse students with special education, whether appropriate or not.

First, poverty and its many associated effects (e.g., compromised health, reduced academic gains, high dropout rates) are disproportionately associated with families from diverse backgrounds in this country. In 1994 the Children's Defense Fund reported that 53 percent of all young African-American families with children live in poverty, as well as 40 percent of such families with Hispanic heritage. In general, 24 percent of Native Americans are in poverty, but those living on reservations face a poverty rate of 42 percent (Quality Education for Minorities Project, 1990). In addition, the U.S. faces the largest immigration wave in history (U.S. Bureau of the Census, 1990). Students from recent immigrant groups (e.g., Nicaraguan, Vietnamese, Hmong) are often poor and have often experienced violence, war, and other traumatic situations, in addition to adjusting to new role delineations and cultural expectations (Wei, 1983). Each of these factors may multiply the impact of poverty on learning capacities.

Second, several researchers have noted that administrators and teachers carry lower expectations for students from diverse backgrounds than for those from the mainstream, and thus see special education as a viable placement option (Gersten, Brengelman, and Jimenez, 1994; Gottlieb, Alter, and Gottlieb, 1994). Apparently, students from diverse cultures and languages are disproportionately placed into special education programs because it represents an inferior education that the system believes meets their needs. Dumping diverse students into special education reinforces the apparent validity of the diagnostic and remedial classification systems and reduces the pressure for general education to create meaningful programs for these students. As a result, overidentification of learning disabilities may occur readily among culturally and linguistically diverse students.

Third, societal forces throughout the history of the United States, unintentionally or with intent, have played out a love-hate relationship with culturally and linguistically diverse groups. While recognizing the varied native and immigrant groups that developed this nation, the policies and practices within our broad institutions (social, educational, and particularly economic) conversely have oppressed those diverse groups when their needs or interests were perceived to be conflicting with those of the dominant culture. Thus, individuals from different cultures historically have shared similarities in discriminatory treatment with people who have disabilities.

Definitions

Weismantel and Fradd (1989) described students who may speak only English but come from families with dominant languages other than English as having non-English language background (NELB). "Non-English language" may be more appropriate than "first" or "native" language, since students in the United States often learn another language simultaneously with English (not necessarily implying either is taught or learned well). "English for speakers of other languages" (ESOL) is the term used for English instruction programs using only that language, while "bilingual education" refers to the use of a non-English language to support learners while they develop their English language skills (Weismantel and Fradd, 1989).

Weismantel and Fradd (1989) defined "multicultural" persons as individuals from various ethnic groups (e.g., African-American, Native American, Hispanic) and other native-born children of immigrant and nonimmigrant families; they reported this term as the one advocated by the Council for Exceptional Children. "Culturally and/or linguistically diverse" (CLD) students are those whose backgrounds encompass a range of cultural, ethnic, racial, or language elements beyond the traditional Euro-American experience; "language-different" signifies the same as "linguistically different."

Identification Issues

The Education for All Handicapped Children Act (P.L. 94–142) set the stage for nonbiased assessment of language–different students who were suspected of having disabilities. Its reauthorization as IDEA maintained a strong mandate in this area. The interdisciplinary team that determines disability must include at least one person knowledgeable about the student's culture or language. However, Cummins (1984) noted major questions by professionals about the true impact of the law's provisions due to conceptual disagreements about learning disabilities and a philosophical perspective that located such problems solely within the student.

Dodd (1992) and Mercer (1987) outlined some concerns involved in differentiating language learning disabilities from language differences. For instance, any group of students, regardless of shared characteristics, is going to be very heterogeneous, making it difficult to tell the difference easily between the disability and the language difference. Another concern was that certain learning behaviors readily characterize English language learners (ELLs) or other groups as easily as they typify students with Learning Disabilities (see Table 9.1). One caveat or guideline

TABLE 9.1

Indicators of Learning Disabilities That Are Also Behavioral Characteristics of Students in the Process of Learning English

Indicator	Cultural or Linguistic Explanation
Discrepancy between verbal and performance measures on intelligence tests	This discrepancy is predictable because those who are not proficient in the language of the test are often able to complete many of the nonverbal tasks correctly (Cummins, 1984).
Academic learning difficulty	Students in the process of learning a new language often experience difficulty with academic concepts and language because these terms and ideas are more abstract, less easily understood and experienced than ideas and terms that communicate social interactions and intents (Cummins, 1984).
Language disorders	When second-language learners enter into meaningful communication, they often appear as language disorders because of disfluencies that are a natural part of second-language development (Oller, 1993).
Perceptual disorders	Even the ability to perceive and organize information can be distorted when students begin to learn a new language (DeBlassie, 1983).
Social and emotional problems	Students in the process of learning how to function successfully in a new language and culture predictably experience social trauma and emotional problems (DeBlassie and Franco, 1983).
Attention and memory problems	When students have few prior experiences on which to relate new information, they may find it difficult to pay attention and to remember (DeBlassie, 1983).
Hyperactivity or hypoactivity; impulsivity	When students have little prior knowlege or experiences on which to base present information, they frequently become restless and inattentive (DeBlassie, 1983).

Source: Fradd, S.H., and Weismantel, M.J. (1989). Developing and evaluating goals. In S.H. Fradd and M.J. Weismantel (Eds.), *Meeting the needs of culturally and linguistically different students: A handbook for educators.* Austin: PRO-ED.

in the midst of this confusion is the agreement among researchers and practition-ers alike that learning disabilities must exist in both languages or cultures of the student in order to be real (Fradd, Barona, and Santos de Barona, 1989). For example, the student must have difficulty with sentence structure, naming objects, or idioms—whatever the specific learning disability is—in both Vietnamese and English. A student would have to show social perception problems (if that were the learning disability) in *both* Nicaragua and the United States.

Overrepresentation, Underrepresentation, and Misdiagnoses Numerous stud-ies have found that learners from non-mainstream cultures are overrepresented in disability categories. This overrepresentation means that students are diag-nosed with learning or other disabilities in numbers far above what their pro-portion in the general population would indicate (Figueroa, 1989; Mercer, 1973; Moecker, 1992). Few assessment experts believe that standardized diag-nostic and achievement tools can truly be culture-free (Wei, 1983). Even *infor-mal* assessment procedures can be fraught with problems if the evaluating professional is uninformed about cultural and linguistic differences (Schiff-Myers, Djukic, McGovern-Lawler, and Perez, 1993). For example, Anderson and Anderson (1983) reported that many Native Americans are labeled with exceptionalities due to cultural differences. These differences, which tradition-al environments may turn into academic difficulties, involve communication styles and behavior patterns, as well as aspects of response to assessment. A his-torical emphasis on shaping the U.S. education system to serve as the accultur-ation agent for Native Americans resulted a century ago in an English-only policy and a refusal to recognize and validate any cultural beliefs or practices other than those of the mainstream. These perspectives, while no longer offi-cially endorsed, continue to pervade the atmospheres of school settings. Adding insult to injury, few teachers of Indian students historically have been Native Americans themselves (10 to 15 percent in recent studies), and most teachers of native students are unfamiliar with the cultures or languages of the group(s) they serve (Anderson and Anderson, 1983).

Students with non-English language backgrounds, such as many American Indians or Asian Americans, run even greater risk for misdiagnosis of learning disabilities than those fluent English speakers from different cultures, such as African-Americans. Reasons for this risk include (1) the language of adminis-tration of the majority of tests used in evaluations; (2) the fact that many U.S. tests, although possibly translated into one's dominant language, are still cul-turally linked to the mainstream experience; (3) arrested development of the first language in so many students who quit speaking it once they enter school, (Schiff-Myers, et al., 1993); and (4) the relative scarcity of translated versions of many widely accepted diagnostic tools. However, diagnostic procedures and team decision-making may also be guilty of influencing misdiagnoses. Moecker (1992) recently found that LD diagnoses were made, based on only achieve-ment test scores and intelligence test scores administered in English, with no room allowed for discussion about second language issues in the assessment process. Another factor leading to misdiagnoses may be simply the referral itself: studies have shown that referrals of diverse students result in special education placements at an alarmingly high rate (Ortiz and Yates, 1983). This finding is particularly unsettling, given that such referrals are often due either to the monolingual teachers' beliefs they cannot teach students who are learning English or to the student's failure to progress (Gersten and Woodward, 1994).

> When school personnel merely acknowledge the potential relationship between environmental, cultural, and linguistic factors and students' failure to achieve at grade-level expectations, but refrain from exploring the causes of learning problems that can be addressed by modifications within the school, then NELB . . . students can be expected to be identified for special education services at rates that are disproportionate to their mainstream peers (Fradd, Barona, and Santos de Barona, 1989, p. 90).

Significantly large populations overrepresented in the learning disabilities category include Native Americans and Hispanics (Anderson and Anderson, 1983; Mercer, 1973). However, contradictory findings about overrepresentation in the LD category have occurred across states (Fradd, Weismantel, Correa, and Algozzine, 1988), so some inconsistencies exist. Some states apparently do a better job in identifying students with learning disabilities than others.

Underrepresentation due to reluctance to make referrals has recently emerged as an alarming trend in some locales in the United States. Gersten, Brengelman, and Jimenez (1994) described several studies that concluded: "far too many language-minority students with clear learning problems simply are ignored or are provided with cursory tutorial services, often by a paraprofessional" (pp. 4–5). Fears that many students will not show the IQ/achievement discrepancy required in many states for a learning disabilities diagnosis, when in fact they may truly have a learning problem, have kept some bilingual educators from referring students for review, while others fear that some students will be misdiagnosed with more severe disabilities (Bozinou-Doukas, 1983). Researchers have suggested that the intelligence scores of bilingual/ESOL students may be depressed due to language constraints as well as their academic scores (Fradd, Barona, and Santos de Barona, 1989).

Prereferral and Assessment Process The prereferral and assessment process is of critical importance for any student suspected of having a learning disability; it becomes doubly important for learners from different cultures and languages. Garcia and Ortiz (1988) have developed a comprehensive model for protecting the rights and capacity-building of students from diverse cultural and linguistic backgrounds who are suspected of having learning problems. This model, entitled "Preventing Inappropriate Placements of Language Minority Students in Special Education: A Prereferral Process" has become one of the standards in the field, offering eight thoughtful steps that result in special education placement only as a last resort (see Figure 9.1).

Multiple assessment measures are recommended for testing learners with learning disabilities, including native language interview, portfolio assessment, phonological tests, and vision and hearing screening (Schwarz and Burt, 1995).

FIGURE 9.1

Preventing Inappropriate Placements of Language Minority Students in Special Education: A Prereferral Process

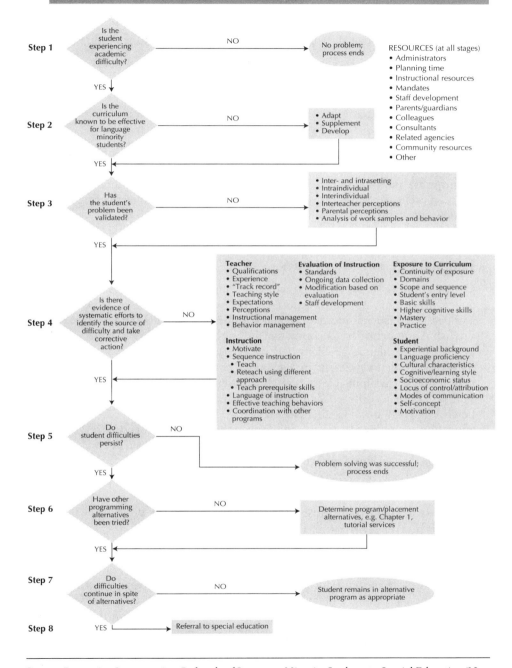

Source: *Preventing Inappropriate Referrals of Language Minority Students to Special Education* (New Focus Series, No. 5), by S.B. Garcia and A.A. Ortiz, 1988, Wheaton, MD: National Clearinghouse for Bilingual Education. Reprinted by permission.

Norm-referenced standardized academic tests, observations in diverse settings, and individual language assessment procedures are also urged (Fradd, Barona, and Santos de Barona, 1989). A comprehensive description of the latter is provided by Fradd, Barona, et al. (1989) through the following components:

- Sampling language - at least three oral (10-15 minutes each) and 2-3 written samples in classrooms and other settings, by experienced educators, and

- Observations across settings, through a variety of methods (checklists, anecdotal records, oral samples, videotapes, reading selections, writing samples, language experience dictations, or other means).

Fradd and Weismantel (1989) developed a checklist for evaluating different sources of information as a way to ensure that data collection procedures are appropriate and to minimize bias in the assessment process. Figure 9.2 portrays this comprehensive checklist useful for both developing and evaluating intermediate program goals; a range of personnel can use and/or modify the checklist to make sure that teaching is well-grounded in knowledge about the student.

Language Acquisition Issues

Until Cummins' (1984) seminal work on bilingualism and exceptionality, language proficiency for the purpose of placement was commonly assessed by competence in social interactions only. Students with adequate conversational English were identified as competent in English and placed in general classes; any further academic problems led staff to suspect learning disabilities rather than the problems inherent in learning a new language while trying to learn new content. Cummins (1984) concluded that basic interpersonal communication skills (BICS) differed significantly from cognitive/academic language proficiency (CALP) and led the fields of bilingual education and bilingual special education in renewed support for thorough assessment procedures and dual language instruction. Language evaluations were expanded to include both academic and social language skills in both written and oral formats (Fradd, Barona, and Santos de Barona, 1989).

IEP Issues and Strategies: Planning for Culturally/ Linguistically Appropriate Instruction

Planning to meet the needs of diverse students requires a "marriage" of three (sometimes separate) systems of education: general education, bilingual/ESOL education, and special education. General education is considered the core, with bilingual, ESOL, and special education perceived as support systems. All disciplines in education have learned that no single system can do the job by itself when students present a range of diverse strengths and needs. Fradd and Weismantel (1989) outlined a process to help connect these three systems for the important purposes of (1) student screening, (2) assessment and diagnosis, (3) placement, (4) instructional design and implementation, and (5) program and student evaluation. Table 9.2 specifies the types of information that each

FIGURE 9.2

Checklist for Evaluating Bilingual/ESOL and Special Education Sources

Student Identification
Before students are considered for special education referral, the following information should be collected.

_____Home language survey is given to all new students.

_____Teacher observations include language use in a variety of settings and ethnolinguistic groups.

_____Observations in English

_____Observations in non-English language

_____School records are kept to reflect:

_____Previous school enrollment _____attendance achievement

_____norm-referenced tests _____grades received

_____Parent interviews: _____English _____non-English

_____General health observation _____vision screening

_____hearing screening

_____Clear records were kept indicating the interventions implemented and the outcomes of these interventions prior to formal referral assessment.

Assessment and Diagnosis
Language assessment is completed before intellectual and academic assessment is begun.

Language Assessment

_____Language measures indicating language dominance

_____Language measures indicating language proficiency

_____Productive and respective language measures:_____English _____non-English

_____Language samples of several tasks were collected under similar conditions and periods of time _____English _____non-English

_____Equivalent tests were used in English and non-English

_____Equivalent methods were used in English and non-English

_____Equivalent observations were made

_____Translators and interpreters were trained and skillful in conducting assessment procedures under standardized-like conditions.

_____Documentation of every effort made to locate bilingual professionals before translators and interpreters were used.

Placement

_____Copies of assessment results were made available to all personnel including parents on child study team: _____English _____non-English

_____All team members understood the results.

_____All team members participated in discussion and decision making.

_____Informal conversations held after the meeting indicated that participants all felt that their input was valued.

(continued)

FIGURE 9.2

continued

Instructional Planning

_____Copies of assessment results were made available to all personnel, including parents, on child study team: _____English _____non-English

_____All team participants understood the results and the implications of results for planning instruction.

_____All team members participated in discussion and decision making.

_____Informal conversations held after the meeting indicated that participants felt that their input was valued and useful.

_____Plan includes opportunities for both English and non-English language development.

Curriculum and Materials Development

_____A consistent plan is implemented for developing both English and non-English language skills and concepts.

_____A framework is used for integrating language and skill development.

_____Instructional plans emphasize students' strengths, specify their current level of language and cognitive skill development, and begin at these specified points to move the students from concrete to abstract language and skills.

_____Plans accommodate both U.S. and non-English culture.

_____Plans promote academic and social skill development.

Achievement Review

_____Progress was measured in terms of academic and social skills development;

_____Progress was made in integrating students into U.S. culture;

_____Progress was measured in terms of both English and non-English language accomplishments;

_____Measurements of progress include parents' evaluation.

_____Progress was made in terms of the plan that was devised.

_____Other factors not considered when the plan was developed were also considered in evaluation progress.

Source: Fradd, S.H., and Weismantel, M.J. (1989). Developing and evaluating goals. In S.H. Fradd and M.J. Weismantel (Eds.), *Meeting the needs of culturally and linguistically different students: A handbook for educators* (pp. 51–52). Austin: PRO-ED.

support system typically gathers for each of the five functions, so that a transdisciplinary team can learn about and build on each other's scope of work. Each teacher can enhance the others' effectiveness by becoming familiar with current insights about their particular focus in education.

Special educators should learn from their bilingual/ESOL colleagues some of the learning and social behaviors that characterize various cultural groups in

TABLE 9.2

Coordination and Integration of Bilingual/ESOL and Special Education Services: The Overall Perspective

ESOL Education	Bilingual/ESOL Special Education	Special Education
Student Identification		

Home language survey
Teacher observation
School records
    Enrollment
    Attendance
    Achievement
    Norm-referenced tests
    Daily work and grades
Parent interviews [a]
	Combined data confirm or refute presence of learning and behavior difficulties requiring in-depth assessment and determine the language(s) of further interaction and assessment[b]	General health observations
		Vision screening
		Hearing screening
		Teacher observation
		Parent interviews
		School records
		    Enrollment
		    Attendance
		    Achievement
		    Norm-referenced tests
		    Daily work and grades

Assessment and Diagnosis[c,d]		
Language dominance assessment Dominance Proficiency (Bilingual/ESOL programs do not consider intellectual ability, except in the extreme) Reading inventories Math skills Focused observation Language samples	(Compilation of information on language use, form, and function in non-English and English) Intellectual assessment (may be bilingual or include nonverbal measures) Academic assessment (may be in both languages) Social skills assessment (information should be obtained by personnel sensitive to linguistic/culture differences)	Intellectual assessment Reading inventories Math skills Focused observation Language samples Adaptive behavior Social and emotional assessment
Placement[e]		
Bilingual/ESOL personnel	(Integrated group including balanced participation from bilingual/ESOL general and special education, and support services)	Special educational personnel
Instructional Planning and Curriculum Materials Development[f]		
Does not require an individual plan, but instruc-	Language assessment data included	Written plan includes Present performance

(continued)

TABLE 9.2

continued

ESOL Education	Bilingual/ESOL Special Education	Special Education
tion can include suggestions from special education Non-English and English language development Content-area instruction	Dual language plan Mode of service indicated Language(s) of instruction indicated Person(s) responsible Non-English and English development adapted to individual needs Learning strategy instruction Content area instruction adapted to individual needs Social skills instruction adapted to individual needs	Specific needs Goals Placement time Duration of services Specific academic skill instruction/remediation Learning strategy instruction Social skill development/remediation

Achievement Review

ESOL Education	Bilingual/ESOL Special Education	Special Education
Teacher observation Language assessment (annual review is usually carried out, not always required) Academic tests Dominance and proficiency tests skills developments Progress in mainstreaming English language	Annual review Language samples Progress on areas remediated in non-English Progress in mainstreaming English language development Academic and social skills development	Annual review Academic skills Progress on areas of remediation in English Progress in mainstreaming Academic and Social development

[a]Parent participation and input is sought in every aspect of the assessment, instruction, and reevaluation process.

[b]If data indicate potential handicapping condition, initiate prereferral activities, including language assessment and instructional interventions.

[c]Language of assessment is determined before assessment of academic, intellectual, and social skills begins.

[d]Presence of handicapping condition must be found in performance obtained in dominant language or in both languages.

[e]Whether special education placement is deemed to be the most appropriate or not, placement and instructional planning should be integrated so as to meet the social and academic needs of the students.

[f]Legal precedent exists for the use of non-English language instruction in meeting the needs of handicapped LEP students.

Source: Fradd, S.H., and Weismantel, M.J. (1989). Developing and evaluating goals. In S.H. Fradd and M.J. Weismantel (Eds.), *Meeting the needs of culturally and linguistically different students: A handbook for educators* (pp. 41–43). Austin: PRO-ED.

order to avoid reacting negatively to students or families out of ignorance. Uninformed teachers may lower their judgments about Native American students, for instance, because the students may avoid public recognition, respond to authority figures by looking down or away, speak little in class, or choose cooperative rather than competitive activities (Anderson and Anderson, 1983). Professionals also may erroneously assume that students' and families' failure to enthusiastically embrace the education program signals their apathy about education, when in fact they may resist or resent the imposition of Anglo values and customs in the schools.

> The apathy develops when the school curriculum fails to prepare Native American students for anything they see as relevant, i.e., skills necessary for a living or for an occupation . . . suited to the specific skills used in different Native American settings and cultures . . . . There is also a need for evaluation of education for occupations not available in the tribal area. Often, schools force the young Native American to choose the tribe, job, or education. If Native American students realistically are not able to find jobs suited to their academic preparation, then attending school, for them, is pointless (Anderson and Anderson, 1983, pp. 166–167).

Ochoa and Palmer (1995) have documented similar behavior patterns (e.g., tendency toward cooperation in learning, an appearance of apathy) among Mexican-American students with learning disabilities. They cite Ogbu's (1987) research when suggesting that some Mexican-American students may not have a strong tradition of academic achievement, perhaps due to a belief that their chances of succeeding in that arena are inequitable in comparison to Anglo peers. Few individuals enjoy continually "losing" in any type of activity.

The concerns expressed above highlight the necessity of including individual cultural experiences and expectations as part of individualized planning. Long-range goals must acknowledge community expectations and parental dreams as well as the goals of the learner. The student, having been raised with those spoken and unspoken expectations among elders and relatives, may not realize that educators are not knowledgeable about those elements of one's life. It is incumbent upon educators to ensure that the lines of communication about such wishes are open and flexible in order for students and families to feel safe talking about personal goals.

Developing a Language Use Plan   Garcia (1995) recommended that direct attention to language development issues be a paramount consideration in each diverse student's instructional program. She advocated a "language use plan" that addresses the following components of instruction:

1. Language of instruction—for academic content areas, literacy development, and functional academics instruction

2. Parties responsible—bilingual educator, ESL specialist, general educator or special educator with ESL training

3. Types of language intervention needed—language enrichment (either language), language development (either), ESL (English only), or language remediation (again, either language).

Fradd, Barona, and Santos de Barona (1989) illustrated a comprehensive checklist for educators to monitor students' progress on language development components of the IEP. This checklist includes eleven questions on language skills developed by interpersonal/social experiences (e.g., "retells a familiar story," "appropriately answers basic questions") and twenty-five questions about skills developed through academic, structured instruction (e.g., "asks for clarifications during academic tasks," "uses sound-symbol association," "writes from dictation"). The format and questions appear easy for students, parents, and educators to understand and use.

Partnerships with Families Parents, siblings, and other critical family members should be valued partners among professionals serving students from diverse backgrounds. Their participation is important due to the influence and support generated from families, communities, and cultures throughout the learner's lifespan, but more importantly because their insights about their children helps save scarce time and maximize resources (Gersten, et al., 1994a). Input from families is essential for planning and development of relevant individualized programs at every age level (IFSPs, IEPs, transition plans, and rehabilitation plans if applicable). While special education should integrate parents (and students) as partners in all decision-making, from ethical, legal, and professional bases, special education as a system has been user-friendly only in theory (i.e., legal mandates), not typically in practice.

A recent study showed that African-American parents of young preschoolers with disabilities consistently tried to support their children's educational programs until they became disillusioned with the system's separation from nondisabled peers and from parental influence (Harry, Allen, and McLaughlin, 1995). In this study, professionals deterred parental advocacy through features such as late notices about meetings, rigid and brief schedules for parent conferences, emphasis on documents rather than participation, use of jargon, and power structures that favored the professionals over the parents. Three additional studies cited by Harry and colleagues observed similar behaviors in parent-professional interactions, where systems controlled how parents could participate in such a way as to delegitimize their viewpoints and confuse or alienate them. Rather than getting involved passively as earlier studies reported (Turnbull and Turnbull, 1990), parents appear to find themselves virtually getting shut out by the formal structure.

Strategies for involving families more actively include:

- establishing relationships early through home visits or other informal meetings (preferably away from school)
- scheduling realistic time periods for meaningful meetings
- scheduling meetings at times convenient for family members
- listening, listening, and more listening
- clarifying perceptions about and impact of labels, jargon, etc.
- recognition of the diverse contributions families make to their children's educational programs.

Gersten et al. (1994a) described successful attempts to integrate families more fully, such as systematically sharing information on student progress and homework expectations, along with specified ways to help at home, and collectively agreeing on desired learning outcomes. Harry (1992) also recommended greater structure to support parental participation, including (1) informing parents in advance of specific issues about which their input will be needed, (2) including parents in the assessment process, and (3) systematically adding to the IEP meeting agenda a parent report on his/her child's progress and needs.

Teaching Approaches for Language/Literacy Development

Recent critics of the skill-building, parts-to-whole approach historically used in special education have warned that critical language development of linguistically diverse students with learning disabilities will be impaired within such a "bottom-up" approach (Cummins, 1984; Gersten and Woodward, 1994; Yates and Ortiz, 1991). As a result, movement toward increased use of whole language approaches has emerged in an effort to facilitate greater enjoyment and understanding and to link with approaches being used in mainstream classrooms.

Gersten, Brengelman, and Jimenez (1994) outlined essential components of effective instruction for students from diverse linguistic backgrounds, listed in Table 9.3. Many of the constructs they advocated are described briefly below, under "Instructional Approaches."

Instructional Approaches A number of strategies were suggested by Gersten et al. (1994a) to increase "comprehensible input" (Yates and Ortiz, 1991), or input that one understands, for English language learners. For example, free access to high-interest storybooks in English was found to double the rate of reading and listening comprehension among English learners. Certain strategically applied adaptations can ensure that students grasp teachers' messages, including:

- eliciting or providing relevant background information (as much as is needed)
- intentional redundancy with minor variations in words and instances
- more simple or declarative sentences
- controlled (but not constricted) vocabulary
- frequent checks for comprehension
- physical gestures
- visual cues (e.g., graphic organizers or actual objects).

"Explicit instructional conversations" (Echevarria, 1994; Goldenberg, 1992/1993) offer guidelines that enhance natural language use on a systematic basis. They are described as intense twenty- to thirty-minute sessions focusing on language learning and language concepts; sessions are teacher-directed but conversational in format. The teacher asks questions, probes, coaxes, or listens, through the following conversational elements:

TABLE 9.3
Constructs for Effective Teaching of Language-Different Students

1. Scaffolding and Strategies
   a. Provide story maps and visual organizers
   b. Encourage transfer of native language skills
   c. Elicit or provide relevant background knowledge
   d. Stress and reiterate underlying big idea with range of examples

2. Challenge

3. Involvement
   a. Provide extended discourse
   b. Use complex linguistic structures
   c. Foster active engagement of all

4. Success

5. Mediation and Feedback
   a. Make it frequent and comprehensible
   b. Focus on meaning
   c. Use recall strategies
   d. Ask for supporting evidence

6. Responsiveness to Cultural and Individual Diversity
   a. Link content to experience
   b. Use personal experience

Source: Gersten, R., Brengelman, S., and Jimenez, R. (1994). Effective instruction for culturally and linguistically diverse students: A reconceptualization. *Focus on Exceptional Children, 27* (1), p. 9. Denver: Love Publishing. Reprinted with permission.

- Promotion of reasoning to support an argument ("How do you know?" or "What makes you think that?")
- Multiple interactive turns that build upon and extend previous student contributions
- Promotion of complex language and expression through invitations to expand ("Tell me more about. . . ," "What do you mean by. . .?")

Cooperative learning is another strategy that appears to serve CLDE students well. Several benefits of this approach within bilingual special education programs have been noted, including:

- creating opportunities to use language in meaningful but safe ways
- building on prior language skills while developing second language skills (especially true if other English language learners collaborate)
- facilitating higher-order cognitive and linguistic discourse
- encouraging peer modeling and feedback rather than correcting errors more formally (Gersten, et al., 1994a).

Students with learning disabilities may still require extra support due to their (frequently) limited language capacities (Ruiz, 1989). Such teaching enhancements of group success may take the forms of vocabulary development, provision of background knowledge, and programming practice with cooperative learning strategies.

Selection and Evaluation of Materials Garcia (1995) questioned specific features of materials to guide in their selection, such as "Will the instructional strategies accommodate student characteristics and needs?" The checklist below provides additional guidelines for selecting and evaluating materials for use with CLDE students (see Table 9.4).

TABLE 9.4

Checklist for Selection and Evaluation of Materials

• Are the perspectives and contributions of people from diverse cultural and linguistic groups—both men and women, as well as people with disabilities—included in the curriculum?

• Are there activities in the curriculum that will assist students in analyzing the various forms of the mass media for ethnocentrism, sexism, "handicapism," and stereotyping?

• Are both men and women, diverse cultural/racial groups, and people with varying abilities shown in both active and passive roles?

• Are both men and women, diverse cultural/racial groups, and people with disabilities shown in positions of power (i.e., the materials do not rely on the mainstreams culture's character to achieve goals)?

• Do materials identify strengths possessed by so-called "underachieving" diverse populations? Do they diminish attention to deficits, to reinforce positive behaviors that are desired and valued?

• Are members of diverse racial/cultural groups, men and women, and people with disabilities shown engaged in a broad range of social and professional activities?

• Are members of a particular culture or group depicted as having a range of physical features (e.g., hair color, hair texture, variations in facial characteristics and body build)?

• Do materials represent historical events from the perspectives of the various groups involved or solely from the male, middle class, and/or Western European perspective?

• Are materials free of ethnocentric or sexist language patterns that may make implications about persons or groups based solely on their culture, race, gender or disability?

• Will students from different ethnic and cultural backgrounds find the materials personally meaningful to their life experiences?

• Are a wide variety of culturally different examples, situations, scenarios, and anecdotes used throughout the curriculum design to illustrate major intellectual concepts and principles?

• Are culturally diverse content, examples, and experiences comparable in kind, significance, magnitude, and function to those selected from mainstream culture?

Source: Garcia, S.B., and Malkin, D.H. (1993). Toward defining programs and services for culturally and linguistically diverse learners in special education. *Teaching Exceptional Children*, 26(1), pp. 52–58.

Strategies for Transitions to Adulthood Few researchers have examined the relationship of cultural and language diversity to adult adjustment outcomes. As with IEP planning, the most important facet of planning school to post-school transitions involves student and family input regarding their goals, dreams, and needs. In order for that input to be present and meaningful, advance planning must occur, often beginning in middle school. Educators who plan vocational training options and work experiences need to be mindful of trends in the labor market, both locally and regionally. Of concern are descriptions of recent trends that have resulted in the majority of new jobs being very low-skilled service jobs with low pay and no benefits. Chapter 7 offers additional guidelines in this area.

Challenges for Educators

Two major issues are critical for teachers and related personnel in training for special education programs and services. These issues are (1) the impact of shortages of culturally/linguistically diverse educators on students' learning, and (2) educators' development of intercultural competencies.

Impact of Shortages of Diverse Educators Severe shortages of teachers from diverse backgrounds exist in bilingual/multicultural education and special education. The consequences of such shortages mean that most diverse students are taught in English only, which often results in language delays in both languages, reading and cognitive delays, behavior problems, increased risk for school failure and dropping out, problems with cultural identity and lowered self-esteem (Maldonado, 1994).

Developing Intercultural Knowledge and Skills Saparani, Abel, Easton, Edwards, and Herbster (1995) studied 832 preservice teacher trainees' grasp of issues associated with diversity and exceptionality in five states. Their findings, stratified by beginning, middle, and end of the training programs, indicated that preservice teachers felt comfortable and knowledgeable about multicultural education and parent partnerships. Such findings hold promise for future students with diverse backgrounds, suggesting that crosscultural awareness and skills will be more widespread among general educators.

Collier (1986) developed competencies for bilingual special educators. These address areas such as language assessment, individualized instructional planning and implementation, crosscultural knowledge and expertise, program evaluation and reporting, and collaboration with parents and professionals. Poplin and Phillips (1993) stressed that teachers must understand multiple viewpoints from diverse cultural groups, as well as know the characteristics of languages among their students, in order to provide appropriate assessment and instruction and avoid misdiagnoses of learning disabilities. Burstein and her colleagues (1993) described their teacher preparation program which systematically infused those competencies critical to serving CLD students with learning disabilities. Similarly, Grossman (1992) reported the descriptions and outcomes of the Bilingual/Multicultural Special Education Program at San Jose State University. Competency areas in that program involved language skills, crosscultural skills, nondiscriminatory assessment techniques, language assessment, instructional strategies, counseling, consultation, advocacy, referral skills, and classroom management techniques.

Gersten and Woodward (1994) noted that many special educators receive training that supports constricted, rather than expansive, use of language. The Council for Learning Disabilities is currently developing a Code of Ethics in which statements that ensure non-discrimination and equal opportunity for students and families and promote their welfare and rights will be incorporated (Council for Learning Disabilities, 1995).

The requirement to provide assessment and instruction in one's native language will often require staff development for existing staff, including the preparation and use of bilingual paraprofessionals (Weismantel and Fradd, 1989). Such efforts appear to be worthwhile. Maldonado (1994) studied the impact of an integrated bilingual special education program involving dual language instruction on ten bilingual Hispanic elementary students with learning disabilities. This three-year program involved primarily native language instruction with one ESL period daily for year one, half Spanish and half ESL during the transition year, and ESL only during the last year. Results indicated significantly higher levels of English proficiency among the experimental group compared to the control group.

Gersten and Woodward (1994) vigorously described the challenges faced by administrators and teachers in today's schools, most of whom were not prepared to educate NELB students: students with serious and unfamiliar learning needs, severe shortages of appropriately trained staff in both general and special education, and lack of certainty about special education's role in addressing the challenges. Although common, relying on special education was also noted as an unsatisfactory solution based on that discipline's general lack of expertise in assessing and instructing language-different students. As a result of these demands, many states and districts are finding that preparation of personnel to meet the needs of all students in general education programs is a viable alternative to identifying ESL students with disabilities (MacMillan, Hendrick, and Watkins, 1988). An additional characteristic about which all students vary, their socioeconomic levels, is discussed in the next section.

▶ SOCIOECONOMIC CORRELATES AND LEARNING DISABILITIES

Learning disabilities cannot be attributed directly to a family's or a child's socioeconomic status (SES). However, poverty-level incomes and their typical correlates directly threaten the health of children, which in turn can create permanent disruptions in the learning process. In addition, socioeconomic differences are quite pronounced in this nation and directly affect perceptions about children by others and by themselves.

Poverty's Relationship to Disability

Each year, an estimated one million babies are born into poverty, which is designated as below $12,000 annual income for a family of three by Health and Human Services guidelines; this figure roughly translates into one baby born every thirty seconds. Every two minutes a baby is born at low birthweight. Of those born into poverty, 232,000 babies will be born to women who received late or no prenatal care (Children's Defense Fund, 1994). It is estimated that one in every four children currently lives at the poverty level. Children born into poverty are at greater risk for learning and health problems that may manifest into academic and behavior challenges throughout life; such students are under-represented in classes for those considered gifted and talented. Today, poverty is seen as an insidious condition which seriously exacerbates the learning difficulties of children and which society seemingly can do nothing to correct.

Chapter 5 carefully describes the range of organic and environmental causes that result in learning disabilities. Within this discussion of economic impact on children, however, some mention is warranted about the etiological variables related to learning disabilities that are often linked to low SES. One of these is the abuse of harmful substances, alcohol and drugs, among expecting and practicing parents. Substance abuse can cause a range of mild to severe learning, emotional, and behavioral problems (Stern, Kendall, and Eberhard, 1991; Rhodes and Jasinski, 1990), such as those linked to fetal alcohol syndrome (FAS) and fetal alcohol effects (FAE), the latter of which is more commonly linked to learning disabilities. Substance abuse may, in addition, create situations of abuse and neglect (Risk, 1990). Neglect is another correlate; over twenty-three million children suffer from extreme neglect each year (Children's Defense Fund, 1994). Finally, Chapter 5 describes the dangers of living in impoverished environments, where poor construction, sanitation, air, and water, as well as high lead levels, may cause a host of learning problems, attention disorders, and behavior problems (Ernhart and Needleman, 1987; Lovitt, 1989; Marlow, 1984). Parents in poverty may lack the ability to adequately provide for the physical and emotional needs of their children.

Perceptions about Equity and Outcomes

Grossman (1995) contended that the meritocracy theory drives society's beliefs about children in poverty and plays a major role in effectively stereotyping society's response to such children. According to this theory, the United States is a "meritocracy in which all people have an equal opportunity to succeed" (Grossman, 1995, p. 29). This sentiment has echoed from the early days of immigration and assimilation into the mainstream of society. For those who worked hard enough, upward mobility was the reward; those who failed to get ahead lacked either the intrinsic ability or motivation. Beliefs of schooling tend to follow in the same vein. Within the construct of meritocracy, all children are provided equal opportunity to learn and to advance. We know now that this is not the case. Schools do not provide equal opportunities or resources (Kozol, 1991). Higher socioeconomic status (SES) results in greater resources and more positive outcomes, while lower SES results in deficient resources in both schools and communities. Thus, the theory of meritocracy and the realities of inequitable schooling clash. Grossman (1995) has argued that no justification exists for society's myopic belief that poor students who do not do well in school are responsible for the state of affairs in which they find themselves.

Still, disproportionate numbers of children with disabilities are identified from impoverished environments. Poverty means that critical family needs (e.g. food, clothing, housing, medical care, and early learning support) cannot be met, resulting in "sickness, psychological stress, malnutrition, underdevelopment, and daily hardship that quickly takes its toll on (children's) young minds and bodies" (Reed and Sauter, 1990, K3). Veteran teachers have reported a drastic increase in learning disabilities in poor children over the past 10 years; Reed and Sautter (1990) reported 11 percent of children were placed into special education because of developmental and cognitive problems manifested during the peak developmental period. Many of these difficulties could have been prevented with proper nutrition and health care.

Learning disabilities are defined as disorders that are "intrinsic to the individual" (NJCLD, 1990) and thus have their genesis in an organic etiology. The aforementioned factors ascribed to low SES could influence biological development into the more subtle patterns that typify characteristics of children with learning disabilities (Gelb and Mizokawa, 1986). A burgeoning identification of children with learning disabilities who live in poverty tends to corroborate this belief. Morrison and Hinshaw (1988) found that SES related significantly to achievement and intelligence (when using formal assessment measures) in children with learning disabilities, but SES was not correlated with performance on neuropsychological tests, thus suggesting further research into interrelationships between intrinsic and extrinsic causative factors.

The greater problem remains that we are charged with identifying learning disabilities based on organic causes, and yet a variety of external factors— social, environmental, instructional—are implicated (Gelb and Mizokawa, 1986). Some contend that learning disabilities comprise an outgrowth of society's narrow prescription of what is "normal" (Poplin, 1993; Sleeter, 1986). Assumptions about language, culture, ability, and lifestyle have in essence created an artificial construct of learning disabilities which will (1) continue to provide a rationale for the correlation of poverty and underachievement, and (2) allow families from higher SES a *raison d'être* as to the learning difficulties their children experience without significantly affecting their status in society. In sum, learning disabilities must be viewed as both intrinsic to the individual but strongly related to extrinsic variables. We must take care, when learning disabilities are appropriately identified in children who live in poverty, that we do not use this as a basis for providing education that has lowered expectations, both academically and vocationally, or that our expected outcomes for these children are necessarily lower than for their higher SES peers with LD.

Challenges for Educators

Educators must be sensitive to the risk factors associated with impoverished environments and make every attempt to provide linkages to agencies which can assist with health and nutritional care. The concept of a "single point of entry" that schools can furnish as host sites to an array of human service agencies is gaining popularity in both urban and rural districts. Families can have immediate access to a range of social services that, in the long run, may ameliorate survival needs and allow children to be more productive while at school. Administrators, counselors, and teachers must be knowledgeable about community resources (and their access) that will support families and students. Unfortunately, until society views problems such as substance abuse as health issues, not social issues, anger and blame will impede true assistance for these families.

▶ GENDER ISSUES AND LEARNING DISABILITIES

General Differences of Males and Females

Generally speaking, male and female students, typical or with disabilities, have very different experiences in schools. These differences cut across language, ethnicity, SES, and geographic location. As educators, we are beginning to understand that males and females differ significantly in their biologic and physiologic characteristics, cognitive processes, problem-solving abilities, linguistic abilities, approaches to social situations, and locus of control and attribution factors. Males and females are rewarded constantly through their life experiences by acting in gender-stereotypic ways that develop gradually throughout the lifespan. There are both obvious and subtle differences which separate female from male behavior patterns.

Grossman and Grossman (1994) have provided a commendable summation of the basic gender differences observed in school-aged children. These include *generalizations* about emotional differences, relationships, communication style, motivation to avoid success, school participation, and behavior problems. Although these summaries may not accurately describe any single individual, they are worth noting. Briefly, females tend to exhibit more fearful and anxious behaviors but are also more altruistic and helpful. They tend to try to avoid conflict but also tend to talk indirectly or inferentially about issues concerning them. They are responsive to both genders in conversation and tend to see resolution to moral conflicts in terms of interrelatedness and sensitivity to the situation. They tend to allow males to dominate the conversation; they also tend to delay decision-making until they feel comfortable that adequate information has been gathered. Females respond to failure in an intrinsic manner, i.e., failure is ultimately their fault due to lack of competence. They are uncomfortable with overt success and tend to explain it as a cause of extrinsic variables ("the test was too easy"). They also tend to choose less rigorous academic and vocational courses aimed at traditionally female occupations.

Males do not tend to express their feelings as openly, but when they do, it is often with more intensity. Their behaviors are more competitive, but they are able to resolve differences more easily and move on with less emotion. Males' morality adheres to the principles of justice and fairness on a more impersonal level as standards by which decisions are made. They tend to ask questions and respond in a more direct manner, interrupt more, use commands and give more direct information. Males are better able to disregard old solutions and apply flexible thinking to find new solutions. They tend to see failure more often in extrinsic terms which may save them the internal suffering common among females but may not realistically inform them about their abilities. However, they enroll in more challenging academic courses, take greater risks, and exhibit higher aspirations across SES strata.

It is obvious in our dominant culture that these broad differences have been culturally assimilated to such a degree that they are considered the "norm." When females or males stray across the gender gap, they may be ostracized or viewed as "different." The introduction of learning disabilities into this equation may further complicate the situation.

Physical and cognitive anomalies differ between males and females as early as conception. Twice as many males are conceived, but only half survive to birth, and complications of pregnancy and birth are more common with males (Nass, 1993). Females tend to mature, both physically and cognitively, earlier than males, thus reducing their organic risk for learning problems in school settings. Learning disabilities tend to run in families and frequently appear to be sex-linked. When females are identified with learning disabilities, they tend to be affected more severely. Males tend to have "clusters" of learning disabilities, while females more often exhibit a single learning disability (Nass, 1993).

Prevalence and Characteristics of Learning Disabilities Across Gender

Traditionally, a preponderance of males have been identified as having learning disabilities. While some neurological studies confirm the disproportionate ratio of males to females from a biophysical perspective, other researchers feel that the inappropriate underidentification of females with learning disabilities has been paid scant attention. A number of studies are now reporting the results of investigations into the male to female discrepancy.

Most estimates place the male/female ratio at four to one (Vogel and Walsh, 1987). In a study to learn the underlying reasons, Harmon et al. (1992) concluded that several phenomena contribute to disproportionate representation in special education, gleaned from both survey data and a thorough literature review:

1. *Biological differences* As stated earlier, females have more early biological advantages (e.g., fewer birth defects, more rapid maturation).

2. *Learned differences* Traditional gender roles are most commonly acquired by imitating same-sex adults, siblings, and peers. Because women tend to have primary responsibilities at home and elementary school teachers are more often

female, it is hypothesized that young girls have more opportunity to learn same-sex behavior at an earlier age and subsequently demonstrate this "approved" behavior in school settings.

3. *Different reactions of boys and girls to school* Boys and girls respond differently in school. Because elementary schools value obedience and compliance, boys are thought to be referred for suspected disabilities more often due to their gender roles of independence, activity, and aggressive behavior, which tend to oppose prevailing desired behaviors. Girls, on the other hand, tend to respond more passively and compliantly and may be overlooked in the referral process because these behaviors fit the school norm.

4. *Different reactions of teachers to boys in comparison to girls* Teacher characteristics may directly influence gender referral biases. For example, if a teacher has little tolerance for misbehavior, he or she may make a larger number of referrals. A closer similarity in the teacher's gender and race to the student decreases referral rates. Some teachers are reluctant to refer girls to special education because they perceive that girls will have emotional difficulties dealing with the stigmatizing effects of labeling as well as the special education program itself.

5. *Flaws or weaknesses in criteria, procedures, and tests* Definitions of learning disabilities vary widely from state to state and may be confounded by interpretation by local districts and teachers. Also, studies have revealed that some identification teams rely more heavily on comments by the referring teacher than to actual assessment evidence (see #4 above).

In gender studies of male and female college students with learning disabilities, Vogel and Walsh (1987) determined females to have been underidentified throughout their schooling. When assessed for IQ, it was found that females consistently had lower Full Scale IQ scores on the WISC-R/WAIS-R than their male counterparts. Further probes determined that females with higher IQ scores were not referred as often and seemed to cope more readily with their disabilities within general classroom settings. Vogel and Walsh speculated that much of what we may know about the nature of learning disabilities may be describing male attributes only; appropriate identification of females with learning disabilities needs to be more carefully scrutinized.

Instructional Considerations and Strategies

These data reveal that much remains to be done to ameliorate the disparities in referral, identification, and instruction of males and females with disabilities. Thoughtful and systematic changes need to be made at administrative, school, and classroom levels. Harmon et al. (1992) provided recommendations to help resolve gender disparities:

• Develop a state policy on gender equity in special education and implement it as an element of compliance monitoring.

• Provide inservice training to raise awareness of the law, to understand the adverse effects of gender bias, and to avoid labeling children inappropriately.

- Improve and strengthen classroom interventions prior to or instead of referral.
- Improve the referral and identification processes.
- Improve the quality of special education programs so that teachers are not reluctant to refer girls (p. ix).

In order to achieve both cultural and gender equity in classrooms, Grossman and Grossman (1994) suggested that teachers use techniques that include both field independent and field sensitive methods (see Table 9.5). By becoming more aware of students' learning styles, teachers can modify their instruction to include elements and strategies that allow students to learn optimally. Teachers also have to become more aware of their own teaching styles and gender-role assumptions if they are to promote gender equity in their classrooms. It is suggested that teachers videotape themselves to examine patterns of teaching which may unconsciously promote gender bias. Grossman and Grossman (1992) created a self-quiz for teachers to asssist them in such reflection (see Table 9.6).

TABLE 9.5

Field Independent and Field Sensitive Teachers

Field Independent Teachers

Maintain formal relationships with students.

Assume the role of the authority figure.

Stress instructional over interpersonal objectives. Emphasize individual effort.

Focus on facts and principles.

Teach mathematics and science abstractly.

Foster competition between students.

Stress independent student functioning.

Field Sensitive Teachers

Demonstrate approval and warmth toward students.

Use personalized rewards.

Are sensitive to students in need of help.

Stress cooperation and group work.

Humanize the curriculum.

Assist students in using concepts to label their personal feelings.

Encourage learning through modeling.

Help students to see how concepts being learned are related to their personal experiences.

Source: Grossman, H. and Grossman, S.H. (1994). *Gender issues in education.* (p. 141). Boston: Allyn and Bacon. Copyright 1994 by Allyn and Bacon. Reprinted/adapted by permission.

TABLE 9.6

Self Quiz on Teaching Style by Gender

Teaching Style

Does your teaching style favor one gender over another? Do you use a gender-stereo-typical teaching style or is your style androgynous? Rate your teaching style in terms of the following instructional characteristics. Videotape yourself, or ask a colleague to observe and rate you. You should not expect to conform to the stereotypical teaching style of your gender because these are only generalizations that do not apply to all female or male educators.

Male Teaching Style

- Direct with students
- Subject-centered
- Lectures a lot
- Has students discuss things strictly among themselves
- Less likely to praise students for answering correctly
- More likely to criticize wrong answers
- Offers explanations designed to help students correct their responses
- Gives students multiple chances to respond correctly
- Less sensitive to students' needs and feelings
- Positively reinforces young boys for stereotypical male behaviors
- Often reprimands students for misbehaving
- Publicly and harshly reprimands students for misbehaving
- Allows students to form their own groups

Female Teaching Style

- Indirect with students
- Student-centered
- Frequently asks questions
- Gets involved with students in classroom discussions
- Praises students for answering correctly
- Less likely to give students feedback when their answers are wrong
- Less likely to criticize wrong answers
- Sensitive to students' needs and feelings
- Negatively reinforces young boys for stereotypical male behaviors
- Seldom reprimands students for misbehaving
- Reprimands students privately and softly for misbehaving
- Assigns students to specific groups

Source: Grossman, H., and Grossman, S.H. (1994). *Gender issues in education.* (p. 140). Boston: Allyn and Bacon. Copyright ©1994 by Allyn and Bacon. Reprinted/adapted by permission.

▶ SEXUAL ORIENTATION AND LEARNING DISABILITIES

An estimated one in ten people in the United States is considered lesbian or gay (Clay, 1991). The majority of gay and lesbian individuals discover their sexual orientation by the time they reach the age of 15. Although they are attending school, sexuality and especially sexual orientation are forbidden subjects. Controversies abound in many districts regarding the teaching of sex education and sexuality; officially sanctioned discussions of sexual orientation are virtually nonexistent.

Student Issues

Because students are exposed to homophobia at home, school, and the community, there is little opportunity to find positive portrayals of gay and lesbian individuals. Many students struggling with their sexual orientation are given messages that homosexuality is evil, sick, and disgusting (Grossman, 1995). It comes as little surprise, then, to discover that gay and lesbian teenagers are two to three times more likely to attempt suicide than other teenagers (National Education Association, n.d.); suicide already stands as a leading cause of death for that age group. These statistics are particularly alarming in light of data cited by Pipher (1994) that the overall suicide rate of youth ages 10 to 14 climbed 75 percent from 1979 to 1988.

As a result of sexual orientation remaining a taboo subject in today's schools, it is difficult to estimate the number of students who may be wrestling with their emotions in this area. What we do know is that the difficulties of dealing with and accepting sexual orientation are exacerbated with race and culture. Anecdotal evidence suggests that students with severe emotional difficulties may be grappling with issues of sexual orientation (Grossman, 1995). At present, we have no clear indications as to the prevalence of gay and lesbian students who have learning disabilities. We can assume, however, that the combination of learning disabilities and homosexuality or bisexuality creates special challenges for students. For this reason, it is critical that teachers are sensitized to the hidden and conflicting emotions harbored by youth.

Grossman (1995) offered suggestions for helping teachers to work with students concerned about their sexual orientation:

- Resist community pressure to avoid relating to the needs of students who are concerned about their sexual orientation.

- Refer students to community agencies and resources where they can obtain assistance.

- Protect students from harassment, criticize such incidents when they occur, and express disapproval of jokes about gay persons.

- Modify homophobic attitudes. Teach students to accept each other regardless of sexual orientation by modeling acceptance.

- Include homosexual role models (pp. 249-250).

Teacher education must include a focus on cultural and linguistic diversity and learning disabilities.

Personnel Preparation Issues

A number of organizations provide information and support for professionals who work with gay and lesbian individuals. The National Education Association (NEA), the National Association of School Psychologists (NASP), and Parents and Friends of Lesbians and Gays (P-FLAG) are three organizations which have strongly endorsed the civil rights of these individuals. NEA offers a Human and Civil Rights Action Sheet entitled "Teaching and Counseling Gay and Lesbian Students" that provides basic information, recommendations for action, and a list of resources. NASP distributes a Teachers' Handout on "Addressing Prejudice Against Gay, Lesbian and Bisexual Youth in School" (Eversole, n.d.) with similar content. P-FLAG has compiled a list of suggestions for persons who work with gay and lesbian youth. Finally, the Gay/Lesbian/Straight Teachers Network focuses on the needs of teachers as well as students (address: 122 West 26th St., Suite 1100, New York, NY 10001, 212/727-0135). As with issues of disability, homosexuality and bisexuality are components of diversity and should be respected as such. Teaching, counseling, and administrative preparation programs must provide the leadership that propels educators in the field to manifest acceptance in nonintrusive ways for students of diversity. Similarly, district and building administrators must recognize and implement staff development programs that provide accurate and supportive information for professionals, paraprofessionals, parents, and students alike.

SUMMARY

This chapter has presented information on learning disabilities and diversity, emphasizing issues that educators need to be sensitive toward. The following points summarize the major areas included in the chapter:

- Increasing numbers of students with learning disabilities will come to school with different experiences or backgrounds than those of their "typical" peers, based upon variables such as culture or ethnicity, language, socioeconomic status, gender, and sexual orientation, simply due to the changing demographic profile of the U.S. population.

- Those differing backgrounds translate into individualistic student strengths, needs, goals, interests, constraints, and supports, any or all of which may interact with one's learning disabilities.

- While some of these variables are not risk factors in and of themselves (such as cultural and language differences), the response of the educational system to those differences can indiscriminately create academic and, sometimes more seriously, affective difficulties for many students; the meritocracy theory so prevalent in our society may work to their detriment.

- Educators, to help their students succeed (maybe even survive), will need to understand, acknowledge, and integrate their diversity issues into programs.

- Sensitivity to each learner's reality will foster more and higher quality student-teacher communication, more effective planning, greater partnerships with family members, and interventions with longer-lasting and greater impact, than forging ahead as if every student were the same.

- Special educators are particularly equipped to pay attention to uniqueness and thus may move (or have already moved) into addressing diversity issues very readily.

- Designing and delivering school curricula that are relevant and sensitive to students' cultures and experiences should enhance their achievements and graduation rates.

- Separate systems or sub-systems of education (e.g., special education, bilingual education, general education) must work together to adequately examine, and develop and implement interventions for, students' educational needs.

Chapter 10

LEGAL ISSUES AND LEARNING DISABILITIES

The objectives for this chapter are as follows:

- To know the reason laws are important for services to persons with learning disabilities.

- To understand the purposes of Section 504 of the Rehabilitation Act of 1973.

- To know the definition of disability used in Section 504.

- To compare the population of persons with learning disabilities covered under Section 504 with those served through IDEA.

- To compare services required for students with learning disabilities under Section 504 and IDEA.

- To understand the purposes of the Americans with Disabilities Act.

- To know the definition of disability used in the Americans with Disabilities Act.

- To compare Section 504 and the Americans with Disabilities Act.

- To describe protections under Section 504 and the Americans with Disabilities Act related to persons with learning disabilities in employment settings.

Lori: Equal Opportunities to Work

Lori wanted to work at the local watch factory more than anything. She graduated from high school with her peers and wanted to stay in her home community, at least for the beginning of her adult life. The best place to work in her hometown was the watch factory. Employees started out making more than minimum wage, and the benefits were very good. In July following Lori's high school graduation, she was thrilled to learn that the factory was hiring thirty-five new employees.

Lori immediately went to the personnel office to apply for one of the openings. When she got the job application, she panicked because she could not read some of the words and did not understand some of the questions. Lori has a learning disability. She was identified as having a learning disability in the second grade and was provided services in a resource room for the rest of her school years. She was always included in general education classes for most of the day, but went to the resource room one or two hours each day for special assistance.

Lori knows that she is qualified to do the jobs that are being advertised. Her older sister has worked at the watch factory for three years and Lori knows she can do the same tasks that her sister does. However, she is concerned that if she cannot complete the job application without assistance, she may not get a chance to show how well she can do the job that is advertised.

For Lori, and many other persons with learning disabilities, job discrimination is a real problem. Section 504 of the Rehabilitation Act of 1973 and the Americans with Disabilities Act both prohibit discrimination based on a disability. If Lori can perform the *essential job functions* of the position, her problems with completing the job application should not be a barrier to her getting the job. Legal protections for individuals with learning disabilities have greatly assisted this group in securing equal opportunities.

There are many legal issues surrounding learning disabilities. Most of these issues are related to one of three laws: the Individuals with Disabilities Education Act (IDEA), the Rehabilitation Act of 1973, and the Americans with Disabilities

Act. IDEA, originally passed as Public Law 94-142, primarily focuses on public education. This legislation has resulted in a significant increase in appropriate educational programs for all students with disabilities, including those with learning disabilities. Section 504 of the Rehabilitation Act of 1973 is much broader than Public Law 94-142 (Streett and Smith, 1996). It is primarily civil rights legislation for persons with disabilities. Finally, the Americans with Disabilities Act (ADA) is the most recent and broadest federal legislation affecting individuals with learning disabilities. As will be described later, this law impacts most segments of our society. Turnbull (1993) noted that the ADA "is the most important disability law enacted since at least 1975 (when Congress enacted Education for All Handicapped Children Act, P.L. 94-142) or, arguably, ever" (p. 23).

The three laws that will be described in this chapter have had a profound impact on persons with learning disabilities. Prior to their passage, many children and adults with learning disabilities were discriminated against, provided inappropriate educational programs, or often not even identified as having a disability. These laws, in conjunction with litigation, have resulted in major services and opportunities for individuals with learning disabilities.

▌ INDIVIDUALS WITH DISABILITIES EDUCATION ACT

The Individuals with Disabilities Education Act (IDEA) was originally passed in 1975 as Public Law 94-142. Known as the Education for All Handicapped Children Act, Public Law 94-142 resulted in significant changes in the way children with learning disabilities were educated in public schools. The legislation focused on the provision of a free appropriate public education for students with disabilities. It had four major purposes (Ballard, 1987):

1. Guarantee the availability of special education programming to children with disabilities.
2. Assure fairness and appropriateness in the decisions made about providing special education to children with disabilities.
3. Establish auditing and management requirements.
4. Provide financial assistance to states and local education agencies.

Prior to the passage of P.L. 94-142, many children with disabilities were not receiving any special education, or their education was considered less than appropriate. Congress found that of the estimated eight million children in the United States with disabilities, as many as one million were totally excluded from the educational system, while another three million were being underserved (Smith, Price, and Marsh, 1986). Public Law 94-142 changed the status of special education forever.

Numerous major advances in special education resulted from PL 94-142. These included:

The Individuals with Disabilities Education Act (IDEA) requires schools to provide a free appropriate public education for students with learning disabilities eligible for special education.

- identification of children with learning disabilities and other types of disabilities who had not been identified;
- provision of appropriate special education and related services to children with learning disabilities and other disabilities;
- application of due process procedures for children with disabilities and their families;
- training of general education and special education teachers to meet the needs of children with learning disabilities and other disabilities; and
- establishment of learning disabilities as a legitimate category of disabilities for special education.

For students with learning disabilities, P.L. 94-142 was especially important because its passage marked the first inclusion of learning disabilities as an identified disability eligible for special education services. In 1977, two years after P.L. 94-142 was passed, federal regulations for definition and identification criteria for learning disabilities were published in the *Federal Register* (Smith, Polloway, Patton, and Dowdy, 1995). (see Chapter 2).

Congress reauthorizes Public Law 94-142 approximately every five years. In 1990 the reauthorization included several changes, including changing the name of the law to the Individuals with Disabilities Education Act (IDEA). IDEA includes the basic provisions found in the original public law, with some modifications. The focus of the legislation continues to be the provision of a free appropriate public education for students with disabilities, including students with learning disabilities.

IDEA defines disabilities using a categorical model. Students are considered to be *disabled* and thus eligible for special education and related services under IDEA if they have (1) mental retardation, (2) learning disabilities, (3) serious emotional disturbance, (4) hearing impairment, (5) visual impairment, (6) orthopedic impairment, (7) other health impairment, (8) autism, (9) traumatic brain injury, or (10) speech impairment, and the disability results in their needing special education. For children who meet these eligibility requirements, numerous provisions are required. Chapter 4, as well as several other chapters, have described some of these provisions in detail. These include definition of disability, child find, referral and evaluation, individual educational programming, least restrictive environment, transition programming, and due process procedures.

Child Find

IDEA requires schools to *find* children with disabilities, including those with learning disabilities. Schools cannot wait until a child is referred by families for services, but are expected to develop and initiate procedures to locate children with suspected disabilities. Child find activities were more important immediately after the passage of Public Law 94-142 than currently because of the vast numbers of children who were excluded from the public education system at that time. Also, there were many children who were in public schools but who had not been identified as having a disability. Because of the hidden nature of the disability, children with learning disabilities were more likely to be in school, but without appropriate services, than excluded from the school system.

Referral and Evaluation

Children who are suspected of having a disability covered under IDEA are referred for services. The referral can be made by any person, including school personnel, parents, or even self-referrals. Following a referral, schools are required to provide a comprehensive evaluation of the child to determine if the child is eligible for services, and to determine strengths and weaknesses that will enable the development of an individual educational program (IEP). The evaluation must be nondiscriminatory and follow specific procedures included in IDEA. For students with learning disabilities, additional evaluation requirements must be implemented. Chapter 3 included a discussion regarding the legal requirements of this assessment process.

Individual Educational Program

Following the evaluation, an individual educational program (IEP) must be developed for children who are eligible for special education and related services. Procedures for developing IEPs as well as legal requirements for IEPs were described in Chapter 4. The primary intent of the IEP is to define and set up a mechanism for a student with a disability to receive a free appropriate public education.

Least Restrictive Environment

One of the most significant requirements of IDEA is that students with disabilities should be educated in the least restrictive environment. This means that students with disabilities should be educated with their nondisabled peers as much as possible, and should be removed from general education settings only when necessary to provide an appropriate education. Prior to the passage in 1975 of Public Law 94-142, many children with disabilities, as noted previously, were totally excluded from public education. Also, for students with disabilities provided educational services, many of these services were provided in segregated settings, apart from general education classrooms.

A continuum of placement options was developed in most school districts to respond to the least-restrictive-environment mandate. This continuum includes full-time general education placements as the least-restrictive placement option, and institutional placements as the most restrictive. Between these two extremes are a variety of options, including part-time special education class and full-time special education class. For students with learning disabilities, the vast majority are educated, at least a portion of each school day, with their nondisabled peers in general education classrooms. The 17th Annual Report to Congress on the Implementation of IDEA noted that 34.8 percent of all students with learning disabilities were educated in general education classes, while another 43.9 percent were educated in resource rooms and general education classrooms during the 1992–1993 school year. This means that nearly 80 percent of all students with learning disabilities receiving special education spend at least a large portion of each day with nondisabled peers in general education classrooms (U.S. Department of Education, 1995).

Transition Programming

One of the changes in IDEA from the original law focused on transition programming. IDEA requires schools to implement transition planning for students with disabilities 16 years of age, or younger if appropriate. The specific requirements for transition planning were discussed extensively in Chapter 7. The intent of the transition requirement is to improve the status of young adults with disabilities after they exit high school programs.

Due Process Procedures

IDEA provides many due process rights for students with disabilities and their families. Prior to the passage of Public Law 94-142, "school personnel often made unilateral decisions about a student's education, including placement and specific components of the educational program; parents had little input and little recourse if they disagreed with the school" (Smith, et al., 1995, p. 18). The due process requirements of IDEA now require schools to provide notice to and often to get permission from parents before taking certain actions on behalf of students with disabilities. Table 10.1 summarizes the due process requirements of Public Law 94–142 and the IDEA. As can be seen from the table, a major result of the act was to make parents *equal partners* with school personnel in the education of students with disabilities.

The Individuals with Disabilities Education Act has made, and continues to make, a significant impact on the educational system for students with all types of disabilities. The act includes many different provisions for children with

TABLE 10.1

Due Process Requirements of IDEA

Requirement	Explanation	Reference
Opportunity to examine records	Parents have a right to inspect and review all educational records.	Sec. 121a.502
Independent evaluation	Parents have a right to obtain an independent evaluation of their child at their expense or the school's expense. The school pays only if it agrees to the evaluation or is required by a hearing officer.	Sec. 121a.503
Prior notice; parental consent	Schools must provide written notice to parents before the school initiates or changes the identification, evaluation, or placement of a child. Consent must be obtained before conducting the evaluation and before initial placement.	Sec. 121a.504
Contents of notice	Parental notice must provide a description of the proposed actions in the written native language of the home. If the communication is not written, oral notification must be given. The notice must be understandable to the parents.	Sec. 121a.505
Impartial due process hearing	A parent or school may initiate a due process hearing if there is a dispute over the identification, evaluation, or placement of the child.	Sec. 121a.506

Source: Final regulations, P.L. 94–142

learning disabilities. Many of the components of IDEA have been discussed in previous chapters. Table 10.2 summarizes the major components of the act.

▶ SECTION 504 OF THE REHABILITATION ACT

For most children with learning disabilities, IDEA provides the protections necessary to ensure appropriate educational programs. There are some children with learning disabilities, however, who are not eligible for services under IDEA but who still need accommodations or modifications in schools. These include children who do not meet the significant discrepancy criterion imposed by some school districts (Martin, 1992), as well as other children who have problems in school but who are not identified as having a learning disability using the criteria established by IDEA. Also, IDEA only provides protections and services in public schools for children with learning disabilities until their twenty-second birthday. Adults with learning disabilities do not stop experiencing problems after leaving high school (Gerber and Reiff, 1994). Indeed, problems for this group continue and may cause significant adjustment problems (Patton and Polloway, 1996) (see Chapter 8). The result is that adults with learning disabilities continue to need protections and services to ensure their equal opportunities in postsecondary education and employment (Brinckerhoff, Shaw, and McGuire, 1993). Without these protections, discrimination will likely add to the problems experienced by this group of individuals. For these

TABLE 10.2

Key Components of IDEA

Provisions	Description
Least restrictive environment	Children are educated with nondisabled children as much as possible.
Individual education program	All children served in special education must have an individualized education program (IEP).
Due process rights	Disabled children and their parents must be involved in decisions about special education.
Due process hearing	Parents and schools can request an impartial hearing if there is a conflict over special education services.
Nondiscriminatory assessment	Students must be given a comprehensive assessment that is nondiscriminatory in nature.
Related services	Schools must provide related services, such as physical therapy, counseling, and transportation, if needed.
Free appropriate public education	The primary requirement of P.L. 94-142 is the provision of a free appropriate public education to all school-age children with disabilities.

two groups of individuals, children with learning disabilities who are ineligible for services under IDEA and adults with learning disabilities, Section 504 of the Rehabilitation Act of 1973 provides important protections and services.

Section 504 of the Rehabilitation Act of 1973 is major federal legislation that impacts entities that receive federal funding. It is primarily civil rights legislation for persons with disabilities, designed to prevent any form of discrimination based on disabilities (Ballard, 1987). Section 504 is turning out to have an incredible impact on public schools across the country. Originally this section, which was part of the broader Rehabilitation Act, rarely affected public schools. Public Law 94-142 was the federal legislation that was the focal point of schools in serving children with disabilities, including learning disabilities. Section 504, which did not provide any funding, was often not considered as important for schools (Streett and Smith, 1996). And, as previously noted, most children with learning disabilities were identified and served through IDEA programs.

Recently, the role played by Section 504 in schools has increased to the point that schools are not able to continue to ignore this legislation. As parents and advocates for children with disabilities learn more about Section 504, schools are having to respond to requests for services under this Act. And, although schools do not receive any additional funds to provide services under 504, they are still mandated to do so for students who are eligible for protections under this Act. For adults with learning disabilities, Section 504 has become a very important legislative mandate.

Section 504 is a major component of the Rehabilitation Act which was passed in 1973. The statute "grants the right to be free from discrimination to a diverse array of people." It prohibits discrimination against individuals who meet the definition of disability in the Act by entities that receive federal funds. Wegner (1988) stated that the primary objective of Congress in enacting Section 504 was to "honor the requirements of 'simple justice' by ensuring that federal funds not be expended in a discriminatory fashion" (p. 398). Although originally targeting programs dealing with employment and the enhancement of employment for persons with disabilities, the act was amended in 1974 to "extend its protections to handicapped students seeking access to federally supported public schools" (Kortering, Julnes, and Edgar, 1990, p. 8). It is this extension of the act that is important for school personnel.

The Rehabilitation Act of 1973 impacts on many different aspects of rehabilitation. Section 504 is the component that deals primarily with discriminatory practices toward individuals with disabilities. Unlike some federal legislation which is written in lengthy, complex formats, Section 504 is a relatively simple part of the Rehabilitation Act. It is only one sentence long. Section 504 states that

> No otherwise qualified individual with a disability . . . . shall solely by reason of her or his disability, be excluded from the participation in, be denied the benefits of, or be subjected to discrimination under any program or activity receiving Federal financial assistance.

There are several different components of the Rehabilitation Act; the primary areas that public schools must deal with are those that focus on employment practices, program accessibility, and preschool, elementary, and secondary education. The main requirement for schools related to students "is to afford students with handicaps equal opportunity to obtain the same result, to gain the same benefit, or to reach the same level of achievement," as students without disabilities (Jacob-Timm and Hartshorne, 1994, p. 29).

Section 504 only applies to entities that receive federal funds. A recipient of federal funds means "any state or its political subdivision, any instrumentality of a state or its political subdivision, any public or private agency, institution, organization, or other entity, or any person to which Federal financial assistance is extended directly or through another recipient, including any successor, assignee, or transferee of a recipient, but excluding the ultimate beneficiary of the assistance." Most public schools, K-12 as well as postsecondary, receive substantial federal funds through their participation in various federally supported activities, and are thus covered under the act (Katsiyannis, 1994; Podemski, Marsh, Smith, and Price, 1995; Wegner, 1988).

Eligibility for Section 504

Section 504 only applies to persons considered to have a disability, as defined in the Act. As a result, the question of eligibility is a critical issue. Eligibility for Section 504 is not the same as eligibility for IDEA. Several key points to remember when determining eligibility include:

- Section 504 eligibility is very broad and covers many different types of disabilities and disabling conditions, many of which are not covered under IDEA.
- Eligibility is based on the definition of disability, as defined in Section 504.
- Eligibility is not based on clinical categories, such as mental retardation or learning disabilities.
- Eligibility for protections under 504 is not related to eligibility under other federal or state laws, such as IDEA.
- As with IDEA, schools are required to locate students in their districts who may be eligible for protections under 504.

For the purposes of public schools, OCR (1988) described a qualified student with a disability as one who is:

1. Of an age during which persons without disabilities are provided such services;
2. Of any age during which it is mandatory under state law to provide such services to students with disabilities; or
3. A student for whom a state is required to provide a free appropriate public education under IDEA.

Several types of students who may not be eligible for IDEA services may be eligible for services and protections under Section 504. These include:

- students with attention deficit hyperactivity disorder (ADHD),
- children considered to be socially maladjusted;
- children who are slow learners, but who do not meet the eligibility criteria for mental retardation; and
- children with learning disabilities but whose discrepancy between ability and achievement is not significant enough to warrant special education.

Children with these types of problems may not be considered to have a disability under the definition used in IDEA, and may therefore not be eligible for special education services under IDEA. There are many children who just do not fit into one of the "neat" categories required in the IDEA but could still benefit from modifications and accommodations and may be eligible for protections and services under Section 504.

Many of the students noted above, who could be eligible for services under Section 504, may have "hidden disabilities." These are disabilities that are not readily apparent to others by simply looking or talking to the child (OCR, 1989b). A learning disability definitely fits into the category of a hidden disability. So also does attention deficit hyperactivity disorder, various reading problems, and some behavior problems. Unfortunately, many hidden disabilities, including learning disabilities, are not properly diagnosed (OCR, 1989b), which often leads to children who are eligible for services, and who could benefit from services, not identified as needing those services under IDEA.

Definition of Disability Under Section 504

Unlike an eligibility system that is based on clinical categories of disabilities, such as IDEA, Section 504 is based on a more functional model (Streett and Smith, 1996). Under 504, a person is considered to have a disability if that person (29 U.S.C. Sec. 706(8)):

1. Has a physical or mental impairment which substantially limits one or more of such person's major life activities,
2. Has a record of such an impairment, or
3. Is regarded as having such an impairment.

The Act defines a physical or mental impairment as (34 Code of Federal Regulations Part 104.3): (A) any physiological disorder or condition, cosmetic disfigurement, or anatomical loss affecting one or more of the following body systems: neurological; musculoskeletal; special sense organs; respiratory, including speech organs; cardiovascular; reproductive; digestive; genito-urinary; hemic and lymphatic; skin; and endocrine; or (B) any mental or psychological disorder, such as mental retardation, organic brain syndrome, emotional or mental illness, and specific learning disabilities. Section B is similar to the categorical definition of disability found in IDEA. However, Section A, while including some of the categories found in IDEA, goes well beyond those disability areas in defining *disability*. IDEA requires that individuals have a categorical disability, and that the disability results in the student's needing special education. Section 504 requires that the person have a *disorder* or *condition* that *substantially limits one or more of the person's major life activities.* A child can be determined to have a disability under Section 504 without any specific disability category.

The second part of the definition relates to the impact of the disability or condition on a *major life activity.* The act defines a *major life activity* using a very functional approach. Major life activities include a wide variety of daily activities, including (34 Code of Federal Regulations Part 104.3) ". . . functions such as caring for one's self, performing manual tasks, walking, seeing, hearing, speaking, breathing, learning and working."

For many school-age children, especially those with learning disabilities, the major life activity affected is learning. The determination of whether or not a disability *substantially limits* a life activity is subjective, since 504 does not provide any operational criteria of *substantial limitation* (Reid and Katsiyannis, 1995). School personnel must use their professional judgment, collectively, to make this determination. For students with learning disabilities, this determination is "particularly complex" (Scott, 1990). *Substantially limits* can be defined as:

1. Unable to perform a major life activity that the average person in the general population can perform, or

2. Significantly restricted as to the condition, manner or duration under which an individual can perform a particular major life activity as compared to the condition, manner, or duration under which the average person in the general population can perform that same major life activity.

Schools should remember that simply because a student is considered for 504 services does not mean the student is eligible. Likewise, just because a student is determined to have a disability does not automatically result in eligibility for 504 services. However, it is the school's responsibility to make a determination of 504 eligibility in the above situations. Specific actions for schools regarding referral, evaluation, and programming are included in a later section.

The diagram in Figure 10.1 depicts the different populations eligible for IDEA and Section 504. As can be seen, all children eligible for services under IDEA are eligible for protections under Section 504; however, many children protected under 504 are not eligible for services under IDEA. Therefore, children identified as having a learning disability under IDEA are still protected under Section 504 of the Rehabilitation Act.

Requirements of Section 504

There are two primary requirements of Section 504 that impact on school-age children with learning disabilities who have been determined eligible for protection and services under the statute. These include *nondiscrimination* and the provision of a *free appropriate public education.* Protections against discrimination include a wide variety of areas as they relate to treating students with learning disabilities fairly. Section 504 "specifically prohibits schools from dis-

FIGURE 10.1

IDEA and Section 504 Populations

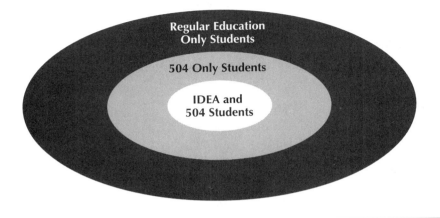

criminating on the basis of handicap in providing any aid, benefit, or service, either directly or through contractual arrangements." (Jacob-Timm and Hartshorne, 1994, p. 29) For example, students with learning disabilities should be allowed to participate in all activities that are available for students without disabilities. These include participation in the same academic curriculum, as well as non-academic, extra-curricular activities. Students protected under 504 must have equal access to health services, recreational activities, athletics, student employment, clubs, specific courses, and field trips.

The provision of a free appropriate education may require that schools provide appropriate modifications and accommodations for students with learning disabilities, as well as ensure that programs are *accessible* for these students (Conderman and Katsiyannis, 1995). This is actually an outgrowth of the nondiscrimination requirement because without appropriate modifications and accommodations, discrimination may occur. In general, there are numerous things that schools have to do to meet the requirements of Section 504 for children with learning disabilities and other disabilities. OCR (1989) describes the following requirements:

- Undertake annually to identify and locate all unserved handicapped children;

- Provide a "free appropriate public education" to each student with handicaps, regardless of the nature or severity of the handicap. This means providing regular or special education and related aids and services designed to meet the individual educational needs of handicapped persons as adequately as the needs of nonhandicapped persons are met;

• Ensure that each student with handicaps is educated with nonhandicapped students to the maximum extent appropriate to the needs of the handicapped person;

• Establish nondiscriminatory evaluation and placement procedures to avoid the inappropriate education that may result from the misclassification or misplacement of students;

• Establish procedural safeguards to enable parents and guardians to participate meaningfully in decisions regarding the evaluation and placement of their children; and

• Afford handicapped children an equal opportunity to participate in nonacademic and extra-curricular services and activities (p. 8).

The nondiscrimination requirement of Section 504 includes both physical accessibility and program accessibility. Program accessibility should be a strong consideration for students with learning disabilities. Simply placing students in a classroom without making modifications and accommodations that enable them to benefit from the class may be discriminatory under 504. Program accessibility, therefore, may require that certain modifications and accommodations be made for students with disabilities (Conderman and Katsiyannis, 1993). Program accessibility is part of the Section 504 requirement of a free appropriate public education (FAPE).

Section 504 defines FAPE as the provision of regular or special education and related aids and services that are:

1. Designed to meet individual educational needs of handicapped persons as well as the needs of a non-handicapped person are met and

2. Are based on adherence of procedural safeguards outlined in the law (Section 104.33(b)).

The FAPE requirement under 504 is thus more broadly defined than under IDEA. It requires schools to implement those measures that are necessary to "avoid" or "eradicate" discrimination caused by the disability (Underwood and Mead, 1995). These measures can include a variety of services, including education in general education classes, education in general education classes with supplementary aids, or special education and related services outside the general education setting (Jacob-Timm and Hartshorne, 1994). Regardless of the accommodations or modifications used, they should be individualized to meet the needs of students protected under Section 504.

Section 504, like IDEA, requires that students with disabilities be educated with their nondisabled peers, to the maximum extent appropriate, while meeting the needs of the students with disabilities. This is part of the FAPE requirement. Schools should always place students with disabilities with their nondisabled peers, unless it can be demonstrated by the school that the student's educational program cannot be achieved satisfactorily, with or without supplementary aids and services, in the general education setting. In making placement decisions, schools should always document reasons for placing students in more restrictive settings outside general education classrooms.

Accommodations and Modifications

Section 504 requires *reasonable accommodations* for persons protected under the act (Conderman and Katsiyannis, 1995). Just as an appropriate education is based on individual student's needs in IDEA programs, reasonable accommodations provided under 504 are determined on an individual basis. The requirement of providing a *free appropriate public education* (FAPE) in 504 is similar to the requirement in IDEA in that it intends to provide programs based on individual needs.

As defined, a free appropriate education under 504 differs to some degree from the FAPE requirement of IDEA. However, in both cases, programs should be designed to meet the needs of individual students. While schools do not have to develop IEPs for students served under 504, they do have to develop individuals plans for students. Section 504 does not specify the contents of the plan, but it must be designed to meet the needs of individual students, including specific accommodations and modifications that are necessary to meet the FAPE requirement. A sample Section 504 Accommodation Plan is depicted in Figure 10.2

Services in Public Schools

Students with learning disabilities who are protected under Section 504, but not eligible for IDEA services, must be afforded a FAPE through a designated

Section 504 requires that schools provide appropriate accommodations and modifications for students with learning disabilities, even if they are not eligible for special education services.

FIGURE 10.2

Sample Accommodation Plan

504 Accommodation Plan

Name: _____

School/Class: _____

Teacher: _____Date of Plan: _____
General Strengths:

General Weaknesses:

Specific Accommodations:

Accommodation #1   Class:

Accommodation(s):

Person Responsible for Implementing Accommodation:

Accommodation #2   Class:

Accommodation(s):

Person Responsible for Implementing Accommodation:

Individuals Participating in Development of Accommodation Plan:

_____

_____

_____

_____

process (see Figure 10.3). This includes referral, evaluation, programming planning, placement, and re-evaluation. Schools should establish written policies that spell out steps that should be taken to provide these services. Figure 10.3 summarizes the contents that should be included in these policies.

Due Process Procedures and Section 504

Schools that serve students under 504 are also required to establish and implement procedural safeguards related to the identification, evaluation, or educational placement of children. These safeguards must include

FIGURE 10.3

Outline of School District 504 Plan

Schools should develop and implement a policy regarding Section 504 of the Rehabilitation Act of 1973. This policy should include a variety of components. The following provides an outline of the major components that should be included in the policy.

I. Overview and Purpose of the 504 Policy

Schools should describe Section 504 and how it applies to its local district. This overview should include a detailed explanation of the purpose of Section 504, emphasizing that it is civil rights legislation that is designed to protect individuals with disabilities from discrimination.

II. Eligibility for Services

The policy should describe the types of students that are eligible for services under Section 504. The Section 504 definition of disability should be highlighted, with specific examples of students that might be eligible for services.

III. Procedures

The school policy must provide a detailed description of the procedures used to implement 504 provisions. These procedures must include the following:

Referral Specific steps for referring students suspected of being eligible for 504 services must be described. Referral forms and how to complete them should be included.

Evaluation Specific actions related to the evaluation of students referred for Section 504 services should be described. These should include requirements for nondiscriminatory assessment, individuals who should be involved in the evaluation process, and how to determine which areas should be evaluated. Forms for evaluation reports should be included.

Program Development Specific actions for developing individual accommodation and modification plans should be included. These should include likely areas of accommodations and modifications, personnel who should be involved in the program development, and forms for the 504 plan.

Procedures for Re-evaluation A description of when and how students should be re-evaluated should be included in the plan. This includes the typical time frame between evaluations, as well as examples of other times when re-evaluations are necessary.

Due Process Procedures The 504 plan must include a detailed description of due process requirements. When and how to involve parents as well as due process forms should be an integral part of the plan.

Review Requirements The plan should include a methodology for its review by patrons of the school district and procedures that should be used to modify the plan.

- notice,
- an opportunity for parents or guardian of the student to examine relevant records,
- an impartial hearing, and
- a review procedure.

One of the first things schools need to do when dealing with a child who has been referred for 504 services is to inform parents of their procedural rights. Table 10.3 summarizes due process safeguards required by Section 504.

Unlike IDEA, Section 504 does not require consent prior to initial evaluation or for the development of the accommodation plan. However, it is good practice for the school to request such permission. Notice, however, is required. The best advice for schools related to notice and consent is to follow the procedures for IDEA. It is significantly better for schools to do more than required rather than less. If complaints are filed by parents, schools look much better if they have gone beyond procedural safeguard requirements and have exhausted efforts to gain parental involvement and consent.

There are many similarities and differences between Section 504 and IDEA and the ADA, which is discussed later. Table 10.4 compares these three legislative acts. As can be seen, while these three laws have a great deal in common, the way that they are implemented contains significant differences. School personnel must remember that some students with learning disabilities not eligible for services under IDEA are eligible for protections and services under Section 504 and the ADA.

Section 504 and Adults with Learning Disabilities

Chapter 8 focused entirely on adults with learning disabilities. As noted, some adults with learning disabilities do not need services after they exit from high school. They are able to enter the competitive job market or postsecondary educational program without any assistance. However, there are many young adults with learning disabilities who need assistance in postsecondary education and training opportunities, or in job placement and supports (Minskoff, 1994). For some of these adults, legal protections are necessary to prevent discrimination. Two areas where these protections are often needed are postsecondary education and training opportunities, and employment.

TABLE 10.3

Procedural Rights Under Section 504

- Right to be informed by the district of specific rights
- Right for the child to have access to equal academic and non-academic school activities
- Right for the child to have an appropriate education in the least restrictive setting, which includes accommodations, modifications, and related services
- Right to notice regarding referral, evaluation, and placement
- Right for the child to have a fair evaluation conducted by a knowledgeable person(s)
- Right to an administrative appeals process
- Right to examine and obtain copies of all school records

TABLE 10.4

Comparison of Section 504, ADA, and IDEA

	Section 504	ADA	IDEA
Scope of the Law	Applies to recipients of federal financial assistance.	Applies to employment, public services, transportation and public accommodations, regardless of whether federal funds are received.	States required to have approved comprehensive plans for education of disabled children to be eligible to receive federal funds. Applies to all public and private schools within each state that provide special education and related services.
Who Is Protected?	Individual with a disability that impairs a major life activity, history of such condition, or regarded as having such a condition, and who is otherwise qualified for the job, program or activity to which he or she seeks access.	Same as section 504.	All individuals with disabilities from birth through age 21 (although eligibility for services varies for children from birth to age two, and from age three through 21).
What Is Required?	Equal opportunity to participate in program or activity, or to be employed, with or without reasonable accommodations to the individual's disability in the most integrated setting appropriate.	Schools may not discriminate in their programs or services, unless doing so would fundamentally alter the nature of the program or service.	States must ensure development of comprehensive plans to identify and evaluate children in need of special and related services, develop IEPs for each child, provide procedural safeguards for enforcing their rights. Education must be provided in the least restrictive environment appropriate to the child. Barrier removal mandated to achieve access.
Accessible Facilities	Education programs, when viewed in entirety, must be accessible. Renovation or construction may be required to make facilities accessible, but only when necessary to achieve program access. All new construction must be accessible.	Same as section 504.	Access to programs required to permit students to participate in educational programs in least restrictive environment.

(continued)

TABLE 10.4

continued

	Section 504	ADA	IDEA
Transition Plan	Must identify obstacles that limit access, detail methods to make facility accessible, specify time schedule, and indicate person responsible for implementation.	Same as section 504	Not required.
Enforcement Scheme	Administrative remedies, private right to sue implied in statute. Courts generally do not require private litigants to exhaust administrative remedies before bringing suit (see ¶860).	Title II cites the administrative enforcement under section 504. Private suits permitted for victims of discrimination in public services.	Administrative remedies must be exhausted before bringing suit under IDEA (unless futile or process flawed). IDEA requires extensive due process protections including right to notice of planned changes in program placement, inspection of records, hearing, review by state school agency, right to counsel and to present evidence. Finally, parents have right to bring civil action in court.
Remedies Available	Wide latitude in fashioning equitable remedies, restraining orders, preliminary or permanent injunctions; suspension or termination of federal funds; compensatory damages (see ¶860).	Relief consistent with section 504, but money damages limited to private employers.	Courts may grant such relief as they deem appropriate, including payment for private tuition or other related services.
Attorney's Fees	Available to successful litigants.	Available under section 505 of the act, including litigation costs, expert witness fees and travel costs.	Available to successful claimants in any proceedings under IDEA (administrative hearings and judicial proceedings) since 1986 amendments.

Source: *Handicapped Requirements Handbook*, April 1995, Washington, DC: Author. Thompson Publishing Group. Reprinted with permission of the *Section 504 Compliance Handbook* © Thompson Publishing Group (800)677-3789.

Section 504 of the Rehabilitation Act of 1973 clearly protects students with learning disabilities in postsecondary education and training programs that receive federal funds (Reif and deFur, 1992). These students "must be granted an opportunity to compete with their nondisabled peers" just as they are provided in K-12 educational programs (Brinckerhoff, et al., 1993, p. 27). Colleges or other postsecondary education and training programs may not (Brinckerhoff, et al., 1993, pp. 28-29):

1. Limit the number of students with disabilities admitted.

2. Make preadmission inquiries as to whether or not an applicant has a disability.

3. Use admission tests or criteria that inadequately measure the academic level of applicants with disabilities, unless the measures used have been validated as a predictor of academic success in the education program or activity in question.

4. Give students with disabilities access to examinations that are not administered in the same frequency as tests given to nondisabled students. In addition, any admission test given to an applicant with a disability must be in an accessible location.

5. Give tests and examinations that do not accurately reflect the applicant's aptitude and achievement level without the interference of disability-related factors (e.g., providing additional time on exams or the use of a reader).

6. Limit access or excuse a student with a disability who is "otherwise qualified" from any course of study solely on the basis of his or her disability.

7. Counsel students with disabilities toward more restrictive careers than are recommended for nondisabled students. However, counselors may advise students with disabilities about strict licensing or certification requirements in a given profession.

8. Institute prohibitive rules that may adversely affect students with disabilities, such as prohibiting the use of tape recorders or laptop computers in the classroom. Auxiliary aids, such as four-track tape recorders and hand-held spellcheckers, must be permitted when they are viewed as appropriate academic adjustments that will help to ensure full participation by students with disabilities.

9. Refuse to modify academic requirements that would afford qualified students with disabilities an opportunity for full educational participation. Permitting additional time to meet degree requirements or allowing a student to receive a course substitution for a foreign language requirement are examples of such actions.

10. Provide less financial assistance to students with disabilities than is provided to nondisabled students, or premise financial aid decisions on information that is discriminatory on the basis of disability, thereby limiting eligibility for assistance.

11. Provide housing to students with disabilities that is not equivalent and accessible and at the same cost as comparable housing available to nondisabled students.

12. Prohibit full participation in campus services or activities that are nonacademic in nature, such as physical education, athletics, or social organizations.

Although Section 504 prohibits discrimination against students with learning disabilities in postsecondary educational programs, the law is limited in providing guidance regarding considerations for requests for accommodations. Universities and other postsecondary education and training institutions should be proactive in considering the legal requirements of Section 504 for students with learning disabilities. At the institutional level, policies regarding admissions, financial aid, and housing should be reviewed to ensure that students with learning disabilities are not discriminated against. Program and course requirements must also be reviewed to prevent discrimination against this group of students (Scott, 1994).

One important area for training programs to consider is the determination that a student has a learning disability and is thus entitled to certain accommodations and modifications. Scott (1994) described a decision chart to facilitate this determination. The basic steps, described in Figure 10.4, focus on whether or not a disability exists, appropriate documentation, and the determination of a reasonable accommodation. By following such a process, it is more likely that postsecondary training programs will not discriminate against individuals with learning disabilities who meet the requirements of protections under Section 504.

Regardless of efforts to adhere to the requirements of Section 504 it is likely that litigation related to postsecondary education and training programs will occur. One of the most likely litigative areas is admission to postsecondary programs and the provision of accommodations for students after they are admitted. Other potential questions that will be involved in litigation include who pays for accommodations for students, such as interpreters for the deaf and laptop computers, and what accommodations are *reasonable* (Brickerhoff, et al., 1993; Brickerhoff, et al., 1996). Being proactive and following procedures like those described above by Scott (1994) will diminish the likelihood of litigation and provide more appropriate services for young adults eligible for protections under Section 504.

Employment issues related to adults with learning disabilities were included in Chapter 8. Section 504 protects adults with learning disabilities from employment discrimination (Grossman, 1992; Jacobs and Hendricks, 1992). Prior to the passage of the Americans with Disabilities Act (ADA), Section 504 was the "single most important law prohibiting employment discrimination" for persons with disabilities, including those with learning disabilities (Grossman, 1994). Specific legal requirements of Section 504 related to employment will be discussed in the section on the Americans with Disabilities Act, which has similar provisions related to employment. Regarding employment discrimination, it is important to remember that Section 504 applies to entities that receive federal funds, while the ADA applies to a broader group of entities.

▶ THE AMERICANS WITH DISABILITIES ACT AND STUDENTS WITH LEARNING DISABILITIES

In addition to the Individuals with Disabilities Education Act and Section 504 of the Rehabilitation Act, there is one more federal legislative act that is having an impact on persons with learning disabilities. The Americans with Disabilities Act (ADA) was passed in 1990 and went into effect over the ensuing several years; the law is currently fully operational. The ADA is massive federal legislation. It is similar to Section 504 of the Rehabilitation Act in that it is basically civil rights legislation for persons with disabilities; however, it goes well beyond Section 504 because of its coverage. The purpose of the ADA "is to

FIGURE 10.4

Accommodation Decision Chart for College Students with Learning Disabilities

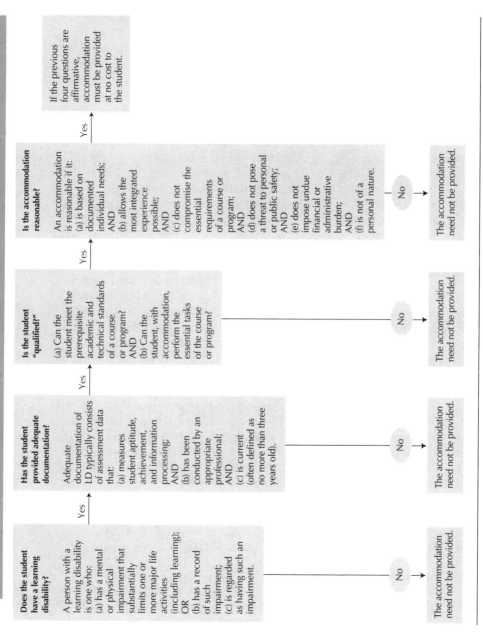

Does the student have a learning disability?

A person with a learning disability is one who:
(a) has a mental or physical impairment that substantially limits one or more major life activities (including learning); OR
(b) has a record of such impairment;
(c) is regarded as having such an impairment.

Yes →

Has the student provided adequate documentation?

Adequate documentation of LD typically consists of assessment data that:
(a) measures student aptitude, achievement, and information processing; AND
(b) has been conducted by an appropriate professional; AND
(c) is current (often defined as no more than three years old).

Yes →

Is the student "qualified"?

(a) Can the student meet the prerequisite academic and technical standards of a course or program? AND
(b) Can the student, with accommodation, perform the essential tasks of the course or program?

Yes →

Is the accommodation reasonable?

An accommodation is reasonable if it:
(a) is based on documented individual needs; AND
(b) allows the most integrated experience possible; AND
(c) does not compromise the essential requirements of a course or program; AND
(d) does not pose a threat to personal or public safety; AND
(e) does not impose undue financial or administrative burden; AND
(f) is not of a personal nature.

Yes → If the previous four questions are affirmative, accommodation must be provided at no cost to the student.

No → The accommodation need not be provided.

No → The accommodation need not be provided.

No → The accommodation need not be provided.

No → The accommodation need not be provided.

Source: Scott, S.S. (1994). Determining reasonable academic adjustments for college students with learning disabilities. *Journal of Learning Disabilities, 27*, p. 409. Used with permission.

provide clear, strong, consistent, and enforceable standards prohibiting discrimination against individuals with disabilities, without respect to their age, nature of disability, or extent of disability." (Turnbull, 1993, p. 128) For children of school age, the ADA like Section 504, is consistent with the IDEA.

Whereas Section 504 only applies to entities that receive federal funding, the ADA applies to all programs, services, buildings, and facilities available to the public. For example, it applies to public schools, universities, department stores, doctors' offices, lawyers' offices, hotels and motels, and day care centers, to name a few. Private clubs and churches are among the few entities not covered by the ADA.

The ADA is composed of five sections, including:

• Title I—Employment. This section of the law prohibits discrimination in employment because of a disability. Persons who are otherwise qualified cannot be discriminated against regarding employment.

• Title II—State and local governments. Title II applies to state and local governments, and their units. It prohibits any form of discrimination against persons because of a disability covered under the ADA. This could be related to employment, access to services, or access to buildings.

• Title III—Public accommodations. This section applies to the nondiscrimination provisions of the act to most facilities and services in the community. Department stores, movie theaters, hotels, private day care centers, and lawyers' offices are a few examples of entities covered under this title. Title III prohibits discrimination, based on disability, from any public accommodation.

• Title IV—Telecommunications. This section targets telecommunication systems, such as the public telephone system.

• Title V—Miscellaneous. Title V deals with methods of securing redress for grievances under the act, as well as provisions for the implementation of the act.

Schools are primarily interested in section one, dealing with employment issues, and section two, since schools are considered a component of state and local governments. Since public schools, and even many private schools, receive some federal funding, Section 504 of the Rehabilitation Act is the federal civil rights for persons with disabilities mandate that is primarily considered. However, the ADA does apply to public schools and some private schools that do not receive any federal funds and is thus linked to educational programs for students with disabilities.

Determining who is eligible for protections under the ADA is again linked to the definition of disability. The ADA uses the same definition of disability used in Section 504. Therefore, the ADA is very broad-based in its coverage and focuses on a functional approach to defining disability as opposed to a categorical model used in IDEA.

Reasonable Accommodation

A person considered disabled under the ADA must be provided the necessary *reasonable* accommodations and modifications that are necessary to ensure

TABLE 10.5	
Ways Schools and Other Agencies Can Ensure Cost Effectiveness When Implementing the ADA	

- Appoint one individual responsible for compliance with the ADA and ensure that individual is well versed in the requirements of the legislation
- Develop and implement a system to determine if an individual is eligible for protections under the ADA
- Provide modifications and accommodations that will enable equal access and treatment, not those that will result in the very best interventions
- Consider accommodations and modifications that will enable equal access and treatment but will not add extensive costs, such as peer readers and tutors, simplified textbooks and directives, time schedules, and homework assignment books
- Provide services, accommodations, and modifications in environment that are natural and are not different from those for nondisabled persons
- Alter schedules and work times when necessary

equal opportunities in jobs, schools, and accessing all sorts of public accommodations. In the area of employment, the ADA, similar to Section 504, prohibits discrimination against individuals with disabilities who would "otherwise be qualified" to perform the "essential functions" of the job, with reasonable accommodations (Turnbull, 1993).

The ADA, again similar to Section 504, impacts schools in numerous ways. First, employment protections afforded under Title I for teachers, maintenance workers, secretaries, etc., who have a disability are similar to those provided under Section 504. A person who is qualified to teach elementary school and is more qualified than other applicants, even if some minor, reasonable accommodations are needed, should be employed as the teacher over other, less qualified candidates.

For students with disabilities, the ADA primarily addresses physical accessibility to the school and program accessibility. Again, similar to Section 504, all school buildings do not have to be remodeled to ensure accessibility, but all programs must be accessible for students, including those with learning disabilities. Again, Section 504 covers students in public schools or even private schools that receive federal funding; however, for schools that do not receive any federal money, the ADA would require reasonable accommodations in the educational process. Table 10.5 provides a list of ways that schools and other agencies can ensure cost-efficient methods of adhering to ADA requirements related to persons with learning disabilities.

▶ EMPLOYMENT ISSUES

In addition to the Americans with Disabilities Act (ADA) affecting school-age children with learning disabilities, there are also legal issues involving adults with learning disabilities. The primary legal concern for adults with learning disabilities focuses on employment issues. Both Section 504 and the ADA are not age-restrictive; they provide protections and guarantees for individuals with learning disabilities of all ages, not just for those of school age. For individuals with learning disabilities, equal opportunities related to employment are provided by both Section 504 and the ADA. Section 504, however, only applies to entities that receive federal funds while the ADA covers public accommodations that do not receive any federal funding.

In addition to Section 504, the Rehabilitation Act includes two additional acts related to employment. Section 501 prohibits discrimination and requires affirmative action for persons with disabilities by federal employers. Section 503 provides similar protections for persons by federal contractors; however, Section 503 does not require affirmative action (Grossman, 1992). Both Section 504 and the ADA prohibit discrimination against persons with disabilities in employment. Persons with disabilities, who are *otherwise qualified* to perform the essential functions of a job with or without reasonable accommodations, are protected from discrimination.

An example would be a young adult who, because of a learning disability, cannot read well enough to complete a lengthy job application for a job that does not require reading. If this person is otherwise qualified for the position, with or without reasonable accommodations, then the person is protected under the ADA or under Section 504 if the employer receives federal funds.

Similar to Section 504, the ADA applies to all aspects of employment, including pre-employment testing and screening, employee selection, employee promotion, pay issues, training issues, employee benefits, and other areas related to employment (Grossman, 1992). The ADA uses the same criteria to determine eligibility as Section 504. Persons must have a disability that substantially limits a major life activity. Working is an example of a major life activity. The ADA, as well as Section 504, requires that employees provide reasonable accommodations for adults with learning disabilities who are *otherwise qualified* to perform the *essential job functions* of a particular job (Grossman, 1992).

Reasonable accommodations may include a wide variety of strategies that employers can use to enable persons with disabilities to be successful in job situations. These include (Grossman, 1992):

- making job sites accessible,
- job restructuring,
- part-time or modified work schedules,
- acquisition or modification of equipment,
- provision of readers and interpreters,
- appropriate modifications or adjustments of examinations, training materials, and policies, and/or
- reassignment to a position that is vacant.

There are many potential discriminatory policies and practices regarding employment and persons with learning disabilities that are prohibited by Section 504 and the ADA. These include (National perspectives on issues in employment, 1992):

- time-limited examinations,
- policies for certification or licensing examinations that do not allow for alternative ways to complete the examination,
- employment based solely on one criterion, such as a written test or oral interview,
- not allowing job restructuring, and/or
- hiring, evaluation, promotion, grievance, termination practices that are discriminatory.

Adults with learning disabilities often are eligible for services provided by state vocational rehabilitation agencies. Initially, individuals with learning disabilities were denied services from vocational rehabilitation agencies because they only served persons with mental retardation and physical disabilities. However, a policy directive by the federal Rehabilitation Services Administration (RSA) in 1981 resulted in the identification of learning disabilities as a medically recognized disability, eligible for VR services (Dowdy, Smith, and Nowell, 1996; Jacobs and Hendricks, 1992). More information on accessing vocational rehabilitation services can be found in Chapter 8.

SUMMARY

This chapter has focused on legal issues related to persons with learning disabilities. The Individuals with Disabilities Education Act (IDEA), Section 504 of the Rehabilitation Act, and the Americans with Disabilities Act (ADA) were described. The following points summarize the major areas included in this chapter:

- Children and adults with learning disabilities are protected by several laws against discrimination.
- Public Law 94-142, reauthorized as the Individuals with Disabilities Education Act (IDEA), provides services for school-age children with learning disabilities.
- Public Law 94-142, passed in 1975, was the first major federal legislation that included learning disabilities as a disability that required appropriate services.
- Schools are required to find children with learning disabilities and initiate procedures to determine if they are eligible for special education services.
- IDEA requires schools to serve students with learning disabilities with their nondisabled peers as much as possible.

- Students with learning disabilities must be provided a free appropriate public education as defined by an individualized education program (IEP).

- Schools must follow specific due process procedures when dealing with students with learning disabilities.

- IDEA meets the needs of most students with learning disabilities.

- Section 504 of the Rehabilitation Act of 1973 is civil rights legislation for persons with disabilities.

- Section 504, unlike IDEA, is not age-restrictive and utilizes a broader definition of disability than IDEA.

- Some children with learning disabilities who are found to be ineligible for services under IDEA are likely protected by Section 504.

- Section 504 only applies to entities that receive federal funds.

- Section 504 uses a functional, non-categorical definition of disability and eligibility.

- Children eligible under 504 must have a disability, as defined by the Act, which must substantially limit a major life activity, such as learning.

- Section 504 requires schools to provide a free appropriate public education (FAPE) to children eligible for protection under the act.

- Similar to IDEA, Section 504 requires schools to educate students with learning disabilities in the least restrictive environment.

- Specific due process safeguards must be afforded children with learning disabilities and their parents under Section 504.

- Section 504 also applies to adults with learning disabilities.

- Adults with learning disabilities are protected in employment and post-secondary education and training programs.

- Universities and other post-secondary training programs should be proactive in implementing Section 504 protections for persons with learning disabilities.

- The Americans with Disabilities Act (ADA) is major civil rights legislation for persons with learning disabilities and other disabilities.

- The ADA applies to most agencies and facilities, including those that do not receive federal funds.

- Through five distinct titles, the ADA prohibits discrimination against persons with disabilities of all ages.

- The ADA uses the same broad definition of disability used in Section 504.

- Persons with learning disabilities, who are otherwise qualified to perform the essential functions of a job, are protected under the ADA and Section 504.

Chapter 11

WORKING WITH FAMILIES OF STUDENTS WITH LEARNING DISABILITIES

The objectives for this chapter are as follows:

- To understand the changing nature of families over the past twenty years.

- To know the history of family involvement in programs for students with learning disabilities.

- To identify various factors that influence the involvement of families with children with learning disabilities.

- To describe present-day families.

- To describe the different reactions families may have when they realize that they have a child with a learning disability.

- To understand the impact that children with learning disabilities have on families.

- To understand the importance for school and family collaboration.

- To describe the legal requirements for involving families in educational programs for students with learning disabilities.

- To identify ways to enhance communication between schools and families.

- To describe ways that schools and families resolve disputes regarding the educational program for students with learning disabilities.

- To describe ways family members can become involved in the educational program for students with learning disabilities.

Jake's Parents: Interested But Not Involved

Jake is fourteen years old and in the seventh grade. He was retained in the third grade because he was so far behind his age peers. He was identified as having a learning disability during his second year in the third grade. Although Jake's achievement levels have continued to fall, school personnel have decided to promote him with his peers rather than holding him back again. They do feel that Jake will never be a very good student and that retention will not result in improved academic success because of his learning disability. What is puzzling to some of Jake's teachers is how bright he seems to be. He tries, even though he gives up more easily now than he did a few years ago, but simply cannot do well. He is reading on the fourth grade level, but his math skills are near average for his age.

Jake's parents have been concerned about his development and lack of success in school since the first grade. They have attended every conference the school has held concerning Jake and consistently agree with school teachers and administrators regarding Jake's IEP. Jake has been in the resource room two periods each day since he was identified in the third grade. Although Jake's parents want to help, they are intimidated by the experts who work at the school. They really do not understand some of the words that are used in the conferences, and they surely do not understand this condition called learning disabilities. However, they are afraid to ask because they think that the school people will think they are not very smart.

Jake's parents are not unlike many other parents of students with learning disabilities. Many do not understand learning disabilities or how they can help their children with this condition. Rather than being equal partners in school decisions made about their child, many of these parents simply participate with their physical presence. School personnel must take the initiative and work to involve parents more. Jake's parents, if they were more involved, might be able to provide some insight that would prove very beneficial to Jake's educational program.

Parents of students with learning disabilities are in a unique position to become involved with the educational intervention of their children. Before the school has even seen the student, a parent, or both parents, have been involved in the child's life for several years. Parents have observed the child's first steps, listened to the child's first words, and provided opportunities for the child to grow and develop intellectually, emotionally, socially, and physically. Often, parents are the first ones who notice developmental delays or other signs of a learning disability. They may realize that a child is not doing some of the things other children of similar age can do. In addition to early involvement with the child's development, many parents continue to be very involved in the child's educational programs throughout public school. They often find themselves as the child's most ardent advocate because they may understand the problems their child is experiencing more than some school personnel.

As noted in earlier chapters, the educational system needs to make accommodations and provide specialized interventions in order to meet the unique learning challenges of students with learning disabilities. Schools are legally responsible for making these accommodations and providing appropriate educational programs for these students. The relative newness of the field of learning disabilities (Bender, 1995) and the fact that a learning disability is often a "hidden disability" (Office of Civil Rights, 1989) are no longer legitimate reasons for schools not providing appropriate services. Also, schools cannot use a lack of trained staff or limited funding to justify less than adequate interventions for this group of students.

Services for students with learning disabilities have changed significantly over the past several years. Students with this disability have gone from not even being identified, to being diagnosed and served in segregated settings, to the current trend of educating them with their nondisabled peers. School personnel have gone from not knowing anything about students with learning disabilities to identifying and providing services to more children with this disability than any other disability group (U.S. Department of Education, 1995). Although services for children and youth with learning disabilities have evolved dramatically, schools still need the involvement of parents in order to meet the unique needs of each child. In order for schools to continue to improve services for this group of children, families must be involved.

▶ PARENTAL INVOLVEMENT

Family members of students with disabilities, including those with learning disabilities, have not always been involved in the education of their children. Often they have been left out of important decisions affecting their child, or they have been included only on a superficial level. There are several reasons for this limited involvement, including the traditional role played by all families related to school activities, lack of knowledge of parents regarding disabilities and their legal rights, and sensitivities related to their child having a disability. Traditionally, parents have left the education of their children to schools. This has not only been the case for parents who have children with disabilities, but all parents. The assumption has been that schools know what is educationally best for children; regarding education, schools know best.

Parents have also lacked information about particular disabilities. Learning disabilities, which have been difficult for professionals to understand, are often very confusing to parents. They know that their child appears to be intelligent and without any obvious problems, but they do not understand why the child has such difficulty in school. Along with understanding the disability, parents of students with learning disabilities have also had problems understanding the law and their legal rights. The Individuals with Disabilities Education Act (IDEA), and now Section 504 of the Rehabilitation Act, both provide opportunities for children with learning disabilities. However, without an understanding of their rights, parents often do not know what services they can request. Finally, parents are often sensitive about their child's problems at school. They may be embarrassed by their child's school problems, or they may think that the school blames them for their child's failures. Whether they take on a defensive posture or one that results in their avoiding the school is of little consequence. Both can result in limited interactions with school personnel.

There are some parents who make the choice not to get involved in their child's educational program (Haring, Lovett, and Saren, 1991). As noted above, one of the main reasons is simply that school personnel have always made decisions about their child and often did not seek their participation in the process. Some parents have thus grown apathetic and simply continue to allow school professionals to make all of the important decisions regarding their child's educational program.

In addition to apathy and giving over decision-making to schools because of tradition, there are other factors related to parental involvement. These include family income, educational levels of parents, and how much time a student spends in special education (Cone, Delawyer, and Wolfe, 1985). The results of one study suggested that family members were more likely to be involved if they were well-educated and had higher family incomes. What this could mean is that many parents, especially those who are having a difficult time making ends meet financially, may simply not have the luxury of taking time out of their work day to meet with school personnel. This problem could be alleviated in some cases by school personnel making an effort to meet with parents during the evening or even on weekends to accommodate the parents' work schedules.

Cone et al. (1985) also found that the amount of time students were in special education was correlated with the level of parental involvement, with more parental involvement associated with students who spend more time receiving services. Since students with learning disabilities often spend less time in special education than those with other disabilities, parents might be less likely to get involved in the educational decision-making process. They might view the limited special services as only a small and fairly insignificant part of the student's educational program and therefore not needing a great deal of their time.

Not only has their involvement often been limited by choice, but frequently school personnel dissuaded parents from taking a more active role in their child's educational program. School personnel often liked to make decisions based on what they thought was best for a child rather than what the parents thought. This attitude by some school personnel, plus the acceptance by some parents of the fact that "they were told by school administrators whether and how their children were to be educated" resulted in their limited involvement (Turnbull and Turnbull, 1990, p. 14). Also, some parents have always chosen not to be very involved in the education of their children. They simply believe that professionals know best how to provide appropriate programs for their children.

Regardless of reasons for limited involvement, more parents are active in educational programs now than previously. Several factors have resulted in the increased level of parental involvement in the education of students with learning disabilities, including:

- legislation, particularly P.L. 94-142;
- growing parental advocacy; and
- growing awareness among professionals of the benefits of parental involvement.

Public Law 94-142, discussed extensively in other chapters, required that schools involve parents in all stages of special education for students with learning disabilities, beginning with the referral of the student for special services. In passing this requirement, it was the basic premise of Congress that "families of children and youth with disabilities could make no assumptions that the public schools would educate their children—that schools would allow parents to enroll their children, much less that schools would educate the children appropriately" (Turnbull and Turnbull, 1990, p. 14). Rather, parents would have to take some of the responsibility for ensuring that their children would receive appropriate services. This legislative act made families and schools equal partners in the education of their children.

In addition to legislation, parents have also learned that banding together into advocacy groups can be beneficial. Beginning in the 1950s with the National Association for Retarded Children (NARC), parents began to realize how they could band together and effect more significant change than they could singularly. In 1963, parents formed the Association for Children with Learning Disabilities. Now named the Learning Disabilities Association of America, this organization has more than fifty thousand members in forty-eight states and seven hundred and fifty local chapters. "LDA has been instrumental in sponsoring legislation and influencing rules and regulations that effect the lives of persons with learning disabilities" (Hammill, 1989, p. 5). LDA, in addition to the Orton Dyslexia Society, has resulted in a strong advocacy movement for children and adults with learning disabilities including more parental involvement in school services (Smith, Polloway, Patton, and Dowdy, 1995).

In addition to support and advocacy groups at the national level, often local support group meetings are held that provide families information and support for specific school systems (Bedard, 1995). Through local LDA chapters or just informal parent support groups, family members have found a network of individuals who provide assistance in meeting the challenges and needs of a child with a learning disability. Often this local support network encourages increased parental involvement in educational programs.

Finally, professionals have begun to realize the contribution that parents can make in their child's educational program by realizing that "families are the constant in their children's lives" (Bedard, 1995, p. 23), not school personnel who change from year to year. This realization has brought about a stronger effort on behalf of some school personnel to include parents in all aspects of the individual educational program (IEP) process for students with learning disabilities, including identification, referral, assessment, program planning, and program implementation. School personnel have also begun to realize that parents and other family members can be invaluable in helping them teach certain concepts to children with learning disabilities. Examples include working with children in whole language experiences (Wener and O'Shea, 1992) and homework activities (Kay, Fitzgerald, Paradee, and Mellencamp, 1994; Patton, 1994).

Many parents want to be involved as much as possible in the educational program of their child with a learning disability. They want to participate in decision-making, IEP development, and progress monitoring. In wanting to be involved, parents want certain things from professionals. For example, they want honesty, commitment, and open communication. And they want desperately to be included as equal members of the team that is developing and implementing programs for their child (Wilson, 1995). Table 11.1 describes several things that parents of students with learning disabilities want from school personnel.

TABLE 11.1

Things Parents of Students with Learning Disabilities Want from School Personnel

- Parents want professionals to communicate without jargon. When technical terms are necessary, they would like to have them explained.
- When possible, they want conferences to be held so both parents can attend.
- They want to receive written materials that provide information to assist them in understanding their child's problem.
- They want to receive a copy of a written report about their child.
- Parents want specific advice on how to manage the specific behavior problems of their children or how to teach them needed skills.
- Parents want information on their child's social as well as academic behavior.

Source: Wilson, C.L. (1995). Parents and teachers: Can we talk? *LD Forum, 20,* p. 31. Reprinted with permission of the Council for Learning Disabilities.

Parents of students with learning disabilities have the opportunity to get involved with school personnel in a variety of activities, including referral, assessment, and development of individual educational programs (IEPs). Although research indicates that participation in IEP meetings is generally high, Turnbull and Turnbull (1990) point out that this involvement might only mean that parents are physically present rather than they are actually participating in decision-making. To achieve the benefit of parental involvement, school personnel must attempt to secure active participation rather than mere presence.

The National Joint Committee on Learning Disabilities (1994) published a series of position papers related to children and adults with learning disabilities. Regarding the involvement of parents of children with learning disabilities, the committee made the following statement:

> Parents of and individuals with learning disabilities should be given maximal opportunities for a meaningful involvement in the educational programs. Regardless of the competence of professional personnel in providing services, programs for individuals with learning disabilities will be limited to the extent that the special commitment and abilities of both parents and affected individuals are not used. Therefore, opportunity must be provided to parents of and individuals with learning disabilities to participate actively in the educational process (p. 19).

This statement makes it very clear the importance of involving parents in educating children with learning disabilities. Even with competent, well-intentioned professionals, the educational programs provided children will not be as optimal as they would with parental involvement.

▶ THE FAMILY

Successfully getting families involved with school intervention programs is not an easy task. Some family members want to be involved while others do not. Some are easy to get to know while others are difficult; and some want to know all that is going on with their child while others want to know very little. In order for professionals to know the best ways to interact with families with children with learning disabilities, they need to have a basic understanding of families and of social changes in the past several decades that impact family interactions with schools. Table 11.2 summarizes some of these changes. For example, the role of friends, the church, and neighborhoods have been altered, and this impacts how parents and schools interact.

The nature of families has changed a great deal over the past several decades. Families of today are generally not like the families of the 1960s and 1970s. Remember the television shows depicting families during this era? They included *Ozzie and Harriet, Father Knows Best, Leave it to Beaver,* and *Lassie.* For the most part, these families included two non-divorced parents and two or more children, and they revolved around family-oriented, group activities. Families that differed from these more traditional families, such as the one depicted in *The Brady Bunch*, still had a focus around family-oriented living.

Single-parent families make up a much larger percentage of families than several years ago.

Whereas families used to be very similar in composition, today's families represent diversity in all aspects. This diversity makes it difficult to even define family. The state of New Mexico has described a family using a broad set of characteristics, including:

- Families are big and small.
- Families are extended, nuclear, multigenerational.
- Families include one parent, two parents, and grandparents.
- Families are formed through birth, adoption, marriage, or a desire for mutual support.
- Family members nurture, protect, and influence each other.
- Families are a culture unto themselves.
- Families create neighborhoods, communities, states, and nations.

The New Mexico description reflects the great diversity of families that exist in the 1990s. Single-parent families, usually headed by single mothers, have become a major family type (Shea and Bauer, 1991). Blended families, where mothers and fathers marry and bring children from previous marriages, are also common. There are even alternative families today in which the parents are of the same gender. Most families are just not like they were 20 years ago. Rather than there

TABLE 11.2

Social Changes that Merit Consideration

Factors	1950s	1990s
Family	Extended, traditional nuclear	Neolocal nuclear
Neighborhood	Personal, cohesive	Impersonal, multicultural
Neighbors	Concerned, responsible, active	Concerned, defensive, passive or indirectly active
Companions/friends	Close, cohesive, socially and emotionally supportive	Often distant or unavailable, nonexistent for many needing social and emotional support
School	Small, in the neighborhood, personal	Large, outside the neighborhood, impersonal
Teachers	Accepted as friends, neighbors, community leaders	Perceived as strangers, professionals, specialists
Knowledge	Limited, manageable within existing standards of behavior and application	Exploding, unmanagable within existing standards of behavior and application
Church	Influential	Relatively less influential
Standards/values	Rigid, widely accepted, emphasizing the normal	Relative, fragmented, emphasizing the bizarre and unacceptable
Work	Simple, personal, available, sufficient to produce needed goods, supportive of artisans	Mechanized, impersonal, automated, specialized, unavailable to many, less supportive of artisans
Material goods	Limited, emphasizing necessities for living	Available to majority, emphasizing luxuries
Mobility	Limited for most people	Nearly unlimited
Communication/transportation	Limited, slow, inefficient	Nearly unlimited, rapid, more efficient
National and world events	Not widely followed or understood	Extensively followed and understood

Shea and Bauer (1991). *Parents and teachers of children with exceptionalities: A handbook for collaboration*, 2nd Ed. p. 6. Copyright 1991 by Allyn and Bacon. Reprinted/adapted by permission.

being a standard family prototype, there currently exists many different types of families. In fact, the only thing that is standard about families today is the uniqueness of each family. Each one differs and is associated with different cultures. "Professionals particularly must be cognizant of cultural lifestyles which influence families of children with disabilities in order to enable families to best meet the needs of the child with disabilities" (Bedard, 1995, p. 23).

While recognizing that the nature of families varies significantly, the key thing for school personnel to remember is that students' parents, or grandparents when they are in the role of parents, should be involved in educational programs regardless of the specific composition of the family. School personnel must put aside any personal feelings they may have about various types of lifestyles and family units and work with students' families to develop and implement appropriate educational programs for students with learning disabilities. Some family involvement is almost always better than no family involvement. Therefore, school personnel must take steps to gain and maintain family involvement. One thing that will facilitate this process is for school personnel to understand the "inner-workings" of each family of a child with a learning disability (Bedard, 1995).

Although families are very different now from what they were twenty and thirty years ago, the family unit is still a significant element in the provision of appropriate educational programs for students with learning disabilities. Parents are at home to provide support for their children, and they are the ones who remain the constant in a child's life from year to year. While this year's teacher may do a superb job with a particular student, it is likely that the student will have other teachers next year. Parents, on the other hand, are present from year to year and must, therefore, be actively involved in the student's educational program over the duration of such services. The continuous involvement of family members is a strength that school personnel should encourage and use for the advantage of the student.

Families and Children with Learning Disabilities

Parents always want their children to be successful in life, including during the school years. They want their children to do well in academic work, be popular with peers, and please their teachers and other school personnel. Many parents also have dreams for their children—college, good jobs, and a happy life. Children with learning disabilities often have problems with many of the hopes of their parents. As noted in previous chapters, they frequently do poorly in school, display poor social skills, and experience problems as adults.

A child with a learning disability frequently results in the entire family making adjustments. Important decisions and the solutions to many problems, such as school failure and low self-esteem, must be made. And, these problems must be dealt with in the context of the child, the child's family, and the environment in which many of the problems are displayed—the school (Falik, 1995). A child with a learning disability generally does not only impact a small part of the family. Rather, the child causes some disruptions among all family members and for many of the family functions.

Children with learning disabilities not only cause parents to rethink their goals and dreams for the future, but also result in parents having to deal with real, day-to-day problems that are often the result of learning disabilities. Some of the day-to-day problems resulting from a learning disability that families have to deal with include:

- helping the child do homework (Kay, Fitzgerald, Paradee, and Mellencamp (1994);
- seemingly endless communication with school personnel (Wilson, 1995);
- teaching the child various skills (Lyytinen, et al., 1994);
- participating in school meetings (Ebenstein, 1995);
- dealing with low self-concepts by students;
- dealing with behavior problems; and
- working with the child in the area of social skills.

These types of problems and activities may cause stresses on the family, often affecting family functions and all members of the family.

Family members who have to deal with these problems first must understand the nature of the disability experienced by their child. This is a very difficult step for some families. The obvious nature of some disabilities, such as severe mental retardation and cerebral palsy, causes significant problems for parents, but at least they are able to understand the nature of the disability. They can see the effects of the disability and realize that it indeed exists and results in major problems. The fact that a learning disability is "hidden" and is not always obvious may make it more difficult for parents to understand and accept. Often parents, along with school personnel, fail to realize that a student's problems are caused by a real disability and are not the result of laziness or a poor attitude. Thinking that students with learning disabilities can do better, but only if they try harder, is an attitude that can only exacerbate problems between students and their teachers and parents.

In order for family members to provide appropriate supports for their children with a learning disability, they first must understand the nature of the disability. This is often a very difficult task since it is even difficult for some professionals to understand and agree upon the nature and causes of learning disabilities. Yet if parents do not understand that, in spite of the child having average or above average intellectual ability, difficulties in attention, achievement, and social skills will be likely, their ability to accept and support the child will be very limited. Without an adequate understanding of the disability, parents are less likely to provide appropriate supports for their child, which makes it more difficult for the school program to be successful.

All families experience reactions when their child has a disability. These reactions range from a denial that a disability exists and that the child will get over the problem, to the full realization and understanding of the disability. Emotions family members experience "range from sadness, rejection, acceptance, protection, fear, and anger, to name a few" (Bedard, 1995, p. 23). Often, family members who cannot understand the nature of a learning disability become depressed and discouraged because they do not know why their child is experiencing difficulty. Possible reactions could include the family not believing that the child has a learning disability and continuing to think that the child is simply not trying. Or the family could be depressed and discouraged because of the major hurdles that the child will have to overcome to achieve his or her dream (Cook, Tessier, and Klein, 1992).

For parents of children with learning disabilities, confusion may be the reaction. Often, parents are simply confused and frustrated to learn that their child, "who appears capable in so many ways, indeed has a disability" (Turnbull and Turnbull, 1990, p. 25). Reactions to a diagnosis of a learning disability may vary from the positive—"Oh I'm so glad that I finally know what's wrong"— to the negative—"Now what is he ever going to be able to do?" As noted, the fact that a learning disability is "hidden" often makes believing that a disability truly exists more difficult for some parents.

Reactions to finding out that a child has a disability of any kind are usually mixed. Some parents deny the disability, others shop for cures, and still others are mired in self-pity and depression. The hope for all family members is that the child's disability will be accepted and that family support systems will develop that will facilitate successful school and post-school experiences. Falik (1995) suggested that family reactions to a child having a learning disability fit into one of four patterns. In the first pattern, *"the adversarial family stance"*, family members indicate that there is nothing wrong with the child or the family except the child's learning problems. Family members want the school to address these problems and not bother them doing so. There is limited family involvement in this pattern. The second pattern suggested by Falik is *"I know something is wrong."* In this pattern, one parent, frequently the mother, identifies the child's problem and becomes very active in getting others to recognize the problem. Often this effort becomes obsessive at the expense of other family needs. This obsession on the part of one parent often antagonizes other family members to the point that they are not supportive of the child with the problem.

The third pattern identified by Falik (1995) is *"If only—, there would be nothing wrong with my child."* While families in this pattern exhibit little resistance to services and appear to be very cooperative, their attitude "is that there is little seriously wrong—other than the child's learning difficulty, which is viewed as a minor irritant that can be easily corrected" by school personnel (p. 339). Family members downplay the problem and want it to hurry up and go away. The final pattern, *"You're the expert; you know better than I,"* results in family members who turn everything over to the school to do. However, while they are compliant with the school requests and decisions, they may not carry through with suggestions made by school personnel. While none of these family patterns leads to optimal family involvement, Falik (1995) recommended that school personnel recognize the pattern and attempt to modify it to the point where family members can become more actively involved in their child's educational program.

Several factors influence the reactions of parents to learning that their child has a disability. These include the nature of the disability, severity of the disability, and the demands of the disability (Turnbull and Turnbull, 1990). For example, disabilities that require extensive medical intervention may cause the family severe financial distress, while disabilities that result in the death of a child require extensive emotional adjustment (Turnbull and Turnbull, 1990).

The severity of the disability also affects the impact on the family (Alper, Schloss, and Schloss, 1994). While it would seem that the more severe the disability the greater impact on the family, the issue of severity is more complex. As noted previously, children with more severe disabilities are identified early and result in families having to deal with the disability early. For children with learning disabilities, recognition of the disability occurs later in life, resulting in the family having to cope with a diagnosis much later than families of children with severe problems (Turnbull and Turnbull, 1990). The timing of finding out that a child has a disability may have an effect on its impact on the family.

Finally, the demands of the disability affect the reaction of family members. Children with disabilities that require extensive family time affect families more than disabilities that result in minimal family demands (Turnbull and Turnbull, 1990). Although learning disabilities might appear to result in low family demand, they may cause family members, especially the mother or father, to spend a great deal of time helping the student with school work. For example, some parents of students with learning disabilities spend hours each evening working on homework to help the student keep up with classroom assignments and preparation for tests. Therefore, while there may be limited demand related to physical needs of the child, there may be significant demands related to homework, academic remediation, self-esteem, and other areas.

Learning disabilities do not generally result in severe financial drain or a major emotional reaction; however, they may cause a great deal of distress among family members over the child's seemingly unexplainable academic decline and inadequate social relationships. Again, the family with a child with a learning disability may just be relieved to know that there is an explanation of the problems the child has been experiencing (Turnbull and Turnbull, 1990). Regardless of reaction, school personnel must be aware of how family members are reacting and how best to develop and implement intervention strategies, taking into consideration these reactions.

▶ FAMILY AND SCHOOL COLLABORATION

As noted earlier, Congress recognized the importance of parental involvement in the education of students with disabilities when it mandated such involvement in Public Law 94-142. "Congress viewed parents as agents for accountability, as persons who should or could ensure that professionals provide an appropriate education." (Turnbull and Turnbull, 1990, p. 14) School personnel must involve parents of students in the entire special education process, beginning with referral and culminating with program development and review. Specific legal requirements for such involvement will be discussed later.

Need for Family and School Collaboration

Schools and parents are partners in the education of children with learning disabilities. As such, there needs to be a great deal of collaboration between school personnel and parents. Epstein (1988) noted five ways that parents are typically involved in school activities. These include (1) basic obligation to provide for the child's health and safety; (2) communication between school and parents about the child's educational program; (3) parent volunteerism and attendance at school activities; (4) parents' involvement in homework and other learning activities; and (5) parents' involvement with school governance. While some parents actively participate in all of these forms of collaboration, others are involved extensively in one or two areas. And there are some parents whose involvement in all areas is extremely limited.

There are many reasons why schools and parents should collaborate on educational issues, especially when children have learning disabilities. Such collaboration can result in benefits to the child, to parents, and to teachers (Shea and Bauer, 1991). Table 11.3 summarizes these benefits. As can be seen from the table, the advantages that result from parent-school collaboration are so extensive that school personnel should work diligently at securing more collaboration.

TABLE 11.3

Benefits of Family and School Collaboration

Advantages for Child

- positive affect on child's academic achievement and enhances probability of academic success
- increases number of individuals to foster child's development
- increases time available for learning and instruction
- communicates to children that school is viewed as important by parents
- school personnel have access to additional knowledge about the child
- parents and teachers' expectations become more common

Advantages for Parents

- parents fulfill their social and ethical obligations
- improves the self-worth of parents
- enhances parents' instructional abilities
- the family environment is enhanced as an educational site

Advantages for School Personnel

- provides new information about the child and family
- support from parents for school goals
- allows teachers to devote additional time to student

Shea and Bauer (1991). *Parents and teachers of children with exceptionalities: A handbook for collaboration, 2nd Ed. p. 6. Copyright © 1991 by Allyn and Bacon. Reprinted/adapted by permission.*

Regardless of the numerous advantages of collaboration, there are always barriers to limit such actions. Shea and Bauer (1991) listed six traits that can affect parent-teacher interactions. These include:

1. *Expertise* Both parents and teachers need to be knowledgeable about children, and in cases where children have disabilities, they must be knowledgeable about the disability. Unshared expertise on the part of school personnel or parents can create barriers to collaboration. To circumvent this barrier, school personnel and parents must share their knowledge and expertise with each other.

2. *Control of Emotions* Emotions can affect the way teachers interact with children as well as the way parents interact with their children and the schools. Dealing with children with learning disabilities can be very frustrating. Lack of emotional control from teachers or parents can create barriers to collaboration. Both parties must work to gain control of their emotions in order to remove this barrier to effective collaboration.

3. *Compassion* Both parents and teachers must be sensitive to the feelings of the other in order to ensure collaboration. Often, teachers think that they are the ones who have to carry the burden of working with these children every day and they forget the important role played by the parents. Likewise, some parents think that they are being asked to help the child every night with work that should have been taught during the day. They may think that they are the only ones really interested in helping the child. Without mutual respect and compassion for the problems and frustrations experienced by all parties, effective collaboration will be difficult to attain.

4. *Patience and Acceptance* Teachers must not only be patient with students with learning disabilities, but also with their parents and other teachers. Likewise, parents have to be patient with the way teachers are interacting with their child. Limited patience will only add to the frustration and negatively impact collaboration.

5. *Honesty* Both parents and teachers must be honest with each other to ensure effective communication and collaboration. An atmosphere of trust can greatly facilitate collaboration between the school and parents. Without a trusting atmosphere, parents and school personnel will not be able to work together effectively for the benefit of a particular child.

6. *Advocacy* Teachers must be advocates for children with learning disabilities. They may have to support the child, at times, against unfair practices at the school. Similarly, parents must be strong advocates for their child. As equal partners they must feel comfortable standing up for the rights of their child to a free appropriate public education.

These barriers can result in significant problems between schools and parents of children with learning disabilities. While the problems are common, they can be overcome. Effective collaboration is a two-way street that requires both school personnel and parents to work toward the benefit of the child.

Level of Collaboration

Barriers to collaboration often influence the level of involvement of parents with schools. Although collaboration between schools and parents is essential in providing appropriate educational programs for students with learning disabilities, the level of collaboration is not always optimal. There are many different levels of school-parent collaboration. Figure 11.1 depicts a continuum of collaboration, with the least intensive and least collaboration being at the written and telephone communication stage and the most intensive and most collaborative being at the activities stage. While collaboration at any level is good, school personnel should attempt to work with parents at the more intensive end of the continuum. There is no comparison between what can be accomplished in face-to-face meetings and in phone calls and written notes.

Legal Requirements for Collaboration

Collaboration between schools and parents is the right thing to do in order to maximize the possibilities of providing appropriate educational programs to students with learning disabilities. In addition to collaboration being the right thing to do professionally, it is also legally required. No longer can schools involve parents at their discretion; there is now a legal mandate for such

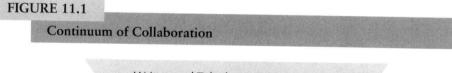

FIGURE 11.1

Continuum of Collaboration

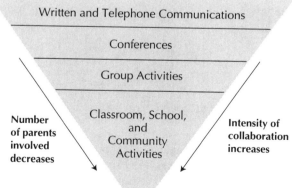

Written and Telephone Communications

Conferences

Group Activities

Classroom, School, and Community Activities

Number of parents involved decreases

Intensity of collaboration increases

Source: Shea and Bauer (1991) Parents and teachers of children with exceptionalities: A handbook for collaboration, 2nd Ed., p. 76. Used with permission. Copyright © 1991 by Allyn and Bacon. Reprinted/adapted by permission.

involvement. School personnel should understand that parents have certain legal and ethical rights regarding their involvement in the educational process for their children. These include (Smith, Polloway, Patton, and Dowdy, 1995):

- the right to be informed regarding educational changes concerning their child,
- the right to be asked for information when evaluating the child's need and right to a special education program,
- the right to be involved in educational decision making about their child,
- the right to be kept informed about the educational progress of their child,
- the right to be asked for their legitimate opinion regarding their child's educational needs,
- the right to be involved in determining appropriate future directions for their child's educational program,
- the assumption that parents desire to be involved in their child's educational program,
- the assumption that parents care about their child's educational program, and
- the assumption that parents will make every attempt to support their child and the school's efforts to provide an appropriate education for their child (p. 455).

School personnel must work diligently to secure the involvement of parents of students with learning disabilities in their educational programs. As previously noted, Public Law 94-142 required schools to involve parents of students with disabilities in the identification, programming, and review of special education programs. The law required schools to seek parental involvement and to take steps to secure such involvement. The Individuals with Disabilities Education Act (IDEA), the 1990 reauthorization of the original Act, continues to require such input. Section 504 of the Rehabilitation Act, described in the previous chapter, also requires the involvement of parents in the education of children protected under that law. While the laws differ in some areas, they generally require schools to inform parents of various actions they are taking and to get their permission for others. Specific due process rights for parents under IDEA and Section 504 are described in Chapter 10. In general, parent permission must be gained before a child is initially evaluated and placed in special education programs. Following these initial actions, schools are required to inform parents of actions they are taking with the child. Schools should always go beyond the minimal requirements regarding notice and permission. Although not always required, it is a good idea to get parental permission before making significant changes in the child's program or before completing extensive evaluations.

Just because a student's parents are unavailable does not mean that the school can take any action it wants regarding a child with a learning disability. When the student's parents are unknown, unavailable, or the student is a ward of the state, a surrogate parent must be appointed for the child. The purpose of the surrogate, or stand-in parent, is to look after the rights of the child just as the child's real parents would do if they were available. If the child's actual parents are known but simply decline to participate in various discussions, then the school does not have to have a surrogate parent appointed before certain actions are taken. They still need to document their attempts to secure parent participation in the child's educational program.

▶ COMMUNICATION BETWEEN SCHOOLS AND PARENTS

A first priority in collaboration between school and family is effective communication among school personnel, parents, and other family members (Wilson, 1995). Without effective communication, successful collaboration will be difficult, if not impossible, to achieve. Effective communication is critical in building positive relationships between families and school personnel (Creekmore, 1988; Turnbull and Turnbull, 1990; Wilson, 1995). As noted by Turnbull and Turnbull (1990), "When family and professionals respect, trust, and communicate openly with one another, a partnership is formed" (p. 144). This partnership cannot be formed without effective communication, and its establishment is essential in providing appropriate educational programs for students with learning disabilities.

Many parents complain that there is simply too little communication between themselves and the school. Even parents who attend conferences about their child often say "that they walk away from meetings not understanding any more about their child's problems than they did before they went into the meeting" (Wilson, 1995, p. 31). Therefore, mere presence at meetings does not mean that effective communication occurs. Too often parents feel that formal conferences are controlled by school personnel and deal too much on general rather than specific issues (Stephenson, 1992). They want better communication for a number of reasons, such as being better able to assist their children with homework assignments (Kay, Fitzgerald, Paradee, and Mellencamp, 1994).

Effective communication requires both parties, in this case parents and school personnel, to understand what has been communicated. It is a two-way street requiring effective communication skills for both parents and school personnel (Bedard, 1995). Wilson (1995) listed several principles of communication that must be addressed when professionals and parents interact about a child with a learning disability. These include (1) accepting parents as equal partners, (2) listening effectively, (3) asking appropriate questions, (4) encouraging parents regarding their child, (5) keeping the conversation focused, and (6) developing a working relationship with parents.

Many parents feel that school personnel are involving them only because they are required to by law. Parents need to feel that they are accepted by school personnel as equal partners in the education of their children with learning disabilities. Introducing parents to other school personnel in a manner that *sets the tone for acceptance* and using understandable language help in making parents feel comfortable (Wilson, 1995).

Being a good listener is also important for effective communication. School personnel need to ensure that parents have time to say what they are interested in talking about. Being an active listener by restating what the parent has said helps clarify the parents' input. School personnel should also ask the right kind of questions of parents to solicit their input. Open questions, beginning with *how, what,* and *tell me about* can help give parents the opportunity to provide information that will be useful for school personnel (Wilson, 1995).

School personnel often need to provide encouragement to family members who are used to hearing only the bad things about their child. Words of encouragement go a long way in increasing parental trust and future involvement. Often, when parents are talking about their children, they tend to get off the subject and discuss issues unrelated to their child's educational program. School personnel should take the opportunity at this point to redirect the discussion to the child and the purpose of the meeting. Finally, all of these strategies will help build a trusting, positive relationship between parents and school personnel. Without such a collaborative effort, programs for children with learning disabilities will not be as effective as they could be (Wilson, 1995).

Regardless of efforts for effective communication between schools and parents, there are barriers that often limit the effectiveness. These include professional jargon, parents feeling like they are being talked down to, and confrontational situations. Terms such as perceptual disability, learning style, learning modality, and whole language may appear to be simple terms for school personnel but be very difficult to understand by some parents. The term learning disability has even been shown to mean different things to parents and school personnel (Stephenson, 1992). Often parents will not feel comfortable asking school personnel what certain words mean. Therefore, it is the responsibility of school personnel to use words and phrases that are understandable for parents (Alper, Schloss, and Schloss, 1994). The use of various acronyms, a popular practice among special educators, should also be limited to avoid misunderstanding by parents. When explaining what certain words and phrases mean, school personnel must be careful not to talk down to parents. Explanations must be given in a way that does not reinforce the parents' view that they are not as knowledgeable as school professionals.

There are many different ways that schools and parents can communicate. These include formal conferences, informal meetings, written notices, telephone conversations, and casual contact. Table 11.4 describes these types of communication modes. Guidelines for effective communication should be addressed in all forms of communication. For example, terms that might not be understood by parents should not be included in written communication unless there is an explanation. Likewise, the use of acronyms that could be meaningless to parents should not be used.

A critical concern when communicating with parents is the cultural and language differences that may exist in some families. School personnel must take these into consideration when dealing with family members from diverse

TABLE 11.4

Different Modes of Communication Between Schools and Parent

Mode	Strengths	Weaknesses
Phone Call	• Can be made often • Contact is immediate	• Person may not be available • Does not have advantage of face-to-face communication • Requires written summary notes for a record
Conferences	• Provides face-to-face communication • Written summary can be made at the time • Time is available for extensive interactions • Misunderstandings can be cleared up easily	• Requires time and scheduling for both parties • Is often difficult to set up • Parents may feel intimidated or out of place
Written Notices	• Record of notice is immediate • Does not require scheduling	• Confusion regarding words or wording may result and may not be cleared up • Notices may not be received • Limited opportunity for immediate response
Casual Contact	• May be less intimidating for family • Does not require scheduling	• Time for interaction may be limited • No written record unless recorded later • Misunderstandings may not be cleared up

cultures to ensure that they do not offend a family member unknowingly. Word choice, as well as other factors related to communication, should be considered. Table 11.5 provides a list for cultural considerations when communicating with families. Regardless of the mode of communication used with families, cultural considerations should always be taken into account.

School personnel must remember that there are simply different values, expectations, and levels of involvement among different cultural groups. Classrooms of the 1990s and beyond include children from a wide variety of cultures. Wilson (1995) listed the following points related to communicating with families from culturally diverse backgrounds:

• Ask parents questions that encourage them to respond rather than waiting for them to ask questions or spontaneously speak their minds.

TABLE 11.5

Suggestions for Cultural Considerations

Cultural Considerations	Examples	May Determine
Meaning of the disability	Disability within a family may be viewed as shameful and disgraceful, or as a positive contribution to the family	The level of acceptance of the disability and the need for services
Attitudes about professionals	Professionals may be viewed as persons of authority or as equals	The level of family members' participation may be only minimal in the partnership out of respect and fear
Attitudes about children	Children may be highly valued	The willingness of the family to make many sacrifices on behalf of the child
Attitudes about seeking and receiving help	Problems within the family may be viewed as being strictly a family affair or may be easily shared with others	The level of denial may work against acknowledging and talking about the problem
Family roles	Roles may be sex specific and traditional or flexible. Age and sex hierarchies of authority may exist	Family preferences may exist for which family member takes the leadership role in the family-professional partnership
Family interactions	Boundaries between family subsystems may be strong and inflexible or relaxed and fluid	The level of problem sharing/solving in families. Family members may keep to themselves and deal with problems in isolation or problem solve as a unit
Time orientation	Family may be present or future oriented	Family's willingness to consider future goals and future planning
Role of the extended family	Extended family members may be close or far, physically and emotionally	Who is involved in the family-professional partnership
Support networks	Family may rely solely on nuclear family members, on extended family members, or on nonrelated persons. Importance of godparents	Who can be called upon in time of need

(continued)

TABLE 11.5

continued

Cultural Considerations	Examples	May Determine
Attitude toward achievement	Family may have a relaxed attitude or high expectations for achievement	The goals and expectations of the family for the family member with the disability
Religion	Religion and the religious community may be a strong or neutral factor in some aspects of family life	Family's values, beliefs, and traditions as sources of comfort
Language	Family may be non-English speaking, bilingual, or English speaking	The need for translators (Smith and Ryan, 1987)
Number of generations removed from country of origin	The family may have just emigrated or be several generations removed from the country of origin	The strength and importance of the cultural ties
Reasons for leaving country of origin	Family may be emigrants from countries at war	Family's readiness for involvement with external world (Valero-Figueira, 1988)

Source: *Families, Professionals, and Exceptionality: A Special Partnership* by Turnbull/Turnbull, © 1990. Reprinted by permission of Prentice-Hall, Inc., Upper Saddle River, NJ.

- Explain to parents the problems associated with test results and specific recommendations.
- Inform parents that there may be several solutions to a situation.
- Encourage parents to bring along family or community members who have experience interacting with schools.
- Involve parents in informal school activities (p. 33).

These suggestions will assist professionals in communicating effectively with parents from culturally diverse backgrounds. Being patient and providing ample time for family members to express their ideas and concerns are important elements in effective communication (Wilson, 1995).

When communicating with parents, school personnel should take steps to ensure that they are doing all they can to encourage increased parent involvement. Schools should:

- send notices to parents in the family's native language;
- send notices by registered mail to make sure that the information is received;
- hold conferences at times and places that are convenient to the parent;
- encourage parents to bring anyone with them to facilitate the interaction;

- provide child care if the parent needs someone to supervise their children; and

- provide transportation if necessary to get the parent to the meeting.

Disagreements Between Schools and Parents

Regardless of the efforts to communicate and collaborate with parents, schools often find themselves at odds with the wishes of parents regarding their child with a learning disability. In situations where disagreements exist, either the school or parent can request a due process hearing. This is a formal hearing where an impartial hearing officer listens to both sides of the dispute and makes a ruling based on the legal issues involved. Although not mandated by law in most states, schools should attempt to mediate disagreements with parents before due process hearings result (Dobbs, Primm, and Primm, 1991).

Due process hearings are a last resort to resolve differences between schools and parents before formal litigation. Unfortunately, hearings often exacerbate an already confrontational situation. This makes it even more mandatory that schools and parents resolve their differences before hearings begin. There are several steps that schools can take to avoid hearings. These include (Podemski, et al., 1995; Smith and Podemski, 1981):

1. *Focus on the child* Schools should always attempt to provide an appropriate educational program for the child. If there is a doubt as to the requirement of a particular service, schools should consider providing the service.

2. *Involve parents* While schools follow specific guidelines to get parents involved, they should go beyond minimal actions to secure involvement. Parents who feel like they are being treated as an equal partner are more likely to work out differences with the school than parents who feel they are being circumvented by school personnel.

3. *Utilize nondiscrimination assessment* Schools must take all steps possible to avoid discriminatory assessment. Assessment that discriminates can only result in inappropriate services.

4. *Document everything* School personnel should keep written records of meetings and conversations with parents about their child. Keeping records of such encounters will add credibility to the account of school personnel regarding past events.

5. *Request mediation* Although not required in some states, schools should be willing to negotiate with parents in trying to resolve disputes before they get to a formal hearing. Regardless of the outcome of a hearing, school personnel and parents must work together to provide appropriate educational programs. This may be more difficult after a due process hearing.

While these actions may not always result in preventing due process hearings, they will go a long way in resolving issues. Due process hearings frequently result in negative feelings between parents and school personnel. Although the ruling favors one side over the other, both parties must work together for the benefit of the child. Animosities that have built up and been reinforced during the hearing process can only add to an already bad situation with the result that the student may continue to suffer negative consequences.

▶ SPECIFIC COLLABORATION ACTIVITIES

There are many different ways parents and other family members can become involved with the education of a child with a learning disability. This includes involvement in planning programs, implementing programs, and evaluating programs. The benefits that result from close parent-school partnerships are numerous. Turnbull and Turnbull (1990) described the following opportunities for families and professionals:

Benefits for the family:

- receiving information about parental rights and responsibilities
- receiving information about the disability
- learning about program activities for the family member with a disability and about ways other family members can be involved
- learning how to bring positive program activities into the home
- learning how to teach new skills to the family member with a disability
- receiving information on other important resources for the family member with a disability

There are many different ways that parents can become involved in the education of their children, including providing instruction.

Benefits for school personnel

- learning more about the strengths and needs of the family as a system
- learning more about the strengths and needs of the family member with a disability
- planning programming activities that may also be carried out at home
- meeting the legislative mandate requiring parental involvement in the family-professional partnership in a way that will provide all parties with the opportunity to work with one another (p. 144-145).

One area in which parents need to become more involved is the IEP process. This is the method that determines what is an appropriate educational program for a particular student. Too often parents sit at the table but do not participate in the meeting as legitimate partners in the process. They may be intimidated by professional educators who use terminology they are not used to, or they may simply not want to speak up with so many *smart* teachers sitting there. Regardless of the reason, school personnel should make every attempt to increase the involvement of parents at IEP meetings. Ebenstein (1995) provided some suggestions to parents on how to get more involved in the IEP process for their children. Some of these suggestions would be effective for professionals to use. They include: (1) review the child's eligibility classification, (2) be sure that evaluation reports are up to date and accurate, (3) work things out with parents before the annual review conference, and (4) treat the annual review meeting as a very important opportunity to review the child's progress with the parents.

Even though significant efforts are made to increase the involvement of parents in the IEP process, school personnel must keep in mind that some parents are simply not interested in getting involved. In these situations, schools should make every effort to keep the parents informed about the status of their child and follow all due process procedures required. A lack of interest on the part of parents does not relieve the school personnel from its responsibilities to follow appropriate procedures.

While some parents choose not to take an active role in their child's education, many parents are eager to get more involved with educational programs. Homework is one area where parental involvement can be extremely beneficial to the student and teacher (Jenson, Sheridan, Olympia, and Andrews, 1994). It is important to note that a typical homework load may prove overwhelming to students with learning disabilities (Turnbull and Turnbull, 1990). Therefore, modifications in homework may need to be a consideration for teachers.

Parents can be very helpful with their children by assisting and supporting them while they perform homework assignments. Specifically, parents can serve in a supportive role to their children doing homework, create a home environment conducive for homework, and encourage and reinforce homework effort (Patton, 1994). Jenson et al. (1994) noted that "in programs to enhance the effectiveness of homework, teachers and parents can share the tasks of (1) identifying the nature of homework problems, (2) developing an effective homework program to be used across home and school settings, (3) systematically monitoring the effects of the intervention on academic and nonacademic skills, (4) determining the need for modifications of the program, and (5) evaluating overall outcome in relation to stated academic objectives" (p. 546).

In order to be the most helpful, parents need to understand the classroom teacher's expectations of homework and have a method of communicating with teachers about homework assignments (Kay, Fitzgerald, Paradee, and Mellencamp, 1994). This requires close collaboration and effective communication on the part of teachers and parents. Meeting periodically to review homework expectations may be necessary to ensure adequate communication between parents and teachers. Table 11.6 provides suggestions for supporting parents with homework for students with learning disabilities.

Parents can also play an important role in carrying out certain instructional strategies (Lyytinen, Rasku-Puttonen, Poikkeus, Laakso, and Ahonen, 1994). Enlisting the support of parents in home instruction can greatly assist teachers by helping them teach new skills or reinforce skills learned at school. An example of an area where parents can become involved is with a whole language curriculum. Including children in creating shopping lists, playing word games such as Hangman, doing crossword puzzles, and finding articles in newspapers are ways that parents can support a whole language approach used in the school (Wener and O'Shea, 1992).

The involvement of parents of children and youth with learning disabilities with school personnel is critical to the success of these children. Without such involvement, professionals will have a much more difficult task of developing and implementing appropriate intervention programs. As previously noted, there are some barriers that can impede the development and implementation of such partnerships. Bedard (1995) suggests the following strategies to facilitate the school-parent partnership:

TABLE 11.6

Suggestions for Supporting Parents with Homework

- Provide parents up-to-date information about school curriculum
- Provide parents with information regarding unique teaching methods that are used
- Provide detailed teacher expectations of the child to parents
- Provide detailed teacher expectations of the role of parents
- Individualize homework assignments with respect to child and family needs
- Make homework experiential and practical
- Develop and implement an effective two-way communication system, including homework notebooks and face-to-face interactions

---

Source: Kay, Fitzgerald, Paradee, and Mellencamp (1994). Making homework work at home: The parent's perspective. *Journal of Learning Disabilities, 27,* 550–561.

1. Recognize emotions which families experience when raising a child with a disability and be responsive to those emotions;

2. Identify coping strategies which a parent employs and capitalize upon these strategies;

3. State the child's strengths and use the strengths to develop areas of need;

4. Listen to how the child interacts at home and in the community as a way of gaining a better understanding of the whole child and recognizing the family's dreams for their child;

5. Identify informal support systems which can enable and empower the family;

6. Explain to families their rights and responsibilities under the law thus enabling and empowering families;

7. Develop goals with the family and fully include them in the educational planning process; and

8. Acknowledge both parental and professional contributions in the child's progress (p. 25).

SUMMARY

This chapter has focused on families of children with learning disabilities. The nature of families, reactions of families to the presence of a child with a learning disability, and ways school personnel can enhance parental involvement in school programs were included. The following points summarize the major areas included in the chapter:

- Parents of students with learning disabilities are in a unique position to become involved in the educational program for their child.
- Parents are often the first persons to notice that a child is having developmental problems.
- Services for students with learning disabilities have changed dramatically over the past fifteen years.
- Family members of students with learning disabilities have not always been involved with the child's educational program.
- Parents often are confused about learning disabilities.
- Some parents choose not to get involved in their child's educational program.
- Public Law 94-142 required schools to involve parents of students with learning disabilities in decisions.
- Parents formed advocacy groups, such as the Association for Children and Adults with Learning Disabilities, and strengthened their influence over school programs.
- Families have changed a great deal in our society since the 1950s.

- There is not a singular model of a family in our society today.
- Families are very diverse.
- Having a child with a learning disability results in major adjustments for the entire family.
- Parents react in many different ways to the realization that their child has a learning disability.
- Parents must first understand what a learning disability is before they can provide appropriate supports.
- The severity of a learning disability impacts parental reactions.
- Families and schools must work together for optimal educational programming for children with learning disabilities.
- There are many barriers that must be overcome to facilitate parent and school collaboration.
- The Individuals with Disabilities Education Act (IDEA) and Section 504 of the Rehabilitation Act both require parental involvement with educational decisions and programs.
- Parents have legal as well as ethical rights.
- A key factor in parent and school collaboration is the level of communication that occurs.
- Many parents complain that there is too little communication with school personnel.
- When communicating with parents, school personnel must be aware of the cultural background of the family.
- Disagreements between schools and parents are common when dealing with children with learning disabilities.
- Disagreements should be mediated when at all possible.
- Schools and parents can always request an impartial, due process hearing if they cannot resolve differences.
- Parents can become involved in many different activities related to school work, including homework, IEP committee participation, and instruction.

Chapter 12

CONCOMITANT EXCEPTIONALITIES[1]

The objectives for this chapter are as follows:

- To understand that some individuals who have other disabilities may also experience learning disabilities.

- To understand that individuals with learning disabilities will in some instances also be identified as having another exceptionality.

- To use the term *dual diagnosis* cautiously in describing individuals with varied problems.

- To conceptualize individuals' complex learning needs in a functional fashion.

- To identify areas of potential overlap and special needs of students with learning disabilities and emotional and behavioral disorders, attention deficit disorder, and communication disorders.

- To understand conceptual aspects and implications of the relationships between learning disabilities and other respective disabilities.

- To appreciate the fact that many students with learning disabilities may also have special gifts and talents.

[1] The authors acknowledge the assistance of Kevin Seeley in researching several sections of this chapter.

Twice Exceptional

From an early age, Dayle Upham remembers feeling like two persons. The person on the inside was quick and competent and would always know the right answers in school. The person on the outside kept getting in the way.

It wasn't until Dayle reached her forties that she discovered why she may have felt that way. Dayle is "twice exceptional"; she is both gifted and learning disabled. That students like Dayle exist at all may come as a surprise to some educators.

"If you ask a lot of educators, they will say that's kind of like an oxymoron," says Upham. "You can't be gifted and learning disabled at the same time."

Half the students [in the sample] were held back one or more grades in school. Most were not identified as learning-disabled until middle school, high school, or college. Yet, many had been tested for a disability at some earlier point in their schooling.

In Upham's case, educators did not figure out she was dyslexic until she reached seventh grade. She knew something was wrong in first grade. But she was able to get along memorizing entire stories that her mother read to her, using the pictures on each page as cues.

"I also learned very quickly to become much more observant than other kids, picking up body language signals and changes in tone of voice," she says. "I always knew when teachers had had enough."

Another student, whom reseachers gave the pseudonym "Peggy," recalls elementary school teachers who yelled at her to "shape up" and who kept her after school when she could not memorize her multiplication tables.

And "Joe," another subject, told the researchers how other students threw rocks at him and called him a "retard" during recess.

"It would've been sad for any group of youngsters but, because these young people were so bright, they caught every nuance," Reis says. "They recognized whenever someone was making fun of them."

Source: Viadero, D. Twice exceptional: Gifted students with learning disabilities get lost in schools. Reprinted with permission from *Education Week,* Vol. 14, No. 36, May 31, 1995.

The nature of learning disabilities as discussed in the previous chapters outlines the conceptual basis for this condition. The difficulties that are experienced by individuals with learning disabilities are clearly significant and thus they require specialized instruction and, frequently, curricular adaptations.

For an important subset of students who may experience learning disabilities, the nature of their needs may be further complicated by the presence of another exceptionality. These individuals may experience other disabilities that also may impair learning. These additional conditions are important to consider in order to appreciate the full profile of individuals who may present as needing special education. Further, the consideration of exceptional learning needs is not simply a reference to learning disabilities interacting with other concomitant difficulties. Rather, it is equally important to consider that some students who are learning disabled may also be appropriately identified as gifted and talented and consequently also require specialized intervention strategies.

▶ DUAL DIAGNOSIS

For students who experience learning disabilities along with another disability, it has been said that this interaction of multiple factors can have an exponential effect on the learning challenges that are faced. However, it is of central importance that the reality of dual diagnosis (e.g., LD/ED) not become the basis for typecasting an individual in such a unique way that further stigma and potential isolation from inclusive settings are the result.

Dual diagnosis serves a useful purpose only when it alerts professionals to the potential difficulties related to the possible interaction of two (or more) disabilities. This attention should become the basis for moving beyond a focus on a root or primary disability to an emphasis on a comprehensive view of assessment, instructional interventions, and integrated service delivery systems (Rock, Fessler, and Church, in press).

On the other hand, the consideration of dual or multiple diagnoses becomes counterproductive when the outcome is not clearly to the advantage of the child, adolescent, or adult who is affected. Consideration also should be given in particular to the fact that the reality of an accurate dual diagnosis may be the consequence of conceptual overlaps across disabilities rather than unique patterns of problems. For example, it has been common to contend that learning disabilities, emotional disturbance, and mild mental retardation may reflect such an overlap (Hallahan and Kauffman, 1976, 1977). Ultimately it is the functionality of the individual rather than the validity of the labels that will predict success.

This concept is perhaps best understood within the context of a multidimensional model. For example, while academic underachievement, uneven patterns of ability, and processing deficits are commonly included within a diagnostic profile of individuals with learning disabilities, other conditions that may be present ultimately may dictate one's adult adjustment and quality of life (e.g., medical and health concerns, emotional and behavioral factors). In these instances, the consideration of other conditions provides a further view of the individual's potential needs. Hence we are then in the position of determining the levels of supports that a person requires in order to achieve success in educational, vocational, and social environments. It is within this broad context that the interactions between LD and other conditions are reviewed in this chapter.

▶ EMOTIONAL AND BEHAVIORAL DISORDERS

The most commonly discussed potential interaction of two disabilities is that between learning disabilities and emotional and behavioral disorders (EBD). To a great extent, the relationship is an expected one. For example, difficulties in one domain in school are often accompanied by difficulties in the other. It is tempting even to hypothesize directionality for this relationship; there are numerous instances when a thesis that learning problems resulted in subsequent emotional or behavioral problems could be posited or instances where a child's problems in the behavioral area subsequently interfere with learning could be supported. For example, Polloway, Patton, Epstein, Acquah, Decker, and Carse (1992) reported that 9.5 percent of the students in their sample not only experienced emotional and behavioral problems but were eligible for services under the area of behavioral disorders. Similarly, Epstein, Kinder, and Bursuck (1989) reported a high percentage of students with behavioral disorders experienced serious learning (i.e., academic) problems while Epstein, Patton, Polloway, and Foley (1992) reported that 31.5 percent of students with behavior disorders experienced significant academic problems.

In their review of concomitance, Rock et al. (in press) summarized the results of numerous studies on this question. They concluded that reasonable estimates for the percentage of individuals with learning disabilities who also experience significant emotional, behavioral, and social problems range from 24 percent to 52 percent. From the reverse perspective, the percentage of students with EBD who also experience significant learning problems ranges from 38 percent to 75 percent. While these studies do not confirm dual diagnosis in the high percentage of cases, they do point to the relationship of the problems associated with these two exceptionalities. Regardless of the research study considered, therefore, it is clear that comorbidity for these two respective disabilities is an issue of some applied importance rather than simply the subject of a series of basic research questions.

Conceptual Issues

The two most common definitions of emotional/behavioral disorders are the modification of the Bower definition of "serious emotional disturbance" cited in federal statutes and the recent "emotional and behavioral disorder" definition developed by a coalition of professionals within these areas (Kauffman,

1993). Both of these definitions acknowledge adverse effects of the condition on academic performance and thus certainly leave open consideration of concomitance with learning disabilities. On the other hand, while the learning disability definitions (see Chapter 2) commonly do not accept consideration of emotional and behavioral disorder as a primary cause of the learning disability, nevertheless they do not preclude the association of an emotional and behavioral disorder as contributing further compounding variables.

The relationship between LD/EBD is clearly far more complex than the interactions between two definitions can ever convey. Rock et al. (in press) presented a useful model for conceptualizing the interaction of characteristics of individuals who experience these two disabilities. Their model includes a set of interrelated critical functioning domains and areas of potential impairment (see Figure 12.1). The double arrows are intended to convey the multi-directional effects of these areas on the development of the individual. The model focuses on consideration of six domains including:

- cognitive processing (e.g., problem-solving, abstract reasoning)
- executive functioning (e.g., metacognition, self-regulation)
- language functioning (e.g., in form, content and use)

FIGURE 12.1

A Conceptual Model of LD/EBD

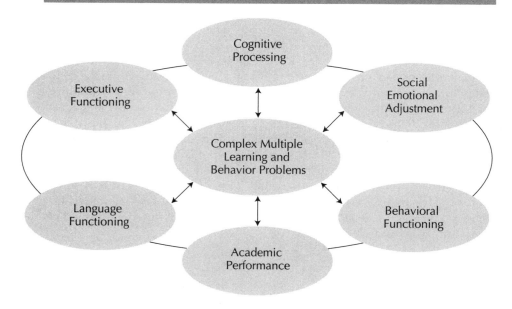

Source: Rock, E.E., Fessler, M.A., and Church, R.P. (in press). The concomitance of learning disabilities and emotional/behavioral disorders: A conceptual model. *Journal of Learning Disabilities*. In press.

- behavioral functioning (e.g., externalizing behaviors including disruptive, aggressive actions)
- social-emotional functioning (e.g., internalizing behaviors such as mood, anxiety, and social interaction)
- academic achievement (e.g., reading, math)

In an identification sense, the model in Figure 12.1 is operationalized by Rock et al. (in press) as follows:

> The child with concomitant LD/EBD is one who manifests problems which (a) occur in two or more of the critical functioning domains, including academic and either social/emotional adjustment or behavioral functioning; (b) are each of a severity as to be considered clinically significant by themselves; (c) interact to substantially impair functioning in school and/or in the community; and (d) may be compounded by difficulties in additional areas which may or may not be clinically significant (p. 13).

While a full discussion of these elements is beyond the scope of the chapter, the model provides an excellent conceptualization of variables that should be considered in determining the educational and life needs of individuals who experience learning disabilities and emotional and behavioral disorders.

Characteristics

A number of research studies have focused on the possible overlap in programs for EBD and LD. For example, Price, Johnson, and Evelo (1994) summarized research reports in learning disabilities confirming "feelings of inadequacy, loneliness, isolation, frustration, anger, hostility, shyness, excessive dependency, and low self-esteem" (p. 82). At the same time, a listing of common academic difficulties experienced by students with learning disabilities (e.g., reading recognition, reading comprehension, math computation) would likewise fit the pattern of many children identified as EBD who exhibit significant academic achievement problems (Kauffman, 1993).

The relationship between LD and EBD can also be conceptualized as one which is a function of lack of school success rather than a correlation between the two areas of exceptionality in a formal sense. For example, Vaughn and Haagen (1994) compared students with learning disabilities to two groups of non-learning disabled students, those who were low achievers and those who were average or high achievers. While students with learning disabilities differed from the latter group on two measures of social competence (i.e., social skills, behavior problems), they did not differ from the former in any of the other five measures used (also peer acceptance, self-concept, and friendships).

On the other hand, Ziegler (1981) argued for the presence of emotional and behavioral disorders as a function of reactive adaptations by the child with a learning disability to the mismatch between environmental demands and the capacities and needs of the child. He posited a three-stage response: an initial reaction of quiet withdrawal or negative motoric response due to frustration; a second phase of disengagement with learning tasks; and a third phase in adolescents of defensiveness characterized by an "I don't care" attitude, apathy, and denial of the importance of schoolwork. While this model implies directionality that often will remain nonverifiable, it highlights the potentially interactive nature of characteristics associated with the two disabilities.

A variety of emotional and behavioral patterns may be observed in students who are learning-disabled. These may include problems associated with both acting-out, disruptive behaviors as well as those associated with withdrawal and anxiety (see Epstein, Bursuck, and Cullinan, 1985; Epstein, Cullinan, and Lloyd, 1986).

One area of potential overlap and particular importance is depression. As noted by Wright-Strawderman and Watson (1992), the relationship between learning disabilities and depressive disorders has been assumed for some time. While these researchers reported depression among non-disabled children as a prevalence of under 10 percent, their review of research indicated a range of 26 percent to 40 percent for students with learning disabilities. Similar elevated percentages were reported by Huntington and Bender (1993).

As Wright-Strawderman and Watson (1992) noted, those high rates are of particular significance due to the association of depression and suicide, with the former implicated as cause in 60 percent of suicides. Elevated suicide rates thus have also not surprisingly been reported for students with learning disabilities (Huntington and Bender, 1993). However, while these findings would clearly be of great concern if confirmed, it is important to consider more recent and cautionary research with alternative methodology which calls into question the strength of the learning disabilities/ depression association. Maag and Reid (1994) reported that in their study of over two hundred teenagers that the rate of depression for students both with and without learning disabilities was found to be approximately 10 percent. They caution citing "severe" characteristics for students with learning disabilities when research may not clearly support such a conclusion.

Implications

The implications for curriculum and instruction are significant. For example, consider the topic of independent work completion. Epstein, Polloway, Foley, and Patton (1993), focusing on the area of homework, noted that the literature suggests that students with behavior disorders often evidence academic deficits and may display deficiencies in organizational (e.g., identifying main ideas and details, test-taking skills) and time management skills (e.g., scheduling, prioritizing tasks). Consequently, these students typically need to increase time on task and develop academic survival skills. At the same time, they noted that students with learning disabilities may have difficulty with tasks demanding high levels of voluntary attention, may exhibit underselective attention, may require assistance in self-monitoring behavior, may require strategy training to mediate learning tasks, and may have problems accepting personal responsibility for their work while exhibiting an external locus of control. While reasons for work completion may vary in general for students with E/BD and learning disabilities, the combination of disorders certainly bodes poorly for this aspect of achievement. By just

A variety of behavioral and emotional problems may be found in students with learning disabilities.

considering this one example of school functioning, the need for a comprehensive approach to academic programming becomes apparent.

The broader implications relate to considerations of outcomes for individuals who are LD and E/BD and to the resultant implications for programming. Rock et al. (in press) note that this combination is likely to be associated with poor grades, restrictive class placement, and elevated school dropout rates. It would be reasonable to point out that, given that students who are EBD are (among individuals with disabilities) most at risk for dropping out and having poor prospects for employment or postsecondary education success, those who are also learning disabled will represent a group very likely to experience serious difficulties both within and beyond the school setting. In considering students identified as having both disabilities, it is clear that for students, teachers, and parents a significant educational and life planning challenge has to be faced.

ATTENTION DEFICIT/HYPERACTIVITY DISORDER

There is a clear relationship between the history of the study and treatment of individuals with learning disabilities and those with attention deficit disorder (or attention deficit hyperactivity disorder). In fact, both areas derived to a significant extent from the early research done by Strauss, Lehtinen, and others on individuals with learning and attentional problems (Epstein, Shaywitz, Shaywitz, and Woolston, 1991) (also see Chapter 1). It is therefore not surprising that some degree of overlap would be anticipated involving these two respective conditions.

Conceptual Issues

The reluctance of the federal government to include attention deficit disorder as a disability group under the Individuals with Disabilities Education Act (IDEA) was due at least in part to the assumption that individuals with ADD or ADHD could receive services through one of the existing categories, including in particular learning disabilities and emotional and behavioral disorders. However, it is increasingly being postulated that ADHD and LD, for example, are distinct, though often co-existing disabilities (Lyon, 1995). Though estimates of co-existence range significantly, it has been hypothesized that from 25 percent up to 80 percent of all students with ADD or ADHD experience learning problems in school and that perhaps 10-20 percent of them may qualify under the learning disability label. At the same time, in the inverse relationship, it has been estimated that one-third or more of all students with learning disabilities may also be accurately identified as ADHD (Cantwell and Baker, 1991; McKinney, Montague, and Hocutt, 1993; Reeve, 1990). Further, an important subgroup of students with ADHD may present a pattern of characteristics quite similar to those individuals who may experience both learning disabilities and emotional and behavioral disorders (Rock, et al., in press).

Various rationales for this comorbidity have been posited. Perhaps the most common assumption is that attentional problems experienced by children result in subsequent learning disabilities that are identified within the various academic domains. However, such a relationship does not preclude the fact that some specific etiological variable may cause both the attentional and learning problems coincidentally. Most often, neurological hypotheses predominate within such a view. Additionally, it cannot be discounted that students who experience learning difficulties in school may very likely find that these problems serve as the genesis for increased levels of distractibility and decreased attention to task focus.

Characteristics

When considering possible characteristics, it is useful to consider clinical diagnoses associated with ADD. Dykman and Ackerman (1993) identified the following three clinical types:

• ADD/WO: attention deficit without hyperactivity (or the "pure" form of the traditional ADD)

• ADDH (ADHD): attention deficit with hyperactivity (the most commonly referred-to type of ADD)

• ADDHA: attention deficit with hyperactivity and aggression (the most recently identified form and the one with the greatest risk of psychopathology)

In each of these three subtypes, the possible presence of a learning disability remains a significant consideration.

Following the ADD model provided by Zentall (1993), particular emphasis in understanding the nature of needs of students identified as attention deficit disorder and learning disabled would focus on:

- *attentional "bias"*—an understanding of the context (i.e., task, setting, conditions) within which deficits in attention arise.
- *activity level*—a focus beyond the noticeable evidence of loudness or frequency but also with the variable occurrence of high levels of activity. Such activity levels may be associated with interference with the establishment of learning routines and diverting of energy from learning to inhibiting behavior.
- *impulsivity*—difficulty in withholding responses, blurting our answers, dealing with only the immediately available information, failure to work, and lack of attention to problem-solving. The implications for planning and organization and ultimately learning are apparent.

Gender trends are also of particular interest; Lyon's (1995) summary of research indicates, for example, that the higher occurrence of ADHD in males combined with the co-existence of ADHD and LD has contributed to "spuriously inflating the gender ratio in favor of males" in students with learning disabilities (p. 11).

Implications

The key area of concern for students with learning disabilities and ADHD is treatment. Initially, one can consider whether the directionality of the two disabilities has treatment implications. If so, for example, then the treatment hypothesis may be to focus on the attentional deficit with the assumption that it will in turn enhance the learning patterns. Such a view might be consistent with the use of chemical intervention such as Ritalin.

The issues surrounding the use of stimulant medications are discussed at length by Swanson, Cantwell, Lerner, McBurnett, and Hannon (1991) and by Swanson et al. (1993). Table 12.1 provides a particularly helpful perspective on the effects of such interventions.

For stimulants such as Ritalin, teachers should be alert to possible side effects including:

- appetite loss
- headaches
- stomachaches
- lethargy
- tics
- irritability
- nervousness
- sadness (Smith, et al., 1995).

Other non-medical interventions would reflect less sensitivity to the directionality of cause and have been used extensively with individuals with both LD and ADHD (Dowdy, Patton, Smith, and Polloway, 1995). Structured classrooms (e.g., physical and temporal arrangements) is one key area of emphasis. The varied tools common within the field in behavioral interventions such as

TABLE 12.1

Treatment of Children with Attention Deficit Disorder with Stimulant Medication

What Should Be Expected

1. Temporary Management of Diagnostic Systems
   a. Overactivity (improved ability to modulate motor behavior)
   b. Inattention (increased concentration or effort on tasks)
   c. Impulsivity (improved self-regulation)
2. Temporary Improvement of Associated Features
   a. Deportment (increased compliance and effort)
   b. Aggression (decrease in physical and verbal hostility)
   c. Social interactions (decreased negative behaviors)
   d. Academic productivity (increased amount and accuracy of work)

What Should Not Be Expected

1. Paradoxical Response
   a. Responses of normal children are in same directions
   b. Responses of normal adults are in same directions
   c. Responses of affected adults and children are similar
2. Prediction of Response
   a. Not by neurological signs
   b. Not by physiological measures
   c. Not by biochemical markers
3. Absence of Side Effects
   a. Infrequent appearance or increase in tics
   b. Frequent problems with eating and sleeping
   c. Possible psychological effects on cognition and attribution
4. Large Effects on Skills or Higher Order Processes
   a. No significant improvement of reading skills
   b. No significant improvement of athletic or game skills
   c. No significant improvement of positive social skills
   d. Improvement on learning/achievement less than improvement in behavior/attention
5. Improvement in Long-Term Adjustment
   a. No improvement in academic achievement
   b. No reduction in antisocial behavior or arrest rate

Source: Swanson et al., (1993) Effects of stimulant medication on children with ADD: A "review of reviews," *Exceptional Children*, 60, p. 159.

reinforcement, extinction procedures, and selected use of punishment represent another focus. Additionally, cognitive strategies, inclusive of self-management techniques (e.g., self-monitoring, self-instruction) are attractive considerations for students with learning and attentional problems given their emphasis on the precise nature of the problems exhibited by these students (e.g., impulsivity, behavioral inhibition). However, it is important to evaluate their effectiveness in particular cases especially in light of the efficacy concerns for students with ADD which have been raised (Abikoff, 1991).

▶ COMMUNICATION DISABILITIES

An important consideration for individuals with learning disabilities is the possible overlap with communication disabilities. Such a consideration should not be unexpected given the fact that many learning disabilities are presumed to have a linguistic basis. In fact, in a study of IEPs, Polloway et al. (1992) reported that over 80 percent of a sample of students with learning disabilities also experienced speech and language problems, with greater than one-third receiving therapy for these concerns. In their review of research, Schoenbrodt, Kumin, and Sloan (in press) noted that estimates of co-occurrence of language disorders and learning disabilities may range as high as 35 to 60 percent, with language impairment representing the most common problem among individuals with learning disabilities. When all communication disorders were considered, Gibbs and Cooper (1989) indicated initially all students with learning disabilities experienced some problem, with approximately 90 percent having some disorder of language, and 23 percent articulation problems, 12 percent voice disorders, and 1 percent fluency (e.g., stuttering) difficulties. It is likely that the issue of severity is the key to understanding these discrepant data; for example, in Gibbs and Cooper's (1989) study, only 6 percent of the sample were actually receiving speech-language services.

Conceptual Issues

The co-occurrence figures cited above merely serve as prelude to issues of overlap between communication disorders and learning disabilities. In fact, common definitions for both disabilities (i.e., NJCLD, 1988; ASHA, 1982) reflect similar foci and both indicate the difficulty experienced by the identified individual in responding effectively to the spoken or written word and, terms used in the respective fields (e.g., language learning disabilities, language-based learning disabilities) add to the sense of common joint diagnosis. Schoenbrodt et al. (in press) further accentuated this interaction when they stated:

> Whether we agree that learning disabilities and language disorders are two distinct classifications, represent manifestations of the same underlying problem, or are the same problem defined differently at different times during the life span, the fact is that both disabilities can be present within the same person (p. 14).

A valid approach for understanding the reason for this overlap is to consider an age-related continuum. With such a model, preschool children may be seen as exhibiting a developmental communication disorder, as noted by parents or others in the child's environment. After school entry, the focus shifts to academic functioning and teachers may raise questions about achievement which ultimately may result in identification as learning-disabled. Finally, in adolescence, more specific language problems which manifest in both academic (e.g., writing) and social (e.g., pragmatic aspects of conversation) may be noted (Schoenbrodt, et al., in press).

Characteristics

The high degree of overlap between these two disabilities logically suggests that common characteristics of individuals with the dual diagnosis would largely be reflective of characteristics seen under the learning-disabled label. Nevertheless, it is important to note the types of problems that may be found across the language components of phonology, morphology, syntax, semantics, and pragmatics. Specific concerns of note are highlighted in Table 12.2 (derived from Fad, 1995; Schoenbrodt, et al., in press; Wallace, Cohen and Polloway, 1987).

TABLE 12.2

Characteristics of Communication Disorders and Learning Disabilities

- Phonology
    - Delayed acquisition
    - Difficulty with phonological awareness
    - Difficulty understanding auditory signals
- Morphology/Syntax
    - Incorrect or immature grammatical forms
    - Limited sentences
    - Problems with correct pronoun usage
    - Following multiple-step directions
- Semantics
    - Word-finding problems (dysnomia)
    - Multiple word meaning difficulties
    - Late and/or limited vocabulary
    - Problems with recall of information
    - Comprehension of classroom vocabulary
- Pragmatics
    - Redundancy in patterns
    - Problems in shifting style to meet changes in social situations
    - Interference with social skills development due to pragmatic difficulties
    - Difficulty in effectively communicating in classroom (e.g., asking for help, seeking clarification)
    - Problems with adolescent social interactions (e.g., understanding jokes)

Implications

For students with learning disabilities who experience communication disabilities, there is a vast array of interventions which have been developed. Schoenbrodt et al. (in press) emphasized the following areas of emphasis for the design of intervention programs:

* enhancing language environments (e.g., physical setting, opportunities for interaction, teacher responsiveness);

* targeting vocabulary development (i.e., words that are relevant, functional and individualized);

* enhancing the learning of content through semantic organizers (e.g., webs, maps);

* developing the ability to be successful in narrative discourse (e.g., public speaking strategies); and

* enhancing conversational discourse (e.g., teaching awareness of rules, use of social cues).

▶ VISUAL IMPAIRMENTS

Impairments in hearing and vision are often described as low incidence disabilities in the general population. In fact, common occurrence figures are typically of the magnitude of 1.0 percent for hearing impaired and 0.40 percent for visually impaired with significant variance only for older (i.e., geriatric) individuals. However, the possibility of etiological overlap with LD not only creates risks of higher incidence rates but more importantly special challenges for individuals. These instances are cases where the sensory impairment is not primary to the learning disability, as precluded by definition, but are caused by some other variable.

Conceptual Issues

In their review of the literature, Erin and Koenig (in press) indicated that most research in the area of visual impairment indicates that a sizeable percentage of individuals identified as VI would also qualify for identification under the label learning-disabled. Such a finding would be particularly likely with the case of procedures based on a discrepancy formula. Specifically, in their review, they found that the range of individuals with VI who could also be classified as learning disabled was from 14 percent to 65 percent. However, the accuracy of such figures is obviously in question and the determination of the number of individuals who would qualify under the dual diagnosis is definitely fraught with definitional problems. On the other hand, the percentage of individuals who are learning-disabled that may also be visually impaired would be expected to be quite low[2] (Polloway, et al., 1992).

[2]The discussion here refers to visual acuity. Many more students with learning disabilities, however, would be likely to have difficulties related to visual perception.

Characteristics and Implications

While the source of the problems would vary, Erin and Koenig (in press) noted that there are several academic characteristics that are commonly observed in both individuals with learning disabilities and those with visual disabilities. These include frustration experienced at prolonged reading tasks, difficulty in the recognition and identification of letters and words, and potentially poor performance on tasks which require eye-hand coordination and/or the use of spatial relationships (e.g., handwriting).

Smith et al. (1995) noted the following considerations relative to characteristics of students with visual impairment. These commonalities will be ones to consider in relationship to their further interaction with learning disabilities. In terms of intellectual and linguistic attributes, their review of the literature indicated:

- intellectual abilities are similar to those of sighted peers;
- concept development depends more heavily on tactile experiences;
- the development of integrated concepts can be negatively influenced by the visual impairment;
- students are generally behind their sighted peers academically; and
- individuals are relatively unimpaired in language abilities.

Assessment issues are particularly important when it comes to the evaluation of individuals who may have both a visual impairment and a learning disability. Given the fact that assessment is already problematic for students with visual disabilities, it is not surprising to note that this problem is aggravated when a learning disability is also considered. To illustrate this quandary, Erin and Koenig (in press) identified a series of concerns that are associated with the use of assessment tools. These include the following (p. 11-14):

- Any modification of a standardized test or the procedures used to administer it will affect validity and reliability.
- The acculturation of students with visual impairments is likely to vary from that of students with normal vision.
- The modification of a given test may inadvertently change the actual skill or skills that the test was intended to measure.
- Some test items related to purely visual phenomena may be inappropriate for students with visual disabilities, particularly those who are functionally blind, and therefore may place them in an assessment disadvantage.
- Modified achievement tests that contain eliminated items may fail to match the curriculum adopted by a school district.
- Elimination of items from a test affects reliability and content breadth.

When students with the dual diagnosis of VI/LD are considered, these concerns are further accentuated.

In order to accommodate the educational needs of students with both visual impairment and learning disability, a variety of educational programs and instructional modifications should be considered. These include especially modifications that address the visual impairment (Erin and Koenig, in press):

- adapting instruction in the use of Braille;
- using environmental adaptations (e.g., color contrasts, additional time, additional illumination);
- designing developmentally appropriate visual training activities which correspond to visual demands of the individual's daily life;
- teaching compensatory skills (e.g., use of a talking calculator); and
- using visual and graphic organizers (e.g., large print, tactile charts and maps).

▶ HEARING IMPAIRMENT

The existence of a relationship between hearing impairment and learning difficulties could be predicted given, for example, that causes of hearing impairment can also affect the functioning of the central nervous system and thus impair learning (Roth, 1991). Further, it is clear that educational history is no doubt replete with instances of children with hearing impairment being labeled underachievers or learning-disabled due to an inaccurate understanding of their educational difficulties.

Conceptual Issues

Research on the overlap between HI and LD indicates that a substantial number of students who are hearing impaired are also learning disabled, when the definition of learning disabilities is based on an underachievement emphasis (i.e., discrepancy formula). Roth (1991) noted that, dependent on research methodology used, the possible percentage of students with hearing impairment who also have a learning disability ranges from 6 to 23 percent. These estimates generally are consistent with the conclusion drawn by Mauk and Mauk (1992) from their review of research.

The alternative way to view this relationship is from the perspective of the universe of students who have the high incidence disability of learning disabilities. One estimate of the percentage of students with learning disabilities who also have hearing impairments indicated that over 7 percent of students with learning disabilities also had some degree of hearing deficit (Gibbs and Cooper, 1989).

A key consideration is the type of hearing loss that affects the child. The types of hearing impairment include the following: conductive (i.e., interruption in transmission of sound from outer ear to inner ear); sensori-neural (i.e., damage or problems with the cochleas or auditory nerve); mixed (i.e., evidence of both conductive and sensorineural loss); and central auditory processing (i.e., difficulty in understanding information arriving to brain).

One condition which traditionally has been assumed to illustrate the relationship between hearing impairment and learning disabilities is early bilateral otitis media, a condition affecting young children between two to four years old in which an inflammation in the middle ear is accompanied by an accumulation of liquid. Interestingly, research indicates that it is approximately twice as prevalent in learning-disabled vs. non-learning-disabled populations, with common estimates of 20 to 25 percent of students with learning disabilities experiencing the problem (Reichman and Healey, 1983). Thus it is likely that one in four elementary children with learning disabilities will have this problem.

Persistent otitis media commonly has been associated with speech and language problems as well as achievement deficits (Peters, Grievink, von Bon, and Schilder, 1994; Reichman and Healey, 1983). However, Peters et al. (1994), reporting on their study of 946 children, found relatively small effects were noted in spelling and writing ability but not in reading ability. They concluded that the problems derived from otitis media thus were often not of significant concern. Nevertheless, elementary school teachers should be alert to the possible presence of otitis media and be sensitive to its potential effects on an individual basis.

Characteristics and Implications

A brief review of the common characteristics of students with hearing impairments serves as a foundation for considering the needs of the child who is both hearing impaired and learning-disabled. Most relevant to considerations of overlap between HI and LD are in the academic arena where characteristics include (Smith et al., 1995):

- Achievement levels significantly below those of their hearing peers;
- Reading ability is most significantly affected;
- Written language production is limited; and
- Discrepancy between capabilities and performance in many academic areas.

The problem for identification when a student has both disabilities is that teachers may not note the key indicators of hearing loss, rather assuming that, at least in some cases, these are a function of diminished learning ability. Indicators include:

- requests information on regular basis
- uses loud voice
- responds incorrectly to questions
- does not respond when spoken to
- appears inattentive/confused
- difficulty following directions
- misarticulates
- withdraws from social interactions (Smith et al. 1995).

In outlining characteristics and implications of young children with both disabilities, Mauk and Mauk (1992) drew on the work of Restarino (1982).

Specifically they indicated the following assumptions about the needs of children who were HI/LD:

1. Children with HI/LD move through the stages of development in the same sequence as other children and they must be provided with the opportunities to do so.

2. The child with HI/LD is seriously hindered in meeting the demands of classroom learning without prerequisite skills. The demands of classroom learning in academic areas are such that subordinate skills must be mastered before any child can be expected to succeed in them.

3. Limited experience with elements in the environment leads the child with HI/LD to display greater rigidity of behavior than other children, and the structuring of the environment by the teacher to ensure progress in motor, perceptual, and conceptual skills may exacerbate such rigidity. Such deliberate structuring may provide little opportunity for the child to adapt to even small changes that confront him or her.

4. The classroom experiences of the child with HI/LD constitute a greater proportion of his or her opportunities for learning than they do for other children. Consequently, the interaction between the child with HI/LD and the teacher is more critical to that child's education than it may be for other children in the class.

5. The child with HI/LD has experienced failure to a greater degree than other children. Thus, the educator's attention must be directed not only toward progress in motor, perceptual, and conceptual skills, but also toward enhancing the child's self-esteem, self-efficacy, and pleasure in trying.

6. There is, within the subgroup of children with HI/LD, as wide a range of individual differences as in the group of deaf children with no concomitant disability. As important as it is for teachers and other members of the multidisciplinary team to observe individual children intensively to identify abilities and disabilities in perceptual, motor, and cognitive areas, it is also essential that these educators study the behavior of children with HI/LD for clues to the kinds of communication and interaction patterns that appear to be productive or obstructive to their learning (p. 188–189).

▶ MENTAL RETARDATION[3]

For years, there has been a clear, though artificial, conceptual distinction between learning disabilities and mental retardation primarily based on the individual's IQ. Smith, Polloway, and Smith (1978) emphasized the dilemma which results from the rather large group of students whose IQ scores may have been above the cut-off level for mental retardation of approximately 70–75 while

---

[3]This section is adapted from: Polloway, E.A., Patton, J.R., Smith, T.E.C., and Buck, G.H. (in press). Mental retardation and learning disabilities: Conceptual and applied issues. *Journal of Learning Disabilities*. Used with permission.

still falling below the common base levels often used in the schools for eligibility for learning disability services (i.e., 80–85). While the size of the "IQ gap" varies significantly dependent on, for example, state guidelines, nevertheless, in most jurisdictions, overlap would be somewhat artificially prevented by the governing agency's regulations. Thus the discussion below merely highlights some important conceptual considerations relative to these two conditions.

Conceptual Issues

While the two categories may seem to be mutually exclusive in the conceptual sense, there has been disagreement about the validity of this distinction. Hallahan and Kauffman (1976, 1977) contended that significant overlap between the categories could be found in the areas of characteristics, etiology, and relevant educational methodology, a perspective consistent with the non-categorical (or cross-categorical) concept. Under this assumption, these groups of students could benefit from similar educational programs. However, limited research support exists to confirm the assumption of similarities between students identified as learning disabled or mentally retarded (e.g., Polloway, Epstein, Polloway, Patton, and Ball, 1986). In fact, some educationally relevant cross-categorical differences have been empirically determined (e.g., Affleck, Edgar, Levin, and Kortering, 1990; Cullinan and Epstein, 1985; Edgar, 1987; Polloway, et al, 1986). Finally, the question of possible categorical distinctions is further confused by the fact that some students initially labeled mildly retarded subsequently have been classified as learning-disabled (e.g., Gottlieb, Alter, Gottlieb, and Wishner, 1994; MacMillan, Siperstein, and Gresham, 1994; Patrick and Reschly, 1982; Tucker, 1980). The reader is referred to Polloway et al. (in press) for a more comprehensive discussion of the conceptual issues which tie or separate these two fields.

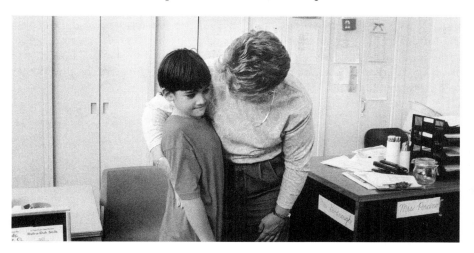

Many students with low intelligence test scores display many characteristics associated with learning disabilities.

▶ NEUROLOGICAL AND HEALTH CONDITIONS

A variety of other conditions are important to consider as possible concomitant problems with learning disabilities. These include the selected examples briefly discussed below.

Cerebral Palsy

The relationship between learning disabilities and cerebral palsy (CP) has been a long one, reaching back, for example, to mutual research roots in the work of William Cruickshank. The relationship between CP and LD is not unexpected given the fact that learning disabilities are, by definition, presumed to be caused by central nervous system dysfunction (see Chapter 5) and CP is clearly the result of neurological problems.

Cerebral palsy is a neurological, educational, and psychological condition caused by a non-progressive brain disorder. In addition to motor problems, deficits that are a common result of this brain disorder also include visual defects, hearing loss, disorders of comprehension, and cognitive dysfunctions. These last two effects are the most notable herein as the neurological cause of CP may also result in the presence of learning disabilities.

There are two characteristics of children with CP that are commonly observed in children with learning disabilities and are worthy of special note. The first is an attention deficit that is likely to be related to the brain damage associated with CP. This deficit may lead to learning problems as individuals may focus on the unimportant details of a lesson instead of the overall meaning. In response to this concern, supports similar to those required for children with learning disabilities (e.g., structured environment, structured curriculum, self-monitoring strategies) should be considered.

The second common element is that of being regarded as passive and dependent learners. Consequently they have difficulty thinking strategically, which ultimately results in problem-solving deficiencies. Children with CP are at a disadvantage as they may be dependent on others for help with some basic functions. These children need help in becoming independent and active learners. Children with CP also are likely to require educational interventions such as intensive skill instruction and the building of daily life skills that will lead to the most independent and empowered life possible.

Convulsive Disorders

Convulsive disorders, or epilepsy, are also associated with neurological dysfunction and thus again may be present in individuals with learning disabilities due to the possibility of some coincidental variable influencing development. For example, Epir, Renda, and Baser (1984) noted an increased occurrence of perceptual motor and language difficulties within a population of children who had epilepsy.

While the interaction of learning disabilities and convulsive disorders presents no unique educational considerations, professionals clearly need to be able to use appropriate procedures for handling seizures. The professional should:

- protect the individual's head and body;
- not force any object or liquid in the individual's mouth;
- not restrain the body in any way;
- lay the person on his side;
- stay with the person through the seizure;
- start CPR only if breathing stops during the seizure;
- let the person rest after the seizure;
- be reassuring to them after the seizure;
- seek emergency assistance if a seizure lasts over five minutes, or if seizures occur repeatedly

Tourette Syndrome

One neurological condition that has received significant attention in recent years is Tourette Syndrome. Tourette Syndrome is a genetically transmitted disorder which is characterized by multiple motor tics (e.g., twitches of the body, blinks, grimaces), vocal tics (e.g., involuntary utterances), the intermittent presence of symptoms, and a variance in symptoms over time (Bronheim, 1991).

A common observation has been that approximately half of individuals with Tourette Syndrome may also have a learning disability. In their research on elementary students, Burd, Kauffman, and Kerbesham (1992) reported that 51 percent of their sample of children with Tourette Syndrome exhibited a discrepancy between ability and achievement in at least one academic area sufficient to be classified as LD. On the other hand, however, they also reported that children with these two disabilities tended to be undiagnosed as having a learning disability and perceived as poorly motivated or resistant to instruction. In instances where children also experienced ADHD, another common correlate of TS (Fisher and Collins, 1991), such observations by teachers were even more common. In terms of educational patterns, Harris, Silver, and Sekhon (1993) reported that the most common academic problems were in spelling and writing, affecting the majority of students while approximately half also experienced math difficulties. Reading difficulties were least pronounced, affecting approximately one fourth of their sample.

Educational implications for the child with Tourette Syndrome and learning disabilities include the following (Burd, et al., 1992; Bronheim, 1991; Lerer, 1987):

- inservice training for teachers on Tourette Syndrome;
- developing understanding and sensitivity among peers;
- instruction in compensation skills;
- special attention to handwriting problems—a common difficulty of children with Tourette Syndrome;

- allowing the child to sit near the door in order to facilitate taking a break, to assist in discharging tics;
- taking tests in a private room to focus on performance rather than suppression of tics; and
- careful monitoring of medication used to control the effects of Tourette Syndrome.

Health Disorders

A variety of health disorders have also been associated with learning disabilities. Although a full discussion of the numerous specific impairments that may be associated with learning disabilities is beyond the scope of this chapter, it is illustrative to consider that in one study approximately one-half of a sample of students who were learning-disabled were adjudged to experience some health-related concerns (i.e., hyperactivity, allergies, hygienic concerns) with 21 percent receiving medication as treatment on a regular basis (Polloway, et al., 1992), a confirmation of the frequent finding of medication prescription in individuals of learning-disabled populations (Gadow, 1986). Several specific health disorders are of particular significance, either owing to their serious nature and/or their concomitance with learning disabilities.

A consistent hypothesis has been that many children with chronic illnesses are at a significantly greater risk to experience learning problems in school settings than their healthy peers. However, the etiology for these learning outcomes differ from one illness to another with a primary concern being the varying degree of neurological deficits contributing to a learning disability as an actual result of the respective illness. The specific health impairments discussed below are diabetes, leukemia, and sickle cell disease.

It has long been recognized that adults with diabetes may have particular neuropsychological impairments which affect sensory and memory abilities and decrease mental and motor efficiency. This helps to explain the fact that 19.6 percent of children diagnosed with diabetes are placed in a special program (Rovet, Ehrlich, Czuchta, and Akler, 1993). This figure is over twice the norm and lends immediate concern to the effects of the acquisition of diabetes. However, as Rovet et al. (1993) reported, these deficits often result from poor control of one's illness over a long period of time. Children who acquire diabetes before the age of five are affected more neuropsychologically than those who develop it later, specifically in the areas of visuospatial and verbal functioning impairments. Therefore it is not the actual acquiring of diabetes, but instead the effects that the illness may have on development that is significant. Holmes and Richman (1985) specified a "duration hypothesis," reporting that neuropsychological differences were quite evident in children who had had diabetes for at least a duration of seven years. Rovet et al. (1993) found that those children with early onset had significantly lower achievement levels in reading and spelling. The key variables to consider relative to learning for children with diabetes are age of onset and prompt, consistent medical control of the diabetes.

Leukemia is also a chronic illness that can adversely affect the learning outcomes of a child. However, unlike diabetes, researchers have discovered that the neurological deficits found in children with leukemia that lead to these outcomes are not a result of the illness itself, but may instead stem from the radiation therapy that is commonly used in the treatment for the illness (Brown and Madan-Swain, 1993).

Pekham et al. (1988) studied twenty-three long-term survivors of leukemia who had received radiation treatment and found that these individuals achieved below their respective chronological age peers. These individuals characteristically had specific difficulties in attention, memory, and comprehension, attributes also often found in persons with learning disabilities (Brown and Madan-Swain, 1993). However, as with diabetes, the neurocognitive effects are greatly influenced by the age of onset (in this case, the onset of the radiation treatment). Consequently, chemotherapies without radiation have recently begun to be used with children who have a favorable prognosis. To date, insufficient research has been reported to fully evaluate the effects of this new procedure.

Sickle cell disease (SCD) is a chronic, hereditary disease that is disproportionately found in African-Americans. While the relationship between SCD and neuropsychological functioning remains under study, Brown et al. (1993) concluded that children with SCD are at risk for subtle cognitive impairments. The most common deficits found were those involving perceptual skills and fine motor skills. They also suggested other factors such as poverty backgrounds that may be associated with SCD can also effect the child's learning and thus may bias the results.

▶ GIFTEDNESS

The above discussions have focused on the relationship between learning disabilities and other disabilities. However, an important, and too often overlooked, relationship is between learning disabilities and giftedness. Perhaps the most underidentified group of gifted and talented children are those who are learning disabled. When an individual is from a minority group, there is even more likely to be a risk of failing to identify the special talents of a child with a learning disability. It has been estimated that as many as 180,000 gifted students may have learning disabilities (Viadero, 1995). Many of these are likely to not be receiving an appropriate education.

Conceptual Issues

The interaction between giftedness and learning disabilities is a complex one. Problems in identification simply emphasize the conceptual problems that a dual diagnosis of an individual being learning-disabled and at the same time gifted may create. Brody and Mills (in press) underscored this concern when they identified three potential sub-groups of individuals falling within the overlap between giftedness and learning disabilities. The first group would be those who are identified as gifted and yet exhibit difficulties in learning. Such students are likely to be perceived as underachievers and may develop a low self-concept. The paradoxical performance pattern that the students present may often lead teachers to have a lack of understanding of their abilities and needs and may lead them to be labeled as lazy or non-compliant.

The second group of individuals may experience learning disabilities of such a severe nature that the difficulties in school preclude the awareness of professionals of the gifts and talents that the individual may have. Brody and Mills (in press), in their review of the literature, estimated that as many as 33 percent of students with learning disabilities may potentially be identified as gifted. Within this sub-group, the most significant problem is the underestimation of the abilities of the individual children.

The third group, and in some ways the most intriguing, are those individuals whose abilities and disabilities tend to mask each other. In a sense, their special talents in one area perhaps serve to counterbalance their difficulties in a related area. Consequently, these students may be identified as neither learning disabled nor gifted and may be perceived simply as average students. Unidentified, they function on perhaps grade level in academic achievement and their true talents and potential may not be recognized. Such students may eventually be labeled as learning-disabled, especially if, over a period of time, their special abilities have not been developed while their disabilities have become more pronounced or apparent.

Characteristics

Brody and Mills (in press) conceptualized the dual diagnosis of giftedness and learning disability as inclusive of the following core characteristics:

- substantial evidence of an outstanding talent or unique ability;
- discrepancy between the level of expected performance and the actual achievement level of the student; and
- evidence of some processing deficit (e.g., visual processing, auditory processing).

The initial point of these three stresses the essence of what giftedness has been defined as and would further reference the specific aspects of a definition of gifted and talented. The second point emphasizes a key element of learning disabilities that is reflected in the most popular definitions and more common diagnostic processes within that field. The third characteristic (i.e., the inclusion of a processing deficit) is an interesting one. For Brody and Mills (in press), the processing deficit element provides further stipulation of the unique problems evidenced by a student with learning disabilities and a possible rationale for the nature of the underachievement they experience. Processing deficits are of particular merit in a discussion of the interaction between giftedness and learning disability given the otherwise high rates of underachievement in gifted children.

Implications

Along with the disability areas, the field of giftedness has experienced a discussion of the implications of the inclusion movement for educational programs. Perhaps more than any other area of exceptionality, advocates within the field of giftedness have persuasively argued that full inclusion may not be in the best interest of students so identified. The basis for this argument is essentially that students will be unable to reach their full potential without specific programs that build on their unique talents and abilities. Most commonly, the schools have responded to the needs of gifted children with programs of acceleration (e.g., moving students through material at a more rapid pace), enrichment (e.g., adding breadth to the curriculum studied by students), or homogenous grouping (e.g., special classes). At the same time, some advocates in the field of learning disabilities have questioned the acceptance of a full inclusion model for students experiencing learning problems (see Kauffman and Hallahan, 1994; Polloway, et al., in press). As these authors described, a number of professional and parent-oriented organizations within the field of learning disabilities have called for a commitment to the continuum of services for students so that, for example, pull-out programs would continue to be available.

In addition to placement issues, several curricular and instructional considerations are relevant. Southern and Swart (1995, p. 49) highlighted three central recommendations for working with students who are gifted and learning disabled:

• Focus on the development of the students' strengths. In programs for students with LD, the emphasis is on remediation. For students who are GT/LD, areas of strength can be used to reinforce weaker skill areas.

• Encourage the students to be aware that all people have areas of strength and weaknesses. The students should learn to value their own strengths and those of others.

• Encourage the development of positive compensation mechanisms. If, for example, the student has difficulties in reading, provide assistance to find other media that can provide similar information.

Of particular importance is the need for programs that emphasize compensation rather than just remediation (Viadero, 1995). As gifted students with learning disabilities themselves related, the over-focus on remediation can become particularly problematic:

> "I kind of wondered why I was there, because everything they had me do was so simple. I kind of felt like I was doing it for them," recalls one subject. "I would go into this room, and the teacher would have me read this story that I had read ten times already in second grade, and fill in questions about it, and it seemed so obvious."

> "We just worked on vocabulary and spelling," recalls another student. "I figured I guess they would teach you to spell better, then your disability would go away." (Viadero, 1995, p. 36).

Finally, one last consideration highlighted by Southern and Swart (1995) is particularly cogent. Students with these two exceptionalities need to understand the nature of the discrepancy between their ability and performance. Appreciating that the difficulties are not primarily a function of motivation or personal choice can reduce frustration and assist them in realizing their potential.

SUMMARY

This chapter focused on other disabilities that can occur in conjunction with learning disabilities. The combination of problems in such situations can create special challenges for the learner. The following points summarize the major areas included in the chapter:

- The merits and dilemmas posed by dual diagnosis.
- The commonality of LD and E/BD overlap in school settings with the natural relationship between the two exceptionalities.
- The overlap between LD and ADHD with the resultant needs for both academic and behavioral management.
- The paradoxical question of overlap between LD and MR and related issues.
- The high relevance of communication disorders in students who are learning disabled-resulting in the need for a multifaceted intervention strategy.
- The unique challenges faced by individuals who have learning disabilities as well as a sensory impairment (i.e., hearing impairment, visual impairment).
- The relationships between learning disabilities and cerebral palsy, convulsive disorders, Tourette Syndrome, and other health disorders.
- The important challenges faced by educators in designing appropriate programs for students who are learning disabled and also are gifted.

Chapter 13

EMERGING CONSIDERATIONS FOR THE FUTURE

The objectives for this chapter are as follows:

- To understand demographic considerations affecting the schools of the 1990s.

- To consider the implications of ongoing societal transformations.

- To evaluate emerging directions in the conceptualization and identification of learning disabilities.

- To critically review the validity of educational interventions in the field.

- To consider the implications of the inclusion movement.

- To evaluate the merits of a supports model for learning disabilities.

- To consider the implications of technology for enhanced lives for individuals with learning disabilities.

Perspective of an Adult with Learning Disabilities

Prof. Rosel Schewel

Lynchburg College

1501 Lakeside Drive

Lynchburg, Virginia 24501

Dear Prof. Schewel,

Thank you for sending me a copy of the manuscript you wrote based on your research into adults with learning disabilities. I'm sorry it's taken me so long to get back to you; things have just recently slowed down a little bit.

You invited us to pass on our reactions, and I'm taking you at your word. First of all, I'm shocked that there may be any debate in the special education community about the fact that many, if not most, learning disabled students carry their disabilities to adulthood. My personal experience and my observation is that it is the rule rather than the exception that disabilities remain with one. It is my experience that one is not "cured" of a learning disability, rather one learns coping skills. Coping skills should not be confused with a "cure."

If a student just needs extra help to overcome a disadvantaged background or something of that nature, then he or she may not have ongoing problems after several years of special education, but for students who have actual problems such as dyslexia, there is no doubt that the problems remain. Training may overcome some obstacles, but many remain. Again, I'm amazed that there would be any doubt about this point in your field.

I was interested in your finding that few learning-disabled adults believed that special education teachers had a significant impact on their education. Were I you, I would find this quite disturbing. My experience bears this out; the special education teachers were not much help to me. I had always believed this was because I was unusual in the special education classes because I was college-bound, came from a family that was supportive, etc. In light of your findings, however, I'm reevaluating this assumption. If it is true that your study's respondents are the more successful ones (by whatever criteria one uses to measure success), it becomes even more important to note that this group did not believe their special education teachers were particularly helpful.

Another interesting point was the importance of strong family support. I believe strong family support of education is important for any child, but I believe it is especially important for a learning disabled child. I'm glad your research confirmed that.

You may be interested to know that I recently completed a graduate course in sociology. I found the experience of returning to the classroom after being out of school several years interesting. As far as my learning disability was concerned, nothing had changed. I did find, as I'm sure everyone does, that the improved work skills I had gained while working were helpful. However, this experience makes me more sure than ever that one is not "cured" of a learning disability. I was more aware of my learning disability in the class than I have been at work, which may explain why many people don't think about their learning disabilities as much after they finish school.

Thank you for your attention to this issue. I believe that we must study learning disabled adults in order to determine what learning disabled students need most. We can also use the experiences of learning disabled adults as a measure of the success of special education. If I can help in any way with future research, please let me know.

Sincerely,

[Name Withheld]

A common observation is that "the present is merely a precursor to the future." Because the simplicity of this observation is indisputable, it provides a useful framework for the inevitable task of attempting to project events in the future for the field of learning disabilities and for individuals with learning disabilities. However, rather than taking a prediction or foretelling approach, we have ample evidence of activities in the present and emerging directions to obtain a reasonable portrait of what the future may hold without relying on a Jean Dixon-type approach. Hammill (1993) sounded this theme when he considered possible future directions for the field of LD. As he noted:

> Predicting the future . . . is a risky business that is best left to clairvoyants who can depend on their crystal balls for insight. It is fairly easy, however, to identify present-

day events or ideas that are important and that might exert a continuing influence on the future of learning disabilities. Regrettably, one cannot tell which of these will significantly influence the future or to what extent they will be influential (p. 303).

The focus of this chapter is thus on contemplating which directions and trends of the current time provide us with the most likely picture of the future of the field of learning disabilities.

In order to paint this portrait, we rely on two approaches in discussing specific topics. First, we identify emerging directions that are particularly fruitful avenues and which bode well for the future (e.g., the empowerment movement) as well as those trends which are so powerful that they cannot be overlooked even if they may not bode well for the future of persons with learning disabilities (e.g., economic trends). Second, we also focus on issues which warrant consideration as we participate in the molding of this future. Initially, the chapter begins with discussions of demographics and of societal transformations.

▶ DEMOGRAPHICS

Increasingly it becomes clear that our future will be shaped to a large degree by demographic trends. Whether seen as straightforward facts of society to consider (e.g., Hodgkinson, 1985) or as frightening evidence of dangerous trends (e.g., Herrnstein and Murray, 1994), there remains little question that any view of the future must begin with consideration of such societal trends.

The data that have been presented in recent years certainly give pause for careful contemplation. Bursts of demographic data that has awakened Americans from complacency in recent years include information such as the following:

- One in four Americans lives below the poverty line; nearly half are children.
- One in five Americans does not have health insurance.
- Child abuse cases are estimated to exceed 450,000 per year.
- Over 10 percent of children are born exposed prematurely to illegal drugs.
- Fetal alcohol cases have risen dramatically.
- Over 100,000 children are homeless on a given night.
- Over 1.5 million teenagers become pregnant yearly.
- Thirty percent of babies are born to unmarried mothers; in some cities, the figure is over 60 percent.

An even bleaker micro-view is illustrated by Table 13.1.

While these data summaries do not provide clear direction for recommendations, let alone solutions, they should be kept in mind when consideration is given to the future of the field of learning disabilities. As Moats and Lyon (1993) noted, the overwhelming national concerns which such data reflect may make the problems of individuals with learning disabilities pale by comparison,

| TABLE 13.1 |
| Children at Risk |

One Day in the Lives of American Children

Every day in America:
- 638 babies are born to mothers receiving late or no prenatal care
- 742 babies are born at low birth weight (less than 5.5 pounds)
- 2,685 babies are born into poverty
- 107 babies die before their first birthday
- 2 children younger than 5 are murdered
- 1,340 babies are born to teen mothers
- 2,754 babies are born out of wedlock

Source: Adapted from *The Catholic Virginian*, February, 1992 and the Children's Defense Fund (1992).

particularly as long as individuals with learning disabilities suffer from the "myth of mildness" (Ellis and Cramer, 1994) which hinders the acceptance of the seriousness of the learning problems of individual children (Mather and Roberts, 1994). It thus becomes important that professionals understand the significance of learning problems, validate attention to their importance to our society, and advocate a continued commitment to their prevention and remediation while parallel efforts focus on the multitude of other challenges reflected in the above list. The data summaries in Table 13.2 provide a basis for underscoring the valid needs of persons with learning disabilities within overall demographic concerns in the future.

Learning disability is not a concept that should be considered apart from the context of society. Hence, for example, the increase in the prevalence of learning disabilities in the schools and the challenges of adulthood for students with disabilities (discussed later in the chapter) should be contextualized within our society's trends in the area of demography. There is increasing evidence that such a view will become widely accepted in the future.

▶ SOCIAL TRANSFORMATION

Against this backdrop of demographics, we next consider the sweeping societal transformations of the twentieth century. Drucker (1994) outlined a number of emerging directions which have clear implications for the field of learning disabilities and for persons with learning disabilities in the near future and in the twenty-first century. Those include:

- The rise of a knowledge society and knowledge workers as the central focus of our nation and our workforce

TABLE 13.2

Demographic Data on Learning Disabilities

- Fifty percent of juvenile delinquents tested were found to have undetected learning disabilities.
- Up to 60 percent of adolescents in treatment for substance abuse have learning disabilities.
- Sixty-two percent of students who are learning disabled were unemployed one year after graduating.
- Fifty percent of females with learning disabilities will be mothers (many of them single) within 3–5 years of leaving high schools.
- Thirty-one percent of adolescents with learning disabilities will be arrested 3-5 years out of high school.
- Learning disabilities and substance abuse are the most common impediments to keeping welfare clients from becoming and remaining employed.

Source: Ellis, W., and Cramer, S.C. (1994). *Learning disabilities: A national responsibility.* Washington, D.C.: National Center on Learning Disabilities (p. 5–6).

- The need for a substantial amount of formal education and, perhaps more significantly, the need for continuous learning
- The diminishing importance of skills that are gained through apprenticeship versus those acquired through formal schooling and training
- The role of the schools continuing to come under the scrutiny of society as a whole as non-educators grapple with the performance and the values of the schools
- Increasing pressure on education to move to the use of vouchers for varied schools
- Redefinition of an "educated person" as one who has learned to learn and continues to learn rather than as one who has acquired a prescribed knowledge base
- Team-based work increasingly serving as the norm as individuals with certain specialties work together to solve multifaceted problems. Such teams obviously demand both knowledge and social skills of their members
- Continuing reduction in community "roots" due to the population's mobility in terms of homes, jobs, and affiliations

What does this mean in the future for professionals in the field of learning disabilities? Clearly, the key element is the acknowledgement of change and the acceptance that such changes will necessitate new approaches to traditional problems faced by children, adolescents, and adults who are learning-disabled. One encouraging finding is that American society has experienced an impressive change in their acceptance of the needs of persons with disabilities, as most notably reflected in the passage and enactment of the Americans with Disabilities Act (ADA). The data in Box 13.1 further underscore this emerging

| Box 13.1 | *Public Attitudes Toward People with Disabilities* |

The following data are summarized from the 1991 Louis Harris Poll. The percentages refer to the citizens surveyed who agreed with these points.

- Ninety-two percent believe economic benefits accrue if people with disabilities are assimilated.
- Ninety-eight percent believe persons with disabilities should have equal opportunity.
- The majority see persons with disabilities as an underused potential in the workplace.

- Ninety percent believe that society benefits from the productivity of persons with disabilities (versus welfare).
- Ninety-six percent support access to public places.
- Ninety-three percent support access to public transportation.
- The most common emotions expressed about people with disabilities are pity and admiration.

Source: Adapted from *AAMR Newsletter,* 5(1), Jan–Feb, 1992.

trend. These data signal a key transformation toward societal acceptance that holds significant promise for the future. At the same time, it represents only the "first battle of the war"—after equity and acceptance, issues of competence will become even more prominent.

▶ CONCEPTUALIZATION AND IDENTIFICATION

It is a safe wager that the concept of learning disabilities and the subsequent identification and diagnostic processes and procedures will continue to be held under scrutiny in the future. The challenges in this area are significant and critical to the survival of the field. Moats and Lyon (1993) emphasized this and related points:

> Learning disabilities in the United States is at a critical juncture where, if we are ever to understand this tremendously heterogeneous array of disorders, we must establish precise definitions for research purposes and a theoretically based classification system that is open to empirical scrutiny. Such a classification system must not only provide a valid framework for clinical scientists to identify different types of learning disabilities, but also be robust enough to recognize the distinctions and interrelationships (comorbidities) between LD and other childhood disorders (p. 283).

Problems related to precision in the definition and classification system thus continue to represent significant problems for the future (Lyon, 1995). As Adelman (1992, p. 17) noted:

> Failure to differentiate underachievement caused by neurological dysfunctioning from that caused by other factors has been cited specifically as a major deterrent to important lines of research and theory and is certainly a threat to the very integrity of the LD field (p. 1).

All other variables aside, the trends in school prevalence rate alone will dictate such an ongoing review. Consider, for example, both the absolute percentage of students being identified as having a learning disability as well as the relative percentage of all students with disabilities who are labeled learning-disabled. In Table 13.3, we present the most recent federal data on the prevalence of learning disabilities in the schools. As can be seen in the table, the trend reflects an increasing percentage of students in general being identified as learning disabled and a parallel increase in the percentage of students with disabilities who are labeled LD (through 1992–1993). These changes come after an increase of approximately 60 percent in the number of students identified as learning-disabled between 1976–1977 and 1987–1988. It could be argued that learning disabilities virtually has become the noncategorical special education approach for which many have clamored. Extrapolations from Table 13.3 would seem to imply that in the future, the clear majority of all children with disabilities will be identified as learning-disabled.

In terms of the effects of these trends, reactions are already being noted and will likely continue. For example, the proposal of the U.S. Department of Education (1995) to fund states based on their school population rather than the numbers of students identified is one obvious such response to the increased prevalence of students identified as learning disabled. In a quite different arena, the number of needed teachers for LD programs remains significant, representing 27.4 percent of the reported national shortage of special education teachers (with an additional 23.4 percent of the shortage being for cross-categorically certified teachers—presumably including learning disabilities) (U.S. Department of Education, 1995).

TABLE 13.3

Prevalence Trends in Learning Disabilities (Ages Six-Seventeen)

Year	LD as Percent of School Population	LD as Percent of Special Education
1987–1988	4.41	48.6
1988–1989	4.55	49.3
1989–1990	4.79	50.1
1990–1991	4.89	50.5
1991–1992	N/A	51.3
1992–1993	5.25	52.4
1993–1994	5.28	51.1

Source: U.S. Department of Education (1990, 1991, 1992, 1993, 1994, 1995). *Annual reports to Congress on the implementation of the IDEA.* Washington, D.C.: Author.

It has been argued that definitional and classification difficulties have been major contributors to the trend toward higher prevalence figures in the field of learning disabilities. While the argument would be that change continues to occur in the definition (see NJCLD, 1988), the numbers continue to move forward and suggest a greater discrepancy between the concept of learning disabilities (i.e., intrinsic disabilities, presumed to be due to CNS dysfunction) and the nature of the population of students as labeled. Moats and Lyon (1993) suggested that:

> Thus, learning disabilities in the United States appears to be a systemic problem: It is an educational category into which children are channeled when the learning-teaching interaction is no longer productive or rewarding for one or both parties. The reality of learning disabilities in schools is thus removed from the abstract issues of definition, classification, and experimental criteria that might provide the cornerstones of a science of developmental learning disorders (p. 284).

Whether such a trend should be cause for serious concern (due to the blurring of the lines between learning disabilities and learning problems) (Adelman, 1992) or whether these increases likely could reflect the relative newness of the field and the social/cultural changes in America (Hallahan, 1992) awaits further attention. In addition, the recent federal initiatives advocating a noncategorical approach to eligibility will also add to this identification quandary. As proposed by the 1995 IDEA Amendments, the emphasis would be to

> promote less categorical approaches to eligibility determinations by eliminating the requirement that States classify children by particular disability category, so long as all children who are currently eligible are served. This would permit states to move toward less categorical eligibility criteria and promote a focus on what children know and what services they need rather than on what disability label they should be given (U.S. Department of Education, 1995, p. 4).

The challenges for the future are thus clear. Either the field of learning disabilities must establish a defensible system of conceptualization, definition, classification, and identification or it will continue to risk the dangers explicit in the attacks on the field (e.g., Coles, 1987) or implicit in the modification of state and federal regulations. What seems most clear is that maintenance of the status quo will not be possible. Professionals must therefore be proactive or allow their field to be shaped by outside, and often less-informed, forces.

▶ INTERVENTIONS

Of greatest significance to professionals in the field of learning disabilities are the emerging directions in the area of interventions. While it is beyond the scope of this chapter to highlight, for example, specific strategies with promise, we focus instead on general considerations in the areas of curriculum and instruction, inclusion, adult support, and technology that will be components of our considerations in the coming years.

Curriculum and Instruction

The foundation of the field of special education in general, and learning disabilities in particular, is the provision of appropriate educational interventions to individual students who need them in order to achieve their maximum potential. If there is one area where virtually every professional can affect the future of this field, it is here. However, it is unfortunate that, to date, we have not found a way to wrestle with the issue of most effective practices and resolve what is best for the students with learning disabilities for whom we advocate.

Kauffman (1994), borrowing from Fritz Redl, refers to the quandary we are in as "implementational sins," that is, failing to place into practice what we know to be true or valid. He further notes that therefore the field is justifiably

> vulnerable to severe criticism from others—and should be severely self-critical—for. . . not delivering the high-quality, individualized, effective instruction that we promised to students with learning disabilities and other disabling conditions. We have not applied to the daily practice of special education what we know, on the basis of reliable empirical evidence, to be the best practices in instruction and behavior management, nor have we insisted on what we believe to be the best practices in teacher education, teacher certification, or program administration (p. 611).

Consistent with these concerns, Moats and Lyon (1993) provide an apt challenge for the future:

> A science of learning disabilities will ultimately rest on our ability to show that once a disorder is identified, we know what to do to help the individual. Building a foundation of validated interventions will be a very complex and challenging task, one that will not be accomplished even in a few years... Directly put, what are the instructional conditions that must be in place for a child to learn, retain, and generalize concepts? (p. 290)

These challenges provide a focus for the future of the field as it relates to curriculum and instruction. Given the primary attention that has always been given to educational aspects of learning disabilities, it becomes increasingly urgent that the field coalesce into some level of agreement as to what constitutes best practices. The LD field seems particularly vulnerable from both of its sides: on the one hand, it has too often acquiesced to pseudo-scientific quack responses to problems that reflect quick cures to significant problems (Worrall, 1990) (see Chapter 4) while on the other hand it functions within the broader field of education where non-validated instructional methods and curriculum are virtually legendary and where social and political changes regularly take precedence over research and validated practice in the design of instructional programs.

One area that currently, and for the foreseeable future, presents a special dilemma is the debate between those advocating direct instruction, skills-based educational approaches (e.g., DISTAR) versus those advocating holistic instructional approaches (e.g., whole language). These two seemingly oppositional positions have been argued extensively elsewhere (see Mather, 1992). However, the focus of the future should be to still the rhetoric and develop ways to integrate validated aspects from both approaches. The challenge, thus restated, is for a reasoned empirical effort to validate effective practices (Lyon, 1995) and then move on to the equally daunting task of insuring the adoption of such approaches to meet childrens' needs in the classroom. Lovitt (1992, p. 25) succinctly noted this:

> Currently, hundreds of practices and procedures designed for youngsters with disabilities are available. Whereas there was a great need to devise tactics and techniques for children with learning disabilities in the 1960s, for there were few of them, there is not as pressing a need today. What we need now are educators and researchers to sort through those ideas, identify ones that are effective, paraphrase them, and publish or otherwise present them in places where practitioners can find them (p. 25).

Central to the efforts sketched above should be the acceptance of the fact that no single method will work for all students with learning disabilities (Mather and Rhia, 1994) or, it could also be argued, for any student all of the time. While there is little evidence to date of the predominence of designing interventions based on a true research-to-practice model, there is no doubt that accountability issues will become more pronounced in the future. Particular responsibility falls on teacher educators to help effect this match, by stressing the implementation of validated interventions and by training teachers to view themselves as classroom researchers. Recent initiatives, such as action research, offer promise for the future in this regard.

School Inclusion

Individuals with learning disabilities have been a focal point in the debates concerning the most appropriate placement of students with special needs and presumably this will be likely to continue. With the mandate in the Individuals with Disabilities Education Act to serve students in the least restrictive environment, service delivery systems increasingly have included greater reliance on resource rooms and general education classroom combinations. The movement to integrate students with disabilities was based on several reasons, including the failure of efficacy studies to demonstrate clear benefits for segregated programs (Polloway, 1984), the need for opportunities for interaction between students with disabilities and their nondisabled peers (Roberts, Pratt, and Leach, 1991), the hope of improved opportunities for social interaction, and the presumed improved academic performance for students educated in the mainstream (Stevens and Slavin, 1991).

Federal data reflect the fact that most students with learning disabilities continue to be served with part-time placement in resource rooms and, implicitly, the majority of their school day in general education classes (U.S. Department of Education, 1994) (see Table 13.4). In fact, recent research from general education teachers is consistent with those findings, with 97 percent of these teachers indicating they had taught students with learning disabilities in their classes (Bursuck, Polloway, Plante, Epstein, Jayanthi, and McConeghy, in press). To look into the future, it would appear that extrapolation from the data in Table 13.3 would suggest that within the next five years that perhaps

The inclusion of students with learning disabilities in general education classes continues to be the predominant trend in placement.

half or more of students with learning disabilities will receive virtually their entire education in the general education classroom and that a decreasing number will be offered resource or separate class services.

TABLE 13.4

Placement Trends for Students with Learning Disabilities (Ages Six–Twenty-One)[1]

	Regular Class	Resource Room	Separate Class	Separate Facilities	Residential Facilities
1986–1987[2]	15.8	60.4	21.4	1.7	0.1
1987–1988	17.6	59.2	21.7	1.4	0.1
1988–1989	19.6	57.9	20.9	1.3	0.1
1989–1990	20.7	56.1	21.7	1.3	0.1
1990–1991	22.5	53.7	22.4	1.1	0.1
1991–1992	24.7	54.2	20.0	0.9	0.1
1992–1993	34.8	43.9	20.1	0.8	0.2

Sources: U.S. Department of Education (1990, 1991, 1992, 1993, 1994, 1995). *Annual reports to Congress on the implementation of the IDEA.* Washington, D.C.: Author.

Notes: [1]All numbers are percentages, rounded to one decimal place. [2]Based on ages 3–21.

These data represent an outcome of the trend begun in the 1980s when the Regular Education Initiative (REI) was introduced as a way to "normalize" the lives of students with disabilities. As Polloway et al. (in press) noted, this movement called for the dismantling of the dichotomous educational system (general education and special education) and for serving most students with disabilities in general education programs, with the REI's particular initial focus being students with learning disabilities and other students with mild disabilities (Will, 1984; Wang, Reynolds, and Walberg, 1989). By the late 1980s, the concept expanded to include calls for the inclusion of all students with disabilities in general education. The full inclusion movement has been particularly driven by attention to students with severe disabilities (Fuchs and Fuchs, 1994; Snell and Drake, 1994) although it clearly also has, and will have, important implications for students with learning disabilities (Mather and Roberts, 1995).

The full inclusion movement has received varied professional receptions (see Kauffman and Hallahan, 1994) which are reflected in the positions on inclusion which several professional and advocacy groups have taken. Table 13.5 briefly summarizes the positions of several of these groups. As can be seen, it is interesting to note that typically the most cautionary approaches have been taken by the organizations that focus on learning disabilities while what might be deemed the pre-eminent pro-inclusion stances have been advocated by a parents' organization in mental retardation (i.e., the ARC) and a professional organization in the severe disabilities field (i.e., TASH). These latter groups have an apparent focus on social integration as opposed to the focus of LD advocacy groups which rather appear to be emphasizing more academic and curricular issues and reflecting more serious concerns for the educational success of inclusion. In fact, for example, a recent survey indicated that 98 percent of parents of children with learning disabilities believed that general educators were not adequately trained to educate their children (Ellis and Cramer, 1994).

The inclusion concept has evolved from a philosophical ideal to increasingly become at least implicit public policy. This process has dismayed many as they review the effects on special education and students with disabilities and as they project future outcomes. Kauffman (in press) has been a particularly strident critic. He observed:

> For decades, special educators have found coherence, unity, and mutual support in the notion that we should celebrate the diversity of the characteristics of children and youth. We have been, to be sure, congregated and united by our dedication to the task of changing for the better the characteristics of our students who have disabilities. Yet we are in no way disparaging of the students whose characteristics we hope to change. We value these young people in all their diversity for who they are. I hope our profession will soon stop disparaging special placements and see renewed value in promoting a diversity of alternatives. For a variety of reasons, our profession has been seriously divided, and therefore weakened, by the ideology of full inclusion. The doctrine of full inclusion defines diversity of placement as morally suspect.... It seeks the elimination of placement options under the assumption that only one environment can be least restrictive, that the regular classroom is the promised land of all children (p. 25).

TABLE 13.5

Comparison of Positions of Advocacy Groups on Inclusion

Organization	Continuum of Services	Full Inclusion
The Arc (formerly Association for Retarded Citizens)	not required	strongly support
Division on Mental Retardation and Developmental Disabilities (MRDD, CEC)	maintain	based strictly on individual needs
Learning Disabilities Association (LDA)	maintain	based strictly on individual needs
National Joint Committee on Learning Disabilities (NJCLD)	maintain	based strictly on individual needs
The Association for Persons with Severe Handicaps (TASH)	not required	strongly support

Source: Polloway, E.A., Patton, J.R., Smith, T.E.C., and Buck, G.H. (in press). Mental retardation and learning disabilities: Conceptual and applied issues, *Journal of Learning Disabilities*.

In the future, it is clear that inclusion must represent more than just a philosophical ideal but a careful plan for the successes of every student as well. In order to achieve this, the National Center on Educational Restructuring and Inclusion (as cited by AEL, 1995) reported that successful programs were characterized by the following general factors:

- visionary leadership that is positive and optimistic
- collaborative assistance between teachers with team planning
- refocused use of assessment to emphasize student needs
- sufficient support for staff
- alternative funding formulae that are not derived from enrollment in separate programs
- active and effective parent involvement

One key element from the above list that deserves special mention is collaboration. The increasing evidence of true cooperative endeavors in education between special and general education teachers represent the most promising future for inclusive schooling (see Bauwens and Hourcade, 1995). Such efforts must be refined and promoted in order to not only benefit students on an ongoing basis but, also to ensure that the future does not lead to a reduction of special education positions (due to perceived lack of need given the inclusion of students with learning disabilities), a distinct possibility in challenging economic times.

In addition to the above, another obvious factor is to design programs that provide appropriate accommodations for students. One way to focus on this is to consider the concept of supports.

Supports. Increasingly, in the 1990s, the concept of supports has been used to refer to approaches which facilitate successful inclusion. For example, the recent classification system of the American Association on Mental Retardation (AAMR; Luckasson et al., 1992) focuses on consideration of levels of *supports* rather than on levels of *severity* as in previous systems. This approach presents an intriguing model for possible consideration and adaptation within the field of learning disabilities. The respective levels of support are as follows (Luckasson, et al., 1992, p. 26):

- *Intermittent:* Supports on an "as-needed basis." Characterized by episodic nature, person not always needing the support(s), or short-term supports needed during life-span transitions.
- *Limited:* An intensity of supports characterized by consistency over time, time-limited but not of an intermittent nature, may require fewer staff members and less cost than more intense levels of support (e.g., time-limited employment training or transitional supports during the school to adult period).
- *Extensive:* Supports characterized by regular involvement (e.g., daily) in at least some environments (such as work or home) and not time-limited (e.g., long-term support and long-term home living support).
- *Pervasive:* Supports characterized by their constancy, high intensity; provided across environments; potential life-sustaining nature.

A supports model formally shifts the focus away from a deficit-oriented emphasis and more toward an emphasis on potentials, with clear applications into adulthood. Further, this approach presumes that successful outcomes are not linked just to educational and other related services but clearly are based on familial, societal, and technological considerations that comprise a broader concept of supports. In the field of learning disabilities, there has been periodic mention of the concepts of mild and severe learning disabilities, but these terms never have been effectively operationalized or widely used. However, the emerging concept of levels of supports provides an attractive classification alternative to a severity model particularly when it is considered within the context of school inclusion. For example, much of the concern that has been raised about full inclusion for students with learning disabilities could be productively re-channeled if the alternative concept of "supported education" (Hamre-Nietupski, MacDonald, and Nietupski, 1992; Snell and Drake, 1994) was substituted. Under this concept, the focus is logically placed not solely on the achievement of integrated placement but rather on the quality of supports (e.g., by collaboration with special education teachers, by paraprofessionals, through peers) that is needed and subsequently provided within general education to ensure that students make appropriate educational progress. The compelling aspect of this concept is that students placed in general education classes can have their needs defined in a way that outlines necessary supports (e.g., time-limited for instruction on sight words; intermittent in terms of follow-up for generalization training or retention of study skill strategies). Such a perspective is preferable to views which either presume deficits are too significant to allow inclusion or presume that placement alone generates success. For the future, a supports model also offers a philosophical basis for affirming the essential nature of collaboration.

Emphasis on Adulthood[1]

One key concern within the area of interventions will be to ensure that programs effectively prepare students for the transition into adulthood. The trends within federal data on school exit provide a useful way to view the future challenges in this area. These data are in Table 13.6. Of particular importance is the data on school dropouts; clearly school completion is critical for adolescents and young adults who are disabled. When the data on drop-out rates are combined with unknown exit—likely to include drop-outs as well—the overall trend is not a positive one for students with learning disabilities (i.e., 34.2 percent in 1986–1987 vs. 39.0 percent in 1991–1992). The clear challenge is to increase the number of students receiving diplomas—a trend that recently can be described as flat at best—while decreasing the number of students leaving early via the drop-out route.

These outcomes data are most important when placed in the context of subsequent challenges for adult adjustment. Recently many professionals in the field

[1]Portions of this section were adapted from Polloway, Patton, Smith, and Buck (in press) and are used with permission.

TABLE 13.6

Basis for Exit From School for Students with Learning Disabilities

	Diploma	Certificate	Age Out	Drop Out	Unknown Exit
1986–1987	54.5	10.2	1.0	26.1	8.1
1987–1988	47.8	8.5	0.7	26.7	16.3
1988–1989	50.1	6.9	1.3	26.7	15.0
1989–1990	51.9	10.0	0.5	26.8	10.9
1990–1991	51.7	10.8	0.7	22.2	14.7
1991–1992	49.7	10.8	0.5	21.3	17.7
1992–1993*					

*Data for 1992–1993 were modified in reporting format and are not comparable.

Sources: U.S. Department of Education (1990, 1991, 1992, 1993, 1994, 1995). *Annual reports to Congress on the implementation of the IDEA.* Washington, D.C.: Author.

Note: All numbers are percentages, rounded to one decimal place.

of learning disabilities have been championing the lifelong needs of persons who
are disabled. One clear example is the incorporation of adult concerns into the
1990 NJCLD definition stating that learning disabilities "may occur across the
life span" (NJCLD, 1994, p. 65). This awakening has occurred for various reasons, most notably the heightened attention to the postschool needs of adults.
The need to qualify for services such as those provided by the disabilities programs of postsecondary education institutions or those afforded thorough vocational rehabilitation accentuates the need for advocacy for the fact that a learning
disability does not end with childhood. The excerpts from interviews with adults
with learning disabilities in Box 13.2 clearly underscore this fact.

The emphasis on adulthood has become particularly noticeable in recent
years in the learning disabilities literature. For example, Patton and Polloway
(1992) illustrated the trend toward increased attention to such a pattern in their
analysis of papers published in the field (see Figure 13.1). An extrapolation of
these data would suggest that the field of LD increasingly will attend to adult
needs in the future.

The emerging focus on adulthood will take on several manifestations. A
first key consideration in the future will be on a careful review of the vocational
and non-vocational demands of adulthood. To function successfully as an
adult, one must display varying degrees of competence in dealing with those
events or activities typically encountered in everyday life. Specific competencies
can be organized in a variety of ways such as areas of major life activity, adaptive skills areas, or adult domains. These competencies apply to all adults.

The area of employment is obviously particularly significant for a consideration of the demands of adulthood. As discussed earlier in the book, the commitment to transition planning for successful careers has increased dramatically
in the field of learning disabilities in recent years. The future promises a more
refined process of transitioning from school to work, further development of
employment alternatives, and availability of subsequent postsecondary training
to develop and/or enhance job success.

Adulthood demands are best considered within the context of needed supports. One way to conceptualize the different types of supports (as defined earlier) available or potentially needed is to consider various options as concentric
circles emanating from the center. If the individual is at the center of this
model, the next circle is family and friends followed by non-paid supports,
generic services, and specialized services across a variety of community contexts. This idea fits well with looking comprehensively at the many demands
presented in adulthood for persons with learning disabilities. The movement
toward the concept that individuals may need different types and degrees of
support is an important one for the future.

Most individuals with learning disabilities have always had family and
friends, non-paid services (e.g., volunteers), and generic services (i.e., those
available to all citizens) at their disposal. However, these options often have not
been extremely useful because they were not accessed, not helpful, or not utilized properly. Enhancements will be necessary here if the future is to write
most positive outcomes for adults with learning disabilities.

| Box 13.2 | *Voices of Adults with Learning Disabilities* |

- I have an extremely supportive family who has helped me through my educational goals. I also had a tutor for eight years who helped me reach my fullest potential. My tutor was an inspiration. . . we became great friends. In high school I had to stop working with the tutor because they thought I was too dependent. My tutor built my self-confidence. . . concentrated on what I could do. I had ideas but couldn't write them so she taped them and then I listened and wrote them. . . had a wonderful guidance counselor in high school who was "tough love."

I get very defensive still. . . and am afraid to ask questions in fear that I will be wrong. Every teacher should remember their worst class when they were in school and realize that that's how LD kids feel all of the time.

- I faked my way through school because I was very bright. I resent most that no one picked up my weaknesses. Essentially I judge myself on my failures. . . have always had low self-esteem. In hindsight I feel that I had low self-esteem in college. . . I was afraid to know myself. A blow to my self-esteem when I was in school was that I could not write a poem or a story. . . I could not write with a pen or pencil.

- I didn't finish school the normal way. . . Quit college. . . went out West. . . stayed 4–5 years. . . was a ski bum. . . waitress. I knew I wanted to do something else. . . Met a guy who wanted to experiment by hiring a person with a limited education. Then he realized that I needed a college education so I went back to school. . . worked as a sales assistant. Now I am a portfolio manager.

I don't think I've ever given myself enough credit. . . 50 percent of the time the guy I now work for doesn't make me feel good. I'm still dealing with all of this.

- When I was in school, someone knocked all of my confidence out of me when I was little. . . so I'm always working on that. That can still hurt me. . . I think about it a lot. . . I think of my whole school experience as being a bad experience. . . horrifying. Thank God for swimming. . . that kept me going. This gave me two-sidedness in my personality. . . I have lots of confidence in some situations and none in others. I was so lucky to have a mother who was as astute as she was. . . She encouraged me into swimming. . . she could see how frustrated I was and she was helpful.

- I do remember feeling different. . . It didn't seem like anyone else was the same. . . I felt stupid, so I didn't ever want to tell anyone [I was learning disabled].

- Now I wish I could go to community college, but I don't have the money. I'm stuck in my job. . . I have four kids and it's rough! . . . Nothing in my school classes helped me in the job market. . . my memory of the programs is that they just kept me going enough to pass. . . I tried to do it but just couldn't keep up in English.

- Sports helped me make contacts. . . I played baseball with a man who is my boss. . . so I made contacts that helped me later. . . Went to Vo-Tech to take food service. . . I liked it. . .

- Because I'm aware of my problems I live with a dictionary. . . Sometimes I can spell the word correctly but not have the confidence that it's correct. I'm very much a perfectionist because of my disability. I want the best. . . I check everything over.

- I remember feeling dumb. . . One teacher told me I'd never go to college. I can't wait to go back to show her my degree. I had moments of discouragement. This was not reinforced by my parents or friends that mattered. . .

- My LD class experience has never been memorable. . . the majority weren't positive. LD teachers were into remediation not accommodation. Accommodation is me taking my time to get things done correctly. . . If I write very slowly I can make legible letters.

Source: Adapted from Polloway, E.A., Schewel, R., and Patton, J.R. (1992). Learning disabilities in adulthood: Personal perspectives. *Journal of Learning Disabilities, 25*, p. 520–522.

FIGURE 13.1

Adult Focus in the LD Literature

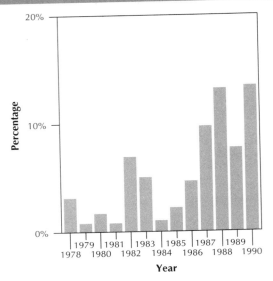

LDQ Articles

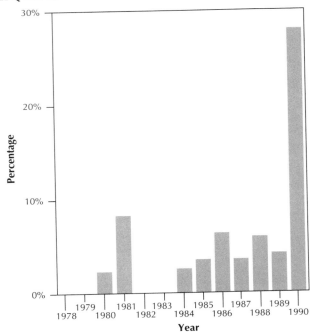

Source: Patton, J.R., and Polloway, E. A. (1992). Learning disabilities: The challenges of adulthood. *Journal of Learning Disabilities, 25*, p. 411–412.

The ultimate focus of instructional programs and adult support systems should be the empowerment of the individual. Clearly the focus on empowerment and self-determination has been a significant achievement of the 1990s in shifting emphasis from what can be done for the individual to what can be done by the individual. Polloway, Smith, Patton, and Smith (in press) presented a working model for empowerment (see Figure 13.2) based on the work of Geller (1990). In the model, specific aspects of life that enhance the empowerment of the individual are identified. Since the literature on empowerment and the related concept of self-determination is a relatively recent development, it is in the future when we can anticipate fully realizing its promise. In particular, the results of a series of federal research programs on self-determination will soon begin to impact on practice. One key aspect will be self-advocacy, a critical necessity for individuals with learning disabilities. There is already increasing evidence that self-advocacy is an emerging focus of many curricula for adolescents and young adults who are learning disabled. Another important area will be consumer empowerment, as individuals with learning disabilities

FIGURE 13.2

Model of Empowerment

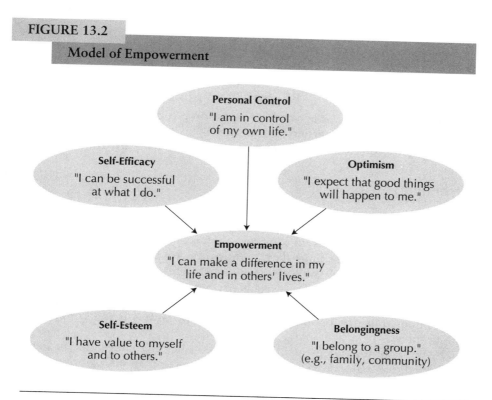

Source: Geller, S. E. (1994b). Ten principles for achieving a total safety culture. *Professional Safety*. Adapted by Polloway, Smith, Patton, and Smith (in press). Historic changes in mental retardation and developmental disabilities. *Education and Training in Mental Retardation and Developmental Disabilities.*

The empowerment of adults with learning disabilities should be the ultimate focus of instructional programs and adult support systems.

will increasingly define the nature of services and supports that they require. Ultimately, the future will be determined by the success of the individual with learning disabilities; his or her ability to develop competence will become the key variable as artificial barriers created through discriminatory attitudes and non-responsive educational and employment environments are transformed.

Technology

Clearly, a major factor in shaping the future will be the increased reliance on technology. To date, technology has been both challenge and boon to persons with disabilities. Thus, in some areas it has decreased the need for additional employees in positions that might otherwise have been occupied by those with disabilities. In addition, lack of widespread training opportunities in technological fields has been particularly problematic in general, and even more so for those with disabilities. At the same time, assistive technology has created numerous new opportunities for others by addressing their functional limitations.

The future of technology and the field of learning disabilities was the focus of Raskind, Herman, and Torgesen's (1995) report on an international symposium in this area. Raskind et al. indicated six purposes for technology: remediation, instruction, compensation, assessment, information access, and the fostering of special talents and abilities (p. 177). These authors summarized the views of symposium presenters in noting that future attention needs to be given to the following issues:

- the social benefits of technology in enhancing peer relationships around common interests;
- the risk of social isolationism due to reliance on computers in lieu of social interactions;
- the potential power of computers to overcome learned helplessness and to enhance self-concept;
- the use of the computer to extend the role of the teacher rather than re-place her;
- the beneficial impact of technology on assessment, especially with the in-creased use of new medical technologies (e.g., magnetic resource imaging); and
- the importance of technology access to all persons with learning disabilities who could benefit from such access.

Perhaps the central principle of future use of technology is the need for deliberate ethical considerations of the implications of technology on the lives of individuals with learning disabilities. Raskind et al. (1995, p. 183) conclud-ed by noting the obligation that professionals will have in the future "to care-fully consider the full ramifications of technology use with individuals with learning disabilities, cautioning against blindly promoting its utilization without adequate reflection and research." While it is virtually impossible to project the future with any confidence in terms of how technology will influence our lives, there is little doubt that developments in this field will represent major deter-minants in the future lives of persons with learning disabilities.

▶ CONCLUSION

In her discussion of research directions for the future of the field, Keogh (1994) identified priorities that should be addressed for the year 2000. In doing so, she quoted from Kauffman (1981, p. 10) when he said that "change is a commod-ity special educators have seen in abundance—progress has always been in short supply." This perspective is a useful one as we view the future. The needs of persons with learning disabilities will best be served if we accept necessary changes that have demonstrated the power to positively affect the individual and help them progress to reaching their potential and a possible quality of life.

SUMMARY

This chapter has presented information about some emerging issues in the field of learning disabilities. The following points summarize the major areas includ-ed in the chapter:

- While the future is difficult to predict, extrapolations from current trends provide useful ways to consider likely future outcomes.

- Demographic trends in the United States suggest major changes and provide a foundation for understanding learning disabilities in the future.
- Societal transformations must be considered as a basis for appreciating demands on persons with learning disabilities in the future.
- Definitional and identification issues continue to be in flux but are critical to the survival of the field.
- Curriculum and instruction orientations are often seen as in opposition to each other while a balanced approach is most fruitful.
- Inclusion is the key trend in the field of the 1990s.
- Collaboration between special and general education teachers is an essential component of inclusion.
- The concept of supports is an important one for the field of learning disabilities to embrace in the future.
- Adult concerns must be paramount in any consideration of the needs of individuals with learning disabilities.
- Technology advances represent boons and challenges to the field of learning disabilities. Careful consideration of the use of technology will be critical to the assurance of future benefits.

References

Abikoff, H. (1991). Cognitive training in ADHD children: Less to it than meets the eye. *Journal of Learning Disabilities, 24* (4), 205–209.

Ackerman, P.T., and Dykman, R.A. (1993). Phonological processes, confrontational naming, and immediate memory in dyslexia. *Journal of Learning Disabilities, 26* (9), 1993.

Adelman, H.S. (1992). LD: The next 25 years. *Journal of Learning Disabilities, 25,* 17–22.

Adelman, P.B., and Vogel, S.A. (1990). College graduates with learning disabilities—employment attainment and career patterns. *Learning Disability Quarterly, 13,* 154–167.

Adelman, P.B., and Vogel, S.A. (1993). Issues in the employment of adults with learning disabilities. *Learning Disability Quarterly, 16* (3), 219–232.

AEL (1995). National survey identifies inclusive education practices. *The Link, 14* (1), 7–8.

Allen, K.E. (1992). *The exceptional child: Mainstreaming in early childhood education* (2nd Ed.). Albany, NY: Delmar Publishers.

Alper, S.K., Schloss, P.J., and Schloss, C.N. (1994). *Families of students with disabilities: Consultation and advocacy.* Boston: Allyn and Bacon.

American Council on Education and Education Commission of the States. (1988). *One-third of a nation: A report by the Commission on Minority Participation in Education and American Life.* Washington, DC: Author.

American Council on Education. (1987). *American freshman: National norms.* Los Angeles: University of California.

Americans with Disabilities Act, P.L. 101–336, signed into law July 26, 1990.

Anderson, A.H., and Novina, J. (1973). A study of the relationship of the tests of Central Auditory Abilities and the Illinois Test of Psycholinguistic Abilities. *Journal of Learning Disabilities, 6,* 167–170.

Anderson, B. W. (1992). [Letter to the editor]. *American Journal of Psychiatry, 149,* 148-149.

Anderson, G.R., and Anderson, S.K. (1983). The exceptional Native American. In D.R. Omark and J.G. Erickson (Eds.), *The bilingual exceptional child* (pp. 163–180). Boston: College-Hill.

Arc (1995, Summer). Center reports more babies being born with FAS. *The Arc Today, 44* (2), 1, 3.

Astin, A., Green, K., Korn, W., Schalit, M., and Berg, E. (1988). *The American freshman: National norms for 1988.* Los Angeles: University of California.

Atkinson, R.C., and Shiffrin, R.M. (1971). The control of short-term memory. *Scientific American, 225,* 85–90.

Baca, L.C., and Almanza, E. (1991). *Language minority students with disabilities.* Reston, VA: Council for Exceptional Children.

Baca, L., and Lane, K. (1974). Dialogue on cultural implications for learning. *Exceptional Children, 40,* 552.

Bakker, D.J. (1990). *Neuropsychological treatment of dyslexia.* New York: Oxford University Press.

Barsch, R.H. (1992). Perspectives on learning disabilities: The vectors of a new convergence. *Journal of Learning Disabilities, 25,* 6–16.

Bateman, B. (1992). Learning disabilities: The changing landscape. *Journal of Learning Disabilities, 25,* 29–36.

Bauwens, J., and Hourcade, J. (1995). *Cooperative teaching: Rebuilding the schoolhouse for all students.* Austin: PRO-ED.

Bear, G.G., Juvonen, J., and McInerney, F. (1993). Self-perceptions and peer relations of boys with and boys without learning disabilities in an integrated setting: A longitudinal study. *Learning Disability Quarterly, 16* (2), 127–136.

Becker, J.T., and Sabatino, D.A. (1973). Frostig revisited. *Journal of Learning Disabilities, 6,* 180–184.

Bedard, E. (1995). Collaboration in educational planning: A parent's perspective. *LD Forum, 20,* 23–25.

Bell, D., Feraios, A.J., and Bryan, T. (1991). Learning disabled adolescent's knowledge and attitudes about AIDS. *Learning Disabilities Research and Practice, 6,* 94–111.

Belmont, I., Flegenheimer, H., and Birch, H.G. (1973). Comparison of perceptual training and remedial instruction for poor beginning readers. *Journal of Learning Disabilities, 6,* 230–236.

Bender, B. G., Puck, M. H., Salbenblatt, J. A., and Robinson, A. (1986). Cognitive development of children with sex chromosome abnormalities. In S. D. Smith (Ed.), *Genetics and learning disabilities* (pp. 175–201). San Diego: College-Hill Press.

Bender, B., Puck, M., Salbenblatt, J., and Robinson, A. (1984). Cognitive development of unselected girls with complete and partial X monosomy. *Pediatrics, 73,* 175–182.

Bender, B. (1995). *Introduction to learning disabilities.* Boston: Allyn and Bacon.

Bibace, R., and Hancock, K. (1969). Relationship between perceptual and conceptual cognitive processes. *Journal of Learning Disabilities, 2,* 17–25.

Binkard, B. (1985). A successful handicap awareness program-Run by special parents. *Teaching Exceptional Children, 18,* 12–16.

Blachman, B.A. (1994). What we have learned from longitudinal studies of phonological processing and reading, and some unanswered questions: A response to Torgeson, Wagner, and Rashotte. *Journal of Learning Disabilities, 27* (5), 287–291.

Blalock, G., and Patton, J.R. (1996). Transition and students with learning disabilities: Creating sound futures. *Journal of Learning Disabilities, 29,* 7–16.

Blalock, G. (1996a). Community transition teams as the foundation for transition services for youth with learning disabilities. *Journal of Learning Disabilities, 29* (2), 148–159.

Blalock, G. (1997). Transition education. In D.D. Smith and D.P. Rivera, *Teaching students with learning and behavior problems* (3rd ed.). Boston: Allyn and Bacon.

Blalock, G. (1996b). Transition of youth with learning disabilities to early adulthood. In J.R. Patton and E.A. Polloway (Eds.), *Learning disabilities: The challenges of adulthood.* Austin, TX: PRO-ED.

Blalock, G., Brito, C., Chenault, B., Detwiler, B., Hessmiller, R., Husted, D., Oney, D., Putnam, P., and Van Dyke, R. (1994). *Life span transition planning in New Mexico: A technical assistance document.* Santa Fe, NM: N.M. State Department of Education.

Blalock, J. W. (1987a). Auditory language disorders. In D. J. Johnson and J. W. Blalock (Eds.), *Adults with learning disabilities* (pp. 81–105). Orlando: Grune and Stratton.

Blalock, J. W. (1987b). Problems in mathematics. In D. J. Johnson and J. W. Blalock (Eds.), *Adults with learning disabilities* (pp. 205–217). Orlando: Grune and Stratton.

Blalock, J. W. (1981). Persistent problems and concerns of young adults with learning disabilities. In W. M. Cruickshank and A. A. Silver (Eds.), *Bridges to tomorrow: The best of ACLD,* (Vol. 2, pp. 53–54). Syracuse, NY: Syracuse University Press.

Blalock, G., and Dixon, N. (1982). Improving prospects for the college-bound learning disabled. *Topics in Learning Disabilities, 2* (3), 67–78.

Bluechardt, M.H., and Shephard, R.J. (1995). Using an extracurricular physical activity program to enhance social skills. *Journal of Learning Disabilities, 28* (3), 160–169.

Boder, E. (1973). Developmental dyslexia: A diagnostic approach based on three atypical reading-spelling patterns. *Developmental Medicine and Child Neurology, 15,* 663–687.

Bogdan, R. (1986). The sociology of special education. In R.J. Morris and B.Blatt (Eds.), *Special education: Research and trends* (pp. 344–359). Elmsford, NY: Pergamon Press.

Bos, C.S., and Vaughn, S. (1994). *Strategies for teaching students with learning and behavior problems* (3rd ed.). Boston: Allyn and Bacon.

Bosch, H. (1994). Independent living services and programs: Integration into the community. In C. A. Michaels (Ed.), *Transition strategies for persons with learning disabilities* (pp. 213–238). San Diego: Singular Publishing Group, Inc.

Bozinou-Doukas, E. (1983). Learning disability: The case of the bilingual child. In D.R. Omark and J.G. Erickson (Eds.), *The bilingual exceptional child* (pp. 213–232). Boston: College-Hill.

Brinckerhoff, L.C., Shaw, S.F., and McGuire, J.M. (1993). *Promoting postsecondary education for students with learning disabilities.* Austin, TX: PRO-ED.

Brinckerhoff, L. C. (1985). Accommodations for college students with learning disabilities: The law and implementation. In *Support services for LD students in Postsecondary education: A compendium of readings* (pp. 1–7). Columbus, OH: Association on Handicapped Student Service Programs in Postsecondary Education.

Brinckerhoff, L. C., Shaw, S. F., and McGuire, J. M. (1992). Promoting access, accommodations, and independence for college students with learning disabilities. *Journal of Learning Disabilities, 25,* 417–429.

Brinckerhoff, L.C., Shaw, S.F., and McGuire, J.M. (1996). Promoting access, accommodations, and independence for college students with learning disabilities. In J.R. Patton and E.A. Polloway (Eds.), *Learning disabilities: The challenges of adulthood.* Austin, TX: PRO-ED.

Brody, L.E., and Mills, C.J. (in press). Gifted children with learning disabilities: A review of the issues. *Journal of Learning Disabilities.*

Brolin, D.E. (1995a). *Career education: A functional life skills approach* (3rd ed.). Englewood Cliffs, NJ: Prentice Hall.

Brolin, D.E. (1995b). Foreword. In P.J. Schloss, M.A. Smith, and C.N. Schloss, *Instructional methods for adolescents with learning and behavior problems* (2nd ed.). Boston: Allyn and Bacon.

Brolin, D.E. (1993). *Life-centered career education: A competency-based approach (4th Ed.).* Reston, VA: The Council for Exceptional Children.

Bronheim, S. (1991). An educator's guide to Tourette syndrome. *Journal of Learning Disabilities, 24,* 17–22.

Brooks-Gunn, J., McCarton, C., and Hawley, T. (1994). Effects of in utero drug exposure on children's development. *Archives of Pediatrics and Adolescent Medicine, 148,* 33–39.

Brotherson, M.J., Berdine, W.H., and Sartini, V. (1993). Transition to adult services: Support for ongoing parent participation. *Remedial and Special Education, 14* (4), 44–51.

Brown, R.T. (1993). An introduction to the special series: Pediatric chronic illness. *Journal of Learning Disabilities, 26,* 4–6.

Brown, R., Armstrong, F.D., and Eckman, J.R. (1993). Neurocognitive aspects of pediatric sickle cell disease. *Journal of Learning Disabilities, 26,* 33–45.

Brolin, D.E. (1995). *Career education: A functional life skills approach* (3rd ed.). Englewood Cliffs, NJ: Prentice Hall.

Brown, D., and Moore, L. (1992). The bama bookworm program. *Teaching Exceptional Children, 24*, 17–21.

Brown, R. and Madan-Swain, A. (1993). Cognitive, neuropsychological and academic sequelae in children with leukemia. *Journal of Learning Disabilities, 26*, 74–91.

Brownell, M.T., Mellard, D.F., and Deshler, D.D. (1993). Differences in the learning and transfer performance between students with learning disabilities and other low-achieving students on problem-solving tasks. *Learning Disability Quarterly, 16* (2), 138–156.

Bruck, M. (1987). The adult outcomes of children with learning disabilities. *Annals of dyslexia, 37*, Baltimore: The Orton Dyslexia Association.

Bruck, M. (1986). Social and emotional adjustments of learning disabled children: A review of the issues. In S.J. Ceci (Ed.), *Handbook of cognitive, social, and neuropsychological aspects of learning disabilities* (Vol. 1, pp. 361–380). Hillsdale, NJ: Erlbaum.

Bryan, T.H. (1986). Self-concept and attributions of the learning disabled. *Learning Disabilities Focus, 1*, 82–89.

Bryan, T.H., and Bryan, J.H. (1978). Social interactions of learning disabled children. *Learning Disability Quarterly, 1* (1), 33–38.

Bryan, T., and Nelson, C. (1994). Doing homework: Perspectives of elementary and junior high school students. *Journal of Learning Disabilities, 27* (8), 488–489.

Bryan, T., Pearl, R., and Fallon, P. (1989). Conformity to peer pressure by students with learning disabilities: A replication. *Journal of Learning Disabilities, 22* (7), 458–459.

Buchanan, M., and Wolf, J. S. (1986). A comprehensive study of learning disabled adults. *Journal of Learning Disabilities, 19*, 34-38.

Burd, L., Kauffman, D., and Kerbeshian, J. (1992). Tourette syndrome and learning disabilities. *Journal of Learning Disabilities, 25*, 598–604.

Bursuck, W., Polloway, E., Plante, L., Epstein, M.H., Jayanthi, M., and McConeghy, J. (in press). Report card grading and adaptations: A national survey of classroom practices. *Exceptional Children.*

Bursuck, W. (1989). A comparison of students with learning disabilities to low achieving and higher achieving students on three dimensions of social competence. *Journal of Learning Disabilities, 22*, 188–193.

Burstein, N., et al (1993). Teacher preparation for culturally diverse urban students: Infusing competencies across the curriculum. *Teacher Education and Special Education, 16* (1), 1–13.

Butler, R., and Marinov-Glassman, D. (1994). The effects of educational placement and grade level on the self-perceptions of low achievers and students with learning disabilities. *Journal of Learning Disabilities, 27* (5), 325-334.

Cawley, J.F., Fitzmaurice, A.M., Goodstein, H.A., Lepore, A.V., Sedlak, R., and Althaus, V. (1976). *Project math.* Tulsa, OK: Educational Development.

Cantwell, D.P., and Baker, L. (1991). Association between attention deficit-hyperactivity disorder and learning disorders. *Journal of Learning Disabilities, 24*, 88–95.

Cardon, L. R., DeFries, J. C., and Fulker, D. W. (in press). Quantitative trait locus on chromosome 6 predisposing to reading disability. *Science.*

Chelser, B. (1982). Association for Children with Learning Disabilities Vocational Committee complete survey on LD adults, *ACLD Newsbriefs,* No. 146, 5, 20–23.

Children's Defense Fund (1992). *The state of America.* Washington, D.C.: Author.

Children's Defense Fund. (1994). *Annual report.* Washington, DC: Author.

Clark, G.M. (1996). Transition planning assessment for secondary-level students with learning disabilities. *Journal of Learning Disabilities, 29* (1), 79–92.

Clark, G.M., Carlson, B.C., Fisher, S., Cook, I.D., and D'Alonzo, B.J. (1991). Career development for students with disabilities in elementary schools: A position statement of the Division on *Career Development. Career Development for Exceptional Individuals, 14,* 109–120.

Clark, G.M., Field, S., Patton, J.R., Brolin, D.E., and Sitlington, P.L. (1994). Life skills instruction: A necessary component for all students with disabilities. A position statement of the division on career development and transition. *Career Development for Exceptional Individuals, 17* (2), 125–134.

Clay, J.W. (1991, April). Respecting and supporting gay and lesbian parents. *The Education Digest, 51*–53.

Cohen, S.A. (1971). Dyspedagogia as a cause of reading retardation. In B. Bateman (Ed.). *Learning disorders* (Vol. 4). Seattle, WA: Special Child Publications.

Coles, G. (1987). *The learning mystique: A critical look at learning disabilities.* New York: Pantheon Books.

Collective perspective on issues affecting learning disabilities. (1992). Austin, TX: PRO-ED.

Collier, C. (1986). Mainstreaming and bilingual exceptional children. In L.M. Baca and H.T. Cervantes, *The bilingual special education interface* (pp. 284–313). Columbus, OH: Merrill.

Conderman, G., and Katsiyannis, A. (1995). Section 504 accommodation plans. *Intervention in School and Clinic, 31,* 42–45.

Conderman, G. (1995). Social status of sixth- and seventh-grade students with learning disabilities. *Learning Disability Quarterly, 18* (1), 13–24.

Cone, J.D., Delawyer, D.D., and Wolfe, V.V. (1985). Assessing parent participation: The parent/family involvement index. *Exceptional Children, 51,* 417–424.

Cook, R.E., Tessier, A., and Klein, M.D. (1992). *Adapting early childhood curricula for children with special needs.* New York: Merrill Publishing.

Corneliussen, G., Lund, M., and Nilsen, E. (1989). Children with cerebral palsy: An educational guide. In H. Rye and M. Skjorten (Eds.), *Guides for education no. 7,* 36–48. United Nations Educational, Scientific, and Cultural Organization. Paris, France.

Cotman, C.W., and Lynch, G.S. (1988). The neurobiology of learning and memory. In J. F. Kavanagh and T. J. Truss, (Eds.), *Learning disabilities: Proceedings of the national conference* (pp. 1–66). Parkton, MD: York.

Coughran, L., and Liles, B.Z. (1974). *Developmental syntax program.* Austin, TX: Learning Concepts.

Council for Learning Disabilities (1995, October). Principles of ethics: Draft #5. Paper presented at the Council for Learning Disabilities Annual Conference, Chicago.

Council of Administrators of Special Education, Inc. (n.d.). *Student access: A resource guide for educators, Section 504 of the Rehabilitation Act of 1973.* Reston, VA: CASE.

Creekmore, W.N. (and students). (1988). Family–classroom: A critical balance. *Academic Therapy, 24,* 207–220.

Crocker, A.C. (1992a). Introduction: Where is the prevention movement? *Mental Retardation, 30* (6), iii–v.

Crocker, A. C. (1992b). Data collection for the evaluation of mental retardation prevention activities: The fateful forty-three. *Mental Retardation, 30,* 303–317.

Cronin, M., and Gerber, P. (1982). Preparing the learning disabled adolescent for adulthood. *Topics in Learning and Learning Disabilities, 2*(3), 55–68.

Cronin, M.E. and Patton, J.R. (1993). *Life skills instruction for all students with special needs.* Austin, TX: PRO-ED.

Cruickshank, W.M. (1967). The education of the child with brain injury. In W.M. Cruickshank and G.O. Johnson (Eds.). *Education of exceptional children and youth,* 2nd ed. (pp. 238–283). Englewood Cliffs, NJ: Prentice-Hall.

Cruickshank, W.M. (1975). The education of children with specific learning disabilities. In W.M. Cruickshank and G.O. Johnson (Eds.), *Education of exceptional children and youth,* 3rd ed. (pp. 242–289). Englewood Cliffs, NJ: Prentice-Hall.

Cullinan, D., Lloyd, J.W., and Epstein, M.H. (1981). Strategy training: A structured approach to arithmetic instruction. *Exceptional Education Quarterly, 2* (1), 43–44.

Cullinan, D., and Epstein, M.H. (1985). Teacher-related adjustment problems of mildly handicapped and non-handicapped students. *Remedial and Special Education, 6,* 5–11.

Cummins, J. (1984). *Bilingualism and special education: Issues in assessment and pedagogy.* Cleveland, Avon, England: Multilingual Matters, Ltd.

Das, J.P., Mishra, R.K., and Kirby, J.R. (1994). Cognitive patterns of children with dyslexia: A comparison between groups with high and average nonverbal intelligence. *Journal of Learning Disabilities, 27* (4), 235–242.

deBettencourt, L.U. (1990). Cognitive strategy training with learning disabled students. In P.I. Myers and D.D. Hammill, *Learning disabilities: Basic concepts, assessment practices, and instructional strategies (4th Ed.)* Austin, TX: PRO-ED.

deBettencourt, L., Zigmond, N., and Thornton, H. (1989). Follow-up of postsecondary age rural learning disabled graduates and dropouts. *Exceptional Children, 56* (1), 40–49.

deBettencourt, L.U. (1987). How to develop parent relationships. *Teaching Exceptional Children, 19,* 26–27.

Decker, S. N., and DeFries, J. C. (1980). Cognitive abilities in families with reading disabled children. *Journal of Learning Disabilities, 13,* 517–522.

DeFries, J. C., Fulker, D. W., and LaBuda, M. C. (1987). Evidence for a genetic aetiology in reading disability of twins. *Nature, 329,* 537–539.

Dennis, R.E., Williams, W., Giangreco, M.F., and Cloninger, C.J. (1993). Quality of life as context for planning and evaluation of services for people with disabilities. *Exceptional Children, 59* (6), 499–512.

Deshler, D.D., Ellis, E.S., and Lenz, B.K. (1996). *Teaching adolescents with learning disabilities: Strategies and methods (2nd. Ed.).* Denver: Love Publishing.

Dickson, S.V., Simmons, D., and Kameenui, E.J. (1995). Instruction in expository text: A focus on compare/contrast structure. *LD Forum, 20* (2), 8–15.

DiGangi, S.A., Maag, J.W., and Rutherford, R.B. (1991). Self-graphing of on-task behavior: Enhancing the reactive effects of self-monitoring on on-task behavior and academic performance. *Learning Disability Quarterly, 14* (3), 221–230.

Dobbs, R.F., Primm, E.B., and Primm, B. (1991). Mediation: A common sense approach for resolving conflicts in education. *Focus on Exceptional Children, 24,* 1–12.

Dodd, J.M. (1992, November). Preventing American Indian children from overidentification with learning disabilities: Cultural considerations during the prereferral process. Paper presented at the Council for Exceptional Children Division for Early Childhood Topical Conference on Culturally and Linguistically Diverse Exceptional Children, Minneapolis. (ERIC Document No. 352 794).

Dowdy, C. A., and McCue, M. (1994). Crossing service systems: From special education to vocational rehabilitation. In C. A. Michaels (Ed.), *Transition strategies for persons with learning disabilities* (pp. 23–52). San Diego: Singular Publishing Group, Inc.

Dowdy, C.A., Patton, J.R., Smith, T.E.C., and Polloway, E.A. (in press). *Students with attention deficit disorder: A practical guide for teachers.* Austin, TX: PRO–ED.

Dowdy, C.A., and Smith, T.E.C. (1994). Serving individuals with specific learning disabilities in the vocational rehabilitation system. In P.J. Gerber and H.B. Reiff (Eds.), *Learning disabilities in adulthood.* Boston: Andover Medical Publishers.

Dowdy, C.A., Smith, T.E.C., and Nowell, C.H. (1996). Learning disabilities and vocational rehabilitation. In J.R. Patton and E.A. Polloway (Eds.), *Learning disabilities: The challenges of adulthood.* Austin, TX: PRO-ED.

Dowdy, C.A., and Smith, T.E.C. (1991) Future-based assessment and intervention. *Intervention in School and Clinic, 27,* 101–106.

Downey, J., Elkin, E. J., Ehrhardt, A. A., Meyer-Bahlburg, H. F. L., Bell, J. J., and Morishima, A. (1991). Cognitive ability and everyday functioning in women with Turner syndrome. *Journal of Learning Disabilities, 24,* 32–39.

Drucker, P.F. (1994). The age of social transformation. *The Atlantic Monthly, 274,* 53–80.

DuChossois, G., and Michaels, C. A. (1994). Postsecondary education. In C. A. Michaels (Ed.), *Transition strategies for persons with learning disabilities* (pp. 79–118). San Diego: Singular Publishing Group, Inc.

Dunn, L., Smith, J.O., and Smith, D.D. (1992). *Peabody language development kit-Revised.* Circle Pines, MN: American Guidance Service.

Dunst, C.J., Johanson, C., Trivette, C.M., and Hamby, D. (1991). Family-oriented early intervention policies and practices: Family-centered or not? *Exceptional Children, 58,* 115–126.

Dudley-Marling, C., and Dippo, D. (1995). What learning disabilities does: Sustaining the ideology of schooling. *Journal of Learning Disabilities, 28,* 408–414.

Dunn, C. (1996). A status report on transition planning for individuals with learning disabilities. *Journal of Learning Disabilities, 29,* 17–30.

Dykman, R., and Ackerman, P. (1993). Behavioral subtypes of attention deficit disorder. *Exceptional Children, 60,* 132–141.

Ebenstein, B. (1995). IEP strategies. *Exceptional Parent, 27,* 62–63.

Echevarria, J. (1994). Altering teacher discourse style to match the needs of Spanish-speaking students in special education. Unpublished research report, Loyola Marymount University, Los Angeles. (ERIC Document Reproduction Service No. 371 532)

Edgar, E. (1987) Secondary programs in special education: Are many of them justifiable? *Exceptional Children, 53,* 555–561.

Edgar, E., and Levine, P. (1987). *A longitudinal follow-along study of graduates of special education.* Seattle: University of Washington, Experimental Education Unit, Child Development and Mental Retardation Center.

Ehlers, V.L., and Ruffin, M. (1990). The Missouri project—Parents as teachers. *Focus on Exceptional Children, 23,* 1–14.

Eliason, M.J. (1986). Neurofibromatosis: Implications for learning and behavior. *Journal of Developmental and Behavioral Pediatrics, 7,* 175–179.

Eliason, M.J. (1988). Neuropsychological patterns: Neurofibromatosis compared to developmental learning disorders. *Neurofibromatosis, 1,* 17–25.

Elksnin, N., and Elksnin, L.K. (1991). Facilitating the vocational success of students with mild handicaps. *The Journal for Vocational Special Needs Education, 13* (2), 5–11.

Elliott, L. L., and Bosse, L. A. (1987). Auditory processing by learning disabled adults. In D. J. Johnson and J. W. Blalock (Eds.), *Adults with learning disabilities* (pp. 107–129). Orlando: Grune and Stratton.

Ellis, W., and Cramer, S.C. (1994). *Learning disabilities: A national responsibility.* Washington, D.C.: National Center on Learning Disabilities, (5–6).

Engelmann, S., Becker, W.C., Hanner, S., and Johnson, G. (1980). *Corrective Reading Program.* Chicago: Science Research Associates.

Engelmann, S., Becker, W.C., Hanner, S., and Johnson, G. (1988). *Corrective reading program* (revised). Chicago: Science Research Associates.

Englert, C.S., Garmon, A., Mariage, T., Rozendal, M., Tarrant, K., and Urba, J. (1995). The Early Literacy Project: Connecting across the literacy curriculum. *Learning Disability Quarterly, 18* (4), 253–275.

Englert, C.S., and Raphael, T.R. (1988). Constructing well-formed prose: Process, structure, and metacognitive knowledge. *Exceptional Children, 54,* 513–520.

Epir, S., Renda, Y., and Baser, N. (1984). Cognitive and behavioral characteristics of children with idiopathic epilepsy in a low-income area of Ankara, Turkey. *Developmental Medicine and Child Neurology, 26,* 200–207.

Epstein, M.H., Bursuck, W.D., and Cullinan, D. (1985). Patterns of behavior problems among the learning disabled: Boys aged 12–18, girls aged 6–11 and girls aged 12–18. *Learning Disability Quarterly, 8,* 123–129.

Epstein, M.H., Cullinan, D., and Lloyd, J.W. (1986). Patternsof behavior problems among the learning disabled: III. Replication across ages and sexes. *Learning Disability Quarterly, 9,* 43–54.

Epstein, M.H., Kinder, D., and Bursuck, B. (1989). The academic status of adolescents with behavior disorders. *Behavioral Disorders, 14,* 157–165.

Epstein, M.H., Shaywitz, S., Shaywitz, B., and Woolston, J. (1991). The boundaries of attention deficit disorder. *Journal of Learning Disabilities, 24,* 78–86.

Epstein, M.H., Patton, J., Polloway, E., and Foley, R. (1992). Educational services for students with behavior disorders: A review of individualized education programs. *Teacher Education and Special Education, 15,* 41–48.

Erikson, E. H. (1968). *Identity. Youth and crisis.* New York: W. W. Norton and Company.

Erin, J.N., and Koenig, A.J. (in press). The student with a visual disability and a learning disability. *Journal of Learning Disabilities.*

Ernhart, C.B., and Needleman, H.L. (1987). Lead levels and child development: statements by C. B. Ernhart and H. L. Needleman. *Journal of Learning Disabilities, 20,* 262–265.

Eversole, T. (no date). Addressing prejudice against gay, lesbian and bisexual youth in school: Teachers' handout. National Association of School Psychologists.

Fad, K. (1995). Communication disorders. In T.E.C. Smith, E.A. Polloway, J.R. Patton, and C.A. Dowdy (Eds.), *Teaching students with special needs in inclusive settings,* (pp. 248–285). Boston: Allyn and Bacon.

Falik, L.H. (1969). The effects of special perceptual-motor training in kindergarten on reading readiness and on second reading grade performance. *Journal of Learning Disabilities, 2,* 395–402.

Falik, L.H. (1995). Family patterns of reaction to a child with a learning disability: A mediational perspective. *Journal of Learning Disabilities, 28,* 335–341.

Farfard, M., and Haubrich, P. (1981). Vocational and social adjustment of learning disabled adults: A follow-up study. *Learning Disability Quarterly, 4,* 122–130.

Federal Register. (1991, July 26). 56 (144), 35735, et seq.

Feingold, B. F. (1976). Hyperkinesis and learning disabilities linked to the ingestion of artificial food colors and flavors. *Journal of Learning Disabilities, 9,* 19–27.

Felton, R. (1993). Effects of instruction on the decoding skills of children with phonological-processing problems. *Journal of Learning Disabilities, 26* (9), 583–589.

Felton, R., and Wood, F.B. (1992). A reading level match study of nonword reading skills in poor readers with varying IQ. *Journal of Learning Disabilities, 25*, 318–326.

Fernald, G.M. (1943). *Remedial techniques in basic school subjects.* New York: McGraw-Hill.

Figueroa, R.A. (1989). Psychological testing of linguistic-minority students: Knowledge gaps and regulations. *Exceptional Children, 56* (2), 111–119.

Fisher, R., and Collins, E. (1991). Tourette syndrome: Overview and classroom interventions. ERIC Document Reproduction Service No. ED 339 182.

Fletcher, J. (1985). Memory for verbal and nonverbal stimuli in learning disability subgroups: Analysis of selective reminding. *Journal of Experimental Child Psychology, 40,* 244–259.

Flowers, D. L. (1993). Brain basis for dyslexia: A summary of work in progress. *Journal of Learning Disabilities, 26,* 575–582.

Forest, M., and Pearpoint, J.C. (1992). Putting all kids on the MAP. *Educational Leadership, 50,* 26–31.

Forness, S.R. (1988). School characteristics of children and adolescents with depression. *Monographs in Behavioral Disorders, 10,* 177–203.

Forness, S.R., and Kavale, K.A. (1991). Social skills deficits as primary learning disabilities: A note on problems with the ICLD diagnostic criteria. *Learning Disabilities Research and Practice, 6* (1), 44-49.

Fourqurean, J.M., Meisgeier, C., Swank, P.R., and Williams, R.E. (1991). Correlates of postsecondary employment outcomes for young adults with learning disabilities. *Journal of Learning Disabilities, 24,* 400–405.

Fradd, S.H., Barona, A., and Santos de Barona, M. (1989). In S.H. Fradd and M.J. Weismantel (Eds.), *Meeting the needs of culturally and linguistically different students: A handbook for educators* (pp. 63-105). Boston: College-Hill.

Fradd, S.H., and Weismantel, M.J. (1989). Developing and evaluating goals. In S.H. Fradd and M.J. Weismantel (Eds.), *Meeting the needs of culturally and linguistically different students: A handbook for educators* (pp. 34–62). Boston: College-Hill.

Fradd, S.H., Weismantel, M.J., Correa, V.I., and Algozzine, B. (1988). Developing a personnel training model for meeting the needs of handicapped and at risk language minority students. *Teacher Education and Special Education, 11,* 30–38.

Friend, M., and Bursuck, W.(1996). *Including students with special needs: A practical guide for classroom teachers.* Boston: Allyn and Bacon.

Frostig, M. (1967). Education for children with learning disabilities. In H.R. Myklebust (Ed.), *Progress in Learning Disabilities.* (pp. 234–266) New York: Grune and Stratton.

Fuchs, D., and Fuchs, L. (1994). Inclusive schools movement and the radicalization of special education reform. *Exceptional Children, 60,* 294–309.

Gadow, K.D. (1986). *Children on medication (Vol. II): Epilepsy, emotional disturbance, and adolescent disorders.* San Diego: College Hill Press.

Gajar, A. (1992). Adults with learning disabilities: Current and future research priorities. *Journal of Learning Disabilities, 25* (8), 507–519.

Galaburda, A. M. (1990). The testosterone hypothesis: Assessment since Geschwind and Behan, 1982. *Annals of Dyslexia, 40,* 18–38.

Garcia, S.B. (1995, October). Bilingual exceptional students: An assessment and intervention model. Paper presented at the New Mexico Learning Disabilities Association 1995 Fall Conference, Albuquerque, NM.

Garcia, S.B., and Malkin, D.H. (1993). Toward defining programs and services for culturally and linguistically diverse learners in special education. *Teaching Exceptional Children, 26* (1), 52–58.

Garcia, S.B., and Ortiz, A.A. (1988). *Preventing inappropriate referrals of language minority students to special education* (New Focus Series, No. 5). Wheaton, MD: National Clearinghouse for Bilingual Education.

Gargiulo, R.S. (1985). *Working with parents of exceptional children.* Boston: Houghton Mifflin.

Gargiulo, R.S., O'Sullivan, P., Stephens, D.G., and Goldman, R. (1989–1990). Sibling relationships in mildly handicapped children: A preliminary investigation. *National Forum of Special Education Journal, 1,* 20–28.

Garmezy, N., and Rutter, M. (1983). *Stress, coping, and development in children.* New York: McGraw–Hill.

Gaylord-Ross, R., and Browder, D. (1991). Functional assessment: Dynamic and domain properties. In L. H. Meyer, C. A. Peck, and L. Brown (Eds.), *Critical issues in the lives of people with severe disabilities* (pp. 45–66). Baltimore: Paul H. Brookes.

Geary, D.C., and Brown, S.C. (1991). Cognitive addition: Strategy choice and speed-of-processing differences in gifted, normal, and mathematically disabled children. *Developmental Psychology, 27,* 398–406.

Geary, D.C., Brown, S.C., and Samaranayake, V.A. (1991). Cognitive addition: A short–term longitudinal study of strategy choice and speed-of-processing differences in normal and mathematically disabled children. *Developmental Psychology, 27,* 787–797.

Gelb, S.A., and Mizokawa, D.T. (1986). Special education and social structure: The commonality of "exceptionality." *American Educational Research Journal, 23,* 543-557.

Geller, E.S. (1994). Ten principles for achieving a total safety culture. *Professional Safety, 39* (9), 18–24.

Gerber, P.J., and Reiff, H.B. (1994). Perspectives on adults with learning disabilities. In P.J. Gerber and H.B. Reiff (Eds.), *Learning disabilities in adulthood.* Boston: Andover Medical Publishers.

Gersten, R., Brengelman, S., and Jimenez, R. (1994). Effective instruction for culturally and linguistically diverse students: A reconceptualization. *Focus on Exceptional Children, 27* (1), 1–16.

Gersten, R., and Woodward, J. (1994). The language-minority student and special education: Issues, trends, and paradoxes. *Exceptional Children, 60* (4), 310–322.

Geschwind, N., and Behan, P. O. (1984). Laterality, hormones, and immunity. In N. Geschwind and A. M. Galaburda (Eds.), *Cerebral dominance* (pp. 211–224). Cambridge: Harvard University Press.

Gettinger, M. (1991). Learning time and retention differences between nondisabled students and students with learning disabilities. *Learning Disability Quarterly, 14* (3), 179–189.

Gibbs, D., and Cooper, E. (1989). Prevalence of communication disorders in students with learning disabilities. *Journal of Learning Disabilities, 22,* 60–63.

Gillingham, A., and Stillman, B. (1970). *Remedial training for children with specific disability in reading, spelling, and penmanship* (7th ed.). Cambridge, MA: Educators Publishing Service.

Ginsberg, R., Gerber, P. J., and Reiff, H. B. (1994). Employment success for adults with learning disabilities. In P. J. Gerber and H. B. Reiff (Eds.), *Learning disabilities—Persisting problems and evolving issues* (pp. 204-213). Stoneham, MA: Andover Medical Publishers.

Gold, S., and Sherry, L. (1984). Hyperactivity, learning disabilities, and alcohol. *Journal of Learning Disabilities, 17,* 3–6.

Goldenberg, C. (1992/1993). Instructional conversations: Promoting comprehension through discussion. *Reading Teacher, 46* (4), 316–326.

Goldman, S.R., Mertz, D.L., and Pellegrino, J.W. (1989). Individual differences in extended practice functions and solution strategies for basic addition facts. *Journal of Educational Psychology, 81,* 481–496.

Goldman, S.R., Pellegrino, J.W., and Mertz, D.L. (1988). Extended practice of basic addition facts: Strategy changes in learning disabled students. *Cognition and Instruction, 5,* 223–265.

Goldstein, H. (1974). *The social learning curriculum.* Coumbus, OH: Merrill.

Goldstein, S., and Turnbull, A.P. (1982). Strategies to increase parent participation in IEP conferences. *Exceptional Children, 48,* 360–361.

Goodman, K.S. (1982). Revaluing readers and reading. *Topics in Learning and Learning Disabilities, 1* (4), 87–93.

Gottesman, R. L. (1994). The adult with learning disabilities: An overview. *Learning Disabilities—A Multidisciplinary Journal, 5* (1), 1–14.

Gottlieb, J., Alter, J., and Gottlieb, B.W. , and Wishner, J. (1994). Special education in urban America: It's not justifiable for many. *Journal of Special Education, 27* (4), 453–465.

Graham, S., Harris, K.R., and MacArthur, C.A. (1995). Introduction to special issue: Research on writing and literacy. *Learning Disability Quarterly, 18* (4), 250–252.

Greenan, J.P., and Jarwan, F.A. (1994). The relationship between student self-rating and teacher ratings of special needs students' reasoning skills. *The Journal for Vocational and Special Needs Education,* (Number 3, Spring), 38–42.

Greenberg, J. R., and Mitchell, S. A. (1983). *Object relations in psychoanalytic theory.* Cambridge, MA: Harvard University Press.

Greenwood Genetic Center (1984). *Counseling aids for geneticists.* Greenwood, SC: Author.

Gregg, N. (1983). College learning disabled writer: Error patterns and instructional alternatives. *Journal of Learning Disabilities, 16,* 334–337.

Gresham, F.M., and Reschly, D.J. (1986). Social skill deficits and low peer acceptance of mainstreamed learning disabled children. *Learning Disability Quarterly, 9* (1), 23–32.

Gripp, N.G. (1995). Neurofibromatosis. Unpublished manuscript, Lynchburg College, Lynchburg, VA.

Grossman, H.J. (1983). *Classification in mental retardation.* Washington, D.C.: AAMR.

Grossman, P.D. (1992). Employment discrimination law for the learning disabled community. *Learning Disability Quarterly, 15,* 287–329.

Grossman, H. (1992). *The San Jose State University Bilingual/Multicultural Special Education Personnel Preparation Program: A report on 13 years of experience.* San Jose, CA: San Jose State University. (ERIC Document Reproduction Service No. 364 092)

Grossman, H. (1995). *Special education in a diverse society.* Boston: Allyn and Bacon.

Grossman, H., and Grossman, S.H. (1994). *Gender issues in education.* Boston: Allyn and Bacon.

Gugerty, J.J. (1994). The School-to-Work Opportunities Act. *Tech Prep Advocate, 2* (1), 1, 6–7.

Guterman, B.R. (1995). The validity of categorical learning disabilities services: The consumer's view. *Exceptional Children, 62* (2), 111–124.

Hallahan, D.P., Kauffman, J.M., and Lloyd, J.W. (1996). *Introduction to learning disabilities.* Boston: Allyn and Bacon.

Hallahan, D.P. (1992). Some thoughts on why the prevalence of learning disabilities has increased. *Journal of Learning Disabilities, 25,* 523–528.

Hallahan, D.P., and Kauffman, J.M. (1977). Labels, categories, behaviors: ED, LD and EMR reconsidered. *Journal of Special Education, 11,* 129–149.

Hallahan, D.P., and Kauffman, J.M. (1991). *Exceptional children: Introduction to special education* (5th ed.). Eglewood Cliffs, NJ: Prentice Hall.

Hallahan, D.P., and Sapona, R. (1983). Self-monitoring of attention with learning disabled children: Past research and current issues. *Journal of Learning Disabilities, 16,* 616–620.

Halmhuber, N.L., and Paris, S.G. (1993). Perceptions of competence and control and the use of coping strategies by children with disabilities. *Learning Disability Quarterly, 16* (2), 93–111.

Halpern, R. (1982). Impact of P.L. 94–142 on the handicapped child and family: Institutional responses. *Exceptional Children, 49,* 270–273.

Halpern, A.S. (1993). Quality of life as a conceptual framework for evaluating transition outcomes. *Exceptional Children, 59* (6), 486–498.

Halpern, A.S. (1994). The transition of youth with disabilities to adult life: A position statement of the Division on Career Development and Transition, The Council for Exceptional Children. *Career Development for Exceptional Individuals, 17* (2), 115–124.

Halpern, A.S., Yovanoff, P., Doren, B., and Benz, M.R. (1995). Predicting participation in postsecondary education for school leavers with disabilities. *Exceptional Children, 62* (2), 151–164.

Hammill, D.D. (1989). *A brief history of learning disabilities.* Austin, TX: PRO-ED.

Hammill, D.D. (1993). A brief look at the learning disabilities movement in the United States. *Journal of Learning Disabilities, 26,* 295–310.

Hammill, D.D. (1979). The field of learning disabilities: A futuristic perspective. Presented at the National DCLD Conference on Learning Disabilities, Louisville, Kentucky, October 6, 1979.

Hamre-Nietupski, S., McDonald, J., and Nietupski, J. (1992). Integrating elementary students with multiple disabilities: Challenges and solutions. *Teaching Exceptional Children, 24* (3), 6–11.

Harris, D., Silver, A., and Sekhon, H. (1993). Tourette's syndrome and learning disorders. ERIC document Reproduction Service No. ED 356 614.

Hamstra-Bletz, L., and Blote, A.W. (1993). A longitudinal study on dysgraphic handwriting in primary school. *Journal of Learning Disabilities, 26* (10), 689–699.

Haring, K.A., Lovett, D.L., and Smith, D.D. (1990). A follow-up study of recent special education graduates of learning disabilities programs. *Journal of Learning Disabilities, 23,* 108–113.

Haring, N.C. and Gentry, N.D. (1976). Direct and individualized instructional procedures. In N.G. Haring and R.L. Schiefelbusch (Eds.), *Teaching special children.* New York: McGraw-Hill.

Haring, K.A., Lovett, D.L., Haney, K.F., Algozzine, B., Smith, D.D., and Clarke, J. (1992). Labeling preschoolers as learning disabled: A cautionary position. *Topics in Early Childhood Special Education, 12* (2), 151–173.

Haring, K.A., Lovett, D.L., and Saren, D. (1991). Parent perceptions of their adult offspring with disabilities. *Teaching Exceptional Children, 23,* 6–10.

Harmon, J.A,. et al. (1992). *Gender disparities in special education.* Madison, WI: Wisconsin State Department of Public Instruction, Madison Bureau for Exceptional Children. (ERIC Document Reproduction Service no. ED 358 631)

Harris, K.R., and Graham, S. (1992). *Helping young writers master the craft.* Cambridge, MA: Brookline Press.

Harris, E. (1986). The contribution of twin research to the study of the etiology of reading disability. In S. Smith (Ed.), *Genetics and learning disabilities* (pp. 3–19). San Diego: College Hill.

Harry, B. (1992). Restructuring the participation of African–American parents in special education. *Exceptional Children, 59*, 123–131.

Harry, B., Allen, N., and McLaughlin, M. (1995). Communication versus compliance: African-American parents' involvement in special education. *Exceptional Children, 61* (4), 364–377.

Hasazi, S. B., Gordon, L. R., and Roe, C. A. (1985). Factors associated with the employment status of handicapped youth exiting high school from 1979 to 1983. *Exceptional Children, 51*, 455–469.

HEATH (1988, Winter). LD update. *Information from HEATH*. Washington, DC: Author.

HEATH (1989, Fall). Facts you can use. *Information from HEATH*. Washington, DC: Author.

Herrnstein, R. and Murray, C. (1994). *The bell curve: Intelligence and class structure in American life*. New York: The Free Press.

Hoffman, F.J., Sheldon, K.L., Minskoff, E.H., Sautter, S.W., Steidle, E.F., Baker, D.P., Bailey, M.B., and Echols, L.D. (1987). Needs of learning disabled adults. *Journal of Learning Disabilities, 20*, 43–52.

Holmes, C.S., and Richman, L.C. (1985). Cognitive profiles of children with insulin-dependent diabetes. *Developmental and Behavioral Pediatrics, 6*, 323–326.

Huntington, D.D., and Bender, W.N. (1993). Adolescents with learning disabilities at risk? Emotional well being, depression, suicide. *Journal of Learning Disabilities, 26*, 159–166.

Hynd, G., and Cohen, M. (1983). *Dyslexia: Neuropsychological theory, research, and clinical differentiation*. London: Grune and Stratton.

Jacob-Timm, S., and Hartshorne, T.S. (1994). Section 504 and school psychology. *Psychology in the Schools, 31*, 26–39.

Jacobs, A.E., and Hendricks, D.J. (1992). Job accommodations for adults with learning disabilities: Brilliantly disguised opportunities. *Learning Disability Quarterly, 15*, 274–286.

Jenson, W.R., Sheridan, S.M., Olympia, D., and Andrews, D. (1994). Homework and students with learning disabilities and behavior disorders: A practical, parent-based approach. *Journal of Learning Disabilities, 27*, 538–548.

Johnson, D. (1988). Review of research on specific reading, writing, and mathematics disorders. In J.F. Kavanagh and T. J. Truss (Eds.), *Learning disabilities: Proceedings of the national conference* (pp. 79–161). Parkton, MD: York.

Johnson, D.J., and Myklebust, H.R. (1967). *Learning disabilities: Educational principles and practices*. New York: Grune and Stratton.

Johnson, M. J., and Scruggs, T. E. (1981). *All our children: Handicapped and normal*. (ERIC Document Reproduction Service No. ED 217 674)

Jones, K. L., Smith, D. W., Ulleland, C. N., and Streissguth, A. P. (1973). Pattern of malformation in offspring of chronic alcoholic mothers. *Lancet, 1*, 1267–1271.

Jordan, D. (in press). *Overcoming dyslexia*. Austin, TX: PRO-ED.

Jordan, N.C., Levine, S.C., and Huttenlocher, J. (1995). Calculation abilities in young children with different patterns of cognitive functioning. *Journal of Learning Disabilities, 28* (1), 53–64.

Karge, B.D., Patton, P.L., and de la Garza, B.M. (1992). Transition services for youth with mild disabilities: Do they exist, are they needed? *Career Development for Exceptional Individuals, 15,* 47–68.

Katims, D.S. (1994). Emergence of literacy in preschool children with disabilities. *Learning Disability Quarterly, 17* (1), 58–69.

Katims, D.S. (1991). Emergent literacy in early childhood special education: Curriculum and instruction. *Topics in Early Childhood Special Education, 11* (1), 69–84.

Katims, D.S., and Pierce, P.L. (1995). Literacy-rich environments and the transition of young children with special needs. *Topics in Early Childhood Special Education, 15,* 219–234.

Katsiyannis, A. (1994). Individuals with disabilities: The school principal and Section 504. *NASSP Bulletin, 45,* 6–10.

Kauffman, J. (1989). *Characteristics of emotional and behavioral disorders of children and youth (5th ed.).* New York: Merrill.

Kauffman, J.M. (1994). Places of change: Special education's power and identity in an era of educational reform. *Journal of Learning Disabilities, 27,* 610–618.

Kauffman, J.M. (1993). *Characteristics of emotional and behavioral disorders of children and youth (5th ed.).* New York: Merrill.

Kauffman, J.M., and Hallahan, D.P. (1994). *The illusion of full inclusion.* Austin, TX: PRO-ED.

Kavale, K.A., and Forness, S.R. (1985). The historical foundation of learning disabilities: A quantitative synthesis assessing the validity of Strauss and Werner's exogenous versus endogenous distinction of mental retardation. *Remedial and Special Education, 6,* 18–24.

Kavale, K.A., Forness, S.R., and Bender, M. (1987). *Handbook of learning disabilities: Dimension and diagnosis (Vol. 1).* Austin, TX: PRO-ED.

Kavale, K.A., Forness, S.R., and Lorsbach, T.C. (1991). Definition for definitions of learning disabilities. *Learning Disability Quarterly, 14,* 257–266.

Kavale K. and Mattson P.D.(1983). One jumped off the balance beam: Meta-analysis of perceptual-motor training. *Journal of Learning Disabilities, 16,* 165–173.

Kay, P.J., Fitzgerald, M., Paradee, C., and Mellencamp, A. (1994). Making homework work at home: The parent's perspective. *Journal of Learning Disabilities, 27,* 550-561.

Keilitz, I., and Dunivant, N. (1986). The relationship between learning disability and juvenile delinquency: Current state of knowledge. *Remedial and Special Education, 7* (3), 18–26.

Keogh, B., and Weisner, (1993). An ecocultural perspective on risk and protective factors in children's development: Implications for learning disabilities. *LD Research and Practice, 8,* 3–10.

Keogh, B.K. (1994). What the special education research agenda should look like in the year 2000. *Learning Disabilities Research and Practice, 9,* 62–69.

Kephart, N.C. (1971). *The slow learner in the classroom, 2nd Ed.* Columbus, OH: Charles Thomas.

Kline, F.M., Schumaker, F.B., and Deshler, D.D. (1991). Development and validation of feedback routines for instructing students with learning disabilities. *Learning Disability Quarterly, 14* (3), 191–207.

Kopp, K. H., Miller, J. H., and Mulkey, S. W. (1984). The paradox of learning disabilities: A stumbling block to rehabilitation. *Journal of Rehabilitation, 50* (2), 4–6.

Kortering, L., Julnes, R., and Edgar, E. (1990). An instructive review of the law pertaining to the graduation of special education students. *Remedial and Special Education, 11,* 7–13.

Kozol, J. (1991). *Savage inequalities.* New York: Harper Perennial.

Krauss, M.W. (1991). New precedent in family policy: Individualized family service plan. *Exceptional Children, 56,* 388–395.

Kronick, D. (1988). *New approaches to learning disabilities: Cognitive, metacognitive, and holistic.* Philadelphia: Grune and Stratton.

Kulak, A.G. (1993). Parallels between math and reading disability: Common issues and approaches. *Journal of Learning Disabilities, 26* (10), 666–673.

Lacelle-Peterson, M.W., and Rivera, C. (1994). Is it real for all kids? A framework for equitable assessment policies for English language learners. *Harvard Educational Review, 64* (1), 55–75.

Lachiewicz, A., Harrison, C., Spiridigliozzi, G.A., Callanan, N.P., and Livermore, J. (1988). What is the Fragile X syndrome? *North Carolina Medical Journal, 49,* 203–208.

La Greca, A.M., and Stone, W.L. (1990). LD status and achievement: Confounding variables in the study of children's social status, self–esteem, and behavioral functioning. *Journal of Learning Disabilities, 23,* 483–490.

LDA Newsbriefs. (1994, September/October). Adults with learning disabilities—Preliminary analysis of survey data. *LDA Newsbriefs,* 3–4.

Leigh, J., Huntze, S.L., and Lamorey, S. (1995). Topical issues education: Teaching controversial or sensitive topics to students with learning disabilities. *Journal of Learning Disabilities, 28,* 353–363.

Lenz, B.K., Ellis, E.S., and Scanlon, D. (1996). *Teaching learning strategies to adolescents and adults with learning disabilities.* Austin, TX: PRO-ED.

Lerner, J.W., Ganschow, L., and Sparks, R. (1991). Critical issues in learning disabilities: Foreign language learning. *Learning Disabilities Research and Practice, 6* (1), 50–53.

Lerner, R.M., and Galambos, N.L. (1984). The adolescent experience: A view of the issues. In R.M. Lerner and N.L. Galambos (Eds.), *Experiencing adolescents: A sourcebook for parents, teachers, and teens.* New York: Teachers College Press.

Lerner, J., Lowenthal, B., and Lerner, S. (1995). *Attention deficit disorders: Assessment and teaching.* Pacific Grove, CA: Brooks/Cole Publishing Company.

Lerer, R. (1987). Motor tics, Tourette syndrome, and learning disabilities. *Journal of Learning Disabilities, 20,* 266–267.

Lewis, K., and Taymans, J.M. (1992). An examination of autonomous functioning skills of adolescents with learning disabilities. *Career Development for Exceptional Individuals, 15* (1), 37–46.

Lipper, K. (1995). Proudest moments. In C.G. Tuttle and G.A. Tuttle, *Challenging voices: Writings by, for, and about individuals with learning disabilities* (pp. 65–66). Los Angeles: Lowell House.

Litowitz, B. (1987). Problems of conceptualization and language: Evidence from definitions. In D. J. Johnson and J. W. Blalock (Eds.), *Adults with learning disabilities* (pp. 131–143). Orlando: Grune and Stratton.

Little, S.S. (1993). Nonverbal learning disabilities and socioemotional functioning: A review of recent literature. *Journal of Learning Disabilities, 26* (10), 653–665.

Lombardino, L., and Mangan, N. (1983). Parents as language trainers: Language programming with developmentally delayed children. *Exceptional Children, 49,* 358–361.

Lovitt, T.C. (1989). *Introduction to learning disabilities.* Boston: Allyn and Bacon.

Lovitt, T.C. (1992). Reflections on Barsch's perspectives, and a few of my own. *Journal of Learning Disabilities, 25,* 23–28.

Luckasson, R., et al. (1992). *Mental retardation: Definition, classification and systems of supports.* Washington, D.C.: AAMR.

Lusthaus, C.S., Lusthaus, E.W., and Gibbs, H. (1981). Parents' role in the decision process. *Exceptional Children, 48,* 256–257.

Lyon, G.R. (1995). *Research in learning at the NICHD.* Bethesda, MD: NICHD.

Lynch, E.W., and Stein, R.C. (1987). Parent participation by ethnicity: A comparison of Hispanic, Black, and Anglo families. *Exceptional Children, 54,* 105–111.

Lyon, G.R., and Flynn, J.M. (1991). Assessing subtypes of learning abilities. In H.L. Swanson (Ed.), *Handbook on the assessment of learning disabilities: Theory, research, and practice* (pp. 59–74). Austin, TX: PRO-ED.

Lyytinen, P., Rasku-Puttonen, H., Poikkeus, A., Laakso, M., and Ahonen, T. (1994). Mother-child teaching strategies and learning disabilities. *Journal of Learning Disabilities, 27,* 186–192.

Mangrum, C. T., and Strichart, S. S. (1984). *College and the learning disabled student: A guide to program selection, development, and implementation.* Orlando: Grune and Stratton.

McBurnett, K., Lahey, B.B., and Pfiffner, L.J. (1993). Diagnosis of attention deficit disorders in DSM-IV: Scientific basis and implications for education. *Exceptional Children, 60,* 108–117.

McCue, M. (1994). Clinical diagnostic and functional assessment of adults with learning disabilities. In P. J. Gerber and H. B. Reiff (Eds.), *Learning disabilities in adulthood—Persisting problems and evolving issue* (pp. 55–71). Stoneham, MA: Andover Medical Publishers.

McCue, M. (1987). The role of assessment in rehabilitation of LD adults. *Proceedings from the State of the Art Conference on Adults with Learning Disabilities.* Washington, DC: The National Institute on Disability and Rehabilitation Research.

McCue, P. M., Shelly, M. A., and Goldstein, G. (1986). Intellectual, academic and neuro-psychological levels in learning disabled adults. *Journal of Learning Disabilities, 19,* 233–236.

McDonnell, J. J., Hardman, M. L., McDonnell, A. P., and Kiefer-O'Donnell. (1995). *An introduction to persons with severe disabilities—Educational and social issues.* Needham Heights, MA: Allyn and Bacon.

McKinney, J., Montague, M., and Hocutt, A. (1993). Educational assessment of students with attention deficit disorder. *Exceptional Children, 60,* 125–131.

McKinney, J.D., Osborne, S.S., and Schulte, A.C. (1993). Academic consequences of learning disability: Longitudinal prediction of outcomes at 11 years of age. *Learning Disabilities Research and Practice, 8* (1), 19–27.

McLeod, T., and Armstrong, S. (1982). Learning disabilities in mathematics: Skill deficits and remedial approaches. *Learning Disability Quarterly, 5,* 305–311.

McLeskey, J. (1992). Students with learning disabilities at primary, intermediate, and secondary grade levels: Identification and characteristics. *Learning Disability Quarterly, 15* (1), 13–19.

McNaughton, D., Hughes, C.A., and Clark, K. (1994). Spelling instruction for students with learning disabilities: Implications for research and practice. *Learning Disability Quarterly, 17* (3), 169–185.

MacArthur, C.A., Graham, S., Schwartz, S.S., and Schafer, W.D. (1995). Evaluation of a writing instruction model that integrated a process approach, strategy instruction, and word processing. *Learning Disability Quarterly, 18* (4), 278–291.

MacMillan, D.L., Gresham, F., and Siperstein, G.M. (1993). Conceptual and psychometric concerns about the 1992 AAMR definition of mental retardation. *American Journal of Mental Retardation, 98,* 325–335.

MacMillan, D.L., Hendrick, I.G., and Watkins, A.V. (1988). Impact of Diana, Larry P., and P.L. 94-142 on minority students. *Exceptional Children, 54,* 426–432.

Maag, J.W., and Reid, R. (1994). The phenomenology of depression among students with and without learning disabilities: More similar than different. *Learning Disabilities Research and Practice, 9,* 91–103.

Maldonado, J.A. (1994). Bilingual special education: Specific learning disabilities in language and reading. *The Journal of Educational Issues of Language Minority Students, 14,* 127–147.

Mann, L. (1973). *The first review of special education.* Austin, TX: PRO-ED.

Mann, L. (1979). *On the trail of process.* New York: Grune and Stratton.

Mannix, D. (1995). *Life skills activities for secondary students with special needs.* New York: The Center for Applied Research in Education.

Martin, J., Marshall, L.H., Maxson, L., and Jerman, P. (1993). *The self-directed IEP.* Colorado Springs, CO: University of Colorado at Colorado Springs, Center for Educational Research.

Martin, R. (1992). *Continuing challenges in special education law.* Urbana, IL: Carle Media.

Marlowe, M., et al. (1984). Hair mineral content as a predictor of learning disabilities. *Journal of Learning Disabilities, 17,* 418–421.

Masutto, C., Bravar, L., and Fabbro, F. (1994). Neurolinguistic differentiation of children with subtypes of dyslexia. *Journal of Learning Disabilities, 27* (8), 520–526.

Mather, N. (1992). Whole language reading instruction for students with learning disabilities: Caught in the cross fire. *Learning Disabilities Research and Practice, 7,* 87–95.

Mather, N., and Roberts, R. (1994). Learning disabilities: A field in danger of extinction? *Learning Disabilities Research and Practice, 9,* 49–58.

Mauk, G., and Mauk, P. (1992). Somewhere, out there: Preschool children with hearing impairment and learning disabilities. *Topics in Early Childhood Special Education, 12,* 174–195.

May, D., Kundert, D., and Akpan, C. (1994). Are we preparing special educators for the issues facing schools in the 1990s? *Teacher Education and Special Education, 17,* 192–199.

Meichenbaum, D. (1977). *Cognitive behavior modification: An integrative approach.* New York: Plenum.

Mellard, D.F., and Hazel, J.S. (1992). Social competencies as a pathway to successful life transitions. *Learning Disability Quarterly, 15* (4), 251–271.

Mercer, C.D., Algozzine, B, and Trifiletti, J. (1988). Early identification—An analysis of the research. *Learning Disability Quarterly, 2,* 12–24.

Mercer, C.D., and Miller, S.P. (1991). *Strategic math series.* Lawrence, KS: Edge Enterprises.

Mercer, C.D. (1987). *Students with learning disabilities* (3rd ed.). Columbus, OH: Merrill.

Mercer, J.R. (1973). *Labeling the mentally retarded.* Berkeley: University of California Press.

Messerer, J., and Meyers, G. (1983). *The adequacy of high school preparation on the adult adjustment of learning disabled youth.* Eric Document Reproduction Service No. ED 248 681.

Meyer, L. H., Peck, C. A., and Brown, L. (1991). Definition of the people TASH serves. In L. H. Meyer, C. A. Peck. and L. Brown (Eds.), *Critical issues in the lives of people with severe disabilities* (p. 20). Baltimore: Paul H. Brookes.

Michaels, C.A. (1994). Transition issues. In C.A. Michaels (Ed.), *Transition strategies for persons with learning disabilities* (1–22). San Diego: Singular Publishing Group, Inc.

Michaels, C.A. (1997). Preparation for employment: Counseling practices that promote personal competency. In P.J. Gerber and D.S. Brown (Eds.), *Learning disabilities and employment.* Austin: PRO-ED.

Michaels, C.A. (1994a). Preface. In C.A. Michaels (Ed.), *Transition strategies for persons with learning disabilities* (ix–xiii). San Diego: Singular Publishing Group, Inc.

Michaels, C.A. (1994c). Employment issues: Transition from school to work. In C.A. Michaels (Ed.), *Transition strategies for persons with learning disabilities* (119–152). San Diego: Singular Publishing Group, Inc.

Michaels, C.A. (1989). Employment: The final frontier. *Rehabilitation Counseling Bulletin, 33,* 67–73.

Michaels, C.A., and Lazar, J.W., and Risucci, D.A. (1995). *A neuropsychological approach to the assessment of adults with learning disabilities in vocational rehabilitation.* Manuscript submitted for publication.

Michaels, C.A., Lee, M., Grosso, C., and Reiser, F. (1991). *Social skills for the world of work and beyond—A curriculum designed to promote social skill development in college students with learning disablities.* Albertson, NY: Human Resources Center.

Michaels, C.A., Thaler, R., Zwerlein, R., Gioglio, M., and Apostoli, B. (1988). *From high school to college: Keys to success for students with learning disabilities.* Albertson, NY: Human Resources Center.

Millon, T. (1983). *Millon Clinical Multiaxial Inventory.* Minneapolis, MN: Interpretive Scoring Systems.

Minskoff, E.H., and DeMoss, S. (1993). Facilitating successful transition: Using the TRAC model to assess and develop academic skills needed for vocational competence. *Learning Disability Quarterly, 16* (3), 161–170.

Mistler, S. (1978, March). *Planning for the implementation of Section 504 at colleges and universities.* Washington, DC: George Washington University.

Mithaug, D.E., Horiuchi, C.N., and Fanning, P.N. (1985). A report on the Colorado statewide follow-up survey of special education students. *Exceptional Children, 51,* 397–404.

Mithaug, D.E., Martin, J.E., Agran, M., and Rusch, F.R. (1988). *Why special education graduates fail: How to teach them to succeed.* Colorado Springs: Ascent.

Mithaug, D.E., and Horiuchi, C.N. (1983, September). *Colorado statewide follow-up survey of special education students.* Colorado Springs: Colorado State Department of Education.

Moats, L.C., and Lyon, G.R. (1993). Learning disabilities in the United States: Advocacy, science, and the future of the field. *Journal of Learning Disabilities, 26,* 282–294.

Moecker, D.L. (1992, November). Special education decision processes for Anglo and Hispanic students. Paper presented at the Council for Exceptional Children Topical Conference on Culturally and Linguistically diverse Exceptional Children, Minneapolis.

Mokros, H.B., Poznanski, E.O., and Merrick, W.A. (1989). Depression and learning disabilities in children: A test of a hypothesis. *Journal of Learning Disabilities, 22,* 230–233.

Montague, M., Bos, C., and Doucette, M. (1991). Affective, cognitive, and metacognitive attributes of eighth-grade mathematical problem solvers. *Learning Disabilities Research and Practice, 6* (1), 145–151.

Montgomery, M.S. (1994). Self-concept and children with learning disabilites: Observer-child concordance across six context-dependent domains. *Journal of Learning Disabilities, 27* (4), 254–262.

Moore, K. L. (1982). *The developing human: Clinically oriented embryology* (3rd ed.). Philadelphia: W. B. Saunders Company.

Morrison, D.C., and Hinshaw, S.P. (1988). The relationship between neuropsychological/perceptual performance and socioeconomic status in children with learning disabilities. *Journal of Learning Disabilities, 21,* 124–128.

Mount, B. (1992). *Person-centered planning: Finding directions for change using personal futures planning.* New York: Graphic Futures, Inc.

Myklebust, H.R. (1965). *Development and disorders of written language. Volume one: Picture Story Language Test.* New York: Grune and Stratton.

Nass, R.D. (1993). Sex differences in learning abilities and disabilities. *Annals of Dyslexia, 43,* 61–77.

National Education Association (no date). *Teaching and counseling gay and lesbian students.* Washington, DC: Author.

National Joint Committee on Learning Disabilities. (1996). Secondary to postsecondary education transition planning for students with learning disabilities. *Learning Disability Quarterly, 19* (1), 62–64.

National Joint Committee on Learning Disabilities. (1992, September). *Learning disabilities and the Americans with Disabilities Act (ADA).*

National Joint Committee for Learning Disabilities. (1988). [Letter to NJCLD member organizations].

National Joint Committee on Learning Disabilities. (1994). *Collective perspectives on issues affecting learning disabilities.* Austin, TX: PRO-ED.

National Joint Committee on Learning Disabilities (NJCLD). (1990). Learning disabilities: Issues on definition. In National Joint Committee on Learning Disabilities, (1994). *Collective perspectives on issues affecting learning disabilities,* pp. 61–64. Austin, TX: PRO-ED.

National Joint Committee on Learning Disabilities (1994). Secondary to postsecondary education transition planning for students with learning disabilities. In NJCLD, *Collective perspectives on issues affecting learning disabilities: Position papers and statements.* Austin, TX: PRO-ED.

National Joint Committee on Learning Disabilities (1988). *Position statements on learning disabilities.* Austin, TX: Author.

Nativio, D. G., and Belz, C. (1990). Childhood neurofibromatosis. *Pediatric Nursing, 16,* 575–580.

Needleman, H.L. (1987). Lead levels and child development. *Journal of Learning Disabilities, 20,* 264–265.

Needleman, H. L., Gunnoe, C., Leviton, A., Reed, R., Peresie, H., Maher, C., and Barrett, P. (1979). Deficits in psychological and classroom performance of children with elevated dentine lead levels. *New England Journal of Medicine, 300,* 689–695.

Neely, C. W. (1991). Family bonds: A mother's story about a family affected by Fragile X syndrome. *LDA/Newsbriefs, 26* (4), 3, 6–7.

Neisworth, J.T., and Greer, J.G. (1975). Functional similarities of learning disability and mild retardation. *Exceptional Children, 42,* 17–21.

Nichols, P. L., and Chen, T. C. (1981). *Minimal brain dysfunction: A prospective study.* Hillsdale, NJ: Lawrence Erlbaum Associates.

Obrzut, J. E., and Hynd, G. W. (1987). Cognitive dysfunction and psychoeducational assessment in individuals with acquired brain injury. *Journal of Learning Disabilities, 20,* 596–602.

Ochoa, S.H., and Palmer, D.J. (1991). A sociometric analysis of between-group differences and within-group status variability of Hispanic learning disabled and non-handicapped pupils in academic and play contexts. *Learning Disability Quarterly, 14* (3), 208–218.

Ochoa, S.H., and Palmer, D.J. (1995). Comparison of the peer status of Mexican-American students with learning disabilities and non-disabled low-achieving students. *Learning Disability Quarterly, 18* (1), 57–63.

Offer, D. (1969). *The psychological world of the teen-ager.* New York: Basic Books.

Office of Civil Rights (1988). Free appropriate public education for students with handicaps: Requirements under Section 504 of the Rehabilitation Act of 1973. Washington, D.C.: Office of Civil Rights.

Office of Civil Rights. (1989). Student placement in elementary and secondary schools and Section 504. Washington, D.C.: Office of Civil Rights.

Office of Civil Rights (1989). The civil rights of students with hidden disabilities under Section 504 of the Rehabilitation Act of 1973. Washington, D.C.: Office of Civil Rights.

Ogbu, J.U. (1987). Variability in minority school performance: A problem in search of an explanation. *Anthropology and Education Quarterly, 18,* 312–334.

Okolo, C.M. (1992). The effect of computer-assisted instruction format and initial attitude on the arithmetic facts proficiency and continuing motivation of students with learning disabilities. *Exceptionality, 3* (4), 195–211.

Olson, R., Wise, B., Conners, F., Rack, J., and Fulker, D. (1989). Specific deficits in component reading and language skills: Genetic and environmental influences. *Journal of Learning Disabilities, 22,* 339-348.

O'Neil, J. (1994). Getting a head start on a career: School-to-work programs demand new curriculum. *Update, 36* (8), 1, 3–4.

Opp, G. (1994). Historical roots of the field of learning disabilities: Some nineteenth-century German contributions. *Journal of Learning Disabilities, 27,* 10–19.

Ortiz, A.A., and Yates, J.R. (1983). Incidence of exceptionality among Hispanics: Implications for manpower planning. *NABE Journal, 7,* 41–54.

Ouellette, E. M. (1984). The fetal alcohol syndrome. *In developmental handicaps: Prevention and treatment, II* (pp. 34–50). (ERIC Document Reproduction Service No. ED 276 193).

Osborne, A.G. (1992). Legal standards for an appropriate education in the post-Rowley era. *Exceptional Children,* 488–493.

Palinscar, A., and Brown, A. (1988). Teaching and practicing thinking skills to promote comprehension in the context of group problem solving. *Remedial and Special Education, 9,* 53–59.

Palincsar, A.S., Brown, A.L., and Campione, J.C. (1991). Dynamic assessment. In H.L. Swanson (Ed.), *Handbook on the assessment of learning disabilities: Theory, research, and practice* (pp. 75–94). Austin, TX: PRO-ED.

Palincsar, A., and Klenk, L. (1992). Fostering literacy learning in supportive contexts. *Journal of Learning Disabilities, 25,* 211–225.

Patrick, J.L., and Reschly, D.J. (1982). Relationship of state educational criteria and demographic variables to school-system prevalence of mental retardation. *American Journal of Mental Deficiency, 86,* 351–360.

Patton, J.R., and Polloway, E.A. (1996). Adults with learning disabilities: An emerging area of professional interest and public attention. In J.R. Patton and E.A. Polloway (Eds.) *Learning disabilities: The challenges of adulthood.* Austin, TX: PRO-ED.

Patton, J.R. (1994). Practical recommendations for using homework with students with learning disabilities. *Journal of Learning Disabilities, 27,* 570–578.

Patton, J.R., and Polloway, E.A. (1992). Learning disabilities: Challenges in adulthood. *Journal of Learning Disabilities, 25,* 410–415, 427.

Pearl, R. (1987). Social cognitive factors in learning disabled children's social problems. In S.J. Ceci (Ed.), *Handbook of cognitive, social, and neuropsychological aspects of learning disabilities* (Vol. 2, pp. 273–294). Hillsdale, NJ: Erlbaum.

Pearl, R., Bryan, T., Fallon, P., and Herzog, A. (1991). Learning disabled students' detection of deception. *Learning Disabilities Research and Practice, 6* (1), 12–16.

Pearpoint, J., Forest, M., and Snow, J. (1992). *The inclusion papers: Strategies to make inclusion work.* Toronto: Inclusion Press.

Pearpoint, J., O'Brien, J., and Forest, M. (1992). *PATH Planning alternative tomorrows with hope—A workbook for planning better futures (Version 1.2).* Toronto: Inclusion Press.

Pekham, V.C., Meadows, A.T., Bartel, N., and Marrero, O. (1988). Educational late effects in long term survivors of childhood acute lymphocytic leukemia. *Pediatrics, 81,* 127–133.

Pennington, B. F. (1990). Annotation: The genetics of dyslexia. *Journal of Child Psychology and Psychiatry, 31,* 193–201.

Peters, S.A.F., Grievink, E.H., vanBon, W.H.J., and Schilder, A.G.M. (1994). The effects of early bilateral otitis media with effusion on educational attainment: A prospective cohort study. *Journal of Learning Disabilities, 27,* 111–121.

Pipher, M. (1994). *Reviving Ophelia: Saving the selves of adolescent girls.* New York: Ballantine Books.

Plumridge, D., Barkost, C., and LaFranchi, S. (1982). *Klinefelter syndrome: The X-tra special boy.* Oregon: Health Sciences University.

Podemski, R.S., Marsh, G.E., Smith, T.E.C., and Price, B.J. (1995). *Comprehensive administration of special education*, 2nd Ed. Columbus, OH: Merrill.

Polloway, E.A., Epstein, M.H., Polloway, C.H., Patton, J.R., and Ball, D.W. (1986). Corrective Reading Program: An analysis of effectiveness with learning disabled and mentally retarded students. *Remedial and Special Education, 7* (4), 41–47.

Polloway, E., Patton, J., Epstein, M., Acquah, T., Decker, T., and Carse, C. (1992). Characteristics and services in learning disabilities: A report on elementary school programs. ERIC Document Reproduction Service (No. ED 342 158).

Polloway, E.A., Patton, J. R., Smith, T.E.C., and Buck, G.H. (in press). Mental retardation and learning disabilities: Conceptual and applied issues. *Journal of Learning Disabilities.*

Polloway, E.A., Schewel, R., and Patton, J.R. (1992). Learning disabilities in adulthood: Personal perspectives. *Journal of Learning Disabilities, 25,* 520–522.

Polloway, E.A. (1987). Transition services for early age individuals with mild mental retardation. In R.N. Ianacone and R.A. Stodden (Eds.), *Transition issues and directions* (pp. 11–24). Reston, VA: CEC-MR.

Polloway, E.A., Bursuck, W.D., Jayanthi, M., Epstein, M.H., and Nelson, J.S. (1995). Treatment acceptability: Determining appropriate interventions within inclusive classrooms. *Intervention in School and Clinic, 31* (3), 133–144.

Polloway, E.A., and Patton, J.R. (1996). *Strategies for teaching learners with special needs* (6th ed). Columbus, OH: Merrill.

Polloway, E.A., and Smith, J.D. (1994). Causes and prevention. In M. Beirne-Smith, J.R. Patton, and R. Ittenbach (Eds.), *Mental Retardation* (pp. 136–210). Columbus, OH: Merrill.

Poplin, M., and Phillips, L. (1993). Sociocultural aspects of language and literacy: Issues facing educators of students with learning disabilities. *Learning Disability Quarterly, 16,* (4) 245–255.

President's Committee on the Employment of People with Disabilities. (1990). *From paternalism to productivity—Whatever it takes.* Washington, DC: Author.

Price, L. (1993). Psychosocial characteristics and issues of adults with learning disabilities. In L. C. Brinckerhoff, S. F. Shaw, and J. M. McGuire (Eds.), *Promoting postsecondary education for students with learning disabilities* (pp. 137–168). Austin, TX: PRO-ED, Inc.

Price, L.A., Johnson, J.M., and Evelo, S. (1994). When academic assistance is not enough: Addressing the mental health issues of adolescents and adults with learning disabilities. *Journal of Learning Disabilities, 27,* 82-90.

Pueschel, S. M., Kopito, L., and Schwachman, H. (1972).Children with an increased lead burden: A screening and follow-up study. *Journal of the American Medical Association, 222,* 462–466.

Quality Education for Minorities Project. (1990). *Education that works: An action plan for the education of minorities.* Cambridge: Massachusetts Institute of Technology.

Ramey, C.T., Bryant, D.M., Sparling, J.J., and Wasik, B.H. (1985). Project CARE: A comparison of two early intervention strategies to prevent retarded development. *Topics in Early Childhood Special Education, 5*(2), 12–25.

Rapp, D. J. (1978). Does diet affect hyperactivity? *Journal of Learning Disabilities, 11,* 383–389.

Raskind, M.H., Herman, K.L., and Torgesen, J.K. (1995). Technology for persons with learning disabilities: Report on an international symposium. *Learning Disabilities Quarterly, 18,* 175–184.

Reed, S., and Sautter, R.C. (1990). Children of poverty: The status of 12 million young Americans. Kappan Special Report. *Phi Delta Kappan, 71,* 1–11.

Reeve, R.E. (1990). ADHD: Facts and fallacies. *Intervention in School and Clinic, 26,* 71–78.

Rehabilitation Act (1973). Section 504 (P.L. 93-112), as amended, 29 U.S.C.794.

Rehabilitation Services Administration. (1985). RSA Program Policy Directive. RSA-PPD-85-7, March 5.

Reichman, J., and Healey, W. (1983). Learning disabilities and conductive hearing loss involving otitus media. *Journal of Learning Disabilities, 16,* 272–278.

Reid, D.K., and Hresko, W.P. (1980). A developmental study of the relation between oral language and early reading in learning disabled and normally achieving children. *Learning Disability Quarterly, 3* (4), 54–61.

Reid, R., and Katsiyannis, A. (1995). Attention-deficit/hyperactivity disorder and Section 504. *Remedial and Special Education, 14,* 44–52.

Reiff, H. B., and Gerber, P. J. (1994). Social/emotional and daily living issues for adults with learning disabilities. In P. J. Gerber and H. B. Reiff (Eds.), *Learning disabilities in adulthood* (pp. 72–81). Stoneham, MA: Andover Medical Publishers.

Reiff, H.B., and deFur, S. (1992). Transition for youths with learning disablties: A focus on developing independence. *Learning Disability Quarterly, 15,* 237–249.

Rhodes, S.S., and Jasinski, D.R. (1990). Learning disabilities in alcohol-dependent adults: A preliminary study. *Journal of Learning Disabilities, 23,* 551–556.

Rice, F.P. (1987). *The adolescent: Development, relationships, and culture.* Boston: Allyn and Bacon.

Richardson, S.D. (1992). Historical perspectives on dyslexia. *Journal of Learning Disabilities, 25,* 40–47.

Rieth, H.J., and Polsgrove, L. (1994). Curriculum and instructional issues in teaching secondary students with learning disabilities. *Learning Disabilities Research and Practice, 9,* 118–126.

Rist, M.C. (1990). The shadow children. *American School Board Journal, 177,* 19–24.

Rock, E.E., Fessler, M.A., and Church, R.P. (in press). The concomitance of learning disabilities and emotional/behavioral disorders: A conceptual model. *Journal of Learning Disabilities.*

Roffman, A. (1994). Social skill training. In C. A. Michaels (Ed.), *Transition strategies for persons with learning disabilities* (pp. 185–212). San Diego: Singular Publishing Group, Inc.

Roth, V. (1991). Students with learning disabilities and hearing impairment: Issues for the secondary and postsecondary teacher. *Journal of Learning Disabilities, 24,* 391–397.

Rourke, B.P., Young, G.C., and Leenaars, A.A. (1989). A childhood learning disability that predisposes those afflicted to adolescent and adult depression and suicide risk. *Journal of Learning Disabilities, 22,* 169–175.

Rousseau, F., Heitz, D., Biancalana, V., Blumenfeld, S., Kretz, C., Boue, J., Tommerup, N., Hagen, C. van der, DeLozier-Blanchet, C., Croquette, M. F., Gilgenkrantz, S., Jalbert, P., Voelckel, M. A., Oberle, I., and Mandel, J. L. (1991). Direct diagnosis by DNA analysis of the Fragile X syndrome of mental retardation. *New England Journal of Medicine, 325,* 1673–1681.

Rovet, J., Ehrlich, R., Czuchta, D., and Akler, M. (1993). Psychoeducational characteristics of children and adolescents with insulin-dependent diabetes mellitus. *Journal of Learning Disabilities, 26,* 7–22.

Rovet, J.F. (1993). The psychoeducational characteristics of children with Turner syndrome. *Journal of Learning Disabilities, 26,* 333–341.

Ruiz, N.T. (1989). An optimal learning environment for Rosemary. *Exceptional Children, 56* (2), 130–144.

Salvia, J., and Ysseldyke, J.E. (1985). *Assessment in special and remedial education,* 3rd ed. Boston: Houghton Mifflin Company.

Saparani, E.F., Abel, F.J., Easton, S.E., Edwards, P., and Herbster, D.L. (1995, February). Pre-service teacher education majors' understanding of issues related to diversity and exceptionality. Paper presented at the Annual Meeting of the Association of Teacher Educators (75th), Detroit, MI. (ERIC Document Reproduction Service No. 379 280)

Savage, R.C. (1994). Guide to brain and brain injury. In R.C. Savage and G.F. Wolcott (Eds.), *Educational dimensions of acquired brain injury. Austin,* TX: PRO-ED.

Schalock, R.L. (1996). Reconsidering the conceptualization and measurement of quality of life. In R. L. Schalock (Ed.), *Quality of life: Conceptualization and measurement (volume 1)* (pp. 123–139). Washington: American Association on Mental Retardation.

Schalock, R.L. (1986). *Transition from school to work.* Washington, DC: National Association of Rehabilitation Facilities.

Schiff-Myers, N.B., Djukic, J., McGovern-Lawler, J., and Perez, D. (1994). Assessment considerations in the evaluation of second-language learners: A case study. *Exceptional Children, 60* (3), 237–248.

Schoenbrodt, L., Kumin, L., and Sloan, J. (in press). Learning disabilities existing concomitantly with communication disorder. *Journal of Learning Disabilities.*

Schulze, K.A., Rule, S., and Innocenti, M.S. (1989). Coincidental teaching: Parents promoting social skills at home. *Teaching Exceptional Children, 21,* 24–27.

Schumaker, J. B., and Ellis, E. (1982). Social skills training of learning disabled adolescents: A generalization study. *Learning Disabilities Quarterly, 5,* 409–414.

Schumaker, J.B., Hazel, J.S., Sherman, J.A., and Sheldon, J. (1982). *Social skill performance of learning disabled, non-learning disabled, and delinquent adolescents* (Research Report No. 60). Lawrence, KS: University of Kansas Institute for Research in Learning Disabilities.

Schunk, D.H., and Rice, J.M. (1992). Influence of reading comprehension strategy information on children's achievement outcomes. *Learning Disability Quarterly, 15* (1), 51–64.

Schwarz, R., and Burt, M. (1995). ESL instruction for learning disabled adults. ERIC Digest (January), 1–2. (ERIC Document Reproduction Service No. 379 966)

Scott, E.M. (1995). An overview of Prader-Willi syndrome. Unpublished manuscript, Lynchburg College, Lynchburg, VA.

Scott, S.S. (1990). Coming to terms with the "otherwise qualified" student with a learning disability. *Journal of Learning Disabilities, 23,* 398–405.

Scott, S.S. (1994). Determining reasonable academic adjustments for college students with learning disabilities. *Journal of Learning Disabilities, 27,* 403–412.

Scruggs, T.E., and Mastropieri, M.A. (1990). Mnemonic instruction for students with learning disabilities: What it is and what it does. *Learning Disability Quarterly, 13* (4), 271–280.

Scruggs, T.E., and Mastropieri, M.A. (1986). Academic characteristics of behaviorally disordered and learning disabled students. *Behavioral Disorders, 11,* 184–190.

Segalowitz, S. J., and Lawson, S. (1995). Subtle symptoms associated with self-reported mild head injury. *Journal of Learning Disabilities, 28,* 309–319.

Scuccimarra, D.J., and Speece, D.L. (1990). Employment outcomes and social integration of students with mild handicaps: The quality of life two years after high school. *Journal of Learning Disabilities, 23,* 518–520.

Seidel, J.F., and Vaughn, S. (1991). Social alienation and the learning disabled school dropout. *LD Research and Practice, 6,* 152–157.

Seidenberg, P.L. (1989). Relating text-processing research to reading and writing instruction for learning disabled students. *Learning Disabilities Focus, 5* (1), 4–12.

Seidenberg, M.S., Bruck, M., Fornarolo, G., and Backman, J. (1985). Word recognition processes of poor and disabled readers: Do they necessarily differ? *Applied Psycholinguistics, 6,* 161–180.

Seidenberg, M.S., Bruck, M., Fornarolo, G., and Backman, J. (1986). Who is dyslexic? Reply to Wolf. *Applied Psycholinguistics, 7,* 77–84.

Sell, E. J., Gaines, J. A., Gluckman, C., and Williams, E. (1985). Early identification of learning problems in neonatal intensive care graduates. *American Journal of Diseases of Children, 139,* 460–463.

Selz, M.J., and Wilson, S. L. (1989). Neuropsychological bases of common learning and behavior problems in children. In C. R. Reynolds and E. Fletcher-Janzen (Eds.), *Handbook of clinical child neuropsychology.* (pp. 129–145). New York: Plenum Press.

Semel, E.M., and Wiig, E.H. (1982). *Clinical language intervention program.* Columbus, OH: Merrill.

Serna, L.A., and Lau-Smith, J. (1995). *Learning with PURPOSE.* Honolulu: University of Hawaii.

Shapiro, E.S., and Lentz, F.E. (1991). Vocational-technical programs: Follow-up of students with learning disabilities. *Exceptional Children, 58,* 47–59.

Shaywitz, S. E., Escobar, M. D., Shaywitz, B. A., Fletcher, J., and Makuch, R. (1992). Evidence that dyslexia may represent the lower tail of a normal distribution of reading ability. *New England Journal of Medicine, 326,* 145–150.

Shea, T.M., and Bauer, A.M. (1991). *Parents and teachers of children with exceptionalities: A handbook for collaboration.* Boston: Allyn and Bacon.

Shepard, T., and Adjogah, S. (1994). Science performance of students with learning disabilities on language-based measures. *Learning Disabilities Research and Practice, 9* (4), 219–225.

Shokoohi-Yekta, M., and Kavale, K.E. (1994). Effects of increased high school graduation standards on college entrance examination performance of students with learning disabilities. *Learning Disabilities Research and Practice, 9* (4), 213–218.

Shprintzen, R. J., and Goldberg, R. B. (1986). Multiple anomaly syndromes and learning disabilities. In S. D. Smith (Ed.), *Genetics and learning disabilities* (pp. 153–174). San Diego: College-Hill Press.

Siegel, L.S., and Ryan, E.B. (1989). The development of working-memory in normally achieving and subtypes of learning disabled. *Child Development, 60,* 973–980.

Siegel, S., Robert, M., Greener, K., Meyer, G., Halloran, W., and Gaylord-Ross, R. (1993). *Career ladders for challenged youths in transition from school to adult life.* Austin, TX: PRO-ED.

Singer, L T., Garber, R., and Kliegman, R. (1991). Neurobehavioral sequelae of fetal cocaine exposure. *Journal of Pediatrics, 119,* 667–671.

Sitlington, P.L. (1996). Transition to living: The neglected component of transition programming for individuals with learning disabilities. *Journal of Learning Disabilities, 29* (1), 31–39.

Sitlington, P.L., and Frank, A.R. (1990). Are adolescents with learning disabilities successfully crossing the bridge into adult life? *Learning Disability Quarterly, 13,* 97–111.

Sleeter, C.E. (1986). Learning disabilities: the social construction of a special education category. *Exceptional Children, 53,* 46–54.

Smith, D.D., and Lovitt, T.C. (1982). *The computational arithmetic program.* Austin, TX: PRO-ED.

Smith, D.D., and Luckasson, R. (1995). *Introduction to special education: Teaching in an age of challenge.* (2nd ed.). Boston: Allyn and Bacon.

Smith, J.D. (1994). The revised AAMR definition of mental retardation: The MRDD position. *Education and Training in Mental Retardation and Developmental disabilities, 29,* 179–183.

Smith, J.E., Polloway, E.A., and Smith, J.D. (1978). The continuing dilemma of educating children with mild learning problems. *Special Children, 4,* 52–63.

Smith, S. D. (Ed.), (1986). *Genetics and learning disabilities.* San Diego: College-Hill Press.

Smith, S. E. (1993). Cognitive deficits associated with Fragile X syndrome. *Mental Retardation, 31,* 279–283.

Smith, T.E.C., Finn, D.M., and Dowdy, C.A. (1993). *Teaching students with mild disabilities.* Ft. Worth: Harcourt Brace.

Smith, T.E.C., and Dowdy, C.A. (1992). Future-based assessment and intervention and mental retardation. *Education and Training in Mental Retardation, 27,* 23–31.

Smith, T.E.C., and Podemski, R.S. (1983). Special education hearings: How to do them correctly. *Executive Educator, 3,* 19–24.

Smith, T.E.C., Polloway, E.A., Patton, J.R., and Dowdy, C.A. (1995). *Teaching students with special needs in inclusive settings.* Boston: Allyn and Bacon.

Smith, T.E.C., Price, B.J., and Marsh, G.E. (1986). *Mildly handicapped children and adults.* St. Paul: West Publishing

Snell, M.E., and Drake, G. (1994). Replacing cascades with supported education. *Journal of Special Education, 27,* 393–409.

Snow, J. A. (1994). *What's really worth doing and how to do it.* Toronto: Inclusion Press.

Southern, W.T., and Jones, E.D. (1991). *Academic acceleration of gifted children.* New York: Teacher's College Press.

Southern, W.T., and Swart, G. (1995). Twice exceptional: Gifted children with learning disabilities. *LD Forum, 20,* 48–49.

Spear-Swerling, L., and Sternberg, R.J. (1994). The road not taken: An integrative theoretical model of reading disability. *Journal of Learning Disabilities, 27* (2), 91–103, 122.

Spekman, N.J., Goldberg, R.J., and Herman, K.L. (1993). An exploration of risk and resilience in the lives of individuals with learning disabilities. *Learning Disabilities Research and Practice, 8* (1), 11–18.

Spekman, N.J., Goldberg, R.J., and Herman, K.L. (1992). Learning disabled children grow up: A search for factors related to success in the young adult years. *Learning Disabilities Research and Practice, 7,* 161–170.

Stanford, L.S., and Hynd, G.W. (1994). Congruence of behavioral symptomatology in children with ADD/H, ADD/WO, and learning disabilities. *Journal of Learning Disabilities, 27* (4), 243–253.

Stanovich, K.E. (1988). Explaining the differences between the dyslexic and the garden-variety poor reader: The phonological-core variable-difference model. *Journal of Learning Disabilities, 21*, 590–604.

Stanovich, K.E., Nathan, R.G., and Vala-Rossi, M. (1986). Developmental changes in the cognitive correlates of reading ability and the developmental lag hypothesis. *Reading Research Quarterly, 21*, 267–283.

Stephens, T.M. (1978). *Social skills in the classroom.* Columbus, OH: Cedars Press.

Stephenson, J. (1992). The perspectives of mothers whose children are in special day classes for learning disabilities. *Journal of Learning Disabilities, 25*, 539–543.

Stern, R., Kendall, A, and Eberhard, P. (1991). Children of alcoholics in the schools: Where are they? Their representation in special education. *Psychology in the Schools, 28*, 116–123.

Stone, A., and Michals, D. (1986). Problem-solving skills in learning-disabled children. In S.J. Ceci (Ed.), *Handbook of cognitive, social, and neuropsychological aspects of learning disabilities* (Vol. 1, pp. 291–315). Hillsdale, NJ: Lawrence Erlbaum Associates.

Stone, C.A., and Reid, D.K. (1994). Social and individual forces in learning: Implications for instruction of children with learning difficulties. *Learning Disability Quarterly, 17* (1), 72–86.

Stone, W.L., and LaGreca, A.M. (1990). The social status of children with LD: A reexamination. *Journal of Learning Disabilities, 23*, 32–37.

Super, D. (1953). A theory of vocational development. *American Psychologist, 8*, 185–190.

Streett, S., and Smith, T.E.C. (1996). *Section 504 and public schools: A practical guide.* Little Rock, AR: The Learning Group.

Streissguth, A. P., Martin, D. C., Barr, H. M., Sandman, B. M.,Kirchner, G. L., and Darby, B. L. (1984). Intrauterine alcohol and nicotine exposure: Attention and reaction time in four-year-old children. *Developmental Psychology, 20*, 533–541.

Strodden, R. (1980). *Vocational assessment for special needs individuals* (Project Final Report, Phase I 1979–1980). Upton, MA: Blackstone Valley Regional Vocational School District.

Sutherland, G. R., Gedeon, A., Kornman, L., Donnelly, A., Byard, R. W., Mulley, J. C., Kremer, E., Lynch, M., Pritchard, M., Yu, S., and Richards, R. I. (1991). Prenatal diagnosis of Fragile X syndrome by direct detection of the unstable DNA sequence. *New England Journal of Medicine, 325*, 1720–1722.

Swanson, H.L. (1989). Strategy instruction: Overview of principles and procedures for effective use. *Learning Disability Quarterly, 12* (1), 3–14.

Swanson, H.L. (1994). The role of working memory and dynamic assessment in the classification of children with learning disabilities. *Learning Disabilities Research, 9* (4), 190–202.

Swanson, H.L. (1991). Operational definitions and learning disabilities: An overview. *Learning Disability Quarterly, 14*, 242–254.

Swanson, J.M., Cantwell, D., Lerner, M., McBurnett, K., and Hanna, G. (1991). Effects of stimulant medication on learning in children with ADHD. *Journal of Learning Disabilities, 24,* 219–230.

Swanson, J.M., McBurnett, K., Wigal, T., Pfiffner, L.J., Lerner, M.A., Williams, L., Christian, D.L., Tamm, L., Willcutt, E., Crowley, K., Clevenger, W., Khouzam, N., Woo, C., Crinella, F.M., and Fisher, T.D. (1993). Effect of stimulant medication on children with attention deficit disorder: A "Review of Reviews." *Exceptional Children, 60,* 154–162.

Swanson, H.L., Christie, L., and Rubadeau, R.J. (1993). The relationship between metacognition and analogical reasoning in mentally retarded, learning disabled, average, and gifted children. *Learning Disabilities Research and Practice, 8 (2)* 70–81.

Switzer, L.S. (1985). Accepting the diagnosis: An educational intervention for parents of children with learning disabilities. *Journal of Learning Disabilities, 18,* 151–153.

Tallal, P. (1988). Developmental language disorders. In Kavanagh, J.F., and Truss, T.J. (Eds.), *Learning disabilities: Proceedings of the national conference* (pp. 181–270). Parkton, MD: York.

Taylor, S. J., and Bogdan, R. (1996). Quality of life and the individual's perspective. In R. L. Schalock (Ed.), *Quality of life: Conceptualization and measurement (volume 1)* (pp. 11–22). Washington: American Association on Mental Retardation.

Thurston, L.P. (1989). Helping parents tutor their children: A success story. *Academic Therapy, 24,* 579–587.

Turnbull, A.P., and Turnbull, H.R. (1990). *Families, professionals, and exceptionality: A special partnership,* 2nd Ed. Columbus, OH: Merrill.

Turnbull, H.R., Turnbull, A.P., Bronicki, G.J., Summers, J.A., and Boeder-Gordon, C. (1989). *Disability and the family.* Baltimore: Brooks Publishing Co.

Turnbull, A.P., and Turnbull, H.R. (1990). *Families, professionals and exceptionality* (2nd ed.). Columbus, OH: Merrill.

Turnbull, H.R. (1993). *Free appropriate public education,* 4th Ed. Denver: Love.

Tur-Kaspa, H., and Bryan, T. (1995). Teachers' ratings of the social competence and school adjustment of students with LD in elementary and junior high school. *Journal of Learning Disabilities, 28* (1), 44–52.

Underwood, J.K., and Mead, J.F. (1995). *Legal aspects of special education and pupil services.* Boston: Allyn and Bacon.

U.S. Department of Education (1995). *Making a good law better: Summary of IDEA amendments for 1995.* Washington, DC: Author.

U.S. Department of Education (1989, 1990, 1991, 1992, 1993, 1994, 1995). *Annual reports to Congress on the implementation of the IDEA.* Washington, D.C.: Author.

U.S. Office of Education (1976). Proposed rulemaking. *Federal rulemaking, 41* (230), 52404–52407.

U.S. Department of Education (1993). *Fifteenth annual report to Congress on the implementation of the Individuals with Disabilities Education Act.* Washington, DC: Author.

U.S. Department of Education (1995). *Seventeenth annual report to Congress on the implementation of the Individuals with Disabilities Education Act*. Washington, DC: Author.

U.S. Department of Commerce. (1990). *U.S. Census*. Washington, DC: Bureau of the Census.

U.S. General Accounting Office. (1987). Bilingual education: Information on limited English proficient students. Briefing report to the Chairman, Committee on Labor and Human Resources, United States Senate. Washington, DC: Author.

Van Baar, A., and deGraaff, B. M. T. (1994). Cognitive development at preschool age of infants of drug-dependent mothers. *Developmental Medicine and Child Neurology, 36,* 1063–1075.

Van Dyke, D. C., and Lin-Dyken, D. C. (1993). The new genetics, developmental disabilities, and early intervention. *Infants and Young Children, 5* (4), 8–19.

Van Reusen, A.K., Bos, C.S., Schumaker, J.B., and Deshler, D.D. (1994). *The self-advocacy strategy*. Lawrence, KS: Edge Enterprises, Inc.

Vaughn, S., McIntosh, R., and Spencer-Rowe, J. (1991). Peer rejection is a stubborn thing: Increasing peer acceptance of rejected students with learning disabilities. *Learning Disabilities Research and Practice, 6,* 83–88.

Vaughn, S., McIntosh, R., Schumm, J.S., Haager, D., and Callwood, D. (1993). Social status, peer acceptance, and reciprocal friendships revisited. *Learning Disabilities Research and Practice, 8* (2), 82–88.

Vaughn, S. and Schumm, L.S. (1995). Responsible inclusion for students with learning disabilities. *Journal of Learning Disabilities, 28,* 264–270, 290.

Vaughn, S., and Hogan, A. (1994). The social competence of students with learning disabilities over time: A within-individual examination. *Journal of Learning Disabilities, 27* (5), 292–303.

Vaughn, S., and Haager, D. (1994). Social competence as a multifaceted construct: How do students with disabilities fare? *Learning Disability Quarterly, 17,* 253–266.

Vellutino, F.R. (1991). Introduction to three studies on reading acquisition: Convergent findings on theoretical foundations of code-oriented versus whole-language approaches to reading instruction. *Journal of Educational Psychology, 83,* 437–443.

Vellutino, F. R. (1987). Dyslexia. *Scientific American, 56,* 34–41.

Viadero, D. (1995). Beating the odds. *Education Week* (March 29), 32–33.

Viadero, D. (1995). Twice exceptional: Gifted students with learning disabilities get lost in schools. *Education Week* (May 31), 35–36.

Vocational Evaluation and Work Adjustment Association. (1978). *Vocational evaluation and work adjustment standards with interpretive guidelines and VEWAA glossary*. Menomonie: University of Wisconsin-Stout, Material Development Center.

Vogel, S. A., and Walsh, P.C. (1987). Gender differences in cognitive abilities of learning-disabled females and males. *Annals of Dyslexia, 37,* 142–165.

Wadsworth, S.J., DeFries, J.C., and Fulker, D.W. (1993). Cognitive abilities of children at seven and twelve years of age in the Colorado Adoption Project. *Journal of Learning Disabilities, 26* (9), 611–615.

Wagner, M. (1989). *The transition experiences of youth with disabilities: A report from the national longitudinal transition study.* (USDOE, DSEP contract #300-87-0054). Menlo Park, CA: SRI International.

Wagner, M. (1993, June). *Trends in postsecondary youth with disabilities: Findings from the National Longitudinal Transition Study of special education students.* Paper presented at the meeting of the Transition Research Institute at Illinois Project Directors' Eighth Annual Meeting, Washington, D.C.

Wagner, M., Newman, L., D'Amico, R., Jay, E.D., Butler-Nalin, P., Marder, C., and Cox, R. (1991, September). *Youth with disabilities: How are they doing? The first comprehensive report from the National Longitudinal Transition Study of special education students.* Menlo Park, CA: SRI International.

Walker, H.M., McConnell, S., Holmes, D., Todis, B., Walker, J., and Golden, N. (1983). *The Walker social skills curriculum: The accepts program.* Austin, TX: PRO-ED.

Wallace, G., Cohen, S.B., and Polloway, E.A. (1989). *Language arts: Teaching exceptional students.* Austin, TX: PRO-ED.

Wang, M.C., and Gordon, E.W. (Eds.) (1994). *Educational resilience in inner-city America: Challenges and prospects.* Hillsdale, N.J.: Lawrence Erlbaum Associates.

Ward, M.J. (1992). Introduction to secondary special education and transition issues. In F.R. Rusch, L. Destefano, J. Chadsey-Rusch, L.A. Phelps, E. Szymanski (Eds.), *Transition from school to adult life: Models, linkages, and policy* (pp. 387–389). Sycamore, IL: Sycamore Publishing.

Warren, K. R., and Bast, R. J. (1988). Alcohol-related birth defects: An update. *Public Health Reports, 103,* 638–642.

Webb, K.W. (1995). *My plan for success: A college preparation manual.* Freeport, IL: Peekan Publications.

Wegner, J.W. (1988). Educational rights of handicapped children: Three federal statutes and an evolving jurisprudence. Part I: The statutory maze. *Journal of Law and Education, 17,* 387–457.

Wei, T.T.D. (1983). The Vietnamese refugee child: Understanding cultural differences. In D.R. Omark and J.G. Erickson (Eds.), *The bilingual exceptional child* (pp. 197–212). Boston: College-Hill.

Weismantel, M.J., and Fradd, S.H. (1989). Understanding the need for change. In S.H. Fradd and M.J. Weismantel (Eds.), *Meeting the needs of culturally and linguistically different students: A handbook for educators* (pp. 1–13). Boston: College-Hill.

Wener, D.L., and O'Shea, D.J. (1992). School professionals and parents encouraging whole language experiences for children with language disabilities. *LD Forum, 17,* 7–9.

Westling, D.L., and Koorland, M.A. (1988). *The special educator's handbook.* Boston: Allyn and Bacon.

Weinstein, G., and Cooke, N.L. (1992). The effects of two repeated reading interventions on generalization of fluency. *Learning Disability Quarterly, 15* (1), 21–28.

Werner, E.E. (1993). Risk and resilience in individuals with learning disabilities: Lessons learned from the Kauai Longitudinal Study. *Learning Disabilities Research and Practice, 8* (1), 28–34.

Werner, E.E., and Smith, R.S. (1992). *Overcoming the odds: High risk children from birth to adulthood.* Ithaca, NY: Cornell University Press.

West, T. G. (1991). *In the mind's eye: Visual thinkers, gifted people with learning difficulties, computer images, and the ironies of creativity.* Buffalo, NY: Prometheus Books.

Westman, J. C. (1990). *Handbook of learning disabilities: A multisystem approach.* Boston: Allyn and Bacon.

White, W.J. (1992). The postschool adjustment of persons with learning disabilities: Current status and future projections. *Journal of Learning Disabilities, 25,* 448–456.

White, W.J., Alley, G.R., Deshler, D.D., Schumaker, J.B., Warner, M., and Clark, F.L. (1982). Are there learning disabilities after high school? *Exceptional Children, 49* (3), 273–274.

White, W. J., Schumaker, J. B., Warner, M. M., Alley, G. R., and Deshler, D. B. (1980). *The current status of young adults identified as learning disabled during their school career* (Research Report No. 21). Lawrence: The University of Kansas Institute for Research in Learning Disabilities.

Whitman, T.L., Borkowski, J.G., Schellenbach, C.J., and Nath, P.S. (1987). Predicting and understanding developmental delay of adolescent mothers: A multidimensional approach. *American Journal on Mental Retardation, 92,* 40–56.

Wiederholt, J.L., and Hale, G.B. (1982). Indirect and direct treatment of learning disabilities. *Topics in Learning and Learning Disabilities, 1* (4), 79–86.

Wiederholt, J.L. (1974). Historical perspectives on the education of the learning disabled. In L. Mann and D. Sabatino (Eds.), *The second review of special education* (pp. 103–152). Austin, TX: PRO-ED.

Wiener, J., Harris, P.J., and Shirer, C. (1990). Achievement and social-behavioral correlates of peer status in learning disabled children. *Learning Disability Quarterly, 13,* 114–127.

Wiig, E.H. (1989). An interview with Dr. Donald D. Hammill, scholar and publisher. *LD Forum, 14,* 1+.

Wiig, E. H., and Fleischmann, N. (1980). Prepositional phrases, pronominalization, reflexivization and relativization in the language of learning disabled college students. *Journal of Learning Disabilities, 13,* 45–50.

Wiig, E.H. (1990). Linguistic transitions and learning disabilities: A strategic learning perspective. *Learning Disability Quarterly, 13* (2), 128–140.

Wiig, E.H. (1989). *Steps to language competence: A figurative language program.* San Antonio, TX: The Psychological Corporation.

Will, M. (1984). *OSERS programming for the transition of youth with disabilities: Bridges from school to working life.* Washington, DC: Office of Special Education and Rehabilitative Services.

Wilson, C.L. (1995). Parents and teachers: Can we talk? *LD Forum, 20,* 31–33.

Wilson, G.L. (1994). Self-advocacy skills. In C.A. Michaels (Ed.), *Transition strategies for persons with learning disabilities* (pp. 153–184). San Diego, CA: Singular Publishing Company, Inc.

Wilson, P. G., and Mazzocco, M.M.M. (1993). Awareness and knowledge of Fragile X syndrome among special educators. *Mental Retardation, 31,* 221–227.

Winn, J.A. (1994). Promises and challenges of scaffolded instruction. *Learning Disability Quarterly, 17* (1), 89–104.

Winstead, T. (1995, Fall). I am my learning disability—I am learning disability. We are one. We are inseparable. *The Missing Piece,* 7, Redmond: Quarterly Newsletter of the Learning Disabilities Association of Washington.

Wolery, M., Holcombe, A., Brookfield, J., Huffman, K., Schroeder, C., Martin, C.G., Venn, M.L., Werts, M.G., and Fleming, L.A. (1993). The extent and nature of preschool mainstreaming: A survey of general early educators. *Journal of Special Education, 27,* 222–234.

Wolery, M., Werts, M.G., and Holcombe, A. (1994). Current practices with young children who have disabilities: Placement, assessment, and instruction issues. *Focus on Exceptional Children, 26* (6), 2–12.

Wong, B.L. (1994). Parameters promotiong transition of learning strategies in students with learning disabilities. *Learning Disability Quarterly, 17,* 110–120.

Wong, B.Y.L., Wong, R., Darlington, D., and Jones, W. (1991). Interactive teaching: An effective way to teach revision skills to adolescents with learning disabilities. *Learning Disabilities Research and Practice, 6,* 117–127.

Worrall, R. S. (1990). Detecting health fraud in the field of learning disabilities. *Journal of Learning Disabilities, 23,* 207–212.

Wright-Strawderman, C., and Watson, B.L. (1992). The prevalence of depressive symptoms in children with learning disabilities. *Journal of Learning Disabilities, 25,* 258–264.

Yanok, J., and Derubertis, D. (1989). Comparative study of parental participation in regular and special education programs. *Exceptional Children, 56,* 195–199.

Yates, J.R., and Ortiz, A.A. (1991). Professional development needs of teachers who serve exceptional language minorities in today's schools. *Teacher Education and Special Education, 14* (1), 11–18.

Young, G. (1995, Fall). Success and IDEA's importance—Testimony of Glenn Young. *The Missing Piece,* 4–5, Redmond: Quarterly Newsletter of the Learning Disabilities Association of Washington.

Zigmond, N. (1990). Rethinking secondary school programs for students with learning disabilities. *Focus on Exceptional Children, 23* (1), 1–22.

Zigmond, N., and Thornton, H. (1985). Follow-up of postsecondary age learning disabled graduates and dropouts. *Learning Disabilities Research, 1* (1), 50–55.

Zirkel, P.A. and Kincaid, J.M. (1994). *Section 504 and the schools.* Horsham, PA: LRP Publications.

Ysseldyke, J.E. (1973). Diagnostic-prescriptive teaching: The search for aptitude-treatment interventions. In L. Mann and D. Sabatino (Eds.), *The first review of special education.* Austin, TX: PRO-ED.

Zentall, S. (1993). Research on the educational implications of attention deficit hyperactivity disorder. *Exceptional Children, 60,* 143–153.

Ziegler, R. (1981). Child and context: Reactive adaptations of learning disabled children. *Journal of Learning Disabilities, 14,* 391–393.

Zwerlein, R. A., Smith, M., and Diffley, J. (1984). *Vocational rehabilitation for learning disabled adults: A handbook for rehabilitation professionals.* Albertson, NY: National Center on Employment of the Handicapped at Human Resources Center.

Index